WHAT WORKS FOR WHOM?
A Critical Review

o

h

G

DS

© 1996 The Guilford Press
A Division of Guilford Publications, Inc.
72 Spring Street, New York, NY 10012

Printed in the United States of America

This book is printed on acid-free paper.

Last digit is print number: 9   8   7   6   5   4

Library of Congress Cataloging-in-Publication Data

Roth, Anthony.
  What works for whom?: a critical review of psychotherapy research/
Anthony Roth and Peter Fonagy, with contributions from Glenys
Parry, Mary Target, and Robert Woods.
      p.   cm.
  Includes bibliographical references and index.
  ISBN 1-57230-125-2   ISBN 1-57230-355-7 (pbk.)
  1. Psychiatry—Differential therapeutics. 2. Psychotherapy—
Evaluation. 3. Psychotherapy—Research. I. Fonagy, Peter, 1952–
RC480.52.R669   1996
616.89′14—dc20   96-22624
                                                          CIP

Contributing Authors

Anthony Roth, Ph.D., Clinical Tutor, University College London Doctoral Programme in Clinical Psychology; Honorary Research Fellow, University College London; Coordinator, Adult Mental Health Clinical Psychology Services, Camden and Islington Community NHS Trust

Peter Fonagy, Ph.D., Freud Memorial Professor of Psychoanalysis, University of London; Director, Subdepartment of Clinical Health Psychology, University College London; Director, Psychoanalysis Unit, University College London; Director of Research, Anna Freud Centre, London; Director, Child and Family Center, Menninger Foundation, Topeka, Kansas

Glenys Parry, Ph.D., Director of Research and Development, Community Health Sheffield NHS Trust; Professor Associate, Department of Psychology and School for Health and Related Research, University of Sheffield; Senior Psychological Officer, National Health Service Executive, Department of Health, London

Mary Target, Ph.D., Senior Research Fellow, Anna Freud Centre, London; Lecturer in Psychology, University College London

Robert Woods, M. Phil., Senior Lecturer, University College London Doctoral Programme in Clinical Psychology; Head of Clinical Psychology Services for Older People, Camden and Islington Community NHS Trust

Acknowledgments

This book is based on a report commissioned by Professor Glenys Parry, on behalf of the National Health Service Executive of the English Department of Health, which formed a part of the Department's Strategic Policy Review of Psychotherapy Services.

We are grateful to the Department of Health for their commission, and especially grateful for the support and encouragement extended to us by Professor Parry throughout all stages of the project.

An initial draft of our work was peer-reviewed by international experts in the field, solicited by the Department. These were David Barlow, Ellen Frank, John C. Markowitz, Michael King, Marsha Linehan, Paul A. Pilkonis, Mark Aveline, Isaac Marks, Jane Milton, Jan Scott, Chris Freeman, Paul Crits-Christoph, Eugene Paykel, Digby Tantum, Ivy Blackburn, and Ray Hodgson. We should like to thank our reviewers for their often very detailed, helpful, and pertinent comments, which contributed invaluably to a revised version of the report, and consequently to this book. We should like also to thank Professor David Shapiro for his coordination of these reviews.

A number of colleagues contributed observations and comments on drafts of chapters; for this we should like particularly to thank Chris Barker, John Clarkin, Keith Hawton, Rose Kent, Deborah Lee, Emanuelle Peters, and Anne Richardson for their comments on work-in-progress. We should also like to thank Tom Price for his help in identifying and retrieving source material.

Foreword

ALAN E. KAZDIN

Since the early 1900s, when psychotherapy began to emerge as a formally recognized intervention within medicine and the mental health professions, the effectiveness of treatment and demonstration of the impact of therapy were not high priorities. Proponents of various forms of therapy provided case studies and claimed dramatic improvements. These case studies (e.g., Dora, Anna O.), many of which remain well known today, seemingly attested to the effectiveness of treatment and the role of therapy in unlocking processes leading to change. The case study approach set a standard for reporting treatment, evaluating its effects, and making decisions of what to apply to whom. In this tradition, clinical work from many different theoretical approaches has been able to continue on threads of therapist testimony and clinical judgment regarding what treatments are appropriate for various clinical problems and how the treatments ought to be applied. In this approach, the individual clinician or clinical service decides the duration, goals, and methods of treatment. The decision-making process is rarely explicit and itself suffers from rather well-documented limitations and biases of human perception and judgment. Research can serve as a basis for informing practice by testing theoretical propositions about the processes underlying clinical problems and their modification and, more directly, by testing the effects of treatment on clinical outcomes. Central features of research (e.g., explicitness of procedures and methods, replication across researchers and sites) overcome some of the frailties of judgment, even though research itself has its own frailties.

Concerns regarding the financing of mental health services by government and insurance companies have led to increased scrutiny of what sorts of treatments are practiced. To contain spiraling costs of health care, those who pay for treatment are concerned about the effectiveness and efficiency of these services. Since those who ultimately pay for treatment and those who receive treatment are us—the public at large—it is surprising and regrettable that the demand for greater accountability in services has peaked only now. In any case, the question of what treatments work for whom and under what conditions is no longer academic. Hundreds of forms of psychotherapy are available. Selecting which treatment to use based on clinician preference, training experiences, or views about what is effective is less tolerable now. We know that most of the treatments and treatment combinations in use have not been carefully studied or shown to be effective. Clearly, we would profit immensely from a thorough, balanced, and incisive review of how research might guide clinical services. This book provides that review.

The goals of this book are to review psychotherapy research and to draw implications for clinical practice and service delivery. An extraordinarily large number of controlled treatment outcome studies are reviewed and encompass a broad range of clinical problems and interventions. Considering the findings, the status of treatment is canvassed and the implications for clinical practice and service delivery are stated. The book is well conceived, thorough in its coverage, and appropriately cautious in the conclusions about what currently is known. As a statement of the status of psychotherapy outcome research, *What Works for Whom?* is without peer.

The book makes three major contributions. First, the conclusions about the effectiveness of treatment will further underscore the advances in psychotherapy research. The past 40 years have generated a vast amount of research and evaluations of that research. The book covers meta-analytic and narrative reviews of the field as well as key studies across a broad range of clinical problem areas. From this coverage, we can see that many therapy techniques are effective; delineating effective techniques and the clinical problems to which they have been applied is quite important. At the same time, the review reveals that many techniques currently used in clinical practice have little or no evidence in their behalf. Although the absence of evidence is not tantamount to ineffectiveness, clinical work and reimbursement agencies ought to be guided by techniques that have a research base. The present book comprehensively evaluates the state of the evidence and can serve as a basis for treatment selection.

Second, the book conveys the limitations of current research. How we currently conceive of treatment and treatment evaluation may be limited and not provide the sorts of answers we need to guide clinical services. For example, the outcome criteria to evaluate effectiveness often are restricted to symptom reduction and omit evaluation of domains (e.g., impairment in daily functioning, quality of life, family functioning, physical health) that are critically important. Similarly, relatively few studies have examined follow-up. Among the studies that have, information beyond 1 year after treatment is rare. The long-term effects are very important to see if improvements are maintained and to identify if there is a preventive function in relation to other problems that may emerge. In addition, the treatments studied in clinical research often depart considerably from those that are conducted in clinical practice. To serve as a guide for clinical practice, research ought to draw further on strategies that are used clinically and considered important in that context.

Finally, the contribution of the book also stems from the attention it draws to clinical practice. The improvement of patient care and service delivery will not automatically result from using empirically based treatments. Integrating systematic methods of monitoring and evaluating treatment delivery and patient progress will be essential. The accountability that reimbursement parties wish and the quality of services to which patients are entitled call for new methods of evaluating treatment implementation and patient progress. Feasible methods for large-scale use are only beginning to be explored, but they are available. This book is pregnant with implications that can influence the quality of research and clinical practice, well beyond the research findings that have accumulated.

What Works for Whom? is stellar in its presentation of current accomplishments and advances in research. At this time, we may not know precisely what techniques work for whom, but we do know that selected treatments can achieve change and some of the therapeutic processes and patient and therapist characteristics that influence outcome. This knowledge is very important. From the meticulous review of progress provided by the authors, we can see how much more work is needed and, in my view, how very different that work ought to be. Controlled trials of therapy remain essential as a method of establishing treatment effects. Yet, the trials can be improved by (1) reflecting the complexity of clinical problems seen in clinical work, (2) evaluating a broader range of outcomes, (3) studying treatments that can be applied in clinical practice, and (4) providing methods to monitor treatment implementation and patient progress that can be extended to practice. No less significant is the need to improve the quality of clinical practice. The quality of clinical practice does not derive merely from using techniques of demonstrated efficacy, but also from evaluating and systematic monitoring of patient progress. This book charts the course of therapy research to the present and provides a vision to guide and to improve future research, clinical practice, and service delivery.

Alan E. Kazdin, Ph.D., is Professor of Psychology, Yale University, and Director, Yale Child Conduct Clinic.

Foreword

DAVID A. SHAPIRO

It is a pleasure to introduce the work of Anthony Roth, Peter Fonagy, and their colleagues. They set out to meet a need for a comprehensive, balanced, and authoritative account of the evidence demonstrating the benefit of psychotherapeutic interventions to patients with mental health disorders. No existing account of research in psychotherapy quite does this. Prior reviews were restricted to single diagnostic groups or treatment approaches and lacked the breadth and detail required to derive recommendations to policymakers and those paying for psychotherapy.

What, then, is the yield of 50 years' research on the outcomes of psychotherapy, as presented in this work? If there was ever a classic example of the glass that is either half full or half empty—depending on your point of view (or your score today on the Beck Depression Inventory)—this is it.

On the positive side, the glass is (at least) half full, because there is more, and better quality, scientific evidence to support psychotherapy than for many other interventions in health care today. The beliefs and claims of practitioners in this field have been more critically and searchingly challenged than in any other, and the response to this challenge has been vigorous, creative, and effective.

To take but one example, meta-analysis, the systematic, quantitative approach to reviewing empirical literature, was introduced to the health care domain in 1977 by the classic work of Smith and Glass. This work demonstrated convincing benefits from psychological treatment. For some years, meta-analysis remained unknown to most medical researchers. Now, however, this approach is the cornerstone of evidence-based practice across health care. Work in other areas follows the precedent set by psychotherapy research that meta-analysis is an essential step in the process of translating research findings into effective practice.

Impressive evidence is marshaled in the pages that follow, from both primary research and meta-analytic reviews, for the efficacy of psychological treatments across the field of mental health. Most of this evidence has been obtained through a process of specifying both the goals or targets of treatment and the nature of the intervention. Psychotherapeutic approaches following this strategy may be expected to prosper, such are the demands from purchasers, policymakers, and service users.

On the negative side, the glass is half empty. Many, if not most, of the cherished beliefs of theorists and practitioners of particular methods of psychotherapy remain largely unsupported by the kinds of evidence preferred by those who control the budgets of health care systems across the globe. Where treatment approaches compete, those whose adherents have comprehensively followed the research strategy of most of the work reviewed here are well supported by evidence. Others are in relative limbo. Although there have been enormous investments in training and practice, they are less well grounded in evidence. With notable and commendable exceptions, there has been relatively little progress in developing an evidence base for psychodynamic therapies and for longer-term treatments. Both of these make important claims whose validity urgently requires evaluation.

Roth, Fonagy, and colleagues identify the importance of redressing these imbalances. However, "head-to-head" comparisons among treatments differing in the strengths of their respective evidential support show surprisingly modest differences. For most of the disorders reviewed here, there is little evidence to take us beyond the paradoxical "Dodo bird verdict" of equivalent outcomes from very different treatment methods. In addition, evidence for the specific mechanisms (sometimes termed, perhaps misleadingly, "active ingredients") adduced by adherents of seemingly effective therapies is typically surprisingly limited.

Another clear caveat to emerge is that there is ample room for improvement in the efficacy of psychological treatments in mental health. More severely disordered patients are often found to be less responsive. In major depression, the exciting prospect that successful psychotherapy can protect against subsequent relapse or recurrence may prove confined to cognitive-behavioral treatment and, even here, this effect is not uniformly found.

There are, of course, methodological and strategic problems in this field of research, to which the authors have given us an invaluable guide. Their chapter on evidence-based practice may prove seminal in its conceptualization of how practice is informed both by research-derived guidelines and by the professional consensus arising from audit of service delivery. Clinical practice in turn informs theory development and, hence, innovative practice, which helps set the research agenda. This is an enormous advance on the simplistic assumption, guaranteed to deter clinicians from the consumption or production of research, that the flow of influence from research to practice should be in just one direction.

This book also teaches us that scientifically strong randomized designs are now beginning to provide the basis for determining the appropriate mix of therapies for a population. In sum, we learn both how much, and how little, we know. On the one hand, psychotherapies have an established place in mental health treatment; on the other, the promulgation of lists of empirically validated treatments for specific disorders is at best hazardous, and at worst may mislead and retard progress. Anyone seeking such a list would do well to consult the one offered, with due circumspection, in this volume.

The present book, with its unprecedented scope, quality, and sophistication, invites us to compare anew the scientific standing of psychotherapies in mental health with that of other health care interventions. Just as psychotherapy research led the way 20 years ago with the development and application of systematic reviews, so now it may be ahead of other fields in its critical appreciation of the limits of current empirical methods and its creative initiation of new ways to build a scientific base for clinical practice. If such is the judgment of future commentators, much of the credit for this will belong to Anthony Roth, Peter Fonagy, and their colleagues for this truly monumental book.

David A. Shapiro, Ph.D., is Professor of Clinical Psychology and Director, Psychological Therapies Research Centre, University of Leeds, and Director of Research and Development, Leeds Community and Mental Health Services (Teaching) NHS Trust.

Contents

Introduction

In this book we aim to examine evidence that can help us answer the following questions:

- Which psychotherapeutic interventions are of demonstrated benefit to which patient groups?
- Is there research evidence that would help funders of health care decide on the appropriate mix of therapies for their populations?
- To what extent can one draw on evidence of demonstrated efficacy in controlled research conditions and clinical effectiveness in services as delivered?

Two forces combine to make these particularly pertinent questions: (1) the rapid development and prominence of psychological therapies within mental health systems, and (2) the increasing demand across all fields of health care for evidence-based practice—a demonstration that the procedures adopted by a profession are safe, effective, and cost-effective.

Since Freud's pioneering work in the 19th century, psychotherapy has undergone a process of evolution. Rather than being a single entity, it is now more accurate to talk of a range of psychological therapies, each employing more or less distinctive techniques. Some have retained the models of unconscious motivation of psychoanalysis, others have eschewed it; some focus on the remoter aspects of the patient's past, others are interested only in present experience and functioning. Arguments have long raged over which approach is the "fittest," not only among clinicians but also among researchers. To a great extent this has been helpful and creative, forcing an examination of practice and leading to the development of further methods of intervention.

For many years this has been a debate conducted largely among clinicians; now they have been joined by the agencies responsible for funding the supply of therapy. Both in America and in Europe these

1

organizations seek information that would help them direct money to approaches of proven benefit. To this end they are turning to the large body of research evidence that has been accumulating on relative treatment efficacy. However, the questions posed by researchers (and the techniques used to answer them) rarely produce data that are directly applicable to funders of health care (Parry, 1992). Readers need to understand that there is no direct relationship between research and clinical practice—the one needs translation into the other. We believe that research evidence can be used to improve the structure and planning of psychotherapy services. We also recognize that, without careful interpretation, this evidence could be misconstrued, to the detriment of all parties.

The book begins with a description of the theory and practice of the major schools of psychological therapy. In Chapter 2 we outline the methodologies used by psychotherapy researchers and the way in which these limit the application of research findings to clinical practice. In the final introductory chapter, Chapter 3, we try to place research in the context of health care delivery systems, and present a model relating research findings to clinical practice. In many ways the model is a guide to interpretation of all that follows.

The body of the book contains research evidence relating to the treatment of each of a wide range of psychological problems. Our strategy has been to examine available reviews of treatments, together with individual studies where these are relevant. On methodological grounds we have had to be selective, making judgments about the form of study that we consider contributes best to our task. For this reason the majority of trials in this book represents controlled studies of psychotherapy outcome; less frequently, open trials; and only rarely, case reports. After reviewing this evidence, we present a number of conclusions and consider their implications for service delivery.

CHAPTER 1

Defining the Psychotherapies

Psychosocial treatments are common in the mental health field—indeed, almost any intervention could be seen as assisting patients to cope with impairments in their psychological functioning. Psychotherapies are inevitably psychosocial treatments but usually share a set of distinguishing characteristics. Strupp's (1978, p. 3) well-known definition describes psychotherapy as "an interpersonal process designed to bring about modifications of feelings, cognitions, attitudes and behaviour which have proved troublesome to the person seeking help from a trained professional." This definition draws attention to three characteristics of psychotherapy: the presence of a therapist–patient relationship; the interpersonal context of the psychotherapies; and, implied by the notion of training and professionalism, the sense that therapies are conducted according to a model that guides the therapist's actions. Psychotherapies are defined in part by their setting and in part by the presence of an explicit model of psychopathology, which in turn generates procedures for relieving distress.

Within this broad definition, it is worth noting that a large number of interventions can be described as psychotherapeutic; Kazdin (1986) identifies over 400 different therapies. The diversity of interventions is hard to encompass in any single review, though the task is made easier by the fact that many of these therapies represent subclasses of a smaller number of major orientations. In this book we differentiate therapies primarily in terms of the following major classes:

- Psychodynamic psychotherapy
- Behavioral and cognitive-behavioral psychotherapy
- Interpersonal psychotherapy
- Strategic or systemic psychotherapies
- Supportive and experiential psychotherapies
- Group therapies

Each of these orientations provides a model of human behavior as well as a heuristic focus for the level to which an intervention is ideally addressed. We recognize that in clinical practice few practitioners make use of orientations in their pure form. By contrast, most recent outcome investigations concern themselves with treatment approaches clearly nested within the theoretical framework of one of these orientations. Less is known about the value of combining orientations, even though this might be more representative of everyday practice.[1]

A further parameter distinguishing treatment approaches is the context or format within which treatment is offered. Psychotherapeutic treatment may be offered to individuals, to families, or to groups. It may be offered for relatively short periods or be open-ended. The format of treatment will also differ in terms of intensity (e.g., five times a week as against once a week or once a month), the setting (inpatient or community based), and the extent to which nonpsychosocial treatments (such as medication) are offered adjunctively.

Whereas it is clear that a comprehensive psychotherapy service would cover a range of orientations, it is less evident that significant benefit may accrue from a single individual's mastery of a range of approaches. Nonetheless, it seems reasonable to argue that a therapist's capacity to intervene flexibly with a range of problems requires at least rudimentary knowledge of a number of the orientations listed above.

PSYCHODYNAMIC THERAPY

The origin of the psychodynamic approach is a relatively brief, focused therapy (Freud & Breuer, 1895/1955). Classical psychoanalysis developed into a long-term, intensive treatment aimed not at removing single symptoms or troublesome problem behaviors but at attempting to restructure the entire personality. More pertinent to providing managed care services are the focal therapies designed by pioneers such as Alexander and French (1946), Sifneos (1972), Mann (1973), Malan (1976),

---

[1] It is worth noting that over the past 20 years considerable efforts have been made to systematically integrate differing components of psychotherapies within a coherent theoretical framework; in the United Kingdom the most notable such development is that of cognitive analytic therapy (CAT; Ryle, 1990). Practitioners of CAT are likely to use intervention techniques belonging to, for example, psychodynamic or cognitive-behavioral therapies. However, intervention strategies follow from a formulation of the patient's difficulties. This coherent and planned eclecticism is distinct from therapies in which techniques are "borrowed" in the absence of a guiding theoretical framework.

Davanloo (1978), Luborsky (1984), and Strupp and Binder (1984). Such focal approaches no longer aim at pervasive transformations of the personality, but assume that cognitive understanding of personal problems may initiate symptomatic change, which continues after termination of the formal treatment. Long-term exploratory psychodynamic psychotherapy may span 1 year or more. Its focal implementation is more likely to compromise 4 to 6 months of once- or twice-weekly sessions. Whereas long-term exploratory therapy aims to consider a wide variety of transference distortions, focal therapy tends to be aimed at circumscribed character change. Both exploratory and focused treatment have the resolution of unconscious conflict as their goal; unlike cognitive and behavioral psychotherapies, these are not primarily or only concerned with achieving symptomatic change.

The technique of psychodynamic therapy is a focus on the provision of conscious understanding, primarily through the use of interpretation of the patient's verbalizations and behavior during the session. Modern psychoanalysis also highlights the experience of problematic internal states of feelings, desires, and beliefs in conflict, encoded into relationship patterns that are exposed to scrutiny within the therapeutic situation and in relation to the therapist. Conscious insight may not be as important a component of the treatment as previously thought; the emotional experience associated with the therapist tolerating thoughts and feeling previously considered intolerable by the patient may be equally, or even more, important. Other potentially therapeutic aspects of the treatment include promoting the assimilation of emotionally painful and previously warded-off experiences (catharsis), suggestion, and support. The more structured approach of the focal therapist calls for a more active therapist, who identifies for the patient recurring patterns of behavior consistent with the presence of a hypothesized unconscious conflict.

BEHAVIORAL AND
COGNITIVE-BEHAVIORAL THERAPIES

The roots of behavioral and cognitive-behavioral interventions are in classical learning theory (conditioning and operant learning) and in social learning theory. Wolpe's systematic desensitization method was probably the first rigorous attempt to adapt Pavlovian conditioning to a clinical situation. At the same time, Skinner and colleagues used operant conditioning techniques to modify the behavior of psychotic inpatients. Largely for epistemological reasons, behavioral approaches ignore the importance of cognitive processes. Under the influence of Bandura, Ellis, Michenbaum, and Beck, the balance has been redressed, and cognitions (both conscious and unconscious) have come to occupy an increasingly prominent role in models of psychopathology (as indeed is the case in the academic discipline of psychology as a whole). Cognitive therapies share with dynamic therapies the assumption of irrational cognitive processes. However, within cognitive therapy, cognitions are seen as having been learned and to be maintained through reinforcement; challenges to these assumptions may therefore be made directly rather than via unconscious determinants as implied by dynamic theory. In addition, the proposed links between symptomatology and specific cognitions are somewhat less complex in cognitive than in dynamic approaches. Nevertheless, there is considerable overlap between modern cognitive therapy and traditional psychoanalytic ideas, and indeed many cognitive propositions derive from analytic formulations. Examples of overlap between these two traditions include the notion of helplessness; the discrepancy between the perceived self and the ideal self; the self-destructiveness of negative cognitions implied in the negative view of the self, the world, and the future; and the tendency defensively to avoid the scrutiny of painful cognitions.

At least traditionally within this orientation, the clinician is less concerned than his or her dynamic counterpart with how maladaptive ideas and behaviors have emerged. Behavioral and cognitive-behavioral clinicians focus on how these maladaptive aspects of functioning are maintained by the individual's environment and through properties inherent to their belief systems. In the early days of cognitive therapy, considerable emphasis was placed on the primacy of cognitions over emotional responses—in other words, the proposition that emotional reactions could be predicted on the basis of beliefs and expectations. More recently there has been a general recognition by both dynamic and cognitive theorists that the separation of these two modes of functioning is an oversimplification of little heuristic value, and one that has no credibility either within philosophical tradition or in modern cognitive science.

Because of the intellectual roots of this orientation in positivist epistemology, the focus of behavioral interventions is on definable behaviors that can be readily monitored and addressed in therapeutic interventions. Cognitive-behavioral treatments represent an integration of this level of analysis with consideration of thoughts and beliefs that may lead to dysfunctional behavior. The goal of such interventions is to change maladaptive beliefs, using a wide range of techniques at the clinician's disposal. These commonly include elements of self-monitoring, identifying, and challenging negative thoughts and assumptions that maintain problematic behavior and experiences; decatastrophization; and scheduling activities that, in turn, aid further self-monitoring and challenge to dysfunctional beliefs. Although interpretation may at times be a part of the cognitive therapist's armamentarium, finding reasons for particular beliefs is not regarded as an essential or necessarily very effective component of the intervention. The goals of intervention tend to be clear, and the patient's motivation is strongly reinforced by suggestion and support from the therapist.

The distinction between cognitive and behavioral interventions is a controversial one. Clinicians from a primarily behavioral tradition consider that interventions such as cognitive restructuring may be effective only through their impact on the patient's behavior, which in turn modifies their subjective state. By contrast, "pure cognitivists" consider directly induced behavioral changes (e.g., through selective reinforcement, or *in vivo* exposure) to have a long-term impact only in that they force a change in the patient's expectations. In this review we will not concern ourselves with this distinction, which is of limited relevance to technique, although it may have implications for training.

INTERPERSONAL PSYCHOTHERAPY

Interpersonal psychotherapy (IPT) is based on the ideas of the interpersonal school (Sullivan, 1953), and was initially formulated as a time-limited weekly therapy for depressed patients. It makes no assumptions about etiology, but uses the connection between the onset of depressive symptoms and current interpersonal problems as a focus for treatment. It therefore focuses on current relationships rather than enduring aspects of the personality, and therapists take an active and supportive stance.

IPT is normally a brief treatment, usually administered in the acute phase of depression. Therapy starts with a diagnostic phase, where the patient's disorder is identified and explained. The therapist highlights the ways in which the patient's current functioning, social relationships, and expectations within these relationships may have been causal in the depression. There is an educational aspect to this process whereby the therapist links depressive symptoms to one of four interpersonal areas: grief, interpersonal role disputes, role transitions, or interpersonal deficits. In the second phase of treatment the therapist pursues strategies specific to one of these problem areas—for example, he or she may facilitate mourning and help the patient to find new relationships and activities to compensate for the loss. Role disputes may be tackled by helping the patient explore problem relationships and consider options available to resolve them. In the final phase of the treatment, the patient is helped to focus on therapeutic gains and to develop ways of identifying and countering depressive symptoms, should they arise in the future.

Though originally intended for application only to depression, IPT has more recently been adapted for use with a wider range of disorders (Weissman & Markowitz, 1994).

SYSTEMIC ORIENTATIONS

Whereas the roots of both dynamic and cognitive approaches date back to the turn of the last century, the systemic approach is a relatively new model of psychological disturbance. The intellectual roots of the approach lie in anthropology as well as cybernetics. Early workers in this field (such as Bateson, Haley, and Erickson) identified some general properties of human systems that ran across a number of domains. A basic assumption of the model is that neither symptoms nor insight can be an appropriate focus for treatment interventions. Rather, the system that generates the problem behavior is the appropriate target for intervention. The approach is most usefully applied to the system of the family, where each family member is seen as a unit within the system and the client's problem behavior is generated by its malfunctioning. The therapist's task is to identify the strategic role that the client's problem has in maintaining the family system, and addressing this aspect of its functioning. Although symptomatic change is not seen as an appropriate goal, a change in symptomatic behavior may help toward identifying dysfunctional aspects of the system. Thus, systemic therapists also use a number of techniques for directly tackling symptomatic behavior as a preliminary to bringing about systemic modification. Although the setting of systemic therapy often includes the entire family, this is neither a necessary nor a sufficient condition for systemic change.

Systemic therapists use advice, suggestion, paradoxical injunctions, symptom prescription, marking of boundaries, and an emphasis on the positive value of symptoms for the whole family as ways of bringing about change to the family system.

SUPPORTIVE AND EXPERIENTIAL THERAPIES

The philosophical tradition behind supportive and experiential therapies has roots in the humanistic, existential, and phenomenological ideas proposed by Nietzsche, Sartre, and Husserl. In different ways all these authors reject the mechanistic philosophies underpinning psychodynamic, behavioral, and systemic therapies. The roots of disturbance are seen to lie in the dehumanizing and disintegrative effect of social conditions. In their view any therapy that imposes directive and mechanistic methods compounds rather than solves this problem. Supportive and experiential therapists eschew intellectual solutions and prescribe interventions aimed at reinforcing and validating spontaneous and immediate experience, which is seen as facilitating the integrity of the self and a sense of personal authenticity. Emotional problems arise when circumstances prevent an individual from actualizing his or her potential and force the individual to inhibit essential aspects of his or her personality. Supportive and experiential approaches do encourage self-awareness, but not awareness of unconscious forces (rather, awareness of experience itself, including emotional reactions and the experience of interactions with others). The therapist's role is one of a facilitating observer, who will aid clients in extending their awareness of their subjective world. Again, insight and symptomatic improvement are not seen as appropriate goals for therapy. Instead, clients are offered support in their natural striving toward self-determination, personal meaning, and self-awareness.

Because of its nonmechanistic philosophy, technique plays a less important part in experiential treatments than it does in many therapies. Experiential therapists place emphasis on intuitiveness, openness, receptiveness, empathy, and unconditional regard for the patient as key elements that facilitate change. However, the very insistence that psychotherapy is not a "treatment" but rather a growth experience represents a technical stance, as is the focus on therapist attitudes rather than on specific maneuvers. Specific exemplars of this orientation, such as psychodrama, Gestalt therapy, or the client-centered approach, do make use of specific techniques, such as role play and strategies for encouraging various forms of abreaction.

GROUP THERAPIES

Group psychotherapy has been used to address the needs of children, adolescents, adults, and the elderly. It was developed particularly during World War II, when understaffed military hospitals were forced to use group treatment to attend to the overwhelming number of psychiatric casualties.

The growth of group therapy to some degree transcends theoretical orientations. While it has common roots with psychoanalysis, even in its early days it was associated with clinicians who became disillusioned with Freud's ideas. Yalom's (1975) influential contribution came from a Sullivanian perspective and focused on correcting here-and-now interpersonal problems. Group sessions were seen as enabling the expression and understanding of such problems as mistrust, anger, and dependency.

The mechanisms of change were seen as hope, corrective emotional experience, modeling, and the promotion of self-awareness. Alongside this interpersonal tradition, the psychoanalytic influence continued, with an emphasis on eliciting the interpersonal derivatives of unconscious conflicts through the manifestations of transferences both to the group leader and to other group members (Slavson, 1964). Foulkes (1975) originated group analysis based on the concept of the "group matrix," a hypothetical web of communication in which the group serves to represent the feelings of individuals. Other therapists developed innovative action-based group methods. For example, Moreno's (1953) emphasis on spontaneity and action led him to develop the technique of psychodrama. This and other methods were adopted by Gestalt and experiential therapies and the encounter group movement, including role playing, doubling, role reversal, and vicarious therapy.

Group therapies encompass clinical outpatient groups and their derivatives, such as psychoeducational, human development, and self-help groups. The community mental health movement in the United States in the early 1960s led to a further rapid growth in the application of group techniques and the development of short-term group therapies with a limited focus on the enhancement of ego functioning and social competence. In addition, modified group approaches were developed that did not require specialist training in psychotherapeutic techniques and that are frequently found in mental health settings, such as drama, art, and dance therapies.

The many theoretical positions listed above represent a small sample of those that exist in contemporary group psychotherapy. Further, many group therapists practice in a pluralist fashion using theories drawn from a wide range of orientations (Scheidlinger, 1994). Consequently, it is not surprising that group therapy research is hard to examine as an entity in and of itself.

Many treatments originally described for use with individuals are also administered in group formats. The current review includes a number of group-based interventions, though within the context of the patient groups for which treatments were delivered and the theoretical orientation guiding the therapy.

DIFFERENTIATION AND INTEGRATION OF TREATMENT APPROACHES

The above discussion represents prototypes of therapeutic orientations that rarely exist in pure form. Psychodynamic intervention is probably impossible to carry out without a substantial supportive, experiential component. Similarly, cognitive and strategic interventions overlap. Some approaches (e.g., Kohutian psychoanalytic psychotherapy; Kohut, 1977) deliberately combine supportive and dynamic components. Other therapies (e.g., Ryle, 1990) aim deliberately to integrate orientations. In a clinical setting, the orientation adopted by a clinician will depend to a large measure as much on the characteristics of the client as on the therapist's own training and orientation. A psychologically minded individual may well demand expanded self-understanding, whereas a less psychologically minded person may insist on practical help and advice. Certain problems lend themselves well to specific treatment approaches— for example, a monosymptomatic phobia is readily addressed by simple behavior techniques. Dysthymic disorder may require a wider repertoire of approaches to tackle the interpersonal problems associated with this form of disorder. Although there have been attempts at providing a theoretically coherent integration of techniques derived from these orientations, there are as yet few satisfactory theories to provide the clinician with a rationale for integrating these approaches.

In the United Kingdom, Ryle's (1990) cognitive analytic therapy, based on his procedural sequence object relations model, has recently gained increasing acceptance. The primary value of this technique is that it offers a structure for intervention by requiring the therapist to offer a parsimonious formulation of the patient's difficulties within an interpersonally focused schema–oriented framework. In the United States, cognitive therapists working with individuals with personality disorders are in the process of expanding cognitive therapy using schema theory. A particularly significant contribution has been made with borderline patients by Young and Lindeman (1992), whose approach extends the traditional cognitive framework in terms of both theory and technique. Theoretically, the additional focus is on the origins of maladaptive and preverbal cognitive structures; in terms of technique, these workers recommend long-term structured interventions, which sometimes come close to psychodynamic therapies. However, in clinical practice, considerations for integration tend to be pragmatic.

Of course, therapists and the theories that guide them do not exist in isolation from each other. To some degree the techniques applied determine the kind of data to which therapists of particular orientation are exposed, and indeed to which they are responsive. Nonetheless, there is considerable cross-fertilization between treatment approaches, in terms of both theory and technique. Currently, for example, there is a degree of convergence among clinicians rooted in psychoanalytic practice and those whose interests lie primarily in cognitive-behavioral techniques. While the latter are increasingly interested in nonconscious processes and the impact of the therapeutic relationship, the former have shown more concern about the nature of knowledge representation and the significance of cognitive factors that may account for slow progress within psychotherapy. Ultimately, theoretical orientations will have to be integrated, since they are all approximate models of the same phenomenon: the human mind in distress. For the moment, however, integration may well be counterproductive, as theoretical coherence is the primary criterion for distinguishing false and true assertions in many psychotherapeutic domains. To the extent that it removes the applicability of this criterion, integration would create confusion rather than clarify controversies. There may be notable exceptions to this objection among emerging integrative psychotherapy approaches—for example, Ryle's (1990) cognitive analytic therapy. In any case, this objection does not apply to the desirability of integration at the level of technique. In everyday clinical practice there is much that is "borrowed" from different orientations, by all practitioners. From the point of view of evaluation, what remains crucial is that all such borrowed techniques should make sense in the context of the theory into which they are borrowed.

CHAPTER 2

Translating Research into Practice
Methodological Considerations

Research into psychotherapy necessarily and inevitably changes the nature of the therapy it investigates—quantification requires a compromise between the usual procedures of the clinic and the demands of scientific inference. Clear thinking about the applicability of research findings rests on an understanding of these compromises.

CLINICAL EFFICACY AND CLINICAL EFFECTIVENESS

At the outset, a clear distinction needs to be drawn between the *efficacy* of a therapy (the results it achieves in the setting of a research trial) and its *clinical effectiveness* (the outcome of the therapy in routine practice). Clinical trials are required to conform to a number of criteria to demonstrate reliability and validity (Cook & Campbell, 1979). In particular, they usually aim to achieve a high degree of *internal validity*. This can be defined as the extent to which a causal relationship can be inferred among variables, or where the absence of a relationship implies the absence of a cause. If internal validity is low, *statistical conclusional validity* is compromised, and the results of a study would be hard to interpret. However, achieving internal validity requires the use of techniques rarely seen in everyday practice, examples of which would be studying highly selected, diagnostically homogenous patient populations; randomizing the entry of these patients into treatments; and employing extensive monitoring of both patients' progress and the types of therapy used by therapists. All of this poses a threat to *external validity*—the extent to which we can infer that the causal relationship can be generalized. In the present case this translates into the problem of inferring clinical effectiveness from any demonstrations of efficacy.

The contrary demands of internal and external validity pose a considerable problem to clinical researchers, and not only in the field of psychotherapy. For example, while a medication may show efficacy under controlled conditions, in the world of clinical practice any number of factors may militate against its effectiveness—the simplest of which would be patients who forget to take their pills. Whereas in a treatment trial drug levels may be monitored (thus enhancing adherence to a treatment protocol), in ordinary clinical settings there is rarely an opportunity to monitor this aspect of treatment integrity. Similar considerations apply to the offer of psychological treatment. For example, outcome studies frequently assess the efficacy of a clear and well-delivered intervention, though this may be unrepresentative of the quality of that intervention as it is generally offered in clinical practice. Equally, there may be times when the effectiveness of therapy in clinical practice could be enhanced by procedures not found in clinical trials—for example, by matching a therapy to patient preference and hence reducing premature dropout.

The bridge between research trials and routine treatment is even more difficult to span because of the vicissitudes of biology and individual psychological differences in treatment response. Psychotherapy is a highly complex interchange in which a large number of factors interact, any one of which could be significant to outcome. Patients differ along many dimensions, in terms of their socioeconomic circumstances, the stage of their disorder at the time of presentation, and in their premorbid psychological functioning. Similarly, therapists vary in their personality, their skills, their motivation, their ability to comprehend their patients' problems, and their adherence to treatment modalities. Service provision also varies in important ways, including the length of treatment offered, the quality of liaison with other services, the support and supervision offered to practitioners, and the physical resources available.

All these factors are known to interact in a highly complex manner, and are subjected to systematic scrutiny in research on *psychotherapy process*. In principle, such work is beyond the scope of this review. Orlinsky et al. (1994) provide a comprehensive overview of progress in this field. However, they note that the distinction between process and outcome research can become blurred. Indices of therapeutic process can often be informative of outcomes in the course of therapy, which in turn contribute to measures of end-state functioning employed in outcome research. The conclusions that can be drawn from trials of therapeutic efficacy will be influenced and modified by these considerations. Thus, where possible, we have attempted to identify some critical process factors in our review of treatment outcome.

We have organized the appraisal of outcome according to client groups, rather than according to treatment modalities.[1] To some degree our findings justify this problem-oriented approach, since specific interventions appear to have particular applicability to certain disorders, and considerations of the relative efficacy of treatment techniques are nested within major groups of disorders. This strategy has its own limitations, particularly that service provision is currently largely organized according to specific approaches rather than mental health problems. However, as the results of this review suggest, advantages for a multimodal psychotherapeutic service, we feel that our appraisal is service-relevant. A further advantage of the approach we have taken is to be found in the obvious fact that the challenge a disorder presents to psychotherapy services greatly depends on its prevalence, comorbidity, and natural history, both in the clinic and in the community. In organizing the review according to clinical problems, we have considered these as critical parameters of our evaluation.

SPONTANEOUS REMISSION

It is a matter of common clinical observation that some patients will recover without intervention. Given that this is so, all clinical trials face the problem of demonstrating that treatments have a gain beyond natural recovery; in other words, this is the hurdle over which they need to pass. Eysenck (1952) was the first investigator to attempt to quantify this phenomenon, claiming that although around two-thirds of patients undergoing therapy demonstrated improvements in their functioning over a 2-year period, a similar proportion of untreated patients showed equal improvements over the same period.

Eysenck's work has been heavily criticized for its reliance on methodologically flawed studies and for problems in the interpretation of these studies (detailed in Bergin, 1971; and Lambert, 1976). Further, McNeilly and Howard (1991) have conducted a probit analysis of rates of improvement within Eysenck's treated and untreated patient samples. This analysis suggests that approximately 50% of treated patients improved within 8 weeks, in contrast to only 2% of untreated patients over this time, a result clearly running counter to the claims made by Eysenck.

On the basis of their reviews, Bergin (1971) estimates a range for spontaneous remission of between 30 and 40%, while Lambert (1976)

---

[1] We discuss the advantages and disadvantages of this approach later in this chapter.

proposes a median rate of 53% for minimally treated and 43% for untreated patients. A major problem with these figures is that they are based on studies of mixed patient populations with differing diagnoses of widely varying severity and duration. Lambert (1976) reported remission rates ranging from 8 to 73%, dependent on the clinical condition under study. In an important paper, Subotnik (1975) identified the implications of the chronic (cyclical) course of many psychological disorders for the study of psychotherapy outcome. The rate of observed spontaneous remission will depend on the point in time, over the natural cycling of a disorder, at which treatment is offered. Subotnik's study speaks not only to the importance of randomized controlled assessment but also to the value of long-term follow-up.

Spontaneous remission might best be seen as a reflection of the natural history of a disorder, and statements regarding outcome for any particular client group can only be made in the context of knowledge about its course. In this review we attempt to consider all interventions in the light of what is known about the natural course of a disorder and the extent to which an intervention may be considered to influence its evolution.

METHODOLOGIES AND STRATEGIES IN PSYCHOTHERAPY RESEARCH

The choice of a particular research methodology will always be a compromise, reflecting the intents, interests, and resources of investigators. Major approaches will be considered in turn, together with their strengths and weaknesses. A full account of methodological issues in psychotherapy research is given in Kazdin (1994).

Single-Case Studies

In these designs the focus is on the individual patient rather than a group average, even where a group of patients are studied. Single-case studies may be descriptive or quantitative. Within this latter group some are naturalistic reports of outcome or quasi-experiments (Cook & Campbell, 1979), others reports of the experimental manipulation of interventions. In cases where appropriate baseline measures are taken, or where treatments are applied and withdrawn in a controlled manner, the patient acts as his or her own control. This methodology has been widely used by behavioral and cognitive-behavioral researchers (Morley, 1987,

1989), but is equally applicable to psychodynamic investigators (e.g., Fonagy & Moran, 1993) and to the investigation of process factors (e.g., Parry et al., 1986).

Single-case studies have a number of attractive features. They can be carried out in routine clinical practice, do not (necessarily) require the facilities associated with more complex research, and can be conducted fairly quickly. While of great importance in the demonstration or refinement of clinical technique and especially in treatment innovation, their results can be difficult to generalize to the broader clinical population (indeed, the design is not intended for such a purpose). Patients are often highly selected (necessarily so where studies are aiming to show the effectiveness of a technique for particular clients). More fundamentally, however, interpretation of results is limited by the fact that (as will become evident in the body of this book) therapeutic interventions have both general and specific impacts on the welfare of patients. A contrast intervention is required in order to be clear that any demonstrated benefits are attributable to specific therapeutic techniques—a strategy adopted in the randomized control trial.

Randomized Controlled Trials

In contrast to the single-case study, randomized controlled trials (RCTs) explicitly ask questions about the comparative benefits of two or more treatments. Patients are randomly allocated to different treatment conditions, usually with some attempt to control for (or at least examine) factors such as demographic variables, symptom severity, and level of functioning. Attempts are made to implement therapies under conditions that reduce the influence of variables likely to influence outcome—for example, by standardizing factors such as therapist experience and ability, and the length of treatments. The design permits active treatments to be compared, or their effect to be contrasted with no treatment, a waiting list, or a "placebo" intervention. Increasingly, studies also ensure that treatments are carried out in conformity with their theoretical description—for example, ensuring that cognitive-behavioral treatments do not include psychodynamic elements, and vice versa. To this end many treatments have been "manualized" (a process that specifies the techniques of the therapy programmatically), and therapist adherence to technique has been monitored as part of the trial.

Though this design has the potential to distinguish the impact of treatments (and to provide a control for the effects of spontaneous remission), there are inherent limitations to this approach.

Problems of Control Groups

Although the ideal design of a treatment would be to contrast treatment to no treatment, it is rarely the case that this is either ethically or practically possible. The alternative of offering a placebo treatment—one which is considered inactive, at least from the point of view of the active treatments offered—is beset by the difficulty of finding an activity which could be guaranteed to have no therapeutic element, which controls for the effect of attention and which is also viewed by patients as being as credible as the active interventions. Many recent studies restrict themselves to the comparison of active treatments; as evidence has accumulated for the general efficacy of therapy, ethical committees have become unwilling to sanction trials which could be seen to deprive patients of help (e.g., see Elkin, 1994).

Length of Therapy

Setting up an RCT is a major undertaking and consequently a great expense. Although there are exceptions, most trials limit the amount of intervention offered (frequently to around 16 weeks). While this may be appropriate for some therapies (principally behavioral or cognitive-behavioral approaches), psychodynamic therapists (e.g., Fonagy & Higgitt, 1989) could and do argue that the techniques they employ were never designed for delivery over such a short time frame.

Generalizability

Few RCTs monitor the implementation of psychological therapies under conditions that obtain in routine practice. As noted above, because they are characterized by a concern to maintain internal validity, their applicability could be seen as limited. For example:

- Patients will have been selected to conform to diagnostically precise categories.
- Patients will have been exposed to multiple assessments.
- Therapies will be applied with some precision, often under supervision.
- Researchers will often be particularly enthusiastic and particularly expert in the techniques they employ.

Patient Preference and Random Allocation to Treatment

Patients are not passive recipients of treatment, and their preferences for differing forms of treatment may be critical to their participation in clinical trials (Brewin & Bradley, 1989). The bias introduced by consequent attrition from treatment is invisible within studies, but may be particularly relevant to clinical practice.

Open Trials

This methodology is intermediate between the single-case design and the randomized control trial. Although entry to treatment may be governed by strict criteria, there is no control group. Such designs often reflect a more naturalistic treatment protocol than is the case with RCTs. Frequently two or more treatments for the same disorder, as practiced in different settings, are contrasted. In principle, such a design could answer the question, "What kind of patient benefits most from particular treatment protocols?" In reality, differences in case mix and the failure to control specific components of treatment usually place drastic limitations on the implications that may be drawn from such studies. Given a sufficiently large data set, it may be possible to derive conclusions about the relative value of treatments even in the absence of random assignment. However, studies on such a large scale are not yet available. In the meantime, RCTs provide the only valid—albeit limited—source of evidence for the efficacy of various forms of psychological treatment.

RESOLVING CONFLICTS BETWEEN INTERNAL AND EXTERNAL VALIDITY IN RESEARCH DESIGNS

We have already noted that a major problem for psychotherapy researchers is the tension between satisfying the demands of internal and external validity when developing research strategies. Current designs have to reach a compromise between these factors; bridging the gap between them requires innovative attempts at integrating an apparent incompatibility between scientific rigor on the one hand and generalizability on the other. Single-case designs may come to play a more important role in this respect, since external validity is not an inherent problem in designs of this type (Kazdin, 1994). When replicated across randomly sampled cases, they have considerable generalizability. They can be employed to answer most of the questions that concern researchers, such as the appropriateness of a particular form of treatment, the length of treatment required to achieve a good outcome, the relative impact of treatment on particular aspects of the problem, or the relevance of particular components of treatment. However, there is one critical exception: within this research strategy, client and therapist factors are difficult to study. If there is no replication across subjects (clients and therapists), the design will not yield information about their influence on outcome. Thus methodology that is truly adequate to the task of simultaneously assuring internal and external validity in psychotherapy research has probably yet to be developed. In the meantime, the best—though possibly inadequate—answer lies in reviews (such as the present one), which include critical appraisal of likely threats to external validity posed by current research.

MEASUREMENT TECHNIQUES

There is some consensus (Kazdin, 1994) that single measures of outcome are unsatisfactory, that measures should be unreactive to experimenter demand, and that they should be drawn from the following:

- Differing perspectives (such as those of the patient, close relatives, or friends of the patient, and those of the therapist or independent observers)
- Differing symptom domains (such as affect, cognition and behavior)
- Differing domains of functioning (such as work and social and marital functioning)

There is, however, little consensus on the precise measures to be employed. This leads to some difficulty in comparisons among studies, and on occasion problems of interpretation within trials where measures assumed to converge on similar target areas give discrepant results.

For many therapists this reduction of outcomes to a series of scores is unsatisfactory because it fails to capture the complexity of their work. There is undoubtedly merit in this objection, since the majority of current measures do not capture the subtleties of individual presentations or the significance of particular changes to particular patients. Many psychoanalytic clinicians are impressed by the way in which, in some patients, psychotherapy promotes the unfolding of developmental processes, step by step, in an ordered and progressive way. However, the appropriateness of the developmental metaphor is by no means universally accepted by psychoanalysts (Mayes & Spence, 1994). In addition, psychodynamic therapists have noted that a focus on symptomatic change is inappropriate where personality change—which may be hard to measure—is the object of therapy. Techniques considered to measure this dimension have been developed (e.g., Malan, 1976; Malan & Osimo, 1992), though the degree to which they are truly independent of symptomatic change is less clear (Mintz, 1981). The eschewal of existing reliable and valid measures by practitioners of psychodynamic treatment is a regrettable fact which will only be corrected by a concerted effort on the part of psychodynamic therapists to identify, in a consensual and measurable way, the outcomes their treatment aims to bring about, and to validate these against criteria that other stakeholders (such as patients, funders, and other practitioners) see as important.

Finally, there may be legitimate concern that some measurement techniques may tap domains of change close to those targeted by the therapies employed, and may therefore indicate greater degrees of success than would be found using broader assessments. For example, the Beck Depression Inventory (BDI) assesses the level of depression largely through more cognitive representations of this disorder. In contrast, the Hamilton Rating Scale for Depression (HRSD) has more of a focus on biological symptoms. It may be that trials of cognitive therapy could achieve better outcomes using the BDI, and trials of medication better outcomes using the HRSD, reflecting less the "true" outcome than the bias of scoring instruments.

FOLLOW-UP

For many conditions the success of therapy may be measured by its ability both to improve patient functioning and to maintain that improvement after therapy ends. Although most trials report follow-up data, the length of follow-up can vary markedly between studies, sometimes being only a matter of weeks, sometimes years. The length of follow-up required to demonstrate a clinical effect is governed by the natural history of a disorder, which will suggest both the probability of relapse and the usual length of time between episodes. Therapeutic efficacy can only be demonstrated in the context of both factors and, for example, 3-month follow-up for a condition known to show greatest relapse over a period of 1 year would clearly be inadequate.

Although this suggests that extended follow-up periods should be the norm, the longer a patient is followed up, the more difficult it is to ascribe change to original treatment. In part this is because patients will often seek further treatment in the intervening period (e.g., Shea et al., 1992), and also because the relative impact of treatment in the context of life experiences decreases over time. Ironically, the results of very prolonged follow-up, while desirable, may be difficult to interpret.

Finally, the stability of symptomatic change over the follow-up period may be an issue of concern in its own right. The monitoring of individual patients suggests that a proportion will change their symptom status more than once (e.g., Shapiro et al., 1995; Brown & Barlow, 1995). Reporting of group averages tends to obscure this variability, leading to an overestimation of longer-term outcomes in clinical practice.

ATTRITION

All clinical trials will lose patients at various points in treatment; the point at which they are lost will have differing impacts on validity. Early loss from an RCT may disrupt the randomization of treatment, threatening internal validity. Even where there is no differential attrition from treatments, it may be the case that significant attrition could lead to results applicable only to a sub-group of persistent patients, threatening external validity. Alternatively, attrition rates across treatment conditions may not be random and may reflect the acceptability of therapies, suggesting that attrition may be an important variable in its own right.

Significant levels of attrition will restrict the conclusions that can be drawn from a study, and complicate reporting of results. A number of statistical solutions to this problem are available to researchers that utilize the last available data point to estimate the likely bias introduced by loss of patients (e.g., Flick, 1988; Little & Rubin, 1987). Alternatively, data can be reported on the basis of an "intention-to-treat" sample, including all subjects entered into the trial, as well as presenting separate data for those completing all or a specified length of therapy (e.g., Elkin et al., 1989).

META-ANALYSIS

In the past 15–20 years, techniques have been developed to enable quantitative review of psychotherapy studies. Meta-analysis is a procedure that enables data from separate studies to be considered collectively through the calculation of an effect size from each investigation. Effect sizes are calculated according to the formula

$$\text{Effect size} = \frac{M_1 - M_2}{SD}$$

where M_1 is the mean of the treatment group, M_2 is the mean of the control group, and *SD* is the pooled standard deviation. The terms M_1 and M_2 can stand for the means of any two groups of interest, such as psychotherapy contrasted against a waiting-list control, or equally could be the comparison of two forms of psychotherapy. Because this technique converts outcome measures to a common metric, individual effect sizes can be pooled. In addition to examining the contribution of main effects such as therapy modality, effect sizes for any variable of interest can be calculated, such as the impact of methodological quality or investigator allegiance on reported outcomes (e.g., Smith et al., 1980; Robinson et al., 1990).

Effect sizes refer to group differences in standard deviation units on the normal distribution. Their intuitive meaning is made clearer by translating them into percentiles, indicating the degree to which the average treated client is better off than control patients. A table giving this information and an explanatory guide to interpretation is included in the Appendix at the end of the book.

Meta-analysis is a powerful research tool, but some researchers have been critical of the technique (e.g., Wilson & Rachman, 1983). Common criticisms include:

- The fact that reviews do not include single-case studies
- The inclusion of studies of questionable methodological adequacy
- The inclusion of studies not directly relevant to clinical issues, such as analogue studies, and trials of patients whose symptoms are not clinically significant or of great severity
- The fact that analyses can multiply sample measures taken from the same patient and from the same study leads to effect sizes computed on the basis of dependent data
- The fact that using average Z scores assumes that outcome measures are appropriately measured on an interval scale, and that their distribution may be assumed to have insignificant skewness and kurtosis
- Sampling will be biased by the tendency for editors and authors to favor positive results
- Not all meta-analyses weight the means for sample size

Meta-analyses cited in this report are consistently selective in their choice of clinically relevant studies; though not all exclude methodologically unsound trials, many examine the impact of this selection criterion. A major difficulty is, however, that the effect size statistic can only speak to treatment effects for the average client, and though this is informative of general treatment effects, further elaboration of therapeutic impacts is usually required to detail the more specific effects of treatment.

PROBLEMS ASSOCIATED WITH THE USE OF STATISTICAL TESTS IN PSYCHOTHERAPY RESEARCH

Clinical and Statistical Significance

Much of this report is based on journal articles examining the truth of the null hypothesis—in essence the proposition that psychological therapies have no effect, or no effect greater than a placebo. It is conventional to report the statistical significance of differences between treatments in terms of a confidence level of $p < .05$ or $< .01$. However, researchers may be able to reject the null hypothesis at relatively high levels of statistical significance without simultaneously demonstrating that this finding is worthy of clinical attention (Kukla, 1989). Demonstration of statistical effects may not be equivalent to a clinically significant therapeutic change, and a number of strategies have been used to detect this (discussed further in Kazdin, 1994).

- Comparison of patient change with normative samples
- Measurement of the extent of individual change by reference to a criterion measure of change—for example, that treated clients should be 2 SD from the mean of the untreated group (Jacobson & Truax, 1991)
- The use of a criterion of recovery which enables categorical rather than continuous scoring of outcomes—for example, using a BDI score ≤9 to indicate treatment response (e.g., Elkin et al., 1989)

The clinical significance of change is central to the evaluation of psychotherapy outcomes; though recent investigations are more likely to report data in this form, such measures are not always available.

Multiple Data Sampling and Type I Error

Researchers frequently report numerous results of statistical significance without being clear how each test relates to the prediction they are examining. Dar et al. (1994) illustrate this problem by suggesting a hypothetical study in which two treatments for flying phobias are contrasted, with levels of anxiety and coping skills being the dependent variables. In practice there may be a number of procedures for measuring these variables, all of which are likely to be intercorrelated. Each of these variables could be examined separately, though in reality there are only two hypotheses under investigation—the impact of the treatment on anxiety, and its effect on coping skills. More than two statistical analyses are therefore redundant and represent an overstatement of the data available to the researchers. A real-life example of this process is the much cited National Institute of Mental Health study of treatments for depression (Elkin, 1994), which shows statistical significance on only some of a relatively large family of variables pertaining to dysfunctional emotional states.[2] A consequence of multiply sampling related data sets is to increase the risk of Type I errors—rejecting the null hypothesis when that hypothesis is false (e.g., in practice, claiming that one treatment works better than another when in reality the two work equally well).

Because it is well recognized that a series of measures tapping similar domains may be interrelated, investigators often employ multivariate tests, which permit some understanding of relationships between dependent measures. Though this procedure overcomes some of the problems noted above, problems can arise where multivariate tests that indicate overall significance are then followed by univariate tests. Not only does this increase the risk of Type I error, but results can be difficult to interpret, once again because of possible relationships among variables under test.

Atheoretical Analysis

Dar et al. (1994), in a review of the use of statistical tests in psychotherapy research from the 1960s to the 1980s, note a high level of inappropriate significance testing, which they attribute to the pragmatic concerns of psychotherapy researchers. The determination to find statistically significant associations is seen by them as motivated by "a flight from theory into pragmatics." As psychotherapy research frequently has very little theoretical guidance leading to meaningful hypotheses and testable predictions, there has been an explosion of exploratory procedures, leading to a state of affairs where, even in the best journals, "much of the current use of statistical tests is flawed" (Dar et al., 1994, p. 80).

---

[2] This study is discussed in full in Chapter 4; a caveat to this criticism (Ogles et al., 1995) should be noted.

Statistical Power

Statistical power is the extent to which an investigation is able to detect differences between samples when such differences exist in the population—in other words, when there is a true difference among the groups under test. Power is a function of the criterion for statistical significance, or alpha level; the sample size; and the effect size, or the magnitude of the difference that exists between the groups. Statistical power in perhaps the majority of psychotherapy trials may be relatively weak, primarily because of low sample sizes (Kazdin, 1994). Cohen (1962) distinguished three levels of effect size (small = 0.25, medium = 0.50, and large = 1.0) and evaluated the ability of published studies to detect such differences at the conventional alpha level of $p < .05$. Power within these studies was generally low—for example, studies had a 1 in 5 chance of detecting small effect sizes, and less than a 1 in 2 chance of detecting medium effect sizes. Despite the cautionary note struck by Cohen's (1962) paper and the date of its publication, Dar et al. (1994) found that a significant proportion of even recent research continues to neglect these issues. Most particularly, there continues to be a neglect of measures of effect size in favor of citing statistical significance. The problems inherent in this procedure can be readily illustrated by considering a study with a large sample but a small effect size; although statistical significance may well be achieved, this does not speak to the magnitude of the effect, nor its likely reliability or validity.

It should be clear that all of the above issues threaten the external validity of psychotherapy research; Dar et al. (1994) detail a number of strategies for ensuring that such threats are minimized—for example, by employing theory-guided predictions, planned rather than post hoc statistical decisions, reduced use of omnibus multivariate techniques, stricter control of type I error rates by using single rather than multiple tests, employing "families" rather than a multiplicity of hypotheses, the avoidance of stepwise statistical procedures and testing of hypotheses not against a difference of zero but rather against a predetermined interval.

STRUCTURE OF THE REPORT AND USE OF THE *DIAGNOSTIC AND STATISTICAL MANUAL OF MENTAL DISORDERS*

This report considers treatments for major categories of psychological disorder in separate sections. These disorders are classified using the *Diagnostic and Statistical Manual of Mental Disorders*. The most recent revision of this manual (DSM-IV; American Psychiatric Association,

1994) represents an advance on earlier versions of the manual, as well as introducing comparability with the forthcoming revision of the major alternative classificatory scheme, the *International Classification of Diseases and Related Health Problems* (*ICD-10*). However, because of inevitable publication lags, most of the studies we review base their diagnostic criteria on the *Diagnostic and Statistical Manual of Mental Disorders*, third edition, revised (DSM-III-R; American Psychiatric Association, 1987) or in some cases earlier versions of this manual. In order to indicate the categories of disorders researched in each section, full DSM-IV descriptions are given together with a description of significant changes to these definitions from DSM-III-R.

The DSM system classifies patients on five axes. Axis I represents clinical syndromes, Axis II, developmental disorders and personality disorders; Axis III, physical disorders and conditions; Axis IV, severity of psychosocial stressors; and Axis V, a global assessment of functioning. This report largely considers Axis I and Axis II disorders.

There have been many criticisms of the behavior-based descriptive approach DSM represents. A number of authors point to the philosophical roots of DSM in logical positivism and operationalism (Millon, 1987; Schwartz & Wiggins, 1986; Schwartz, 1991), by now a discredited epistemological approach (Leahey, 1980). Leading philosophers of science (e.g., Polanyi, 1958; Kuhn, 1970) have demonstrated that scientific observations cannot be independent of theory to the extent that they represent theoretical constructs, and obtain their meaning through their placement in a network of concepts. Thus an atheoretical classification may be an epistemological oxymoron (Millon, 1987). In fact, many have pointed out that the operationalism of DSM favors behavioral and biological orientations (Frances et al., 1990) over other, potentially equally useful perspectives in the realm of psychopathology (Jacobsen & Cooper, 1993). In particular, there is a more or less complete absence of psychodynamic considerations in diagnosis, such as unconscious mental processes and defenses (Shapiro, 1991).

A related problem is an implicit shift of focus from the etiological perspective of many clinicians to the phenomenological/behavioral orientation of administrators and researchers. For example, clinicians frequently encounter, and are asked to treat, adult sequelae of childhood deprivation and, increasingly frequently, childhood abuse. Although there are many common etiological features in such cases, their diagnoses may be diverse, ranging across anxiety, depression, eating disorder, posttraumatic stress disorder, and severe personality disorder (or combinations of these diagnoses). On this basis it could be argued that an etiological orientation would be more appropriate, at least insofar as it may better define both technique and expected outcome. On the other hand, it is well known that the outcome of any single stressful event is mediated by a large number of intervening variables, which may ultimately be of greater significance in determining outcome than the original stressful event itself (Rutter, 1994). An approach based on diagnosis assumes that these mediating variables play a part in determining the kinds of clinical presentation that confront the clinician, and thus may be an equally appropriate method for summarizing clinical knowledge regarding the individual. Nonetheless, readers should be aware that diagnostic labels have a tendency to create an illusion of homogeneity which fails to mirror the complexity of clinical work. Any particular diagnosis may have a wide variety of clinical implications, depending on the circumstances of its presentation. For example, depression immediately postpartum may call for a different clinical strategy from a chronic depression intensifying in midlife, a level of complexity not adequately addressed by current psychiatric nosology.

In response to this issue of complexity, some orientations—particularly psychodynamic—consider that "suitability for therapy" is more important than formal diagnosis when considering which patients to accept into therapy. This leads psychodynamic therapists to eschew diagnostic criteria in favor of structural or meta-psychological considerations relevant to treatability.

There are some empirical data to back this claim. For example, Piper et al. (1994) report that individuals with high scores on tests of psychological mindedness and quality of object relationships were more likely to benefit from psychodynamic psychotherapy, for a range of disorders. Findings such as these may be regarded as implying that patients should be grouped not according to descriptive criteria but by underlying psychic mechanisms. However, we see both theoretical and practical problems with this position, because the issue of suitability is nested within a particular psychodynamic context, as indeed would be the case with any other therapy when considering which patients are likely to respond to treatment. Thus, family therapists would generally recognize that their approach may be ill-equipped to tackle family systems in intense and violent conflict. Pharmacotherapy may be undermined by a patient's refusal to comply with medical recommendations. Suitability, in these contexts, clearly does not amount to a generally applicable diagnostic system, but only to a series of pragmatic considerations concerning the application of a theoretical orientation.

Considerations of suitability for any one theoretical approach cannot be considered to be of the same order as a reliable and valid system of classification for disorders, whatever the limitations of that classification with regard to specific orientations. In fact, where such studies have been performed, diagnostic considerations were found to be important predictors for suitability for psychodynamic treatment (Target & Fonagy, 1994a,b; Baruch, 1995). In favor of DSM are, in particular, its operationalized diagnostic criteria (with concomitant enhancement of reliability) which, together with its multiaxial system, provide a clear conceptual structure for looking at state–trait interactions as well as social and biological influences on psychopathology. This represents a major advance over previous psychiatric diagnostic systems. Its primary value in the present context is in the vast impact it has had on mental health research worldwide including, naturally, psychotherapy research (Wilson, 1993). Since most recent research on outcome employs DSM as the basis for patient selection, there is some congruence between the structure of the report and the research it reviews. Research findings that precede DSM are difficult to interpret precisely because observations about therapeutic effectiveness are hard to link to specific patient populations, which leads to insurmountable problems in the generalization of results from such studies. We recognize the limitations of DSM, but find ourselves unable to identify a suitable alternative framework that would meet our objective of providing a scientific context for recommendations regarding psychotherapy practice and training.

LIMITATIONS OF THIS REVIEW

Methodological Quality of Research Studies

In this chapter we have detailed the many issues relating to the methodology underpinning research trials. In carrying out our review, we note that the quality of studies is improving as the research community recognizes the standards to which they need to aspire. However, many of the trials we review do have methodological problems—some minor, some more serious. We have made a decision, largely on the grounds of limitations of space, not to identify or itemize the deficiencies of each study, except where these seem especially relevant. Instead, we rely on the discussion contained in this and the next chapter to alert readers to the general problems likely to be contained in studies, and trust that they will examine individual studies and reviews where these seem particularly pertinent to their practice or interests.

The Range of Disorders

Readers of this review will note a number of omissions. Because of limitations of time and resources, we have had to exclude discussion of a number of disorders—treatments within the health psychology setting (psychophysiological disorders), obesity, treatment for marital difficulties, substance abuse other than alcohol dependence, forensic problems, and treatments for people with learning disabilities.

We realize that coverage of these areas would undoubtedly make our contribution more valuable. However, it is our view that providing a thorough report on a limited number of disorders will be more valuable than a less comprehensive review of a wider range of mental health problems and techniques for managing them. Our focus has been on difficulties most commonly encountered within psychotherapy service settings; many of the disorders omitted are most commonly treated within specialist settings.

Literature Covered

Our review is heavily dominated by English-language journals, most frequently reporting trials carried out in the United States. Unfortunately, we had no resources for translating non-English-language papers. We are aware of a substantial body of literature (from France, Germany, and some Scandinavian countries in particular) relevant to this review but inaccessible to us. This naturally raises questions about the degree to which our report is culturally representative. We have no definitive response to this question. However, a number of the trials we have reviewed were performed in European centers, but have been published in English-language journals. Informal comparison between these and equivalent English or American studies we have examined suggests that findings from outcome studies are generalizable across national boundaries, despite the apparent diversity of cultures covered by the research.

Contrasts of Psychopharmacological and Psychological Treatments

Many of the conditions we discuss are commonly treated using both medication and psychological interventions. Many researchers have contrasted the relative benefits of these treatments, both alone and in combination, and we consider these studies at a number of points in this review. Our comments regarding medication are based on these contrasts; it is beyond our brief to provide definitive statements regarding the benefits of psychopharmacology, nor are we qualified to do so. In chapters discussing conditions where medication is particularly relevant to treatment, we have tried to indicate sources of further information for the interested reader.

The Problem of Comorbidity

Throughout this review we find that comorbidity of Axis I and Axis II disorders is extensive. Both clinicians and researchers are increasingly recognizing the importance of comorbidity in the application of therapeutic technique and its impact on efficacy. As noted by Clarkin and Kendall (1992), there is irony in the fact that as awareness of this challenge to the efficacy of therapy grows (and is becoming the focus for research), the pressures of resource management dictate shorter treatments. It is clear from evidence we review that comorbidity will impact on treatment delivery, usually resulting in more difficult therapies with poorer outcomes (Grunhaus, 1988; Coryell & Noyes, 1988; Coryell et al., 1988). Comorbid conditions are also likely to lead to poorer end-state functioning, because at the end of treatment patients may continue to exhibit symptomatology related to the untreated comorbid condition—an example of which would be panic disorder with comorbid generalized anxiety disorder (Brown & Barlow, 1992).

This fact makes the relationship between diagnosis and treatment planning more complex than might be indicated by research we have reviewed, and certainly makes it unlikely that data from trials can be transferred directly into the clinical context. For example, existing manualized treatments used in clinical trials that focus on a specific disorder are likely to pay little attention to comorbid conditions.

Patients with comorbid conditions are particularly likely to be seen in specialist mental health settings. They are also likely to constitute the majority of patients receiving long-term therapy or multiple episodes of short-term therapy. This creates a major problem, in that recommendations regarding appropriate treatment (e.g., their modality and length) must be considered in the context of patients who present with multiple and possibly changing diagnoses. We are uncertain whether appropriate treatment length is best considered as an additive or multiplicative function of the number of diagnoses, or if particular combinations of diagnoses may be better treated as separate disorders from the point of view of psychotherapeutic treatment.

Different therapeutic orientations take very different views of this problem, and it may be impossible to arrive at a formulation of comorbidity that is genuinely independent of the theoretical orientation of particular practitioners. Some Axis II diagnoses, such as borderline personality disorder, are so constructed as to inevitably include multiple

Axis I disorders—such as depression and anxiety. No clinician would mistake problems of depression in such individuals with those presented by a patient without significant Axis II pathology. Thus the applicability of findings from randomized controlled trials fails even at the level of face validity with such patients. Given the current state of research-based knowledge, caution should be shown in generalizing research results to those with comorbid Axis I disorders and severe deficits in personality functioning.

Biased Representation of Theoretical Orientations in the Research Literature

In the previous chapter we identified the range of commonly practiced psychological therapies. However, there is a marked variation in the extent to which these differing orientations have been subjected to systematic evaluation. The consequence of this fact is that, relative to the frequency with which they are employed, certain orientations—most particularly psychodynamic therapy—are underrepresented in this review.

Treatment trials of psychodynamic treatments have been particularly constrained by:

- An absence of a quantitative research tradition within this orientation
- The related fact that appropriately trained clinicians are rarely available to participate in research trials
- The expense and difficulty of mounting trials of long-term treatment
- The absence of appropriate measures to encompass the more ambitious aims of these treatments

It would be inaccurate to claim that no research on the efficacy of psychodynamic therapy has been carried out, but it should be acknowledged that it is limited in volume. Svartberg and Stiles (1991) present a meta-analytic review of 19 studies of short-term psychodynamic psychotherapy. Crits-Christoph's (1992) meta-analysis reviews 11 trials of brief psychodynamic psychotherapy. Curiously, there is little overlap between the studies sampled in these reviews. It should also be noted that Crits-Christoph's (1992) review inappropriately includes data from the National Institute of Mental Health study of treatments for depression,[3] where psychodynamic treatments were not employed.[4]

Both reviews indicate that, on the whole, brief psychodynamic psychotherapy shows greater efficacy than waiting-list control, though they differ in their judgment of its efficacy relative to alternative treatments. Svartberg and Stiles (1991) suggest that psychodynamic treatments perform less well than alternative therapies (usually cognitive-behavior therapy); Crits-Christoph (1992) finds them equally effective. However, both reviewers acknowledge that these conclusions are based on a relatively small number of studies and that firmer conclusions await a larger research base.

Some individual studies do suggest that brief psychodynamic treatments show efficacy. For example, Thompson et al. (1987) have shown brief psychodynamic therapy to be equally effective to behavioral therapies in the treatment of depression in older people. Shapiro et al. (1994) demonstrated psychodynamic therapy to be equally effective to cognitive therapy in the treatment of outpatient depression. Woody et al. (1990) found that psychodynamic therapy added to the benefits of drug counseling with opiate addicts, and a further two studies (Piper et al., 1990; Winston et al., 1991) showed it to be superior to a waiting-list control group for heterogenous patient groups. However, many trials tend to be small in size, do not address themselves to specific diagnostic groups or clinical problems, use nonstandard measures of clinical outcome, and examine the efficacy of quite different procedures. Thus, the amount of data available for examining the efficacy of psychodynamic treatment for specific disorders is very limited indeed.

There are a number of approaches taken by psychodynamic therapists to address the skew inherent in the research literature and its corollary, the lack of research representative of actual clinical practice. The first is to rely on clinical intuition and judgment. There is a feeling, prevalent among clinicians of all orientations, that their clinical experience, rather than research findings, guides their clinical practice (Morrow-Bradley & Elliot, 1986). This may be a realistic perception in terms of research on psychotherapeutic process, but it does not seem to us either pertinent or viable as a response to the absence of outcome research. No single clinician can accumulate experience sufficient in quan-

---

[3] Reviewed in Chapter 4.

[4] This inclusion is justified on the grounds that interpersonal psychotherapy (IPT) has at least some theoretical roots in psychoanalysis. However, it is clear that its proponents do not view it as a psychodynamic therapy (Weissman & Markowitz, 1994).

tity to ensure generalizability. A second strategy, commonly used to describe outcomes in psychodynamic journals, is the use of case reports. Although of great clinical interest, these cannot be used as evidence for effectiveness, since they rely on a small group of clinicians and nonrandomly sampled patients, which necessarily limits the possibility of generalization to other settings and other therapists. Ultimately, and perhaps unfortunately, in the absence of data, clinicians tend to rely on their intuition, which when put to empirical test tends to lack both reliability and validity (Garb, 1989).

There have been objections to randomized controlled trials for long-term treatment because of the ethical implications of withholding treatment from needy individuals for a long period. In our view there is no special ethical problem presented by RCTs for psychodynamic psychotherapy, particularly since the limited availability of these services implies that very few of the individuals who may need such treatments would ever receive them. Furthermore, maintenance therapy is an effective control for most long-term interventions (e.g., Frank et al., 1991). We do, however, see an ethical problem in administering a treatment to patients without firm evidence of the absence of negative effects. Open trials are not an appropriate alternative (for reasons considered above) since they fail to avoid many of the problems associated with RCTs while adding the ambiguity inherent in nonrandom assignment to treatment groups.

Thus, while we can see that the absence of evidence of efficacy cannot and must not be equated with absence of evidence of effectiveness, this scientific review can only draw conclusions from the evidence available. It cannot use different evidential criteria for different orientations. In the absence of evidence, broader organizational and less formal considerations may be used to guide policy, but these are beyond the scope of the present review.

Cost–Benefit Analysis

We have not systematically considered economic analyses as they relate to the psychological therapies. This issue has been given detailed attention considered in a recent report commissioned by the English Department of Health (Healy & Knapp, 1995).

However, it is relevant to note that research on the efficacy of psychotherapy only rarely addresses the economic impacts of interventions, particularly with regard to their wider, societal impacts (Krupnick & Pincus, 1992). Measures of outcome employed by researchers are seldom useful for econometric analysis, and there is as yet no consensus on the pertinent variables that would form the basis for cost-effectiveness or cost–benefit analyses. Reaching a consensus is made more difficult not only because of the differing languages of psychotherapy researchers and economists, but also because any such analysis would need to include data drawn from a wider perspective than that of the consulting room or hospital. While it is inevitable that this endeavor will be both complex and controversial, the costs to the community of mental health problems per se are demonstrable (e.g., Katon, 1991; Stroudemire et al., 1986).

Central to questions of cost is the concept of therapeutic effort (Newman & Howard, 1986), which addresses the issue of both the type and amount of treatment required to restore functioning. This concept encompasses (1) the dosage of therapy required, (2) the degree to which therapy requires resources such as hospital care or additional staff input (termed restrictiveness), and (3) the cumulative cost of resources involved in care, such as the degree of skill required of therapists or the material resources they consume.

Of these, dosage is the most easily measured. There is evidence that patients exposed to more treatment derive more benefit than those receiving less therapy (Orlinsky et al., 1994), though it is less clear what the optimum treatment might be for any different condition. Howard et al. (1986) conducted a meta-analysis of 15 trials comprising data from 2,431 patients, suggesting that, for outpatients, 52 once-weekly sessions provided a maximum effective dosage. At this point 85% of patients were improved; beyond it there was point of diminishing returns. Data from this study also indicate that by the eighth session 50% of patients are measurably improved, and that this increases only to 75% by the end of 6 months. Although this suggests that the measurable rate of change is fastest in the earlier stages of therapy, there is still room for debate about the point at which optimal change has occurred.

Further data from Orlinsky and Howard (1986) indicates, as might be expected, that different client groups respond differentially, with, for example, depression and anxiety disorders responding faster than personality problems. Kopta et al. (1992; cited in Lambert & Bergin, 1994) examined the dose–effect relationship in relation to different types of symptoms, finding that, for example, chronic distress was alleviated in around 80% of patients by the 52nd session, whereas characterological symptoms improved more slowly, with only 60% of patients responding significantly by the 52nd session.

Techniques for assessing the impact of therapeutic dosage in individual clients are developing, though these are currently more apparent in research than in clinical settings. Howard et al. (1993) present a model that permits the tracking of therapeutic change in the areas of remoralization, resolution of symptoms, and restoration and rehabilitation of functioning. The model appears powerful in that case tracking clearly identifies different and reliable patterns of change associated with successful and unsuccessful therapies. This has the potential to provide feedback relevant to decision making about likely outcomes at relatively early stages of therapy.

Assessing the cumulative costs of therapy can be complex; Newman and Howard (1986) discuss the use of procedures to assess the cumulative episode cost. Some costs will relate to patient characteristics, such as the likelihood of missed appointments or the need for more restrictiveness in treatment. Secondly, it may be the case that some patients require more skilled (and therefore more expensive) therapists, whereas others could be treated under supervision by workers with less expertise. Direct contact time will vary depending on whether patients are seen individually or in groups, and the need for indirect contact will vary according both to the type of therapy and the needs of the patient. Finally, all these costs will need to be related to outcome; it should be clear that being cost-efficient is not equivalent to being cost-effective. A brief but ineffective treatment is likely to be less cost-effective than one that has greater cumulative costs but better outcomes. Choice of treatment will therefore reflect the balancing of costs against outcomes.

Although there is little research that directly examines these issues, there are the beginnings of a database on which to build such work. Krupnick and Pincus (1992) make a number of suggestions about variables that should be included in trials to facilitate economic analysis. Future trials of psychotherapy will inevitably have to consider cost and benefit in relation to one another.

CHAPTER 3

Psychotherapy Research, Funding, and Evidence-Based Practice

ANTHONY ROTH
PETER FONAGY
GLENYS PARRY

HEALTH SERVICE DELIVERY SYSTEMS AND RESEARCH ON PSYCHOTHERAPY EFFECTIVENESS

Research on psychotherapy effectiveness takes place, and its findings are exploited, within the context of a health service delivery system. Although there are major differences in how psychotherapy services are funded and provided internationally, concerns about the accountability of health care professionals and the costs and effectiveness of psychotherapy are universal (Miller & Magruder, 1996). A comparison of the common issues of the American and British health systems illustrates this. In both countries, there have been significant changes in how health services are delivered over the past 20 years.

Between 1967 and 1980, the proportion of the U.S. population using mental health services increased from 1% to 10%, with outpatient services accounting for this; the proportion of mental health reimbursements relating to outpatient services rose from less than 1% to 12% in the same time period (Klerman, 1983). Government and employers pay for 80% of health-related expenditure (Austad & Berman, 1991), and these interests, with the health insurance industry, have been increasingly concerned to contain mental health costs. In 1978, the subcommittee on health of the U.S. Senate Finance Committee heard evidence relating to expanding coverage of mental health under Medicare–Medicaid programs. Senators were surprised at the amount of disagreement among mental health professionals about who was adequately trained to provide what types of care and under what conditions. There was even disagreement about whether psychotherapy had any positive benefit at all (Inouye, 1983). The Finance Committee asked the Federal Office of Technology Assessment (OTA) to evaluate which of 130 known psychotherapies were effective or ineffective. The OTA report was published in 1980 and found evidence that psychotherapy generically was effective; its outcomes could not be accounted for by spontaneous remission or placebo effects (Office of Technology Assessment, 1980). However, psychotherapy research was not able to indicate which therapies could be recommended for specific problems, which is what was needed from the insurers' perspective (Banta & Saxe, 1983). Senators Matsunaga and Inouye proposed a legislative mechanism whereby an independent, interdisciplinary commission including clinical and scientific experts would decide on which therapies would be reimbursable under Federal insurance plans. The proposal was modeled on Federal requirements for safety and efficacy of drugs and was "a source of discomfort and controversy amongst practitioners" (DeLeon et al., 1983), not only because clinicians felt their own practices threatened. Strupp (1986) expressed the view of many psychotherapists when he wrote that the emphasis of policy makers and third-party payers on safety and efficacy promotes a medical drug metaphor which fundamentally misrepresents the purpose and methods of psychotherapy.

Although the Matsunaga/Inouye proposal foundered, the issues are enduring. A variety of health maintenance organizations and other models of managed health care have proliferated in the United States and mental health care is included by a Federal statute requiring an HMO to offer short-term outpatient mental health evaluation and crisis intervention services as well as 60 days of inpatient psychiatric care (DeLeon et al., 1985). Professional responses have been to provide pragmatic, brief interventions and to seek more cost-efficient ways of treating chronically mentally and emotionally disabled patients in prepaid health care systems (Austad & Berman, 1991). Whether or not psychotherapy researchers or clinicians approve, research evidence now influences which forms of therapy are reimbursable for which presenting conditions. Concurrent reimbursement review causes clinicians deep concern about their ability to provide optimal treatment (Gabbard et al., 1991) and psychotherapy practices may be particularly vulnerable (Cummings, 1987).

The National Health Service (NHS) in Britain provides health services to the public free of charge at the point of delivery, funded through government revenue. Health care, including mental health care, is provided by family physicians (known as general practitioners) and staff they employ, and by NHS hospital and community trusts. Despite a different infrastructure for funding, the themes of containing costs and ensuring clinical effectiveness are just as salient within the British NHS (see Parry, 1996). Recent changes to the funding and management structures of the NHS have led to increased scrutiny of psychotherapy services. Local health authorities act as "purchasers" of health care and are charged with the responsibility of assessing the needs of the local population and allocating resources on behalf of the public to achieve the best services for the lowest cost. Managers of NHS services also strive to increase the volume of clinical activity to meet contractual targets. Most recently, some general practitioners have been afforded a portion of government revenue to purchase these services on behalf of their patients. These "fund-holding" doctors have started to exert considerable influence as third-party payers for mental health services in general and psychotherapy services in particular.

These inevitable pressures to examine value for money and cost-effectiveness have led to the debate that took place in the United States in the early 1980s being recapitulated in Britain. Health authorities are beginning to question the existing pattern of resource investment in trying provide optimum noninstitutional health and social care for people with severe and enduring mental illness living in community settings. There are worries that scarce resources have been appropriated for less disabling conditions (Patmore & Weaver, 1991) and that psychotherapy services are sometimes seen as providing expert help to those with mild difficulties while those with more severe and complex mental health needs are relatively neglected. There are also concerns about efficacy and cost effectiveness of psychotherapy, and some U.K. health authorities are beginning to examine more closely the types and lengths of psychological treatments they purchase.

THE MEANING OF RESEARCH
TO DIFFERENT STAKEHOLDERS

Clinicians and funders have different concerns, interests, and needs, and they view research from contrasting standpoints. Clinicians sometimes complain that research fails to capture the complexity of the clinical situation, where permutations of diagnosis, psychological characteristics, and social circumstance make the choice of treatment a complex decision-making process. Each patient could be seen as presenting a unique puzzle, rendering research evidence that suggests matching treatment to diagnosis irrelevant, because it is seen as oversimplistic. In contrast, those paying for psychological therapy would like to identify treatments that are both effective and cost–effective, and from this standpoint it is unhelpful to be told that planning should be constructed on the basis of each individual case. As research evidence begins to be collated, there is a temptation to turn to these findings as though they provide a definitive answer, without noting the cautions researchers almost universally attach to them. Where payers yield to this temptation in the design of managed care programs and directives regarding first-line treatments, the reaction of many clinicians is to become suspicious of moves toward (or demands for) evidence-based practice. This adversarial process threatens to set those paying for care against those providing it, and indeed, providers against researchers. In this context, there are clear perils along the path of applying research findings to clinical practice. On the one side, the risk that practitioners reject psychotherapy research out of hand; on the other, the possibility that purchasers embrace it uncritically, leading to a cookbook approach to planning.

UNCRITICAL APPLICATIONS OF RESEARCH: IMPLICATIONS FOR INNOVATION IN THE PSYCHOTHERAPIES

In this chapter, and at many points in this book, we detail our concerns about the limitations of the research literature, and note the caveats of most researchers about their own work. Some may feel impatient with this caution, and consider that enough is now known to permit authoritative statements about appropriate psychotherapy provision. However, we feel that overconfidence at this point carries with it the risk not only of penalizing underresearched (but possibly effective) therapies, but also of freezing therapeutic innovation.

The last 40 years have been a period of rapid growth in the field of psychotherapy, during which we have learned a great deal about techniques that may be powerful in combating mental health problems. From some perspectives, the very richness of this development represents a major obstacle for rational health care—there are over 400 different named therapies, which can be seen as variations on the basic themes within a smaller number of families of theories and techniques. The vast majority of these "brand name" therapies are totally unevaluated. However, it is doubtful if such creativity would have been possible had there been in place a rigorous scientific gating mechanism to ask the question, "Is your new therapeutic orientation really necessary?" Such a challenge is far from inappropriate; outcome research challenges the assumption that each of these approaches is uniquely beneficial. Process–outcome research, especially "dismantling" studies, has the potential to clarify the degree to which an innovative technique is truly distinctive, or best seen as part of an already established family of therapies. However, a premature demand for rigor may discourage clinical curiosity; clinicians often work toward diversification and elaboration of technique in an attempt to meet the needs of particular patients. Sometimes this results in genuine and generalizable innovation, sometimes in applications appropriate only to a single case. The critical task is to establish systems capable of distinguishing between these two outcomes—but ones that also manage the tension between clinical creativity and the need for demonstrable outcomes.

The history of clinical practice over the past 20–30 years suggests that this is not an empty, abstract point. Most psychotherapists recognize that clinical practice has seen major developments in this time. Perhaps few would have seen the light of day had overenthusiastic purchasers constrained treatments to those available and validated during the 1960s; clinicians would have been restricted to a narrow range of behavioral techniques, effective but of limited application. In fact, cognitive therapy has greatly extended the potential scope and potency of behavior therapy, and even those relatively few practitioners who decry what is often referred to as the "cognitive revolution" recognize the enormous stimulus to practice, research, and innovation arising from these newer developments. For us this represents both a powerful caution against premature foreclosure on therapy provision, and a model of practice; cognitive therapy has developed in the context of a strong commitment to research, a factor that might also be relevant to its current status.

THE ROLE OF CLINICAL JUDGMENT IN RESEARCH AND CLINICAL PRACTICE

In many respects the correspondence between the aims of researchers and clinicians—to shed light on questions about best practice—is more apparent than real. Their activities *en route* to this aim are not the same, and the temptation to consider them isomorphic can quickly lead to confusion. It is important to bear in mind that these parties adopt the methods that best address their particular lines of inquiry, and hence each field is constructed and equipped to answer differing questions—one through clinical psychological therapy, the other through the use of systems aimed at testing hypotheses.

The priority of researchers undertaking clinical trials is to show underlying causal relationships between improvement and intervention. The researcher requires tight controls on the way the treatment is structured and administered, the way the sample is selected, and how outcomes are assessed. By contrast, the clinician's priority is usually more pragmatic, concerned less with the demonstration of which component of a complex intervention is responsible for change than with achieving change itself.

This disjunction of priorities means that the manner in which therapy is conducted within research trials may differ from therapy as conducted in the clinical setting. To take one example, research trials boost inferential clarity by trying to ensure that treatments adhere closely to treatment protocols or manuals. In research trials, greater adherence can sometimes be shown to relate to improved clinical efficacy (e.g., Frank et al., 1991; O'Malley, 1988; Foley, 1987; for an exception see Strupp et al., 1988, discussed below). An uncritical reading of this work could lead to the erroneous conclusion that greater effectiveness would be achieved simply by insisting that therapists adhere to a manual. However, in the research cited above the capacity of the therapist to achieve adherence depended, at least to some extent, on the patient's orientation to and willingness to accept the technique. The same therapist sometimes carried out the therapy "well," sometimes less so.

Though it is a truism to state that psychological therapy requires the active participation of the patient, this fact may sometimes be overlooked. It should be unsurprising to discover that carrying out a therapy "as planned" requires a coordination of effort between patient and therapist. A number of patient characteristics are associated with better outcomes, such as their capacity for thinking about their problems, their readiness for therapy, their motivation, and their general adjustment (Garfield, 1994). Undoubtedly some patients are more responsive to treatment than others. However, the skill of the good therapist may lie in his or her ability to detect obstacles that would make it difficult to implement therapy—in other words, a capacity to monitor and maintain the therapeutic alliance.

The alliance is often referred to as a common factor across therapies. Though this is undoubtedly the case (e.g., Horvath & Symonds, 1991), most recent models of the alliance (e.g., Gaston, 1991) note that it is more than a reflection of a bond between patient and therapist; it also involves a series of technical factors which are related to the implementation of the particular therapy—not only how to achieve this implementation, but in what areas. In this context the therapist's ability to apply clinical judgment and to formulate become critical, and the importance of these factors to successful outcome is recognized across the spectrum of therapeutic orientations. Thus, Persons (1989, 1991) has criticized research into cognitive therapy because of its neglect of case formulation in favor of manualization, with the attendant risk that therapy becomes formulaic (and by implication less effective). More empirically, Strupp et al. (1988) monitored the progress of trainees in psychodynamic therapy, finding that though they showed increased technical adherence, they also showed decreased efficacy. Though at first sight this result is surprising, it appears that as trainees focused on becoming "good" therapists (implementing the therapy well), they seemed to neglect the alliance.

Therapeutic effectiveness therefore appears to rest on more than narrow technical competence. There is a risk that the technical sophistication of research trials, which demand clear causal inference, can overregulate therapy content and underemphasize the freedom of action available to individual clinicians. This could widen further the gap between clinical trials and clinical practice in terms of a relative neglect of clinical judgment. Paradoxically, the task of applying research findings may call for precisely this capacity on the part of the clinician—in other words, the ability to see the pertinence of specific discoveries to the individual case.

To summarize, achieving evidence-based practice in the psychotherapies is not simple. Basing payment decisions on research evidence of efficacy is an apparently straightforward and justifiable process but one that needs to be undertaken with care if it is not to do more harm than good. In particular there are dangers in funding, purchasing, or reimbursing for only a limited range of treatment "packages" which meet a stated efficacy criterion in relation to certain specified diagnostic groups. The most obvious concern with this funding pattern is that it overlooks the very high rates of comorbidity found in clinical settings (e.g., Kessler et al., 1994) as well as the many other important variables known to be helpful in predicting which psychotherapeutic approach is likely to be of most benefit.

There is the further danger that in a system where public sector or insurance-based funding is the determining influence on psychotherapy service delivery and research, overprescriptive purchasing or reimbursement could stifle innovation and development. As noted above, one has only to imagine the negative consequences of having implemented such a policy in the 1960s.

We also take seriously the possibility that those reimbursing for therapy or commissioning services preempt, through funding decisions, clinical judgments on, for example, treatment length and modality. Ironically, rather than encouraging clinical assessment and formulation to be based on research evidence and fostering a model of evidence-based practice, such a policy could actually delay its development.

THE CASE FOR UNDERRESEARCHED THERAPIES

This research review could be seen as providing backing for the claim that there is no good efficacy evidence, one way or the other, for many clinical practices—for example, many psychoanalytic interventions and the eclectic approach, which characterizes much psychotherapeutic treatment in practice. Although outcomes of eclectic practice have been underresearched, there is good evidence for the importance of nonspecific, pantheoretical factors. It is possible to argue (e.g., Goldfried, 1995) that the difference in effectiveness of therapies may lie in the differential extent to which they allow common curative factors to come into operation rather than in the extent to which specific factors are brought to bear. Where the appropriate research has not yet been done, the absence of evidence for efficacy is not evidence of ineffectiveness, and valuable approaches that offer appropriate and clinically effective care should not perish for lack of funding.

This argument has particular force in relation to psychodynamic therapies which, while widely practiced, are hard to justify solely on the basis of existing outcome research. For example, two meta-analyses[1] (Crits-Cristoph, 1992; Svartberg & Stiles, 1991) appear to suggest that psychodynamic therapies have at best equal, and at worst less, efficacy than cognitive-behavioral therapies, particularly in relation to some diagnostic categories, such as depression. In response, psychodynamic therapists would probably present two arguments against the relevance of these findings. First, their priority is to address the needs of the patient through a formulation of their difficulties that includes symptoms (and therefore diagnoses) only insofar as symptoms are seen as expressing underlying pathology. Secondly, and consequently, because their work transcends narrow diagnostic categories, psychodynamic therapists are particularly well placed to address cases characterized by complexity and comorbidity.

In our judgment, the particular value of psychodynamic formulations is the degree to which they locate the present functioning of a patient in the context of the individual's life experiences. In contrast (at least initially), cognitive-behavioral therapy took a relatively narrow focus in formulating patient's difficulties. Increasingly, however, theoreticians within this framework recognize that the way patients learn to represent their sense of self and knowledge about the world is often relevant to their symptoms and hence to treatment (e.g., Persons, 1989; Safran & Segal, 1990). These workers attempt to produce a model that is recognizably derived from cognitive therapy, but which includes formulations of sufficient breadth and complexity to account for and manage comorbidity. In doing so, both theorists introduce concepts derived from psychodynamic thinking, such as noting the importance of cognitive processing out of the patient's conscious awareness.

---

[1] These meta-analyses, and their limitations, are discussed further in the next chapter.

It is ironic that well-researched therapies are beginning to modify their practice by incorporating one of the strengths of psychodynamic therapy—a well-constructed, rigorous formulation. There may be a further irony in the fact there are an increasing number of systems for producing replicable psychodynamic formulations (e.g., Luborsky & Crits-Christoph, 1990; Perry et al., 1989; Horowitz, 1989; Horowitz et al., 1989), with good evidence for their reliability and construct validity (Luborsky et al., 1994) and for a link between the capacity of a therapist to utilize these formulations accurately and outcome (Piper et al., 1991, 1993).

Some may see this useful cross-fertilization simply as a process whereby a newer therapy takes the best from and thereby supplants an older method. Alternatively, it may be prudent to bear in mind that one reason for this borrowing of technique and method is the development and application of cognitive methods to people who do not easily fit diagnostic categories, or whose presentations are themselves highly complex (e.g., patients with severe personality disorders). As such, these service-driven demands may give rise to more call on the expertise and methods of psychodynamic therapy, which is in many ways adapted to the needs of precisely this type of patient. An illustrative case example may be useful here.

> Ms. A, a 23-year-old woman, was referred for psychodynamic therapy following unsuccessful attempts at both family therapy and cognitive-behavioral therapy. There was an immediate requirement to deal with her chronic mismanagement of her diabetes; she had over half a dozen hospital admissions for ketoacidosis in the past year and refused to administer her insulin injections even though she was fully aware of her need. She was severely depressed, bulimic, parasuicidal, and self-harmed using a razor blade, usually on her legs. Her doctors were greatly concerned for her safety, although she refused both inpatient treatment and medication to help her with the depression. In her therapy the early loss of her mother at the age of 7 became a major theme, as well as the serious physical deformity of her sister. She came to recognize that through constantly keeping herself close to death (by mismanaging her illness) she was protecting herself from fully mourning the loss of her mother and attempting to live out an unconscious belief that the only way to be loved was to be physically ill. The achievement of this understanding helped her come to terms with her illness, and both her diabetes and her bulimia quickly improved. She found a sexual partner, continued her university education, and had no further problems during a prolonged follow-up of 4 years (Fonagy & Moran, 1993).

In this case it appears that the perspective of the psychodynamic therapist was helpful. We acknowledge, however, that arguing for the benefits of a particular school of therapy on the basis of a single case is generally unconvincing, because there is no control for simple differences between therapists; for example, had Ms. A's previous therapists been more alert to these underlying factors, they may have achieved a similar outcome with different methods. (More broadly, differences between therapists are known to influence outcomes as much as or even more than the schools they follow [e.g., Luborsky et al., 1985, 1986; Beutler et al., 1994].) Perhaps the most intellectually honest position would be to acknowledge that we cannot be sure that treatment success was based on choice of therapeutic orientation. Equally, however, we cannot be sure that it was not.

This lack of clarity is crucial. While we would argue against preemptive funding on the basis of therapy orientation and outcome research alone, this does not justify the hostility of some psychodynamic therapists to evidence-based practice. Historically psychodynamic therapists have tended to be antipathetic toward scientific investigation on the grounds that the product of such therapy was beyond measurement, or that the changes detected by empirical methods would be so inappropriately unsophisticated as to be not worth collecting. We view this position as demonstrably untenable; there is a growing body of empirically sophisticated high-quality outcome and process–outcome research conducted by a number of research teams. In this book we detail work conducted by (among others) Lester Luborsky, William Piper, Mardi Horowitz, Leonard Horowitz, and Hans Strupp. Even without this research, it would be curious to suggest that *none* of the products of a successful psychodynamic therapy would be measurable. For example, even if the aim of therapy with a depressed patient was to improve functioning rather than symptoms, we might still expect to see a decrease in scores on a depression inventory without this doing damage to the philosophy of the therapy (which might wish to claim success beyond—but still including—symptomatic change). Even if there is an interaction between psychological processes involved in the completion of such inventories and the process of therapy (e.g., an individual in psychodynamic therapy might become more, rather than less, aware of his or her depression), other concurrent measurements should nevertheless reveal therapeutic effects in the domains of, for example, social adaptation, interpersonal relationships, and personality functioning.

To summarize, there is no doubt that the relative paucity of good-quality outcome evidence for psychodynamic therapies hampers arguments for their retention. However, it is beholden on payers to measure carefully what evidence is available. There is little negative evidence to argue against the efficacy of psychodynamic therapies; the major problem is simply one of an absence of studies. On this basis any discussion about the comparative benefits of psychodynamic therapy is effectively rendered into a matter of opinion—a judgment that applies equally to purchasers and practitioners. Until research effort and service evaluations provide us with more data, both parties would be well advised to recognize this fact and to act with appropriate caution.

ACHIEVING EVIDENCE-BASED PSYCHOTHERAPY PRACTICE

Psychotherapy research (particularly outcome research) can only be expected unequivocally to answer a very narrow range of questions. Researchers, practitioners, and purchasers all have different and internally coherent requirements of the literature but sometimes act as if these were the same, rather than overlapping. Research findings cannot be "all things to all people"; we need to recognize research as one part of a process, capable of offering useful insights to all parties.

In this section we suggest a way of resolving the conflict between researchers, funders, and clinicians to the benefit of the patient, by presenting a model (see Figure 1) whose end point is the improvement of patient care, and which tries to locate and integrate the differing domains, interests, and concerns of all stakeholders in psychotherapy provision. The model relates clinical innovation to research and research to evidence-based practice, and locates the role of evidence-based practice in maintaining and improving the quality of a clinician's work.

The key to our approach is to see the relationship of clinical work and research as part of a broader process, one that takes place across time and across settings. The model locates the different phases of development for a therapy, and its workings may be best understood if we imagine how a new clinical idea could come to be widely implemented in clinical practice.

FROM CLINICAL INNOVATION TO RESEARCH

The starting point for our model is the clinician's wish to improve patient care. Observations from clinical practice, sometimes in combination with theoretical development, result in the perfection of techniques or innovation. This can result in new approaches to traditional clinical problems, or the application of therapies to new areas. Two illustrative examples (reviewed in this book) are the development of cognitive-behavioral techniques specifically oriented to the management of panic disorder, and the extension of ideas from cognitive

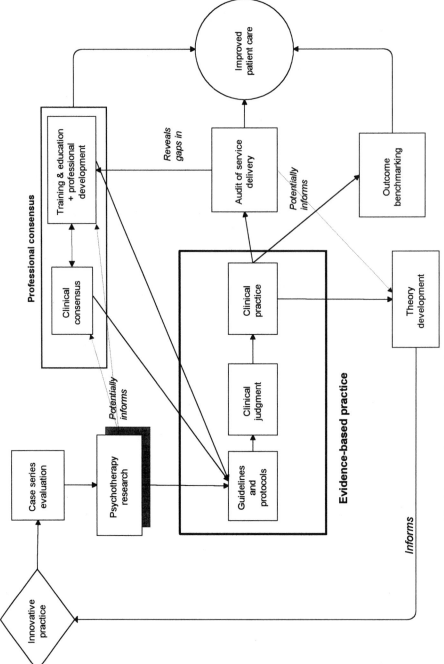

FIGURE 1. Achieving evidence-based practice in the psychological therapies.

therapy to the management of delusions and hallucinations in people with schizophrenia.

CASE SERIES EVALUATION

Although the discovery of new therapeutic approaches ultimately calls for formal evaluation, in practice this is often preceded by a phase of small-scale research aimed at developing the theory and practice of the technique. Salkovskis (1995) describes this process of clinical development in his "hourglass" model, within which initial ideas abut technique are tested through single-case study. Sometimes relatively less stringent methodological criteria are used at this stage, reflecting both the exploratory nature of the work and likely constraints on time and resources. However, once initial development is complete, there is a requirement for research that conforms to the most rigorous standards of enquiry—equivalent to the pinch in the hourglass. Salkovskis (1995) notes that at this point considerations of internal validity take priority, recognizing the fact that this raises questions about generalizability (or external validity) but that these can be answered in a subsequent phase of research which returns to an externally valid form of inquiry. These phases of development are well illustrated in Salkovskis's (1995) account of the development of panic control therapy along the lines of the hourglass model.

FROM RESEARCH TO EVIDENCE-BASED PRACTICE

Evidence-based practice rests largely, but not exclusively, on formal research evaluation, itself a process involving several well-recognized and distinct phases. For example, evaluation frequently starts by comparing a new treatment with an established treatment or a no-treatment control group. Only at a later stage does it involve more refined analysis—for example, varying the components of treatment to see which are necessary and sufficient, examining what new components may be added to enhance the likelihood of change, or exploring how much of any particular component (such as number of sessions or intensity) is optimally required. Even later in the research cycle comes the question, "Which of two reasonably well-optimized treatments is more effective for a particular population?" And later still come questions about patient or therapist characteristics (or other individual-difference factors) which significantly moderate the effectiveness of an approach. Alongside all these lines of inquiry run questions of process—at each of the levels distinguished above we may legitimately ask, "What processes occur within treatment which may contribute to the treatment outcome?"

Clearly this body of research takes considerable time to accumulate, and few if any psychotherapies have been programmatically taken through this full cycle. It would be impractical and indeed unnecessary to insist that research findings should be integrated across all these levels before being applied to clinical guidelines and standards of practice.

In reality, as evidence becomes available it is used for a variety of purposes, and its shortcomings are overcome through interpretation—as is the case in this volume. In recent years a number of professional bodies have interpreted research evidence to provide protocols and standards (e.g., the American Psychiatric Association's [1993] practice guidelines on depression, or the American Psychological Association's identification of a range of empirically validated treatments [Task Force on Promotion and Dissemination of Psychological Procedures, 1995]). The protocols that result have themselves been the subject of debate in part because they are not seen as being sufficiently responsive to the variety of patients' presentations (e.g., Munoz et al., 1994; Rush, 1993; Schulberg & Rush, 1994). Ideally, guidelines should be informed by clinical consensus, to meld training and experience with information gleaned from research findings. Without this, guidelines may be inappropriately narrow and risk so many cases falling outside their range of application that they are seen as clinically unhelpful (hence weakening moves toward achieving the acceptance of evidence-based practice).

The development of research-based clinical guidelines can take place at a number of levels. For example, trainers make decisions on which of a range of potentially important areas of psychotherapeutic expertise would be most relevant to incorporate in prequalification and postqualification training of mental health professionals, and this process is both informed by and has an influence on clinical guidelines. While psychotherapy research evidence might be thought to guide these decisions, in practice there is little evidence that this is the case (Crits-Christoph et al., 1995). There is also no reason why the development of guidelines should not be carried out at local level, through reviews carried out by individual clinical teams or services.

IMPLEMENTING TREATMENT GUIDELINES AND PROTOCOLS: THE ROLE OF CLINICAL JUDGMENT

A clinical guideline could state that a person with a particular diagnosis should receive a particular therapy. Though for some individuals this may be entirely appropriate, ideally the guideline should include patient presentations that may be the "exception to the rule." However, the advantages of widening a protocol has to be balanced against the possibility that directives are diluted to the point where they become inappropriately broad and flexible. The challenge of protocol-driven practice is to ensure that clinicians combine clinical experience and sensitivity together with their knowledge of the research base, recognizing the value and limitation of each resource.

Our view is that clinical protocols represent the default position for treatment, a statement about the treatment most likely to benefit the average patient presenting with a particular principal diagnosable condition. This statement is consonant with the research base, most of whose conclusions are derived from statistics, and by definition therefore rest on findings that are known to apply to perhaps a majority of, but certainly not all, patients in any trial. Against this background, clinicians should be making judgments about whether or not a particular presentation is normative, and if it is not, whether factors can be identified that militate against the recommended treatment.

This judgment can only be made in the context of a clear formulation of the patient's difficulties, and requires the integration of skills training, theoretical knowledge, and past clinical experience, as well as an acquaintance with the research literature. This, in combination with the protocol, allows for the fact that, as Kazdin (1991) has commented, no manual (or indeed protocol) of psychological therapy can ever reflect the complexity of treatment and scope of the exchanges between therapist and patient.

In our view the critical step in this process is the derivation of a formulation of the patient's problems, which the clinician derives through the initial assessment and at subsequent points during the course of an intervention. Formulation is the process of constructing explanations of current and past behavior in terms of mental attributes, beliefs, emotions, goals, and intentions—arriving at a set of hypotheses that offer a psychologically coherent model for the patient's problems, and which suggest the most appropriate mode of intervention.

CHALLENGES TO PROTOCOL-DRIVEN PRACTICE: COMORBIDITY, COMPLEXITY, AND "READINESS FOR TREATMENT"

Clinicians frequently—and rightly—point out that the discrete diagnostic categories used in psychotherapy research are often unrecognizable in clinical practice, where an admixture of comorbidity and complexity is the norm. While there is much to be said for this observation, it is only partially true; the patient mix of most secondary care services is likely to be quite varied in terms of diagnostic clarity, complexity, and chronicity. Nonetheless, there is evidence (discussed in the body of this book) that these factors are likely to influence both the outcome and the difficulty of treatment, and their impact needs to be considered as a part of service planning. By design, research trials underestimate the impact of factors often seen in clinical practice, where patients may be poorly motivated, be suffering severe social stress, have few social and economic resources, and so on. How might these elements be conceptualized to achieve balanced and realistic treatment planning?

There are a number of integrative pantheoretical models of psychotherapy (e.g., Frank, 1961; Prochaska, 1984; Mahrer, 1989). Howard et al.'s (1995) model is particularly helpful because its description of patients' progression through therapy is derived empirically. In essence the model suggests that all successful psychological therapies are characterized by the stages of remoralization, remediation, and rehabilitation. The process of beginning therapy is seen as helping patients to regain some sense that they may be able to overcome their problems. For some clients this phase of remoralization is sufficient for them to regain contact with their own coping resources, and no further work is required. Others will require a period of remediation, focused on work oriented toward symptom relief and correction of the underlying difficulties.

Again, this may be sufficient for some patients; for others a further phase of rehabilitation is necessary, focused on identifying and changing the patterns of thoughts and behavior which lead the patient to suffer recurrent psychological problems. Most clinicians will recognize in this model a description of the pattern and duration of therapeutic input required by different patients. Importantly it may also characterize the differing readiness of patients for therapy. For some patients the phase of remoralization may be more significant than the model suggests, especially where the presenting problem is chronic. This has important implications for setting guidelines about appropriate therapeutic input.

CLINICAL EXAMPLES OF
EVIDENCE-BASED PRACTICE

Thus far our discussion has been rather abstract, and three case examples may be helpful to illustrate not only how complex presentations should lead to variations in technique, but also how formulation needs to be built into (and hence vary) practice essentially informed by clinical guidelines.

A direct interpretation of our review of treatments for patients presenting with a primary diagnosis of posttraumatic stress disorder (PTSD) suggests that relatively short-term exposure-based interventions together with anxiety management strategies are often successful. Though appropriate for some patients, guidelines based on this "default" option will need to be modified to match the needs of the individual case.

> Ms. B was a young woman who had been severely injured in an unprovoked and savage physical assault, as a result of which she was unable to walk for several months. She had refused an offer of counseling immediately after the attack, but requested referral for psychological help nearly a year after the incident. At assessment she described feeling both ready for therapy and determined to overcome her difficulties, which consisted of frequent intrusive thoughts and nightmares about the assault, severe panic disorder with agoraphobia, and depression. Her comorbid symptomatology was considered secondary to her primary diagnosis, and therapy proceeded rapidly and successfully, employing exposure together with anxiety management techniques.

> Mr. C was a 30-year-old man who was first seen 7 years after being injured in an industrial accident. He presented with symptoms of PTSD, but also suffered from depression and panic disorder with agoraphobia. In addition he had been unemployed since the accident, and at the point of referral was in danger of becoming homeless. Mr. C presented in a manner that made compliance with standard treatment unlikely. His circumstances had led him to a chronic state of demoralization and hopelessness, leading in turn to social withdrawal, which itself contributed to the development of symptoms of depression and agoraphobia (the presence of which further deepened his sense of demoralization). A number of sessions were required to help him manage his basic needs (such as finding secure accommodation and stabilizing his economic situation), work that focused on giving him a sense that he could retrieve himself from his situation. Not only did this relieve some of his depression and agoraphobia, but crucially it enabled symptomatic management according to standard practice.

Though his diagnostic presentation was similar to Ms. B, it is unlikely that Mr. C could have received treatment aimed at symptom relief without a fairly prolonged period of "remoralization." This phase, described within Howard's model as relatively short-term, could be seen as pivotal to the success of the therapy; it is unlikely that treatment could have adhered to a clinical guideline until "readiness" had been achieved. For Ms. B a period of remoralization was hardly apparent; her entry into therapy marked this phase of her recovery.

In other cases the patient may present in a manner that is diagnostically uncomplicated, but it becomes apparent on formulation that the standard treatment protocol requires modification.

> Mr. D was referred to a specialist trauma unit[2] following unsuccessful treatment for PTSD using exposure-based anxiety management techniques. He had entered an elevator with a stranger and had been both physically assaulted and threatened with a knife; his previous therapist noted that attempts at debriefing appeared to make him worse. At assessment his new therapist identified a certain evasiveness in his account of the incident. The therapist's familiarity with the PTSD literature alerted her to the possibility that his trauma reaction was "complex"; rather than reflecting simple fear, she speculated that his adverse reactions were based on issues connected to self-esteem and shame. It became apparent that Mr. D had lost bowel control during the assault, and felt such deep shame (both about the event and its meaning) that he had previously been unable to reveal this fact. In this light it is clear that simple exposure had served only to reinforce his sense of humiliation.

In this case, reformulation indicated the importance of exploratory psychotherapeutic work to manage these feelings; successful therapy required a deviation from protocol-driven practice.

MONITORING THE EFFECTIVENESS OF CLINICAL PRACTICE

We have argued that while research can identify potentially useful interventions, and hence should influence the design and strategic direction of services, it says little about how effectively therapies are implemented in any particular setting, and local data collection concerning effectiveness (clinical audit) is crucial to answer this question. Without this, the quality of service delivery may actually be poor—for example, in trying uncritically to apply research findings of little relevance to work at ground level, by therapist errors in delivery of a potentially effective therapy, or by ignoring potentially useful research-based information altogether. The clinical guideline, informed by research findings, states "the right thing to do," but there are three important matters we need

---

[2] We are grateful to Deborah Lee for this case example.

to establish: whether the right thing has been done, whether it has been done right, and whether it resulted in the right outcome. Psychotherapy research has severe weaknesses in relation to external validity, and these questions can only be answered by clinical audit and service evaluation methods (Parry, 1996).

AUDITING THERAPY DELIVERY AND BENCHMARKING OUTCOMES

Clinical audit of therapy delivery involves choosing the *criteria* for judging service quality, defining the *norms* for good care, and setting specific *standards* of performance. Adherence to these standards is then monitored to establish whether the therapy has been delivered to an acceptable quality. This process should yield relatively quick feedback for the audit cycle to reveal useful information about what steps can be taken by psychotherapists to improve their practices. The audit of therapy delivery will reveal gaps in therapists' skills and knowledge, and this in turn should help to set the agenda for continuing professional development of the clinicians involved. Though an audit of therapy process might appear to be beyond the resources of many services, in practice it can be achieved by drawing up a set of guidelines for the broad characteristics of a particular intervention, and establish the degree to which these matched the methods employed by therapists—for example, through a process of peer-review or self-administered checklists.

As well as monitoring the process of service delivery, there is a role for outcomes monitoring. Routine monitoring of outcomes in clinical practice is far from common, and indeed some would argue that, where the quality of delivery of a well-researched therapy is well monitored, it is uninformative to report on outcomes across the service (Donabedian, 1980). The costs of doing so are certainly prohibitive in many instances. However, outcome benchmarking may reveal to clinicians that, for whatever reason, practice recommendations based on research findings are ineffective in their local context. There may be a number of reasons for this, and an audit of how the therapy is actually delivered is necessary to eliminate the most obvious: that procedures are not being implemented as prescribed.

There is increasing interest in the concept of "report cards" for psychotherapy outcomes, where services agree to use the same core battery of measures and performance indicators that allows comparability across services. Payers welcome such developments, and work is under way in both the United States and Europe in terms of service level evaluation of outcomes.

Where outcomes in clinical practice are poorer than those predicted by research, and this cannot be accounted for in terms of an audit of service delivery, attention is drawn to gaps in our knowledge concerning that treatment method. Considering ways of accounting for these discrepancies yields further research questions—for example, in terms of either the client therapist variation or the necessary and sufficient components of a treatment strategy. Ideally, further clinical development and innovation follow, as does refinement of the clinical protocol.

The evaluation process as a whole should permit a more general evaluation and planning of a service on the part of management. Naturally this should include lead clinicians as well as purchasers of services. Given that all these groups have improvement of patient care as their collective priority, there is *a priori* little need for conflict in making appropriate change to a service in line with data obtained. Even more important, a good-quality service becomes defined as the end result of a process of integration, linking research with clinical findings arising from clinical practice, and using this as a springboard to further innovation, in this way ensuring a fully recursive process and that improvements in patient care are continuous.

SUMMARY

Changes in the health care delivery system in the United States, United Kingdom, and other Western European countries have inevitably led to increased concern with the effectiveness of all medical interventions. Psychological therapies, along with other forms of mental health intervention, are increasingly subject to scrutiny from funders of these services. They, along with clinicians and service managers, raise questions about the likely efficacy of therapy for particular patient populations. Though at root these are the same questions psychotherapy research has attempted to answer from a scientific stance, because the motives for asking the question are quite distinct, the criteria for judging the answers as helpful or not will also be different.

No single answer can meet the requirements of these stakeholders; each is addressing different issues within an ongoing process, which we describe in our model of evidence-based practice. For research to be put to effective use requires other components, such as the achievement of a professional consensus and the preparation of guidelines and protocols for good practice. Through studies of clinical practice and effectiveness this should lead to further theoretical developments. It is our view that if these components are in place, improvements in patient care will be the result.

CHAPTER 4

Depression

DEFINITIONS

DSM-IV describes a number of subcategories of depression; those particularly relevant to research studies are defined as follows (adapted from Wells, 1985).

Major Depressive Disorder

Major depressive disorder (MDD) is characterized by one or more major depressive episodes and the absence of manic episodes. A major depressive episode is defined by depressive mood or loss of interest or pleasure in almost all usual activities, accompanied by other depressive symptoms. These include disturbances in appetite, weight, and sleep; psychomotor agitation or retardation; decreased energy; feelings of worthlessness or guilt; difficulty concentrating or thinking; and thoughts of death or suicide or suicidal attempts. DSM-IV specifies that at least five of nine specific depressive symptoms must be present nearly every day for at least 2 weeks to make a diagnosis of MDD, and that the symptoms cause clinically significant distress or impairment in social, occupational, or other important areas of functioning. Depressive episodes are distinguished from normal bereavement reactions.

Dysthymic Disorder/Dysthymia

This condition is referred to as "dysthymic disorder" in DSM-IV and "dysthymia" in DSM-III-R. As in MDD, dysthymic disorder is characterized by depressed mood or loss of interest in nearly all usual activities. However, the depression is not of sufficient severity to meet the criteria for a major depressive episode.

Dysthymic disorder is characterized by depressed mood for most of the day, for more days than not, together with at least two of the following six symptoms: poor appetite, insomnia or hypersomnia, low energy, low self-esteem, poor concentration, and feelings of hopelessness. For diagnostic purposes, these symptoms should be severe enough to cause clinically significant distress or impairment in social, occupational, or other areas of functioning (a criterion absent in DSM-III-R), but not of sufficient severity or persistence to meet the criteria for major depression. For adults the disorder should be present for at least 2 years, but there may be periods of normal mood lasting a few days or weeks. A diagnosis of dysthymic disorder cannot be made if patients are symptom-free for more than 2 months in any 2-year period. Patients with dysthymic disorder frequently present with a superimposed MDD; this is usually referred to as "double depression."

PREVALENCE, INCIDENCE, AND COURSE

Prevalence

Two recent large-scale community surveys provide data on the prevalence of depression. The National Institute of Mental Health (NIMH) Epidemiologic Catchment Area (ECA) was a five-site project sampling 15,000 adults (Robins & Regier, 1991). The National Comorbidity Survey (Blazer et al., 1994) interviewed 8,098 adults between ages 18 and 54; together these surveys give the best current estimates of the prevalence of psychiatric disorders in the United States. The ECA study estimated that during a 6-month period 6% of the population have a DSM-III-R diagnosis of an affective disorder. The most prevalent types of disorders are MDD and dysthymia, each affecting about 3% of the population. The National Comorbidity survey estimates a 30-day prevalence for MDD of 4.9%, and lifetime prevalence at 17.1%.

Angst (1992), reviewing 17 studies, suggests that 1-year prevalence rates for MDD lie between 2.6 and 6.2%, and for dysthymia between 2.3 and 3.7%. Lifetime prevalence rates vary between 4.4 and 19.5%. Angst reports data from a Swiss prospective community survey carried out (to date) over 10 years. This was based on multiple interviews and hence avoided problems of estimating prevalence based on recall. Lifetime prevalence to age 30 of MDD was 14.5%, with around half of affected individuals seeking treatment.

The prevalence of depression varies by gender and age; prevalence of MDD in the ECA and National Comorbidity surveys was almost twice as high in women as men and greater in younger adults. In part this may reflect the greater willingness of younger adults to admit to mental health problems (Taube & Barrett, 1985; Weissman et al., 1988b), or problems of recall when older respondents are interviewed in cross-sectional surveys (Fombonne, 1994). However, there is evidence that prevalence within younger age groups is increasing (Burke et al., 1991), though the degree to which this is associated with comorbid substance abuse is unclear. Furthermore there is some agreement that overall rates of depression are increasing (Klerman & Weissman, 1989), though the extent to which this is occurring is uncertain (Fombonne, 1994).

Natural History

The natural course of depression is difficult to document independent of treatment, though data from the ECA study suggest that only 31% of those with depressive disorders present to a mental health clinic in the 6-month period for which the study was concerned (Taube & Barrett, 1985).

One strategy for detecting the likely course of depression comes from the longitudinal study of patients offered "treatment as usual." Wells et al. (1992) report data from the Medical Outcomes Study (MOS), in which 626 outpatients were followed over a 2-year period. These patients were diagnosed using DSM-III-R categories, and the sample comprised not only patients with MDD, dysthymia, and double depression but also clients with subthreshold depressive symptoms. All patients were attending health practices and remained in care over the period of the study, though the nature of the treatments they received is not specified. There was a trend for patients who were more symptomatic at the start of the study to be receiving antidepressant medication; preliminary analyses showed a significant association between medication use and favorable outcome. However, controlling for initial severity of symptoms (which acts to control the bias introduced by selective treatment), no association was found. No information is given about psychological treatments for these patients.

Of some importance is the finding that both dysthymic patients and those with subthreshold symptoms of depression were at considerable risk of suffering an episode of MDD over the study period. Half the patients with an initial diagnosis of dysthymia and 25% of patients with subthreshold symptoms of depression (with or without a prior history of depression) experienced an episode of MDD over the 2-year period. Data from patient samples in field trials for DSM-IV confirm this pattern; 79% of dysthymics eventually developed MDD (McCullough et al., 1992).

Patients with MDD had a 42% probability of remission[1] in the first year, and a 60% probability of remission in the second year if none had occurred in the first year. Clients with double depression had a rather different course, dependent on the severity of their symptoms. Those with more severe symptoms had a 37% likelihood of remission in the first year; if no remission occurred by this point, there was only a 16% probability of remission in the second year.

The poorest clinical outcomes were found in patients with double depression; there was a particularly low rate of remission in patients with both double depression and high initial symptom severity. Patients with dysthymia (even in the absence of MDD) had higher levels of depressive symptoms over the 2-year period of the study than patients with MDD alone, despite the fact that dysthymia is defined by the presence of less severe (if persistent) depressive symptoms. In addition patients with dysthymia were rated as having poorer social and emotional functioning than those with MDD.

Piccinelli and Wilkinson (1994) review 50 naturalistic follow-up studies of unipolar in- and outpatient depressed patients carried out between 1970 and 1993. They report that although recovery rates increase over time (on average 53% of patients will recover at least briefly by 6 months), a quarter of the patients will have suffered a reccurence of the index episode within 1 year. Seventy-five percent of patients followed up for 10 years suffered a further episode of depression, and 10% of patients suffered persistent depression. However, 30 of the 50 studies examined by Piccinelli and Wilkinson were concerned with the course of depression in inpatients, and these figures may therefore reflect the course of more severely depressed individuals.

A number of studies suggest that outcome even after treatment can be poor. Keller et al. (1982) report data on 75 patients who had reached a criterion of recovery (no or only mild symptoms for 8 weeks), finding

---

[1] Recovery and relapse are problematic terms unless specified, and are used inconsistently in the literature (Prien et al., 1991). Frank et al. (1991) have proposed the adoption of the following definitions, many of which have been adopted by researchers but (where relevant) with somewhat differing time courses:

Partial remission: A period when improvement of a sufficient magnitude is observed, but during which the patient continues to show more than minimal symptoms.

Full remission: A relatively brief period during which the individual is asymptomatic.

Recovery: A remission of a longer period, usually indicating recovery from the index episode (though not from the illness per se).

Relapse: A return of symptoms satisfying criteria for the full syndrome that occurs during the period of remission, but before recovery.

Recurrence: The appearance of a new episode of MDD arising during a period of recovery.

that around 25% of their sample had relapsed within 12 weeks, and of these half had relapsed in the first 4 weeks (though these results may be somewhat pessimistic given that only low doses of medication were employed). As reported by Wells et al. (1992), a higher rate of relapse was found for double depression. In addition, those with three or more previous episodes of depression had a 43% relapse rate by 12 weeks, compared with 11% of those with 0–2 previous episodes. A similar pattern has been reported by Gonzales et al. (1985), who studied 113 patients, finding that overall 30% relapsed within the first year. However, recovery was more likely for those with MDD (70%) compared to those with double depression (27%).

Additional studies by Keller and Shapiro (1982) and Keller et al. (1983) suggest that patients with double depression tend to have a shorter episode of MDD, but are also more likely to relapse quicker than those with MDD alone. Double depressives appear to have a faster "cycle time"; over a 2-year period 62% of them had completed a cycle of recovery and relapse, compared to 33% of the MDD group.

Summary

- Although precise estimation is difficult, it is clear that depression is a syndrome affecting at least 6% of the population.
- The likely course of depression appears to differ according to subtype (MDD, dysthymic disorder, or double depression) and its chronicity. Overall it is characterized by a high probability of relapse: 75% of patients followed up over 10 years will suffer a further episode of MDD, and 10% of these will have endured persistent depression.
- It is likely that 80% of patients with dysthymic disorder will eventually develop an MDD, suggesting that dysthymic disorder and acute depression are variants of a similar condition.
- The probability of MDD relapse is greatest in patients with a diagnosis of dysthymic disorder; these patients show a faster cycle of recovery and relapse than those with MDD alone.
- The probability of relapse is increased in patients with more than three previous episodes of MDD.

Implications

- The results of treatment trials need to be interpreted with reference to the high probability of relapse in depression. The effectiveness of treatments cannot be judged simply by the management of an index episode; reduction in relapse is a more pertinent and informative guide to success.

- On the basis of figures given above, long-term follow-up of at least 2 years would be necessary to provide a conclusive result that is not confounded with the natural history of this disorder.
- Outcome in clinical trials will depend on the case mix, and particularly the presence of patients with double depression or a history of recurrent major depressive disorder.
- Because of the exclusion criteria frequently applied in research trials, it is likely that the clinical population will contain comparatively more chronically depressed and dysthymic patients. This biasing of data in the direction of overestimating treatment effects is likely to lead to poorer outcomes in clinical practice than in trials.

OVERALL TREATMENT EFFECTIVENESS: INDIVIDUAL STUDIES

Subsequent chapters in this review place individual studies within a framework established by meta-analyses and quantitative reviews. When considering treatments for depression, however, a different strategy is warranted. Some of the largest and most methodologically rigorous psychotherapy trials have been conducted in this area, and the four studies that follow set the agenda for consideration of the broader body of evidence.

The NIMH Treatment of Depression Research Program

This major research program represents a benchmark against which other studies can be judged. It has been reported in a number of papers (discussed below) and summarized by Elkin (1994). The intention of this project was to examine the efficacy of cognitive-behavioral psychotherapy (CBT; Beck et al., 1979) and interpersonal psychotherapy (IPT; Klerman et al., 1984). IPT is based on the ideas of the interpersonal school (Sullivan, 1953) and, while making no assumptions about etiology, "uses the connection between the onset of depressive symptoms and current interpersonal problems as a treatment focus" (Weissman et al., 1994, p. 600). It deals with current rather than past relationships and maintains a clear focus on the patient's social context and dysfunction rather than their personality. Both CBT and IPT had been developed to treat depressed outpatients, both were designed to be delivered over a brief period of time, data were available supporting their efficacy, and both were standardized in the form of a manual (enabling them to be implemented reliably). The research plan was to test the psychological interventions against a standard reference condition of (presumed) known efficacy—imipramine. This strategy is important to understand, since the study has been widely misinterpreted as a test of therapy against medication (Elkin, 1994). Rather, the medication condition was intended as a control condition of known effectiveness, against which to compare the psychological therapies.

Research was carried out at three research sites in the United States. Five hundred sixty outpatients were initially screened on a number of criteria, essentially to include those with a DSM-III-R diagnosis of unipolar depression. Two hundred fifty patients, all moderately to severely depressed, were selected for the trial; 239 actually entered it. Of these, 60% had been depressed for more than 6 months; for only 36% was this a first episode of depression.

Patients were randomly assigned to four treatment conditions: CBT, IPT, imipramine plus clinical management (IMI-CM), or placebo plus clinical management (PLA-CM). Clinical management consisted of a weekly meeting of 20–30 min to discuss medication, side effects, and the patient's clinical status. In addition, and where necessary, support, encouragement, and direct advice were also offered. It is therefore clear that both medication conditions contain psychotherapeutic elements.

Treatments were carried out by experienced therapists (10 each in IPT and pharmacotherapy, 8 in CBT) who had been chosen for their expertise in applying their respective therapy and who were supervised regularly throughout the clinical trial. To ensure that therapies were conducted as intended, sessions were taped and the process of therapy was checked against measures of therapy adherence.

Though there were some differences in attrition from each condition, these were not statistically significant. Rates of dropout across treatment modalities were as follows: 23% ($n = 14$) for IPT, 32% ($n = 19$) for CBT, 33% ($n = 19$) for IMI-CM, and 40% ($n = 25$) for PLA-CM.

Patients were assessed before treatment and at 4, 8, 12, and 16 weeks and followed up at 6, 12, and 18 months. During therapy a number of standardized measures of symptomatic status were employed (including the Hamilton Rating Scale for Depression [HRSD] and the Beck Depression Inventory [BDI]). After discharge, progress was assessed using a semistructured interview designed to assess the longitudinal course of psychiatric disorders (the Longitudinal Interval Follow-up Evaluation II [LIFE-II]; Keller et al., 1987).

Analyses were carried out on three overlapping sets of patient samples: a completer sample ($n = 155$) who had received at least 12 sessions or 15 weeks of therapy; the sample of patients who had entered treatment and received at least four sessions of therapy ($n = 204$); and the total (intent-to-treat) sample of patients who had entered the trials ($n = 239$).

Posttherapy the general direction of results was similar on all measures and in all samples (Elkin et al., 1989), with patients who received IMI-CM having the lowest symptomatic scores, PLA-CM the most symptomatic, and the psychotherapies in between and usually closer to IMI-CM. The magnitude of these differences was not large, and pairwise comparison of treatment conditions revealed no differences between therapies or between therapies and IMI-CM.

In addition to comparisons of relative scores, a comparison of "recovery rates" was carried out—clearly a more stringent and clinically relevant analysis. Recovery was defined as an HRSD score ≤ 6 and a BDI score ≤ 9. No significant differences between treatment groups were found employing the BDI data, though in part this seems to reflect the degree of improvement in the PLA-CM condition. Using HRSD data, significant differences were apparent. Pairwise comparisons using the complete sample of patients indicated that clients who received IMI-CM and IPT were significantly more likely to recover than those who had received PLA-CM; a trend toward significance was apparent in the other two patient samples. There were, however, no significant differences between therapies or between therapies and IMI-CM in any patient sample.

All treatment conditions resulted in a significant improvement pre- to posttreatment—perhaps surprisingly, this included PLA-CM. Outcome for patients in the therapy conditions was equivalent to that in other treatment trials (reviewed below). The lack of significant differences seems attributable to the good performance of PLA-CM. However, as already noted, PLA-CM does contain a number of nonspecific therapeutic elements; in a sense comparisons between it and the psychotherapies may reflect differences between such elements and the technical interventions embodied in the therapies.

Ogles et al. (1995) reanalyzed data for the completer sample of patients, arguing that Elkin et al.'s (1989) analysis did not consider the reliability of change from pre- to posttherapy, that there was no attempt to consider the clinical significance of multiple measures simultaneously, and that the possibility of reliable deterioration was not determined. Using Jacobson and Truax's (1991) method, it is apparent that the proportion of clients showing reliable change was statistically equivalent across treatments, with little evidence of deterioration—in fact, observed at a rate of between 2% and 5% dependent on the measure employed. If clinically significant change is determined by movement into the functional distribution of scores across instruments (within 2 *SD* of the mean for the normal population), the immediate impact of therapy across all treatments was equivalent when using the BDI and HRSD. This further emphasizes the substantial improvements achieved by clients within the PLA-CM group (e.g., 62% achieved clinically significant change using the BDI as a measure). However, there were significant differences across treatments on measures of general symptomatology (using the Hopkins Symptom Check List (HSCL-90; Lipman et al., 1979), equivalent in most respects to the SCL-90 (Derogatis, 1977). Thus on this instrument, 78%, 93%, and 87% of the CBT, IPT and IMI-CM groups were placed in the functional distribution, contrasted to 65% of the PLA-CM group.

Although (as noted above) Elkin et al.'s analysis found statistically significant differences between treatments only when the HRSD was employed as a measure, Ogles et al. (1995) note that reanalysis for both clinical significance and concordance across measures shows a high level of agreement. Thus for 118 (73%) of 162 clients, all three measures were in agreement regarding the clinical significance of the change pre- to posttreatment.

A secondary analysis (Elkin et al., 1989) considered the degree to which initial symptom status influenced outcome. Two definitions of severity were employed. In the first, severity was defined as an HRSD score of ≥ 20; in the second, a Global Assessment Scale (GAS) score of ≤ 50 was used (the GAS tapping both depressive symptomatology and functional impairment). The results suggested that for the less depressed group there were no significant differences between treatments. However, for the more depressed group (and contrasting the three patient samples), pairwise comparisons using the HRSD revealed consistently lower scores for IMI-CM than for PLA-CM, and some significant differences for IPT compared to PLA-CM. Using the recovery criterion, there were no significant differences between treatment groups for less severely depressed patients, but again patients receiving both IMI-CM and IPT were significantly more likely to recover than those in PLA-CM. However, no significant differences were found between therapies.

Recent reanalysis of these data (Elkin et al., 1995), using more powerful statistical techniques (random regression models), confirms the equivalence of intervention methods for less depressed patients but indicates greater differentiation among the therapies for the more depressed sample. For these patients, using both HRSD and BDI scores as outcome measures, IMI-CM and IPT appeared equally effective. IMI-CM was significantly more effective than CBT or PLA-CM; IPT showed a trend ($p < .08$) toward greater efficacy. CBT was no more effective than PLA-CM. When the GAS was used as an outcome measure, a different pattern emerged, with IMI–CM being more effective than the other three interventions, all of which showed equal relative efficacy.

These analyses are exploratory, but they do suggest that initial patient severity may be an important factor in considering treatment allocation—particularly the finding that for patients with lower levels of depression, PLA–CM (which could be considered a "minimal support" intervention) was as effective as the active therapies. Although there is evidence that IMI–CM was particularly effective with more severely depressed and functionally impaired patients, it should be noted that it was no more effective than IPT where patients were symptomatically rather than functionally impaired. A number of researchers have interpreted these results to indicate that medication is necessarily the treatment of choice in more severe depression (Elkin, 1994). These results suggest that some caution should be advanced in this regard.

Further comment on the relative efficacy of IPT and CBT is also in order. There are suggestions that CBT performed much better at one site, and IPT performed more poorly at another (Elkin, 1994). Though this has been attributed to variations in the quality of treatment administered (Hollon et al., 1994), there is no published evidence with which to weigh these claims. Certainly studies by Hollon et al. (1992) and Evans et al. (1992) do provide strong evidence for the efficacy of CBT under equivalent conditions to those obtaining in the NIMH trial, suggesting that it may be premature to draw definitive conclusions about appropriate treatment modalities on the basis of the NIMH trial.

Follow-up of patients continued over 18 months and is reported in Shea et al. (1992). In this analysis the question of interest was the fate of the patients who had met a stringent criteria for recovery—at least 8 weeks following completion of treatment with minimal or no symptoms. Relapse was defined as the presence of at least 2 weeks of MDD-level symptoms over the 18-month follow-up period.

Only 20% of the original sample and 24% of the patients with follow-up data met the criteria for recovery with no relapse. Of those entering therapies, 24% of those receiving CBT remained recovered without relapse at 18 months, compared with 23% for IPT, 16% for IMI–CM, and 16% for PLA–CM. Of those with follow-up data at 6 months, 30% in CBT, 26% in IPT, 19% in IMI–CM, and 20% in PLA–CM were recovered without relapse at 18 months. Despite the presence of a trend for psychotherapy to be superior to IMI–CM, there are no statistical differences in these rates. However, it should be noted that, as is the case for any study that attempts a naturalistic long-term follow-up, there are problems in interpreting the data statistically: because the groups no longer benefit from the original randomization, attributions about effects cannot be traced to the treatment modality employed (Shea et al., 1992).

Overall, it is clear that rather few patients recover and remain well with 16 weeks of treatment, and a clear conclusion from this study is that interventions of this length are not sufficient to maintain functioning in the majority of patients. This result is not, perhaps, surprising in the light of evidence considered earlier regarding the natural course of depression.

University of Minnesota Study of Cognitive Therapy and Pharmacotherapy

Hollon and colleagues at the University of Minnesota have carried out research which, in many respects, follows the same design and attention to methodological detail as was evident in the NIMH study (Hollon et al., 1992; Evans et al., 1992). Because this research provides important evidence about the efficacy of CBT when contrasted with medication, it merits separate description.

One hundred seven moderately to severely depressed patients (all with BDI scores ≥ 20) were randomly assigned to one of four treatment conditions. In three conditions patients received 12 weeks of active treatment: imipramine and clinical management alone; CBT alone; or CBT and imipramine. In a fourth condition patients continued to receive imipramine for 12 months after the initial 12-week period of imipramine and clinical management.

Sixty-four patients completed all treatments; although attrition was high, there was no significant difference in the rate between conditions. Treatments were administered by experienced therapists and were somewhat more intensive than in the NIMH study, with 20 sessions planned for the 12-week period. Clinical management was similar to that employed in the NIMH trial.

At the end of treatment (and at this stage considering both medication conditions together), all three treatments showed equal efficacy, though with a nonsignificant trend toward better results for the combined treatment group. In contrast to the NIMH study, there was no indication of a differential response with more severely depressed patients (although the sample size was perhaps too small to allow this comparison).

At 2-year follow-up, clear differences were found between treatment groups. Recovery was defined along the same lines as the NIMH trial, though relapse was indicated by a consistently elevated BDI score. Although 44 patients (of the 64 completing treatment) were followed up, the low number of patients in each treatment cell necessitates some caution in interpreting the treatment results. Nonetheless, adjusting for patient attrition from the study, patients receiving medication without continuation showed the greatest rate of relapse (50%), all within the first 4 months of follow-up. In contrast, the relapse rate of patients receiving cognitive therapy (either alone or in combination with medication) was 18%. Most of these relapses occurred later than in the medication–no continuation condition; mean survival times were 17.4 ± 1.2 months and 3.3 ± 0.4 months, respectively. Relapse rate in the medication continuation condition was intermediate, with a 32% relapse rate and a mean survival time of 17.3 ± 2.1 months. A secondary analysis indicated that relapse rates in the two cognitive therapy conditions were not different from one another.

This study provides evidence supporting the prophylactic value of a relatively short period of CBT during the acute phase of depression, but the high dropout rates result in small sample sizes at follow-up, which inevitably restricts its generalizability.

University of Pittsburgh Study: Long-Term Maintenance Therapy

Frank and colleagues (Frank et al., 1989, 1990, 1991; Kupfer et al., 1992) report a major study which advances understanding of maintenance treatments for depression. The study was designed to examine the effects of continued treatment in patients whose index episode had been intensively treated and who had maintained recovery from this episode. It is therefore one of the few studies to concern itself explicitly with relapse prevention.

Two hundred thirty patients were selected for inclusion in the trial on the basis of a history of recurrent depression. All had experienced at least three previous episodes of depression, with the preceding episode being no more than 2½ years before the index episode (the mean number of episodes was 6.8, with a median of 4). All were selected on the basis of a clear DSM-III-R diagnosis of MDD in the absence of other Axis I disorders. Those with double depression were excluded, as were patients with severe Axis II disorders.

All patients received short-term treatment with imipramine and interpersonal psychotherapy. Psychotherapy sessions were scheduled weekly for 12 weeks, then biweekly for 8 weeks, and then monthly. At whatever point patients achieved remission (defined as a HRSD score or a Raskin depression scale score ≤5 for 3 consecutive weeks), a further 17 weeks of treatment was offered, during which Hamilton and Raskin scores had to remain stable. At this point a third evaluation was carried out, and the 128 patients who had reached the recovery criteria were assigned to one of five maintenance treatments for 3 years, or until the recurrence of depression; treatments were offered monthly and consisted of (1) medication clinic/clinical management and imipramine, (2) medication clinic/clinical management and placebo, (3) IPT and imipramine, (4) IPT and placebo, or (5) IPT alone (see Table 1). It should be noted that all patients had been receiving IPT; those assigned to medication conditions alone continued to see their original therapist, though the nature of their interaction changed from one of therapy to clinical management, along the lines of the NIMH study (Frank & Kupfer, 1994).

Unusual both in research studies and probably in clinical practice, imipramine continued to be prescribed at high levels (a mean of 207 mg daily). Attrition from the maintenance phase of the study was relatively low; only 22 (17%) of patients assigned to this phase failed to complete the 3-year protocol.

Results are reported at 3 years for the main trial (Frank et al., 1990) and at 5 years for a further group of patients maintained on imipramine or placebo alone (Kupfer et al., 1992). At 3 years, and contrasted with patients receiving placebo, medication or the combination of medication with IPT resulted in a significant reduction in the relapse rate ($p <$ .0001). Maintenance therapy with IPT or IPT and placebo also resulted in a significant though less marked reduction in relapse ($p <$ .043). There was no advantage to combination treatment over imipramine alone.

Overall, a 22.6% recurrence rate was found for patients treated with imipramine, contrasted with 78.2% for placebo over 3 years. Patients treated with IPT (with or without placebo) had a 44.2% recurrence rate over the same period. Further analysis suggests that where the quality of treatment delivered was high, relapse rates with IPT were

TABLE 1. Mean and Median Survival Times in Five Maintenance Conditions for 3 Years (Frank et al., 1990)

Treatment condition	Mean ± *SD* survival time (in weeks)	Median survival time (in weeks)
Medication clinic and imipramine	124 ± 13	[a]
IPT and imipramine	131 ± 10	[a]
Medication clinic and placebo	45 ± 11	21
IPT	82 ± 13	54
IPT and placebo	74 ± 12	61

[a] Since 50% of these subjects did not have a relapse no median can be calculated.

equal to those achieved with imipramine. Frank et al. (1991) examined audiotapes of 38 of the 52 patients receiving maintenance IPT (either alone or in combination with placebo) and used rating scales of therapy adherence to determine the degree to which this therapy was implemented as intended. Therapies were defined as high quality if the patients received IPT above the median of adherence ratings, or low quality if delivered below the median. Results were striking; patients receiving high-quality therapy had a median survival time to relapse of approximately 2 years, while those receiving low-quality therapy had a median time of only 5 months.

The quality of therapy delivered was not a reflection of "good" or "bad" therapists, since individual therapists implemented IPT accurately with some patients and with less success with others. Although requiring further study, accuracy of implementation seemed to reflect an interaction between patient and therapist factors.

Patients completing the 3-year protocol who had been receiving active medication (with or without maintenance IPT) were invited to continue a further 2-year randomized trial of active medication against placebo (Kupfer et al., 1992). Twenty patients entered this trial, either continuing to receive the high-dose imipramine regime, or being transferred to placebo medication. Thirteen patients continued to receive monthly IPT, evenly split across placebo and medication conditions. Again survival times were significantly greater for patients receiving active medication (99.4 ± 4.4 weeks) than those assigned to placebo (54.0 ± 14.6 weeks, $p < .006$). Only one-third of patients receiving placebo survived the study period without relapse; 78% of placebo survivors were receiving continuation IPT. Only 11% of patients receiving neither medication nor IPT survived without experiencing a relapse.

The Second Sheffield Psychotherapy Project

The second Sheffield Psychotherapy Project (Shapiro et al., 1994) is a comparative trial of prescriptive psychotherapy (which may be taken as analogous to CBT) and exploratory therapy (a psychodynamic/interpersonal therapy). As well as representing a substantive investigation of therapeutic impacts with a British sample, the study was designed to permit exploration of additional methodological and clinical issues raised by prior research:

1. *Impact of investigator allegiance.* As will be discussed later in this chapter, statistical control of investigator allegiance seems to abolish

differential outcomes in comparative trials (Robinson et al., 1990). The authors of the Sheffield study claim equal allegiance to both cognitive-behavioral and psychodynamic approaches, and hence might be expected to be less biased in their assessment of the efficacy of each therapy.

2. *Impact of symptom severity.* Data from the NIMH study (Elkin et al., 1989) suggest that patients with severe depression may be more refractory to psychotherapy. However, this finding is based on a second-ary analysis of their data. In the Sheffield study initial symptom severity was included as a factor from the outset.

3. *Speed of recovery.* Howard et al. (1986) examined data from approxi-mately 300 patients on whom session-by-session reports were available. Their analysis suggests that most treatment gains are made within the first eight to 16 sessions, with improvements in subsequent sessions showing a negatively accelerating "dose–response relationship." Patients in the Shef-field study were given either eight or 16 session treatments in an effort to explore directly the relationship of dose and effect.

The study was therefore concerned with (1) the efficacy of the two different therapies, (2) the influence of initial symptom severity, and (3) the impact of offering differing lengths of treatment (and relatedly, any evidence for a differential speed of action between the therapies).

A total of 257 patients were assessed; 169 met the study criteria of a DSM-III-R diagnosis of MDD and a Present State Examination (PSE; Wing et al., 1974) index of definition of ⩾5. Thirty-nine percent were referred by their family physicians or mental health services; the remain-der were self-referred. Clients were stratified into those with low (BDI score 16–20), moderate (BDI score 21–26), or high (BDI score ⩾27) levels of depression.

Treatment was either CBT or psychodynamic/interpersonal ther-apy; therapy was administered for either 8 or 16 weeks. Following assessment, patients were randomly allocated to treatment. The design has 12 "cells" formed by the interaction of symptom severity, type of therapy, and duration of treatment. Patient allocation continued until each cell had been occupied by 10 patients (see Table 2).

TABLE 2. Allocation of 120 Patients to Treatment Cells in Shapiro et al. (1994)

Severity level	Treatment type	Length of treatment
High depressed	CBT *or* psychodynamic/exploratory	8 *or* 16 sessions
Moderately depressed	CBT *or* psychodynamic/exploratory	8 *or* 16 sessions
Low depressed	CBT *or* psychodynamic/exploratory	8 *or* 16 sessions

Overall, both therapies were found to be equally effective, to exert their effects with equal rapidity, and to have equivalent results for clients at all three levels of symptom severity. However, an interaction was found between initial symptom level and duration of therapy. Patients with mild or moderate depression did equally well with either 8 or 16 weeks of therapy. In contrast, those with severe depression showed significantly better outcomes when they received 16 weeks of therapy, compared to those who received only 8 weeks.

One hundred three of the 117 completer patients were followed up at 1 year (Shapiro et al., 1995) and classified as recovered (at least 4 months asymptomatic, defined as a BDI score <9), as having relapsed (having a BDI score ≥15 during a period of remission from the previous episode but before meeting the criterion for recovery), or as having a recurrence (a BDI score ≥15 after the criterion for recovery has been met). Of the 103 patients, 52% were treatment responders: 57% maintained their gains, 32% partially maintained gains, and 11% relapsed or had a recurrence. Thus the proportion of all patients entering the trial and remaining asymptomatic from posttreatment to 1 year follow-up is 29% (a figure comparable with that found in the NIMH study).

No overall differences were found in outcome or maintenance of gains between CBT and psychodynamic–interpersonal therapy, nor was the interaction between initial symptom severity and duration of therapy maintained. However, there was an interaction between treatment type and duration, with those patients receiving eight sessions of psychodynamic/interpersonal therapy doing less well at 1 year on all measures. In addition, there was a nonsignificant trend toward better maintenance of gains with 16-session CBT, contrasted to the three other treatment combinations. Further, there was some evidence that the patients who were more depressed initially tended not to maintain their gains, regardless of treatment modality or duration.

Shapiro et al. (1994) tentatively raise a number of questions about the degree to which their findings have direct implications for service delivery. Their posttherapy data suggest that patients with mild or moderate depression will gain no more from 16 sessions than they would from eight; only patients with severe depression would derive extra benefit from (and hence justify) longer therapy. However, follow-up data suggest a more cautious interpretation, since the pattern of maintenance of gains suggests that simple recovery is not an adequate measure of the efficacy of brief interventions. In particular, eight sessions of exploratory therapy appears to be too little, and there is some evidence favoring 16 sessions of CBT. Overall, poorer maintenance was evident in patients with greater levels of initial distress. This may caution against too marked a contraction of therapy contact, particularly for more depressed patients.

A further concern regarding this study is the extent to which its results can be generalized from a research to a clinical sample. Although it is clear that patients met study criteria for depression, the majority (approximately 60%) were self-referred or referred through occupational sources, raising some questions about the comparability of these patients to the usual clinical population. This question has been partially addressed by the Collaborative Psychotherapy Project (CPP; Barkham et al., 1994), an explicit attempt to replicate the Sheffield project within a standard clinical context. This was carried out by researchers in close contact (and overlapping with) workers involved in the Sheffield project, and, though (for practical reasons) smaller-scale, used a similar methodology and research design. Thirty-six patients of low, medium, and high depression severity were allocated to CBT or psychodynamic/interpersonal therapy for eight or 16 sessions (see Table 2).

Two main effects were found. CPP patients fared significantly better in therapies carried out over 16 sessions than in eight-session treatments. Secondly, while posttherapy gains made by patients in the CPP and the Sheffield project were similar, at 3-month follow-up there was strong evidence that CPP patients were failing to maintain their gains. The severity × duration interaction found at posttherapy in Shapiro et al. (1994) was not replicated, though there is good reason to believe that the low statistical power of the CPP study may have contributed to this null finding (Barkham et al., 1994).

Taken together, the Sheffield study and the CPP provide evidence that both therapy modalities under study are—broadly—equally effective and equally rapid in their initial response. However, some caution is necessary in considering "dose–response" relationships found in the Sheffield project, particularly where these appear to indicate that very brief periods of therapy may be effective at posttherapy. Longer periods of therapy appear to be associated with better longer-term outcomes, particularly in the case of interpersonal/psychodynamic therapy. In addition, more severely distressed individuals have a greater risk of relapse, and, while there is no clear indication as to why, there is some evidence from the CPP that clinic sample patients may be more at risk of relapse than those usually found in research populations.

Summary

- Studies that meet the most stringent criteria of methodological rigor confirm the efficacy of certain structured psychotherapies for depression.
- The best studies in the field demonstrate that interpersonal therapy and CBT are effective in the treatment of depression.

- In the single trial in which there was a contrast of dynamic exploratory therapy and CBT, the two modes of treatment were equivalent in their efficacy.
- Posttherapy, significant effects are observed in from as little as eight sessions for less severely depressed patients, and 16 sessions for more severely depressed individuals.
- In the first application of these effects to clinical settings, the briefer treatments were found to be less effective.
- These effects are both statistically and clinically significant.
- The long-term effectiveness of acute treatments is relatively poor for the majority of these patients: only between one-third and one-quarter of any sample can be expected to remain recovered without relapse after 18 months.
- The contrast of imipramine and psychotherapy tends to favor imipramine, particularly for the more seriously depressed individuals.
- Both medication and psychotherapy may face problems of patient acceptability. Immediate dropout rates may be higher for psychotherapy because of its delayed treatment effects, whereas some antidepressants (e.g., imipramine) produce side effects that may be poorly tolerated.
- Both the Pittsburgh and the Minnesota studies indicate that the quality of therapy delivered may be critical in maintaining patients functioning.
- There is relatively good evidence to suggest that psychotherapy both in combination with imipramine and alone can contribute to a significant reduction in relapse rates, particularly when the therapy is delivered to high standards.

Implications

- CBT, IPT, and exploratory dynamic therapy appear to be useful in treating acute episodes of MDD.
- There is evidence that IPT has a useful role in the prevention of relapse.
- Purchasers of psychotherapy services should be aware that while these modes of intervention are effective at alleviating a single episode of depression, patients treated in this way are likely to need further treatment.
- Continued drug treatments are helpful in reducing the likelihood of subsequent episodes of depression.

- Psychotherapy may be a viable alternative in prolonging the periods between depressive episodes in some patients.
- The pattern of dropouts in studies contrasting pharmacological and psychological treatment suggests that education about the efficacy of medication and psychotherapy may be helpful for both treatments to prevent mounting patient dissatisfaction leading to attrition.
- Although some of the studies reviewed were designed to contrast psychological and pharmacological treatment in terms of efficacy, the two should in no sense be seen as mutually exclusive. There is accumulating evidence (reviewed below) to suggest that their combination may be the treatment of choice for many severely depressed patients.
- Notwithstanding evidence concerning efficacy, there may be clinical factors (including patient choice, adverse medical reactions, and social/cultural factors) that contribute to the greater acceptability of specific treatment forms to particular populations. These need to be taken into consideration in the provision of mental health services.
- Purchasers should be aware that the evidence suggests that the long-term effectiveness of treatments in delaying subsequent episodes of depression relates strongly to the quality of therapy offered—that is, the better the quality of the treatment, the more likely that it will help delay relapse. Thus in costing services, a lower-quality service may generate a group of inadequately treated "revolving-door" patients who make further demands on health care provision.
- The literature implies that long-term, low-frequency psychotherapeutic maintenance of these patients may offer benefits, in terms of both enhancing adherence to drug regimens and contributing independently to diminished relapse rates.

REVIEWS OF TREATMENTS FOR DEPRESSION

Meta-Analyses

The most thorough, and hence perhaps the most significant, review of psychopharmacological and psychotherapeutic treatments for depression has been conducted by the U.S. Public Health Service's Agency for Health Care Policy and Research (AHCPR; Depression Guideline Panel, 1993a,b,c). The AHCPR was mandated to develop clinical practice guidelines for primary care practitioners and other health care practitioners, and has attempted to establish these guidelines on the basis of a comprehensive review of treatment trials. Thirty-nine treatment reviews were commissioned by a steering panel, covering 3,500 studies published in peer-reviewed journals between 1975 and 1990. Inclusion–exclusion criteria restricted the range of studies to those in which patients were selected on the basis of a DSM-III-R diagnosis of depression, where the research design was a randomized controlled trial, and where treatment effects were measured using a standardized method which permitted assessment of depressive and/or functional status before and after treatment. Meta-analyses were then conducted to ascertain the efficacy of treatments. The majority of trials considered examined the efficacy of psychopharmacological interventions.

Schulberg and Rush (1994), who were members of the steering panel, note that the methodology adopted has certain restrictions that are relevant to the applicability of the AHCPR findings to primary care settings. In particular, most studies of depression are conducted in tertiary rather than primary care units. This raises questions about the generalizability of findings, particularly since there is little direct research evidence that speaks to the treatment of the mild depressive conditions frequently seen in primary care. The high internal validity of studies included in the review was considered by the steering panel to overcome the problem of external validity (Schulberg & Rush, 1994), though this is a view which has not gone unchallenged (e.g., Munoz et al., 1994).

The published depression guidelines (Depression Guideline Panel, 1993a,b,c) advise practitioners on the treatments that are most likely to be effective, together with a rating of the strength of supporting evidence. One difficulty in assessing the guidelines is that the literature review on which they are based has not yet been published, though we are grateful to Professor A. John Rush (Chair of the Guideline Panel) for advancing us a draft of this report, covering evidence for the efficacy of psychological therapies (Jarrett & Down, in press).

In addition to the AHCPR report there have been six meta-analytic reviews of treatments for depression in which psychological treatments for depression are contrasted (1) against one another, and (2) in comparison to psychopharmacological interventions. These reviews usually examine comparative controlled trials of therapy which include either a waiting list or a placebo therapy comparison group and hence also provide data on the untreated course of depression.

Three reviews have focused on the efficacy of psychotherapy as contrasted with pharmacotherapy (Quality Assurance Project, 1983; Steinbruek et al., 1983; Conte et al., 1986). These reviews excluded research examining the benefits of psychotherapy alone. Dobson (1989) and Neitzel and Russell (1987) include more of such studies, but restrict their analysis to trials using the BDI. Robinson et al.'s (1990) review is perhaps the most comprehensive, examining a wider range of studies using multiple outcome measures and more diverse forms of therapy.

One problem with meta-analyses is that different conclusions can be reached because varying the sampling criteria leads to the inclusion or exclusion of different studies. Equally, more reviews of the same database would not advance our understanding, and hence it is important to be clear how far the meta-analyses to be discussed overlap. Unfortunately, this can be difficult to ascertain. While Jarrett and Down (in press), Robinson et al. (1990), and Dobson (1989) all provide a full list of studies included, this is not the case for the Quality Assurance Project (1983), Steinbruek et al. (1983), or Neitzel et al. (1987). Since the AHCPR guidelines and Robinson et al. provide the most comprehensive reviews, these will be described in some detail below. It should be noted, however, that with only 11 studies in common, there is only marginal overlap between these two reviews. The earlier meta-analyses will be summarized first, together with some indication of the degree of overlap between them.

The Quality Assurance Project (1983) analyzed data from 200 studies in which a variety of therapies were employed, of which only 10 involved the use of psychotherapy; the majority were concerned with the efficacy of medication. On the basis of this (rather limited) sample, an effect size of 0.69 was found for psychotherapy of any type, contrasted with a mean effect size for tricyclics of 0.55 and for monoamine oxidase inhibitors (MAOIs) of 0.39.

Conte et al. (1986) reviewed 17 studies published between 1974 and 1984 in which psychotherapy in combination with medication was contrasted with another treatment; all bar two are included in Robinson et al.'s (1990) review. A statistical weighting procedure was used to reflect methodological adequacy, the results of which were used in the assessment of treatment effects. This procedure makes a number of assumptions about the link between methodological quality and outcome that have not been supported by more conventional meta-analyses (Smith et al., 1980), and its use may be questioned. No distinction among different types of therapy was made. Conte et al. conclude that there is some limited evidence for the greater effectiveness of combination treatments, as against psychotherapy or pharmacotherapy alone.

Steinbruek et al. (1983) examined 56 studies published between 1962 and 1981 where psychotherapy alone or pharmacotherapy alone was contrasted with a control group. A significantly larger mean effect size was found for psychotherapy (1.22) contrasted with medication

(0.61). Although an effect size for tricyclic medications was derived (0.67), no separate analyses are given for the differing categories of psychotherapy. Further, contrasting therapies against waiting lists would be expected to give a different result from comparison with placebo; in this study both groups are subsumed under a single heading ("control group"). These considerations limit the usefulness of this review.

Both Dobson et al. (1989) and Neitzel et al. (1987) conducted reviews of trials where the BDI was used as an outcome measure. This restriction on outcome measures was introduced to increase the uniformity of comparisons, and also on the grounds that the BDI appears to be a more conservative measure of change than therapist-rated instruments (Lambert et al., 1986).

Neitzel at al. (1987) collected their database from all studies included in the Steinbruek et al. (1983) analysis together with additional studies published subsequently. Forty-five outcome studies were identified, of which 31 used the BDI and were included in the analysis. Their results indicated that the type of therapy did not influence outcome, and that individual therapy produced larger effect sizes than group treatment. Pooling data from across studies, the clinical significance of treatment effects was computed by contrasting treated and control patients to two reference groups for which normative data for the BDI had been obtained. The first of these reference groups was specifically selected as a nondistressed group; the second, a general population sample.

Using these contrasts, the average treated client moved from 4.79 SD units above the mean for the nondistressed group to 1.62 SD units posttreatment; using general population norms the comparable figures are 2.9 SD units and 0.71 SD units. Control subjects had similar pretreatment scores to treated patients, but showed little gain posttreatment. (Their posttreatment scores were 3.97 SD units and 2.96 SD units when contrasted to the nondistressed and general population samples.) Gains were maintained at follow-up, though it is worth noting that the mean follow-up period was only 16 weeks (range 4 to 52).

These figures can be expressed, perhaps more meaningfully, in terms of percentiles. On this basis the average treated client moves from a pretreatment level at the 99.9th percentile to the 94.7th percentile of the nondistressed group at posttreatment. Contrasted to the general population sample the gains are more striking—from the 99.8th percentile to the 76.1th percentile. Although there can be some debate about the clinical significance of these scores, they do indicate that the average treated client will have an approximate posttreatment BDI score of 10, which would place him or her at the boundary between a normal and a mildly depressed level of functioning.

Dobson's (1989) review identified 28 studies in which cognitive therapy was contrasted with other therapies, and (as with Nietzel et al.)

in which the BDI was included as an outcome measure. Given that Nietzel et al. do not cite the studies included in their review, the degree of overlap between the two analyses cannot be readily ascertained (though it is likely to be considerable). In contrast to Nietzel et al., Dobson found mean effect sizes favoring cognitive therapy as contrasted with pharmacotherapy (0.53), behavior therapy (0.46), and other psychotherapies (0.54). Comparing cognitive therapy to waiting list or no-treatment controls gave a mean effect size of 2.15, indicating that the average treated client did better than 98% of control subjects. No follow-up data were analyzed; nor were data for clients who dropped out of treatment.

Robinson et al. (1990) reviewed 58 studies up to 1986, all focused on outpatient psychological treatments of depressive disorder (excluding subthreshold cases). Eleven of these studies were not examined by Dobson (1986), and 40 were not covered by Nietzel et al. (1987). Therapies were classified as behavioral, cognitive (where treatments focused on the evaluation and modification of cognitive patterns), cognitive-behavioral, or general verbal.

Rather few studies utilized standard outpatient samples. Around half used media announcements to recruit subjects, and a further quarter solicited students. Twelve percent did not report on the source of their patients, leaving only nine studies unambiguously focused on out-patient attenders. In addition, only 35% of investigations require patients to meet formal diagnostic criteria for depression. The analysis is further weakened by the fact that most of the results are reported using posttreatment rather than follow-up data, on the basis that the figures for each data point were very similar (34 of the 58 studies had follow-up, but the mean length of follow-up was only 13 weeks, with a range of 2 to 52 weeks).

Contrasting therapy of any kind against no therapy (defined as placebo or waiting-list control) gives an effect size of 0.73 at posttherapy and 0.68 at follow-up. As might be expected, effect sizes are higher where the contrast is against waiting list (0.84); when compared to placebo, the effect size is nonsignificant (0.28).

Overall, behavioral, cognitive, and cognitive-behavioral treatments showed moderate effect sizes (1.02, 0.96, and 0.85, respectively). Verbal therapies showed a more modest effect size (0.49), though this figure is based on only six studies.

A better measure of the relative efficacy of different classes of therapy is afforded by comparative studies that include differing treatments and therefore allow direct comparison among them. Using data from these trials there is evidence of a modest superiority for cognitive-behavioral over behavioral treatment (0.24), and a moderate superiority of cognitive and cognitive-behavioral treatments over verbal treatments (0.47 and 0.27, respectively). Fifteen studies examined the implementation of these therapies in group or individual settings, finding equal efficacy for all approaches.

Interpretation of these results is made difficult by the fact that ratings of allegiance of the investigators correlated highly and significantly ($r = .58$) with the results of direct comparisons between treatments. Using a regression analysis to partial out this effect reduced the effect sizes almost to zero. Longer treatment or the number of sessions did not contribute to a greater effect size, though the mean length of treatments was only seven sessions, and this may not be sufficient to test this variable.

There was little evidence of any specific client characteristics that influenced treatment outcome. Effect sizes did not vary reliably when examining outcomes in relation to the initial severity of depression (as measured by BDI), the presence or absence of diagnosed depression, or the source of referral of the client.

To examine the clinical significance of the gains made by patients (Jacobsen et al., 1984), Robinson et al. identified 39 studies reporting normative data on the BDI, in order to contrast the level of depression after treatment with that obtaining in the general population. One problem with this approach is that it is difficult to know against whom patients should be compared. Some studies have established norms on the basis of samples selected because of the absence of pathology; unsuprisingly, these norms are more stringent than those obtaining from general population surveys. Using these estimates, therapy appears to shift the average client from 2.4 *SD* above the mean for the general population to 0.8 *SD* above the mean. Comparison with a nondistressed population gives an equivalent pre–post therapy shift (from 3.4 to 1.4 *SD* above the mean) but does suggest some residual distress. Nonetheless, the clinical effect of treatment is clear.

As noted earlier, there is only marginal overlap between the AHCPR review and Robinson et al.'s (1990) meta-analysis. The AHCPR review identified 22 randomized controlled trials of cognitive therapy, 13 of behavioral therapy, four of interpersonal therapy, eight of brief dynamic therapy, and one of marital therapy. Studies included in the analysis involved treatment of both adult and elderly populations, and for both behavioral and cognitive therapy used both individual and group formats. Data were analyzed using "intent-to-treat" samples (contrasting outcomes for all patients entered into the trial, regardless of whether a full course of therapy was given).

Rather than using conventional meta-analytic methodology (as described in the introduction to this report), the guideline panel employed techniques based on Bayesian models—the Confidence Profile Method (CPM; a full account is given in Eddy et al., 1990). Bayesian statistical methods can be described as a formal framework within which data from available studies are used to produce the best fit to a hypothetical, perfectly performed study. Existing data form a "prior distribution," which describes our present state of knowledge about, for example, outcomes for a particular therapy. The addition of further studies describes a "posterior distribution," representing our new state of knowledge as a consequence of the addition of further evidence. The application of Bayesian statistics results in a series of probability functions, which in essence describe the likelihood of a particular intervention having a particular result—for example, the probability that a treatment will be successful in resolving depression. It is argued that these methods are more sensitive and appropriate than conventional statistical techniques, and allow more scope for the management of possible bias in the studies forming the meta-analysis (Eddy et al., 1990).

The CPM method can be employed for continuous data (e.g., differences in BDI scores). However, while of interest to researchers, such data do not give a result that is easy to interpret if asking questions such as, "What is the probability that patients can be expected to get better when therapy A is used?" Here it is necessary to employ categorical scoring, in which cutoff points are applied to scores, below and above which patients are deemed to be, for example, better or not better. Because categorical scoring has an obvious utility for practitioners, it was adopted by the guidelines panel. An important consequence of this decision is that not all the trials identified by the panel could be included in the meta-analysis, because outcomes were not reported in a categorical form. In addition, some studies did not report the number of patients randomized to each cell. This further reduces the number of analyzable studies markedly. Only six studies of brief dynamic therapy were meta-analyzed, and estimates of the efficacy of interpersonal therapy rest on the NIMH study alone. No trials of marital therapy were appropriate for analysis. Finally, it should be noted that the CPM method does not declare a conventional effect size; rather, it derives an expected response rate for each therapy.

Table 3 shows the likely overall efficacy of all therapies combined and of each treatment alone (Depression Guidelines Panel, 1993b). The

TABLE 3. Meta-Analyses of Psychotherapy Trials (Depression Guidelines Panel, 1993b)

Therapy	Overall efficacy	Number of trials analyzed
Behavioral therapy alone	55.3%	10
Brief dynamic therapy alone	34.8%	6
Cognitive therapy alone	46.6%	12
Interpersonal therapy alone	52.3%	1
All therapies	50.0%	29

AHCPR report also computes response rates contrasting each of the therapies against waiting-list control, other psychological therapies, placebo control, and medication administered alone (these latter two comparisons are discussed further below). All therapies combined yielded an estimated overall efficacy of 50%; contrasted to waiting list there was a 26% advantage to therapy, and contrasted to placebo a 15.7% advantage. A more meaningful contrast is the impact of each of the psychotherapies, though for some therapies there are few appropriate studies on which to base these computations.

For behavioral therapy, the overall efficacy was 55.3%. Contrasted to all other forms of psychotherapy it was 9.1% more effective (six studies). Compared to waiting list (five studies), it was 17.1% more effective. Brief dynamic therapy had an overall efficacy of 34.8%; contrasted to other therapies it was slightly less effective (-7.8%; eight studies). Cognitive therapy was found to have an overall efficacy of 46.6%, with approximately equal efficacy to the other therapies (-4.4%, six studies). For interpersonal therapy, the NIMH study provides the only appropriate data for meta-analysis; on this basis it has an overall efficacy of 52.3%, and exceeds the efficacy of cognitive therapy by 13.3%.

Undoubtedly the Confidence Profile Method is statistically sophisticated and (from this perspective) superior to other forms of meta-analysis. However, this considerably restricts the number of studies appropriate for inclusion in this form of analysis. As discussed in the introduction to this book, studies meeting the inclusion criteria for conventional meta-analysis may not be representative either of clinical work or even of research trials, a criticism that may apply even more strongly to the CPM technique. This may lead to the emergence of misleading conclusions. Thus, few clinicians would accept that behavior therapy alone was the most effective treatment method for depression. Although achieving a high ranking in the meta-analysis of the depressions guidelines panel, this is most likely an artifact of sampling and of the six contrasts performed. Although CPM meta-analysis is an exciting development, it will require a considerable extension of the database to ensure that specific contrasts of therapies with one another can be interpreted reliably.

Comparison of Psychotherapy, Medication, and Combination Treatments

Robinson et al. (1990) examined 15 studies comparing the effectiveness of psychological interventions alone, medication alone, and the combination of these treatments. The majority of these studies employed cognitive-behavioral or behavioral psychotherapies. However, basic methodological requirements were not always met—not all studies ensured that therapeutic levels of medication were prescribed, and although most trials utilized antidepressants, two (surprisingly) employed benzodiazepines.

When contrasted to the use of tricyclic antidepressants, psychotherapy showed a significant, though small advantage, with an effect size of 0.12. There was no evidence of a significant advantage to combination treatments contrasted with psychotherapy alone or medication alone. However, if the effect of investigator allegiance is controlled statistically (as described earlier), the advantage to psychotherapy disappears.

In the AHCPR report, contrasting psychological therapies to medication alone showed an advantage to psychological therapy of 14% (based on eight studies). More specifically, the comparison of behavioral therapy to medication indicated that it was 17.1% more effective than medication (based on two studies). The contrast of cognitive therapy to placebo and clinical management (in the NIMH study alone) suggests that it was 9.4% more effective, and to medication alone 15.3% more effective (three studies). Brief dynamic therapy compared to medication was 8.4% more effective (two studies). For interpersonal therapy, using data from the NIMH study alone, its efficacy exceeds that of placebo and clinical management by 13.3% and of medication and clinical management by 12.3% (based on the BDI as the outcome measure and using data from the intent-to-treat sample).

Summary

- There have been a number of reviews of psychotherapy outcome studies on MDD, which appear to exhaustively cover the literature up to 1990.
- Up to this time evidence has accumulated to indicate that therapy is considerably better than no therapy. Cognitive-behavioral treatment, in particular, is superior to less structured forms of psychotherapeutic intervention.
- When comparison is made with placebo psychotherapy treatments, the effectiveness of treatment is less marked, though this contrast is weakened by the variable definitions of placebo therapy employed across trials.
- Direct comparisons among different forms of therapy show small differences, but nevertheless the superiority of cognitive-behavioral treatments over other verbal treatments remains.

- The superiority of psychotherapeutic treatment over pharmacological treatment is small and unreliable across studies, and is confounded by the lack of control over the nature of the medical treatments offered.
- Reviews include few well-structured studies of psychodynamic treatments.
- Estimates of effect sizes differ across meta-analyses as a function of the sampling frame of the original studies, the dependant measures used, the statistical principles of the meta-analysis, and the original date of the investigation. Broadly speaking, larger effect sizes are observed with patient samples who are likely to have been less severely impaired, on clinician ratings as opposed to self-report measures, and with studies carried out by the proponents of techniques.
- There is little evidence of an advantage to treatments combining pharmacotherapy and psychotherapy, though the adequacy of implementation of medications in studies examined is questionable and the study designs tend not to be comparable. In particular, differential dropout rates between treatment conditions make the size of the difference between treated and untreated groups a poor index of relative effectiveness. Nevertheless there seems to be a consistent value added by psychotherapy to the medical regimen, although the magnitude of this is hard to estimate.
- Posttherapy follow-up periods are probably too brief to permit clear conclusions about long-term effectiveness.

Implications

- There are encouraging data from these meta-analyses suggesting that episodes of depression may be relieved by psychotherapeutic interventions, particularly when this is of a structured form.
- There is less evidence to suggest that the therapies administered reduce the likelihood of subsequent episodes, as would be expected on the basis of the natural history of the disorder.
- The studies are not representative of standard clinical practice, which most commonly combines psychotherapeutic and drug treatments, or where patients' preference for one or other form of therapy reduces the options available to the clinician.
- Most studies antedate the introduction of newer, more specific antidepressants, with somewhat fewer side effects and greater patient acceptability. During the same period there has also been a cultural change, which may have made drug treatments more

acceptable. The relative usefulness of pharmacology and therapy should not therefore be judged using meta-analytic data.

SPECIFIC COMPARISONS

In addition to the general problems associated with meta-analytic studies detailed in the introduction, a particular problem in this context is that for some contrasts there are too few studies to yield meaningful effect sizes. Examination of qualitative rather than quantitative reviews is necessary to overcome this limitation.

Comparison of Psychotherapy Alone, Medication Alone, and the Two in Combination

Wexler and Cicchetti (1992) review treatment trials contrasting psychotherapy alone, pharmacotherapy alone, and combination treatments, identifying eight relevant studies. Manning et al. (1992) review 17 trials in which there is a contrast of combination treatment with any specified psychotherapy against any single component of the combination. There is considerable overlap between the two reviews, with six of the studies included in the Wexler and Cicchetti (1992) review considered by Manning et al. (1992).

In three primary studies considered by Wexler and Cicchetti (Blackburn et al., 1981; Hersen et al., 1984; Murphy et al., 1984), all three possible treatment modalities were compared; five further studies contrasted at least two interventions. Psychological treatments were not analyzed separately but included cognitive therapy, behavioral therapy, psychodynamic therapy, or interpersonal therapy. Medication was invariably a tricyclic antidepressant.

All studies used the BDI and broadly similar cutoff points to indicate recovery (usually a BDI score of less than 8), but different criteria were used to indicate nonresponse to treatment (ranging from a BDI score of >16 to one of >23).

Two of the three studies contrasting all treatment modalities (Blackburn et al., 1981; Murphy et al., 1984) suggested that combination treatments had the greatest efficacy, with intermediate efficacy for psychotherapy, and the lowest for medication. The third (Hersen et al., 1984) showed a nonsignificant trend favoring psychotherapy over combination, with medication showing the least efficacy. Combined data from these studies suggested a trend indicating that combination treatments were the most effective, followed by psychotherapy alone and medication alone. Overall, however, there was no statistically significant evidence demonstrating the greater efficacy of any one treatment over the other two.

Three studies compared psychotherapy alone to medication alone (NIMH, 1994; Elkin et al., 1989; McLean & Hakstian, 1979, 1990; Rush et al., 1977). In two of these, psychotherapy showed a higher response rate; in the NIMH trials similar response rates were obtained. Beck et al. (1985) contrasted psychotherapy alone to combination, producing results favoring psychotherapy over medication. However, these studies may form a poor basis for comparison of medication and psychotherapy. The Rush et al. study (1977) has been criticized for poor implementation of medication regimens; Beck et al. (1985) employed relatively low doses of amitriptyline for short periods; and in the NIMH (1994) trial, medication was offered in combination with clinical management.

Using data from the studies in their review Wexler and Cicchetti (1992) estimate that of 100 patients treated, the success rate will be 29% for medication, contrasted with 47% for both psychotherapy alone and combination treatments. These figures suggest a strong advantage for psychotherapy or its combination with medication. However, it is clear that each therapy modality shows a high rate of partial or nonresponse—42% with psychotherapy alone and 52% with medication alone, suggesting that treatment strategies based exclusively on either modality will show little benefit to a significant number of patients.

Manning et al. (1992) review a larger set of 17 studies. The most frequent comparison was of combination treatment against psychotherapy alone (12 comparisons) or psychotherapy and placebo against psychotherapy (12 out of 41 comparisons). Combined therapy was compared with medication alone or drug attention control 11 times. No studies were conducted by investigators with a primary interest in medication. Therapies were psychoanalytic, behavioral, cognitive, interpersonal, and marital. Amitriptyline was employed in six studies, imipramine in seven, and nortriptyline in two; two further studies employed diazepam or alprazolam. Only seven studies employed placebo conditions, leaving unresolved the question of whether the combination treatment using active medication reflected an augmented placebo response.

Small sample sizes, and hence low statistical power, were identified as a problem by these reviewers. Only two studies had more than 30 patients per treatment cell. In addition, most trials (15 of 17) focused on the acute phase of antidepressant treatment. Only seven included follow-up data (varying from 3 to 24 months), and four focused on maintenance therapy.

The efficacy of therapies was examined using a "box score" method, contrasting the relative outcomes associated with each treatment modality rather than their absolute impacts. In no study was combined therapy less effective than its component treatments. However, although some advantage was found to combination treatment, no clear superiority was evident. Summing across studies, combined treatments outperformed medication alone in four of 10 instances (40%), and outperformed psychotherapy alone or with placebo in seven of 18 instances (39%). Not enough trials were available to examine the impact of specific psychotherapies.

Data from a number of studies have suggested that both treatment failure and rate of dropout were highest for patients receiving medication. Given that the cited success rate of most studies usually reflects treatment completers, these factors are important to any consideration of clinical effectiveness. There is some evidence to suggest that dropout reflects dissatisfaction with treatment rather than clinical improvement. Weissman et al. (1979) reported that 92% of patients dropout because of dissatisfaction with treatment; in the NIMH study (Elkin et al., 1989) 77% of dropouts were for similar reasons. Fawcett et al. (1989) report that 98% of drop out was because of problems with medication side effects or dissatisfaction with treatment. Wexler and Cicchetti (1992) estimate the rate of dropout at 52% for medication, 30% for therapy alone, and 34% for combination treatments. In contrast, Manning et al. (1992) report that of 11 authors reporting attrition rates, only one study found attrition rates varied between single and combined treatments.

Two methodological issues, each contrasting in its implications, also caution against drawing firm conclusions on the basis of current literature. Firstly, medications may not have been adequately prescribed, or indeed therapies may have been contrasted against arguably inappropriate medications, such as anxiolytics, reducing the likely impact of pharmacotherapy. Secondly, rather few trials employed placebos, and none employed an active placebo (which mimics known side effects of the experimental medication), potentially inflating the impact attributable to medication.

Two studies included in both reviews illustrate the problems of inadequate prescription of medication. Rush et al. (1979) employed low doses of medication which were then rapidly withdrawn before outcome measures were taken. Blackburn et al.'s (1986) study was carried out in both an outpatient and a primary care setting; patients in primary care showed an unusually low response to medication against which therapy inevitably showed a superior outcome. Meterissian and Bradwejn (1989) suggest that comparative trials of psychotherapy and medication should be interpreted with caution because of poor or absent controls on medication levels and few checks on compliance. These authors examined 11 comparative studies carried out between 1977 and 1987, finding that only in around half were optimal levels of antidepressants employed; only three measured drug plasma levels. Of five studies using adequate doses, one reported psychotherapy to be superior to medication; the remainder found it equivalent. In those studies using lower doses of medication, two indicated that psychotherapy was superior, one that it was equivalent, and one that a combination treatment was best.

Turning to problems with placebo control, Greenberg et al. (1992) suggest that the performance of antidepressants in clinical trials is usually overestimated. Because of side effects, double-blind studies of antidepressants against placebo may be more transparent than intended; patients and clinicians are often able to guess correctly the form of medication they have been offered (e.g., Bystritsky & Waikar, 1994). For this reason, Greenberg et al. (1992) examined 22 studies of antidepressants in which trials compared both newer and standard antidepressants as well as a placebo control. Under these conditions effect sizes for medication fell to between one-half and one-quarter those usually reported. In addition, patient-rated change in these studies suggested no advantage for medication beyond that exerted by placebo. A similar effect has been noted in studies that employ an "active" placebo (Greenberg & Fisher, 1989; Thomson, 1982).

A related problem is the absence of attention control conditions in all but two studies. Patients receiving therapy as opposed to medication alone are likely to receive more time with their therapists (typically three or four times as much time), making it hard to distinguish the relative benefits of attention as opposed to therapeutic interventions.

On the basis of the Wexler and Cicchetti, and Manning et al. reviews it seems appropriate to conclude that there is no clear advantage to combination treatments. It may—tentatively and in line with the findings of the NIMH study—be appropriate for milder disorders to be treated with therapy alone and for more severe disorders to be treated with medication, with the later addition of therapy if needed. For patients between these extremes it may be helpful to use combination treatments. However, there is as yet little research evidence to underpin this view, particularly since most patients in the trials discussed above were diagnosed as having only mild or moderate depression.

Summary

- The relative efficacy of cognitive therapy and imipramine is controversial and unclear from studies directly comparing the two treatments.

- There are a number of apparently well-controlled studies which show medication to be at least equal, or superior; in studies that show the psychotherapy to be superior, the dosages tended to be lower and drug plasma levels were not monitored.
- The comparisons are confounded by the possibility of overestimating drug effects; patients and assessors are rarely genuinely blind to their treatments because of the side effects of their medication.
- The comparison of the two treatments simply in terms of symptomatic improvement may conceal important differences between them in terms of patient acceptability, which is reflected in the differential dropout rates.
- These studies yield very little information concerning the comparative effectiveness of medication and psychotherapy, other than for cognitive or cognitive-behavioral treatment.

Brief Dynamic Therapy

There are few controlled trials of brief dynamic therapy. Of those available, few have been carried out by proponents of the technique; usually dynamic therapy has been employed as a contrast to alternative therapies with which the investigators were professionally identified. Treatment periods are usually short—a mode of 12 sessions (range 12–36) in the studies reviewed below, which may be too short for this technique. Therapists in these trials were unlikely to administer dynamic therapy appropriately because of their lack of commitment to the method. These methodological problems, taken together with the likely bias introduced by investigator allegiance, suggests that results from these studies should be viewed with caution.

A number of these trials suggest that dynamic therapy is significantly less effective than other forms of intervention. Thus Steuer et al. (1984) found it less effective than cognitive therapy; McLean and Hakstian (1979), that it performed more poorly than behavior therapy; and Covi and Lipman (1987), that it was less effective than both cognitive therapy alone and cognitive therapy combined with medication.

Kornblith et al. (1983) contrasted behavioral self-control methods against dynamic therapy; all treatments were administered in groups and were found to be equally effective. However, small sample sizes and variations in sample size across treatment conditions make interpretation of this study difficult.

Bellack and colleagues (Bellack et al., 1981; Hersen et al., 1984) treated 50 depressed women with either amitriptyline, social skills training and medication, social skills training and placebo, or dynamic therapy with placebo (designated as a "nonspecific therapy"). All treatments resulted in equivalent gains.

Thompson et al. (1987, 1990) contrasted dynamic therapy cognitive therapy and behavioral therapy against a wait-list control; all treatments were delivered in group formats and with elderly depressed patients. Dynamic therapy was more effective than a wait-list control, and all three treatments were equally effective both posttherapy and at 1- and 2-year follow-up.

These results are at best equivocal. No study favors dynamic over other therapies, a number suggest it performs more poorly, and the best-designed study (Thompson et al.) was conducted in a group format with older people, which cautions against generalization. Firm conclusions regarding the efficacy of brief dynamic techniques are not possible without further and better-designed research.

Contrasts between Cognitive, Behavioral and Cognitive-Behavioral Therapy

Distinctions can be drawn between pure cognitive treatments, pure behavioral therapy, and interventions that employ a range of cognitive and behavioral techniques (such as the combination of cognitive restructuring and activity scheduling). In her review, Blackburn (1988) reserves the term cognitive therapy for therapies that use Beck's approach to treatment (which focuses on modifying maladaptive thoughts and beliefs), and CBT for those that incorporate other components.

Shaw (1977) contrasted the effects of cognitive therapy, behavior therapy, an attention control group, and a waiting-list. Treatment was biweekly for 4 weeks; posttherapy cognitive therapy was more effective than other conditions, but the result was not sustained at 1 month follow-up. Taylor and Marshall (1977) (whose "patients" were mildly depressed students) compared cognitive therapy, behavior therapy, cognitive-behavioral therapy, and a waiting-list control group, finding that while cognitive therapy was as effective as behavior therapy, cognitive-behavioral therapy was more effective than either alone. Zeiss et al. (1979) found that cognitive therapy, social skills training, and techniques aimed at increasing pleasant activities were all equivalent in efficacy, and all showed gains relative to a waiting-list control group. Wilson et al. (1983) found behavior therapy and cognitive therapy to be equally effective when contrasted with patients in a waiting-list control group.

There are few studies in which cognitive therapy is contrasted with other treatments, and these tend to use recruited subjects, to have small numbers of patients, and to use variations from Beck's model. The relative importance of cognitive and cognitive-behavioral techniques is not yet clear.

Relapse with Cognitive and Cognitive-Behavioral Treatments

A claim often made for CBT is that it acts prophylactically against recurrence of depression; most (though not all) studies support this contention.

Kovacs et al. (1981) followed up patients in the Rush et al. (1977) study; after 1 year treatment gains both with CBT and medication were maintained, though patients treated with CBT had significantly lower levels of depression than those treated with medication, and there was a trend for more of them to be judged as being in remission. Beck et al. (1985) found improvement to be stable over 6 and 12 months in patients who had received CBT or CBT in combination with medication. There was a trend for the combination group to be doing better than the CBT group at 12 months. Simons et al. (1986), reporting follow-up data from a study by Murphy et al. (1984), found that at 12 months patients who had received CBT had a significantly lower relapse rate than those receiving medication. Blackburn et al. (1986), reporting follow-up of Blackburn et al. (1981), found significantly greater relapse in patients who received medication than in patients receiving CBT at 6 months, though this reduced to a trend at 2 years. Rotzer-Zimmer et al. (1985, cited in Williams, 1992) and Evans et al. (1992) also found a significantly reduced rate of relapse in patients treated with CBT, as compared to those receiving medication. In contrast the follow-up phase of the NIMH study (Shea et al., 1992) suggested no significant advantage to CBT over other interventions.

Summary

- There seems to be a prophylactic effect of CBT when administered by those responsible for the development of the technique.
- This effect does not generalize to trials which were not conducted exclusively by proponents of CBT.

DYSTHYMIC DISORDER/DYSTHYMIA

Markowitz (1994) has written a comprehensive review of evidence for the efficacy of psychotherapies for dysthymic disorder; much of the following discussion is based on this work. Although the clinical picture of dysthymic disorder has been recognized for many years, most quantitative research follows its reclassification in DSM-III-R as an Axis I mood disorder rather than a personality disorder.

Approximately 3% of Americans have dysthymia (Robins & Regier, 1991), and there is evidence that these individuals are at elevated risk of developing an episode of MDD (McCullough et al., 1992). There is also evidence that approximately half of dysthymics do not respond to medication or refuse it (Markowitz, 1994). As a group they have a low placebo response rate, of around 15% (Kocsis et al., 1988), which increases the salience of treatment trials showing positive outcomes.

Psychodynamic and Psychoanalytic Studies

There are no quantitative psychoanalytic studies of dysthymic disorder, though historically there has been extensive qualitative discussion of the depressive personality. As a consequence there is little evidence to support—or to disprove—the efficacy of psychodynamic methods in treating this condition.

Interpersonal Psychotherapy

Markowitz and colleagues at Cornell University are investigating the effectiveness of interpersonal psychotherapy (IPT) for dysthymia; pilot data from three small samples is promising (Markowitz, 1994). Mason et al. (1993) have treated nine subjects with 12 sessions of IPT, and obtained a significant reduction in HRSD scores. Overall, of 17 patients treated by this group, none have worsened and 11 have achieved remission, with most gains maintained at 2-year follow-up.

Cognitive-Behavioral Therapy

Markowitz reviews data from seven studies; in these, largely open trials the mean response rate is 41% (which is close to that obtained using medication in RCTs). Only two of these have examined substantial numbers of patients.

Gonzales et al. (1985) report a trial of 113 patients treated with 12 2-hour individual or group "psychoeducational" sessions over 2 months, with follow-up at 1 month and at 6 months. Results varied according to diagnosis, with more improvement for those with acute MDD (75% reaching a recovery criterion) than those with chronic intermittent depression (43%) or double depression (27%).

De Jong et al. (1986) treated 30 unmedicated inpatients over 3 months. A combination of activity scheduling, social competence training, and cognitive restructuring achieved a higher response rate (60%) than cognitive restructuring alone (30%) or a waiting list (10%). However, data from dropouts from treatment was not analyzed. At 6 months follow-up of half the sample, gains were maintained. One problem with this study is that response was defined as a BDI score ≤14, or by a 50% reduction in pretreatment BDI scores. The clinical significance of gains defined in this way is arguable.

Fennel and Teasdale (1982) treated five patients with long-term depression, all of whom had failed to respond to previous treatment. One patient showed clear improvement, though the remainder showed some reduction in BDI scores.

Harpin et al. (1982) report the treatment of 12 patients who had failed to improve with medication. Patients either received 10 weeks of twice weekly CBT ($n = 6$) or were allocated to a waiting-list control group ($n = 6$). A significant drop in HRSD scores was found in the active treatment group as contrasted to the control group, though results were poorer with more severe levels of depression. Two of the six treated patients showed significant pre–post improvement, but only one maintained this at 6 months.

Stravynski et al. (1991) treated six patients with 15 weekly sessions of CBT; significant improvements in HRSD scores were obtained, and four patients no longer met criteria for dysthymic disorder following treatment.

McCullough (1991) treated 10 dsythymics over a rather longer period than the above studies, with a range of 14 to 44 weekly sessions. All reached the recovery criterion of a BDI score ≤10, and nine remained in remission at 2 years follow-up. These results are perhaps less promising than they appear, in that an original cohort of 20 patients was treated, of whom four did not complete treatment and six were unavailable to follow-up.

Mercier et al. (1992) report a 12- to 16-week trial with 15 chronic dysthmics; four booster sessions were offered over the 6-month follow-up period. Three of eight dysthymics and three out of seven double depressives responded, and of the six responders four remained well over the follow-up period. Given that all responders had been depressed for 7 years or longer, this is an impressive result.

Combined Treatment Studies

Only three combined treatment studies have been carried out, all with sample sizes that limit their statistical power. Miller et al. (1985) report that two of four patients responded to a combination of CBT, social skills training, and medication. Becker et al. (1987) allocated 39 mildly symptomatic patients either to social skills training or crisis-supportive psychotherapy, along with either nortriptyline or placebo. After 16 weeks of treatment, gains were evident in all conditions. A similar result was obtained by Waring et al. (1988), with 12 mildly depressed patients given either cognitive marital therapy or supportive therapy and also doxepin or placebo; all patients improved.

Overall, the research literature is limited. Studies are few in number and often employ small samples; therapies are not always well defined, and not infrequently only one therapist is employed. There is some evidence of the efficacy of both IPT and CBT in treating this condition, and certainly the results obtained are comparable to those obtained with medication (Howland, 1991). Markowitz (1994) makes the interesting observation that there is a clear interpersonal focus in these treatments and that both CBT and IPT involve some remoralization and social reactivation in the patient. The degree to which these factors contribute to outcome requires further investigation.

Clearly more research is required not only into the results of acute treatment but also into the long-term outcome of such patients. Given that 79% of dysthmics will eventually develop an MDD (McCullough et al., 1992) and that there is a natural course of remission and recurrence (Keller & Shapiro, 1982; Keller et al., 1983), adequate follow-up periods are a *sine qua non* of outcome trials with dysthymic patients.

Summary

- There is a large group of patients suffering from chronic depression of somewhat lesser severity than MDD who are nonetheless statistically likely to experience episodes of MDD.
- Until recently research has not differentiated this group, and the variability of many early findings of psychotherapy outcome may be attributable to this ommision.
- Treatment studies specifically aimed at this group are few in number and small in size.
- There is accumulating evidence for the efficacy of IPT and CBT for dysthymia.

- Studies indicate that the rates of improvement in IPT and CBT are lower than that in MDD patients.
- There is evidence that longer treatments are more effective for these individuals.
- Evidence for the efficacy of combination treatments is currently very limited, though it is clear that medication and psychotherapy play an important part in the management of this condition.

Implications

- Although dysthymic patients may present as less symptomatic than those with MDD, the long-term nature of their disorder implies that clinical services are appropriately directed toward this group.
- As dysthymic patients respond less well to psychological interventions, this group should be distinguished from those with MDD in all reporting of outcomes, including research trials and clinical audit.
- There is some evidence that psychotherapy is effective for these individuals but that, paradoxically, longer-term treatment is likely to be required than for patients with MDD.

CBT WITH INPATIENTS AND PATIENTS WITH SEVERE DEPRESSION

Although many trials of CBT with inpatients have been reported, five recent studies are of particular interest in that they examine the use of CBT with patients with more severe depression and with associated behavior likely to exclude them from other treatment trials, such as suicidal behavior.

Thase et al. (1991) treated 16 unmedicated inpatients characterized by an HRSD score of ≥ 15 and with an index episode of MDD of less than 2 years' duration. All were drug-free for at least 7 days before the trial commenced. Twenty-six patients were assessed as suitable for the trial; 16 of these completed treatment, while the remainder had electroconvulsive therapy (ECT) or medication, either because of noncompliance with therapy or because of the emergence of severe symptomatology before therapy commenced.

Intensive CBT was offered five times a week over 4 weeks; on average patients received 13 sessions of therapy. Response was defined by reduction in HRSD scores of at least 50% and a final score of ≤ 10, and 13 patients (81%) reached this criterion. Follow-up therapy was offered, but only seven patients received more than 1 month of outpatient CBT; though the follow-up period is not specified, Thase et al. (1991) report that of these patients only one relapsed, compared to three out of four patients who refused further therapy and whose progress was monitored.

Thase and colleagues (1993) report an extension of this work to larger samples in three research trials (Thase et al., 1991; Simons & Thase, 1992; Nofzinger et al., 1993). In total, 142 unmedicated patients were treated either as outpatients ($n = 110$) or inpatients ($n = 32$). Outpatients received up to 20 sessions of CBT over 20 weeks; inpatients received more intensive therapy—20 sessions over 4 weeks (as reported in detail above; Thase et al., 1991). Across all three patient samples significant reductions in HRSD scores were found, though higher initial levels of depression were associated with poorer response rates. This effect was most marked for patients with HRSD scores above 20.

Bowers (1990) conducted a comparative trial of nortriptyline alone, relaxation in combination with nortriptyline, or CBT and nortriptyline, offered to 30 inpatients in addition to the usual hospital milieu. Therapy was conducted in groups, and 12 therapy sessions were offered. Forty-one patients were approached, eight declined, and one patient per group dropped out "because of violation of the protocol."

Patients were moderately to severely depressed; the mean pretreatment BDI scores for the CBT, relaxation, and medication groups were 24.2, 25.8, and 31.2, respectively (giving a nonsignificant trend toward greater initial severity in the medication group). All therapies were offered by the same therapist.

Symptoms were assessed using the BDI, the HRSD, and measures of cognitive adjustment at sessions 1, 6, and 12 and at discharge. All groups improved, but patients receiving CBT or relaxation had significantly fewer depressive symptoms and negative cognitions than in the medication-alone condition. In addition, patients receiving CBT were less likely to be judged depressed at discharge than in the other treatment conditions. A recovery criterion of an HRSD score of $\leqslant 6$ was achieved by 8 of 10 patients in the CBT group, compared with 1/10 and 2/10 in those receiving relaxation or medication alone.

The degree to which this result reflects the specific impact of CBT is not clear. Using a criterion based on a BDI score of $\leqslant 9$, patients receiving relaxation showed similar gains to those in the CBT group. Interpretation of this study is also made more difficult by the fact that there was no control for the additional attention therapy patients received contrasted to those on medication alone.

Miller et al. (1989) assigned 47 patients to one of three conditions—standard treatment (hospital milieu, medication, and medication management), CBT and standard treatment, or social skills training and standard treatment. All patients had BDI scores ⩾17 and HRSD scores ⩾17. Therapies were conducted daily while the patients were in the hospital, and continued weekly after discharge. CBT was offered daily while patients were in the hospital and weekly after discharge. All therapies led to significant gains on a range of measures. At discharge there was a trend for patients receiving combination treatments to be categorized as responders; after outpatient treatment the trend reached significance. However, there were significant differences in the dropout rate between conditions—41% from standard treatment, 31% from CBT, and 14% from social skills. In addition, all patients from the standard treatment group had dropped out by week 8 of follow-up, leading to problems in interpreting the follow-up data.

Scott and colleagues in Newcastle present data from two open trials of combined medication and CBT, offered to chronically depressed inpatients who had previously failed to respond to standard antidepressants and had been depressed for at least 2 years. Pharmacotherapy comprised phenelzine, L-tryptophan, and lithium. In the first trial (Barker et al., 1987), 20 patients were randomly assigned either to pharmacotherapy alone or to combination treatment with CBT over 12 weeks. This was initially offered twice weekly for 3 weeks, followed by 9 weekly sessions. Though 11 patients showed a 50% reduction in HRSD scores (all within the first 6 weeks), there was no evidence for an additional benefit from CBT. In a second trial (Scott, 1992) with a similar population, 24 patients were divided into two cohorts. The first ($n = 8$) received 12 weeks of combined pharmacotherapy and CBT as described in Barker et al. (1987), achieving similar outcomes to those described above. The second cohort ($n = 16$) was offered a modified CBT package offering a "milieu" treatment; patients were admitted to a dedicated inpatient unit, and therapy was more intensive and prolonged—approximately 26 inpatient sessions followed by at least 6 months of outpatient treatment. Percentage change scores on the BDI and HRSD were greater for patients receiving the modified package (52 and 57% respectively) than for those receiving standard CBT (42% on both measures), and significant change was observed in 69% of patients. Although suggestive, the small sample sizes and the open nature of this trial limit the conclusions that can be drawn.

Summary

- There is good evidence that CBT, particularly when delivered intensively, can be a useful adjunct to treatment in inpatient settings and with more severe cases of depression.

- Usually these treatments have been used in the context of other treatments, such as social skills training, bibliotherapy, and relaxation; the specific effects of CBT are not well established. However, the effect of therapy is likely to reduce the severity of depression on discharge and follow-up, and lead to better levels of adjustment.

PRIMARY CARE TREATMENTS FOR DEPRESSION

Evidence for the efficacy of treatments for depression delivered in primary care settings is scant. There are few trials, most of those that exist are small-scale, and few specify the nature of the treatments offered or the qualifications of the therapists. Thus Sheldon et al. (1993) have identified 12 randomized controlled trials for depression in primary care. In only four was a therapy identified (in all cases CBT); two further trials considered the impact of counseling from social workers or health visitors, and the remaining six were trials of medication. It is relevant to note that in many clinical settings counselors may not have received formal training; for example, Sibbald et al. (1993) found that, of counselors employed to work alongside family physicians in the United Kingdom, only one-third had training in counseling.

Blackburn et al. (1981) carried out a trial of CBT alone, medication alone, and its combination delivered in an outpatient clinic and by family physicians in a primary care setting. Forty-nine hospital and 39 primary care patients (all with BDI scores of ≥ 14) were treated over 12–15 weeks; results differed among sites. Defining response as a BDI or HRSD score of ≤ 8 or ≤ 9, respectively, there were no differences between treatments in the hospital setting.

However, in the primary care setting the medication-alone group did significantly (and perhaps inexplicably) worse—of completers, only 1/7 patients recovered in this condition, contrasted with 8/9 and 8/8 for the combination and CBT group, respectively. Treatments continued with six weekly appointments for 6 months; follow-up was naturalistic, and continued for 2 years (Blackburn et al., 1986). At this point attrition made separate analysis of the hospital and primary care samples impossible; overall, patients on medication showed a significantly greater rate of relapse.

Teasdale et al. (1984) treated 17 patients with BDI scores ≥ 20, contrasting them with 20 patients receiving "treatment as usual." Although CBT led to a significant difference in the number of patients judged recovered posttreatment (indicated by a BDI score ≤ 10), at 3 months follow-up the treatment as usual group had also improved, leading to no between-group differences at this point.

Ross and Scott (1985) treated 51 patients with BDI scores ⩾14; patients continued to receive treatment as usual from their family physician, but were additionally allocated either to individual or group CBT, or to a 3-month waiting-list control group (who subsequently received CBT). A 64% reduction in BDI scores was found for the CBT group, contrasted to a 13% reduction in the wait-list group. However, no figures using a recovery criterion are given in the study, and relapse was defined as a BDI score ⩾16, which is markedly less stringent than that usually adopted. Partial data from a 12-month follow-up suggested that no patients receiving CBT relapsed on this criterion.

Scott and Freeman (1992) requested 63 family physicians from 14 primary health care practices to refer patients with a depressive disorder. One hundred ninety-four patients were referred and 121 were accepted into the trial. The study design was such that some patients would be assigned to treatment with medication; of some interest is the fact that most patients who declined to take part in the study cited as a reason a reluctance to take medication.

Patients were randomly assigned to one of four conditions for 16 weeks of treatment. Help was offered either by a psychiatrist (for amitriptyline), a clinical psychologist (for CBT), or a social worker (for supportive counseling). In the remaining condition patients were reassigned to their family physicians for treatment as usual (which included referral to other agencies).

One difficulty in this study is that randomization of patients to treatment conditions was not successful; only 11/29 (38%) of patients seeing the social worker had HRSD scores ⩾16, suggesting that most clients in this group did not achieve a level of "caseness" for depression (contrasted to 22/30 [73%] in the family physician group). In addition, only 2/29 (7%) of patients seeing the clinical psychologist had a previous episode of depression.

At the end of treatment, only social work counseling showed a greater reduction in depressive symptoms when contrasted to care from the physician. It has already been noted, however, that patients in each of these groups differed markedly in their initial levels of depression, which makes it difficult to interpret this result. Patient satisfaction was greatest with social work counseling, though the fact that only one therapist offered each treatment modality increases the likelihood of therapist-specific effects.

Summary

- CBT seems to be a useful adjunct to primary health care treatment of depression.

- There is some very preliminary evidence that supportive counseling may be useful.
- In the light of the increasing use of counselors in primary care, this is an area for urgent further study.

OVERALL SUMMARY

- Depression is a common disorder which has been addressed psychotherapeutically in outpatient, inpatient, and community settings.
- When considering the likely response to psychotherapy, there are important diagnostic distinctions to be made in this group of patients. In particular, patients with acute episodes of depression should be distinguished from those who suffer from depression in a less intense form but with a more chronic course (dysthmics). Further, patients with severe depression are less likely to respond to psychological therapies.
- Depression appears to be a chronic disorder in many patients, and the likelihood of complete recovery is low.
- The best-designed outcome studies underscore the efficacy of CBT, IPT, and dynamic exploratory therapy (as employed in the Sheffield Psychotherapy Project).
- Brief treatment has a relatively large effect when assessed posttherapy, but on the whole this impact is relatively short-term.
- The efficacy of brief interventions is poor in the longer-term; the efficacy of longer term psychological treatments, as frequently practiced clinically, has not been adequately examined.
- Long-term pharmacological treatment is so far the only method shown to be unequivocally effective in the prevention of relapse. There is suggestive evidence that psychotherapeutic techniques, particularly IPT, may be a useful adjunct in the prevention of relapse. More research is necessary to establish the value of psychotherapy in this context.
- Meta-analytic studies in this field, when taken in combination, suggest that patients derive clinically significant benefit from psychotherapeutic interventions, although in the majority of cases, they may be expected to remain both symptomatic and vulnerable at the end of acute treatment.
- The relative efficacy of treatments is hard to establish because of the limitations of the available database. Nevertheless, CBT emerges across studies as a powerful and useful method for treating the acute symptoms of depression. IPT also emerges as valu-

able in a number of contexts, both in tackling severe symptoms and as an adjunct to pharmacological treatment. Work on dynamic therapies is just beginning, though a unique large-scale U.K. trial (the Sheffield Psychotherapy Project) indicates that it may be comparable in efficacy to CBT.

- Evidence for the superiority of combination treatments over psychological intervention alone is weak, with the exception of its use with intensive structured (CBT) techniques in an inpatient context.
- The superiority of psychotherapeutic treatment over medical treatment is small and unreliable across studies, and confounded by the lack of control over the nature of the medical treatments offered.
- The absence of long-term controlled follow-ups in the majority of trials undermines conclusions concerning both long-term effectiveness and generalizability.
- The value of psychotherapy in primary health care settings is less well established, but the data provide little evidence to suggest that studies in an outpatient setting would not be generalizable to this population.
- Data on dysthymic patients support the need to consider patient mix, particularly the prevalence of double depression in clinical trials and service evaluations.
- There is some indication in the literature that the quality of therapy delivered correlates with long-term outcome, suggesting that the maintenance of high-quality therapy may be an important consideration for service providers.
- There are as yet too few data to draw conclusions about the effectiveness of counseling.

OVERALL IMPLICATIONS

- In the light of the high prevalence of depressive conditions and the availability of specific psychological interventions strategies, it seems desirable that there should be specific service provision for these patients.
- The poorer responsiveness of severely depressed and dysthymic patients suggests that services should monitor their patient mix in auditing and evaluation of psychological therapy services for depressed individuals.
- Research has highlighted both the efficacy and the limitations of brief intervention, and it is clear that many individuals presenting with depression will require long-term maintenance therapy.

- Chronicity should be a critical factor in designing treatment programs. Brief therapy may be less appropriate for individuals with more than two episodes of major depressive disorder: longer-term maintenance therapies should be considered for this group.
- The literature on the use of medication alongside psychological therapy suggests that, to be effective, treatment, particularly of severely depressed individuals, may require a combination of pharmacotherapy and psychotherapy in order to maximize the therapeutic potential of both forms of intervention.
- Cost–benefit tradeoffs of psychological therapies, medical treatments, and their combination can at this stage only be guessed at. There is no doubt that for medication to be effective in reducing relapse, long-term administration with ongoing physician monitoring is essential. The cost advantage of older (and cheaper) antidepressants, and certainly that of the newer and more expensive serotinergic antidepressants, is thus lessened in comparison to brief therapies. The value added by medication to psychological therapy and vice versa should also be costed.
- The literature review indicates that there may be a danger were the balance of service provision to be skewed too far in the direction of brief interventions. Our review suggests that a cascade or stepwise mode of service provision may be more appropriate, and that patients who fail to respond to brief treatments should be offered longer-term therapy. It should be noted that, though we have not been able to identify evidence that would substantiate the value of long-term therapy for this group of patients, it is clear that very brief treatment regimens (of around 10 sessions) may not be adequate for more severely depressed individuals.
- A good service should offer a range of therapies. Provision of CBT and other structured forms of verbal interventions (such as IPT and exploratory dynamic therapy) should be a priority.
- The review suggests that psychiatric and psychological therapy services should work together to develop treatment programs combining medication with psychological interventions. Clinically it is not unusual for individuals who could benefit from psychological intervention to receive exclusively medical treatment; equally, patients receiving psychological treatment may be undermedicated or have received no psychiatric assessment when this might have been indicated.
- Better-integrated treatment provision has a number of advantages. Not only would it facilitate greater patient choice; greater efficacy is also likely, since it should ensure that patients are not treated over long periods with methods to which they are not responsive, or to which their response could be optimized.

- Research on outcome after psychological therapy underscores the importance of regular follow-ups for this patient group, in either a specialist or primary care setting.
- Referrers should be cautioned that recurrence of a depressive episode is quite likely even after full remission, and this is not a counterindication to further psychological intervention.
- The literature suggests that better-quality therapy may be associated with better long-term outcome, and therefore the quality of treatments offered should be carefully monitored and maintained.
- More research is required in a number of key areas to provide a closer match between research data and everyday clinical practice. Such studies should examine the effectiveness of the longer-term psychological therapies, and studies of the effectiveness of structured dynamic therapies and counseling.

CHAPTER 5

Bipolar Disorder

DEFINITIONS

Bipolar disorder—sometimes referred to as manic depression—has as its essential feature one or more manic episodes, usually alternating with one or more major depressive episodes. Depressive episodes have been defined in Chapter 4, which discusses treatments for depression.

DSM-IV defines the essential diagnostic features of a manic episode as a period lasting at least 1 week (or any period if hospitalization is required) during which the predominant mood is either elevated, expansive, or irritable, and there are associated features of the manic syndrome. The disturbance is sufficiently severe to cause marked impairment in social and occupational functioning or to require hospitalization to prevent harm to self or others. At least three of the following characteristic symptoms should be present: inflated self-esteem or grandiosity (which may be delusional), decreased need for sleep, pressure of speech, flight of ideas, distractibility, increased involvement in goal directed activity, psychomotor agitation, and excessive involvement in pleasurable activities that may have a painful outcome that the person does not recognize.

Only when the severity of symptoms is such that there is a marked impact on functioning can a diagnosis of a manic episode be made. Individuals without delusions and with milder symptoms who are able to function socially and occupationally without a need for hospitalization would receive a diagnosis of hypomanic episode.

DSM-IV distinguishes bipolar I disorders and bipolar II disorders, as follows:

Bipolar I Disorders

These describe the form of the current episode in the context of a previously diagnosed manic or depressive episode. The possible variants of bipolar I disorder are therefore: 1) most recent episode hypomanic (but where there has been at least one previous manic episode), 2) most recent episode manic, 3) most recent episode mixed and 4) most recent episode depressed. A further category of bipolar disorder I, single manic episode, is characterized by only one manic episode and no past major depressive episodes.

Bipolar II Disorders

This diagnosis is reserved for individuals who present with major depressive disorders accompanied by hypomanic episodes, in the absence of any previous manic episode. This presentation is classified under DSM-III-R as bipolar disorder not otherwise specified.

Summary

This organization differs from DSM-III-R, which classified bipolar disorders as "bipolar disorder, mixed" (where the current episode involves the rapid alternation or intermixing of symptoms of both mania and depression: "bipolar disorder, manic" (where the person is currently in a manic episode); and "bipolar disorder, depressed" (where the individual is currently in a depressed episode, having had at least one previous manic episode).

Cyclothymia

Some individuals show a pattern of chronic mood disturbance characterized by numerous hypomanic episodes and depressive episodes which do not meet criteria for a major depressive episode. To meet diagnostic criteria, such a pattern should be present for more than 2 years, and the individual should not have been without hypomanic or depressive symptoms for more than 2 months at a time. It is worth noting that the boundaries between cyclothymia and bipolar disorder are not well specified.

Bipolar Disorder Not Otherwise Specified

These are disorders with manic or hypomanic features that do not meet the criteria for any specific bipolar disorder. Examples might include patients showing rapid alternation between manic and depressive symptoms which never reach the minimal duration criteria for a manic episode or major depressive episode, or recurrent hypomanic episodes without intercurrent depressive symptoms.

PREVALENCE

Data from the Epidemiologic Catchment Area survey (ECA; Weissman et al., 1988a) suggest a 1-year prevalence rate of 1.0%, with men and women almost equally affected. Angst (1992) cites 1-year prevalence rates of bipolar disorder in community samples at between 1.0% and 1.7% in the adult population.

COMORBIDITY

Data from the ECA survey (Regier et al., 1990) indicate that approximately half of patients with bipolar illness have comorbid alcohol or drug abuse at some point during their lifetime. Recent data also suggest that a significant subset meet criteria for schizoaffective disorder, borderline personality disorder, panic disorder, obsessive–compulsive disorder, or generalized anxiety disorder (NIMH, 1994).

NATURAL HISTORY

Bipolar disorder is usually recurrent disorder (Goodwin & Jamison, 1990), with more than 80% of individuals presenting with one manic episode going on to have further episodes. Both the manic and depressive episodes are more frequent than the major depressive episodes in major depressive disorder. Frequently a manic episode is followed by a short depressive episode, or vice versa. In 5–15% of individuals with bipolar I disorder there are four or more mood episodes within a year; such cases of rapid cycling are associated with a poorer prognosis.

Although the majority of individuals with bipolar disorder return to a functional level between episodes, some 20–30% of patients continue to display some lability and interpersonal and occupational difficulties. Untreated, there is significant mortality associated with bipolar disorder; Müller-Oerlinghausen et al. (1992) estimate that without treatment, mortality rates are two to three times higher than that obtaining in the general population.

TREATMENT APPROACHES

Since the first report of its benefits in the prophylaxis of bipolar illness (Cade, 1949), lithium has become the standard treatment for bipolar disorder, with approximately 80% of patients showing some favorable response. Lithium has become the current treatment of choice (Goodwin & Jamison, 1990), with evidence that it reduces the frequency and severity of episodes of mania and stabilizes mood between episodes (Prien & Potter, 1990). However, it appears to be a better prophylactic agent for mania than depression (Prien et al., 1984; Shaw, 1986). Further, despite its efficacy, it is estimated that over a 2-year period of follow-up, between 41% and 60% of patients will experience a manic or depressive relapse, even if maintained on lithium or adjunctive medications (Prien et al., 1984). More recently there has been increasing interest in the use of the anticonvulsant medications carbamazapine and valproate. Data from a number of double-blind trials suggest that both are as effective as lithium in controlling acute manic states and in maintaining patients between episodes (Goodwin & Jamison, 1990; Prien & Potter, 1990; Gelenberg & Hopkins, 1993; Bowden et al., 1994). Standard antidepressant medications also show efficacy during depressive phases of the disorder (Gelenberg & Hopkins, 1993).

Until recently there has been little investigation of the impact of psychological and psychosocial interventions for bipolar disorders. Two factors appear relevant to an increasing research effort in this area. Firstly, despite the efficacy of medications for this disorder, their clinical effectiveness is reduced by noncompliance, estimated at between 25% and 50% of bipolar patients receiving medication (Prien & Potter, 1990). Even with adequate compliance and optimal treatment response, the impact of medication on social functioning is usually limited (Clarkin et al., 1990). Secondly, recent work with people with a diagnosis of schizophrenia (reviewed in Chapter 10) has demonstrated the potential efficacy of psychological interventions even with a disorder where the primary treatment of choice is recognized to be pharmacological. Such work emphasizes the role of psychosocial stress, and there is increasing evidence that this model is relevant to treatment outcomes in people with bipolar disorder (Johnson & Roberts, 1995). For example, Miklowitz et al. (1988) found that greater levels of family stress predicts clinical outcomes for bipolar patients. Twenty-three recently hospitalized patients and their families were assessed using a combined measure of expressed emotion (EE)[1] together with assessment of their affective style and fol-

---

[1] Expressed emotion is a measure of family functioning, most thoroughly researched in relation to people with a diagnosis of schizophrenia, and more fully discussed in Chapter 10. In brief, a number of studies indicate that relapse is more likely if patients live with, or have extensive contact with, relatives who are excessively critical and/or overinvolved.

lowed up for 9 months after discharge. Marked differences in relapse rates were found between families rated low on the combined measure (17%) and contrasted to families with high ratings (94%).

There is as yet only a limited body of research in this area; Scott (1995, in press) offers a comprehensive discussion of the rationale for psychosocial treatments for bipolar patients and reviews the available outcome research. Much of it is small-scale, and for the most part comprises single-case studies, case series, or open trials. However, major controlled trials of psychosocial interventions are currently in progress both in the United Kingdom (Scott, personal communication) and in the United States (Weissman & Markowitz, 1994; NIMH, 1994).

Individual Therapies

While there are a number of anecdotal and single-case reports of psycho-analytic and cognitive-behavioral therapies for bipolar disorder, there are few substantive studies (Scott, 1995). Benson (1975) describes a case series of 31 patients meeting Feighner criteria (Feighner et al., 1972). Patients received either individual, group, or couples therapy, which appears to have been psychodynamically oriented. Over 41 months in an open trial, 24 were reported to have a good clinical outcome, of whom 19 continued with the maintenance treatment, and five discontinued medication but continued psychotherapy. Though Benson suggests that this level of functioning is higher than that usually found in follow-up studies of medication alone, measures of functioning were determined by the author acting alone, a procedure open to bias.

Cochran (1984) examined the impact of six sessions of cognitive therapy on lithium compliance rates and outcomes for 28 newly diagnosed patients meeting research diagnostic criteria (RDC) for bipolar disorder (Spitzer et al., 1978). Patients were randomly assigned either to therapy or to treatment as usual; compliance both at 6 weeks and 6 months was significantly better in patients receiving the intervention. There were problems in the criteria adopted for rating compliance, which depended both on measurement of serum levels and (potentially highly reactive) ratings by the patient and treating physician. Poor intercorrelations between these ratings suggest that the reliability of the overall measure of compliance is poor. Nonetheless, only three (21%) cognitive therapy patients discontinued medication, and two (14%) were hospitalized; in the control group, eight (57%) discontinued medication and eight (57%) were hospitalized.

Group-Based Therapies

In a problematic but widely cited study, Davenport et al. (1977) contrasted outcomes in 65 hospitalized patients meeting RDC criteria for bipolar disorder, all of whom had intact marriages at the start of the trial. Patients were randomly assigned for follow-up either to psychodynamic couples group therapy (12 patients), a lithium clinic (11 patients), or the patients' local community mental health center (CMHC; 42 patients). However, there were significant differences in the ages of couples assigned to each group, with those receiving couples therapy being significantly older and married for longer than those in the other treatment conditions. In addition, while patients in the first two conditions were treated by the researchers, those seen in the CMHCs were not. Relatedly, though lithium was prescribed and compliance monitored in patients seen by the researchers, it is not clear what treatment was given within CMHCs.

Patients were studied retrospectively 2–10 years after hospitalization; those who had received the couples group therapy were functioning best in terms of social and family functioning, and reported no rehospitalization or marital failure. In contrast, the CMHC group had the poorest outcomes, with 16 readmissions and 10 marital failures. However this group was not significantly different from the lithium follow-up clinic. It should be noted that though the researchers found no association between length of illness and outcome, the significant differences between the groups noted above is likely to have selected for marital stability. Hence, though the results of this study appear to demonstrate the benefits of psychological therapy, poor control of both patient assignment and subsequent treatment makes interpretation problematic.

Though there have been no controlled studies of the adjunctive benefits of group therapy in addition to lithium, there have been a number of open trials. Shakir et al. (1979) and Volkmar et al. (1981) report on outcomes at 4 years from 20 participants in a Yalom-style group (Yalom, 1975). All patients were responsive to lithium and had been on medication for a mean of 21 months. Significant differences in functioning were found by contrasting the 2 years prior to and the 2 years subsequent to entry into the group. In particular medication compliance was improved and there was a decrease in hospitalization rates.

Cerbone et al. (1992) treated 43 outpatients in weekly group therapy, with a focus on education about the disorder and on interpersonal problems. Using the year prior to group entry as a baseline, patients evidenced lower rates of hospitalization and shorter inpatient stay and reported higher levels of functioning. There were, however, no reported changes in medication usage.

Kripke and Robinson (1985) describe a group for 14 bipolar patients (13 of whom were male) conducted over 12 years; eight members stayed in the group over this time. The group contained both psychodynamic and problem-solving elements, and there was some evidence of reduced hospitalization and better social functioning.

Wulpsin et al. (1988) conducted a group run in a CMHC for 22 bipolar patients over 4 years. Though there was some reduction in hospitalization, attrition was high, with almost half the group members dropping out.

Van Gent and Zwart (1994) report outcomes for 26 patients in receipt of lithium, treated in group therapy over 10–13 sessions. Group content was largely psychoeducational, together with some interpersonal focus. Contrasted with the period before group therapy and following up patients for 5 years after intervention, there appeared to be some increase in medication compliance and some reduction in hospital admission.

In a small study, Palmer et al. (1995) examined the impact of Newman and Beck's (1993) manualized cognitive-behavioral treatment for bipolar disorder. Four patients received 17 weekly sessions of group therapy; sessions contained psychoeducational elements but largely focused on strategies for managing and coping with the various manifestations of bipolar disorder. Although all patients attended psychiatric outpatient clinics, medication use was not monitored. Symptom status and social adjustment were assessed weekly while the group was running, and monthly for five follow-up visits after the end of active treatment. In addition, the use of outpatient clinics and inpatient facilities in the 12 months prior to the group was contrasted with their use during the period of active treatment and follow-up.

Overall, there was some evidence of improvements during the active treatment phase, though the pattern of change varied among individuals and across measures. Though generalization from such a small sample is inappropriate, three of the four participants showed gains on measures of symptomatic status, greater stability in their condition, and better social adjustment; however, there was evidence of some loss of gains during the follow-up phase. There were no changes in the use of outpatient clinics, and changes in the hospital stay were difficult to assess since only one participant had been an inpatient in the year prior to the trial.

Family-Based Interventions

Clarkin et al. (1990) report data from a large trial of inpatient family interventions. Patients with a range of diagnoses were randomly assigned to receive family intervention in addition to treatment as usual, with treatment as usual acting as a control condition. Family intervention comprised psychoeducation, identification of family stress, explored likely precipitants for the current and future episodes, and considered problem-solving strategies for managing future stress.

Within the total sample of patients, 21 had a diagnosis of bipolar disorder, of whom 13 were manic at admission, seven depressed, and one mixed. Seventeen of the 21 were psychotic, and 14 had previous episodes; 14 (66%) of the sample were female. Twelve received family interventions, and nine, treatment as usual. Follow-up data were collected at 6 and 18 months. For female patients outcome was better following family intervention, with improvements in social and work functioning, and improved family attitudes toward treatment; it should be noted that over 18 months this effect diminished. No benefit to family intervention was seen in males. Statistical analysis of the gender by treatment effect suggests that it is robust. However, the small number of male patients in the sample, and indeed the small overall sample size, cautions against overinterpretation of what the authors themselves considered to be an exploratory study. Although they speculate that male patients may be particularly sensitive to interpersonal stimuli, and hence may find family interventions more stressful, gender differences in outcome from family intervention are not notable in comparable studies of outcome with patients diagnosed as schizophrenic (reviewed in Chapter 10). As such, the clinical implications of the interaction effects noted in this study are unclear in the absence of replication in a larger-scale study.

There are two additional small-scale studies of family interventions in combination with lithium, both pilot studies for larger trials. Miklowitz and Goldstein (1990) describe an adaptation of Falloon's behavioral family management technique (Falloon et al., 1984). Nine recent-onset bipolar patients were treated with 21 family sessions spread over 9 months. Sessions were held weekly for the first 3 months, tapering to biweekly and monthly, and comprised family education, communication skills training, and problem-solving skills training. Outcomes in this group were contrasted with 23 patients who participated in a naturalistic study of outcomes conducted by the same authors (Miklowitz et al., 1988). These patients received lithium alone and were followed-up over 9 months. Among the treatment group one out of nine patients relapsed over 9 months (11%), a significantly lower rate than that found in the contrast group (14 of 23, a 61% relapse rate). Honig et al. (in press) report a small-scale study of a psychoeducational program, again suggesting that reductions in expressed emotion are possible and that this is associated with reduced relapse rates.

SUMMARY

- It is difficult to assess the adjunctive impact of psychosocial to pharmacological interventions in people with bipolar disorder.

Currently the research base is small, and there is only one controlled trial, itself limited by a restricted sample size.

- Evidence from available trials suggests some benefit from psychological interventions, particularly in increasing adherence to medication regimens and reducing hospitalization.
- However, existing trials are flawed; published outcomes from substantive trials in progress are needed before firmer conclusions are possible.

CHAPTER 6

Anxiety Disorders I
Phobias, Generalized Anxiety Disorder, and Panic Disorder with and without Agoraphobia

DEFINITIONS

DSM-IV identifies a number of anxiety disorders, but begins by defining panic attacks, on the grounds that (though not a defined disorder) their ubiquity across anxiety disorders justifies separate definition. A panic attack is characterized by the sudden onset of feelings of intense apprehension, dread, fear, or terror, often associated with feelings of impending doom. During this period at least four of a possible 13 symptoms, such as palpitations, sweating, shaking, shortness of breath, choking, nausea, dizziness, derealization, fear of losing control, or dying, must be present.

Definitions of anxiety disorders relevant to the research that follows (with indications of any significant differences between DSM-IV and DSM-III-R) are given below.

Specific Phobia/Simple Phobia

Specific phobias (termed simple phobias in DSM-III-R) are characterized by a persistent fear of a specific stimulus, and exposure to the phobic stimulus provokes an immediate anxiety response, though the person invariably recognizes that his or her fear is excessive. DSM-IV nomenclature avoids the inference that such phobias are necessarily simple in their nature.

Social Phobia

This is defined by a persistent fear of one or more social situations in which the person fears that he or she may do something or act in a way that may be embarrassing or humiliating. Examples would be concern about being unable to continue talking when speaking in public or choking on food when eating in a restaurant. Situations provoking anxiety are usually avoided, despite the fact that the person recognizes that his or her fear is excessive, and there is disruption of social and occupational functioning.

Generalized Anxiety Disorder

The essential feature of this disorder is persistent, excessive anxiety or worry about a number of life circumstances occurring most days over a period of 6 months or more.[1] For a diagnosis to be made, the person must find it difficult to control the worry, and it must be of a sufficient level to cause clinically significant distress or impairment in functioning. At least three of the following six symptoms also need to be present—restlessness, being easily fatigued, difficulty in concentrating, irritability, muscle tension, and sleep disturbance.

This diagnosis needs to be distinguished from anxiety arising as part of a mood disorder, or where anxiety may be related to another Axis I disorder (such as worry about public eating in a patient with an eating disorder).

Panic Disorder without Agoraphobia

The essential feature of this condition is the presence of recurrent and unexpected panic attacks, accompanied by a month or more of persistent concern and worry about the possibility of additional attacks.[2] These attacks are, at least initially, unexpected; in other words, they do not reflect exposure to a situation that always causes anxiety (as in *specific phobia*). In addition they are not triggered by social attention (as in *social phobia*). Later in the course of the disturbance certain situations, such as driving a car or being in a crowded place, may become associated with panic. These situations then increase the likelihood of panic occurring. Arguably many patients in this group could be seen as nonsevere agora-

---

[1] Within DSM-III-R such worries were required to be "unrealistic"—for example, an excessive concern about one's child (when the child is in no objective danger) or worry about financial misfortune (for no good reason).

[2] DSM-III-R specifies that either four panic attacks have occurred within a 4-week period or, as in DSM-IV, that these attacks have been followed by at least 1 month of persistent worry about future attacks.

phobics within ICD-10, since they manifest panic mainly in public places, even if avoidance is not always present.

Panic Disorder with Agoraphobia

In clinical settings most cases of panic disorder present with agoraphobia—defined in DSM-IV as a fear of being in situations from which escape might be difficult or embarrassing, or in which help might not be forthcoming in the event of a panic. This results either in restrictions on travel or in endurance of situations outside the home in spite of high anxiety. Typical agoraphobic situations include being outside the home alone, being in crowded situations, waiting in queues, and travel by train, bus, or car.

PREVALENCE, COMORBIDITY, AND NATURAL HISTORY

Prevalence

Kessler et al. (1994), reporting data from the U.S. National Comorbidity Survey, suggest a lifetime prevalence for specific phobia of 11.3% and a 12-month prevalence of 8.8%.

Six-month prevalence of social phobia as estimated from two sites in the National Institute of Mental Health's Epidemiologic Catchment Area (ECA) survey was 1.2% and 2.2% (Eaton et al., 1991); surveys in New Zealand estimated 6-month prevalence at 2.6% (Wells et al., 1989). Angst and Dobler-Mikola (1983) cite rates of 1% from their survey.

Wittchen et al. (1994) and Kessler et al. (1994) suggest that generalized anxiety disorder (GAD) is a relatively rare current disorder, with a current prevalence of 1.6%, but a more frequent lifetime disorder, affecting 5.1% of the population between 15 and 54 years; 12-month prevalence is estimated at 3.1%. Other community surveys produce a wide range of estimates; Breslau and Davis (1985), using the DSM-III definition of GAD, found prevalence rates in a sample of 375 women surveyed from the general population of 2.4% and 11.5% for 1 month and 6 months, respectively. One-year prevalence rates of GAD have been reported as 6.4% (Uhlenhuth et al., 1983), 2.3% (Angst et al., 1985) and 2.6% (Dean et al., 1983) and 3.8% (Blazer et al., 1991).

Data from the ECA study give 6-month prevalence rates of 0.8% for panic and 3.8% for agoraphobia. Rates for these disorders vary slightly from study to study: although those quoted seem reasonably representative of a number of investigations (Oakley-Brown, 1991), some authors suggests rather higher prevalence—for example, Reich (1986) suggests that the 6-month prevalence rate for agoraphobia is 6% and for panic disorder 3%. Angst and Dobler-Mikola (1983), using a community sample of 19- and 20-year-olds in Zurich, found 4-week prevalence rates of 2.8% for panic disorder and 1.0% for agoraphobia.

The prevalence of all these disorders is significantly higher in women than men—60% higher for panic, 30% higher for agoraphobia, and 50% higher for social phobia and for GAD (Myers et al., 1984; Weissman et al., 1985; Wittchen et al., 1994).

In many of the community surveys reported above (United States, Germany, and Switzerland) a relatively large proportion of identified cases are untreated for their complaint (in excess of 50%). Although a pattern not unique to this group of disorders, it is perhaps more marked in the case of phobias, panic, and generalized anxiety than many other conditions.

Comorbidity

Comorbidity within the Anxiety Disorders

Between 30% and 80% of patients with a principal diagnosis of anxiety have at least one other anxiety disorder (Weissman et al., 1986; Lesser, 1988). Brown and Barlow (1992) report that of 468 consecutively diagnosed patients, 50% had comorbid anxiety or depressive disorders, with GAD being the most frequently assigned additional diagnosis (at 23%). Data from the ECA study suggest that of patients with social phobia, 45% had specific phobia, 59% agoraphobia, and 5% panic disorder (Schnier et al., 1992). Estimates of comorbidity within clinical samples are probably higher than those based on community surveys; Wittchen et al. (1991) report that 53.8% of anxiety disorders in community surveys are "pure," contrasted to only 37.1% in clinical samples

Depression

There is evidence of extensive comorbidity of anxiety disorders and depression, though estimated rates vary considerably. In the Cross-National Collaborative Panic study (Lesser et al., 1988) there were wide variations in estimates across sites, ranging from 8 to 52% comorbidity for panic disorder with or without agoraphobia. Reviewing this issue, Rapaport and Maser (1992) estimated that rates vary between 15% to

50% for agoraphobia, and between 28% and 68% for GAD. The variability of these rates reflects differing methodologies used to detect depressive symptomatology, differing criteria (lifetime presence of depression or concurrent depression), and differing definitions (largely for detecting the temporal relationship between anxiety and depression, which would alter the diagnosis). Chambless and Gillis (1993) suggest a comorbidity of up to 30% for social phobia and depression. Brown and Barlow (1992) suggest that the highest rates of comorbidity of mood and anxiety disorders may occur with obsessive–compulsive disorder (40%) and panic disorder with agoraphobia (55%).

Personality Disorder

Four reviews (Friedman et al., 1987; Green & Curtis, 1988; Mavissakalian & Hamann, 1988; Reich et al., 1987), suggest that 40–63% of agoraphobics have associated DSM-III-R personality disorders, usually in the avoidant or dependent cluster. Chambless et al. (1992), studying a clinical sample of agoraphobics using the Millon Clinical Multiaxial Inventory, found rates of 91%, again most usually avoidant or dependent personality disorder.

Social Phobia and Avoidant Personality Disorder

Patients with avoidant personality disorder (APD) are characterized by longstanding, pervasive, and active withdrawal from social relationships; they are devastated by disapproval and are vigilant for signs of ridicule. There is some overlap between the description of social phobia and APD, and though it seems that social phobia could occur in a pure form (such as public speaking anxiety), the reverse seems unlikely for APD. It is unclear to what extent these two diagnoses reflect a continuum of severity; Turner et al. (1986) found that patients with a diagnosis of APD had poorer social skills than those diagnosed with social phobia.

Comorbidity between GAD and Other Disorders

The high comorbidity of GAD with other disorders has led to some disagreement as to whether it is best conceptualized as a separate disorder or regarded as a residual or prodrome of other disorders (e.g., Cooper, 1990). Data from the National Comorbidity Survey (Wittchen et al., 1994) suggest that 66.3% of patients with current GAD report at least one other disorder in the previous 30 days, and lifetime comorbidity between GAD and other disorders is 90.4%—most usually with affective disorders (major depression and dysthymia), panic disorder, and (for current comorbidity only) agoraphobia. Though approximately one-third of cases with current GAD did not have additional diagnoses, it is unclear how many of these individuals would suffer a later episode of another disorder. Borkovec et al. (1995) report that of 55 patients entered into an outcome study for GAD, 78% had received at least one additional diagnosis pretherapy, and 31% more than one comorbid diagnosis. Approximately half of the sample also met criteria for past major depressive episodes.

Although estimates of comorbidity vary, there is some concensus that many patients with anxiety are likely to have concurrent Axis I and II disorders. This suggests that, for trials to be fully informative about effectiveness in everyday practice, they will need both to include and to identify such patients. Such conditions are not usually met in clinical trials.

Natural History

Anxiety disorders are usually chronic and persistent. Wittchen (1988) defined remission as an absence of relevant symptoms in the 6 months preceding survey. On this basis remission rates for panic were 14.3%, for agoraphobia 34.6%, and for social phobia 21.9%. Blazer et al. (1991) found that among patients with current GAD, 40% had suffered for more than 5 years and 10% for more than 10 years.

Summary

- Prevalence rates for anxiety disorders suggest that they are relatively common within the general population; the most frequently occurring is panic disorder with agoraphobia, followed by GAD, social phobia, and panic disorder without agoraphobia.
- Prevalence rates are between one-third and two-thirds higher in women than men.
- Anxiety disorders are often seen in combination with other anxiety disorders, affective disorders (particularly depression), and personality disorders. Prevalence figures for individuals who would require treatment for anxiety alone is approximately 50% of those cited above.

• Anxiety disorders represent problems with a wide range of chronicity and severity. The presence of a corresponding Axis II diagnosis may be critical in explaining differences between efficacy and effectiveness.

EVIDENCE OF TREATMENT EFFICACY

The sections below cover evidence for treatment efficacy derived from meta-analyses, general reviews, and specific trials for each anxiety syndrome in turn. As noted in the earlier discussion of meta-analyses for depression, lists of the studies included in analyses are not always available. Without this information, the overlap between reviews and the degree to which they supplement or repeat one another are difficult to determine. Where possible the degree of overlap will be reported.

Specific/Simple Phobia

Emmelkamp (1994) reviews behavioral treatments for specific phobia; systematic desensitization and exposure techniques are usually found to be effective, with a clinically significant improvement achieved in 70–85% of cases (Emmelkamp, 1982; Marks, 1987; Jansson & Öst, 1982). *In vivo* techniques appear to be the most effective, particularly where exposure is prolonged to the point at which anxiety is markedly reduced (Marshall, 1985, 1988).

Where fears are specific and circumscribed, fairly brief interventions can be helpful. Thus dental phobia appears responsive to brief, two-session or four-session interventions (e.g., Smith et al., 1990; Liddell et al., 1994), with results maintained at long-term follow-up (Liddell et al., 1994). Öst (1989) treated 20 animal phobics in one 2-hour session using exposure and modeling, finding that 90% remained recovered after 4-year follow-up. In a second trial, 71% of patients recovered and remained well at 1 year (Öst et al., 1991). Data from this trial strongly suggest that therapist-directed exposure is markedly more effective than self-directed exposure. There is little evidence that cognitive techniques add substantially to efficacy, though there are few studies.

Blood/injury phobics appear to require additional treatment measures when exposed to feared stimuli, because there is evidence that, in contrast to the usual anxiety response, these individuals show bradycardia and a decrease in blood pressure (Connolly et al., 1976; Öst et al., 1984), which may result in fainting. Öst et al. (1984, 1989, 1991) have trained blood phobics to recognize early signs of a drop in blood pressure and to apply tension techniques at this point. Combining this with exposure gives better results than simple exposure; in Öst's (1989) trial, 73% of patients were clinically improved posttreatment, and 77% at follow-up.

Summary

- Phobic symptoms respond best to exposure treatments; a very high percentage of specific phobics—perhaps as many as 70–85%—are effectively treated by this method.
- The addition of cognitive techniques appears to add little to efficacy.
- Blood phobics may need tension exercises as well as exposure.
- There is some limited evidence suggesting that therapist-directed exposure is more effective than self-directed exposure.

Social Phobia

Meta-Analyses

Chambless and Gillis (1993) review 10 trials of behavioral and cognitive-behavioral treatments for social phobia, including anxiety management, exposure, and social skills training. All patients met DSM-III-R criteria for social phobia, though trials varied in the degree to which other anxiety disorders and Axis II diagnoses of avoidant personality were present. This implies that patient samples in these studies are not homogeneous.

Contrasted with control subjects, an average effect size of 0.68 for measures of social phobia and 0.7 for fear of negative evaluation were obtained. Results were maintained at follow-ups varying between one and six months.

General Reviews and Specific Studies

Heimberg (1989), Mattick and Newman (1991), and Heimberg and Juster (1994) review treatment interventions for social phobia. The most common treatments usually include *in vivo* exposure and social skills training, both for patients with social phobia and for patients with APD. Cognitive-behavioral interventions have also been developed, most usually including some form of cognitive restructuring. Increasingly packages of treatment have been developed which include these elements in various permutations.

A number of studies have demonstrated significant effects of *in vivo* exposure for social phobia (e.g., Butler et al., 1984; Mattick & Peters, 1988; Mattick et al., 1989; Turner et al., 1994) and on APD (Alden, 1989; Renneberg et al., 1990; Stravynski et al., 1982, 1994). The relative efficacy of treatments such as social skills training and cognitive therapy, which usually encourage social exposure, is therefore more difficult to ascertain (Heimberg et al., 1987). Nonetheless, there is some, limited evidence for the usefulness of social skills training in patients with APD; three studies have suggested an advantage for skills training over exposure in such individuals (Cappe & Alden, 1986; Öst et al., 1981; Trower et al., 1978), though Alden (1989) found the two equally effective.

There is evidence that packages based on cognitive-behavioral therapy can be effective. Thus, Heimberg et al. (1990) contrasted cognitive therapy with an educational–supportive therapy, which comprised education on topics regarding social phobia (e.g., social skills and models of anxiety) together with opportunities for mutual support. Forty-nine patients were randomly assigned to either therapy over 12 weeks of treatment. At 6 months follow-up, 81% of patients receiving cognitive therapy were judged improved, contrasted with 47% of those receiving the educational package.

The degree to which cognitive techniques enhance outcome when combined with exposure, rather than being effective *sui generis*, is unclear. Though Emmelkamp et al. (1985) have demonstrated the efficacy of self-instructional training and rational–emotive therapy in the absence of directed exposure, most studies are less conclusive. Mattick and Peters (1988) and Mattick et al. (1989) contrasted the effects of cognitive restructuring alone, exposure alone, and cognitive restructuring in combination with exposure, finding that the combination was more effective than either treatment alone on some measures. The effect of combined treatment was more apparent at 3-month follow-up than posttreatment, particularly on measures of fear of appraisal. Mattick and Newman (1991) raise the possibility that self-directed exposure, facilitated by cognitive treatment, resulted in these gains.

Butler et al. (1984) found that exposure alone was inferior to its combination with an anxiety–management package which included relaxation, distraction, and rational self-talk; effects were particularly marked at 1-year follow-up. At this point, 40% of patients receiving exposure alone had requested further therapy, whereas none from the group receiving exposure and anxiety management had done so. However, other researchers have failed to find any additional benefits for CBT or for packages of intervention over gains attributable to exposure-based techniques alone. Scholing and Emmelkamp (1993) and Hope et al. (1990) found no evidence that cognitive therapy and exposure was more effective than exposure alone. Similarly, Mersch (1995) contrasted 34 patients assigned either to exposure alone or to a package of treatment comprising rational emotive therapy, social skills training, and exposure. Equal gains were found for both treatments posttherapy and at 3- and 18-month follow-up. Recent work from Heimberg's research group (Hope et al., 1995) compared outcomes in 33 patients assigned to one of three conditions—cognitive-behavioral group therapy, exposure alone, or a waiting list. Immediately after 12 weeks of treatment, patients given active treatment showed greater gains than waiting-list controls. Using a measure of clinically significant change, 70% of those treated with exposure were classified as responders, contrasted with 36% of those treated with the CBT package, with gains maintained at 6-month follow-up.

Relatively small cell sizes in many of these studies makes it difficult to draw substantive conclusions regarding the relative efficacy of exposure as contrasted to CBT and a range of more comprehensive packages of treatment. While there is only limited evidence that cognitive procedures are helpful (and this suggests more an adjunctive role with behavioral treatments), there is clear evidence for the efficacy of exposure. This raises doubts about the benefits of increasingly complex treatment packages that are being developed for social phobics (e.g., Heimberg, 1991; Turner et al., 1994), particularly when these are evaluated in open trials without contrast to exposure (e.g., Turner et al., 1994, 1995).

A small number of trials have contrasted pharmacotherapy and cognitive techniques. Gelernter et al. (1991) contrasted cognitive therapy with phenelzine, alprazolam, and pill placebo in 65 patients. However, all patients were encouraged to expose themselves to feared situations; more accurately, the study is a contrast of these treatments in combination with exposure. All treatments conferred some gains; though patients treated with phenelzine showed greater gains than those in other treatment groups, these were not significant. In addition, only patients treated with phenelzine and cognitive therapy maintained their gains at follow-up.

A further major study in progress, reported by Heimberg and Juster (1994), contrasts cognitive therapy, phenelzine, the educational–supportive package described above in Heimberg et al. (1990), acting as a control treatment, and pill placebo. Treatments were administered for 12 weeks, with a subsequent period of maintenance therapy over 6 months. While preliminary results from 133 patients entered into the trial suggest that both treatments are effective posttreatment, more detailed conclusions will only be possible after full publication.

Although trials suggest that gains are possible for social phobics, few studies address the issue of clinically significant improvement. Using a criterion of high end-state functioning to determine the clinical significance of change in CBT, 37% and 33% of patients in Mattick and Peters (1988) and Mattick et al. (1989) achieved high or very high end-state functioning. Of the 58 treatment completers in Gelernter et al.'s (1991) study, 34% achieved scores below the mean for the general population on the fear questionnaire (Marks & Mathews, 1979). Alden (1989) treated 48 subjects with exposure or social skills training, finding that though there were significant improvements on a range of measures, only 9% of patients treated for APD rated themselves as completely improved.

Summary

- Meta-analytic studies show moderate to strong effect sizes for cognitive and behavioral treatments of social phobia.
- General reviews of individual studies have yielded significant effects for *in vivo* exposure.
- The effects of social skills training are more equivocal but nevertheless promising, particularly for patients with APD.
- There is some (though limited) evidence that cognitive restructuring in combination with exposure is more effective than exposure alone. Other cognitive techniques such as distraction and rational self-talk also seem to enhance the effects of exposure in some studies.
- Despite these findings, there is no indication that cognitive therapy alone or social skills training alone, without an exposure component, whether self-administered or therapist-directed, can be effective.
- The outcome for APD patients is relatively poor; only a small minority treated achieve high end-state functioning.
- There is limited evidence for the impact of medication on psychological treatment to suggest that, at the least, medication does not detract from the efficacy of exposure. There are some suggestions that phenelzine may enhance the effects of cognitive therapy and exposure.

Generalized Anxiety Disorder

Meta-Analyses

Chambless and Gillis (1993) examine seven studies published between 1987 and 1992 in which GAD was diagnosed to DSM-III-R criteria and which treated patients with CBT. Contrasted to control groups, there is a pre–post treatment effect size of 1.69, and a pretreatment follow-up effect size of 1.95 (follow-up was only reported in four studies, and was either 6 months or 1 year). Control groups in these studies varied, employing pill placebo, nondirective therapy, or waiting list. Presumably because of the small number of studies these are collapsed into one variable, though it is clear that effect sizes would be expected to vary depending on the specific control group against which therapies are contrasted.

General Reviews and Specific Studies

Durham and Allan (1993) review comparative outcome studies published between 1980 and 1991, determining efficacy using the criteria of clinical significance (Jacobson et al., 1984). To determine this with some degree of consistency, 14 studies using the Hamilton Anxiety Scale (HAS) and the State–Trait Anxiety Inventory (STAI-T; Speilberger et al., 1983) were examined. Techniques used in these studies were cognitive and behavioral therapies, relaxation, biofeedback, and nondirective therapy.

The percentage improvement posttreatment varies rather markedly across studies. For all treatments combined there is a 54% reduction for somatic symptoms on the HAS (range across studies 20–76%) and a 25% reduction in "general tendency to worry" on STAI-T (range 6–50%). Usually, but not consistently, the best results were obtained by CBT. Though these improvements are modest, they compare well with results for anxiolytic medication and placebo (which show an average reduction in HAS scores of 47% and 30%, respectively [Barlow, 1988]). Only half the studies followed up patients; where this was reported, follow-up was between 3 and 12 months (mode = 6) and gains were maintained.

Using standardized, categorical criteria to indicate improvement is more clinically meaningful than reporting percentage change. Five studies (all contrasting cognitive therapy and behavior therapy) employed cutoff points on anxiety scales or a reduction of 2 SD from pretreatment scores to gauge clinically significant change. On average, 57% of patients who had received cognitive therapy were in the normative range, compared to 22% of behavior therapy patients.

There was some, limited evidence that studies that included more patients with a first episode of anxiety had better results, though only three studies give any information about this. Comorbidity was described only in two studies; one-third of the sample in Jannoun et al. (1982) had agoraphobia. Butler et al. (1987) report that 47% of their patients had a depressive condition, and 29% panic disorder.

Reviewing almost the same set of studies, Marks (1989) reached similar conclusions, and noted in particular the importance of exposure strategies in managing the tendency to avoidance behavior noted frequently in patients with GAD. Overall, the two reviews indicate that moderate treatment gains are possible, more particularly with cognitive-behavioral techniques, but that many patients will not be symptom-free. Nonetheless, these results are comparable to those obtained with medication.

Hollon and Beck (1994) note that more recent studies of cognitive-behavioral interventions for GAD have shown more promising results than earlier research, perhaps reflecting an increasing sophistication in the application of the cognitive components. A small number of recent trials do indeed show strong evidence for the efficacy of cognitive approaches as contrasted both to behavioral interventions and to waiting-list control.

Durham and Turvey (1987) treated 51 patients with GAD of at least 1 year's duration, assigning them to 16 sessions of either CBT (modification of maladaptive thoughts and assumptions) or behavioral treatment (relaxation, distraction, and exposure). On global ratings by independent assessors, posttreatment gains were similar in each treatment condition; overall, 25% of patients showed no change, 20% showed moderate gains, and 55% had greatly improved. However, the stability of these gains varied across treatment groups; at 6-month follow-up, 62% of CBT patients were rated as greatly improved, contrasted with only 30% of those treated with behavior therapy.

Butler et al. (1991) also contrasted CBT and behavior therapy, but included a waiting-list control group. This study is particularly notable for the care taken to assess treatment integrity, which was assessed by independent observers rating tapes of therapy. Fifty-seven patients participated in the trial; the mean duration of the index episode of GAD was 3 years. Both treatments were superior to waiting list, but CBT was more effective than behavior therapy across a range of symptoms. Clinical significance of change was assessed using as a criterion scores of ≤10 on the HAS, ≤10 on the Beck Anxiety Scale, and ≤6 on the Leeds Anxiety Scale. Thirty-two percent of patients receiving CBT and 16% of those receiving behavior therapy met this target posttherapy. At 6 months follow-up the advantage to CBT was more marked; 42% of CBT but only 5% of behavior therapy patients met the criterion.

Durham et al. (1994) examined the efficacy of CBT, analytically based psychotherapy, and anxiety management training. All patients had a diagnosis of GAD, with a mean duration of 30 months (range 6–60 months). Eighty percent of patients had comorbid Axis I disorders (most usually agoraphobia, panic disorder, social phobia, and dysthymia); 46% also received an Axis II diagnosis, usually of avoidant or dependent personality disorder. Though CBT and analytic therapy were delivered by experienced therapists, anxiety management training was offered by therapists relatively inexperienced in this approach.

Treatment was offered over 6 months, with analytic therapy and CBT delivered either at "high" frequency (essentially weekly) or "low" frequency (essentially fortnightly). Anxiety management training was delivered at low frequency. One hundred ten patients were allocated to treatment groups, of whom 99 began treatment; a further 19 (19%) dropped out of treatment. Attrition was lowest for CBT (10%) and similar for analytic therapy and anxiety management training (24% and 27%, respectively).

Overall, patients receiving CBT showed significant and consistent gains across a range of measures, with improvements maintained at 6-month follow-up. While patients receiving analytic therapy showed significant gains on some measures after treatment, these were not maintained at follow-up. Equivalent results were found for patients treated at both high and low frequency. Contrasting all three treatments, at the end of treatment 81% of CBT patients were at least moderately improved, compared to 80% who received anxiety management training and 74% of those receiving analytical psychotherapy. At 6-month follow-up, 76% of CBT patients were at least moderately improved, contrasted to 49% of those receiving anxiety management training and 42% of those offered analytical psychotherapy. Jacobsen et al.'s (1984) criterion of recovery (a return to functioning within the normal range) was achieved at follow-up by approximately two-thirds of patients receiving CBT, one-third of those receiving anxiety management training and one-fifth of those receiving analytic therapy.

Borkovec and Costello (1993) examined the relative efficacy of CBT, applied relaxation, and nondirective counseling. Fifty-five patients entered the trial from an original total of 508, solicited through health care agencies and advertisements. CBT was perhaps less focused than that offered in Durham et al.'s research, reported above, incorporating as it did applied relaxation together with cue detection, self-control techniques, and "brief cognitive therapy" (Borkovec & Costello, 1993 p. 613). At posttherapy patients treated using applied relaxation and CBT improved to an equivalent extent, and significantly more so than those who received nondirective counseling. At 12-month follow-up, the percentage of patients defined as having a high response to treatment on the basis of eight anxiety measures was 57.9% for those receiving CBT, 33.3% for applied relaxation, and 22.2% for nondirective counseling.

There appear to be rather few contrasts of medication and CBT. Lindsay et al. (1987) contrasted 40 patients assigned to lorazepam, CBT, anxiety management training, and a waiting list. Although lorazepam showed a rapid response, this effect diminished over the 4 weeks of the trial. Patients in both CBT and anxiety management groups showed improvements, though this was greatest for CBT. Power et al. (1989) showed that CBT and relaxation training was superior both to diazepam and pill placebo both at posttreatment and at 12-month follow-up. Power et al. (1990) treated 101 patients assigned to diazepam or placebo alone and also in combination with CBT. Ten weeks of treatment was offered, with control for therapist attention in patients receiving medication alone. Defining recovery as an HAS score of more than 2 *SD* from the pretreatment range, at posttreatment between 83 and 86% of patients in the three groups receiving CBT recovered, contrasted with 68% and 37% in the diazepam and placebo alone groups. At 6-month follow-up patients receiving CBT tended to maintain their gains, while those receiving medication relapsed; at this point around 70% of those receiving CBT had maintained their recovery and had no further subsequent treatment. In contrast, this status was achieved by 40% and 21% of the diazepam and placebo groups.

Summary

- The single meta-analytic review in this area yielded a very large posttherapy effect size for CBT, though follow-up data were sparse and control groups utilized by studies varied significantly.
- CBT delivered by experienced therapists shows good evidence of efficacy. Two-thirds to three-fourths of patients may be expected to show clinically significant improvement at 6 months follow-up.
- These medium-term effects are markedly greater than those observed from analytic therapy, nondirective counseling, and behavioral methods such as applied relaxation training or biofeedback.
- The presence of comorbidity with panic disorders or depression complicates these conclusions but may go some way to explaining the unique efficacy of CBT.
- CBT appears to be the most acceptable treatment in terms of attrition from therapy and outcome on follow-up.
- Benzodiazepines alone appear to have only short-term effects.

Panic Disorder with and without Agoraphobia

Meta-Analyses

A number of meta-analytic reviews consider the efficacy of treatments for panic disorder with and without agoraphobia; although all cover some of the same studies, overall there is little overlap between them. Interpretation is further impeded by different methods used to calculate effect sizes. Some examine within-patient pre–posttherapy changes. Others employ comparisons of outcome with control groups, such as waiting list or placebo. Yet others arrive at effect sizes from comparisons between treated groups. Despite this variation in methodology, there is some consensus across reviews.

Mattick et al. (1990) offer perhaps the most general review, reflecting their intention to integrate the literature from a clinical perspective. Fifty-four studies investigated the efficacy of *in vivo* exposure, medication, or alternative psychological techniques in patients with agoraphobia and panic disorder. All effect sizes were derived from pre–posttreatment scores and follow-up data.

A preliminary finding was the low rate of improvement for patients in waiting-list conditions or placebo treatments; mean effect sizes for measures of panic were respectively 0.32 and 0.29. These figures reflect the chronicity of this disorder and the findings of studies specifically oriented to this question. For example, Michelson and Mavissakalian (1983) monitored patients while they were on a waiting list for 3 months, finding little change in symptoms over this period.

Benzodiazepines showed some effect on symptoms, though this was more marked for alprazolam than for diazepam; on measures of panic, effect sizes were 1.04 and 0.56, respectively. Imipramine showed a similar effect to alprazolam on panic measures (1.01) but had a greater impact on depression (0.89 contrasted with 0.41 for alprazolam).

Although most studies examined *in vivo* exposure, there were nine trials of behavioral therapies not incorporating this technique. Interventions used were relaxation, assertion therapy, cognitive therapy, or imaginal exposure. Assessed by their impact on measures of phobia, these therapies produce a relatively large effect size (0.96); however, on measures of panic their efficacy was low (0.47).

Forty studies of *in vivo* exposure (in various contrasts with other techniques) yielded a substantial effect size on measures of phobia (1.7), while that for panic was 0.96. On measures of anxiety and depression, effect sizes were more moderate (0.68 and 0.69). Improvements were maintained at a mean of 16 months follow-up.

In 16 studies that employed cognitive anxiety management along with exposure, smaller effect sizes were found on measures of phobia (1.43). However, effect sizes were greater on measures of panic (1.29), anxiety (1.04), and depression (0.84), suggesting a broader impact of treatment. Mattick et al. note that in these studies there was less time given to exposure, which may account for these differences in effect sizes.

A smaller number of studies (12) combined imipramine and psychological treatments. Although the effect of combined treatments on measures of phobia is greater than that produced by imipramine alone, combination treatments are no more effective than exposure alone.

Cox et al. (1992) review trials carried out between 1980 and 1990 in which patients with panic disorder with or without agoraphobia received treatment with imipramine, alprazolam, or exposure. Thirty-four studies were reviewed (not detailed in the paper), excluding combination treatments and studies that included agoraphobic without panic. Using global pre–posttreatment ratings by clinicians, the greatest effect size was found for exposure (3.42), followed by alprazolam (2.1) and imipramine (1.16).

Trull et al.'s (1988) review concerns itself with the clinical significance of outcomes after behavior therapy for agoraphobia, restricting its analysis to 19 outcome studies using the Fear Questionnaire (FQ) carried out between 1975 to 1987 (a list of studies examined is not provided). Therapy was usually *in vivo* exposure carried out either individually or in groups, though in some studies imaginal exposure was used, and in a small minority no exposure. Larger effect sizes were found for *in vivo* exposure contrasted with imaginal, and better results were found for more experienced therapists (though the magnitude of these effect sizes is not given). The clinical significance of treatment effects was computed by contrasting treated patients to two reference groups on whom normative data for the FQ had been obtained. The first of these reference groups was specifically selected as a nondistressed group; the second was a general population sample.

Using these contrasts, and using the agoraphobia subscale of the FQ the average treated client moved to within 2.2 *SD* units above the mean for the nondistressed group and to within 0.47 *SD* units of the mean for the general population sample. These figures can be expressed more meaningfully in terms of percentiles. Adopting this criterion, the average treated client moves from a pretreatment level at the 99.9th percentile to the 98.7th percentile of the nondistressed group at posttreatment. Contrasted to the general population sample the gains are more striking—from the 97.3th percentile to the 68th percentile.

Seventy-five percent of studies included follow-up data; of these the median length of follow-up was 18 weeks (range 4–96), which is perhaps rather brief. Effect sizes at follow-up were very similar to those obtained posttreatment.

Two further meta-analyses (Clum et al., 1993; Chambless & Gillis, 1993) contain full lists of studies examined. There is hardly any overlap between these reviews; each uses different study selection criteria, though the two are focused on the same diagnostic group. In addition there is only limited (and inconsistent) overlap with reviews discussed above.

Clum et al. (1993) base their analysis on a larger and broader sample than Trull et al., focusing on 29 studies of treatments for panic disorder with and without agoraphobia published between 1964 and 1990. Treatments examined were behavioral and cognitive-behavioral interventions, medication, and combination treatments. All studies included a control group, which was sometimes a waiting list, placebo, or comparison between treatments. Effect sizes for all treatments ranged between 0.2 and 2.88. Comparing psychological coping techniques and exposure/flooding against placebo gave effect sizes of 1.41 and 1.36, respectively. Antidepressants and benzodiazepines contrasted to placebo gave effect sizes of 0.82 and 0.29. These effect sizes are less meaningful than might appear, since the placebo controls used in studies varied and sometimes included psychological techniques such as relaxation.

Further effect sizes were calculated to determine the relative efficacy of each treatment modality against another, rather than defining overall effect sizes for treatments per se.

Multiple comparison indicated that psychological interventions such as relaxation training, cognitive restructuring, and exposure produced the highest effect sizes, followed by combination treatments. Where medication was used alone, antidepressants had the highest effect sizes; benzodiazepines performed poorly. Combination treatments using antidepressants also performed well; medication makes a small additional contribution to exposure treatments (comparison of exposure alone to combination treatment gives an effect size of 0.34). Few of the studies reviewed included follow-up data (12 of 29), and treatment gains are not commented on. Studies were divided into those that included more than or less than 75% of patients with agoraphobic symptoms; no significant difference in effect size was found (though only in six studies were there less than 75% agoraphobic).

Chambless and Gillis (1993), in a detailed review, contrast the impacts of cognitive and cognitive-behavioral treatments. Comparing cognitive treatments against cognitive treatment combined with exposure for panic disorder with agoraphobia (five studies), combination treatments were more effective than control groups but no more effective than exposure alone; overall, 66% of clients treated using these methods were panic-free at the end of treatment.

Contrasting interventions using combined treatment with control patients receiving pill placebo or waiting-list control, effect sizes between 0.40 and 1.07 were found. On average, 72% of clients receiving these treatments are panic-free posttherapy, contrasted with 25% of subjects in control groups.

Cognitive therapy for panic disorder without agoraphobia, using Clark and Salkovskis's model (1994; discussed further below) is examined in six studies, with effect sizes of 1.0 to 1.73. On average, 85% of clients were panic-free at posttest contrasted with 12% of control subjects, and 88% were panic-free at follow-up (though figures for length of follow-up are not given).

Van Balkom et al. (1995) present a meta-analysis of treatment outcome in panic disorder with agoraphobia. They note that though the meta-analyses discussed above reach similar conclusions in relation to the efficacy of imipramine, alprazolam, panic control therapies, and exposure, they disagree about their relative efficacy and the benefits of their combination. Along with methodological differences, this is attributed to the use of between-study contrasts, which risk confusing a range of confounding variables for true between-treatment effects. To correct for this, Van Balkom et al. identified 25 within-study contrasts published between 1964 and 1993. The bulk of these trials directly compared imipramine and high-potency benzodiazepines ($n = 9$) or contrasted the combination of exposure and panic control therapies against exposure alone or panic control therapy alone ($n = 11$). The remaining studies contrasted cognitive therapy against alprazolam ($n = 1$) and against fluvoxamine ($n = 1$), exposure in combination with alprazolam against alprazolam alone or exposure alone ($n = 1$), and exposure in combination with imipramine against imipramine alone ($n = 2$). It should be noted that each of the Mattick, Cox, and Clum meta-analyses included some of these studies (eight, nine, and seven, respectively); among them 15 of the 25 studies were examined, though between- and within-study contrasts were not presented separately.

Nine trials contrasted imipramine and high-potency benzodiazepines (usually alprazolam). The dropout rate for imipramine was 27%, contrasted with 13% for alprazolam. The mean between-treatment effect size for both completer and intent-to-treat samples was 0.0.

Eleven studies (with a total of 408 patients) contrasted panic management techniques (including paradoxical intention, applied relaxation, cognitive therapy, breathing retraining, and flooding in imagination) against *in vivo* exposure. Results consistently favored exposure *in vivo*, and suggested that the addition of panic control techniques did not enhance efficacy. Thus exposure alone was more effective than panic management alone. Panic management and exposure in combination was more effective than panic management alone, but no more effective than exposure alone.

The remaining contrasts, based on a single trial and sometimes with rather small sample sizes, suggest that cognitive therapy showed superiority over alprazolam. The contrast between cognitive therapy and fluvoxamine was complex. Outcomes varied between intent-to-treat and completer samples; overall, there appeared to be no difference between cognitive therapy and fluvoxamine on measures of panic, though fluvoxamine appeared more effective if measures of anxiety and depression are employed. Alprazolam in combination with exposure appeared more effective than exposure alone; exposure alone was more effective than alprazolam alone. Two studies examined the combination of imipramine with exposure in contrast to imipramine alone, finding large between-treatment effect sizes favoring the combination treatment.

General Reviews and Specific Studies

Behavioral treatments based on exposure and response prevention have been extensively investigated, with evidence both of short- and long-term efficacy (Marks & O'Sullivan, 1988; O'Sullivan & Marks, 1990). In 10 studies reviewed by O'Sullivan and Marks (1990), patients were followed up at between 1 and 9 years (mean 4 years). Combining data from these trials, 76% of patients were judged improved or much improved, with 24% rated as unimproved. This suggests that considerable gains are possible with this treatment. However, it is important to note that, when followed up over the longer term, many patients evidence residual symptoms, though with diminished handicap.

In a cautionary review, Jacobson et al. (1988) reanalyzed data from 11 studies investigating the efficacy of exposure-based treatments for agoraphobia, applying criteria for clinical significance developed by Jacobson et al. (1984). All treatments were trials of *in vivo* or imaginal exposure, flooding or cognitive restructuring in various combinations, all contrasted against a control condition, which was usually one of the above treatments (in 10/11 cases). Follow-up was between 3 and 6 months. Although a statistically significant percentage of cases improved (a weighted mean of 58% pre- to posttreatment) and gains were maintained (60% pretherapy to follow-up), the proportion reaching a criterion of recovery was lower (a weighted mean of 27% posttreatment, and 34% at follow-up). Although the review provides supportive evidence for the efficacy of exposure-based treatments, it also sets a challenge to researchers. By reference to the rigorous test of full recovery employed, these treatments can be seen as less than optimal. Many studies report data on relative rather than absolute improvement, a decision that may be clinically justifiable but that is likely to magnify treatment effects.

Clum (1989) reviews 67 studies of treatments for panic with and without agoraphobia conducted between 1964 and 1988. The meta-analysis by Clum et al. (1993, and discussed above) has some overlap with this review but is more restricted in examining only trials including placebo or waiting-list control groups. The relative merits of psychological and psychopharmacological interventions were determined using as criteria dropout rates, treatment outcome rates, and relapse rates. Success rates were defined by the absence of panic attacks or a 50% reduction in their frequency; relapse was defined as an increase in panic frequency above 50% of the pretreatment baseline, or a return to treatment.

Behavioral interventions have a significantly higher aggregate success rate (71%) than that shown by placebo controls (40%); propanolol and low-potency benzodiazepines show no greater efficacy than placebo, with success rates of 30% and 45%, respectively. The success rate of antidepressants and high-potency benzodiazepines is equivalent to behavior therapy. Combining medication and behavior therapy has little impact on outcome, though there is a trend toward reduced efficacy, a finding more marked with high-potency benzodiazepines (where success rates of 57% were obtained). Wardle (1990) has suggested that benzodiazepines may interfere with the therapeutic process, and there is direct evidence of this from Marks et al. (1993). This issue is discussed further below.

Patients with panic disorder with agoraphobia have somewhat lower rates of success (59%) than those who have panic disorder without agoraphobia (66%). Although this effect is consistent regardless of treatment modality, it is more marked for behavioral therapies and high-potency benzodiazepines.

Only 23 of the 67 studies followed up patients to estimate relapse rates; length of follow-up is not detailed by Clum (1989). However, on the basis of available figures, aggregated relapse rates were lowest with behavioral therapy (12%), contrasted with 28% for high-potency benzodiazepines and 55% for MAOIs. The paucity of data in this review makes firm conclusions difficult.

Dropout rates were higher with medication, particularly tricyclics, than psychological treatment (28% and 14.5%, respectively) and for panic disorder with agoraphobia as contrasted to panic disorder without agoraphobia (24% and 14%, respectively).

Self-Exposure and Therapist-Aided Exposure. Exposure-based treatments may be administered either by therapists accompanying the patient during exposure or by patient-directed ("self-directed") exposure. While decisions about which method to use reflect technical and clinical concerns, it is obvious that the two modes of delivery have very different costs. If the two methods are of equivalent efficacy, self-directed exposure would clearly be the preferred method. At least three controlled trials by Marks and colleagues suggest this to be so (Al-Kubaisy et al., 1992; Ghosh et al., 1987; McNamee et al., 1989).

After assessment, Ghosh and Marks (1987) assigned 46 agoraphobics to receive exposure instructions either from a therapist, via computer instruction, or with reference to a book detailing the management of anxiety using self-exposure. Although all patents were seen by therapists over the period of treatment and all received instruction regarding the rational behind exposure, mean total therapist contact for each mode of delivery was 4.6, 2.7, and 1.5 hours, respectively. Equivalent results were obtained for each treatment condition.

McNamee et al. (1989) assessed 37 housebound agoraphobics over the telephone; 23 agreed to treatment and were assigned either to telephone-guided self-exposure or telephone-guided self-relaxation. Exposure subjects were given a self-exposure manual. Patients using self-exposure improved significantly more than those using relaxation, though remained somewhat symptomatic and improved more slowly than in other trials where therapists guided exposure. In part this may reflect the level of severity and chronicity in this patient group, though it may also suggest that while therapists do not need to accompany their patients, therapist contact may be an important ingredient of therapeutic efficacy.

Al-Kubaisy et al. (1992) examined the efficacy of (1) therapist-assisted exposure combined with self-exposure and (2) self-exposure and relaxation with no exposure. Eighty patients with mixed phobias completed treatment, of whom 30% were agoraphobic, 30% had social phobia, and 40% had a specific phobia. Both exposure conditions resulted in significantly greater gains than did relaxation; the addition of therapist-assisted exposure did not add to efficacy, though there was some evidence that social phobics showed some additional gains from this procedure.

Combination Treatments of Imipramine and Exposure. Five controlled studies have directly examined the relative efficacy of imipramine and exposure (Marks et al., 1983; Mavissakalian & Michelson, 1986; Telch et al., 1985; Zitrin et al., 1980, 1983). Marks et al. (1983) contrasted therapist-assisted *in vivo* exposure and relaxation in combination with either imipramine or placebo, finding that imipramine did not have an effect beyond exposure either posttreatment or at 1 year follow-up. In contrast, the remaining four studies suggest a facilitative effect for imipramine and exposure in combination. Mavissakalian and Michelson (1986) contrasted imipramine and placebo in combination either with therapist-aided exposure or self-exposure in 62 patients over 12 weeks of treatment, finding that the addition of imipramine significantly increased response at termination. However, at 6-month follow-up there were no between-treatment differences, largely attributable to significantly greater relapse rates in the patients receiving imipramine and continued improvement in those receiving placebo. Zitrin et al. (1980, 1983) treated patients with imipramine or placebo for 4 weeks, followed by 10 weeks of *in vivo* exposure and a further 12 weeks of maintenance drug treatment. *In vivo* exposure was conducted in groups, and it is not clear that individual programs were constructed for patients. Global ratings of improvement made by the patient and by an independent evaluator favored patients receiving imipramine, though on therapist ratings there were no differences between imipramine and placebo. At 2-year follow-up there were no indications of differential relapse between treatment groups.

Further studies have examined whether exposure enhances the effects of imipramine. Mavissakalian et al. (1983) contrasted imipramine alone with imipramine and exposure; after 12 weeks of treatment the combined treatment showed statistically greater gains. Using a broadly similar design, Telch et al. (1985) controlled for the possibility that patients receiving medication alone might self-expose by including an additional antiexposure condition. The patients receiving the combination of imipramine and exposure improved significantly more than those receiving medication alone or medication and antiexposure. Posttreatment patients who had been receiving antiexposure showed significant improvement on being given exposure instructions.

These studies suggest that the combination of imipramine and exposure may have beneficial effects, though there is some evidence from follow-up data that the addition of imipramine is at best neutral in relation to exposure; at worst there is some tentative evidence of greater relapse with medication (Mavissakalian & Michelson, 1986; Mavissakalian, 1993).

Exposure Treatments for Agoraphobia in Combination with Benzodiazepines (Alprazolam and Diazepam). Although there is evidence that psychological treatments can combine well with tricyclic antidepressants (though, as discussed above, with mixed evidence as to their differential efficacy), there may be reason to be cautious about the use of high-potency benzodiazepines in combination with exposure.

Marks et al. (1993a) report a cross-national study (carried out in London and Toronto) of *in vivo* exposure in combination with alprazolam. Four treatment conditions contrasted alprazolam with exposure, alprazolan with relaxation, placebo with exposure, and placebo with relaxation. Patients were given active outpatient treatment for 8 weeks, followed by a drug taper from weeks 8–16 and a follow-up at 10 months.

One hundred fifty-four patients entered treatment; mean duration of agoraphobia was 8 years, and 10% had current and 30% previous MDD. However, those patients with a current history of MDD that predated the agoraphobia or predominated over it were excluded from the trials. Attrition was relatively consistent across conditions; 16% dropped out before the end of active treatment, and 50% were followed up at 10 months.

All four conditions resulted in posttreatment improvements on a range of measures of phobias, mood, and adjustment. At 10 months (using a clinician-rated measure of global improvement), the rate of relapse in patients who had shown improvement during treatment was significantly different across treatment conditions. The proportions of patients who both responded to treatment and stayed well were 62% for placebo and exposure, 36% for alprazolam and exposure, 29% for alprazolam and relaxation, and 18% for placebo and relaxation. This suggests that not only does withdrawal of alprazolam result in higher levels of relapse as contrasted with exposure, but also that exposure is less effective when combined with alprazolam.

A possible explanation for this effect has been offered by Wardle (1990), who suggests that benzodiazepines may interfere with therapy through the mechanism of state-dependent learning. However, Wardle et al. (1994) in an RCT and Hegel et al. (1994) in an open trial have demonstrated that concurrent treatment with moderate doses of diazepam did not significantly interfere with exposure treatments for severe, chronic agoraphobics. Further, Spiegal et al. (1993) have criticized Marks et al.'s study on the grounds that excessively high doses of medication were employed, a factor disputed in turn by Marks et al. (1993b). Given that Marks et al. imply that certain medication combinations are contraindicated, further research may be required to clarify this issue.

Applied Relaxation. Applied relaxation has been evaluated in a series of studies reviewed by Öst (1987). This technique focuses on generalizing the patient's ability to apply progressive relaxation techniques. Though essentially a behavioral technique, it does contain cognitive elements in the rationale it offers to patients. In nine studies with populations containing mixed anxiety diagnoses, applied relaxation was contrasted to alternative behavioral techniques such as *in vivo* exposure, social skills training, progressive relaxation, and self-instructional training. Applied relaxation was equivalent in efficacy to these techniques in most studies, though superior to progressive relaxation in patients with panic disorder. Öst (1988) reports a trial of 18 patients, the majority of whom had panic disorder (14) or GAD (4), contrasting applied to progressive relaxation. At posttreatment, 75% of the applied relaxation group and 38% of the progressive relaxation group met a recovery criterion based on a number of anxiety scales. At follow-up (mean length 19 months), 100% of the applied relaxation group were judged recovered, contrasted with 25% of those receiving progressive relaxation. The efficacy of this technique was somewhat poorer in the study conducted by Clark et al. (1994), which is discussed further below. However, these authors made some modifications in the rationale offered to patients, which may have influenced outcome.

Cognitive Treatment. Cognitive models of panic are based on the proposition that otherwise benign bodily cues are misinterpreted as evidence of an imminent catastrophe; the resultant panic is then taken as confirmation of this misperception, and a vicious cycle is set in train. A number of similar interventions have been developed, varying in the extent to which cognitive or cognitive-behavioral techniques are employed (Beck & Emery, 1985; Barlow & Cerny, 1988; Salkovskis & Clark, 1991). Therapies focus on catastrophic misinterpretation and in this sense are an advance on earlier applications of more general cognitive theory to anxiety (Hollon & Beck, 1994). Most studies focus on patients with only mild or moderate levels of agoraphobia.

Panic control treatment (PCT) has been examined in two controlled trials (Barlow et al., 1989; Klosko et al., 1990). In the first study, patients with panic disorder alone or with mild or moderate agoraphobia were allocated either to PCT alone (cognitive restructuring and exposure to introceptive cues), relaxation alone, relaxation and PCT in combination, or a waiting-list control group. Data are presented for 56 completers from an original sample of 72 patients. All treatments were superior to the waiting-list control, but PCT and PCT in combination were superior to relaxation in reducing panic frequency, but not generalized anxiety. Posttreatment, 85% and 87% of patients receiving PCT alone and in combination respectively were panic-free, contrasted with 60% of those receiving relaxation alone, and 36% of those on the waiting list. At 2-year follow-up (Craske et al., 1991), the percentages of patients panic-free were 81% for PCT alone, 43% for PCT with relaxation, and 36% for relaxation alone. However, if measures of general anxiety are adopted, rather less impressive results are obtained, largely accounted for by continuing agoraphobic avoidance in the absence of panic. This result may indicate that separate procedures may be required to alleviate symptoms of panic and avoidance.

Klosko et al. (1990) contrasted PCT to alprazolam, a drug placebo, and a waiting-list control in a sample of 57 patients. PCT was significantly more effective than placebo (87% panic-free) and waiting list (33%), but was not significantly more effective than alprazolam (50%) which, in turn, did not differ significantly from placebo (36%).

Beck et al. (1992) allocated 33 patients (80% with panic disorder without agoraphobia) to either 12 weeks of cognitive therapy or 8 weeks of client-centered supportive therapy, attempting in this way to control for nonspecific effects of therapy contact. Patients who received supportive therapy were then given the opportunity to cross over to cognitive therapy for 12 weeks. When assessed at 8 weeks, cognitive therapy patients were significantly more likely to be panic-free than those receiving supportive therapy (71% and 25%, respectively). Nearly all the patients receiving supportive therapy subsequently received cognitive therapy; at 1 year follow-up 87% of the cognitive therapy, and 79% of the crossover group were panic-free.

Beck et al. (1994) contrasted cognitive therapy, relaxation training, and a minimal contact control group in 64 patients with panic disorder with mild or moderate agoraphobia. Both active treatments were significantly more effective than control, and cognitive therapy was more effective than relaxation. At posttherapy, 82% of those receiving cognitive therapy were classified as treatment responders, contrasted to 68% of those receiving relaxation and 36% of the controls.

Clark et al. (1994) describe a controlled trial of cognitive therapy contrasted with applied relaxation, imipramine, or a waiting list. Sixty-four patients participated; all had panic disorder with mild or moderate agoraphobia, but those with severe agoraphobia were excluded. Twelve sessions of treatment were offered over 3 months, with up to three booster sessions over the subsequent 3 months. Imipramine was withdrawn after 6 months.

All three treatments were effective, though cognitive therapy was markedly more effective than both imipramine and relaxation, both 3 months after treatment and at 1 year. At this point 85% of patients receiving cognitive therapy were panic-free, contrasted with 47% and 60% for relaxation and imipramine, respectively. It is worth noting that 26% of the relaxation group and 40% of those receiving imipramine sought further treatment over the follow-up period, contrasted with 5% of the cognitive therapy group.

In a study that partially replicates Clarke et al.'s trial, Öst and Westling (1995) contrasted the efficacy of cognitive therapy with applied relaxation in a sample of 38 outpatients, 30 of whom had a diagnosis of panic disorder without agoraphobia; the remainder showed mild agoraphobic avoidance. After 12 weeks patients treated with cognitive therapy showed greater gains than those treated with applied relaxation; the proportion considered to have "high end-state functioning" (no panic attacks over a 3-week period and an independent assessor rating them to have low severity of panic disorder) was 74% and 47%, respectively. However, over 12-month follow-up patients treated with applied relaxation continued to improve, such that 82% were now rated as having high end-state functioning, contrasted to 79% of those receiving CBT.

The cognitive model of panic specifies a particular set of intervention procedures. Though there is good evidence for the efficacy of cognitive therapy, there may be some doubt about whether its mode of action flows so specifically from the model. Shear et al. (1994) contrasted 15 sessions of manualized CBT with a "nonprescriptive" therapy (NPT). The study was designed as a test of the efficacy of CBT against a credible control therapy (NPT), in which the therapist's role was largely restricted to reflective listening. The first three sessions for all patients were given over to education about anxiety, together with the identification of stressors that might trigger panic. Forty-five patients completed the treatment; no significant differences were found between treatments, either posttherapy or at 6-month follow-up. These results present a challenge to the CBT model, given that patients receiving NPT were apparently not in receipt of cognitive interventions. However, the priming effect of the initial three sessions may have significantly directed the focus of patients receiving NPT; further work is required to clarify this issue.

The trials reviewed above focus on patient samples treated in research settings and with minimal or moderate levels of agoraphobic avoidance. Robinson et al. (submitted) carried out a trial of group-based cognitive therapy in a panic disorder clinic, with a sample that included patients with severe agoraphobia. Of 115 patients entered into the study, 25% had no or mild agoraphobia, 50% moderate, and 25% severe agoraphobia. Attrition was fairly high, at 52% over the 11 sessions of therapy, though treatment completers were not significantly different from dropouts on pretreatment measures. Forty-five patients were treated with cognitive therapy, contrasted against 20 patients acting as waiting-list controls. Posttherapy 73% of the treatment group were panic-free, contrasted with 5% of the control group, with gains maintained at 9-month follow-up. However, measures of agoraphobic avoidance showed less clear-cut results. Contrasted to controls, measures of avoidance were reduced only when the patients were accompanied, with no significant differences for agoraphobic avoidance when unaccompanied.

Although the percentage of patients classified as moderate or severe agoraphobics reduced pre- to posttreatment, small cell sizes make it difficult to interpret these results (only five patients in the treatment group were classified as severe agoraphobics pretreatment). Such patients show a good response to exposure and response prevention, and some authors have suggested that this is the treatment of choice for this group (e.g., Beck et al., 1994). While cognitive techniques do appear to impact effectively on panic, there is evidence that panic and agoraphobic avoidance improve independently (Basoglu et al., 1994). It seems reasonable to conclude that without further research, it would be premature to advise the extension of cognitive therapy (without exposure) to patients with severe agoraphobia.

Finally, a cautionary note might be appropriate regarding the criteria adopted to indicate successful outcomes over follow-up. Brown and Barlow (1995) present a reanalysis of data from Barlow et al. (1991, reported in Brown & Barlow, 1995), a dismantling study of panic control therapy in which 63 patients with panic disorder with no or mild agoraphobia were assigned to one of four conditions: cognitive restructuring, cognitive restructuring and breathing retraining, cognitive restructuring and interoceptive exposure, or a combination of all four components. Little difference was found between treatment conditions, and 3-month and 2-year follow-up data appeared to indicate continued improvement with time. High end-state (HES) status was defined by the absence of panic attacks in the month prior to evaluation; this criterion was met by 68% of the sample at 3 months and 75% at 2 years. However, these aggregated data obscure shifts in HES status by individual patients. Thus 19 patients who failed to meet HES criterion at 3 months met them at 2 years; equally, eight patients rated as panic-free at 3 months failed to meet this criterion at 2 years. Similarly some patients started and others discontinued medication, such that the population of medication users was not the same at each evaluation point. Finally the HES criterion itself proved misleading in some cases. Thus 34% of patients classified as having HES status at 2 years nonetheless reported having had one or more panic attacks in the previous year.

Brown and Barlow show that outcome for patients in this study varies markedly dependent on the stringency with which criteria for HES status are set. Using aggregated data and the original criterion, at 2 years 75% of patients achieved HES status. However, if HES is defined by no panic in the previous month and no treatment over 2 years, this percentage falls to 48%, and to 21% if a further requirement of no panic in the past year is added. It may be relevant to add that though the presence of comorbid diagnoses was not strongly predictive of outcome (Brown et al., 1995), patients with more severe pretreatment symptomatology were more likely to have poorer outcomes at 2 years, despite evidence of gains at 3 months. Thus, although responsive to treatment, this group showed poor maintenance. Overall, these results confirm the fact that panic disorder tends to be a chronic disturbance, and suggest that over time, outcomes in clinical settings with individual patients may not reflect those achieved in research using shorter follow-ups and aggregated data.

Summary

- This field has been particularly well covered by meta-analytic studies, which yield unusually consistent findings.

- Behavioral therapies using relaxation and exposure procedures have substantial effect sizes for phobic symptoms, and somewhat smaller but still large effect sizes for panic.
- Patients with panic disorder with agoraphobia have a slightly lower rate of success than those with panic disorder without agoraphobia.
- Cognitive techniques appear to benefit panic symptoms in particular.
- Combinations of cognitive treatments and exposure seem effective in treating panic with agoraphobia in two-thirds of cases; for panic disorder without agoraphobia, about 85% improve.
- The impact of behavioral and cognitive-behavioral treatment is statistically highly significant, but across studies the proportion of patients who can expect to reach a criterion of full recovery is only between one-fourth and one-third.
- As cognitive techniques almost invariably include an exposure element, it seems reasonable to conclude that the efficacy of cognitive therapy alone in the treatment of phobia is broadly comparable to behavioral techniques.
- Meta-analyses indicate that treatment gains are, on the whole, maintained with psychological treatments. The impact of medication generally appears to be short-term after discontinuation.
- Low-potency benzodiazepines, propanolol, and psychological and drug placebo show a clinically significant impact in approximately one-third of cases.
- Antidepressants employed alone have lower effect sizes than behavioral or cognitive-behavioral interventions.
- Relapse rates are lowest for behavior therapy and cognitive-behavioral therapy. On discontinuation of medication, relapse rates are somewhat higher for high-potency benzodiazepines and imipramine, and unacceptably high for MAOIs.
- Dropout rates are high for imipramine and relatively low for all psychological treatments.
- Programs that combine antidepressant and psychological treatments show a small improvement in efficacy for the combination treatment. Benzodiazepines have a relatively small impact when employed alone and add little when used in combination with psychological treatment.
- The combination of imipramine and exposure may have beneficial effects, though there is some evidence from follow-up data that the addition of imipramine is at best neutral in relation to exposure, and at worst some tentative evidence of greater relapse with medication.

- There is contradictory evidence concerning the impact of combinations of benzodiazepines and exposure. Studies using moderate doses of diazepam were not able to demonstrate the negative interactions sometimes found between these medications and exposure treatment.
- Self-exposure is as effective as therapist-guided exposure, though there is evidence that therapist involvement in designing the program for the individual patient is helpful.
- Applied relaxation seems more effective than progressive relaxation.
- In most, but not all, trials, panic control therapies are superior to applied relaxation treatments, benzodiazepines, and client-centered supportive therapy.
- The efficacy of panic control therapies with patients with panic disorder with severe agoraphobia is less well established, and this approach may be less effective with these patients.
- These findings should be interpreted cautiously in view of the relatively short follow-up period in the great majority of studies reviewed.
- Studies using stringent recovery criteria suggest that outcomes may be poorer than that reported by many research trials. Results obtained in clinical settings may not reflect those achieved by researchers using aggregated data, which may mask considerable variation in patient's symptomatic status across time.

Implications

- Although less is known about the natural history of anxiety disorders than is the case with depression, epidemiological studies indicate that they represent a clinical problem of high prevalence and great chronicity.
- There is little justification for using anything other than exposure treatments for specific phobias.
- Social phobia and APD should also benefit from exposure; cognitive therapy may enhance outcomes. As there is only limited evidence for the impact of social skills training, this can only be recommended adjunctively.
- Treatment for APD may require longer, and may be associated with relatively poorer, outcomes than treatments for social phobia. Patients with this diagnosis will need to be considered separately in reviews of services with regard to patient mix.

- Of the anxiety disorders, GAD is likely be the most resistant to both psychological and medical interventions. Currently, CBT appears to be the treatment of choice for patients presenting with GAD, particularly those who show comorbidity with panic disorders and depression.
- Panic disorders with and without agoraphobia appear to respond best to a combination of cognitive techniques (PCT) and exposure treatment, and this should be tried in the first instance. Applied relaxation may be a useful adjunct to treatment.
- Patients with panic disorder with severe agoraphobia are more difficult to treat successfully, and should receive exposure treatment; the addition of cognitive therapy may enhance the patient's capacity to deal with panic.
- Individuals with severe anxiety disorders are frequently prescribed anxiolytic or antidepressant medication. There is no compelling evidence that this is likely to interfere with their psychological treatment. Indeed, in the case of panic disorders, antidepressant medication may enhance the effects of psychological interventions.
- Medical treatments should not be seen as alternatives to psychological therapies for anxiety. Overall, medical treatments administered alone tend to be no more effective than psychological, even for chronic and severe conditions. Their therapeutic effects tend to diminish rapidly after discontinuation, leading to relapse.
- Whereas the cost of psychological therapies may be higher relative to medical interventions, considerable progress has been made in designing programs that involve relatively small therapist input and substantially greater self-administration on the part of the patient. This provides a helpful model for the administration of psychological services and should be developed and explored further in the context of psychological interventions with other disorders.
- As evidence indicates that, even after effective treatments, a large proportion of patients will remain impaired relative to a nondistressed sample, both purchasers and providers should be aware that these treatments are not "curative" of these serious disorders. This is particularly important since studies of efficacy are performed largely by those who were responsible for these innovative treatment methods, and therefore the effectiveness of treatment can be expected to be more modest in clinical practice.
- There is a striking absence in the literature of interventions other than behavioral, cognitive, and cognitive-behavioral therapies—indeed, nondirective therapies have been used as attention placebo

controls. In the absence of evidence, we cannot recommend the use of dynamic or humanistic techniques alone for anxiety disorders unless this is justified by (1) The presence of comorbidity, particularly personality disorders, which are known to complicate the implementation of brief structured treatments, and where evidence for the use of dynamic techniques exists; (2) Treatment failure in all the therapeutic modalities for which efficacy has been demonstrated, at which point the clinician may wish to try alternative treatments, given that the treatments of choice have been ineffective.

CHAPTER 7

Anxiety Disorders II
Obsessive–Compulsive Disorder

DEFINITION

Obsessions are defined in DSM-IV as recurrent, persistent, and distressing ideas, thoughts, impulses, or images; these are experienced (at least at some time in the disturbance) as intrusive and senseless, and do not reflect excessive worry about real-life problems. Examples would be a parent having repeated impulses to kill a loved child or a religious person having blasphemous thoughts. The person attempts to suppress or to neutralize such thoughts or impulses with another thought or action. There is clear recognition that the obsessions are the product of the person's own mind and are not imposed from without.

Compulsions are repetitive and intentional behaviors (such as hand washing, ordering, or checking) or mental acts (such as praying, counting, or repeating words silently). These are performed in response to an obsession, according to certain rules that have to be applied rigidly, and are aimed at preventing or reducing distress or preventing a dreaded event or situation. However, the behavior is either not connected in a realistic way with what it is designed to neutralize or prevent, or it is clearly excessive. The act is performed with a sense of subjective compulsion that is (at least initially) combined with a desire to resist. Diagnostic criteria also specify that the obsessions and compulsions cause marked distress, are time-consuming, or significantly interfere with the person's functioning.

Depression and anxiety are commonly associated with obsessive–compulsive disorder (OCD), together with phobic avoidance of situations that involve the content of the obsession (such as dirt or contamination).

PREVALENCE

Prior to the Epidemiologic Catchment Area survey (ECA), OCD was regarded as a relatively uncommon disorder (Marks, 1986). However, the 6-month prevalence rate in the ECA study was 1.5% (Karno et al., 1988); very similar rates of 1.5% and 1.6% were found in Canadian and New Zealand studies (Oakley-Brown, 1991). The disorder appears to be chronic—lifetime prevalence is estimated at 2.5% in the ECA study, and at 3.0% and 2.2% in the Canadian and New Zealand studies, respectively.

NATURAL HISTORY

Data from the ECA study indicate that OCD has an early age of onset and a prolonged duration (Karno et al., 1991). Twenty percent develop the disorder in childhood, 29% in adolescence, and 74% before the age of 30. A similar pattern was found in the Edmonton study (Bland et al., 1988; Kolada et al., 1994), where 46% of men and 58% of women developed the disorder before 20. One-year recovery rates were low; the percentage of people who had met DSM-III-R criteria but who had not had symptoms in the past year was 36% in the ECA study and 38.7% in the Edmonton study.

The degree to which professionals have underestimated prevalence of OCD presumably reflects low presentation rates for treatment, a situation that might be expected to change if patients had greater awareness of the treatability of their condition (Jenike, 1989).

COMORBIDITY

Data from the ECA survey (Karno et al., 1988) indicate that there is high comorbidity of OCD with other Axis I disorders: 46.5% of patients diagnosed with OCD had an additional diagnosis of phobic disorder, 31.7% a major depressive disorder, and 24.1% were substance abusers (usually alcohol abuse).

META-ANALYSES

Christensen et al. (1987) review studies of exposure therapies, nonspecific treatments (such as relaxation), tricyclic medication and psychosurgery carried out to 1984. There were only eight controlled trials from which effect sizes could be calculated, with little overlap in comparison conditions between these investigations. Twenty-seven studies were identified that gave pre- and posttreatment data and therefore permitted calculation of an effect size. Forty-four further studies did not contain sufficient information to make these calculations, and effect sizes were derived through probit transformations.

Considering only trials from which effect sizes could be derived directly, effect sizes for exposure treatments and tricyclic medications were not significantly different (1.22 and 1.4, respectively). Nonspecific treatments gave an effect size of 0.21. It should be noted that effect sizes based on observer ratings were higher than those derived from self-report measures; medication trials were more likely to use these than behavioral interventions.

Contrasting trials containing patients with differing proportions of patients with or without compulsive behavior yields differing effect sizes; treatment of any kind is more successful when compulsions are present than when they are absent (1.13 and 0.41; effect sizes for individual treatments are not reported because only six studies permitted such contrasts).

Ten trials had follow-up data. For exposure therapies the mean effect size at an average of 82 weeks posttreatment did not differ significantly from that found at posttreatment. No follow-up data were available from medication trials.

Van Balkom et al. (1994), in a more recent and extensive meta-analysis, review 86 trials carried out between 1970 and 1993, of which 58 were controlled studies. The majority of trials focused on antidepressants, behavior therapy, and combination treatments, with a very small number of studies ($n = 4$) examining the efficacy of cognitive therapy. As found by Christensen et al. (1987), observer ratings tended to yield larger effect sizes than self-ratings.

Effect sizes associated with serotonergic antidepressants (clomipramine, fluoxetine, and fluvoxamine) were significantly higher than other antidepressants, which had effect sizes equal to or smaller than placebo. As discussed further below, there is consistent evidence for the efficacy of serotonergic antidepressants in OCD.

Results from analyses using self- and observer ratings gave different results. Using self-ratings, and contrasting serotonergic antidepressants alone, behavior therapy alone, and their combination, behavior therapy had a larger effect size than antidepressants alone. Combination treatment had a greater effect than medication alone, but was equivalent to behavior therapy alone. Effect sizes based on observer ratings showed no differences among treatments. Follow-up for the majority of studies was conducted at between 3 and 6 months, with effect sizes tending to remain stable over this period.

All behavioral therapies employed exposure *in vivo*, with variations in technique such as therapist or self-controlled exposure, spousal involvement, therapist modeling, or the addition of cognitive strategies such as thought stopping. No differences in effect size were found among these variants, a finding most reasonably attributed to the common element of exposure *in vivo*.

Though the two meta-analyses are consistent in providing evidence for the efficacy of exposure treatments, they differ in their assessment of the relative efficacy of medication and behavior therapy. This may be attributable to methodological issues which require resolution. The superiority of behavioral therapies over medication indicated in Van Balkom et al.'s (1994) review rests on self-report rather than observer ratings, and this in turn may reflect different assessment strategies adopted by behavior therapists and pharmacotherapists.

QUALITATIVE REVIEWS

Exposure and Response Prevention

Behavioral treatments typically employ exposure or blocking techniques. Exposure techniques include systematic desensitization, paradoxical intention, flooding, and satiation, either *in vivo* or in imagination. Blocking interrupts ruminations or rituals through response prevention, distraction, or thought stopping. Early studies indicated that exposure alone or response prevention alone was associated with poor outcomes and high rates of relapse (e.g., Foa et al., 1980, 1984), and more recent trials almost invariably examine imaginal or *in vivo* exposure and response prevention in combination. Emmelkamp (1994), in an overview of the clinical implementation of this technique, suggests that gradual exposure *in vivo* is as effective as flooding (Boersma et al., 1976; Marks et al., 1975), that modeling by the therapist has no greater effect than self-exposure (Boersma et al., 1976; Marks et al., 1975), and that exposure sessions of long duration (around 2 hours) are more effective than short sessions (Rabavilas et al., 1976).

The relationship between chronicity and severity of symptoms and outcome is unclear; while some studies have suggested that patients with more chronic and more severe symptoms have poorer outcomes (e.g., Foa et al., 1983; Cottraux et al., 1993), others find either no or only weak associations between these variables (e.g., Basoglu et al., 1988; Hoogduin & Duivenvoorden, 1988; Hoogduin et al., 1989; Visser et al., 1991). A more complex picture emerges from Castle et al. (1994), who reviewed outcomes from an audit of 178 patients receiving exposure and response prevention in an inpatient setting. For women, lower initial severity predicted better outcome, though for men the only predictor was living alone (leading to a poorer response). In reviewing this issue, Steketee and Shapiro (1995) note that patients with more severe symptoms may also present with associated comorbid conditions and poorer functioning, a combination that was indeed predictive of poorer outcomes in Basoglu et al.'s (1988) study.

While some studies suggest that patients with compulsions have better outcomes than those with checking rituals or ruminations (Basoglu et al., 1988; Boulougouris, 1977), others find that the type of symptom is only weakly or not predictive of outcome (Castle et al., 1994; Foa et al., 1983; Rachman, 1973). The form of the symptom may relate to outcome; Merckelbach et al. (1988) found that patients with fears that related to more "realistic" anxieties (such as checking for fires) showed fewer gains.

There are fewer comparative treatment trials of OCD than is warranted by its prevalence. Reflecting this, Cottraux (1989), Perse (1988), and Steketee and Cleere (1990) review an overlapping sample of approximately 20 studies of exposure and response prevention alone, carried out between 1974 and 1989. Perse (1988) suggests that 70–80% of patients who accept and comply with treatment will improve. In the Steketee and Cleere (1990), review, an average of 85.8% of clients were rated as improved/much improved posttreatment (range 67–98%). Follow-up (range 3 months to 3 years) showed good maintenance of gains, with 77.8% of patients retaining this rating.

Foa and Kozac (in press) review studies examining outcomes for over 300 patients presenting with rituals, treated by exposure and response prevention. Defining improvement as an improvement over pretreatment symptoms of over 30%, the response rate was 76% (range 60–100%) at 3–6 years posttreatment. In seven studies of the long-term effects of exposure reviewed by Öst (1989), 85% of patients maintained their gains 1–3 years posttreatment. In the same study, more than half the patients required no further therapy. These relatively low relapse rates are particularly impressive when compared with the relatively low proportion (10%) who retained their gains after withdrawal from clomipramine (Pato et al., 1988).

It is important to note that a number of these studies have been carried out in hospital settings using daily treatment (e.g., Hodgson et al., 1972; Marks et al., 1975; Rachman et al., 1971, 1973; Roper et al., 1975). However, comparison of hospital and outpatient treatments suggests that similar results are obtained (Hout et al., 1988; Emmelkamp et al., 1989); Kirk (1983) effectively treated 60% of patients on an outpatient basis using homework assignments.

Cognitive-Behavioral Therapy

Treatment failure with exposure and response-prevention has been linked to patients' attitudes and beliefs about their symptoms. Foa (1979) found that poor responders were those whose beliefs amounted to over-valued ideas—usually that their obsessive fears were realistic. Lelliot et al. (1988) found that one-third of a cohort of 49 compulsive ritualizers saw their obsessive thoughts as rational and believed that their rituals successfully averted a feared event. The more bizarre the obsessive belief, the more strongly it was defended and the less attempt was made to resist the urge to ritualize. Though outcome after treatment with exposure and response prevention was not related to initial fixity of belief, there was evidence that patients who did respond to treatment altered their beliefs about the necessity to perform their rituals.

While pretreatment fixity of belief does not appear predictive of outcome (Steketee & Shapiro, 1995), it is clear that if beliefs remain unaltered, outcome is likely to be poor. In these patients the cognitive component of their problems becomes more salient; the negative conse-quences of a variety of actions are often overestimated. Typically there is an exaggeration of normal concerns regarding health, sex, the welfare of others or religious matters. Relatedly there is often a concern to be perfectly competent in all endeavors, and that failure to live up to such ideals will be punished or will result in catastrophe. This formulation indicates that cognitive interventions may be helpful, given that rituals serve the role of reducing the anxiety consequent on these thoughts.

In response to such observations, treatments based on cognitive models have been developed (Beck, 1976; Creamer, 1987; Reed, 1983), though rather few studies have been carried out to test their empirical validity. James and Blackburn (1995) note that most investigations are single-case or uncontrolled trials, often using more than one treatment modality and hence making it difficult to discern the relative importance of cognitive and behavioral components (Blue et al., 1987; Ellis, 1987; Moore & Burrow, 1991; Ownby, 1983; Willmuth, 1988).

Enright (1991) report on 24 patients treated in four groups over 9 weeks using a range of techniques including thought stoping, exposure, anxiety management, and cognitive therapy. Although significant im-provements were found on a variety of measures of OCD symptoms, mood, and anxiety, only 17% of patients improved using the criterion of improvement of at least 1 *SD* from the group pretreatment mean.

In a single-case study that illustrates the clinical application of cogni-tive techniques, Salkovskis and Warwick (1985) report the treatment of a 25-year-old female with fears of contamination, compulsive hand washing, and a fear of cancer who had had behavior therapy as an inpatient but who had relapsed. Rather than modifying the intrusive thought ("I'll catch cancer"), attention was directed to the negative automatic thought associated with the intrusive thought ("I'll be rejected"; these thoughts often produced low mood and often preceded the intrusive thoughts). This, recombined with behavior therapy, produced almost complete recovery. Given the patient's previous history, this study provides strong evidence for the link between the addition of cognitive elements and outcome.

Hiss et al. (1994) report a small controlled study of a relapse prevention program following an intensive 15-day exposure and response prevention package. Half the sample then received relapse prevention, and the remainder a control placebo treatment ("free-association therapy"). Relapse prevention combined training in self-exposure with anxiety management, goal setting, recruitment of social support, and some additional interventions addressing the anticipated sources of stress, maladaptive patterns of interpersonal interactions, and unrealistic expectations of treatment results. A core part of the program was cognitive restructuring, identifying and challenging cognitive distortions. Although sample sizes were small (18 patients *in toto*), those receiving relapse prevention maintained their posttreatment outcome, whereas those receiving control placebo treatment ("free-association therapy") showed a tendency to relapse at 6-month follow-up. This small study is additionally interesting because it suggests that the combination of effective followed by ineffective treatment may have detrimental effects on long-term outcome.

Emmelkamp and colleagues have carried out a series of controlled studies that contrast the efficacy of behavioral and cognitive-behavioral interventions in OCD. Emmelkamp et al. (1980) contrasted the effects of exposure therapy alone with exposure therapy combined with self-instructional training. Fifteen patients were treated (eight and seven per group); both groups improved and both maintained their gains at 6-month follow-up. Emmelkamp et al. (1988) contrasted nine patients receiving RET to nine treated with *in vivo* exposure; treatments were of equal efficacy, though there was a slight trend for better outcomes with *in vivo* exposure. Both earlier studies used young, well-educated, and nonchronic cases; in contrast, Emmelkamp et al. (1991) used a more clinically representative pool of subjects, 10 receiving RET and self-directed exposure, and 11 *in vivo* exposure. Again, the treatments gave equivalent outcomes.

In a larger study of 71 patients, Van Oppen et al. (1995) contrasted the efficacy of exposure and cognitive therapy. In the latter treatment, patients were initially encouraged to identify negative automatic thoughts regarding their symptoms and to challenge them—for example, by noting that they were overestimating danger or the degree of their own personal responsibility. After six sessions patients were encouraged to carry out behavioral experiments to test their beliefs and assumptions (in itself, of course, a form of exposure). While the two treatments led to significant improvements, using Jacobson and Truax's (1991) criteria for clinically significant change, there was evidence (on some but not all measures) that patients in receipt of cognitive therapy had better outcomes than those receiving exposure. This suggests some additive benefit for cognitive therapy (including an element of exposure) over exposure alone.

Ruminations

There have been few trials of techniques aimed at treatment of ruminations without associated rituals, which reflects the greater therapeutic problem posed by patients presenting with this problem (Rachman, 1983). There have been a number of single-case studies, though few reports of comparative trials. Salkovskis and Westbrook (1989) review six small-scale group comparisons. *In toto* these involved only 50 patients, and though ruminations were the primary problem, a number of patients had associated rituals. Trials have involved the use of thought stopping contrasted with assertiveness training (Emmelkamp & Van der Hayden, 1977), with imaginal exposure (Emmelkamp & Kwee, 1977), with flooding (Hackman & McLean, 1975), and with habituation (Likierman & Rachman, 1982). Others have compared exposure to ruminations to exposure to irrelevant fear-provoking scenes. Emmelkamp and Giesselbach (1981) and Stern et al. (1973) contrasted thought stopping to stopping a neutral thought. Approximately 46% of patients in these trials showed a 50% improvement in symptom frequency, though only 12% showed a 50% reduction in subjective distress.

Salkovskis and Westbrook (1989) present a number of single-case studies of "revised habituation" in which patients record their ruminations onto tapes, taking care to avoid including thoughts that might act to reduce anxiety ("covert rituals"). Listening to the recording then becomes a form of exposure. This and other single-case studies have shown promising results with the technique (Thyer, 1985; Martin & Tarrier, 1992; Roth & Church, 1994). Lovell et al. (1994) carried out a small controlled trial essentially using the same technique; 12 ruminators listened either to their ruminations or to neutral prose. Though the two groups improved equivalently, there were indications that patients who successfully engaged with the technique by becoming anxious while listening to the tape improved more. More research is required to demonstrate the efficacy of this approach.

Combination Treatments

The efficacy of antidepressant medications in treating OCD—typically clomipramine, amitriptyline, or imipramine—has been reviewed by Perse (1988), Marks and O'Sullivan (1988), Zetin et al. (1992), Abel (1993), Klerman et al. (1994) and Piccinelli et al. (1995). There is clear evidence for a good therapeutic response with clomipramine, but little evidence of efficacy for other tricyclics or antidepressant medications. Other serotonergic compounds, such as fluoxetine and fluvoxamine, also appear to have some efficacy, though contrasts of these drugs against clomipramine tend to favor clomipramine (Abel, 1993; Piccinelli et al., 1995).

There are rather few trials of exposure in combination with medication. Neziroglu (1979) treated 10 patients with clomipramine followed by behavioral treatment. Medication reduced symptoms by 60%; behavioral treatment decreased symptoms by a further 20%.

Rachman et al. (1979) administered either clomipramine or placebo to 40 patients in a complex multiple baseline design. After 4 weeks on either clomipramine or placebo, patients received either 15 sessions of exposure and response prevention or relaxation training over 3 weeks. Following this, patients who had received relaxation were trained in exposure and response prevention. Analyses immediately after exposure or relaxation training had been administered suggested that patients administered clomipramine fared better than those given placebo and that exposure was more effective in reducing symptoms than relaxation. The effect of clomipramine was more apparent on more depressed patients and was absent in those with low initial depression scores; it seemed to act more as an antidepressant than against compulsions. Exposure had a significant effect in reducing rituals, though it had no impact on mood. One-year follow-up (Marks et al., 1980) indicated that patients receiving exposure maintained their gains.

Marks et al. (1988) treated 49 patients in a complex design which contrasted clomipramine with placebo and also with three different types of exposure—exposure homework, antiexposure homework, and therapist-aided exposure added to exposure homework. (In antiexposure the patient is directed to avoid contact with the feared situation.) There were four conditions; in three, all patients received clomipramine for 27 weeks, while the fourth received placebo. In the clomipramine conditions, one group received antiexposure and another exposure for 23 weeks; the third received self-directed and therapist-aided exposure. The placebo group received both self-directed and therapist-aided exposure.

Contrasting the impacts of each treatment, clomipramine compared to placebo gave transient benefits in the first 8 weeks only. Self-exposure treatment was markedly superior to antiexposure; the addition of therapist-aided exposure did little to boost improvements. Exposure appeared to be the most effective of the three treatments. Overall, 81% of patients were improved or much improved; there were very similar outcomes with clomipramine and exposure contrasted with placebo and exposure. Gains were maintained at 2 years (Kasvikis & Marks, 1988), though the best outcomes were with patents whose rituals had been less severe initially (Basoglu et al., 1988).

Cottraux et al. (1990), in a trial with 44 patients without major depression, contrasted three groups: fluvoxamine with antiexposure, fluvoxamine with exposure (8 weeks imaginal exposure followed by 16 weeks exposure and response prevention), and placebo with exposure. Some cognitive techniques, such as distraction, were incorporated into exposure instructions, though these are known to interfere with its efficacy (Grayson et al., 1986). After 24 weeks of therapy all groups showed a decrease in symptoms of OCD; exposure and response prevention were of equal efficacy to fluvoxamine.

Freund et al. (1991; cited by Abel, 1993) treated 48 patients either with 15 daily sessions of exposure and response prevention ($n = 13$), clomipramine ($n = 7$), fluvoxamine ($n = 14$), or placebo ($n = 14$). Assignment to therapies was nonrandom in that patients could choose whether to receive exposure. Exposure treatment was superior to placebo on all measures, and both medications were superior to placebo on some measures. Exposure was superior in efficacy to fluoxetine, but not (on all measures) to clomipramine.

FACTORS INFLUENCING OUTCOME IN OCD: DEPRESSION AND INITIAL SYMPTOM SEVERITY

A number of authors have linked poorer outcomes in OCD with the severity of comorbid depression (e.g., Foa, 1979; Foa et al., 1982, 1983; Marks, 1977), though this has not been found in other studies (e.g., Mawson et al., 1982; Basoglu et al., 1988; Hoogduin & Duivenvoorden, 1988).

In a carefully designed study avoiding post hoc analyses, Foa et al. (1992) stratified 38 patients into high and low depressed groups (using a cutoff above or below a BDI score of 20). Patients were in- as well as outpatients, and received either imipramine or placebo, followed by intensive daily treatment exposure with response prevention and supportive therapy over 12 weeks. Although imipramine improved mood, it did not impact on symptoms of OCD symptoms.

Psychological treatment with or without medication was highly effective; significant main effects for treatment only occurred once behavior therapy was initiated. Using a categorical system, at posttreatment 44% of patients were rated highly improved, 44% moderately, and only 10% or so worse. There was evidence of some relapse at 2-year follow-up, at which point 29% remained highly improved, 50% were moderately improved, and 18% were rated as failures. No differences were found between in- and outpatient groups, nor was the initial level of depression related to outcome.

Keisjers et al. (1994) treated 40 patients with exposure and response prevention, examining the relationship between outcome and depression, OCD symptom severity, and duration of OCD symptoms. Higher levels of depression were predictive of poorer outcomes on posttreatment measures of compulsive behavior. A greater duration of symptoms of OCD, lower levels of patient motivation, and a poorer therapeutic relationship were predictive of poorer outcomes on posttherapy measures of obsessive anxiety.

It is difficult to interpret the mixed picture of results found in these reports. It may be reasonable to suppose that more chronic conditions would be more difficult to treat and that there may be associations between chronicity, depression, and level of motivation. More research is required to clarify their impacts on outcome.

SUMMARY

- Exposure in imagination and *in vivo*, in combination with response prevention, is helpful in the treatment of OCD, bringing about a 30–50% improvement in 75% of patients.
- It should be noted that treatments are rarely completely successful, and a significant proportion of patients remain with reduced symptoms but some degree of continued distress.
- Though rather few studies of long-term effects are available, the effects of response prevention and exposure tend to be maintained at roughly posttreatment levels.
- Serotonergic agents—particularly clomipramine—are effective treatments for OCD. Other antidepressants are markedly less effective.
- Relapse after withdrawal of medication is high, and long-term outcomes are clearly inferior to that obtained with exposure treatment.

- The efficacy of drug treatment is broadly comparable to that of exposure and response prevention.
- There is some suggestion that an exposure-based behavioral intervention increases the benefit of clomipramine.
- Psychological treatments that do not include exposure and response prevention (e.g., relaxation training or anxiety management) have been shown to be ineffective with this group of patients.
- Cognitive therapy appears to be an effective adjunct to exposure treatment in the treatment of intrusive thoughts, ruminations, and the prevention of relapse.
- Initial severity of symptoms does not appear strongly to relate to outcome.
- Symptoms of compulsion and checking are, on the whole, better treated than other symptoms of OCD.
- Psychological treatment for OCD is effective in both the inpatient and outpatient context. The critical parameter enhancing the effectiveness of exposure seems to be exposure of a sufficiently long duration, though this is often delivered in the context of a relatively brief but intensive treatment.
- Ruminations respond less well to currently available behavioral techniques, although some innovative procedures show some promise in dealing with this relatively prevalent problem.

IMPLICATIONS

- OCD is a severely handicapping disorder which affects 1–2:100 individuals, who may frequently be unaware that their problem is recognized and is likely to be treatable. Greater efforts could be made to publicize the availability of treatments for OCD.
- OCD should not be treated by non-symptom-specific techniques. The combination of symptom-oriented techniques with more general supportive or expressive techniques could be cautiously explored in the light of the residual distress experienced by many sufferers following behavioral treatment.
- Evidence does not permit a recommendation concerning the combination of psychological and pharmacological treatment, except where severe depression may make response to a psychological intervention unlikely.
- There is no indication that OCD patients benefit additionally from inpatient treatment, and outpatient management is recommended.

- In the light of evidence of the greater effectiveness of massed exposure, daily 1.5-hour treatment sessions may be preferable to the more usual weekly programs.
- More research effort should be exerted toward developing treatment for ruminations.
- In the light of evidence that a proportion of patients do not respond to behavioral treatments, more research should be initiated to identify the combination of treatments most appropriate to this chronic and severely handicapped group.

CHAPTER 8

Anxiety Disorders III
Posttraumatic Stress Disorder

DEFINITION

DSM-IV describes posttraumatic stress disorder (PTSD) as the development of characteristic symptoms following exposure to an extreme traumatic stressor involving direct personal experience of an event that involves actual or threatened death, injury, or a threat to the physical integrity of the self or another person. Though the definition of the traumatic stressor is broad, to guard against diagnostic overinclusiveness,[1] the person's reaction must involve intense fear, helplessness, or horror.

Common directly experienced traumatizing events are rape, military combat, being taken hostage or incarcerated (e.g., in a concentration camp), natural disasters (such as floods), or accidental disasters with associated serious physical injury (such as car accidents or large fires). Common witnessed events include observing serious injury or unnatural death due to violent assault, accident, or war, or accidentally witnessing a dead body or body parts.

Characteristic symptoms usually involve one or more of the following forms of reexperiencing of the event: recurrent and intrusive images, thoughts, or perceptions about the event; recurrent distressing dreams; acting as if the event were recurring; or intense distress at exposure to cues resembling the original traumatic event. Stimuli associated with the event are avoided; there is numbing of general responsiveness, and increased arousal (e.g., difficulty in falling asleep, irritability, or poor

---

[1] Within DSM-III-R the stressor event was defined as one "outside the range of normal human experience." However, literature reviews and field trials for DSM-IV suggested that this phrasing was unreliable and inaccurate since the prevalence of such stressors in the general population is not as low as has been thought.

concentration). Symptoms need to be present for more than 1 month for a diagnosis of PTSD to be made. DSM-IV distinguishes chronic from acute cases,[2] where the duration of symptoms is greater than or less than 3 months, respectively. Symptoms of anxiety and depression are common, and in some cases may be sufficient for an additional diagnosis of anxiety or depressive disorder to be made.

PREVALENCE

Data from the Epidemiologic Catchment Area (ECA) survey of approximately 2,500 people (Helzer et al., 1987) suggest a lifetime prevalence for PTSD of 1% in the general population. A similar figure of 1.3% for lifetime prevalence was found by Davidson et al. (1991), with a 6-month prevalence of 0.44%. Some surveys suggest higher prevalence rates, though this may reflect sampling differences across studies. Thus Shore et al. (1986) report a lifetime prevalence of 2.6%, and Breslau et al. (1991), in a sample of 1,000 adults aged 21–30, estimate lifetime prevalence at 9.2%.

The prevalence of PTSD is greater for individuals who have been exposed to traumatic events—in the ECA survey, those who had been physically attacked had a prevalence of 3.5%, and veterans of the Vietnam War a prevalence of 20%. Kilpatrick and Resnick (1993), in a retrospective study, note that 35% of rape victims and 39% of victims of assault report symptoms of PTSD. Rothbaum et al. (1992), in a prospective study, found higher rates; in the 3 months following a sexual assault, rates of PTSD were 47%, and for nonsexual assault 22%. Curran et al. (1990) report that 50% of survivors of the Enniskillen bombing in Ireland had symptoms of PTSD.

COMORBIDITY

PTSD appears to be associated with high rates of other Axis I disorders, though many studies of comorbidity are based on Vietnam veterans. Rates in patients traumatized by non–combat-related stress may be different. Keane and Wolfe (1990) review surveys of community and clinical samples, and report consistently high rates of depression and substance abuse. In a sample of 50 patients presenting with PTSD, these authors report rates of 70% for alcohol abuse, 68% with a lifetime

---

[2] A distinction not made within DSM-III-R.

diagnosis of depression, and 26% with a diagnosis of personality disorder, most usually antisocial personality disorder or mixed personality disorder.

NATURAL HISTORY

It appears to be the case that PTSD is a common and frequently persistent sequela of traumatic events. Ramsay (1990) examined the natural course of the disorder in 36 survivors of a freighter collision, who were assessed immediately after the accident and again after 4.5 years, with no systematic psychiatric care in the intervening period. Immediately after the incident most of the group had multiple psychological and psychosomatic complaints. At follow-up significant deterioration was found; 12 had been hospitalized, and 26 of the men had received psychiatric help. Holen (1990) followed up survivors of an oil rig disaster; contrasted with a comparison cohort of workers not exposed to trauma, significantly enhanced levels of psychiatric morbidity were still evident 8 years after the disaster. Archibald and Tuddenham (1965) followed up World War II veterans at 20 years, finding an increased incidence of psychiatric presentations over time for problems associated with war experiences. A 40-year follow-up of World War II prisoners of war revealed that two-thirds had suffered from PTSD (Kluznik et al., 1986). Of these, 29% had fully recovered, 39% still reported mild symptoms, 24% showed moderate improvement, and 8% had no recovery. There is also some evidence for the reactivation of trauma. Survivors of the Enniskillen bombing, thought to have recovered 6 months after the event, again showed symptoms at the 1-year anniversary (Curran et al., 1991). Thus, available evidence suggests that untreated PTSD has a chronic course in a significant proportion of individuals exposed to trauma.

Some authors (e.g., Resick & Schnicke, 1992; Turner, 1996) suggest that the natural history of PTSD (and, by implication, the likely response to treatment interventions) may be complicated both by the nature of the trauma, and by the person's response to that trauma. Thus, a precipitating trauma might be categorized as "simple" or "complex," depending on whether it is a one-off event (such as assault or rape), or one that extends over time (e.g., the experience of being taken hostage). The person's response to trauma might also be categorized as simple or complex, depending on whether exposure to thoughts about the trauma evoke fear or a mix of both fear and shame. In the latter case, simple exposure carried out without strategies to manage (for example) self-blame might be expected to show poor results. However, while these propositions may be important clinically, they have not been subjected to systematic evaluation as a part of the studies discussed below.

PREVENTIVE INTERVENTIONS

A detailed review of interventions aimed at preventing the emergence of PTSD is beyond the scope of this review, as are other primary prevention interventions. However, it is now generally accepted that psychological intervention—usually in the form of a debriefing—is an essential component of responses to natural or man-made disasters, as well as traumatic events affecting individuals, such as rape or violent crime (e.g., Ramsay, 1990).

While these interventions are now common, there are problems in evaluating their efficacy, not least because definitions of debriefing vary widely—sometimes referring to minimal opportunities for feedback, sometimes to generic counseling, and sometimes to a specific model, such as Critical Incident Stress Debriefing (Mitchell & Everly, 1994). Understandable pressures to mount a rapid response means that there are few controlled trials of these interventions; consequently the degree to which these responses actually benefit victims is unclear. Further, many trials that do exist are methodologically weak (Solomon et al., 1992). Though some reports suggest positive outcomes (e.g., Stallard & Law, 1994), this is not always the case (e.g., Deahl et al., 1994). Attrition from open trials following disasters makes it difficult to be clear about the effectiveness of these interventions, particularly because there is evidence that survivors who absent themselves from assessment following trauma may represent the most severely affected individuals (Weisaeth, 1989).

GENERAL REVIEWS

Foa et al. (1995), Hacker-Hughes and Thompson (1994), Murray (1993), and Solomon et al. (1992) review treatment approaches. Foa et al.'s review is very comprehensive and provides the framework for much of this section. Most reports focus on two client groups—Vietnam veterans and female rape victims. There are few controlled studies of treatments for the victims of disasters. Solomon et al. (1992) identify 255 studies, 244 of which were individual case studies or (more rarely) open trials; there are currently very few comparative trials.

Pharmacotherapy

There have been three double-blind studies of imipramine and amitriptyline against placebo (Frank et al., 1988; Davidson et al., 1990; Reist et al., 1989). Two of these demonstrated some beneficial effects, though these were modest—for example, in the Davison et al. (1990) study 64% and 72% of the medication and placebo patients respectively still met diagnostic criteria for PTSD. Reist et al. (1989) failed to show any drug efficacy (though this study used smaller doses and short periods of time [4 weeks] on medication). In trials of MAOIs against placebo, Frank et al. (1988) found a positive effect; Shestatsky et al. (1988) did not, though again low dose and short treatment periods may have contributed. The efficacy of serotonin reuptake inhibitors has been examined by Kline et al. (1993) and Rothbaum et al. (1994; both cited in Foa et al., 1995), though both were open trials. There is only weak evidence of the efficacy of alprazolam from open trials.

Psychodynamic Interventions

Although widely used, there is limited evidence for the efficacy of psychodynamic techniques. Most studies reporting data have a number of methodological problems, including a lack of control groups, failure to define treatments, no inclusion and exclusion criteria, a failure to assign patients randomly to treatments, and an absence of objective measures of target symptoms. An equivocal picture emerges from these trials; Bart (1975; reported in Foa et al., 1995) found an increase in symptoms. Grigsby (1987) found no benefit in a single-case study, reporting that psychodynamic elements were less helpful than a form of exposure. Cryer and Beutler (1980) reported mixed results using group therapy with nine rape victims; though a significant reduction in symptoms was found in most group members, some did not benefit, and one patient showed an increase in symptomatology. Perl et al. (1985) found positive benefit in 17 sexual assault victims treated in an open trial using a group approach, though no quantitative measures were used.

Lindy et al. (1983) treated 30 patients 6 months to 1 year after a major fire in a semicontrolled trial employing short-term psychodynamic therapy; 19 of these patients met DSM-III-R criteria for PTSD alone or with comorbid depression, with the remainder receiving diagnoses of depression or complicated bereavement. The therapy was conducted over 6–12 sessions following a standardized protocol that included encouragement of exposure; therapists ranged in experience from advanced trainees to senior clinicians. Patients in the trial were a self-selected subgroup of 147 who had responded to outreach programs established in the wake of the fire. Comparison of treated to untreated patients suggested improvements in symptom ratings, though this was more marked for patients who completed treatment. Patients with a diagnosis of PTSD were less likely to complete treatment than those with a diagnosis of depression alone, though more experienced therapists were more likely to retain patients for the full course of treatment.

Brom et al. (1989) contrasted psychodynamic therapy, hypnotherapy, and systematic desensitization with a waiting-list control. All three treatments led to improvements, though in different areas of functioning; those receiving dynamic therapy showed most reduction in avoidance symptoms, while hypnotherapy and systematic desensitization led to more reduction in intrusive thoughts. However, only 23 of the 112 patients in this sample had experienced a traumatic event; the remainder were bereaved, severely limiting the conclusions that can be drawn from this study.

Cognitive-Behavioral Therapy

Treatments for PTSD include anxiety management, exposure, and additional cognitive techniques.

Systematic Desensitization

Studies with Vietnam veterans have suggested that both flooding *in vivo* (e.g., Johnson et al., 1982) and in imagination (e.g., Keane et al., 1989) appear helpful, though these studies often include other elements such as anger management and relaxation training. Bowen and Lambert (1986) and Peniston (1986) carried out controlled studies of systematic desensitization alone contrasted with a no treatment control. Although treatment showed efficacy on a range of psychophysiological measures, no direct measures of PTSD symptoms were taken. Frank and Stewart (1983, 1984) and Turner (1979; cited in Foa et al., 1995) employed systematic desensitization with victims of rape in open trials. Although effective in reducing anxiety, depression, and social maladjustment, impact on PTSD symptoms was not directly assessed.

A major failing of these studies is that only relatively recent victims of trauma participated in the trials; in the absence of control groups it is possible that any improvements reflect the natural reduction in symptoms that can be expected over time. Becker and Abel (1981) found no evidence for the effectiveness of systematic desensitization in rape victims with chronic PTSD symptoms. There is therefore only very limited evidence for the efficacy of systematic desensitization.

Exposure

Foa et al. review three controlled studies of exposure, all treatments of Vietnam veterans (Cooper & Clum, 1989; Keane et al., 1989, Boudewyns & Hyer, 1990; Boudewyns et al., 1990). Effects were small and results were mixed. Cooper and Clum (1989) found improvements on PTSD symptoms but little effect on depression or general anxiety. In Keane et al. (1989), therapists rated exposure patients as more improved on PTSD symptoms than controls, though self-report on these measures found no difference between groups. Boudewyns and Hyer (1990) contrasted exposure and "conventional" psychotherapy (not further defined by the authors), finding no differences posttherapy. However, at 3-month follow-up the exposure group showed greater improvements in adjustment, and a greater proportion were classified as successful treatments than those receiving psychotherapy (Boudewyns et al., 1990).

Vaughn and Tarrier (1992) employed one session of training followed by nine sessions of self-directed exposure with 10 patients who had experienced a range of traumas; although measures of symptom severity decreased, mean scores remained quite high, suggesting that few patients showed clinically significant improvement.

Richards et al. (1994) administered both imaginal and *in vivo* exposure to 14 patients with chronic PTSD. Half the patients received imaginal exposure for four sessions, followed by four sessions of live exposure to situations they had been avoiding; the remaining patients received these treatments in the reverse order. The majority of these patients had been involved in a shipping disaster, and the remainder had been victims of assault. Equal and significant gains were made by both groups.

In an open-trial, Thompson et al. (1995) offered patients a package comprising one session of critical incident stress debriefing (a procedure which in itself involves a major element of imaginal exposure) followed by eight sessions of imaginal and *in vivo* exposure, along with cognitive interventions. Posttherapy results are reported for 23 patients (from a total of 38) who completed the therapy; 16 of these met DSM-III-R criteria for PTSD. Overall, significant reductions in symptomatology related to PTSD were obtained; half of the patients meeting diagnostic criteria for PTSD no longer did so at the end of the trial.

Anxiety Management Techniques

Studies have employed a range of anxiety management techniques, such as relaxation, biofeedback, and cognitive restructuring, often in combination, leading to difficulties in ascertaining which element is important. Frank et al. (1988) and Frank and Stewart (1984) contrasted cognitive therapy and systematic desensitization in an uncontrolled study with rape victims (some of whom were treated very soon after the assault). Cognitive Therapy had similar outcomes to systematic desensitization; ratings of fear, anxiety, depression, and social adjustment all showed gains, and though delayed treatment seekers were initially more symptomatic, the time elapsed from assault did not relate to outcome.

Stress Inoculation Training

Stress inoculation training (SIT) comprises elements of relaxation, role playing, covert modeling, thought stopping, and guided self-dialogue. Veronen and Kilpatrick (1982; cited in Foa et al., in press) carried out an uncontrolled study of rape victims 3 months posttrauma, showing a decrease in anxiety and depression on multiple measures. Resick et al. (1988) conducted a controlled study of six 2-hour sessions of group therapy for rape-related anxiety, contrasting SIT, assertion training, and supportive psychotherapy against a waiting-list control. Compared to control patients, all three treatments were equally effective on measures of rape-related fear, intrusion, and avoidance, with gains related to fears maintained at 6 months. However, other gains were lost at this point.

Combination Treatments of Anxiety Management Training and Exposure

Foa et al. (1991) treated 45 rape victims (all at least 3 months after the assault), contrasting prolonged exposure, SIT, and supportive counseling against a waiting-list control. The treatment package comprised nine biweekly individual sessions, and PTSD symptoms were assessed directly. (Supportive counseling was almost a control condition, focusing on problem solving which may or may not have been assault-related, but avoiding direct discussion of the assault itself in order not to replicate the exposure treatment.)

SIT produced better results on PTSD symptoms posttreatment than exposure or counseling; 50% and 40%, respectively, of the SIT and exposure patients no longer met diagnostic criteria for PTSD, contrasted to 90% and 100% of the counseling and waiting-list groups. However, at 3-month follow-up, between-treatment differences were nonsignificant, with 55% of both SIT and exposure patients and 45% of the counseling group no longer meeting diagnostic criteria for PTSD.

Foa et al. (1995) report a second study in progress, in which patients with chronic PTSD (patients were on average 4.2 years postassault) received either SIT alone, exposure alone, or SIT and exposure in combination. Posttreatment all active treatments were equally effective. Recovery from a diagnosis of PTSD was found in 71% of exposure group, 67% of SIT, and 73% of those receiving combination therapy, contrasted with no recovery in waiting-list patients. At follow-up combination treatment was superior—91% of this group were rated as recovered from PTSD, compared with 42% and 29% of those receiving SIT and exposure, respectively.

Resick and Schnicke (1992) treated 19 rape victims with exposure and cognitive restructuring over 12 weeks using a group format and a quasiexperimental design with a naturally occurring waiting list. Posttreatment none of the patients met DSM-III-R criteria for PTSD; gains were maintained at 6 month follow-up.

Overall there appears to be stronger evidence for efficacy in female rape victims than Vietnam veterans. This may relate not only to gender but also to the greater comorbidity of Axis I and II disorders in veterans and the fact that veterans may be dealing with guilt at their own actions.

Eye Movement Desensitization and Reprocessing

An increasingly widely used technique in the United States (and to some extent in the United Kingdom and elsewhere), eye movement desensitization and reprocessing (EMDR; Shapiro, 1989a) requires patients to focus on a detailed image of events causing anxiety or traumatic memories (thus EMDR includes a prominent element of imaginal exposure). While simultaneously generating cognitive coping statements patients track the therapist's finger as it is moved rapidly and rhythmically from side to side across their face. Acierno et al. (1994) review eight uncontrolled case studies and case series, detailing the treatment of approximately 100 patients. A major deficiency in these reports is the lack of standardized assessment and a reliance on therapist judgments of improvement.

Shapiro (1989b) contrasted the impact of one session of EMDR with one session of imaginal exposure in 22 subjects. Though significant results were claimed for EMDR contrasted with exposure, assessments were conducted by the therapist, and it is not clear that all patients met DSM criteria for PTSD. Sanderson and Carpenter (1992) employed a single-session crossover design to examine the relative efficacy of EMDR and flooding with 58 phobics (most usually spider phobics). Again, no standardized assessment procedures were used, though similar gains were apparent for the two treatments.

Boudewyns et al. (1993) contrasted EMDR with imaginal exposure and milieu therapy using standardized assessment techniques. Subjects were 20 Vietnam veterans treated as inpatients in two sessions over 2 weeks. Though therapist ratings suggested that patients receiving EMDR improved more than those receiving the other treatments, no intergroup differences were evident on standardized tests, nor were there any improvements over baseline on these tests.

Vaughn et al. (1994a) carried out a small open trial of EMDR with 10 consecutively referred patients, eight of whom had a DSM-III-R diagnosis of PTSD consequent on a range of traumatic events. On average patients received three sessions of treatment (range 1–6). Both standardized measures for rating the presence of PTSD symptoms and judgments from independent assessors suggested considerable improvements in symptoms specific to PTSD. A larger controlled trial by this same group (Vaughn et al., 1994b) allocated 36 patients to one of three treatments—EMDR, image habituation training (a form of exposure), or applied relaxation (Öst, 1987). No significant differences were found among treatments, though there was some evidence that EMDR was more successful at reducing flashbacks and nightmares.

Two dismantling studies of EMDR differ in their assessment of the importance of eye movements to outcome. Renfrey and Spates (1994) report a dismantling study of EMDR in which patients were randomly assigned to EMDR as described by Shapiro (1989a), a variant in which eye movements were induced by a light tracking task, or a procedure in which they focused on a fixed stimulus. Twenty-one of 23 patients met DSM-III-R criteria for PTSD. Though no standardized assessments were employed, all three treatment variants were equally effective in reducing heart rate and ratings of subjective distress, suggesting that eye movements are not a necessary component of this technique. Montgomery and Ayllon (1994) report results from six patients who first received all the elements of EMDR but without eye movements (patients were asked to look at a fixed point). Only when eye movements were instituted was a reduction in anxiety observed (in five of the six patients). Though (in contrast to Renfrey & Spates, 1994) this seems to support the need for the full EMDR treatment package, it should be noted that there is no control for treatment length (which would be met by having patients exposed to treatments in the reverse order). In addition it is not clear how the six patients in the trial were chosen; Montgomery and Ayllon report that they were "selected" from a larger pool of patients but give no criteria for their choice.

Further research is necessary to indicate whether EMDR represents a significant gain over exposure or is in fact a variant of this technique.

SUMMARY

- The prevalence of PTSD is surprisingly high, although exact figures will depend on social and economic conditions and will vary locally.
- The natural history of PTSD suggests that it can be a chronic and disabling condition in a significant proportion of survivors of trauma.
- The course of PTSD may be influenced both by the nature of the trauma and by the person's reaction to it.
- Although symptoms of depression are frequently comorbid with PTSD, the major intervention techniques assessed have primarily focused on symptoms of anxiety.
- Despite more active research over recent years, studies are relatively small in sample size, which precludes definitive conclusions from negative outcomes or failures to demonstrate between-treatment effects.
- There is mixed evidence concerning the efficacy of psychodynamic therapy. The methodology employed by most relevant studies is flawed to the point where unequivocal conclusions cannot be drawn.
- A variety of anxiety management techniques have been shown to be effective, particularly on anxiety-related symptoms.
- Exposure-based techniques alone show limited effects on PTSD symptoms, as the effects on more generalized anxiety and depression are small.
- Stress inoculation training has been shown to be equal or superior to supportive psychotherapy, but the differences are less apparent in long-term follow-up.
- EMDR has been examined with relatively small groups of PTSD patients, but methodological limitations of the studies preclude definitive conclusions concerning the specific contribution of this technique beyond that of exposure.
- The current treatment of choice appears to be a combination of cognitive techniques (SIT and cognitive restructuring) and exposure.
- Short courses of tricyclic antidepressants appear to have moderate effects.

- The effect of these treatments on patients whose symptom profile includes a significant element of depression is unclear.
- The literature leaves open the possibility that treatments may be specific to particular types of traumatic experience.

IMPLICATIONS

- Psychological therapy techniques appear to be valuable in reducing the intensity of PTSD symptoms in a substantial proportion of patients.
- Effective treatments appear to involve relatively complex combinations of treatment methods, which may be best administered at service units specializing in this type of disorder.
- Although we have not reviewed the efficacy of counseling following disasters aimed at the later emergence of PTSD, there is good evidence that generic counseling is not particularly effective in those who develop this condition.
- Because of the small samples involved in most treatment trials, systematic attempts should be made to integrate research findings in meta-analytic reviews.

CHAPTER 9

Eating Disorders

DEFINITIONS

Eating disorders considered in this section are anorexia nervosa and bulimia nervosa. These are defined in DSM-IV as follows.

Anorexia Nervosa

The essential feature of this disorder is a refusal to maintain body weight at or above a minimally "normal" body weight; this is defined as a body weight 15% below that expected for the individual's age and height. To meet diagnostic criteria there must also be an intense fear of becoming fat, even though underweight; a severe restriction of food intake, often with excessive exercising, in order to achieve weight loss; a disturbance in the way in which body weight or shape is experienced, and an undue influence of body weight or shape on self-evaluation; and (in postmenarcheal women) amenorrhea.

There are two subtypes of anorexia nervosa—binge eating/purging type, where there is regular binge eating or purging (self-induced vomiting or use of laxatives or diuretics), and restricting type, where these behaviors are not present.

Bulimia Nervosa

The main feature of this disorder is recurrent episodes of binge eating associated with a lack of control over eating behavior during the binges. Self-induced vomiting, use of laxatives or diuretics, and strict dieting or excessive exercise are often associated features, together with a persistent preoccupation with body size and shape. At least two binges a week over a period of 3 months are required to make this diagnosis. As with anorexia nervosa, self-evaluation is excessively linked to ideas about body weight and shape.

It should be noted that within DSM-IV there is a diagnostic primacy for anorexia nervosa,[1] since a primary diagnosis of bulimia nervosa can only be applied in the absence of anorexic features. DSM-IV subtypes bulimia nervosa to purging type, in which vomiting or purging occurs, or nonpurging type, where excessive fasting or exercise occurs but without purging.

Eating Disorder Not Otherwise Specified

DSM-IV recognizes the presence of "subthreshold" cases of eating disorder, where patients meet some but not all of the criteria for anorexia nervosa or bulimia nervosa. Examples might include women who meet all the criteria for anorexia but have regular menses, or where all the criteria for bulimia are met but compensatory behaviors occur at a frequency of less than twice a week, or for less than 3 months.

DSM-IV also notes a proposed category of binge eating disorder in which binge eating takes place in the absence of other compensatory behaviors characteristic of bulimia nervosa.

PREVALENCE

DSM-IV estimates the prevalence of anorexia nervosa among women in late adolescence and early adulthood at between 0.5% and 1.0%. Presumably because of assumptions about the gender-related nature of this disorder, there are only limited data concerning prevalence rates in males. Crisp et al. (1977) estimate a similar rate of 1% for this age group while Hsu (1990, 1991) estimates a rate of 1–2%. Fairburn and Beglin (1990) review studies of prevalence rates of bulimia nervosa; again, most focus on adolescent and young adult women. A consistent finding is a prevalence rate within this group of 1–3%.

Fairburn and Beglin (1990) caution that methodologies used to detect cases may result in an underestimation of the prevalence of eating disorders. Inclusion of individuals with subthreshold diagnoses greatly increases prevalence rates to between 5% and 15% (Herzog et al., 1991).

---

[1] Within DSM-III-R, individuals presenting with binge eating and purging occurring exclusively during periods of anorexia would have attracted a separate diagnosis of bulimia nervosa.

Similarly, but more cautiously, King (1989, 1991) reports prevalence rates based on combining clear and subthreshold cases, finding rates of 3.9% for women and 0.5% for men. Most studies indicate that the disorder is markedly more frequent in women than men.

COMORBIDITY

Comorbidity of the eating disorders is reviewed by Mitchell et al. (1991). Studies report lifetime prevalence of depression at between 24% and 88%, with similar prevalence rates for anorexia and bulimia. Rates of substance abuse are elevated in bulimia (though not in anorexics), with lifetime prevalence rates varying between 9% and 55%. Anxiety disorders are also common; Laessle et al. (1987) report that 56% of a sample of bulimics had a comorbid DSM-III-R anxiety disorder, most frequently social phobia. Obsessive-compulsive disorder may be more common in anorexic patients (Holden, 1990). Mitchell et al. (1991) report that personality disorder is common in both bulimia and anorexia, though estimates vary markedly between studies. Prevalence rates for the DSM-III-R anxious–fearful cluster range from 2% to 75%, and for the borderline, histrionic, or narcissistic cluster from 16% to 80%.

NATURAL HISTORY

Anorexia Nervosa

The mean age of onset is 17 years, with some data suggesting bimodal peaks at 14 and 18 (DSM-IV). Herzog et al. (1988) and Steinhausen et al. (1991) review between them approximately 70 studies of the longer-term outcome in anorexia nervosa. These studies are most commonly open trials of a variety of treatments with a wide range of (often unstandardized) outcome measures, and with follow-up periods ranging from 1 to 40 years. Although this variability limits reliability, the long-term outlook for anorexia nervosa is likely to be poor. Normalization of eating behavior is found in 44% of patients in more recent trials, with a range of 30–70% across all studies. Some trials suggest even poorer response: Ratnasuriya et al. (1991) followed up 41 patients admitted for treatment between 1959 and 1966; only 9% were classified as eating normally, though 29% were considered to be recovered despite some residual eating difficulties.

There is some evidence that a significant proportion of anorexics develop bulimia, and that bulimia nervosa is the most common diagnosis after anorexia nervosa at follow-up (Hsu, 1988). Reflecting this, Kreipe et al. (1989) followed up a sample of 49 adolescents for an average of 6.5 years after hospital treatment, finding that 49% had developed symptoms of bulimia.

Severe anorexic restriction can lead to physical harm and mortality. Ratnasuriya et al. (1991) found that 15% of their patients had died of causes related to anorexia nervosa. Hertzog et al. (1988) and Steinhausen et al. (1991) report a mortality rate of 10% in older trials, though this has reduced to 4.4% in more recent studies, perhaps reflecting better recognition of the condition and its risks.

Bulimia Nervosa

Bulimia nervosa usually begins in late adolescence or early adulthood (DSM-IV) and appears to be a chronic condition marked by frequent remissions and relapses (Herzog et al., 1991). King (1989, 1991), following progress in a community sample, suggests that untreated patients with full or partial syndromes of bulimia nervosa tend to progress in severity over 1–3 years. Though there appears to be some consensus that the course of bulimia nervosa is chronic, Collings and King (1994) suggest that, at least for treated patients, this may be overly pessimistic. These authors followed up 50 patients 10 years after they had participated in a medication trial; of 37 patients traced, 62% had recovered. Similarly, Fairburn et al. (1995) found that of 91 patients followed up approximately 6 years after psychological treatment, 54% had recovered.

Most information regarding the natural history of these disorders is derived from patients seen in tertiary care settings; the prognosis for individuals with subthreshold symptoms and those seen in primary care or community settings may be more benign.

TREATMENTS FOR ANOREXIA NERVOSA

Inpatient treatment for anorexia nervosa, usually combines medical care with programs aimed at increasing weight. Schwartz and Thompson (1981) review 12 outcome studies for such a regimen, finding that on follow-up there was a 6% mortality rate from self-starvation, and that though 49% had recovered from anorexia, 31% continued to have eating disorders and 18% showed no significant change.

There appear to be few comparative trials of psychotherapies for anorexia nervosa. Hall and Crisp (1987) treated 30 anorexic patients, contrasting 12 sessions of "dietary advice" with psychotherapy. Psychotherapy included both individual psychodynamic and family therapy, depending on the willingness of families to be involved in treatment. There was some overlap between treatment conditions, since dietary advice included discussion of mood and behavior, and psychotherapy included discussion of dietary matters. Both groups showed improvements at 1 year follow-up, though only the dietary group showed significant pre- to posttherapy weight gain. In the psychotherapy group, weight loss in three patients masked overall weight gain in the remaining clients. Those receiving psychotherapy had better social and sexual adjustment, though global clinical ratings were equivalent between treatment groups.

Crisp et al. (1991) report 1-year outcomes for 90 severe anorexics randomly allocated to one of four treatments. Inpatient treatment comprised a package of behavioral techniques aimed at restoring weight, coupled with weekly individual therapy, group therapy, family therapy, dietary advice, and a range of milieu treatments. On discharge, patients were seen for 12 weeks of outpatient therapy. Two outpatient treatments were also offered. In the first, patients received 12 sessions of psychodynamic individual or family therapy. In the second they were given 10 sessions of group therapy, which appear to have been structured and topic-based. Dietary advice was offered in both outpatient conditions. The three treatment groups were contrasted with patients who were seen only for assessment and referred back to their GP or consultant, and who then received a variety of unmonitored treatments.

At 1 year patients in all treatment conditions showed improvements. However, this was most striking for both outpatient groups, which showed significant gains contrasted to patients who had only received assessment. Though inpatient treatment resulted in greater posttherapy gains than the other conditions, significantly greater relapse was evident at follow-up. Gowers et al. (1994) report a 2-year follow-up of patients treated with outpatient therapy and those receiving only a one-off assessment. Gains were maintained by those treated with outpatient psychotherapy, who continued to show better weight maintenance than those receiving assessment alone.

This study raises questions about the relative merits of in- and outpatient treatments. Inpatient treatment is sometimes viewed as the "established" treatment for this group of patients (e.g., Crisp, 1980). Though there may be some prognostic factors, such as very low weight, which would indicate a need for admission (Gowers et al., 1994), effective treatment on an outpatient basis appears to be a viable treatment option.

Channon et al. (1989) contrasted CBT, behavior therapy, and (as a control) routine outpatient treatment in 24 anorexics; given the medical condition of patients, a waiting-list control was felt to be unethical. Both

CBT and behavioral treatment included self-monitoring and dietary planning; behavior therapy also included gradual exposure to avoided foods, whereas CBT identified dysfunctional beliefs about eating. No differences were found between treatment groups or between the treatment groups and routine treatment.

Russell et al. (1987) contrasted family therapy and individual supportive therapy in 80 patients, 57 of whom were anorexic and 23 bulimic, all of whom had been admitted to the hospital for management of weight loss. Individual therapy was eclectic, using cognitive, interpretive, and strategic techniques.

Outcome was assessed on a number of symptom measures and on weight gain. Although mean weights for anorexic patients showed significant gains, categorical assignment to good, intermediate, and poor outcomes on the basis of clinical measures indicated only moderate clinical gains; 23% of patients had a good outcome, 16% an intermediate and 61% a poor outcome at 1-year follow-up. However, there were indications of differential impacts of therapies depending on the age of onset of the disorder. Patients with an age of onset before 18 appeared to respond better to family therapy, whereas those whose difficulties began at 19 or after did better with individual therapy.

Le Grange et al. (1992) attempted to evaluate the salience of differing aspects of family therapy by offering two forms of family-based treatment—conjoint family therapy, or separate supportive therapy for the patient and counseling for the parents. Eighteen patients were randomly assigned to therapy; at 1 year follow-up there were similar benefits from each treatment.

Treasure et al. (1995) treated 30 anorexic outpatients randomly allocated either to cognitive analytic therapy (CAT; Ryle, 1990) or to an educational–behavioral treatment. Behavioral treatment included dietary education, whereas CAT maintained a largely interpersonal focus. Therapies were offered weekly over 20 weeks, and though therapists were supervised weekly, they were inexperienced in the therapies they were delivering. Patients in both treatment groups showed weight gain sustained over 1-year follow-up. Although patients receiving CAT reported greater subjective improvement than those receiving the behavioral intervention, there were no significant differences between treatment groups on measures of weight gain.

TREATMENTS FOR BULIMIA NERVOSA

Meta-Analyses

Hartmann et al. (1992) examined 18 trials of therapies for bulimia nervosa from a potential pool of 243 reports of therapeutic interventions carried out to 1990. These authors note that much of the literature comprises single-case reports or reports of case series, and included in their analysis only studies with a sample of five or more patients. The 18 trials reported on 24 treatment groups (433 patients) and six control groups (61 patients). Most studies utilized cognitive or cognitive-behavioral interventions; five examined the impact of humanistic and psychodynamic interventions.

Because of variability across studies in reported measures, effect sizes were calculated for binging and/or purging. Follow-up data were not used, and all effect sizes quoted are based on pre–posttreatment change. Change in the control groups was negligible (mean effect size 0.18), indicating that there is little spontaneous remission for bulimia nervosa. For therapy of any type, the mean effect size was 1.04. Treatments employing 15 or more sessions had larger effect sizes (mean effect size 1.37); those with less than 13 sessions had a mean effect size of 0.79 (though this effect was restricted to the number of sessions rather than the duration of treatment). There were no statistical differences in effect sizes for different treatment modalities (though as noted above, the sample of studies was rather uniform in terms of this variable).

Laessle et al. (1987) report a meta-analysis of trials of both drug therapy and psychological therapies for bulimia. Perhaps reflecting the earlier date of this review, selection criteria were less rigorous than in Hartmann et al.'s (1992) study. There is little overlap between the two analyses, and Laessle et al. (1987) review a larger number of studies with very few patients and a greater number of uncontrolled studies. Most psychotherapies were cognitive-behavioral; most medication trials employed tricyclic antidepressants.

On the single measure of binge eating, an overall effect size of 0.95 was found. Psychological therapies including dietary management had a higher effect size than those without (1.30 and 1.14, respectively). The mean effect size for medications (0.60) was lower than that for either psychotherapeutic technique.

Individual Treatment Approaches

Exposure and Response Prevention

Procedures in which patients are exposed to food and encouraged to delay vomiting and purging approximate exposure and response prevention strategies. Carter and Bulik (1994) have reviewed these studies, noting that within the literature distinctions are made between exposure to purging cues and exposure to prebinging cues. However, in practice procedures often seem to expose patients to both sets of cues, and this may be more a theoretical than a practical issue.

Leitenberg et al. (1988), with a sample of 47 bulimic women, contrasted exposure and response prevention either in a single setting or in multiple settings, CBT, and a waiting-list control. All three treatments resulted in significant gains, though multiple setting exposure resulted in the lowest rates of purging at 6-month follow-up, followed by single setting and CBT. However, cognitive techniques were employed in the exposure treatments (e.g., patients were taught to identify and challenge distorted thoughts during exposure), and this study might be best viewed as demonstrating the benefits of adding exposure to CBT.

In contrast, Wilson et al. (1986) found only limited, nonsignificant benefit for the addition of CBT, Wilson et al. (1991) found that it had no effect, and Agras et al. (1989), that it had a deleterious effect. These differences in outcome may be accounted for by differing emphases on CBT and exposure in each study—Agras et al.'s (1989) trial, for example, devoted less time to exposure sessions than the other trials reported above, perhaps leading to inadequate implementation of the technique.

There are few studies examining the efficacy of exposure alone as a treatment for bulimia; most are very small-scale or single-case studies (Jansen et al., 1989; Schmidt & Marks, 1988; Rossiter & Wilson, 1985). In two slightly larger trials (Schmidt & Marks, 1989; Jansen et al., 1992), reductions in binging and purging were evident. However, only Jansen et al.'s (1989) study included a control treatment. There is therefore little reliable evidence for the efficacy of exposure and response prevention alone.

Cognitive-Behavioral Therapy

Cognitive therapies typically contain an educational component, self-monitoring and self-regulatory strategies, the examination of dysfunctional attitudes toward eating, the management of purging, and the reestablishment of control over eating. Relapse prevention strategies are usually a part of this package.

There are relatively few controlled studies of CBT for bulimia nervosa. Craighead and Agras (1991), Mitchell (1991), and Wilson and Fairburn (1993) review among them 18 trials; unsurprisingly, there is considerable overlap among these accounts. Most trials contrast highly structured therapies which contain techniques from CBT or behavior therapy. Around half the studies employ group approaches, with the remainder using either individual therapy or, more rarely, a mix of group and individual therapy.

Craighead and Agras (1991) review 10 studies of CBT for bulimia nervosa; using the average of mean reductions in binge eating and purging, across studies there was a mean reduction in purging of 79%, with 59% of patients in remission. However, contrasting measures of outcome based on symptom reduction with measures based on a criteria of clinically significant improvement yields somewhat less striking results. In Mitchell's review the mean percentage reduction in binge eating frequency pre- to posttreatment across 23 studies is 69.9% (range 40–95%), while the mean percentage of patients found to be free of symptoms at the end of treatment is markedly lower, at 32.8% (0–71%). In four of the most recent controlled trials reviewed by Wilson and Fairburn (1993), the mean percentage reduction in binge eating was 73–93% and for purging from 77–94%. Again however, mean remission rates were lower—from 51 to 71% for binge eating and from 36 to 56% for purging (Agras et al., 1989, 1992; Fairburn et al., 1991; Garner et al., 1991; Mitchell et al., 1990).

Contrasts of CBT and Antidepressants

There are three studies contrasting antidepressant medication and psychotherapy. All studies tend to involve self-monitoring of eating behavior, a technique which Agras et al. (1989) suggest has some therapeutic benefit in itself.

Mitchell et al. (1990) employed four treatment conditions: group therapy using CBT principles combined either with imipramine or with placebo, imipramine alone, and placebo alone. Imipramine alone was superior to placebo, but inferior to CBT combined either with medication or placebo. In the two CBT conditions, mean reductions in binge eating were 83% and 92%, contrasted with 34% and 9% for imipramine and placebo alone. Fifty-one percent of those receiving CBT were in remission posttreatment, contrasted with 16% of those receiving imipramine. Though imipramine had no effect on bulimic symptoms, it did improve mood and anxiety symptoms. All patients who had responded to treatment (defined as no more than two purges over the last 2 weeks of treatment) were assigned to a 4-month maintenance program and followed up at 6 months after treatment was initiated (Pyle et al., 1990). Relapse was greatest in patients receiving imipramine (67%) or placebo (83%), and lowest for those receiving CBT (22% and 31%).

Agras et al. (1992) contrasted CBT alone, desipramine alone, and the two treatments in combination. The study design was complex, with medication withdrawn either at 16 or 24 weeks and CBT administered for 16 weeks, leading to a total of five contrasts. At 16 weeks,

CBT and combination therapy were superior to medication alone in reducing binge eating and purging. At 32 weeks, patients receiving CBT alone and CBT in combination with medication (continued for 24 weeks) had better outcomes than those given medication for 16 weeks, suggesting that the addition of CBT acts to prevent relapse. This pattern was maintained at 1 year follow-up (Agras et al., 1994).

Leitenberg et al. (1994) assigned patients to three conditions—CBT alone, desipramine alone, and CBT and desipramine in combination. Although the original design planned for 12 patients in each condition, as the trial progressed it became evident that patients receiving desipramine alone were responding poorly and dropping out. This led the investigators to discontinue the trial early, when only seven patients had been assigned to each condition.

CBT alone was biweekly for 2 weeks, and weekly for a further 18 sessions, and followed Fairburn's (1985) model, with the addition of exposure to feared foods. Patients receiving desipramine alone met once a week for medication management; therapists were scrupulous in avoiding offering any discussion or advice regarding bulimic symptoms. Four of the seven patients dropped out of desipramine-alone condition, contrasted to one in the CBT and two in the combined. The reasons given for dropout usually related to side effects or the patient's expressed wish for a broader treatment approach. On a range of measures, CBT appeared to show benefit at both posttreatment and 6-month follow-up; the combined treatment appeared to confer no greater gains than CBT alone, and the high rate of dropout from the desipramine condition made data analysis meaningless. Overall, these trials suggest that there is no additional treatment benefit from the addition of medication to CBT.

Differential Impacts of CBT and Other Psychotherapies

Two trials have contrasted CBT against supportive psychotherapy in combination with self-monitoring (though as noted above, self-monitoring may in itself be helpful, reducing any likely between-treatment variance). Kirley et al. (1985), employing group therapy, found CBT to be superior in its effect at posttreatment, though at 4 months follow-up there were no between-treatment differences. Agras et al. (1989) found that CBT offered individually was more effective than supportive psychotherapy, both posttreatment and at 6-month follow-up.

Freeman et al. (1988) contrasted CBT, behavior therapy, group psychotherapy, and a waiting-list control, finding that all treatments were equally effective, and all were superior to control patients. Fairburn et al. (1986) found that CBT and a brief focal psychotherapy (focused not on eating problems but on understanding triggers for maladaptive eating) were equally effective in managing binge eating and purging, though CBT appeared to be somewhat more effective in reducing other symptoms such as depression.

Fairburn et al. (1991) contrasted CBT, behavior therapy, and interpersonal psychotherapy (IPT) in 75 patients. Posttherapy, IPT performed more poorly than either behavior therapy or CBT. However, follow-up at 4, 8, and 12 months indicated that behavior therapy patients showed a significantly higher rate of relapse than the other treatment conditions, most usually within the first 4 months of follow-up. In contrast, those receiving IPT continued to improve. At 12 months the proportion of patients meeting a strict criterion of recovery and no relapse were 44% for IPT, 35% for CBT, and 20% for behavior therapy. In addition, 48% of patients treated with behavior therapy dropped out during the trial or were withdrawn because of their worsening condition (Fairburn et al., 1993).

These trends appear to be maintained over the longer term. Ninety-one patients (from studies reported in Fairburn et al., 1986, 1991) were followed up at a mean of 5.8 years (Fairburn et al., 1995). Remission (defined as the absence of any DSM-IV eating disorder) was significantly more frequent in patients who had received either CBT or IPT/focal therapy (63% and 72%, respectively) than those who had received behavior therapy (14%). Much of this difference is accounted for by the high proportion of behavior therapy patients who received a follow-up diagnosis of "eating disorder not otherwise specified"—the proportion of patients diagnosed with bulimia nervosa or anorexia nervosa at follow-up was approximately equal across treatments.

Wilfley et al. (1993) examined the efficacy of group CBT and group IPT in nonpurging bulimics. Fifty-six patients were assigned to waiting-list control or to treatment, which comprised 16 weekly sessions. Posttherapy both treatment groups showed significant and equivalent improvement in binge eating contrasted to controls; these gains were sustained at 6-month and 1-year follow-up.

Garner et al. (1993) contrasted CBT with psychodynamic therapy (supportive–expressive psychotherapy; Luborsky, 1984) in 50 bulimic patients. Both treatments were effective in reducing binge eating, though CBT was more effective in improving purging, and had more impact on attitudes toward eating and on measures of psychological distress. Follow-up data have not been reported, though Fairburn et al.'s (1993) data suggest that this may be critical to any conclusions about differential therapeutic efficacy.

The trials reviewed offer some, though limited, evidence for mode-specific effects for CBT over other therapies. Thus studies show evidence of a reduction in dietary restraint (Fairburn et al., 1991; Garner et al., 1991; Wilson et al., 1991), more food eaten between bulimic episodes (Rossiter et al., 1988), and better attitudes toward body size and shape (Fairburn et al., 1993; Garner et al., 1991; Wilson et al., 1991). However, studies by Fairburn et al. (1993) and Wilfley et al. (1993), though based on slightly different patient populations, suggest that IPT may be equally effective, despite an apparently broader focus.

SUMMARY

- While the point prevalence rate of eating disorders is relatively low (between 1% and 4% for women and 0.5% to 1% for men), the inclusion of those with distorted attitudes to eating and sub-threshold disorders is likely to be substantially higher.
- There is a very high rate of comorbidity with Axis I disorders, particularly depression, but also anxiety, social phobia, and obsessional–compulsive disorder.
- Severe cases may be comorbid with various personality disorders, but the strength of the association seems to vary according to the population studied.
- Examination of the outcome literature is complicated by its focus on tertiary referrals, with a high degree of severity and chronicity. Thus remission rates may be underestimated and relapse rates overestimated.
- Although the evidence is mixed, severe anorexia nervosa appears to be life-threatening in a significant minority of cases, although this risk may be decreasing with increasing recognition and intervention of the condition.
- Approximately a third to a half of severely anorexic patients progress to bulimia nervosa.
- Bulimia nervosa shows little spontaneous change in the short term, although the long-term outcome may be favorable in over half the cases. It should be borne in mind that chronic bulimia nervosa is associated with relatively severe medical complications.
- Inpatient contingency management treatments of anorexia nervosa appear to be effective in ensuring immediate weight gain, but these programs have unacceptably high relapse rates.
- There is preliminary evidence that younger anorexic patients (less than 18) may respond better to family therapy than to individual therapy.
- Patients over 18 are more likely to respond to individual eclectic psychotherapy than to family therapy.

- Psychological techniques (dietary advice, individual dynamic group therapy, family therapy) appear to be effective in facilitating weight gain in anorexic patients and reducing relapse rates.
- There is some indication that outpatient treatment may be more effective with anorexic patients than previously thought, though very low weight at presentation may be a factor in deciding on treatment mode.
- Studies of the psychotherapeutic treatment of anorexia suffer from major methodological weaknesses—in particular, small sample sizes and nonrepresentative (tertiary referral) samples—limiting conclusions about the comparative benefits of differing therapeutic modalities.
- There is a striking lack of systematic investigation of the efficacy of behavioral and cognitive-behavioral methods for anorexics.
- The effectiveness of treatments for bulimia nervosa are better supported by outcome studies, although here, too, evidence is limited.
- Exposure and response prevention strategies alone seem to be of little benefit.
- Dietary education, advice, and monitoring of food intake appear to be important components of treatment effectiveness.
- Cognitive-behavioral therapy techniques incorporating these and other methods (such as addressing dysfunctional attitudes toward eating and reestablishment of control over eating) are effective for two-thirds of patients, although they ensure symptom-free status in only one-third of cases.
- There are a limited number of trials of psychotherapies other than CBT. These include individual and group IPT, supportive-expressive psychotherapy, and cognitive analytic psychotherapy. At the end of treatment the effectiveness of these treatments appears comparable with CBT, and in one study nonbehavioral treatments were shown to be more effective on long-term follow-up.
- Medication, particularly tricyclics, seems to add little to the effects of CBT, and there has been a suggestion that concurrent medication with imipramine increases relapse rates.
- Techniques of CBT are improving, and more recent studies are showing greater impact.
- Longer treatments (contrasting 12 sessions to 6 months) are associated with better outcome.

IMPLICATIONS

- Psychotherapeutic treatment of eating disorders is justified both by the demonstrated efficacy of these interventions and the presumed savings in the costs of treating medical complications frequently associated with the chronic form of these conditions.

- The literature suggests that the group of patients presenting with eating disorders are probably fairly heterogeneous. Some patients are more likely than others to respond to relatively brief interventions. However, there is as yet little evidence available to guide clinicians to specific treatment strategies which may be effective for specific subgroups.
- A variety of treatments may be appropriate for this group, including, for anorexics, family therapy (particularly for younger patients), inpatient management, and eclectic individual therapy, and for patients with bulimia nervosa, CBT, IPT, and dynamic psychotherapy.
- The literature suggests that interventions making use of multiple orientations may be particularly effective for this group. Provider units offering treatments for eating disorders should have expertise in structured approaches, such as CBT, IPT, or structured dynamic therapy, as there is little evidence that supportive treatments alone are effective.
- Services should be structured such that individuals presenting with eating disorders are offered short-term treatment, but longer-term treatment should be made available to those who respond poorly, since there is some (though limited) evidence that better gains are achieved with longer treatment.
- The effectiveness of CBT may be further enhanced by technical developments, and the exploration of therapies integrating CBT with interpersonal therapies should be explored, particularly for chronic cases of bulimia nervosa.
- Concurrent medication cannot be recommended unless justified by the presence of comorbid severe depression.

CHAPTER 10

Schizophrenia

DEFINITION

DSM-IV describes a range of symptoms of schizophrenia. Diagnosis is based on a complex pattern which usually involves disturbance in several of the following areas: content and form of thought, perception, affect, sense of self, volition, relation to the external world, and psychomotor behavior. No one feature is invariably present, or seen only in schizophrenia. The disorder is usually associated (at some point in its course) with severe impairment in social and work functioning and difficulties in self-care. Supervision of the person may be required to ensure that basic needs are met and that they are protected from the consequences of actions deriving from the disorder. Between episodes the extent of disability may range from none to disability so severe that institutional care is required.

A distinction is often made clinically between acute (or positive) symptoms—such as delusions or hallucinations—and residual (or negative) symptoms—such as social withdrawal and marked impairment in social role functioning.

PREVALENCE

Data from the Epidemiologic Catchment Area (ECA) program give 1-month prevalence rates for schizophrenia of 60 per 10,000 and lifetime prevalence of 130 per 10,000 (Regier et al., 1988).

NATURAL HISTORY

The course of this disorder is usually chronic, though in some patients recovery occurs after one or two brief acute psychotic episodes. However, a more chronic course is found in patients who have recurrent

184

episodes of longer duration, and in these individuals a "defect" state can develop, marked by lack of motivation, apathy, and social withdrawal (Kendall, 1993). Florid symptoms may or may not persist between acute episodes, and depressive symptoms are frequent.

PSYCHOLOGICAL INTERVENTIONS

While neuroleptic medication is widely recognized as the treatment of choice for schizophrenia, a substantial proportion of patients will remain troubled by symptoms. There is evidence that despite appropriate levels of medication, many patients continue to experience residual psychotic symptoms which, though often less severe than those occurring in acute episodes, are unresponsive to further medication. Full remission of symptoms occurs in less than two-thirds of patients (Shepherd et al., 1989). In a 3-year follow-up study, 47% of patients continued to experience some psychotic symptoms (Harrow & Silverstein, 1977; Silverstein & Harrow, 1978). Similarly, Curson et al. (1985), in a 7-year community follow-up study, report that 23% of patients continue to experience florid symptoms; in a hospital setting nearly half did so (Curson et al., 1988). The need for psychological interventions also arises from patients' difficulty in maintaining themselves on long-term medication, and the fact that high relapse rates are evident even in patients who continue with this regimen.

Before the introduction of effective antipsychotic medication there were reports of individual case studies examining the usefulness of psychodynamic treatments for schizophrenia. As these studies antedate the development of reliable diagnostic criteria for the disorder, they will not be reviewed here. More recently there have been important developments in two areas: (1) family intervention programs aimed at modification of the support network of the schizophrenic person, and (2) cognitive-behavioral treatment of acute symptoms. The focus of this section will lie largely with these interventions.

Family Intervention Programs

There have been a number of psychosocial intervention programs, initiated partly in the light of relatively high relapse rates for schizophrenia (Leff & Wing, 1971; Johnson, 1976) and also because of the success of measures of expressed emotion (EE) in predicting relapse (Brown et al., 1972; Vaughn & Leff, 1976; Leff & Vaughn, 1985; Bebbington & Kuipers, 1994). In brief, these early studies indicate that relapse is more likely if patients live with, or have extensive contact with, relatives who are excessively critical and/or overinvolved. Two factors appear to be protective and additive in their effect; regular maintenance therapy with neuroleptic medication, and the establishment of a social distance between the patient and relative.

Intervention programs have as an aim the prevention of relapse and improvement in functioning rather than direct amelioration or "cure" of the condition. All assume that it is useful to regard schizophrenia as an illness. Importantly, none regard the family as the cause of schizophrenia, but take as their focus the family burden imposed in attempting to care for their relative. Finally, treatments are offered in conjunction with routine medical management. There are usually two components to intervention programs: (1) education regarding the illness, (2) education and treatment aiming at influencing family functioning. With one exception (Glick et al., 1993), all trials discussed below were carried out on an outpatient basis.

A meta-analytic review of these studies has been carried out by Mari de Jesus and Streiner (1994), and qualitative reviews by Barrowclough and Tarrier (1984), Strachan (1986), Kuipers and Bebbington (1988), and Lam (1991).

Family Education

Six studies reviewed by Lam (1991) have examined the impact of educational packages, delivered either with or without the patient and to a single family, or in multifamily groups (McGill et al., 1983; Berkowitz et al., 1984; Barrowclough et al., 1987; Smith & Birchwood, 1987; Cozolino et al., 1988; Abramowitz & Coursey, 1989). Packages are usually fairly brief, in four studies consisting of two sessions; the longest (Abramowitz & Coursey, 1989) comprised six 2-hour sessions every 2 weeks. Studies have used different educational content, different measures, and differing lengths of follow-up (ranging from 2 to 9 months); some of these follow-up measures are contaminated by intervening treatments. However, with one exception, all studies demonstrated an increase in family knowledge regarding the condition at follow-up, contrasted with controls. In the exceptional case this may relate to the fact that only one 3-hour education session was offered. There was no difference between high- and low-EE families, though there was a trend indicating that relatives of recent-onset patients gained more knowledge from the intervention. There was only limited and inconsistent evidence of change in family belief systems; those receiving education showed some greater optimism about the patient's future and less self-blame, though this effect was not stable over follow-up. There was no evidence that relapse rates—perhaps the most clinically rigorous test of these interventions—differed between experimental and control groups.

Family Intervention

Mari de Jesus and Streiner (1994) identified six studies for meta-analysis. Trials were examined for the efficacy of family intervention programs, and analyses carried out on relapse rates utilizing data as presented in the original studies, intent-to-treat data from 169 patients, and with 181 patients acting as controls. Using data as presented in studies, experimental subjects showed a significantly lower relapse rate than controls (at 9 months a mean relapse rate of 15.6% contrasted to 47.2%); as follow-up progressed, the relapse rate in the two groups of patients increased, though more so among controls (at 2 years mean relapse rates were 24% and 65%, respectively). The pooled odds ratio was 0.3 at 6 months, 0.22 at 9 months, and 0.17 at 2 years, indicating a significant reduction in relapse rates. Intent-to-treat analyses (which treated dropouts as though they had relapsed rather than using end-point data) suggested a more marginal level of efficacy (odds ratios were 0.65 at 6 months, 0.59 at 9 months, and 0.80 at 2 years). Secondary analyses indicated that treated patients showed a significant increase in compliance with medication, and that their families showed a marginally significant reduction in expressed emotion.

Lam (1991) identified five family intervention programs that have been carried out with patients with a diagnosis of schizophrenia based on standard research tools such as the Present State Examination (PSE; Wing et al., 1974) or Research Diagnostic Criteria (RDC; Spitzer et al., 1978), which randomly allocate patients to control or experimental groups and in which some attempt was made to control for the impact of medication (Leff et al., 1982, 1985, 1988, 1990; Falloon et al., 1982, 1985, 1987; Hogarty et al., 1986, 1987; Tarrier et al., 1988, 1989; Kottgen et al., 1984). Four of these studies offered very similar treatments. Despite differences of detail, all focused on positive (rather than negative) areas of family functioning, acknowledging family burden and increasing family structure and stability (e.g., through problem solving, behavioral goal-setting, cognitive restructuring, or techniques derived from family therapy). In contrast, Kottgen et al. (1984) adopted a psychodynamic approach.

Effects of family intervention appear to be marked. With the exception of the Kottgen study, significant reductions in relapse rates were evident. At 9 months to 1 year, rates in patients from treated families ranged from 6–23%, contrasted with 40–53% in patients from control families. Levels of EE within families were usually reduced in these programs, and measures of household, social, and work functioning indicated that patients from treated families had improved relative to control patients.

At 2 years, less dramatic differences were observed; contrasting patients in high EE families (who have the most elevated risk of relapse), rates were 17–44% in patients from treated groups and 59–83% in controls. Although this suggests that intervention delays rather than prevents relapse, in most studies there was only minimal contact between therapists and patients during the follow-up phase. Falloon's group maintained contact once every 6 months over the 2-year follow-up, obtaining a 17% relapse rate. There may be some indication, therefore, that better outcomes would be obtained by use of a maintenance model of treatment.

Glick et al. (1993) report outcomes following a relatively brief family intervention program, offered on an inpatient basis. The study included 169 patients with a range of diagnoses, of whom 92 had a diagnosis of schizophrenia. All patients received standard hospital care, but half received additional family treatment (a mean of 8.6 sessions over a mean hospital stay of 51 days). This comprised an educational package, an examination of family interaction patterns which might exacerbate stress, and training in identifying potential sources of stress. Patients were followed up for 18 months after discharge, with no control on subsequent treatment, though results are reported only for patients who had six or more therapy sessions. Using Jacobson et al.'s (1984) criteria for establishing clinical significance, at discharge 86% of patients receiving family therapy showed significant improvement, contrasted with 63% of controls. As follow-up progressed differential treatment effects diminished, such that at 18 months 54% and 50%, respectively, of the family therapy and control groups showed significant improvement.

Although the success of interventions in this group of studies could be attributable to better adherence to drug regimens and to the nonspecific effects of greater therapeutic input, this seems unlikely. Evidence from Tarrier et al. (1989) suggests that amount of contact with the clinical team and degree of drug compliance was equivalent across treatment and control groups. In addition Kottgen et al. (1984) failed to demonstrate a benefit for their psychodynamic intervention, suggesting that therapeutic contact per se is not sufficient to account for change.

Despite these promising findings, it is important to note that in all the above trials a number of families refused to enter treatment, and that there is a moderate level of attrition from treatment. Tarrier (1991a) discusses this issue, noting that across studies the rate of families refusing treatment is between 7% and 21% (median 13%), the rate of withdrawal from treatment is 7–14% (median 9.5%), and the rate of noncompliance is between 8% and 35% (median 16%). This is a significant problem, in that there is evidence that patients from families that refuse or drop out of treatment have a higher relapse rate than those who follow the intervention program (Hogarty et al., 1986).

Tarrier (1991a) suggests a number of features which may be associated with adherence. There is some—though little—evidence that families high in EE may be more likely to drop out (Tarrier et al., 1989). Other characteristics (e.g., the age of relatives, degree of chronicity in the index patient, or level of family burden) remain unclear; further research in this area would be helpful.

As is usual in research trials, most data on the efficacy of family interventions have been culled in the context of high levels of therapeutic expertise and supervision. Trials conducted closer to everyday practice are few. Brooker et al. (1992) report a pilot study in which psychiatric nurses were trained to deliver intervention packages composed of education and family stress management. In a naturalistic design 54 families were recruited either to experimental or control conditions and followed up for 12 months; control families received treatment as usual from nursing staff. For families receiving the intervention package, significant gains were found in social and personal functioning and in relatives' General Health Questionnaire scores. However, no differences in relapse rates were found.

In a subsequent trial (Brooker et al., 1994) a similar intervention package was employed with families either receiving treatment immediately or after a 6-month delay, thus forming a waiting-list control group. Broadly similar gains in functioning to those found in the earlier trial were achieved, together with a marked reduction in the length of inpatient admissions.

Randolph et al. (1994) report on the impact of behavioral family interventions (as described by Falloon et al., 1984) in a standard clinical setting. Forty-one patients were allocated either to a mean of 21 family sessions over 1 year or to routine care, which comprised monthly sessions of medical management. At the end of this treatment period 15% of the treatment group had an exacerbation of their condition, contrasted to 55% of those receiving routine care. However, there was no difference between the groups in the number of days spent as inpatients.

Though promising, more research will be needed before conclusions can be drawn about the likely effectiveness of family interventions outside research trials. This caution reflects the fact that, as noted above, families who refuse interventions may contain patients at higher risk of relapse.

Family Interventions and Service Costs

It is evident that family intervention programs can reduce relapse rates. Given the high cost of inpatient care and attendant interventions, it seems likely that such programs would be cost-effective. This issue has been investigated in detail by Tarrier (1992b). Eighty-three patients and their families were entered for a treatment trial, receiving either a full family intervention program, an educational program or routine treatment. All contacts with mental health services were monitored and costed. Low-EE families in the control group made no more demands on services than high-EE families in the intervention group. However, comparison between high-EE families in the control and intervention groups revealed significantly greater costs accrued as a result of admission and professional contact time. Although there is a significant cost involved in offering family interventions, high-EE patients in receipt of the program had an estimated mean cost per patient of £1,171 ($1,760), contrasted with £1,603 ($2,400) for high-EE controls and £822 ($1,230) for low-EE controls. Cardin et al. (1986) have reported that over 12 months the costs of family management were 19% lower than individually managed care, attributable to reduced rates of admission and crisis management. Some caution may be required in considering these figures, in that the studies reviewed above suggest that over longer time frames increased relapse would be observed even in treated patients.

Social Skills Training

There are a number of general reviews of social skills training with schizophrenic patients (Gomes-Schwartz, 1979; Wallace et al., 1980; Donahoe & Driesenga, 1989; Halford & Haynes, 1991). However, a number of studies in these reviews include nonschizophrenic patients or fail to ensure that diagnostic inclusion criteria are met. In addition, wide variations in the form and length of interventions make it difficult to draw firm conclusions about efficacy. With some exceptions (Gomes-Schwartz, 1979), reviewers note that although social skills training leads to improvements in role-play tests, these fail to generalize over a longer time span and to situations outside the hospital (Wallace et al., 1980; Emmelkamp, 1994).

Benton and Schroeder (1990) present a meta-analytic review of 23 studies in which at least 75% of subjects had a diagnosis of schizophrenia and had been inpatients for more than 6 months continuously. In addition, social skills training was characterized as containing elements of modeling, rehearsal, and homework assignments; studies not adhering to this specification were excluded. Overall, mean effect sizes based on naturalistic measures of outcome were rather lower than those closely related to treatment process, such as role-play-based measures (0.68 and 0.83, respectively). Self-rated assertiveness yielded an effect size of 0.69. Effect sizes based on measures of general functioning, self-rated symptomatology, and discharge and relapse rates were small and nonsignificant. In concordance with qualitative reviews there appears to be some, rather limited evidence of positive impacts using this technique, though only a modest degree of generalization of skills.

Management and Modification of Psychotic Symptoms

A range of psychological techniques have been applied in an attempt to alleviate psychotic symptoms (Sellwood et al., 1994). Earlier trials examined the efficacy of more behavioral techniques (such as operant methods, exposure, social skills training, and distraction). In recent years a number of research groups have been developing and researching the use of strategies based on cognitive-behavioral techniques. It should be noted that there are some significant differences between these groups in terms of their target groups (ranging from young, acutely ill individuals to patients presenting with chronic, drug-resistant conditions), the clinical context (inpatient through to community settings), the length and intensity of intervention, and the extent to which treatments are offered as part of a broader care plan. Most results have been reported in single-case studies, case series, or uncontrolled trials (e.g., Fowler & Morley, 1989; Chadwick & Lowe, 1990, 1994; Kingdon & Turkington, 1991; Nelson et al., 1991; Tarrier, 1992; Bentall et al., 1994; Alford & Correia, 1994; Chadwick & Birchwood, 1994; Perris & Skagerlind, 1994; Garety et al., 1994; Persaud & Marks, 1995). However, this is an area of active research, and controlled trials are now appearing or under way.

Tarrier et al. (1993a) allocated 27 patients to two forms of cognitive-behavioral treatments aimed at alleviating residual delusions and hallucinations; coping strategy enhancement (CSE), or problem solving. CSE is a method which identifies potential stressors and triggers to psychotic phenomena and which aims to develop patients' skills in controlling both these cues and their reactions to them. Problem solving was selected as a control treatment because, though not directly addressing psychotic processes, it is commonly used in family management trials. Treatment was delivered in 10 sessions over 5 weeks, with no maintenance sessions after this time. Baseline measures of functioning were obtained by monitoring patients over a 6-week period prior to initiating treatment.

Patients showed significant, though specific, improvements in functioning with both treatments, contrasted to base-line. Delusions (but not hallucinations) improved, as did levels of anxiety, but depression, wider areas of functioning, and negative symptoms were not affected. Gains were maintained at 6-month follow-up, though there was evidence of some relapse at this point. There was some, though limited, evidence for the greater efficacy of CSE over problem solving, raising some questions about the mode of action of these techniques (Tarrier et al., 1993b).

Drury et al. (in press a,b) present results from a controlled trial of cognitive therapy for positive symptoms in combination with a stress management package. Of 117 patients with acute nonaffective psychosis, 69 satisfied inclusion criteria and 40 were allocated to one of two groups on the basis of demographic and psychiatric variables. The first was a cognitive therapy program (CT), which comprised four elements in addition to routine supervision and monitoring: (1) individual cognitive therapy designed to challenge and modify delusional beliefs; (2) group cognitive therapy designed to enhance the work undertaken in individual therapy and to develop more general coping skills; (3) family psychoeducation and support, which was offered either in the hospital or in the family home and was aimed at supporting the patient's attempts to manage their symptoms—particularly their delusional beliefs; (4) a "meaningful activity program" away from the ward, aimed at reducing negative symptoms. The control group comprised element (4) of the CT program, and was designed to raise patients activity level and provide informal support. All patients received neuroleptic medication; poststudy checks indicated that the two groups were prescribed this at equivalent levels.

Overall, patients in the CT group showed marked improvement in symptom status, functioning, and speed of recovery, contrasted to the control group. Their stay in the hospital was significantly shorter (a mean of 54 days compared to 119 days), and the mean length of time to full resolution of positive symptoms was also reduced (108 days and 151 days, respectively). Patients in the CT program showed a significantly faster decline in positive symptoms and a significant reduction in the conviction with which they held, and were preoccupied by, core delusional beliefs. These group differences were maintained at 9-month follow-up, with 95% of the CT group, contrasted to 44% of the control group, displaying no or minor positive symptoms. In addition, the rates at which delusional beliefs were reported, and held with conviction, were significantly lower in the CT group.

Though these results are impressive, some caution is warranted. The design of the trial provides only partial control for the impact of cognitive interventions per se, since family interventions are themselves are known to be of demonstrable benefit to patients. There may also be some problems of generalization from this trial to other research, in that the patient group tended to be young and their treatment particularly intensive.

Garety et al. (1994) report a smaller controlled trial that recruited patients who suffered persistent, drug-resistant psychotic symptoms which had been present for at least 6 months. The first 13 patients to be recruited formed the experimental group, with seven subsequently referred patients forming a waiting-list control. Therapy was weekly or biweekly over 6 months, with an average of 16 sessions (range 11–22), and comprised a manualized cognitive-behavioral intervention (Fowler et al., in preparation). Following a lengthy assessment, patients were offered a package comprising cognitive-behavioral coping strategies, modification of delusional beliefs, psychoeducation, and techniques aimed at remoralization. Significant reductions were found in the conviction with which delusional beliefs were held, together with reductions in measures of distress and preoccupation with delusions. However, there were no differences between the treatment and control groups on measures of functioning.

Individual Psychotherapy

Research into the efficacy of expressive, insight-oriented psychotherapy appears to be largely negative (Goldstein, 1991); indeed, there is some evidence that the emotional intensity of psychodynamic treatments may be harmful for at least some patients (Drake & Sedere, 1986; Mueser & Berenbaum, 1990). Illustrative of the few available reports is Gunderson et al.'s (1984) trial, in which psychodynamic–expressive therapy was contrasted with supportive therapy oriented toward coping with problems of daily living. Therapies were carried out over 2 years, and patients were maintained on medication. Supportive therapy appeared to be significantly more helpful, particularly on measures such as relapse and the number of days in employment. This study also indicated, however, that the 31% of patients who remained in their assigned therapy over 2 years had the best outcomes, a similar finding to that of Alanen et al. (1985). However, it is not clear whether better outcomes can be attributed to therapy or to self-selection of patients who were able to maintain extended therapeutic contact and who therefore (by definition) had better levels of functioning. Although these studies indicate that therapy—particularly of a more supportive nature—may be useful to some patients, the very high dropout rate from both studies (over 50% by 6 months) suggests that it may have limited application in practice.

Although formal psychotherapy may not be judged appropriate, there is some suggestion that the development of a good therapeutic alliance between clinician and patient promotes better compliance with medication (Frank & Gunderson, 1990) and may be a helpful adjunct to treatment (e.g., Weiden & Havens, 1994; Liberman, 1994).

Self-Help Groups

There are a number of voluntary agencies offering support to people with a diagnosis of schizophrenia and to their relatives. Though undoubtedly highly valued by consumers, the impact of such organizations has rarely been investigated. Schulze-Mönking (1994) examined the impact of self-help groups (established by a therapy team) for patients with at least two admissions who had been discharged on neuroleptic medication back to their families. Because patients and families were invited to participate in these groups, they clearly differ from the more usual route to a voluntary agency. However, it is of interest that of 333 families contacted, only 99 made initial contact with the groups. Comparison of patients whose families attended the groups with those whose did not suggests that relatives of the most severely ill patients with high levels of EE were most likely to join. Over a period of 2 years there was some indication that, though their EE status did not change, participants in the groups had better levels of social contact and physical and psychological well-being than nonparticipants. There was little indication of direct benefits to patients.

This study gives some, necessarily limited support to the suggestion that carers may be helped by attendance at self-help groups. Though their impact appears to be less than that obtained by both patients and carers following more formal family interventions, there may be significant value attached to the social support obtained by relatives.

SUMMARY

- The symptoms of schizophrenia are effectively treated by neuroleptics in between 50% and 75% of patients.
- Dynamic psychotherapy has been tried, but has not been demonstrated to be effective with this group of patients.
- Family education regarding the nature of the disorder does not lead to a reduction of relapse rates.

- Family interventions aimed at enhancing family structure and encouraging positive social interactions lead, by a factor of 2–3, to a decreased relapse rate for 1–2 years.
- Continued contact with the therapy team may enhance effectiveness, leading to a more prolonged reduction in relapse rates.
- The efficacy of this intervention in everyday clinical practice remains to be demonstrated, particularly since a substantial proportion of patients no longer live with their families.
- Social skills training is effective in treatment-based assessment, but the benefit for the patient in a wider social context remains to be demonstrated.
- Cognitive-behavioral techniques aimed at the modification of delusions are the subject of increasing research effort. Though the database is limited, results suggest it to be of demonstrable benefit to patients.
- The social adaptation of patients who continue to experience florid psychotic symptoms despite adequate medication may be enhanced by stress-management and problem-solving techniques.
- These therapies are of great significance because of their potential to reduce the costs associated with inpatient treatment.
- Whereas supportive individual therapy may be helpful for schizophrenic patients, expressive psychotherapy is unlikely to be of value.
- The usefulness of all these techniques in clinical practice is limited by high rates of refusal to enter treatment and high dropout rates in family interventions.

IMPLICATIONS

- Psychological therapies may be a useful adjunct to medical treatment in the long-term management of schizophrenia.
- Family intervention programs may reduce the cost of services largely as a result of reducing inpatient admissions.
- Promising lines of intervention, which illustrate the potential of psychological interventions to enhance the effects of medication, are the application of behavioral and cognitive-behavioral techniques such as cognitive strategy enhancement, problem solving, cognitive therapy for positive symptoms, and cognitive restructuring for delusional beliefs.
- Despite the absence of studies showing effects on relapse rates in ordinary service provision, we would recommend the widespread

training of psychiatrists, psychologists, and psychiatric nurses in these techniques.

- Although a substantial number of schizophrenic patients do not live in social environments in which systemic interventions could be applied, there may be a role for the range of cognitive therapies discussed above, as an adjunct to neuroleptic treatment.
- Research should focus on identifying which of these treatment combinations will be of maximum benefit to patients. Treatment components such as medication, supportive environments, cognitive-behavioral techniques, and systemic interventions should be tried in various permutations as well as individually, to explore the possibility that therapeutic effects may be additive. In the light of such findings, routine service provision could be modified to incorporate the uniquely effective components.
- As the cost of this group of patients to services is relatively high, more rigorous attempts should be made to audit the impact of psychological and supportive services on relapse rates, using formal survival analyses.
- As existing psychological treatments appear not to be acceptable to perhaps as many as half the patients suffering from this disorder, intensive efforts should be made to develop new treatment methods to facilitate the adaptation of these patients to community life.

CHAPTER 11

Personality Disorders

DEFINITIONS

Axis II of DSM-IV describes three clusters of personality disorders. With the exception of antisocial personality disorder, all are characterized by the development of patterns of behavior in early adulthood. DSM-IV definitions will be summarized briefly.[1]

Cluster A: "Odd–Eccentric"

Paranoid Personality Disorder

The essential feature of this disorder is a pervasive tendency to interpret the actions of others as deliberately demeaning or threatening. People with this disorder are usually argumentative and exaggerate difficulties, "making mountains out of molehills."

Schizoid Personality Disorder

This disorder is characterized by a pervasive pattern of indifference to social relationships. There is little enjoyment of nor desire for close relationships, and people with this disorder tend to be loners, having no (or only one) close friends or confidants. They appear cold and aloof, and display a restricted range of affects.

---

[1] DSM-III-R descriptions of personality disorders are broadly similar to those of DSM-IV, with the exception of *passive–aggressive personality disorder* (a pattern of passive resistance to demands for adequate social and occupational performance), deleted in DSM-IV.

Schizotypal Personality Disorder

In this disorder there is a pervasive pattern of peculiarities of ideation, appearance, and behavior that are not severe enough to meet the criteria for schizophrenia. Disturbances of thought content may include paranoid ideas, ideas of reference, and magical thinking. There may be disturbances of perception or peculiarities of speech content (such as vagueness or impoverishment, but not a loosening of associations). People with this disorder often appear odd and eccentric in their behavior, there may be inappropriate or constricted affect, and social relationships are few and often restricted to first-degree relatives.

Cluster B: "Dramatic–Erratic"

Antisocial Personality Disorder

People with this disorder have a pattern of antisocial and irresponsible behavior beginning in childhood and continuing into adulthood. In adulthood there is a pattern of behavior that often renders the person liable to arrest, such as harassing others, stealing, destroying property, or failing to honor financial obligations. There is a tendency to be irritable or aggressive, often getting into fights or assaulting others. There is rarely expression of remorse for the effects of their behavior on others.

Borderline Personality Disorder

The essential feature of this disorder is a pervasive pattern of instability of self-image, interpersonal relationships, and mood. The person's sense of identity is profoundly uncertain. Interpersonal relationships are unstable and intense, fluctuating between the extremes of idealization and devaluation. There is often a terror of being alone, with great efforts being made to avoid real or imagined abandonment. Affect is extremely unstable, with marked shifts from baseline mood to depression or anxiety usually lasting a few hours. Inappropriate anger and impulsive behavior are common, and often this behavior is self-harming. Suicidal threats and self-mutilation are common in more severe forms of this disorder.

Histrionic Personality Disorder

This disorder is characterized by a pervasive pattern of excessive emotionality and attention seeking. People with this disorder often seek reassurance, approval or praise from others, and often display rapidly shifting and shallow expression of emotions.

Narcissistic Personality Disorder

People with this disorder often display a pervasive pattern of grandiosity, either in fantasy or in behavior together with hypersensitivity to the evaluation of others. There is an exaggerated sense of self-importance which often alternates with a sense of special unworthiness. Self-esteem is very fragile.

Cluster C: "Anxious–Fearful"

Avoidant Personality Disorder

The essential feature of this disorder is a pervasive pattern of social discomfort and timidity, together with a fear of negative evaluation. There is a reluctance to enter into social relationships unless there is a guarantee of uncritical acceptance, and consequently people with this disorder rarely have close friends or confidants. Although there is strong desire for affection, social situations are avoided.

Dependent Personality Disorder

People with this disorder have a pervasive pattern of dependent and submissive behavior, characterized by an inability to make decisions without reassurance from others. There is a sense of helplessness when alone, and there is often great anxiety about abandonment when in close relationships.

Obsessive–Compulsive Personality Disorder

This disorder is characterized by a pervasive pattern of perfectionism and inflexibility. There is an adherence to unusually strict and often unattainable standards which often results in interference with the completion of projects. In addition there is a preoccupation with rules and trivial detail. People with this disorder are always mindful of their status relative to others, often resisting the authority of others and stubbornly insisting that others conform to their own way of doing things. There is frequently a difficulty in expressing affect, and they are often perceived as stilted or "stiff."

PROBLEMS IN THE DEFINITION OF PERSONALITY DISORDER

There is some controversy over the definition and description of personality disorders and over the degree to which accurate diagnosis is possible; indeed, overlap between personality disorders is frequent and explicitly described within the DSM.

A large-scale investigation by Tyrer et al. (1990) has failed to identify any predictive value in terms of response to a variety of treatments associated with categories of personality disorder, implying that current classifications may be erring toward overrefined descriptive distinctions with few practical benefits. Rutter (1987) has proposed abandoning trait-defined personality disorders in favor of identifying a group of patients whose pervasive abnormality seems to be one of establishing and maintaining adequate social relationships.

Many practitioners take issue with the phenomenological approach to the diagnosis of abnormalities of personality, because it underemphasizes developmental perspectives. There exist alternative approaches to the measurement of personality disorders, rooted in the assessment of personality functioning in specific domains, such as work, relationship, and self-care, rather than in terms of an unusual constellation of personality characteristics (Hill et al., 1989). The most promising current work in the area attempts to focus on the ways in which personality reflects the accumulation of individual life choices, made in response to specific key experiences in the course of development (Cicchetti, 1990).

However, as with other areas covered in this review, much of the literature on treatment effectiveness is organized according to Axis II diagnoses. While we do not necessarily regard this as the most appropriate for designing treatment interventions or for assessing effectiveness, it is undoubtedly the most commonly used heuristic device for organizing treatment outcome in this area.

PREVALENCE

Weissman (1993) reviews epidemiological surveys conducted using a range of standardized interview schedules. Overall, around 10–13% of personality disorders were diagnosed in community samples or in samples made up of relatives of patients with psychiatric problems.

Cluster One

Lifetime prevalence rates for paranoid personality disorder vary between 0.4% and 1.8%, for schizoid personality disorder between 0.4% and 0.9%, and for schizotypal personality disorder between 0.7% and 5.6%, with more usual figures in the range 3% to 5.6%.

Cluster Two

Prevalence rates for histrionic personality disorder range between 1.3% and 3.0%; for narcissistic personality disorder rates vary between zero and 0.4%, and for borderline personality disorder between 1.1% and 4.6%. Rates for antisocial personality disorder vary between 1.5% and 3.2%.

Cluster Three

Rates for avoidant personality disorder vary between 1.1% and 1.4%, for dependent personality disorder between 1.5% and 1.7%, and for compulsive personality disorder between 1.7% and 2.2%. Rates for passive–aggressive personality disorder vary between 0% and 1.8%.

Although the percentages suggest that relatively few individuals suffer from personality disorder, the acute nature of their symptoms and the chronicity of their condition lead to their being overrepresented in psychotherapeutic caseloads (Berelowitz & Tarnapolsky, 1993).

COMORBIDITY

Within Personality Disorders

Zimmerman and Coryell (1990) report that paranoid, avoidant, and borderline personality disorders were almost always comorbid; 23% of subjects with borderline disorder also met criteria for schizotypal personality disorder. Antisocial personality disorder was frequently diagnosed in people with borderline or schizotypal personality disorder. Half of those diagnosed with avoidant personality disorder also met criteria for schizotypal personality disorder.

With Axis I Disorders

Swartz et al. (1990) report very high rates of comorbid Axis I disorders in borderline patients. In the year prior to survey, 56.4% had generalized anxiety disorder, 41.1% simple phobia, 40.7% major depression, 36.9% agoraphobia, 34.6% social phobia, 21.9% alcohol abuse, and 6.1% obsessive–compulsive disorder.

NATURAL HISTORY

The course of borderline personality disorder has been more extensively researched than other diagnoses. Although follow-up over 5 years suggests that symptomatic patterns change little (Werble, 1970; Carpenter, 1977; Pope, 1983), follow-up over 15 years suggests that by middle age many borderline patients no longer meet relevant diagnostic criteria, though this does not indicate that recovery is complete (McGlashan, 1986; Paris, 1987; Stone, 1993). At this point approximately 10% of patients will have committed suicide. In this sense borderline personality disorder appears to be a chronic disorder with some moderation in its severity over time. Individual personality disorders consume a significant proportion of psychotherapeutic treatment resources because of their resistance to most forms of psychotherapeutic treatments and the particular tendency of patients in the dramatic–erratic cluster to make simultaneous use of a number of services (Tyrer et al., 1990).

IMPACT OF PERSONALITY DISORDERS ON OUTCOME IN TREATMENT OF AXIS I DISORDERS

Though there are only a limited number of studies directly examining the impact of personality disorders on treatment of Axis I disorders, where studies exist there are indications that treatment efficacy is usually reduced (Shea et al., 1992; Reich & Green 1991; Reich & Vasile, 1993).

Depression

Most trials of major depressive disorder (MDD) exclude patients with major personality disorders, particularly those with borderline personality disorder. Almost invariably, trials that include such patients suggest that poorer outcomes are associated with the presence of any personality disorder (Sullivan et al., 1994). An area of some controversy is the form of presentation of MDD in borderline patients. Some authors suggest that such patients have a distinctive, interpersonally based quality to the depression (e.g., Western et al., 1992). Others (e.g., Sullivan et al., 1994) suggest that psychoticism and poor impulse control are characteristic, with chronic and enduring comorbidity with other Axis I disorders, such as substance abuse.

Shea et al. (1990) report data from the NIMH collaborative research program for depression reviewed earlier. Seventy-four percent of the patients in this sample were diagnosed with a personality disorder, 65% of these being in the anxious–fearful cluster. Contrasted to those patients without personality disorder, they were found to have significantly worse outcomes on measures of social functioning and to be more likely to have residual symptoms of depression.

Burns and Nolen-Hoeksema (1992) conducted a naturalistic trial of cognitive-behavioral therapy for depressed patients, finding that patients with borderline personality disorder improved significantly less than those without personality disorder. This result contrasts with that of Simons et al. (1991), who found no differences between depressed patients with or without any Axis II disorder treated using cognitive-behavioral therapy.

Thompson et al. (1988) and Fiorot et al. (1990) report data from treatment trials with elderly depressed patients, employing behavioral and dynamic therapy or eclectic therapy, respectively. Both studies indicated poorer outcomes for patients with personality disorder.

Diguer et al. (1993) report a trial of 25 patients with major depression treated with 16 sessions of Luborsky's supportive–expressive dynamic therapy. Forty-eight percent of the patients had a diagnosis of personality disorder. Contrasted to patients without personality disorder, these patients had significantly poorer levels of functioning prior to therapy, and though their rate of improvement was equivalent to that of patients with depression alone, they ended therapy with lower levels of functioning and a greater level of depressive symptomatology. This is perhaps most clearly seen in comparison of Beck Depression Inventory (BDI) scores, which reduced from a mean of 29.1 to 17.4 in personality-disordered patients, contrasted to a reduction from 26.7 to 7.3 in those without personality disorder.

A similar pattern was identified in the Edinburgh primary care study (Scott & Freeman, 1992; reported fully in Chapter 4); contrasted to those without personality disorder, depressed patients with mixed personality disorders had elevated levels of depression both before and after treatment, though their rates of recovery were similar. At 18-month follow-up, those with personality disorders showed continued improvement, while those without maintained their gains, leading to approximately equivalent levels of functioning in the two groups (Patience et al., 1995).

Anxiety Disorders

Most reports suggest that patients with personality disorders have poorer outcomes following treatment for anxiety disorders (e.g., Hermesh et al., 1987; Minichiello et al., 1987; Nurnberg et al., 1989; Reich 1988, 1990). Dreessen et al. (1994) report two trials examining the impact of personality disorders on cognitive-behavior therapy with 31 patients with panic disorders and 57 patients with mixed anxiety diagnoses. In both samples the presence of a personality disorder was associated with more severe Axis I pathology, with the consequence that though such patients evidenced similar rates of improvement to those without personality disorders, their outcomes were poorer.

Chambless et al. (1992) assessed the impact of specific personality disorders on treatment outcome in a naturalistic trial of 64 agoraphobic patients receiving cognitive-behavioral therapy. Eighty percent of this sample had a diagnosis in the anxious–fearful cluster; 36% in the dramatic–erratic, and 25% in the odd–eccentric.

Patients with a diagnosis of paranoid personality disorder tended to drop out of treatment earlier. Nine of the 10 subjects with this condition left treatment prematurely, reflecting Mavissakalian and Hamann's (1987) finding that paranoid personality predicted treatment failure. The most consistent predictor of outcome was avoidant personality disorder, which was associated with higher levels of depression and poorer outcomes on three of four measures of outcome. However, it is not clear whether depression contributed independently to poorer outcomes; though controlling statistically for depression abolishes the relationship between avoidant personality disorder and outcome, depression itself fails to predict outcome.

Turner (1987), in a small trial of 13 socially phobic patients, found that the presence of personality disorder (largely schizotypal, borderline, or avoidant) reduced outcomes markedly.However, some personality disorders were associated with a better response to treatment. Clients with histrionic personality disorder showed a better outcome on measures of panic frequency. This may reflect the cognitive style of such patients, whose tendency both to misinterpret and to be reactive to emotional states may be particularly responsive to treatments aimed at relabeling of cognitions. Patients with dependent personality disorder responded better to therapist-aided *in vivo* exposure, but less well with self-directed exposure. Similarly, Steketee (1990), in a trial for patients with obsessive–compulsive disorder, found that clients with this disorder responded better to therapist-aided exposure. However, while they showed more initial gains than other clients, they also relapsed more rapidly over follow-up.

The presence of avoidant, borderline, or paranoid personality disorder appears to reduce the efficacy of treatments for obsessional–compulsive disorder (Jenike, 1990; Cottraux et al., 1993). The impact of some of these disorders appears quite striking. Hermesh et al. (1987) reported that all eight of their borderline patients failed to respond to treatment with behavior therapy or clomipramine because of poor compliance. Patients with schizotypal personality disorder show a similar pattern; Jenike and colleagues (Jenike et al., 1986; Minichiello et al., 1987) report that only 7% of such patients responded to behavioral treatment, contrasted to 90% of patients with no personality disorder.

Other Disorders

Tyrer et al. (1993) examined the impact of personality disorder on 181 outpatients with generalized anxiety disorder (66 patients), panic disorder (66), or dysthymia (56). Patients were randomly allocated either to drug treatment, to cognitive-behavioral therapy or to a self-help program. Overall, patients with personality disorders tended to have poorer outcomes, though there was some interaction with the treatment employed. Outcome for patients with or without personality disorder were equivalent when treated with medication, but there was a trend for those with personality disorders to do more poorly with psychological treatment, particularly for those offered self-help. Tyrer et al. (1994) examined outcomes for 100 patients presenting as psychiatric emergencies. Poorer outcomes were associated with the presence of a personality disorder, whether these patients were treated in a hospital or a community-based setting.

STUDIES OF THE TREATMENT OF PERSONALITY DISORDERS

General Considerations in the Evaluation of Treatments for Personality Disorder

In earlier sections we have observed that the outcome of treatment for Axis I disorders is likely to be varied by the presence of a comorbid personality disorder. Equally, evaluation of treatments for personality disorders is made problematic where, as is frequently the case, Axis I disorders are present. Woody et al. (1985) have demonstrated this influence for antisocial personality disorder (discussed further below). Shea (1993) has suggested that research could control for this by excluding patients with Axis I disorders from clinical trials, but also notes that some disorders, such as borderline personality, are almost always associated with significant Axis I psychopathology. An ideal strategy, but one which no current trial has attempted, might be to assign patients to treatment groups on the basis of matched Axis I disorders.

A further difficulty for evaluation studies is that such comorbidity can be difficult to assess. For example, in studies by Soloff et al. (1987) and Kelly et al. (1992), two cohorts of inpatients with borderline personality disorder were assessed on admission. Though apparent rates of major depressive disorder were between 64% and 75%, depression resolved in a significant proportion of these patients after 2 weeks, and this without any active treatment (intervention being limited to observation without medication). Similar findings under the same "observational" regime have been reported by Siever et al. (1985); depression resolved in 17 of 22 (90%) patients. Such observations raise questions about whether these patients are presenting with comorbid depression or with characterological symptomatology reflective of the borderline syndrome, such as chronically low self-esteem. The extent to which resolution of such problems should constitute a marker for treatment efficacy is therefore a matter for debate.

Psychopharmacological Studies

Pharmacological treatments for patients with personality disorders—almost invariably borderline personality disorder—are reviewed by Zanarini et al. (1988), Stein (1993, 1994), Coccaro (1993), and Soloff (1994). Though there is evidence for the efficacy of pharmacotherapy, Soloff (1994) notes that there is no drug treatment of choice for this condition. Though medication can impact on differing aspects of psychopathology (identified as affective, cognitive–perceptual, anxiety, and impulse control domains), patients vary markedly in the domains in which impairment is presented, and hence the extent to which medication is indicated.

There have been six controlled trials of neuroleptics in patients with borderline personality disorder or schizotypal personality disorder (Brinkley et al., 1979; Leone, 1982; Cowdrey & Gardener, 1988; Goldeberg et al., 1986; Soloff et al., 1986, 1989). Patients with moderately severe schizotypal symptoms appear to benefit most from neuroleptic medication. In addition, neuroleptics have some efficacy on depression (Soloff et al., 1986) and on impulsive behavior (Soloff et al., 1989). Neuroleptics administered tend to be low-dose and contribute to global improvement primarily through addressing psychoticlike symptoms, depression, anxiety, and impulse control.

The efficacy of tricyclic antidepressants tends to be modest (Soloff et al., 1986, 1989; Perry, 1985). Indeed, in some patients the response to tricyclics can be one of increasing anger and poorer impulse control discontrol (Soloff et al., 1986). Even the effect on depressive symptomatology is not reliably demonstrated (Links et al., 1990). MAOIs may be more effective than tricyclics in treating symptoms of depression in patients with borderline personality disorder (Parsons et al., 1989) and are certainly superior to placebo in terms of improving mood (Cowdrey & Garner, 1988). There are no double-blind controlled studies available on serotonin reuptake inhibitors, although open trials of fluoxetine suggest that these drugs may be effective in treating symptoms related to depressed mood (such as suicidal ideation), impulsivity, and aggression (Coccaro et al., 1990; Cornelius et al., 1990; Markovitz et al., 1990, 1991; Norden, 1989).

Early studies indicated that anticonvulsants may be effective in managing anger and discontrol (Stephens & Schaffer, 1970). Cowdry and Gardener (1988) noted an unequivocal effect of carbamazepine over placebo on the frequency of impulsive and aggressive behaviors. By contrast, anxiolytics appear to increase behavioral discontrol (Gardener & Cowdrey, 1985).

Waldenger and Frank (1989) surveyed 40 American clinicians in private practice with experience of psychotherapy with borderline patients; 90% of these clinicians prescribed medication; 87% of the therapists reported problems of patients abusing their prescribed medication at some time. Anecdotal reviews of clinical experience indicate that specific problems may arise when psychotherapy is combined with pharmacological treatment, as many of these individuals have specific problems with dependency on drugs and on individuals, and have a potential for abusing both (see Perry, 1990; Elkin et al., 1988a,b). Trials of long-term maintenance therapy have shown little additional benefit beyond the acute phase (e.g., Cornelius et al., 1993). Nonetheless, short-term adjunctive use of medication may be important in the management of these patients (Soloff, 1994).

Uncontrolled Studies of Psychotherapy

Overall there are few controlled trials of psychotherapy for personality disorders per se, though there are many open trials and single-case reports.

The Menninger study (overviewed in Wallerstein, 1989) treated 42 patients with intensive psychodynamic psychotherapy. The trial was carried out in the 1950s, and follow-up has continued since that date. Although it antedates the development of diagnostic systems, clinical descriptions suggest that the majority of patients would merit a diagnosis of borderline personality disorder. Patients were treated with psychoanalysis, expressive psychotherapy, or supportive psychotherapy. Reports from therapists indicated that rarely was analysis carried out in a pure form, and that (presumably pragmatically) therapy was characterized by a significant degree of supportive (ego-building) elements. Of 27 patients for whom full follow-up data were available, good outcomes were obtained in 11, and a partial resolution in a further 7. Better outcomes were obtained in patients with higher levels of ego strength. Those with high levels of ego strength and better quality of interpersonal relationships seemed to respond better to psychoanalytic or expressive therapy than supportive. In contrast, those with low ego strength responded better to supportive psychotherapy combined, where necessary, with hospitalization.

Waldinger and Gunderson (1984) report a survey of analysts who had treated between them 78 moderately impaired patients with borderline personality disorder. Treatments were either psychoanalysis or psychoanalytic psychotherapy, and were intensive; patients averaged three sessions per week over 4.5 years. Therapist reports indicated significant improvements in all areas, with some relationship between the duration of therapy and better outcomes.

Stevenson and Meares (1992) report an open trial for 48 borderline patients receiving twice-weekly outpatient therapy over 12 months using a dynamic therapy which, while not manualized, was based on a model of borderline functioning which emphasized the importance of the maintenance of the therapeutic alliance. Significant improvements in a range of measures of functioning were found in 30 patients who had completed the therapy and for whom data were available; 30% no longer met DSM-III-R criteria for borderline personality.

Tucker et al. (1987) report data on 40 of 62 inpatients treated for between 6 months and 1 year in a specialized unit for borderline personality disorders. Treatment included individual and group therapies in a milieu which seems to correspond to a therapeutic community setting. Moderate improvements were found at 2-year follow-up, particularly in a reduced rate of suicidal behavior, together with some improvement in social functioning.

All studies with borderline patients emphasize the importance of extremely long follow-up, as the benefits of therapy may not be apparent upon discharge. Of course, longer-term follow-ups are very hard to interpret because of intervening variables, and none of these studies can be considered much more than studies of prognosis. A 5-year follow-up of treatment offered at the Cassel Hospital in London showed that patients who on admission showed borderline pathology tended to be those who showed a poor response to the inpatient psychotherapeutic program, and did no better than at a standard psychiatric institution (Rosser et al., 1987). Stone's (1993) report of follow-up of 550 patients at the New York State Psychiatric Institute indicates that, regardless of mental state at discharge, many patients appear to have utilized long-term hospitalization and inpatient therapy as a springboard toward normal functioning, autonomy, and independence. At up to 20 years' follow-up, 66% of patients were functioning well. Individuals successfully treated with psychotherapy probably fall into a higher-order, less dysfunctional group.

Additional studies using manualized treatments are reported in Shea (1993), though these are uncontrolled and often complicated by the presence of Axis I disorders. Henry et al. (1990) treated 54 patients with avoidant personality disorder and other "mixed" personality disorders. Treatment comprised 25 sessions of dynamically oriented therapy, and significant improvements in global functioning were reported. Woody et al. (1985) report outcome in a subgroup of patients with antisocial personality disorder from a trial of psychotherapy for opiate-dependent men. Patients with antisocial personality disorder with depression showed more improvement than those with personality disorder but no depression; in these patients there was little gain from therapy.

Turkat and Maisto (1985) report results from a case series of 35 patients with a range of personality disorders. Treatment was based on the derivation of detailed formulations for each patient's problems, and cognitive-behavioral interventions were employed. Of 16 cases with outcome data, only four showed a good outcome.

High rates of dropout have been reported in these studies. Gunderson et al. (1989) and Skodol et al. (1983) suggest rates varying between 23% and 67%.

Higgitt and Fonagy (1993), in reviewing the results of follow-up and uncontrolled outcome studies, conclude that (1) psychotherapy is more likely to be effective for less severely borderline patients; (2) in patients under 30, the greatest risk comes from suicide, and the aim of treatment may legitimately be the reduction in this risk, rather than cure; (3) patients with chronic depression, psychological-mindedness, low impulsivity, and good social support appear to be most likely to benefit from expressive therapy; (4) patients with impulse control disorders associated with cluster B diagnoses appear to benefit from a limit-setting group; (5) patients with substance abuse require their dependency problems to be specifically and separately addressed before psychotherapy is likely to be effective.

Controlled Studies

Shea (1993) identifies only nine controlled studies of a standardized psychotherapeutic intervention for personality disorder; some of these take as their focus the amelioration of coexisting Axis I disorders.

Avoidant Personality Disorder

Alden (1989), Cappe and Alden (1986), and Marzillier et al. (1976) have employed behavioral treatments in the treatment of social difficulties encountered by these patients. These studies are reviewed in more detail in the section of this book detailing treatments for social phobia. Briefly, patients were treated using behavioral methods including exposure, social skills training, and systematic desensitization, with resulting improvements relative to waiting-list controls. Though intervention programs are often designated as social skills training, they invariably include exposure procedures and are better described as a behavioral intervention package.

Argyle et al. (1974) found a trend toward improvement for both social skills and psychodynamic treatment in a trial in which patients acted as their own controls in a waiting period. Stravynski et al. (1982) assigned 22 patients to 14 sessions of social skills alone or with the addition of cognitive techniques aimed at challenging maladaptive beliefs. Equal and significant gains were found for both treatment groups. Stravynski et al. (1994) contrasted outcomes in 28 patients assigned to social skills training conducted either in a clinic or in a mix of clinic and real-life settings. The two treatments were equally effective, though only 3-month follow-up data are available. In addition, attrition from the real-life condition was markedly higher than when treatment was conducted in the clinic (58% contrasted with 21%); patients indicated that they found this form of therapy delivery stressful.

Though improvements can be found following treatment using social skills alone or in combination with cognitive techniques, many patients in these studies do not achieve normal levels of functioning, and there was limited generalization of improvements to broader social environments than those tested within studies. Alden and Capreol (1993) suggest that patients with avoidant personality disorder can be distinguished into two groups: those in whom distrustful and angry behavior is prominent, and those who are underassertive. In a trial of 76 patients, those with the former characteristics benefited more from exposure but not from skills training, while the latter benefited from both procedures.

This result, though preliminary, suggests that greater targeting of therapeutic strategies may be associated with better outcomes.

Borderline Personality Disorder

In one of the very few controlled trials of psychotherapy with borderline patients, Linehan et al. (1991) contrasted dialectical behavior therapy (DBT) with treatment as usual. DBT is a manualized therapy (Linehan, 1993) which contains elements of behavioral, cognitive, and supportive psychotherapies. Therapy was conducted weekly, and treatment was offered both individually and in groups over 1 year. By definition, interventions received by patients receiving treatment as usual were not controlled.

Patients were admitted to the trial if they met DSM-III-R criteria and had at least two incidents of parasuicide in the 5 years preceding the trial (with one in the immediately preceding 8 weeks); 22 women patients were assigned to DBT and 22 to the control condition. Assessment was carried out during and at the end of therapy and again after 1-year follow-up (Linehan et al., 1993). Control patients, as contrasted with those receiving DBT, were significantly more likely to make suicide attempts (the mean number of attempts in control and DBT patients respectively was 33.5 and 6.8) and spent significantly more time as inpatients over the year of treatment (mean 38.8 and 8.5 days, respectively). In addition, they were also significantly more likely to drop out of the therapies they were assigned to as part of "treatment as usual"—attrition from DBT was 16.7%, contrasted with 50% for other therapies.

Follow-up was naturalistic, based on the proposition that the morbidity of this group precluded termination of therapy at the end of the experimental period. At 6-month follow-up, DBT patients continued to have less parasuicidal behavior than controls receiving treatment as usual, though at 1 year there were no between-group differences. While at 1 year DBT patients had fewer days as inpatients, at the 6-month assessment there were no between-group differences. Although on some measures (employment performance and anxious ruminations) there were no between-group differences, most assessments of adjustment favored the patients receiving DBT.

There are a number of controlled trials in progress of therapy for borderline patients. Clarkin (1994) reports preliminary data from the Cornell Medical Center study of psychotherapeutic treatment of borderline personality disorder. Treatment follows the manual of psychoanalytically oriented psychotherapy originated by Kernberg et al. (1989).

Interventions focus on the clarification and confrontation of experiences of the self and others which have been dissociated from the core of the personality, and interpretations of the patient's current interactions with others which indicate their habitual overuse of defenses in maintaining these dissociations. Although the treatment method is well documented and treatment integrity can be readily monitored, findings have not yet been reported. Shea (1993) notes that a trial of "relationship management therapy" is in progress at McMaster University, again with results to be reported.

Other Personality Disorders

Liberman and Eckman (1981) report the results of a brief, intensive treatment for inpatients with a range of personality disorders, though the selection criterion of a history of repeated suicide attempts suggests that many would have a diagnosis of borderline personality disorder. Treatment contrasted behavior therapy (which largely comprised social skills training) and insight-oriented therapy; outcome measures at 6- and 9-month follow-up suggested a reduction in suicidal ideation for the behavioral group but no between-treatment differences in the number of suicide attempts.

Winston et al. (1991) treated 32 patients with a range of personality disorders (predominantly in DSM-III-R Cluster C) using two forms of brief psychodynamic therapy (short-term dynamic psychotherapy or brief adaptational therapy), contrasting both with a waiting-list control. Because of ethical constraints, waiting-list subjects began treatment after 15 weeks. Although both therapies used psychodynamic techniques, brief adaptational therapy employed more cognitive strategies. Patients with borderline, schizotypal, and narcissistic personality disorder were excluded from the trial, which comprised weekly sessions over 40 weeks. Contrasted to waiting-list controls, treated patients showed moderate improvements in symptoms and target complaints at posttherapy. Though there were few between-treatment differences, there was more variance in outcome for the patients treated with short-term dynamic therapy, suggesting that for some patients the technique was unhelpful. Gains appeared to be maintained at 18-month follow-up (Winston et al., 1994a).

A larger trial of these therapies by the same authors (Winston et al., 1994b) was conducted with 81 patients (of an original sample of 93). Again the patient sample predominantly constituted those with Cluster C disorders, with approximately one-fifth having Cluster B disorders (primarily hysterical personality disorder). As in the earlier trial, significant and equivalent gains were found with both treatments.

SUMMARY

- There has been considerable progress in clarifying the clinical definition of personality disorders. However, currently used categories remain controversial; the comorbidity of Axis II diagnoses and the degree of heterogeneity within diagnostic groups raise as yet unresolved questions concerning the validity of a diagnostic approach to these disorders.
- Individuals with dramatic–erratic and odd–eccentric personality disorders place considerable pressure on mental health, particularly psychotherapeutic, resources.
- It is well established that the presence of Cluster A and B personality disorders reduces the likelihood of good outcome from symptom-oriented treatments of Axis I disorders, in particular, depression and anxiety.
- Structured treatment procedures for these disorders are at a relatively early stage of evolution, with cognitive-behavioral, interpersonal, and psychodynamic treatments having reached a stage of manualization.
- Uncontrolled studies indicate that psychodynamic and interpersonal approaches may be helpful for these patients, particularly in the long term, although these findings should be interpreted cautiously in the context of the general tendency of these patients to improve with time and the relatively small gains that even long-term treatments are able to achieve.
- The strongest evidence of effective psychotherapeutic treatment in borderline patients comes from dialectical behavior therapy, with demonstrated benefits in reduction of suicide attempts and the need for inpatient services.
- Studies using appropriate control groups are very few in number and tend to be very small in size. Nevertheless, psychodynamic, interpersonal approaches and dialectical behavior therapy appear to be the current treatments of choice for these disorders.
- Studies with relatively brief, noncontinuous follow-up (less than 2 years) are of relatively little interest for this group of patients because of the chronically cyclic nature of their disorder, characterized by a tendency toward periods of almost complete remission followed by episodes of great severity.

- Avoidant personality disorder may be addressed using social skills training or cognitive techniques, but the generalization of improvements to other social contexts is not well demonstrated.
- Medication (particularly neuroleptics and perhaps serotonin reuptake inhibitors) appears to be moderately effective in the short term, reducing suicidal ideation and discontrol. The efficacy of long-term maintenance treatment remains to be demonstrated.
- While specific medications appear to be useful in treating particular symptoms of particular personality disorders, there is no single treatment that can be recommended for treating any one category of disorder.

IMPLICATIONS

- It is not self-evident that a categorical (diagnosis)-based approach to studying the treatment of personality disorder is likely to yield unequivocal results. A problem-focused or dimensional approach may be more helpful in the long run in linking specific treatments to specific problems and specific personality traits.
- There is an urgent need to identify ways of assessing the problems with which personality-disordered patients frequently present, such as aggression, anxious attachment, social avoidance, and lack of impulse control (disinhibition).
- Patients with severe personality disorders may not fit with the brief therapy models of most past outcome research. These individuals may require long-term or even continuous psychotherapeutic treatment, or a schedule of shorter-term but readily available brief treatments to manage crises. The schedule of such treatment and the preferred intervention strategies have yet to be established.
- In view of the major costs to the individual, society, and health services that personality-disordered individuals represent (ineffective work patterns, chaotic family and interpersonal functioning, the social inheritance of mental disorder, the social and personal costs of substance abuse, inappropriate utilization of health care services) the cost-effectiveness of intensive long-term treatment approaches for severely dysfunctional personality-disordered individuals should be a focus of urgent scientific inquiry.
- The chronic nature of these disorders suggest that studies should take a lifespan developmental perspective and treatments should be assessed in terms of their capacity to influence the trajectory

that would be predicted from what is known about the natural history of the disorder.

- In the light of the relatively poor response of these individuals to currently available psychotherapeutic treatment, psychopathological investigations should focus on the preventable causes of these disorders, particularly in ameliorating the effects of early deprivation, and examining the possibility of preventive measures in childhood for high-risk groups.

CHAPTER 12

Alcohol Dependency and Abuse

DEFINITIONS

Within DSM-IV substance dependency is characterized by a maladaptive pattern of substance use leading to clinically significant impairment or distress, as indicated by three or more of the following features occurring in the same 12-month period: (1) tolerance, marked by a need for increasing amounts of the substance, or a decreased effect from taking the same quantity of the substance; (2) withdrawal, as manifested by the characteristic withdrawal syndrome for the substance; (3) the substance is taken in larger amounts and over longer periods than the person intended; (4) a persistent desire or one or more unsuccessful efforts to cut down or control substance use; (5) a great deal of time spent in activities necessary to get the substance, taking the substance, or recovering from its effects; (6) important activities given up because of substance use; (7) continued substance use despite knowledge of personal problems caused by its use.

DSM-IV distinguishes substance abuse from substance dependency[1]; abuse is indicated by evidence of a maladaptive pattern of substance use leading to clinically significant impairment or distress, manifested by one or more of the following occurring within the same 12-month period, but in the absence of criteria for substance dependence: (1) recurrent substance abuse resulting in a failure to fulfil major role expectations (e.g., leading to absenteeism or neglect of household or children); (2) recurrent use in physically hazardous situations (such as driving when impaired by substance use); (3) recurrent substance-related legal problems (e.g., arrests for substance-related disorderly conduct); (4) continued substance use despite social problems caused or exacerbated by the effects of the drug (such as fights).

[1] The clarity of this distinction is the major difference between DSM-III-R and DSM-IV criteria.

216

PREVALENCE

DSM-III-R cites a lifetime prevalence for alcohol dependence of 13%. Warheit and Auth (1993), reviewing data from the Epidemiologic Catchment Area (ECA) survey, report 6-month prevalence rates between 4.5% and 6.1%, with significantly higher rates in men than women (9% vs. 1.5%), and greater prevalence in younger age groups.

COMORBIDITY

Estimated comorbidity rates vary according to the population sample under study (Regier et al., 1992). These authors review 17 studies of patients presenting for treatment of alcohol abuse. Estimates of the lifetime prevalence of major depressive disorder lie within the range 30–40%, with point prevalence between 9% and 27%. Lifetime prevalence rates for panic and phobic disorders were estimated at 2–60%, though most studies yielded rates under 15% for panic and generalized anxiety, with a median rate of about 20% for phobic disorders. Antisocial personality disorder was relatively common, with rates in two studies of 41% and 44%.

Comorbidity rates within community samples are lower. However, based on data from the ECA survey, Regier et al. (1992) note that comorbid Axis I disorders increase attendance for specialist care by a factor of 3 or 4. This suggests that there may be significant differences in the psychiatric profile of clinic attenders and people with drink problems within the community.

TREATMENTS

The focus of treatment for alcohol problems has shifted over the years. As awareness of the risks of excessive drinking has grown, treatment has shifted from provision of services for "alcoholics" toward treatment of patients with a broader range of difficulties with drinking, of which the classical alcoholic picture is one extreme (Thom et al., 1992). Within this context, treatment has moved away from intensive residential treatment and rehabilitation toward brief interventions (Bien et al., 1993), now widely employed both for early intervention with problem drinkers (Heather & Robertson, 1985) and with heavy drinkers (Wallace et al., 1988).

In this context, counseling and cognitive-behavioral techniques such as social skills training, self-management, and self-control techniques have been adapted to help prevent relapse of drinking behavior. A significant contribution has been the development of motivational interviewing (Miller, 1983). This could be described both as an assessment technique for gauging the readiness of patients to deal with their drinking and as a treatment when used to encourage patients to recognize the implications of their dependency for the physical health and family life.

Reviews of Treatments

Three recent reviews of treatment have summarized findings in the field (Miller & Hester, 1986; Holder et al., 1991; Mattick & Jarvis, 1993). Holder et al.'s review is partly based on a cost-effectiveness evaluation of treatment benefits. Effectiveness is defined broadly, to encompass not only reduction in drinking but also improvements in the emotional and physical well-being of the problem drinker. Benefit is defined in terms of a range of measures, reflecting improvements in work performance and problems associated with alcohol abuse such as injury, accidents, and violence. Thirty-three treatment modalities were identified, including interventions such as Alcoholics Anonymous or alternative treatments (e.g., hypnosis or acupuncture). Specifically psychological treatments included aversion therapy, nondirective counseling, behavioral and cognitive therapies (such as behavioral contracting, social skills training, stress management, cognitive therapy, self-control therapies, and motivational interviewing), psychodynamic therapy, and the use of medication. In addition, the impact of treatment settings was examined, an issue of some importance in a field where community support has increasingly replaced residential milieu therapy (Thom et al., 1994; Bien et al., 1993).

Only controlled studies were included in the review, with active treatments contrasted with no-treatment, placebo, minimal alternative interventions, or another treatment. Two hundred comparisons of treatment outcomes were used to construct a table of efficacy. Therapies were assigned a positive score for each demonstration of a successful outcome and a negative score for each instance of poorer outcomes or a failure to demonstrate greater gains than a comparison therapy. In addition, a weighting system was employed to overcome the problem that "five positive outcomes and five negative outcomes for a treatment modality are not equivalent to one positive and one negative result" (Holder et al., p. 522). To reflect this, a "weighted evidence index" was employed, which subtracted the number of positive from the number of negative findings, and added an extra point for every positive finding

TABLE 1. Evidence of Treatment Effectiveness for Alcoholism

Treatments with good evidence of effectiveness (weighted index of ≥6)
  Social skills training
  Self-control training
  Brief motivational interviewing
  Behavioral marital therapy
  Community reinforcement approach
  Stress management training

Treatments that are promising but not proven (weighted index of 0–5)
  Covert sensitization
  Behavioral contracting
  Disulfiram
  Antidepressant medication
  Nonbehavioral marital therapy
  Cognitive therapy
  Hypnosis
  Lithium

Treatments with no evidence of effectiveness (weighted index of −2 or lower)
  Chemical or electrical aversion therapy
  Educational lectures/films
  Anxiolytic medication
  General counseling
  Residential milieu therapy

Note. A further range of treatments for which fewer than three studies were located (and whose efficacy is therefore hard to judge) included antipsychotic medications, Alcoholics Anonymous, and residential milieu therapies. Adapted from Holder et al. (1991).

greater than two.[2] It might be noted that while this procedure recognizes the importance of a positive finding as contrasted to a null result, it also risks underestimating the efficacy of poorly researched areas of treatment. On this basis therapies were classified according to their evidential weighting; a partial list is given in Table 1.

Hodgson (1992) provides a commentary on this review, noting that there is strong empirical support for the efficacy of psychological techniques directed toward improving social and marital relationships. Twenty-one studies in Holder et al.'s (1991) review provide support for the benefits of social skills training, behavioral marital therapy, and community reinforcement. Investigation of factors that predict relapse and recovery suggest that family stability, cohesion, and social support

---

[2] For example, consider a treatment evaluated in four trials; if three trials found a positive benefit for the treatment, and one had a negative result, the treatment would be assigned a score of (3 − 1 = 2), plus an extra score of 1, giving a total weighted score of 3.

are important (Orford & Edwards, 1977; Billings & Moos, 1983). This suggests that, perhaps even more than is the case for many disorders, the social context is critical in preventing relapse. Treatments that facilitate social functioning may therefore be particularly appropriate for this group of patients.

Other psychological techniques show promise; Holder et al.'s (1991) review also identifies positive findings for self-control and stress management techniques; of 27 studies, 18 (67%) were positive. A range of behavioral techniques such as covert sensitization, behavioral contracting, nonbehavioral marital therapy, cognitive therapy, and hypnosis demonstrate some, though less consistently positive, results.

Holder et al. (1991) assessed cost-effectiveness by obtaining information about the costs of treatment from providers, insurance companies, and other agencies. On this basis a "unit charge" for different types of treatment was estimated, which reflects the cost of treatment settings rather than treatment modalities. Unit charges varied considerably—from $6 per visit for a walk-in community recovery program to $585 for acute hospital care. Combining these data with estimations of the typical length of time taken to deliver a particular treatment permitted typical costs for a particular modality to be estimated. Matching this figure against efficacy, Table 2 was derived which contrasted these two variables, giving a range from low-cost, high-efficacy treatments through to high-cost, low-efficacy interventions.

Again, the treatments that focus on improving social skills and relationships appear to have a good profile of costs and benefits. In contrast, some treatments, such as residential milieu therapy, psychodynamic therapy, and some drug treatments appear to have high costs with little evidence of efficacy.

Evidence for the Efficacy of Individual Treatment Approaches

The most comprehensive reviews of evidence for the efficacy of individual treatments are offered by Miller and Hester (1986) and Mattick and Jarvis (1993), the latter forming a part of the Australian Government's Quality Assurance Project for the treatment of drug dependency.

Antidipstrotrophics

Disulfiram (Antabuse) has been widely used in the treatment of problem drinking, both as an implant and as an oral medication. Though earlier

TABLE 2. Treatments by Cost and Effectiveness Categories

	Minimal cost	Low cost	Medium cost	High cost	Very high cost
Good evidence of effectiveness	Brief motivational counseling	Self-control training; self-management	Social skills training; community reinforcement; behavioral marital therapy		
Treatments that are promising but not proven		Behavioral contracting	Covert sensitization; cognitive therapy; antidepressants; nonbehavioral marital therapy	Disulfiram; hypnosis	
Treatments with insufficient evidence	Alcoholics Anonymous			Antipsychotic medication	
No evidence of effectiveness		Educational films and lectures	Group therapy; electrical aversion	Anxiolytics; general counseling	Residential therapies; psychodynamic therapy

Note. Adapted from Hodgson (1992).

studies claimed to demonstrate the superiority of Antabuse contrasted to control, they are characterized by poor methodological quality and short follow-up (e.g., Wallerstein et al., 1957; Reinert, 1958; Gerrein et al., 1973). Later studies provide evidence of a strong placebo effect. Fuller and Roth (1979) allocated 128 patients either to an active dose of disulfiram, an inactive dose, or no medication. At 1 year there was a higher abstinence rate among both the active and inactive medication groups (23%) than among those given no pill (12%). A similar effect has been found for disulfiram implants. Wilson et al. (1978) gave either a disulfiram implant or sham surgery. At 2-year follow-up the implant group showed some advantage to the sham surgery, but there was a clear and substantial placebo effect. The implant group and sham surgery groups had a mean of 367 and 307 days of abstinence, respectively, contrasted with 27 abstinent days for an unoperated control group.

In line with these findings, Mattick and Jarvis (1993) meta-analyzed results from five controlled studies, finding no difference between the impact of oral disulfiram and placebo (effect size of = −0.14), though there was a small difference between the impact of disulfiram and no medication (0.33). However, there was a moderate effect size when contrasting placebo and no medication (0.47), confirming the placebo effect noted above. Meta-analysis of studies of disulfiram implants (four studies) again confirms this pattern.

Peachey et al. (1989) have conducted the only RCT examining the efficacy of citrated calcium carbimide with 128 patients. A crossover design was employed, with subjects receiving either placebo or active medication for 56 days, followed by the alternative for the succeeding 56 days. Active medication reduced levels of alcohol consumption to the same extent as placebo, suggesting no specific impact for this medication.

Trials of metronidazole suggest that it has no greater impact than placebo (e.g., Gallant et al., 1968; Merry & Whitehead, 1968).

Opiate Agonists (Naltrexone)

In contrast to disappointing evidence for the efficacy of disulfiram, and to the relatively low rate of patient compliance associated with its use (e.g., Meyer, 1989; Fuller et al., 1986), there is current interest in the use of naltrexone, an opiate agonist. Two recent controlled trials have investigated its use in conjunction with psychological interventions. Volpicelli et al. (1992) conducted a 12-week double-blind placebo-controlled trial with 70 male alcoholics as an adjunct to outpatient rehabilitation (comprising 1 month of day treatment counseling and psychoeducation, followed by twice-weekly group psychotherapy). Over 12 weeks 23% of those receiving naltexone relapsed, contrasted with 54.3% of those receiving placebo. A particularly marked effect was seen in patients who took alcohol at any point in their treatment; 95% of such patients who had received placebo relapsed, contrasted with 50% of those receiving active medication.

O'Malley et al. (1992) conducted an RCT in which 97 patients received either naltrexone or placebo in combination with a manualized therapy—either coping skills/relapse prevention or a supportive psychotherapy. Coping skills taught were those that assisted self-management in situations associated with relapse and incorporated self-monitoring, social skills training, and a range of CBT methods. Supportive therapy was essentially nondirective and focused on the patient's strategies for managing and maintaining abstinence.

Survival analyses were conducted for each treatment group at 12 weeks. Patients treated with naltrexone were significantly more likely than those receiving placebo to remain abstinent, to show lower relapse rates, and to have fewer drinking-related problems. The impact of therapy was more complex. Abstinence was highest among those who received naltrexone and supportive therapy. Consistent with the findings of Volpicelli et al. (1992), for patients who had at least one drink over the study period, subsequent abstinence was lowest for those receiving naltrexone and coping skills therapy. Further research is required to confirm the value of this approach, and in particular to examine its impact over the longer term.

Psychotropic Medication

Though commonly used in the acute withdrawal phase from alcohol, there appears to be no evidence for the benefits of chlordiazepoxide in sustaining abstinence (e.g., Rosenberg, 1974). Evidence for the benefits of antidepressants is equivocal, though there may be some impact on mood. Kissin and Gross (1968) administered chlordiazepoxide and imipramine in combination, each drug alone, or placebo, finding reduced drinking rates of 28%, 19%, 0%, and 13%, respectively, at 6-month follow-up. Miller and Hester (1986) review the limited number of available studies, noting poor methodology, a failure to control for levels of depression, and inadequate follow-up periods. Investigations of the benefits of lithium carbonate have produced a similarly equivocal picture (e.g., Dorus et al., 1989).

Psychotherapy and Counseling

Evidence for the efficacy of psychotherapy and counseling is limited. Levinson and Sereny (1969) assigned inpatients either to insight-oriented therapy (which included individual and group therapy as well as educational sessions) or to treatment as usual, which comprised occupational and recreational therapy. At 1-year follow-up no differences in drinking behavior were found between groups. In this study somewhat greater improvements were found in control patients; a similar pattern of results has been found by other studies (e.g., Pattison et al., 1967; Tomsovic, 1970; Bjornvoll, 1972, cited in Miller & Hester, 1986).

Though the contrast of dynamic psychotherapy to no treatment yields positive results (e.g., Kissin et al., 1970; Brandsma, 1980), its contrast to minimal intervention strategies indicates that there is little extra benefit to the addition of therapy (e.g., Zimberg, 1974; Crumbach & Carr, 1979). Further studies contrasting psychodynamic therapy and counseling (Ends & Page, 1957) or psychodynamic therapy and behavior therapy (Pomerleau et al., 1978) suggest few differences between therapies or between therapies and controls, and studies that do indicate such differences tend to be characterized by poor methodology (Miller & Hester, 1986).

Marital and Family Therapy

There are few contrasts of marital therapy and minimal intervention. Corder et al. (1972) added a marital therapy workshop to inpatient milieu therapy, finding that at 6 months 42% of this group had relapsed, contrasted with 85% of a previous cohort receiving the milieu therapy alone. Cadogan (1973) assigned 40 inpatients either to an additional outpatient marital therapy group or a waiting-list control group. At 6 months 45% of the marital therapy group and 10% of the controls were abstinent. However, Zweben et al. (1988) found no advantage to eight sessions of marital therapy over one 90-minute session with the drinker and his or her spouse, though this study incorporated a large number of follow-ups which, in effect, may have increased the level of intervention.

Contrasts of marital and individual counseling show mixed results. McCrady et al. (1979) contrasted a control group receiving individual counseling with two treatments: in the first, subjects received outpatient marital therapy; in the second, both patient and spouse were admitted to an inpatient unit. Though significant reductions in drinking were reported for the two treatment groups, effect size analyses by Mattick and Jarvis (1993) suggest that there were no between-group differences in the quantity and frequency of drinking. However, at 4-year follow-up (McGrady et al., 1982), those treated as inpatients evidenced more abstinence and a greater reduction in drinking than either outpatient or individually counseled patients, presumably reflecting the benefit of the greater spousal involvement under this treatment condition. A further study (McGrady et al., 1986) examined the impact of three levels of spousal involvement. In the first, spouses were merely present while the patient received individual cognitive training (acting as a control group). In the second, spouses received the same training, while the spouse was trained in behaviors aimed at reinforcing abstinence. A third group received both these interventions together with behavioral marital therapy. Some advantage to marital therapy was evident.

O'Farrell and colleagues (O'Farrell & Cutter, 1982; O'Farrell et al., 1985) followed up patients receiving marital interventions or individual counseling, finding that though initially there were greater gains for conjoint treatment, these had disappeared at 18-month follow-up.

Reviewing these and additional studies (a total of eight trials), Mattick and Jarvis (1993) conclude, on the basis of effect sizes, that while the impact of marital therapy on consumption is better than no treatment at all, there is little evidence for the long-term impact of marital or family therapies (contrasts of such therapies with control treatments at between 6 and 11 months of follow-up yielding an ES of 0.06). This conclusion contrasts with that of Miller and Hester (1986), who suggest some gains, at least in the short term, for this intervention. Discrepancies between these reviews are difficult to account for, and may reflect differing interpretations of a rather inconsistent literature.

Aversion Therapies

Aversion therapies attempt to countercondition alcohol consumption with an aversive stimulus. Apnea, chemical aversion (emetics), electrical aversion, or covert sensitization have been employed.

Apnea. Laverty (1966) and Vanderhoof and Campbell (1967) induced apnea with succinylcholine, showing some success and no impact, respectively, for this intervention. The combination of these contradictory results and the dangers of the technique make it difficult to recommend the use of this technique.

Chemical Aversion. A number of studies have examined the impact of pairing various emetics and alcohol in open trials (e.g., Smith & Fawley, 1990; Boland et al., 1978) or in RCTs (e.g., Cannon & Baker, 1981; Cannon et al., 1981). These indicate some short-term but no long-term efficacy for this intervention.

Electrical Aversion. Seven RCTs have employed electrical aversion (Mattick & Jarvis, 1993); although results are not consistent across trials, there appears to be only a short-term impact with this technique.

Overall, there is little support for techniques using chemical or electrical aversion. Its use in service settings is made even more difficult to recommend given that there is (unsurprisingly) a high rate of attrition from such therapies.

Covert Sensitization. This approach requires the imaginal pairing of drinking behavior with nausea-inducing scenes. Six RCTs have been conducted (Mattick & Jarvis, 1993); in five of these, covert sensitization is associated with lower drinking at 6 months compared to control groups. The average effect size for all studies is 0.85.

Though there is some evidential support for this approach, good outcomes rest on its successful implementation (Elkins, 1980; Elkins & Murdoch, 1977), and there is little evidence of its greater efficacy over alternative interventions (e.g., Fleiger & Zingle, 1973; Piorkowsky & Mann, 1975).

Social Skills Training and Relapse Prevention

Relapse prevention is focused on the identification and management of high-risk situations in which relapse may occur. As such it is often a component of social skills training programs. There are few studies of this approach alone. Allsop and Saunders (1989) contrasted relapse prevention, a discussion group, and a no-treatment control, finding a strong advantage for relapse prevention in the short term, though this was not maintained at 12-month follow-up.

Consistent gains have been demonstrated for the addition of social skills training to treatment programs. On the basis of 12 studies comparing social skills training to a range of alternative treatments (usually standard treatment and group discussion), Mattick and Jarvis (1993) calculate an effect size of 0.78 at 12-month follow-up.

The benefits of this intervention appear to be robust regardless of whether patients are screened for social skills deficits (Mattick & Jarvis, 1993), and particularly when the focus of this intervention lies in increasing assertiveness (e.g., Freedberg & Johnson, 1978; Chaney et al., 1978; Ferrell & Galassi, 1981).

Cognitive Restructuring in Combination with Social Skills Training

Oei and Jackson (1982) contrasted social skills training alone, social skills with the addition of cognitive restructuring (aimed at modifying beliefs that inhibited assertion), and a group discussion control condition. Both social skills interventions were more successful than control, but at 12 months those who had received additional cognitive restructuring showed the greatest gains. Oei and Jackson (1980) compared the delivery of a combined package of social skills and cognitive restructuring in individual and group formats, finding that alcohol consumption at 12 months was significantly lower for those treated in groups.

There appear to be few studies of cognitive restructuring alone. Brandsma et al. (1980) employed cognitive restructuring in the form of "rational behavior therapy," offered either through self-help manuals or with the aid of professionals. Contrasted to a no-treatment control group, there were significant reductions in the frequency and amount of alcohol consumption.

Stress Management

Relaxation training and systematic desensitization have both been evaluated in nine controlled trials; there is little evidence for the efficacy of either technique (Miller & Hester, 1986; Mattick & Jarvis, 1993).

Community Reinforcement Approaches

There is strong evidence for the efficacy of community support approaches, which combine a broad-spectrum of interventions in one package. Hunt and Azrin (1973) included problem solving, behavioral family therapy, social counseling and (for unemployed clients) job-finding training. This package was added to an inpatient program and contrasted with patients receiving the standard milieu therapy. At 6 months patients receiving the treatment package were drinking on 14% of days, contrasted with 79% in control patients. Broader gains in social adjustment were also evident. All marriages in the experimental group remained intact, contrasted with a 25% rate of separation or divorce in controls. In addition, there were 12 times the number of unemployed days in the control group than the experimental group.

Azrin (1976) added disulfiram, a behavioral program aimed at increasing disulfiram compliance, a "buddy" system, and daily self-monitoring of mood, again contrasting the addition of this program to inpatient treatment to treatment as usual. Again significant gains were obtained in the experimental group, which were maintained at 2-year follow-up.

Azrin et al. (1982) contrasted the full package from their 1976 trial with disulfiram alone (though combined with the behavioral-compliance program), both contrasted with routine outpatient treatment. Drinking in the outpatient group was almost double that in the disulfiram-alone group, but both treatments were significantly inferior to the community reinforcement package. Although Azrin et al. (1982) found that married clients benefited more from treatments than unmarried, this differential effect was not found by Miller et al. (1990; cited in Mattick & Jarvis, 1993).

Meta-analysis of six controlled studies (Mattick & Jarvis, 1993) gives an effect size of 0.87 at 6-month follow-up. While there appears to be good evidence for its short-term efficacy, effect sizes for this intervention diminish almost to zero at follow-up over 1 year, suggesting that long-term impact may be limited.

Length and Setting of Treatment

There is little evidence that longer treatments are more successful than briefer interventions, or that inpatient therapy shows greater efficacy than outpatient treatment. Miller and Hester (1986) review 12 controlled studies of contrasts between in- and outpatient treatment, none of which favored inpatient treatment, and some of which showed greater gains for outpatients. Similarly, five studies of the length of treatment showed no gain for longer treatment, and some advantage for shorter interventions. Contrasts of seven RCTs of in- and outpatient treatments by Miller and Jarvis (1993) yield an effect size close to zero, suggesting no advantage to inpatient regimens.

This picture is complicated by the likelihood of an interaction between inpatient treatment and the use of outpatient aftercare. Pittman and Tate (1972) found that success following inpatient treatment was correlated with subsequent use of outpatient services. Robson et al. (1965) and Smart and Gray (1978) both contrasted high users of outpatient services with patients who attended for only short periods, finding that high users tended to have lower rates of drinking problems. However, these results are based on naturalistic studies using post hoc analysis, and there is the possibility of a confound between motivation and attendance.

Brief Interventions

A large number of studies have examined the relative impacts of brief and more extensive treatment interventions; these have been reviewed by Bien et al. (1993) and by Mattick and Jarvis (1993). Mattick and

Jarvis distinguish among three groups of studies: those in which the patients are alcohol-dependent, those focused on "problem drinkers" (who have difficulties limiting their alcohol intake but who are not alcohol-dependent), and those who are excessive drinkers and not necessarily alcohol-dependent. This distinction is important in clarifying whether the response to intervention is similar or different across the full spectrum of dependency and abuse.

Three trials have been conducted that compare brief and extensive treatments for alcohol-dependent patients (Edwards et al., 1977; Chapman & Huygens, 1988; Chick et al., 1988). A pioneering trial in this area was that of Edwards et al. (1977), who contrasted one 3-hour session of advice with several months of in- or outpatient treatment in 100 married male alcoholics. No differences in outcome were found between these conditions at posttreatment. Although yielding an apparently clear-cut result, this study is open to criticism; subjects were not comorbid and were relatively well adjusted, and there was some blurring in treatment intensity (only one-third of patients randomized to the more intensively treated condition actually continued in treatment). Additionally, there is some evidence from 2-year follow-up data (Orford et al., 1976) that more severely dependent individuals benefited from more extensive interventions.

Chick et al. (1988) and Chapman and Huygens (1988) replicated the Edwards trial using essentially similar research designs. Though Chick et al. suggest some advantage to extended treatment, Chapman and Huygens found no differences in outcome between conditions. However, both studies are flawed by the fact that the minimal intervention condition was, for many patients, relatively extensive. In Chick et al.'s (1988) trial this was because additional treatment was offered to, and accepted by, many patients randomized to minimal intervention. Chapman and Huygen's (1988) study was conducted in the context of a 2-week inpatient detoxification program, and hence more accurately examines the adjunctive impacts of treatments to this program.

Hall and Heather (1991) examine contrasts of minimal and intensive interventions for problem drinkers (those who are not dependent on alcohol). Though many studies suggest that the two interventions are of equal efficacy, this is not a consistent finding. These authors conclude that differences between studies reflect variations in subject motivation, in that self-referred patients may have a better prognosis than those referred for treatment and hence do not respond differentially to additional therapist input.

Patients who are excessive drinkers may or may not run the risk of developing more serious dependency and associated health problems; consequently, this group is rarely targeted for active intervention. There is, however, evidence that those who drink heavily will continue to do so over long periods (Temple & Leino, 1989). Trials of minimal interventions (usually consisting of advice alone, or with the addition of self-monitoring) contrasted with no intervention (treatment as usual) support the proposition that brief interventions in primary care settings can lead to significant reductions in alcohol consumption (Kristenson et al., 1983; Chick et al., 1985; Heather et al., 1987; Wallace et al., 1988; Elvy et al., 1988).

Bien et al. (1993) identified 13 RCTs and 32 controlled studies of brief interventions, covering approximately 6,000 patients. These authors do not distinguish between the target drinking populations as clearly as Miller and Jarvis, with the result that there is some potential for a confound between outcomes and client characteristics (in particular, motivation and levels of dependency). Meta-analysis of 19 studies contrasting brief interventions against control (no or very minimal intervention) yields an effect size of 0.38. Contrasts of brief interventions against extended therapy (13 studies) give an effect size of 0.06, confirming the pattern of results discussed above.

Some caution in interpretation of these studies may be appropriate, in that patients offered brief treatment alone appear to seek further help with some frequency (Bien et al., 1993), and planned follow-up is an important part of many brief interventions (e.g., Elvy et al., 1988; Heather et al., 1987).

In addition, successful interventions appear to have characteristics in common with psychotherapeutic techniques. Consistent common elements in effective brief intervention identified by Miller and Sanchez (1993) are feedback of personal risk, emphasis on personal responsibility for change, clear advice to change, offering a range of options to achieve change, therapeutic empathy, enhancement of client self-efficacy, and optimism. This "package" of factors suggests that efficacy rests on more than the effects of simple advice. Miller and Sanchez (1993) monitored the interventions employed by counselors in a study of brief treatment, finding a close association between the number of confrontational responses from counselors and the amount being drunk by the client at 1-year follow-up.

In summary, there is good evidence that brief interventions will help a significant proportion of patients, though it is important to note that such an approach may not be suitable for all patients, and particularly not for those who are more disabled (Thom et al., 1994). Nonetheless, it may be appropriate for services to ensure that such a service is offered to clients, since there is evidence that allocating patients to a waiting list until therapists become available may result in significant levels of attrition. Leigh et al. (1984), Rees and Farmer (1985), and Thom et al.

(1992) have demonstrated an association between greater waiting time and a reduced probability of patients attending for their first appointment, reinforcing arguments for the utility of relatively rapid and brief interventions.

SUMMARY

- Alcohol dependency and abuse represent a major public health problem.
- People with alcohol dependency presenting in specialist clinics and mental health units are likely to manifest comorbidity with other common Axis I disorders—in particular, depression and anxiety.
- Overall, even the best treatments for alcohol have a relatively poor prognosis.
- The prognosis for patients with greater chronicity is less favorable in terms of both response to treatment and final outcome.
- Over the past two decades, with increasing recognition of the importance of social factors in the maintenance and relapse of alcohol abuse, treatments have shifted away from intensive residential therapy toward briefer interventions which directly address the social context of the drinker.
- The enhancement of social functioning is an appropriate treatment goal in the management of alcohol dependency.
- There is relatively good evidence supporting the value of social skills training, behavioral (but not nonbehavioral) marital therapy, community reinforcement packages, and treatments aimed at enhancing family stability and cohesion.
- There is equivocal evidence for the value of Antabuse and psychotropic medication, particularly from better-controlled studies.
- There is promising evidence for the value of the opiate-agonist naltraxone in combination with psychological treatments (supportive therapy and coping skills therapy), particularly for patients who have relapsed at least once during the course of the treatment program.
- Aversion therapy is associated with good short-term effects but with high dropout rates, and there are few demonstrations of its value in the long term.
- Psychodynamic psychotherapy, stress management, and cognitive therapy appear to be inadequate first-line treatments for individuals presenting with problems of alcohol dependency. It is possible that these therapies could be helpful to deal with residual

comorbid psychiatric disturbance after the alcohol dependence has been addressed.

- Social skills training appears to offer substantial benefit to individuals with dependency problems, particularly where programs focus on assertiveness skills associated with maintaining abstinence.
- Community-based treatments including social counseling, job-finding training, and conjoint behavioral therapy are of great potential value.
- Individuals with alcohol abuse (not necessarily including those with alcohol dependency) problems appear to benefit very substantially from brief intervention, including motivational interviewing that includes nonconfrontational advice on risk and change and an emphasis on personal responsibility.
- There is little justification for offering long-term treatment to most alcohol-dependent individuals.
- The intensity of treatment required appears to be correlated with severity and chronicity.
- Follow-up provision appears to be an important component of effective treatment, particularly for individuals who are motivated to use them.
- The extra cost of inpatient treatment is not justified by differential outcome.

IMPLICATIONS

- Alcohol dependency is a continuum, and treatment may be appropriately directed at both problem drinkers and patients abusing alcohol and those meeting diagnostic criteria for alcohol dependence.
- Where alcohol dependency is comorbid with anxiety and depression, the dependency needs to be addressed before treatment approaches to the other Axis I disorders are implemented.
- Two forms of treatment should be available as part of service provision for this group of disorders:
  - Social skills training and other associated treatments aimed at enhancing social and marital functioning
  - Brief interventions for targeted individuals whose problems are less chronic and more likely to be tractable to intervention
- This group of patients requires rapid treatment response, and long waiting lists are unacceptable.
- Further systematic investigations are needed to identify the specific therapeutic effects of naltrexone, and the value added by

psychological interventions of a specific nature (e.g., social skills training) or of a generic form (e.g., supportive therapy).

- There is good evidence to support a multimodal pragmatic treatment approach addressing a range of social problems faced by the individual, including unemployment, interpersonal, family, or employment difficulties. However, the costs of such broad-range interventions may be prohibitive for health services, and attempts should be made better to integrate social service and health service provision for this group of patients.

- Further research is required to help identify individuals requiring more intensive, long-term input. The presence of comorbidity may be an important indicator.

CHAPTER 13

Sexual Dysfunctions

DEFINITIONS

The essential feature of these disorders, as defined within DSM-IV, is an inhibition in the appetitive or psychophysiological changes that characterize the complete sexual cycle. Two points should be noted—the diagnosis can only be made if the problem is judged clinically significant and causes marked distress or interpersonal difficulty (this criterion was not applied in DSM-III-R). In addition the diagnosis is not made if the dysfunction can be attributed to organic factors or if it is due to another Axis I disorder. Four classes of disorder are distinguished: sexual desire disorders, sexual arousal disorders, orgasm disorders and sexual pain disorders.

Sexual Desire Disorders

Hypoactive sexual desire disorder: persistently or recurrently absent sexual fantasies and desire for sexual activity.
Sexual aversion disorder: persistent or recurrent aversion to, and avoidance of, all or almost all genital sexual contact with a sexual partner.

Sexual Arousal Disorders

Female sexual arousal disorder: persistent or recurrent partial or complete failure to maintain, until completion of the sexual activity, an adequate lubrication–swelling response of sexual excitement.
Male erectile disorder: persistent or recurrent partial or complete failure to maintain an erection until completion of the sexual activity.
Within DSM-IV these diagnoses can only be given where there is a difficulty with physiological arousal. Within DSM-III-R both female

234

arousal disorder and male erectile disorder could be diagnosed where there was a subjective complaint but physiological arousal was present.

Orgasmic Disorders[1]

Female orgasmic disorder: persistent or recurrent delay in achieving orgasm following a period of normal sexual excitement. DSM-IV notes that diagnosis will depend on a clinical judgment that the woman's orgasmic capacity is less than would be expected given her age, sexual experience, and the adequacy of sexual stimulation she receives.

Male orgasmic disorder: persistent or recurrent delay in, or absence of, orgasm following a phase of normal sexual excitement.

Premature ejaculation: persistent or recurrent ejaculation with minimal sexual stimulation, before or shortly after penetration and before the person wishes it.

Sexual Pain Disorders

Dyspareunia: recurrent or persistent pain in either a male or female during, before, or after intercourse, which is not caused by lack of lubrication or by vaginismus.

Vaginismus: recurrent or persistent involuntary spasm of the musculature of the outer third of the vagina that interferes with coitus.

Relevance of Subtypes of Dysfunction to Expected Outcome

All disorders are subclassified in terms of the onset of the dysfunction and the context in which it appears. Individuals who have always suffered from the disorder are distinguished from those where the dysfunction develops after a period of normal functioning (primary or lifelong versus secondary or acquired type). A second subtype differentiates between individuals in whom the disorder is present only in the presence of certain types of stimulation, situations, or partner as opposed to those in whom it is always present (situational versus generalized type).

It is probable that these subtypes reflect different degrees of associated psychopathology (Masters & Johnson, 1970; Kaplan, 1974). It fol-

---

[1] Within DSM-III-R, female and male orgasmic disorder were termed inhibited female and male orgasm disorders, respectively.

lows that expected outcomes for these patients are likely to vary in relation to the particular form of patient presentation.

Problems in Defining Sexual Dysfunctions

While DSM provides a clear framework for classifying sexual problems, decisions about the presence or absence of a dysfunction may at times reflect the values and standards of both clinicians and patients, which in turn are also likely to reflect shifting cultural opinions regarding sexual functioning. The definition and understanding of sexual dysfunctions is complex and at times controversial, especially where dysfunctions imply reference to a normative level of activity or interest.

In addition, the identification of sexual dysfunctions as a separate class of disorder within the DSM could lead to a misleading impression of homogeneity. Almost certainly, there are several etiological routes to each of the dysfunctions; reflecting this, sexual difficulties are often found as part of the clinical picture in both Axis I and Axis II disorders. While diagnosis of a sexual dysfunction is only made where this is considered to be the primary Axis I disorder, there remains the difficulty of ascertaining the role of comorbidity in varying outcomes, both within research and clinical practice.

PREVALENCE

There are few systematic or reliable data regarding the prevalence of sexual dysfunctions; those available show wide variability and probably reflect differences in assessment methods and sampling procedures. Despite this, studies are consistent in suggesting that dysfunctions are relatively common. Spector and Carey (1990) review 23 studies of incidence and prevalence in community samples, suggesting a current prevalence of 4–9% for male erectile disorder, 4–10% for inhibited male orgasm, 36–38% for premature ejaculation, and 5–10% for inhibited female orgasm. Hawton (1985) derives similar figures from community samples and from surveys conducted among patients attending medical clinics. Osborn et al. (1988) present data from a community survey of 436 women aged between 35–39; almost one-third of the sample reported a sexual dysfunction; low sexual desire was reported by 17%, infrequency of orgasm by 16%, and dyspareunia by 8%.

COMORBIDITY AND ASSOCIATED DIFFICULTIES

Sexual problems do not arise in isolation from other psychological difficulties, nor are their effects limited to the sexual arena. However, where comorbidity is present, distinguishing cause from effect can be difficult. Thus while there is evidence that sexual dysfunctions do not necessarily lead to relationship problems, it appears to be the case that sexual difficulties are associated with higher rates of marital separation (Hawton, 1985). There is also evidence to suggest that many individuals with sexual dysfunction are likely to experience distress, reduced self-esteem, and symptoms of anxiety and depression; although studies are not always consistent, a relatively high proportion of patients exhibit psychiatric symptoms and suffer from psychiatric disorders (Hawton, 1985). In some cases psychiatric problems are reactive to sexual problems; in others sexual problems reflect coexisting psychopathology. While distinguishing these patterns may not always be easy, it is obvious that the choice of treatment strategies will be influenced by judgments regarding the relative primacy of the presenting problems.

TREATMENT APPROACHES

The treatment of sexual dysfunctions was revolutionized by the publication of *Human Sexual Inadequacy* (Masters & Johnson, 1970). In an earlier book they described the physiology of normal sexual response (Masters & Johnson, 1966); linked to these studies they developed and described a repertoire of essentially behavioral treatment strategies which are central to most approaches to sex therapy. These methods include information and education about sex, encouraging communication between partners, and using specific techniques such as sensate focus exercises. Patients treated by Masters and Johnson were treated intensively, receiving daily sessions over a 2-week period. Usually patients were seen with their partners by a dual-sex male-and-female therapy team.

Currently there is more variability in the practice of sex therapy. It would be rare for patients to be seen as intensively as Masters and Johnson—weekly sessions being more normative. In addition, resource constraints, perhaps more than research evidence (discussed below), make it more likely that couples will be seen by a single therapist. Finally, sex therapists frequently make explicit use of a variety of alternative behavioral techniques (such as systematic desensitization), and many have adopted an explicitly integrationist approach. Where considered relevant to the presenting problem, therapists may explore conscious and unconscious thoughts and feelings about sex and engage in marital/relationship therapy (e.g., Hartman & Fithian, 1972; Kaplan, 1974).

This deliberate mixing of method introduces uncertainty into studies of therapeutic outcome, since it is not always easy to identify the form of therapy implemented. While this reflects clinical reality, it is important to note that the few studies that "dismantle" the various components of therapy or contrast standard sex therapy with alternative techniques (reviewed below) suggest that some sex therapy approaches may be less specific in their impact than has been supposed.

Limitations of the Research Literature on Treatments for Sexual Dysfunctions

There is only a small outcome literature relevant to the treatment of sexual dysfunctions. Most studies are relatively small-scale, few contrast treatment approaches, and where they do, small sample sizes invariably result in studies of very low statistical power (Bancroft et al., 1986).

Larger studies are usually open trials reporting results from sexual dysfunction clinics. As noted in Chapter 1, in theory very large open trials could overcome the major problems associated with this design—principally that the patient sample is representative only of those patients treated. Unfortunately, available larger-scale reports tend to be problematic, either because outcome data are based on rather crude assessments (e.g., Bancroft & Coles, 1976; Warner et al., 1987) or because their patient samples are demonstrably unrepresentative of the usual clinical population (e.g., Masters & Johnson, 1970).

Even where trials are based on usual clinical populations, differential attrition both before and during therapy appears particularly high during sex therapy. Some of this can be attributed to the fact that not all patients presenting with sexual dysfunctions will be appropriately treated using sex therapy; treatment of a dysfunction is unlikely to succeed where it is secondary to other mental health problems or reflects general relationship difficulties (Hawton, in press). Catalan et al. (1990) report on the fate of 200 consecutive referrals to a sex therapy clinic. Only 55% of this sample were considered suitable for therapy, of whom 30% did not enter treatment. Yet more bias is introduced by the high rates of attrition from sex therapy commonly reported in specialist centers (e.g., Bancroft & Coles, 1976; Warner et al., 1987), a problem compounded by the fact that very few studies cite outcomes for "intent-to-treat" samples.

Three further comments are usefully made. First, some studies classify patients simply on the basis of whether a sexual dysfunction is present and do not present data for individual dysfunctions. Such trials can contribute little to discussion of outcomes, since research discussed below makes it clear that specific dysfunctions are differentially responsive to treatment. Second, not all dysfunctions are equally well researched—the bulk of studies focus on erectile dysfunction. Finally, readers will note that much of the evidence in this chapter is based on studies performed in the 1970s and 1980s, reflecting an apparent decline in research and innovation in this area (Schover & Leiblum, 1994).

Results from Masters and Johnson (1970)

Masters and Johnson (1970) provided information on outcome for patients seen at their research center. Because these data were based on a large sample and appeared to indicate very high rates of improvement for almost all dysfunctions, their work was influential in popularizing sex therapy both with professionals and, particularly in the United States, with the public.

More recent trials of sex therapy tend to report less impressive results, at least for some dysfunctions. The manner in which Masters and Johnson's treatment programs were implemented may go some way to explaining this difference. The therapy programs, as originally devised, were offered on a daily basis over 2 weeks. Since only 10% of the patients lived locally to the research unit, most patients were required to spend this time living in local hotels—to some extent ensuring that only patients committed to the program actually entered into treatment. Though in the early part of the research program treatment was offered free, most patients were middle-class, an unusually high proportion had received higher education (73%), and nearly 20% were physicians or mental health professionals. Taken together, this combination of characteristics undoubtedly favors better outcomes, in part through demographic factors and also because the effort made to physically attend the unit in itself acts as an inclusion factor for patients of higher motivation.

Approximately 800 individuals were assessed over the 11 years of the research program, almost all were seen with their partners. Information about outcomes was collected immediately after treatment and at 5-year follow-up. However, there are a number of problems of analysis and presentation. Masters and Johnson chose to provide details of treatment failure, rather than treatment success, on the grounds that this produces data less prone to subjective bias—the suggestion being that failure is easier to discern unequivocally. Unfortunately this argument is less than persuasive, particularly since no details of assessment procedures are given, without which there are no obvious criteria for defining success or failure. The potential for bias in reporting of results is clear. For example, if only those patients showing a complete absence of improvement were classified as failures, this would inflate the apparent success rate; patients showing a partial response to treatment would have been classified as successes. In summary, significant problems of sample bias and problematic reporting of data necessitate caution in generalizing Masters and Johnson's figures.

Data for outcome are presented at two points—immediately after the 2-week treatment, period and at 5-year follow-up. This is reproduced using DSM categories rather than Masters and Johnson's terminology (see Table 1).

Data for inhibited female orgasm (Table 2) are separately coded by Masters and Johnson, distinguishing women who are orgasmic only during masturbation, those who are anorgasmic during coitus, and a third category described as "random orgasmic inadequacy," which refers to women who are orgasmic but only rarely and who "usually are aware of little or no physical need for sexual expression" (Masters & Johnson, 1970, p. 240). It should be noted that within the DSM these women would probably be seen as suffering from sexual arousal disorder.

Taken as a whole, these data suggest a very high rate of immediate symptom relief for both male and female sexual dysfunctions, together with a low rate of relapse at follow-up. Indeed, for conditions such as premature ejaculation there is almost complete reported success. On publication these figures generated considerable optimism about results likely to be obtained in routine clinical practice. However, results from more recent studies often suggest poorer outcomes, perhaps lending weight to the caution expressed above both about the representativeness of Masters and Johnson's patient samples and their reporting methods.

TABLE 1. Outcome Data following Treatment for Sexual Dysfunctions (Masters & Johnson, 1970)

Complaint	n	Immediate failure (n)	Immediate failure rate (%)	Relapse (n)	Overall failure rate (%)
Primary erectile disorder	32	13	40.6	0	40.6
Secondary erectile disorder	213	56	26.2	10	30.9
Premature ejaculation	186	4	2.2	1	2.7
Inhibited male orgasm	17	3	17.6	0	17.6
Primary inhibited female orgasm	193	32	16.6	2	17.6
Secondary inhibited female orgasm	149	34	22.8	3	24.8
Vaginismus	193	32	16.6	[a]	[a]

[a] Masters and Johnson do not report follow-up data for vaginismus.

TABLE 2. Outcome Data following Treatment for Inhibited Female Orgasm (Masters & Johnson, 1970)

Complaint	n	Failure (n)	Failure rate (%)
Orgasmic only when masturbating	11	1	9.1
Anorgasmic during coitus	106	21	19.8
"Random orgasmic inadequacy"	32	12	37.5

Male Erectile Disorder

This disorder is the most frequent problem in men presenting to sexual dysfunction clinics (Warner et al., 1987; Bhugra & Cordle, 1988; Catalan et al., 1990). Though relatively prevalent, it is important to note that spontaneous remission will be observed in between 14% and 30% of men with psychogenic impotence (Segraves et al., 1982).

A primary and controversial issue is the relative role of physiological or psychological factors in the development of this dysfunction. Though Masters and Johnson (1970) asserted that 95% of erectile failure was psychogenic in origin, more recent studies suggest that approximately 50% of patients presenting with erectile failure have some vascular, neurological, or hormonal involvement. Melman et al. (1988) found that of 406 cases of erectile dysfunction, approximately 30% were purely organic in origin, 40% psychogenic, and 25% combined organic and psychogenic.

Most usually the presence of nocturnal erections is used to differentiate between organic and psychological causes for this dysfunction. Though not always a reliable indicator (Mohr & Beutler, 1990), it appears to be as effective as the complex and expensive investigations sometimes employed to make this distinction (Segraves et al., 1987). However, while etiology is clearly important to treatment planning, it may be a less helpful distinction than at first appears; organic and psychogenic factors may be present to varying degrees and interact with each other to produce the dysfunction. For this reason LoPiccolo and Stock (1986) have suggested that the relationship between these elements is best conceptualized as orthogonal rather than unidimensional.

A number of physical intervention methods have been developed for the treatment of erectile dysfunction. These include penile implants, revascularization for patients with vasculogenic erectile dysfunction, the administration of exogenous testosterone, the use of intracavernosal papaverine injections, and the use of vacuum constriction devices (Gregoire, 1992). Full discussion of the efficacy of these treatments is beyond the scope of this review, though the short-term efficacy of many of these interventions appears to be good (Mohr & Beutler, 1990). However, there are indications that the rate of attrition from somatic therapies—particularly from autoinjection—can be very high. Althof et al. (1991), in a 1-year study of 42 self-injectors, found a dropout rate of 57%, often associated with physical complications. In addition there is evidence that patients with psychogenic erectile dysfunction will respond poorly to such interventions (Hartmann & Langer, 1993).

The major factors considered to underlie psychogenic impotence are performance anxiety or performance demands, distraction, misinformation or inhibition about sex, and relationship problems such as poor communication or hostility (Kinder & Curtiss, 1988). Given this range of issues, it is unsurprising that most psychological treatments are multimodal and employ anxiety reduction techniques in tandem with a focus on communication or relationship issues. These intervention formats are the most frequently studied and have been comprehensively reviewed by Mohr and Beutler (1990). On the basis of 23 studies, they suggest that "approximately two-thirds of men suffering from erectile failure will be satisfied with their improvement at follow-up ranging from 6 weeks to 6 years" (p. 134). These figures are comparable to those obtained by Masters and Johnson (1970). Trials of reasonable sample size and rigor report similar proportions of improved cases both immediately posttherapy and at long-term follow-up (e.g., Hawton et al., 1986, 1992; De Amicis et al., 1985). However, there are exceptions to this picture; Heiman and LoPiccolo (1983) report only modest decreases in the frequency of erectile problems, though their data analysis makes it difficult to ascertain the proportion of men in whom improvement was seen.

Though this conclusion appears broadly favorable, it is not clear what components of the therapy are effective. There are only a small number of studies that focus on deconstructing techniques or contrasting different approaches to treatment. Of these, statistical power is almost invariably low, either because of small total sample sizes or small numbers of patients within treatment cells. As a result their conclusions, while of interest, are in no sense definitive.

A number of studies have contrasted systematic desensitization (either imaginal or *in vivo*) with the sensate focus techniques employed by Masters and Johnson. Everaerd and Dekker (1985) compared these approaches in 24 couples, finding an equivalent improvement in sexual functioning. Mathews et al. (1976) contrasted the relative efficacy of systematic imaginal desensitization and an intervention based on Master and Johnson's method. After assessment both these procedures involved weekly therapeutic contact. To gauge the impact of this aspect of treatment, a third condition offered assessment followed by postal instruction in Masters and Johnson's method. Thirty-six couples with mixed sexual dysfunctions participated in the study; of these the majority of men (13 of 18) had a presenting complaint of erectile dysfunction. At 4-month follow-up there were no significant differences between treatment methods, each showing some benefit. However, the low statistical power of this study makes it important to note a trend in which Masters and Johnson's technique, conducted in conjunction with therapist contact, showed the greatest efficacy. Unfortunately there was no matched assignment of couples to treatment groups on the basis of dysfunctions, nor were dysfunctions distinguished in the data analysis. Consequently it is not possible to be certain whether or not results for erectile dysfunctions followed this overall pattern. A further drawback of this study is the use of imaginal rather than *in vivo* desensitization, a weaker form of intervention. Since *in vivo* desensitization could be seen as approximating to the sensate focus techniques employed by Masters and Johnson, there would be more value in a direct contrast of these techniques.

Cognitive approaches to treatment—almost exclusively rational–emotive therapy (RET)—have also been contrasted to sensate focus. Everaerd and Dekker (1985) examined the relative impact of these techniques in 32 couples. While the two methods produced equivalent improvements in sexual functioning, there was a very high rate of attrition from RET, which makes interpretation of this study more difficult. Munjack et al. (1984) assigned 16 men either to 6 weeks of biweekly RET or to a 6-week waiting-list control group. Though immediately after therapy, treated patients demonstrated some gains relative to controls, at nine months they reported only 25% of attempts at intercourse to have been successful. Contrasted to the overall improvement rates derived by Mohr and Beutler (1990), this is a poor result.

A number of authors (e.g., Mohr & Beutler, 1990; Reynolds et al., 1981; Stravynski, 1986) have suggested that social skills or communication skills training may be helpful in treating erectile dysfunction, on the basis that social and sexual anxiety are likely to be linked. Kilmann et al. (1987) assigned 20 couples to three treatment groups—communication training, sexual technique training, or a combination of the two. In addition there were two control groups—attention-placebo or no treatment. The three treatments produced equivalent gains, though the small sample sizes make it unlikely that any differences would have been detectable. Using post hoc analyses, Hawton and Catalan (1986) found that good long-term outcome was associated with better communication between couples, marked by an ability to discuss difficulties as they arose and to implement appropriate strategies for managing them. However, while suggesting the possible utility of communication training, this result may reflect as much preexisting characteristics of the couples as any benefits from therapy (Hawton et al., 1992).

Treatment of Men without Partners

In the studies reviewed above treatment strategies are largely predicated on the availability and cooperation of the patient's partner. However, some patients will present for treatment by themselves. Some may be temporarily single because their sexual dysfunction has inhibited the development of relationships, or their partners may be unwilling to undergo therapy. Others may have more fundamental difficulties, and there are suggestions that individuals presenting in this way may display significant comorbidity with other mental health problems (Cole, 1986).

A number of treatment strategies have been developed to overcome this problem. Masters and Johnson (1970) employed surrogate partners, and reported satisfactory results, as have other workers (e.g., Apfelbaum, 1984; Dauw, 1988). However, the use of surrogate partners remains controversial and (except in specialized settings) difficult to arrange. Other workers have used structured men's group treatment comprising sex education, group discussion, and homework exercises, usually with a focus on social skills training. Reviewing six studies of such groups, Reynolds (1991) reports improvement rates in open trials varying between 40% and 70%. Price et al. (1981) included a waiting-list control, finding a nonsignificant trend toward greater gains in the treatment group. Across studies there are indications of relatively high relapse rates. Auerbach and Kilmann (1977) contrasted systematic desensitization offered in combination with relaxation with relaxation alone. Sixteen men were treated over 15 sessions, with an improvement rate of 40% for those receiving systematic desensitization, as contrasted to 3% for those receiving only relaxation.

Reynolds (1991) reports three further studies in which patients were treated on an individual basis. In two trials (Csillag, 1976; Reynolds, 1982) biofeedback was employed. Poor results were obtained, perhaps predictably given that this technique is likely to focus attention on performance, and hence to increase performance anxiety. In a third trial Kuruvilla (1984) treated 13 men using sex education, guided imagery, and directed masturbation. At 2-year follow-up, 7 of 11 men (64%) reported continued improvement.

As noted above, men who have never had sexual partners may have comorbid interpersonal problems. Where studies provide separate analyses for men with and without partners, the relevance of this factor to outcome is clear. Everaerd et al. (1982) treated 21 men with erectile or ejaculatory problems in groups, using a mix of RET, sensate focus exercises, masturbation exercises, and social skills training. Thirteen of the 21 men remained dysfunctional; improvements tended to be found only in men who already had partners prior to treatment (Dekker et al., 1985). For partnerless men, social dysfunction may be a more primary problem than sexual difficulties and may account for the rather poor outcomes in most studies (Stravynski & Greenberg, 1990).

Relapse

Relapse rates following treatment appear to be quite high (Mohr & Beutler, 1990), though outcome in erectile dysfunction is better than that for most other forms of sexual difficulty (Hawton & Catalan, 1986). These authors report a naturalistic study of outcomes in a sex therapy clinic, and contrasted rates of improvement in 18 (of an original 31) couples treated using a modified Masters and Johnson procedure and for whom follow-up data at between 1 and 6 years were available. Immediately after treatment 14 of 18 couples (78%) reported the problem wholly or partially resolved. At follow-up, 11 of 18 couples (61%) reported this level of outcome. These figures are similar to those reported by De Amicis et al. (1985), who reported ratings of "improved" functioning in 12 of 18 men posttherapy (66%) and 10 of 17 men (59%) at 3-year follow-up.

Premature Ejaculation

Pharmacological treatments for premature ejaculation are based on two classes of drug—alpha-adrenergic blockers, and medications that increase levels of serotonin, such as clomipramine and paroxetine. While data from a small number of open trials suggest that administration of clomipramine is associated with improved ejaculatory latencies (Grenier & Byers, 1995), there are few controlled trials of these medications. In an exception to this picture, Waldinger et al. (1994) report a small trial in which patients were assigned to either paroxetine or placebo. Those receiving paroxetine showed significant increases in ejaculatory latency over the 6 weeks of the trial. Reviewing this issue, Grenier and Byers (1995) recommend caution in the use of these medications, partly because of the paucity of controlled trials and the absence of long-term follow-up studies, and also because they may interfere with other aspects of sexual functioning.

Very high success rates—between 90 and 98%—have been reported for this dysfunction (e.g., Masters & Johnson, 1970; Yulis, 1976; Kilmann & Auerbach, 1979), and some reviewers consider treatment using the squeeze technique to be highly effective (e.g., LoPiccolo & Stock, 1986). Recent review of this literature (St Lawrence & Madakasira, 1992) suggests a clustering in initial improvement rates between 43 and 65%, with a range of 43 to 100%. However, this conclusion is based on a limited range of studies (Shapiro, 1943; Cooper, 1969; Meyer et al., 1983; Watson & Brockman, 1982), some of which antedate current sex therapy techniques.

Even if the evidence of posttherapy gains were to be taken at face value, there is some suggestion that gains are poorly maintained. Three studies contain data relevant to this issue. In a trial with 21 men, Heiman and LoPiccolo (1983) report significant average increases in the duration of intercourse immediately after therapy (from 1–2 minutes to 5–8 minutes), with some loss of gains at 3 months (with duration of intercourse reducing to 3–6 minutes). Longer-term follow-up suggests poorer results. In De Amicis et al.'s (1985) study, 15 of 20 men reported their dysfunction to have improved immediately following therapy, with a significant increase in mean duration of both intercourse and foreplay. However, this declined by 3 months, and at 3 years had returned to pretherapy levels. Similarly, Hawton et al. (1986) found that at 1- to 6-year follow-up, only two of eight men reported some degree of problem resolution, the remainder reporting the problem to be unresolved or worse.

Inhibited Female Orgasm

Heiman and LoPiccolo (1983) treated women with primary and secondary orgasmic dysfunction (n = 25 and 16, respectively). Posttherapy, women with primary dysfunction showed a significant increase in orgasm during masturbation (from an average rate of 0 to 60%), during manual stimulation (from 0 to 40%), and during coitus (from 0 to 25%), with good maintenance of gains at 3-month follow-up. Women with secondary dysfunction showed little gain in orgasmic frequency during masturbation or manual stimulation, and only a moderate (nonsignificant) increase in the average rate of coital orgasm (from 12 to 30% posttherapy).

De Amicis et al. (1985) followed up 22 women with a mix of primary, secondary, and situational orgasmic dysfunction over 3 years, all treated using procedures described by Masters and Johnson (1970). Across all subtypes, there were posttherapy gains in sexual satisfaction, though there was less evidence of behavioral change. Women with primary dysfunctions showed an increase in orgasmic frequency during masturbation and "genital caress." This improvement was not evident for women with situational dysfunction, and across subtypes there was no improvement in orgasmic functioning during coitus.

Similar results are reported by Libman et al. (1984), who treated 23 couples whose main complaint was secondary orgasmic dysfunction, using either "standard" couple therapy (as described by Masters & Johnson, 1970), group therapy (in which women were treated in groups on a weekly basis, and their partners once a month), or minimal-contact bibliotherapy. A wide variety of measures of sexual functioning were employed, and where there were differences between treatment conditions, these favored the standard treatment over other treatment options. However, though gains in orgasmic frequency were statistically significant, their clinical significance is less clear. Posttherapy women were more likely to achieve orgasm during masturbation (77% were orgasmic at follow-up, contrasted with 55% at intake), though a significant proportion remained anorgasmic in interpersonal contexts. Thus at 3-month follow-up, and dependent on the type of sexual activity engaged in, only between 6 and 27% of women were orgasmic. Further analysis of data from this study (Fichten et al., 1986) suggests that though enjoyment and satisfaction did increase as a consequence of treatment, there was little behavioral change. In addition, daily recording of sexual activity suggested even poorer therapeutic response than when patients were asked to make retrospective judgments of their sexual responsiveness.

Kilmann et al. (1986) report outcomes in 55 couples for whom secondary orgasmic dysfunction was the presenting complaint. Patients were assigned to four treatment groups—communication training, sexual technique training, or two variants of the combination of the two (communication training followed by sexual technique training, or vice versa). In addition there were two control groups—attention-placebo or no-treatment. There was no evidence that treatment formats exerted differential effects. Overall, contrasts between couples receiving therapy and those in control conditions suggest some moderate gains. Improvement was defined in terms of reaching orgasm during coitus more than 50% of the time. Pretherapy no women met this criterion. Posttherapy it was achieved by 9 of 35 of the treated women (26%), with a slight increase in this rate at 6-month follow-up (11 out of 30; 37%). In contrast, no patient from the control groups ($n = 20$) met this criterion at posttherapy, and only 1 of 10 did at follow-up. Longer-term follow-up of these patients at between 2 and 6 years (Milan et al., 1988) suggests that coital orgasmic frequency was reasonably stable over follow-up, though there was a decline in the frequency of intercourse. However, approximately one-quarter of the sample sought additional help during this time. Overall it appears that greater gains can be expected for orgasm during masturbation and manual stimulation—particularly for women with primary dysfunction—than is the case for orgasm during coitus, where most studies suggest only moderate improvements.

Vaginismus

Results from two surveys of outcomes in a sexual dysfunctions clinic are reported by Bancroft and Coles (1976) and Warner et al. (1987); the reliability of ratings of outcome in both are limited by reliance on therapist-based ratings of outcome. Bancroft and Coles (1976) report a successful outcome in six of eight women treated for vaginismus. Of 52 women treated by Warner et al. (1987), 52% had a "good" outcome, and 65% a moderate or better response to treatment.

Hawton and Catalan (1990) examined treatment outcomes in 30 couples; patients were consecutively referred to a sexual dysfunction clinic and were selected on the basis that the main sexual problem was vaginismus. The mean duration of the problem was 5 years. Therapy was based on Masters and Johnson's (1970) procedures and was conducted over an average of 18 sessions. Immediately after treatment 43% of patients reported the problem resolved, with a further 37% reporting it largely resolved. At 3-month follow-up more gains were evident, with 61% of patients reporting the problem resolved and a further 26% that it was largely resolved.

Similar results were obtained in an earlier trial by the same authors (Hawton et al., 1986). Twenty women with vaginismus were followed-up at 1–6 years. Posttherapy 10 women reported that the problem was resolved, and a further seven that it was largely resolved. At follow-up 11 women reported the problem resolved, and seven reported that it was largely resolved, suggesting some stability in therapeutic gain.

Outcomes for women with vaginismus appear to be better than for other sexual dysfunctions. This may relate to patient characteristics. Hawton and Catalan (1990) contrasted patients referred with vaginismus with women referred for other sexual dysfunctions. Though patients with vaginismus tended to be younger and less sexually experienced, they also appeared to be more motivated and more interested in sex, to display less sexual aversion, and to enjoy greater sexual arousal and pleasure from sexual activity prior to treatment.

Sexual Desire Disorders

In the largest survey of outcomes for desire-phase disorders, Schover and Lo Piccolo (1982) retrospectively reanalyzed data from 152 couples who had attended their clinic between 1974 and 1981. However, nearly all these couples had been diagnosed using systems that antedated the recognition of desire disorders. A post hoc classification system was employed to identify such cases on the basis of questionnaire data from the couples' intake interviews, raising some questions about the reliability of diagnoses.

The sample included 58 men and 67 women with a diagnosis of inhibited sexual desire, and 27 women with an "aversion to sex." Treatments were broadly based, with "the usual sex therapy format" supplemented by behavioral, cognitive-behavioral, psychodynamic, and Gestalt techniques. Results for women with an aversion to sex were poor. For patients with inhibited sexual desire there was a modest improvement in ratings of sexual satisfaction and a significant gain in the frequency of intercourse (from a mean of approximately once every 2–4 weeks to once to twice a week). This declined significantly over 3-month follow-up, to around once every 1 to 2 weeks. However, while men appeared to maintain this increase, the pattern for women was of an improvement followed by a decline. Relatedly, though there was an initial increase in the frequency with which the partner with low desire would initiate sex, this declined at follow-up, a trend again more clearly seen in women than men. These data suggest that overall treatment outcomes are modest, with men responding more to treatment than women.

Hawton et al. (1986) report data for 32 couples where the female partner's presenting problem was one of "impaired sexual interest." Though posttherapy 68% of patients reported that the problem was fully or partially resolved, at 1- to 6-year follow-up this proportion had dropped to 34%.

De Amicis et al. (1985) present data on a sample of six men and three women with desire dysfunction. Both posttherapy and at 3-year follow-up there was little improvement in sexual functioning, with some suggestion that the frequency of intercourse decreased over the period of follow-up.

Whitehead et al. (1987) contrasted two treatment approaches for women presenting with a lack of sexual interest or enjoyment. In the first, women were treated with their partners. This conventional treatment, based on Masters and Johnson's (1970) procedures, was contrasted with a "woman-focused" treatment consisting of a graded series of educative elements and exercises designed to encourage sexual self-exploration. Both treatments resulted in a significant posttherapy improvement on measures of the quality of the sexual relationship. Though follow-up data appear to indicate good maintenance of gains, there is some evidence that couples who did worse tended not to return for evaluation.

Marital Therapy and Sex Therapy

Empirical studies suggest a link between marital and sexual difficulties (e.g., Frank & Kupfer, 1976; Schenk et al., 1983), and there are indications that couples showing higher levels of marital adjustment tend to have better clinical outcomes (Leiblum et al., 1976; Abramowitz & Sewell, 1980). However, it is not clear whether this implies that marital therapy is indicated prior to sex therapy for couples with significant relationship problems.

In an attempt to examine whether marital therapy enhanced the impact of sex therapy, Hartman and Daly (1983) carried out a small trial of 12 couples with mixed sexual dysfunctions. Half the couples received standard sex therapy followed by behavioral marital therapy; for the other couples the order of therapies was reversed. Therapy was conducted in small groups, with each form of therapy being offered for 5 weeks. Examining outcomes at the point at which the form of therapy switched suggests that sex therapy had a greater impact on both sexual and marital satisfaction than did marital therapy, though this effect was not significant at the end of therapy. While results from this study broadly suggest that sexual problems can be managed without prior marital therapy, there was some suggestion that couples with major relationship problems did appear to benefit from receiving marital therapy before sex therapy.

Considerable caution is warranted in drawing conclusions from this study; the patient sample is very small, diagnostically heterogeneous, and uncontrolled for levels of marital distress within each condition. A larger-scale examination of these issues was conducted by Zimmer (1987), who selected couples in which the female partner suffered from secondary sexual dysfunction; while a more homogeneous group than Hartman and Daly's, the range of dysfunctions was again fairly diverse, including disorders of sexual desire, sexual arousal, and inhibited orgasm. In the majority of clients, at least one partner had considered separation.

Couples either were placed on a waiting-list ($n = 9$) or received either marital therapy followed by sex therapy ($n = 10$) or a "placebo" treatment (containing relaxation and general discussion of the couple's personal histories) followed by sex therapy ($n = 9$). Contrasted to couples on the waiting list, patients receiving both active treatments showed comparable overall gains. However, on some measures there was evidence of greater and more enduring gains for the couples who received the combination of marital and sex therapy. In addition, marital therapy appeared to have conferred some benefit on sexual satisfaction, whereas sex therapy did not improve marital satisfaction. Overall, the best results were obtained with those couples showing the best marital adjustment.

In this regard it is noteworthy that 16 couples allocated to treatment failed to complete therapy, nearly all because the couples separated.

Apparent discrepancies between these two studies may reflect differences in their samples, since the degree of marital distress in Hartman and Daly's (1983) patients is not clear. Taken together, they provide some support for the clinical contention that marital therapy may be a useful and prior adjunctive treatment for couples presenting with sexual difficulties in the context of acute marital distress. However, this conclusion is weakened by the fact that the most severely maritally distressed couples tended to drop out from Zimmer's study, suggesting that such couples may be particularly hard to help.

Treatment Format

In developing sex therapy, Masters and Johnson employed dual-sex cotherapy teams, working usually, though not exclusively, with couples, and offering treatment daily. Available evidence suggests that more flexible formats are equally effective. Dual-therapist work has obvious resource implications; where studies have explored this issue they suggest that outcome is equivalent whether dual-sex cotherapy teams or single therapists are used (Clement & Schmidt, 1983; Crowe et al., 1981; LoPiccolo et al., 1985). Though the gender of the therapist relative to the patient does not appear to influence outcome (Crowe et al., 1981; LoPiccolo et al., 1985), patient preference is likely to be important in clinical practice. Daily treatment does not appear to confer greater gains than delivering therapy either weekly (Heiman & LoPiccolo, 1983) or biweekly (Clement & Schmidt, 1983).

Beyond examining the structure of therapy, few studies deconstruct Masters and Johnson's techniques. In an exception to this rule, Takefman and Brender (1984) found that the ban on intercourse almost universally imposed at the start of treatment may not be as essential a component of therapy as is usually supposed. In their study, 16 couples in which the male partner presented with erectile dysfunction were assigned to two conditions. Though all patients were asked to focus on communication of sexual likes and dislikes during sexual activity, only in one condition were they asked to refrain from sexual intercourse. Equivalent outcomes were observed with and without the ban. The small sample size renders only tentative the implication that communication is a mutative factor in successful therapies.

SUMMARY

- Sexual dysfunctions are common and represent a serious mental health problem, particularly where they complicate preexisting disorders or lead to the development of psychological disorders, either directly or indirectly through, for example, relationship difficulties.

- Perhaps more explicitly than is the case with psychological approaches to many other disorders, therapeutic approaches to sexual dysfunction often utilize a wide range of treatment procedures and can often be seen as multimodal therapies.
- Reflecting this therapeutic eclecticism, some research reports are not always clear about the form of therapy administered. This leaves open the possibility that variations in the effectiveness of treatment reflect differing combinations of procedures and emphases on technique.
- Findings from studies are rendered ambiguous because focusing on patient's sexual problems without comprehensive descriptions of their psychological functioning and comorbid status can make it difficult to interpret outcomes.
- There have been few large-scale controlled trials on the treatment of sexual disorders. Larger studies are often based on heterogeneous diagnoses of dysfunctions, and are most usually open trials.
- The outcomes for treatments of sexual dysfunction are highly variable, both across different classes and subtypes of dysfunction, and within disorders, presumably because of unmeasured aspects of comorbidity.
- The outcomes from uncontrolled studies should be viewed with caution in the light of relatively high rates of spontaneous remission for erectile dysfunction, and the known situational specificity of other disorders.
- The proportion of *male erectile disorders* with underlying organic pathology has been underestimated by earlier researchers and is likely to characterize approximately half of any unscreened clinical sample.
- Physical treatments are available and relatively effective, but autoinjection in particular is characterized by limited acceptability and high dropout rates.
- A substantial proportion of patients are likely to show a mix of organic and psychological pathology. While it is likely that psychological treatments may have some role in such patients, there is no direct evidence regarding this.
- There is evidence that patients with primarily psychological problems respond poorly to physical treatments.
- Treatment approaches aimed at reducing sexual anxiety and improving communication and the quality of relationships appear to be successful in approximately 60% of cases. In addition there

are suggestions that cognitive approaches and social/communication skills training may be helpful for some patients. Although there is little direct evidence, such approaches may be useful for patients deficient in these skills.

- The few trials that include longer-term follow-up suggest that gains are maintained.
- Most of these success rates are only applicable to men who are already in relationships. Treatments for men without partners appear to be most successful for those who are temporarily outside a relationship rather those who have never had one.
- Problems of *premature ejaculation* in men have been treated using specifically designed behavioral techniques.
- Reported success rates tends to vary considerably across studies; overall, around half the patients tend to improve. However, available data suggest that these gains tend not to be maintained on follow-up.
- Interventions for *inhibited female orgasm* tend to be principally psychoeducational. Findings suggest that women can be taught to achieve orgasm during masturbation, but this does not readily generalize to orgasm during intercourse. However, sex therapy does increase the enjoyment reported by these women.
- *Vaginismus* appears to be an anxiety-related disorder which responds well to exposure-based behavioral techniques; up to 80% of patients will show some or significant improvement, with good maintenance of gains.
- Treatments for *sexual desire disorders* tend to be psychoeducational and behavioral, and while there are indications of some modest initial improvement, outcome is poor in the longer term.
- It is unclear whether marital therapy is always indicated before sex therapy in couples with problematic relationships, though clinical judgment might often suggest this to be an appropriate strategy.
- There is very little research examining the relative importance of widely accepted elements of sex therapy. Such research as exists suggests that techniques such as the use of dual-sex therapy teams and the ban on intercourse during therapy may be less essential to success than has been supposed.

IMPLICATIONS

- Though advocates of sex therapy can make a strong argument for the virtues of a multimodal approach in an area where problems clearly have multiple etiologies, it remains true that sex therapy techniques are often poorly described; a systematic description of the "rules" for combining components of treatment has yet to be developed. More work needs to be done in this area before thorough evaluation of this treatment modality will be possible.

- It may be important to be more specific about the role of emotional disorders—particularly anxiety—in sexual difficulties. The literature suggests that sexual difficulties where anxiety appears to predominate (e.g., erectile dysfunction and vaginismus) are also better treated using behavioral techniques implicity or explicitly based on principles of exposure. Where the etiological role of anxiety is less clear, psychoeducational approaches seem to be somewhat more valuable but outcomes are also more limited.

- Given this limited success, better techniques need to be developed, particularly in relation to premature ejaculation, inhibited female orgasm, and sexual aversion disorder.

- There is a need for well-designed, large, controlled trials with specified dysfunctions and specified therapies.

- Given the heterogeneous nature of patients who receive treatment for sexual problems, and the varied etiologies underlying their presentation, there is also a need for further information on the factors that determine the likelihood of successful outcomes in terms of a range of comorbid factors.

- While particular care should be taken to exclude organic problems in relation to erectile dysfunction, it may also be useful to determine the efficacy of psychological therapies in cases where organic factors significantly contribute to erectile difficulties.

CHAPTER 14

Counseling and Primary Care Interventions

DEFINING COUNSELING AS AN INTERVENTION

The scope of this chapter is somewhat different from earlier sections, which considered the benefits of treatments for defined patient populations.' In the present section, our focus is on evidence for the efficacy of therapies commonly offered in primary care settings. Interventions at this level are often referred to as "counseling," though this is a term that is poorly defined both in clinical practice and in the research literature.

A fundamental problem is the lack of definition of the boundaries between counseling and psychotherapy and, as a consequence, no clear indication of the methods employed or qualifications gained by counsellors (Sibbald et al., 1993). A distinction could be drawn between specialist mental health workers (such as psychiatrists and psychologists) who offer services in primary care locations, and counselors or workers without specialist psychotherapy skills whose methods of working are less easy to determine. However, studies in this area often apply the generic term "counselor" regardless of training. This blurring of professional background and psychological technique makes it difficult to be clear about the relationship between treatment and outcome in these studies. For the purposes of this review we consider three definitions of counseling:

1. Counselors are psychotherapeutically trained practitioners who apply their techniques in a primary care setting with an implicit model of early intervention. In this sense counseling is defined by the setting in which it is offered rather than by the techniques it offers.

2. Counselors are practitioners who use psychological methods but have no specialist training in any one model.

3. Counselors are psychotherapeutically trained practitioners who work in settings where the application of specific theoretical models is unwarranted—for example, where they offer advice or support rather than therapy.

THE STATUS OF COUNSELING IN PRIMARY CARE

Prior to reviewing the available evidence, it is worth noting the implications of the fact, in many health settings, access to specialized mental health services is through a primary care system. This process is analogous to a series of filters through which potential psychiatric patients pass before arriving at specialized care, with some association between the degree of distress and the probability of receiving treatment (Goldberg & Huxley, 1980). Where these filters are removed or diminished—for example, when counselors work alongside family physicians—it is likely that referred patients will be more acutely and less seriously disturbed. This increases the probability of a placebo response to treatment, which assumes a critical significance given that there appear to be few controlled trials that examine the efficacy of counseling as delivered to this group of patients.

Balestrieri et al. (1988) conducted a meta-analysis of the efficacy of "specialist" mental health workers in British primary care settings (though this definition included both individuals with recognized mental health training [such as psychiatrists and psychologists] as well as "counselors" [whose training is undetermined]). All studies contrasted specialist treatment with "treatment as usual" from a family physician. Eleven trials were identified, and a series of effect sizes were calculated for the contrast between treatment as usual and therapy. The overall effect size for any specialist treatment was 0.22, indicating only a slight benefit over routine treatment. Division of treatment into "counseling," behavior therapy, and general psychiatric intervention suggested that all interventions were of equal value (median effect sizes were 0.23, 0.22, and 0.21, respectively).

Trials included in Balestrieri et al.'s (1988) analysis were not only of variable methodological quality, but also covered a wide range of interventions—some specialized both in terms of therapists and treatments, others unspecified on both counts. This is a common characteristic of research in this area (Corney, 1990), and the design of studies often leads to confounds in two major areas. First, their intent is to demonstrate the general efficacy of interventions in primary care; as such, patients of mixed diagnosis are treated. It is clear from our reviews of specific disorders that outcomes cannot be divorced from the natural history of a condition. As such, the degree to which studies are comparable is uncertain. Secondly, the results of treatment are usually compared to standard care from a family physician, though no trial presents a detailed analysis of what this comprises or the degree to which physicians employ treatments known to be or likely to be effective (such as psychotropic medication or referral to specialized care). As a consequence it is difficult to know the extent to which a null result reflects the lack of efficacy of the contrast therapy or the beneficial effects of the control treatment.

THE EFFICACY OF COUNSELING

Cooper et al. (1975) contrasted patients receiving a range of mental health interventions (in addition to treatment as usual) with patients receiving treatment as usual alone. The intervention comprised social work counseling, with some patients also seen by psychiatrists. However, there is no description of the counseling method employed or the duration of treatments. Although there were some indications that experimental patients showed some gains in comparison to controls, the study has serious methodological problems. Control patients were drawn from attenders to a different surgery using different criteria from those selected for treatment, limiting the extent to which between-treatment changes are attributable to therapeutic interventions.

Ashurst and Ward (1983) assigned 726 patients with a range of neurotic disorders either to nondirective counseling or to routine care from family physicians. No differences in outcome were found between groups. Brodaty and Andrews (1983; cited in Corney, 1990) randomly assigned 56 patients with persistent psychological problems either to eight half-hourly sessions of psychodynamic problem–oriented counseling from a trained therapist, to counseling from the physician, or to standard treatment, finding no differences between treatments.

Catalan et al. (1984a,b) contrasted 91 patients randomly assigned either to brief counseling or to treatment with anxiolytics. All patients were selected on the basis that their family physician had diagnosed them as suffering from "minor affective disorders," a description which is less than exact, and which is further confused by the choice of medication. Counseling was offered by the physician after brief training by the investigators, though it is not clear that it comprised any more than an explanation of symptoms, reassurance, and advice on coping. No differences were found between treatment groups, and all patients showed improvements at 7-month follow-up. A secondary analysis

(Catalan et al., 1984b) suggested that poorer outcomes were associated with higher initial levels of symptoms.

Corney (1987) contrasted 80 depressed women receiving either routine treatment from their family physician or social work counseling. No clear model of counseling was followed, though counselors reported using exploration, practical help, and some behavioral goal setting. Overall there was little difference in outcome among treatment groups. The sample was stratified according to the degree of severity of depression and its chronicity. Patients with more acute and less severe problems improved regardless of treatment received, with more moderate outcomes in more severely distressed patients. There were some indications that, contrasted with equivalent controls, those patients with acute but more severe problems had better outcomes when in receipt of counseling.

King et al. (1994) allocated patients either to nondirective counseling or to routine care from their family physician, according to patient preference. This resulted in a counseling group of 19 and a routine care sample of only five, severely limiting any inferences that can be drawn from the study. Patients were moderately to severely disturbed, and those receiving care from their physician appeared to have better outcomes at 6 months than those receiving counseling, in whom very limited change was observed.

Gournay and Brooking (1994) report outcomes for 177 patients drawn from six primary care practices. Patients were offered either routine care from the family physician or treatment by a psychiatric nurse either immediately or after a 12-week wait. Patients' problems varied markedly, and insufficient details are supplied to be clear about their chronicity and severity. In addition, the care offered by the nurses is not specified, though the majority "considered counseling to be an important part of their role" (Gournay & Brooking, 1994, p. 232). Although all patients improved, there was no difference between results obtained by physicians and nurses.

Klerman et al. (1987) describe an intervention in an American primary care setting using a manualized brief counseling treatment—interpersonal counseling (IPC), based on the techniques of interpersonal psychotherapy (IPT). IPC comprises a six-session intervention package, and was offered by nurse practitioners under weekly supervision. One hundred twenty-eight patients were allocated to either IPC or a control group receiving treatment as usual. Counseled patients had significantly greater reductions in symptom scores than controls.

Raphael (1977) examined the efficacy of counseling for bereaved women considered to be at risk of delayed or pathological grief reactions. An initial pool of 200 women were interviewed, on the basis of which

64 patients were selected who demonstrated either marked ambivalence in their relationship to their husbands and/or had poor social support for their grieving. The subgroup of 64 patients were randomly allocated either to counseling or no-treatment groups. Counseling was based on psychodynamic/exploratory methods, was focused on the bereavement, and was offered for the 3 months following the death. At 13-month follow-up, 77% of the counseled group had good outcomes, contrasted with 41% of controls.

Holden et al. (1989) report a trial of counseling for women with acute postnatal depression, delivered by health visitors who had been given a brief (3-week) course in nondirective methods. Forty-eight women were allocated either to eight weekly sessions of counseling in addition to standard health visitor support or to standard health-visitor support alone. Approximately 3 months after treatment started, 69% of the counseled patients no longer met criteria for depression, contrasted with 38% of the control group.

It may be significant that of this series, only Holden et al. (1989), Raphael (1977), and Klerman et al. (1987) demonstrate positive outcomes. Klerman et al. (1987) employed a specific model of counseling based on a therapy of demonstrated efficacy. In Holden et al. (1989) and Raphael (1977), interventions were targeted and specific to a client group with acute difficulties and with therapists who would have been familiar with their patients' presentation. By drawing attention to the very specific characteristics of both counselors and patients, these trials might suggest that focal and focused counseling interventions may be more likely to be successful.

BEHAVIOR THERAPY IN PRIMARY CARE

Marks (1985) reports the efficacy of interventions for 92 phobic and obsessive–compulsive patients randomly allocated to treatment with nurse behavior therapists or standard care from their family physician. At 1-year follow-up patients treated with behavior therapy showed significantly more symptomatic gains than those receiving standard care. At this point control patients were offered behavior therapy, with consequent improvement in their clinical status. Though good results were achieved in this trial, it is worth noting that 254 patients were referred; of the 220 screened, 120 were considered "unsuitable for behavioral psychotherapy" (Marks, 1985, p. 1182). Since the criteria for this decision are not given, it is difficult to be clear about the generalizability of this study.

Robson et al. (1984) conducted a trial in which 429 patients were treated with either routine family physician care or up to 10 sessions of behaviorally oriented therapy offered by clinical psychologists. Patients seen for therapy improved significantly more than controls posttherapy and at 6-month follow-up, though by 1 year improvements in control patients abolished between-treatment effects. Treated patients made significantly fewer visits to their physician in the 6 months after treatment and were prescribed significantly fewer medications of all types over this period. An additional observation was that treated patients required less input than those referred for specialist psychological treatment, perhaps suggesting that these patents were more acutely or less severely distressed.

Teasdale et al. (1984) examined outcomes in 34 moderately to severely depressed patients (with Beck Depression Inventory scores $\geqslant 20$) who received up to 20 sessions of CBT from clinical psychologists or treatment as usual from their physician. Posttherapy, treated patients showed significant gains contrasted to controls. At 3-month follow-up, between-treatment differences were nonsignificant, reflecting improvement in control patients and some relapse in the treated group.

Earll and Kincey (1982) treated 23 patients with behavior therapy delivered by clinical psychologists, contrasted with treatment as usual in 19 patients. No differences were found between treatments, though those receiving behavior therapy had lower prescription rates during the treatment period.

Studies by Ross and Scott (1985) and Scott and Freeman (1992) have already been fully reviewed in Chapter 4. Briefly, Ross and Scott (1985) contrasted 51 depressed patients (with BDI scores $\geqslant 14$) receiving either CBT or treatment as usual from their family physician, finding significant advantages for CBT in the treatment of depression. Scott and Freeman (1992) contrasted 121 depressed patients receiving treatment as usual, tricyclic medication, CBT, or social work counseling. At the end of treatment only social work counseling showed a greater reduction in depressive symptoms when contrasted to care from their physician, though failures of randomization make interpretation of this trial difficult.

Milne and Souter (1988) conducted a naturalistic trial analyzing the response to treatment of 22 consecutive patients referred for up to 18 sessions of CBT with a clinical psychologist. An interrupted time series research design allowed for clients to act as their own controls while waiting for treatment. There was no significant change in symptom measures while clients were on the waiting list; significant improvements were observed posttherapy, with maintenance of gains at 1-year follow-up.

Catalan et al. (1991) allocated 47 patients with a range of psychological symptoms either to 6 weeks of problem-solving therapy or to routine care, finding a significant improvement in those receiving therapy. Patients within this trial were selected on the basis of elevated symptom scores; a contrast group with lower levels of distress were monitored but not treated. This group showed improvement equivalent to that of the treated group, indicating (as in Corney, 1987) that targeting of treatment to more distressed groups of patients is likely to be a more efficient use of resources.

SUMMARY

- The efficacy of counseling is difficult to assess because of the lack of specificity and control in studies, the diversity of patient groups studied, the variation in treatments administered, and the heterogeneity of contrast treatments.
- The success or otherwise of these treatments may depend as much on the quality of treatment as usual as the characteristics of the counseling offered.
- Studies do not preclude the possibility that many (perhaps most) patients currently likely to be treated by counselors are likely to remit spontaneously. This is not to say that such individuals do not value the interventions provided, but little evidence is available that would suggest that remission is accelerated as a result of counseling interventions.
- Very few investigations demonstrate any consistent benefit to patients from counseling, and no studies show generic counseling to add to standard general-practice care.
- The best evidence of efficacy seems to come from studies that target a specific client group (patients with bereavement reactions, acute postnatal depression) or studies that employ a modified version of a specific therapeutic model (IPC, exploratory therapy, and behavior therapy).
- On the whole, counseling seems more effective for milder presentations of the major groups of psychological disorders.

IMPLICATIONS

- If counseling services are to be extended within primary care settings, urgent research is required to examine the efficacy of counseling interventions across a wide range of psychological disorders.

- Counseling training needs to be reviewed in the light of the above studies and reoriented toward specific techniques for particular patient populations.
- While there is little evidence for the value of generic counseling in contrast to treatment as usual, this does not imply that generic counseling is of little value within primary-care settings. Rather, it may suggest that general practitioners have considerable generic counseling skills, though clearly this may not be the most cost-effective use of their time.
- The balance of evidence suggests that generic counseling is most appropriate to the least chronic and least severely impaired individuals within a patient population. This suggests the need for establishing a referral procedure that would enable workers in primary care to refer patients with more serious dysfunction to specialist psychotherapy services.
- Given the current skill profile of counselors, their clinical supervision by mental health professionals seems an essential precondition for the expansion of this service and the implementation of a rational referral strategy.
- The difficulty in evaluating the efficacy of counseling interventions underscores the need for further standardization of mental health care provision in primary care settings and the rigorous periodic audit of these services by an independent agency.

CHAPTER 15

The Psychological Treatment of Child and Adolescent Psychiatric Disorders

MARY TARGET

PETER FONAGY

This chapter covers the following areas: (1) the prevalence and natural history of children's[1] psychiatric disorders; (2) some general considerations in studies of the treatment of children's psychiatric disorders; (3) meta-analytic studies of child therapy outcome; (4) the treatments used for particular disorders, and current evidence on their efficacy; (5) conclusions.

PREVALENCE AND NATURAL HISTORY

Prevalence

Psychiatric impairment among children and adolescents has been estimated at 10–33%, depending on definitions of caseness, whether the population is rural (e.g., Zahner et al., 1993), and on cultural factors (Matsuura et al., 1993). Recent epidemiological studies from several different countries (e.g., Anderson et al., 1987; Bird et al., 1989; Costello, 1989a; Offord et al., 1989; Velez et al., 1989; Zill & Schoenborn, 1990) have reached a fairly close consensus on a prevalence rate of diagnosable disorder of around 20%.

The particular disorders affecting this 20% vary according to age, and to some extent gender. Overall figures from epidemiological studies

---

[1] Throughout this chapter, children and adolescents will be referred to collectively as children, unless a distinction is specifically made.

of children and adolescents spanning 4–20 years of age (reviewed by Costello, 1989b) suggest that diagnosable anxiety disorders affect around 12% of this age range, disruptive disorders around 10%; attention-deficit/hyperactivity disorder (ADHD) perhaps 5%; depression, specific developmental disorders, enuresis, and substance abuse up to 6%, depending on age group. Psychotic and pervasive developmental disorders, such as autistic disorder, are very rare, affecting less than 1%.

Lifetime prevalence of disorders during childhood and adolescence has been estimated by Reinherz et al. (1993) in a longitudinal study of 386 American children followed from 4 to 18 years. Overall, 49% met criteria for at least one disorder during this period.

These proportions are of course much higher than the proportion of children referred for psychiatric help, which has been estimated at 2–3% of the population within this age range in the United States (Knitzer, 1982; Tuma, 1989). The evidence suggests that the referred children are not generally more impaired than the other "cases" identified in epidemiological surveys. However, they have different family influences; specifically, the parental perception and anxiety about the child's behavior is greater in the referred sample, although the severity of symptoms is comparable (Shepherd et al., 1971; Bond & McMahon, 1984). There is also accumulating evidence to suggest that children are perceived as more disturbed by parents at times of marital or other family stress (e.g., Kolko & Kazdin, 1993). It is clear that the "referability" of symptoms differs widely, with children showing disruptive, antisocial behavior much more likely to be referred for treatment than those with anxiety or other emotional symptoms (Weisz & Weiss, 1991; Cohen et al., 1991).

The proportion of children identified as showing significant problems appears to be fairly consistent across different stages of childhood and adolescence, although specific disorders show very different frequencies according to age and gender. For example, Cohen et al. (1993a) found that one-third of all 10- to 20-year olds in a sample of 800 New York families had at least one disorder diagnosable on DSM-III-R. Rates of all specific disorders decreased above age 16, with the exception of substance abuse disorders, which increased through the age range. There were no overall gender differences in prevalence rates, but large differences were found among types of disorder, interacting with age; thus girls over 12 showed far more frequent anxiety and depressive disorders than boys, and up to the age of 16, boys showed far more conduct and attention deficit disorders.

Natural History

Child psychiatric disorders have different natural histories, which parallel their different responsiveness to treatment. Children with autistic and other pervasive developmental disorders tend to remain severely handicapped over several years or throughout life (e.g., Rutter, 1985a; Dahl et al., 1986). A number of studies (reviewed by Gillberg, 1991) have shown that in general, two-thirds of children diagnosed as suffering from an autistic or similar pervasive developmental disorder remain severely impaired, unable ever to lead an independent life. A small proportion (perhaps 5%) do show good outcome; this is related to higher IQ and better early speech development.

Schizophrenia with early onset (usually in adolescence) also has rather a poor prognosis (Gillberg et al., 1993). Werry et al. (1991) found that, among 30 children and adolescents diagnosed as schizophrenic and treated as inpatients, only five (17%) recovered fully over a 5-year follow-up. Premorbid adjustment weakly predicted good outcome (Werry & McClellan, 1992). In the same study, the course of bipolar disorder was found to be more favorable; half of the adolescents showed full recovery at follow-up, and 50% of the variance in outcome could be predicted from IQ, premorbid functioning, and family history.

Disruptive behavioral problems have a better prognosis than autistic or psychotic illnesses, but still present a major problem. They are the most frequent cause of referral of children for treatment, tend to persist over years (see Pepler & Rubin, 1991; Robins & Rutter, 1990) and frequently extend to antisocial behavior in adulthood (e.g., Robins, 1981; Weiss & Hechtman, 1986; Offord & Bennett, 1994). Lefkowitz et al. (1977) investigated the stability of excessive aggressiveness by following up a group of children in New York from the age of 8 to 19 years. Aggression was much less common in girls than in boys, as has been found in every other large-scale study, but in both sexes there were high correlations between aggressiveness at 8 years and again at 19 years (0.38 for boys, 0.47 for girls). Similarly, in a London study by West and Farrington (1973), boys who were rated most aggressive at 8–10 years were far more likely than others to be in this group at 14 (50% vs. 19%), 16, and 18 years (40% vs. 27%), and also had higher rates of serious, violent delinquency (14% vs. 4%).

A large-scale prospective study in New Zealand (White et al., 1990) showed that antisocial behavior at 13 years could be predicted from "externalizing behavior" at 3 years and similar behavior at 5 years. These showed stronger associations with later antisocial behavior than did IQ, mothers' attitudes, or any of many other variables measured. By the time the child was 11 years old, there was very high stability: 84% of those described as uncontrolled at that age met criteria for established, pervasive antisocial disorders at age 13.

Cantwell and Baker (1989) studied the stability of the disruptive disorders (ADHD, conduct disorder, oppositional disorder), as part of a follow-up of former attenders at a clinic for speech and language disorders. Sixty-four children met criteria for at least one disruptive disorder, and it was found that over a 4- or 5-year follow-up, 87% of these children were still psychiatrically ill. ADHD was the most stable, 80% still met criteria for the same disorder, and 9% were well; children with conduct or oppositional disorder were less likely to retain this diagnosis, but only 33% and 7%, respectively, were free of psychiatric disorder. The poor outcome of ADHD has been confirmed in a recent study of 123 children diagnosed at 4–12 years of age (Fischer et al., 1993); 85% of these children still met ADHD criteria at follow-up 8 years later.

Emotional disorders constitute just under half of the overall prevalence of psychological disorders in childhood (Rutter, Tizard, & Whitmore, 1970; Yule, 1981; Esser, Schmidt, & Woerner, 1990), and epidemiological work suggests that they are probably the most common problems across all age groups (e.g., Costello et al., 1988; Kashani & Orvaschel, 1990; McGee et al., 1990; Bernstein & Borchardt, 1991, for review). Children with symptoms of anxiety and depression are less frequently referred for psychiatric attention than those with disruptive disorders (Kazdin, 1985). There is evidence from a longitudinal study of 776 adolescents (Cohen et al., 1991) that young people diagnosed as suffering from major depression or overanxious disorder on DSM-III-R were not significantly more likely to be referred to a mental health professional than children in the rest of the population, in the 2.5-year follow-up period after diagnosis. This was in marked contrast to children with disruptive disorders, who were four or five times more likely than other children to be referred ($p < .01$). They also found that parents were not seeking alternative advice (e.g., from professionals such as teachers, or informally from friends or relatives) about children with emotional disorders, whereas they sought this help as well when children were disruptive.

The information available on the natural history of these disorders is sparse when compared with that available for other diagnostic groups, but has been recently and comprehensively summarized by Clark et al. (1994). It is widely believed that emotional disorders often remit spontaneously (this is often based on pioneering work such as Robins' [1966] follow-up study, which suggested low persistence of emotional disorders). This assumption may account for their underrepresentation in clinical studies (Ollendick & King, 1991). Recent longitudinal investigations (Fischer et al., 1984; Harrington et al., 1990, 1991, 1994; Flament et al., 1990), and retrospective studies (Agras et al., 1972; Francis & Ollendick, 1986) suggest that this may be an overly optimistic view (see review by Ollendick & King, 1994).

There is also evidence that the natural histories of different anxiety disorders differ, so that although separation anxiety and early childhood phobias have a relatively benign course (Husain & Kashani, 1992), over-anxious disorder appears to be more chronic (Last, 1987; Cantwell & Baker, 1989), to be associated with additional depression in adolescence (Strauss et al., 1988) and perhaps to be associated with generalized anxiety disorder in adulthood (Last et al., 1987a). A recent follow-up investigation (Cohen et al., 1993) showed that 47% of children with severe overanxious disorder continued to suffer from the same disorder 2.5 years later, almost all still at a severe level.

Even disorders such as separation anxiety disorder (SAD) may have an unstable rather than a good prognosis; in a small sample followed up by Cantwell and Baker (1989), only one of nine children still had SAD 4 years later, but a further four had a variety of other disorders, two disruptive behavioral disorders and three overanxious disorder; the remaining four children were well. There are tentative suggestions in the literature that SAD is associated with difficulties over separation in adult life: continued separation anxiety disorder and neurotic depression (Flakierska et al., 1988), crises over leaving home or changing jobs (Werkman, 1987), work phobia (Coolidge et al., 1964), and agoraphobia (Gittelman & Klein, 1984). Similarly, in Cantwell and Baker's (1989) study, of 14 children referred for treatment of avoidant disorder, 29% showed the same disorder 4 years later, but overall 64% were still psychiatrically ill (most with overanxious disorder). Overanxious disorder itself had the lowest recovery rate after 4 years in this study: 25% had the same disorder, and 75% were still diagnosably ill with disruptive and emotional disorders.

Other studies have examined the persistence of obsessive–compulsive disorder (OCD). Flament et al. (1990) reported a follow-up of adolescents with symptoms of OCD; in early adulthood, 68% still had an OCD diagnosis, and their adjustment was poor: 48% had diagnosable disorders other than OCD, and they showed difficulties in relationships and in work. In a recent study, Hanna (1995) has examined the demographic and clinical features of OCD in childhood and adolescence, and although this study did not include a follow-up, it was clear that most (84%) of the 31 patients had other diagnosable disorders (most commonly a depressive disorder), and the mean duration of the current disorder was 3.5 years. The majority of the subjects had been clinically impaired for several years, with changing symptoms which might include other anxiety symptoms, depression, tics, or a disruptive behavior disorder. Another recent study, by Thomsen and Mikkelsen (1995), found that half of 23 children and adolescents treated as inpatients or outpatients for OCD still met criteria for OCD diagnosis at 3-year follow-up, and two-thirds of these had suffered from the symptoms continuously (the remainder showed an episodic course). Bolton,

Luckie, and Steinberg (1995) followed up 14 of 15 treated cases after 9–14 years. All but two of these had been treated successfully, using behavioral and family therapy (see below), but at follow-up, six were found again to be diagnosable with OCD, and a further two had had episodes during the follow-up period but were currently in remission. These studies confirm the common clinical view that OCD is a complex and relatively intractable disorder in children, as it tends to be in adults.

There is beginning to be some evidence on the long-term effects of anxiety disorders on general development. Kashani and Orvaschel (1990) studied a community sample of 210 children and adolescents aged between 8 and 17 years. They found that children with anxiety disorders in each age group had higher rates of all other disorders than nonanxious children. They also showed that the anxious children failed to show the improvement with age in peer relationships seen in other children, and that in the area of family relationships, nonanxious children showed a steady level of difficulties across the age range, but the anxious children showed an increasing frequency of problems in the older groups. Other signs of poor adjustment were increasingly prevalent among the older anxious children: at 8 years, the anxious children had more symptoms than others but were reasonably well functioning in other ways; by 12 years, they had more difficulties in school and poorer self-image; at 17 years, anxious children were more likely to be depressed, to show behavioral disorders and somatic complaints, and to have significantly poorer self-esteem than nonanxious peers. It seems that the impact of anxiety disorders can be pervasive, and increasingly so as the child gets older.

The clinical course of childhood depression has been investigated in several studies. Kovacs and Gatsonis (1989) followed up a sample of over 100 cases aged 8–13 with depressive disorders (DSM-III criteria) for a number of years. They found that although nearly all episodes had resolved within 3–4 years (median time to recovery 9.5 months), the majority of children had further episodes of major depression over the following 5 years. There was also a 20–30% risk of secondary anxiety, conduct, or bipolar disorder during these years. A similar pattern has been reported recently for the 14- to 18-year age group (Lewinsohn et al., 1994). In this adolescent group, however, the duration of disorder seems to have been somewhat shorter (6 months on average), and only about a third relapsed within 4 years.

There is accumulating evidence (King & Pittman, 1970; Kandel & Davies, 1986; Garber et al., 1988; Harrington et al., 1990, 1991, 1994) that depressive disorders in childhood and adolescence are associated with significantly greater risk of affective disorders in adulthood. The

Harrington et al. (1990, 1991, 1994) study, for instance, showed that depression in childhood or adolescence was associated with relative risks of psychiatric treatment, hospitalization, and serious suicide attempts in adulthood three times higher than those found among matched nondepressed child psychiatric patients. There seemed to be a specifically increased rate of affective illness (both depressive and bipolar) rather than of psychiatric morbidity in general. The risk of further depressive illness has been found to be greater (Kovacs et al., 1984; Asarnow et al., 1988) where there is dysthymia as well as the index episode of major depression ("double depression"). Kazdin (1990a) summarizes this picture as demonstrating high rates of recovery from episodes, but with high rates of relapse. This is very similar to the situation in adults (see Chapter 4, on depression).

It is often thought that the natural history of childhood disorders is more benign in children who are younger at the onset of symptoms. There is some evidence for this in some disorders; for instance, both Harrington and colleagues (1990) and Kovacs and colleagues (1989) showed that the natural history of depressive illness was more favorable in younger children. Unfortunately, there is no study that provides follow-up data for the full age range and a range of disorders in the same sample, but different investigations of narrower age ranges together suggest that one-third to two-thirds of the children presenting with disorders at any age from 3 years will still show significant disturbance some years later.

Richman et al. (1982) followed a large sample of children up from 3 to 8 years, and found a high level of persistence. Overall, 61% of 3-year-olds who were regarded as showing significant disturbance still had difficulties when clinically evaluated at 8 years. Similar figures have been found in more recent studies of 3-year-olds, with some follow-up periods as long as 12 years (e.g., McGee et al., 1991; Campbell & Ewing, 1990; see review by Campbell, 1995). In the Campbell study, 48% of the children identified as "hard to manage" at 3 years met DSM-III criteria for a disruptive disorder at 9 years (Campbell & Ewing, 1990).

Rutter et al. (1981), in the Isle of Wight study, evaluated children at 10–11 and again at 14–15. The overall rate of persistence of disorder was put at 60%, with lower stability for emotional than for conduct disorders. Esser et al. (1990), in a study of 400 German children followed up from 8 to 13 years, reported that 50% of psychiatric disorders persisted through this period. Again, there was a wide discrepancy between the optimistic prognosis of emotional disorders and the very poor outlook for children with serious disruptive behavior.

Recently, Cohen et al. (1993) have conducted a large-scale epidemiological study assessing the persistence of diagnosable psychiatric problems in older children and adolescents. Cohen et al. (1993) found that "for almost all combinations of diagnosis and severity level, one-third or more of the cases diagnosed at ages 9–18 were still at an equivalent diagnostic level 2.5 years later" (Cohen et al., 1993, p. 876). There was no difference in levels of persistence according to age at the first assessment.

There is increasing enthusiasm for mounting very long-term and sophisticated prospective investigations, to track the natural history and ultimate treatment outcomes of all childhood disorders, and these longitudinal data promise great advances in the understanding of both normal and abnormal development (see e.g., Wierson & Forehand, 1994; Rutter, 1994). However, at present there is no good evidence for the wide belief that earlier psychiatric disorder has a better prognosis.

Summary

- It is likely that at any one time, 20% of children in the United Kingdom and the United States suffer from psychiatric disorder.
- Only 10–15% of these individuals currently find their way to psychiatric services.
- Although the prevalence estimates vary according to social conditions, approximately 10% of children suffer from disruptive disorders, 10% from emotional disorders, and an additional 5% from each of a variety of other psychiatric disorders.
- These figures suggest that there is a relatively high prevalence of comorbidity in childhood mental disorders; this has been confirmed by many epidemiological and clinical studies.
- The natural history of childhood psychiatric disorders has been relatively intensively investigated over recent years.
- The long-term outcome of severe psychiatric disorders of childhood is poor, with 50–100% manifesting psychiatric disorders for many years after initial diagnosis. Disorders with particularly poor outcome include pervasive developmental disorders, childhood schizophrenia, and ADHD.
- The long-term outcome of disruptive disorders of childhood includes a greatly increased risk of antisocial behavior in adulthood, with less than one-third being free of psychiatric disorder 4–5 years later.
- Generalized anxiety disorder and OCD are also likely to persist in two-thirds to three-quarters of cases, and to be associated with other disorders and with major problems of adaptation.
- Depression in childhood shows a relatively high likelihood of resolution in the short term, but runs a cyclical course very similar to that observed for adults.

- Separation anxiety disorder and childhood phobias have the best prognosis, but even these individuals are far more likely to develop other psychiatric disorders than children without psychiatric diagnosis.
- Psychiatric disorders diagnosed at a younger age might have a slightly better prognosis than those of older children, but these differences are not marked, and the evidence is slight.

Implications

- There is a major mental health problem represented by the high prevalence of childhood mental disorders, which is increasingly recognized nationally and internationally.
- Severe childhood psychological disorders do not generally remit spontaneously, and many disorders are associated with poor adjustment in adolescence and adult life.
- The sequelae of childhood disorders include not just a greatly increased risk of mental disorders in adulthood, but also generally poor adaptation, and thus have implications for adult health service resources and the general wealth-creating capacity of these individuals.
- Intervention appears to be justified at all developmental stages as the generally poor long-term prognosis of even early childhood disorder suggests that intervention should be as early as possible, before the disorder is established as chronic.
- The low rate of cases reaching psychiatric services highlights a social problem for this group of psychiatrically disordered individuals, who do not themselves have the resources to seek help. The pattern of referrals (much greater numbers of disruptive children than emotionally disordered children being seen in the clinic) implies that it is the caregiver's rather than the child's needs that are the primary determinants of seeking psychiatric care. Thus in addition to the provision of appropriate services, there seems to be an urgent need to draw caregivers' attention to the possibility that distressed children under their care may not "grow out of it," and may require psychological help. Although adults have different ways of seeking help, children are dependent on adults to perceive the need and to initiate referral. This has major implications for educational programs focused on increasing the awareness of both children and caregivers of the nature of childhood mental disorder, and the possibility of psychological intervention.

• The high prevalence of these disorders implies that attention should be focused on the development of intervention programs which can be integrated with educational initiatives and made as accessible as possible.

SPECIAL PROBLEMS AFFECTING THE EVALUATION OF CHILD THERAPIES

Specific Difficulties in Assessing Symptomatology

Children, even adolescents, do not usually ask for psychiatric help, and even when they are cooperative, they cannot be assumed to be reliable informants. It is now clear in child psychiatry that assessment requires information from the child's parents, and if possible also the teacher. More information does not, however, always solve the problem.

There is consistent evidence (beginning with Rutter et al., 1970; Shepherd et al., 1971) to show that parents and teachers evaluate the same child differently, although the overall rates of reported disorder do not necessarily differ between parents and teachers. Recently studies have generally included child self-report, which diverges even more widely from parent and teacher reports than they do from each other. Kolko and Kazdin (1993), for example, using parallel forms of the Child Behavior Checklist (Achenbach & Edelbrock, 1983, 1986, 1987) with 6- to 13-year olds, found correlations of 0.41 between parent and teacher, 0.34 between child and teacher, and 0.27 between parent and child. Correlations were higher for "externalizing" (disruptive) problems than for "internalizing" (emotional) problems, mainly anxiety and depression; this difference has been confirmed in other investigations (Edelbrock et al., 1986; Phares et al., 1989; Thompson et al., 1993). This low rate of agreement among informants is a particular problem for research on child therapy outcome, as information from each of these sources is relevant to the assessment of referral problems and estimation of change during treatment. As correspondence is generally poor, the overall outcome of therapy is not easy to assess.

Such poor observed agreement probably reflects three factors (see Kolko & Kazdin, 1993): (1) children behave very differently in different settings, and some symptoms (e.g., bedwetting, bullying) are only visible in a particular context; (2) the reports of different informants are susceptible to various biases (e.g., parents' reports have been shown to be more negative where there is marital stress or parental psychopathology; Renouf & Kovacs, 1994); (3) adults are not necessarily aware of how anxious or depressed the child is feeling (e.g., that clinical depression underlies the observed behavior of school refusal and stealing); (4) children's self-awareness is in the process of development, so they may be less reliable observers of their mental states than adults.

Assessment of Change in Relation to Spontaneous Remission Rates and Developmental Course of Disorder

As is the case in studies of adults, the efficacy of treatment, especially long-term treatment, is more difficult to evaluate in conditions with a high spontaneous remission rate. Although the use of an untreated control group is designed to clarify the impact of therapy on natural history, there are additional ethical difficulties with such groups in the case of child disorders and medium- to long-term treatment. However, it is important to bear in mind that treatment may accelerate improvement, provide other benefits (such as improved family functioning), or help to reduce the risk of recurrence. This may be very worthwhile, particularly for children, even if a disorder would be likely to remit spontaneously over a few years. For example, a school phobia that might spontaneously remit within months will nevertheless within that time deprive the child of important educational and social experience, and will distort family functioning if a parent is kept at home by the child's symptoms.

A further complication in the evaluation of treatment efficacy, which is again much more of a problem for longer-term therapies, is that child psychiatric disorders often change predictably as the child gets older. This could lead to spurious findings of change due to therapy. For instance, children with ADHD usually show gross hyperactivity at 3 years; by 5 or 6 years this is commonly much less troublesome, the emphasis having shifted to attention deficit. Similarly, girls who show disruptive behavior before puberty may become anxious or depressed in adolescence, whereas boys show the reverse trend (White et al., 1990). Assessment of treatment outcome needs to take into account the full symptom picture with age: a child whose referral symptom has improved is not necessarily less impaired after treatment, in relation to either their state before therapy or to their expected state given the course of their disorder (Graham, 1993).

Constraints on Treatment Choices in Child Psychology

Far more than is the case with treatment of adult problems, the application of specific treatments in children is limited by the child's developmental stage and context. Thus, for instance, some behavioral anxiety reduction procedures (e.g., relaxation and imaginal desensitization) are difficult for children to practice (Kissel, 1972; Rosenstiel & Scott, 1977). The capacity of children to reflect on their feelings and cognitive processes is limited before puberty, which is likely to restrict the usefulness of cognitive therapy for childhood depression or anxiety states (Kovacs, 1986; Rutter, 1988). Nevertheless, one should note some very promising recent efforts to adapt cognitive procedures for use with younger children (see Kendall, 1994; Hanna, 1995).

On a practical level, it is obviously not possible to conduct family therapy with a child who lives in institutional care or with frequently changing foster families. Similarly, it will only be appropriate to offer family therapy or parent training where family interaction or parenting styles have been identified as unhelpful (Fauber & Long, 1991). It will only be possible to offer school-based intervention where the teacher is able to participate. It may not be helpful to offer family-based treatments to adolescents who are in the process of disengaging from the family. Because many therapies are only relevant when the child's social, emotional, and cognitive levels permit, and when the environment is appropriate, the first choice therapy as judged by research findings on a particular disorder may frequently be inappropriate in a particular clinical situation, even where it is available. It is therefore particularly important in the child field to retain and test a range of specialized therapeutic approaches, so that children of widely differing ages and social contexts can all be offered effective help (Kazdin, 1993c).

The Presence of Concurrent Conditions ("Comorbidity")

It has become clear that the presence of additional disorders can crucially influence the expected course of a disorder. So-called comorbidity (Caron & Rutter, 1991) is the rule rather than the exception in child psychiatry (e.g., Anderson et al., 1987, reported that 55% of children meeting criteria for any DSM-III disorder also met criteria for at least one other disorder). Normally, it appears that children with multiple problems are more likely to remain ill (Verhulst & van der Ende, 1993). Thus, a child showing ADHD will have a considerably worse prognosis if he also shows symptoms of a conduct disorder (e.g., Taylor et al., 1991). This is a complex area with many possible patterns of disorders, and additional diagnoses may not always make the outlook more gloomy. It may be, for instance, that for a child with a conduct disorder, an additional emotional disorder makes the natural history (Verhulst &

van der Ende, 1993) and the response to treatment (Fonagy & Target, 1994) more favorable.

This needs further empirical investigation, and it is encouraging that treatment outcome studies increasingly take comorbidity into account, at least to the extent of describing it (see Ollendick & King, 1994). In some studies, children with additional diagnoses have been excluded. This clarifies the focus of the study, but unfortunately makes it much less clinically useful (Kazdin, 1990b). In other studies, the principal diagnosis of the child is used in selection for treatment, and the results are interpreted without regard to other coexisting disorders. Unfortunately, this could obscure interpretation of treatment efficacy, which may be crucially affected by, for instance, the presence of a conduct disorder or developmental disorder alongside an anxiety state. Kendall et al. (1992) showed that children presenting with concurrent disorders show different developmental pathways and differential responses to a variety of treatment approaches.

Design of Outcome Studies

It is accepted that the blind, randomized controlled trial (RCT) gives the clearest indication of the effectiveness of treatment, for children as for adults. However, until relatively recently, research on psychosocial treatments for children rarely used this procedure, and the field was dominated by single-case reports without an experimental design, often using poorly validated measures and little definition of the treatment provided. There are now more published reports of systematic empirical assessments of child therapy and its effects. Some of these are reports of work with single-subject research designs; others compare groups of treated children or adolescents. However, many of these reports are of treatment of nonreferred, "convenience" samples, and relatively few meet the criteria set down by Barrnett et al. (1991), following a sympathetic but gloomy review of 43 controlled outcome studies of individual child psychotherapy. These authors concluded that the magnitude of flaws in these studies made it impossible to draw reliable conclusions, and listed desirable features of clinical trials: explicit inclusion and exclusion criteria; detailed specification of therapy; appropriate matching procedures and control groups; standardized and objective ratings of outcome, relevant to (but not exclusive to) the subject of study, and carried out by blind assessors.

These desirable features of course apply to the evaluation of treatment of adults, as well as of children, but implementing them raises difficulties that are often greater in the child field. In particular, the specification of inclusion and exclusion criteria was very rarely comparable across studies until relatively recently because of the poor definition of psychiatric disorders in children. This has improved dramatically since the subdivision of child psychiatric syndromes in first ICD-9 (WHO, 1978), and then DSM-III (American Psychiatric Association, 1980).

The use of an RCT design itself is somewhat more problematic in child therapy. Ethical and practical objections arise to random allocation, of which both child and parent must be informed. Children are less able to understand and give valid consent to complex research procedures but must be consulted, and parents may be less willing to consent to a random choice of treatment for their child than they might be for themselves. The choice of an appropriate control group is also difficult: either an untreated (waiting-list) control or an inert (placebo) treatment raises the ethical problems of withholding treatment from disturbed children, particularly from clinical samples, as opposed to children recruited from the community specifically for the study. This is again a more acute problem for treatments that extend over several months, as many child therapies do (the mean length of clinical treatments has been found to be 6–12 months in the United States; Kazdin et al., 1990b; Silver & Silver, 1983). Most studies get round this and other problems by offering much shorter treatment (mean duration 8–10 weeks; Casey & Berman, 1985; Weisz et al., 1987), but this raises questions about the comparability of therapies normally provided with those being evaluated in outcome research (as discussed in the introductory chapter of this book).

The need to follow children up after termination of treatment deserves to be stressed. Levitt (1957) found, as others have since, that treated children may continue to improve considerably at least for some months after the end of treatment, so comparisons between treated and untreated children may look very different depending on the point of assessment. A notable example of this is a study of various school-based treatments for emotional and disruptive disorders in children (Kolvin et al., 1981). At termination, it appeared that neither group of children had benefited substantially from treatment with group therapy or behavior therapy. However, at an 18-month follow-up assessment, both groups showed definite improvement in relation to others. Similarly, as Kazdin (1990b) demonstrated, it can also happen that "the treatment that appeared more or most effective at posttreatment did not retain this status at follow-up." Furthermore, it can appear from follow-up assessment that therapy may not give a long-term advantage: "Treatments that appear effective or differentially effective in the short run may not surpass the impact of developmental changes" (Kazdin, 1990b). Smith et al. (1980), in their very extensive review of adult and child therapy, found that many more studies showed substantial improvement at termination than at follow-up.

Wright et al. (1976) reviewed the outcome literature on individual child psychotherapy and paid particular attention to studies where the assessments distinguished between termination and follow-up. They argued that there was demonstrated improvement in outcome from the end of therapy to follow-up and that this improvement was positively correlated with the number of psychotherapy sessions. They advocated including follow-up assessments as a requirement in the examination of outcome in child psychotherapy.

The other major difficulty, which remains a significant obstacle, is that measures of childhood adjustment and symptomatology are less well developed for children and adolescents than they are for adults. Although much work has been done to correct this, it remains a problem, partly because of the complexity of the interaction between development and psychopathology in childhood. Measures have to have different norms according to age and gender, and perhaps different forms for different stages of childhood. The impact of psychological disorder often involves cognitive and emotional capacities few of which have been systematically assessed in outcome studies. There is also the issue, mentioned earlier, of collecting parallel information from a variety of relevant informants (which could include each parent, a teacher, the child, and peers). The question of suitable outcome measures is especially acute for a treatment such as psychodynamic psychotherapy, which aims to affect overall social, emotional, and cognitive development, rather than specific symptoms.

Summary

- There are major difficulties in evaluating psychological treatments of childhood disorders.
- Measures of symptomatology derived from parents, teachers, and children correlate poorly; thus the overall outcome of an intervention is difficult to assess.
- Assessments of treatment outcome must be made in the context of the natural history of disorders, in particular changing symptom patterns over the course of development.
- The efficacy of treatment for any individual cannot be assessed without attention to the quality of the fit between the specific child's life circumstances and the treatment modality. An inherently effective treatment will be appropriate only if the environment can support it. Thus, for example, some therapies require

cooperation from teachers, or participation in therapy by parents or the whole family. Some children need help partly because of environmental failure or stress, and the degree of support must be considered realistically.

- Comorbidity affects the outcome of treatment in ways that have up till now only been partially identified.
- It is essential to maintain a range of therapies to fit different circumstances and combinations of disorders.
- Available measures of symptomatic outcome are too few in number, and insufficiently well standardized in the United Kingdom for children differing in age, gender, and socioeconomic background.
- There is evidence that treatment outcome varies considerably depending on length of follow-up.
- There are serious ethical problems facing RCTs of children that attempt to contrast long-term untreated outcome with a specific treatment condition.

Implications

- In evaluating studies, changes should be looked at in the context of potential discrepancies between informants. The potential biases introduced by using solely informant-based assessment, as opposed to self-report or independent assessment, should be considered. Wherever possible, all three sources should be used.
- The impact of therapy should not be studied simply in terms of the child's symptomatology, but in terms of the impact of that symptomatology on normal developmental processes, at critical phases of the child's psychological, social, and educational development.
- In view of the predictable changes in symptomatology during development, treatments should be evaluated in terms of their capacity to facilitate change, not just in target symptoms, but across a spectrum of aspects of psychological adaptation. This applies particularly to longer-term therapies.
- One criterion against which treatments should be assessed is the extent to which they are applicable to a wide range of children. In reviewing efficacy, it should be noted how many children were considered for treatment, how many were found suitable, and how many accepted it.
- In looking at outcome, the proportion of children with various types of comorbidity should be noted, and studies looking at

children selected for lack of comorbidity (unrepresentative samples) should be treated with caution.
- In the light of the difficulties in carrying out RCTs, findings from open trials should be given consideration in evaluations of efficacy.
- All outcome studies should include follow-up, for as long a period as is practicable, and with regard to natural history. For example, children treated for depression should be followed up for some years, as the disorder tends to remit spontaneously and then recur.

REVIEWS AND META-ANALYTIC STUDIES OF INDIVIDUAL THERAPY

In this section, the literature on individual psychosocial treatments for childhood disorders is reviewed, drawing on meta-analyses of groups of outcome studies. Since the 1950s, several general reviews or meta-analyses of child and adolescent therapy have been published. The major reviews are described below.

Levitt and Other Early Investigations

The first major effort to assess child psychotherapy was Levitt's (1957) examination of 18 child psychotherapy outcome studies. Levitt contrasted the total percentages of treated and untreated children who improved. He estimated that 78% of the treated children had improved at follow-up, while 72.5% of the untreated children had also improved. This was similar to the findings of Eysenck's (1952) review of studies of adult psychotherapy. Levitt concluded, as had Eysenck, that his results did not support the hypothesis that psychotherapy facilitated recovery from emotional disorders. Levitt's studies have been criticized for a number of reasons, including the facts that his estimate of improvement without treatment was based on two very poor studies, the outcome studies he included were seriously flawed methodologically, and definition of the patient's symptomatology was unavoidably inadequate at that time (see Barrett et al., 1978; Kolvin et al., 1988).

There were a number of further reviews, focusing on methodology in outcome research, by Heinicke and Strassman (1975), Barrett et al. (1978), and Tramontana (1980). This last author reviewed 33 studies of individual, group, and family therapy with adolescents from 1967 to 1977. Only five were regarded as showing adequate methodological scope and rigor. Tramontana concluded that the available evidence did suggest that these forms of psychotherapy were beneficial with these patients.

Smith et al.

Also in the late 1970s, Smith et al. examined 500 controlled studies using the statistical technique of meta-analysis (Smith & Glass, 1977; Smith et al., 1980). Of the 500 studies included in the Smith et al. meta-analysis, approximately 50 assessed the treatment of children and adolescents. The overall analysis revealed significantly better outcome for patients who were being treated than for controls. Unfortunately, however, the approximately 50 children and adolescent studies were not analyzed separately from the original 500 studies, and thus no effect size can be reported. In addition, some of the studies on children and adolescents contained treatments other than individual psychotherapy. They did report, however, in a correlational analysis, that the patient's age had little effect on treatment outcome. Critics of this study have indicated that these authors included studies of very mixed quality (Eysenck, 1978).

Casey and Berman

Casey and Berman (1985) published a review of 75 controlled studies on child psychotherapy outcome, dating from 1952 to 1983. Their review focused on studies with children with a mean age below 13 years at the time of treatment. It included behavioral and cognitive–behavioral treatments together with nonbehavioral psychotherapies, and was restricted to studies that used control groups of untreated children from the same general population. The same meta-analytic techniques used by Smith et al. (1980) were used in this review. A positive effect size of 0.71 was found across outcome measures for the 64 studies. Overall, it was found that those children who had received treatment were better adapted than 76% of the control children. An effect size of 1.00 was obtained for behavioral psychotherapy, 0.40 for nonbehavioral treatment ($p < .001$). Casey and Berman (1985) were concerned that this difference might reflect the fact that behavioral interventions were often judged by tests very similar to therapy tasks (in other words, children were effectively trained to perform better on the posttest assessments). When they excluded studies that had used such criteria, the behavioral–nonbehavioral difference was reduced (mean effect sizes of 0.55 and 0.34, respectively) and no longer significant.

Characteristics of treatment were examined as possible predictors of effect size, but most showed no significant differences. The authors also examined effect size in relation to child characteristics. The highest effect sizes were found where children were presenting with phobic symptoms (1.16) or somatic problems (1.66). Among the various outcome measures, those that assessed anxiety (1.08) and cognitive performance (0.96) showed significantly larger effects than measures of self-concept (0.06) and personality characteristics (0.11). More general assessments showed intermediate effect sizes: measures of global adjustment (0.56), social adjustment (0.48), or achievement (0.35). There was an effect of source of these assessments: ratings from independent observers were highest (1.14), followed by therapists (1.05), parents (0.80), child performance measures (0.74), and peers (0.47), which were all significantly higher than effect sizes obtained from teachers' ratings (0.19) and child self-report (0.16). However, none of these categories was significantly different in mean effect size from those based on expert judges (0.53). Importantly, effect size did not differ as a function of whether the informant knew that the child had received treatment.

A limitation of the Casey and Berman study is that only 24% of the total 75 studies reviewed used samples of children referred for treatment. Thus, it is not clear how representative these results actually are of clinical practice (Saxe et al., 1986).

Weisz et al.

Another important meta-analytic study was conducted by Weisz et al. (1987). These authors examined 163 therapy studies involving children aged 4 to 18 years of age, from 1970 to 1985. Psychotherapy was defined as "any intervention designed to alleviate psychological distress, reduce maladaptive behaviour or enhance adaptive behaviour through counselling, structured or unstructured interaction, a training program or a predetermined treatment plan." In contrast to the Casey and Berman (1985) review, effect size was calculated for each individual comparison by dividing the treatment–control mean differences by the control group standard deviation, rather than by the pooled standard error of the combined treatment and control groups. The rationale for this was that variability in the treatment group might be expected to increase during treatment more than that in the control group (this was in fact found to be the case; Weiss & Weisz, 1990).

Four domains were defined: age group (children aged 4–12 vs. adolescents aged 13–18), therapy type (behavioral vs. nonbehavioral), target problem (overcontrolled vs. undercontrolled), and therapist training (trained professional therapists, paraprofessionals, or graduate students). The main effect of each variable on effect size was tested first, then each main effect for robustness. Across the 163 treatment–control comparisons, a mean effect size of 0.79 was found. Across the various outcome measures used, the average treated child after treatment scored at the 79th percentile of the control group. Only 6% of the treatment-control comparisons yielded negative effect sizes. The effect sizes from behavioral methods (126 treatment–control comparisons) were significantly higher than those from the 27 comparisons of nonbehavioral treatments (means of 0.88 vs. 0.44; $p > .05$). However, withdrawing comparisons in which outcome measures were similar to treatment procedures eliminated 63% of studies, and reduced behavioral–nonbehavioral differences to nonsignificance. Only three studies involved a version of psychodynamic therapy, and the mean effect size here was minimal (0.01).

Focusing on child characteristics, there was a main effect of age of the child, with children under 12 showing larger effects than adolescents ($p < .05$). Age did not interact significantly with therapy type or problem type, but there was a significant age × therapist training interaction ($p < .05$): age and effect size were uncorrelated among professional therapists ($r = .11$) but were significantly correlated among graduate students ($r = .31$; $p < .05$) and paraprofessionals ($r = -.43$; $p < .05$). The difference in mean effect size between studies treating mostly girls (1.11) and studies treating mostly boys (0.80) was nonsignificant.

Focusing on target problems, no significant mean effect size difference was found between the broad categories of overcontrolled and undercontrolled problems. This finding held when age level, therapy type, and therapist training were controlled for. However, there was a marginal interaction with therapist training ($p < .06$). The three therapist types did not differ in their mean effect size with undercontrolled problems; however, with overcontrolled problems, mean effect size did increase with level of professional training (0.53 to 1.03). This suggests the possibility that advanced training makes a bigger difference with overcontrolled problems than with undercontrolled problems.

Kazdin et al.

As a part of a broader survey, Kazdin et al. (1990a) offered a meta-analysis of 108 studies of children from 4 to 18, between 1970 and 1988. The majority of the children had been referred for disruptive behavior. Behavior modification was used in 50% of the studies, cognitive-behavioral approaches in 22%, group therapy in 9%, client-centered therapy in 5%, play therapy in 5%, family therapy in 4%, and other approaches in less than 4% of the studies. The effect sizes were computed similarly to the method used by Casey and Berman (1985). For each study, an effect size was computed for each pair of groups compared, and classified into three categories: treatment versus no-treatment, treatment versus active control group, and treatment versus treatment. For the 64 studies involving treatment versus no-treatment comparisons, a mean effect size of 0.88 was found. For the 41 studies involving treatment versus active control comparisons, the mean effect size was 0.77.

Meta-Analytic Studies of Family Therapy

Two meta-analyses of relatively small groups of studies of family therapy outcome have been reported in recent years (Hazelrigg et al., 1987; Markus et al., 1990). Each of these reviews included about 20 studies; 10 studies were included in both. Hazelrigg and colleagues found moderate mean effect sizes of 0.46 for family interaction measures, and 0.50 for measures of the child's behavior; these effects decreased at follow-up ($r = -.30$). Markus and colleagues reported a larger effect size of 0.70, a superiority they explained in terms of differences between the groups of studies examined, selection of data, and statistical procedures. They offered an interesting exploration of effects at follow-up, which offers a possible explanation of the negative findings reported by Hazelrigg et al. There appeared to be a curvilinear relationship across studies between treatment impact and interval between treatment and follow-up. The effect size increased for intervals up to 10 months after the end of treatment (to 1.14), was still large (0.84) at 18 months, but then declined sharply so that after 4 years no difference could be discerned between treatment and comparison groups.

Shirk and Russell

Shirk and Russell (1992) have pointed out the underrepresentation of nonbehavioral treatments (and specifically psychodynamic therapy) in meta-analyses of child treatment outcome. The neglect of psychodynamic approaches with children is despite the fact that this therapy is the form of nonbehavioral treatment most frequently used and most highly regarded among child psychiatrists and psychologists, at least in the United States (Kazdin et al., 1990b; Koocher & Pedulla, 1977; Silver & Silver, 1983; Snow & Paternite, 1986).

Shirk and Russell (1992) also offered some persuasive criticisms of the negative findings in the few studies addressing this issue. 69% of the 27 nonbehavioral outcome studies examined by Shirk and Russell (1992) concerned treatment administered in groups, whereas several surveys of clinicians have found that they do not regard group therapy as generally useful (Kazdin et al., 1990b; Koocher & Pedulla, 1977), and themselves use individual treatment (Silver & Silver, 1983). They demonstrate that the average effect size for nonbehavioral group treatment is significantly smaller than that for individual therapy (0.27 and 0.56, respectively). They also showed that the majority of evaluations of nonbehavioral treatment had used fewer than 20 shortened sessions, which was not representative of what is normally provided in practice (Kazdin et al., 1990b).

Furthermore, Shirk and Russell (1992) found that over two-thirds of the studies evaluating nonbehavioral treatment had been conducted by investigators with a declared allegiance to behavior therapy, and that investigator allegiance had a very strong effect on effect sizes obtained (0.17 with behavioral allegiance, 0.56 with nonbehavioral allegiance). Thus far, then, psychodynamic therapy has been judged mostly (for want of better evidence) on studies of brief group therapy conducted by behaviorally oriented clinicians.

Although some details of Shirk and Russell's (1992) critique have been convincingly disputed by Weiss and Weisz (1995), it is not in dispute that nonbehavioral treatment has never been adequately evaluated, and that this must be a matter of urgency in therapy outcome research for children and adolescents.

Weisz and Weiss

The Weisz and Weiss study (1989) arose from the observation that other meta-analyses had included studies which did not reflect normal clinic populations or practices. In particular, subjects were recruited rather than referred, samples were chosen for specific problems (e.g., phobias), on which the therapy was focused, and therapists were specially and recently trained in the techniques to be evaluated. It was therefore felt necessary to see whether the good outcomes reported in these studies were also seen in the clinic. The strategy was to compare 93 children who had received at least five sessions of therapy with 60 dropouts from the same clinics, who had been offered treatment but did not attend. There were no significant differences on demographic or clinical variables between these groups when referred. The findings were almost consistently negative. There were no differences in outcome between treated and untreated children; both improved to an extent equivalent to the improvement found in untreated controls in other studies. Various explanations for this are discussed, but the most likely conclusion appears to be that therapy as normally provided, for the type of problems generally referred, does not produce greater improvement than would have occurred without treatment.

This first study of clinic-based treatment has gradually generated increasing interest in the problem of applying laboratory-based outcome findings to clinical practice (see, e.g., Weisz et al., 1992; Hoagwood et al., 1995; Kendall & Southam-Gerow, 1995). Weisz et al. (1995) have reviewed evidence relating to the gulf between efficacy (in lab studies) and effectiveness (in clinic settings) and have attempted to disentangle the reasons behind the difference. The clinic-based studies included in their survey were few (only nine could be found in a thorough search, three of them carried out before 1960) and methodologically very limited; one important point made by the authors is that well-designed effectiveness studies are desperately needed. They then attempted to test eight plausible reasons for the much larger effect sizes found in lab-based outcome studies, by conducting comparisons between over 100 of these studies, according to the presence or absence of possible mediating factors. They found that five of these could not be shown to influence effect sizes obtained (recency of study, special training of therapists, superiority of research therapists over clinicians, specificity of clinical problems included in lab studies, greater structure of research therapy). Three did appear to be relevant (greater severity of clinical problems in clinic samples, greater attractiveness of lab setting, and greater likelihood of behavioral approach in lab studies), although the setting factor was reduced to insignificance once the other two were controlled for.

Summary

- Meta-analyses of child psychotherapy outcome studies have shown that psychotherapeutic treatments for children are associated with significant improvements.
- This conclusion should be qualified in that the pool of controlled studies is far smaller in both number and sample size than the pool of data available for adult treatment reviews.
- The average effect size across studies is comparable to those yielded by meta-analyses of adult treatments. Around three-quarters of children are better off after treatment than untreated controls.

- Treatment effects are greater when measured in terms of psychiatric symptoms than when measured in terms of adjustment or achievement. Personality characteristics show particularly small changes as a consequence of treatment.
- Younger children (those under 12) are likely to show larger changes than older ones, but this is moderated by therapist experience and training, and by type of therapy.
- Specific treatments are broadly equally effective whether contrasted with no treatment or with an active control group.
- There are consistent differences between treatments in terms of effect size. Behavioral treatments show significantly larger effect sizes than nonbehavioral ones, humanistic/existential and family-based treatments obtaining somewhat better effect sizes than individual psychodynamic interventions.
- Between-treatment differences are seriously confounded by the use of measures to assess outcome that favor the behavioral treatment.
- There are very few studies of psychodynamic interventions in the pool available for meta-analysis, and these are unrepresentative of practice because of their brevity and the predominance of group-based treatments.
- The generalizability of these meta-analytic findings is further reduced by the large number of convenience sample rather than clinic-based studies. When the latter are subjected to meta-analyses, there is no clear evidence of treatment effectiveness. Recent efforts to investigate and bridge the gap between laboratory and clinic-based studies are very much welcomed.
- Theoretical allegiance has a strong influence on effect size, indicating the need for close scrutiny of investigators' and clinicians' expectations in studies where treatments are compared.
- Some findings of meta-analytic studies are so inconsistent with clinical experience that they call into question the usefulness (so far) of meta-analytic methodology for this patient group. These include the lack of consistent age and gender effects, and the absence of a difference in outcome between disruptive and emotional disorders.

Implications

- The meta-analyses support the value of these interventions, but only in a context and in a manner that brings the generalizability of the findings into question.

- It is doubtful whether the planning of psychotherapy services for children can be rationally based on the findings of meta-analytic studies.
- The impact of child treatment needs to be looked at in the context of its long-term developmental outcome, particularly in the case of nonbehavioral treatment, and this has implications for the ongoing, audit-based evaluation of children's services.
- Nonprofessional and inexperienced therapists appear to do quite well compared to trained and experienced individuals, but these effects are moderated by age, with experienced paraprofessionals doing better with younger children and graduate students doing better with adolescents. It should be noted that these studies have mostly involved subclinical levels of disorder, and it may be that training and experience become more crucial in treating seriously or multiply impaired children.
- Nonprofessionals may be able to do quite well with disruptive disorders because of the well-structured nature of these treatments.
- Far more controlled studies are required, particularly in the realm of nonbehavioral (psychodynamic and family) therapies. These need to be adequately manualized, and to reflect the conditions of clinical practice as closely as possible.

TREATMENTS USED FOR PARTICULAR DISORDERS, AND CURRENT EVIDENCE OF THEIR EFFICACY

This area has recently been reviewed by Kazdin (1994). This summary draws partly on that review, with details of studies of particular merit or interest.[2]

Depression, Dysthymia, and Bipolar Disorders

The treatment of depression in children and adolescents has been recently and authoritatively reviewed by Harrington (1993).

---

[2] This summary does not cover the treatment of eating disorders, which is detailed in Chapter 9.

Cognitive-Behavioral Interventions

Programs have been devised for children and adolescents using techniques adapted from those developed in cognitive therapy for depressed adults (see Kendall, 1993). Reynolds and Stark (Reynolds & Coats, 1986; Stark, 1990), for instance, describe a package of procedures drawing on social learning theory (Rehm, 1977) and cognitive therapy (Beck, 1967). The program is administered to a group and lasts for 21 sessions. Stark et al. (1987) compared the effectiveness of elements of this package, with 29 9- to 12-year-olds recruited from schools who scored at least 16 on the Children's Depression Inventory (a score of 13 or more is considered indicative of significant depression). One group of children received self-control therapy (modeled on the cognitive therapy approach with adults described by Rehm et al., 1984), the other received behavioral problem-solving therapy, which focused on fostering skills for coping with difficult situations and increasing the frequency of pleasant or rewarding events in the children's lives (Stark, 1990). Children were treated in groups of five for 12 sessions. A third group of children were placed on a waiting list for 5 weeks, then offered the self-control therapy if they wished.

The results of this study are generally taken to show that children in both treatment groups showed significantly reduced depressive symptoms in comparison with those in the control group, and that these gains were maintained over an 8-week follow-up (see Harrington, 1993; Kazdin, 1994). This was the case to the extent that, on individual t-tests, several comparisons of mean differences (for each measure, treatment condition and pair of assessment points) were significant, and favored the two treatments over the waiting-list group. However, with such a large number of comparisons of related measures, and no reported Bonferroni adjustments, the danger of Type I errors is considerable.

The other major analysis reported in this study, an analysis of covariance comparing scores between groups, controlling for pretreatment scores, is more robust and reliable as a procedure. In this multivariate analysis, scores on only one measure (the Children's Depression Inventory) confirmed the reported result to a significant degree. Several additional measures of mood were used, and these did not give such a clear picture. On the other self-report measure of depression, the Child Depression Scale, and the Cornell Dysthymia Rating Scale—Revised (CDRS-R; a semistructured interview on depressive affect), the Coopersmith Self-Esteem Inventory, and the Revised Children's Manifest Anxiety Scale (RCMAS), there were no significant differences among the three groups. Parent report (Child Behavior Checklist [CBCL]) and relevant scales and subscales) also showed no significant effect of treatment. The situation at 8-week follow-up was also complicated;

although on the self-report measures, positive changes during treatment had been maintained, the parents' perception was not entirely in line with child report. CBCL scores on social withdrawal, for example, had returned in the self-control therapy group to the pretreatment level. The waiting-list group (which had dwindled to two to five, depending on the measure, at follow-up) does not provide an indication of the untreated course of these symptoms, since this group had by then also been treated. The only comparison of interest at follow-up was therefore between the two treatment conditions.

This study underlines the points made in an earlier section, about the difficulties of measuring child functioning and change during treatment; it also had a small sample size (9–10 per group at the outset, falling to five or six in the treatment groups at follow-up). The study cannot be seen as providing strong evidence of the effectiveness of these forms of therapy.

No study has yet used these therapies with a group of clinically referred children or adolescents, although Lewinsohn et al. (1990) ran a course of 14 group sessions for adolescents who (while not referred) met DSM-III or Research Diagnostic Criteria (RDC) for major, minor, or intermittent depressive disorder. One group of 19 received just the adolescents' group course; for a second group of 21, there was an adolescents' group course and a simultaneous group for the parents. A third group of 19 were placed on a waiting list and treated later. Adolescents in both treated groups improved significantly more than those on the waiting list; 95% in the waiting-list group were still diagnosable at termination, in comparison with 57% and 52% in the adolescents-only group and adolescents-and-parents groups, respectively ($p < .01$). The gains were generally maintained over a 2-year follow-up.

This was a well-designed study using clinically significant levels of depression, although some caution is appropriate on a number of points. First of all, half of the adolescents did not meet DSM-III criteria for major depression; most of the rest (44% of the total group) met RDC criteria for intermittent depression. Obviously this raises the possibility that they would have been expected to improve spontaneously. This relates to another difficulty, presumably due to the ethical considerations, that the waiting-list group were treated after 7 weeks, and the untreated course of the disorders cannot therefore be compared with outcome in the treated groups, which were followed up for 2 years. A further caution is raised by the finding that although improvement was much greater in the treated groups, over half of the treated individuals still met diagnostic criteria at posttreatment.

A finding to note was that while adolescent report measures improved in both treatment conditions, parent report measures only improved (beyond the improvements found in the waiting-list group) in the second condition, when the parents were also given intensive advice and support. Thus, CBCL scores on the Internalizing scale and the Depression subscale were both rated lower (i.e., more improved) at posttreatment by parents in the waiting-list group than in the adolescent-only treatment group. This raises the question of whether the reported improvements reflected attention as well as symptom change; adolescents reported improvement when they were treated, parents reported improvement in adolescents when they were also helped, but not otherwise.

On the whole, one may conclude that there are important difficulties with these studies, particularly that they have used nonreferred children (even the study by Lewinsohn et al., 1990, recruited from schools, and so was not dealing with the kind of entrenched, polysymptomatic picture that is generally seen in clinics), and that they have used group treatments that are not normally practicable in a clinical setting (Harrington, 1993). Nevertheless, they confirm the possible usefulness of these forms of treatment, developed for adults, in child and adolescent psychiatry.

Social Skills Training

Matson (1989) described the use of a social skills training program using individualized vignettes of difficult situations and evaluated this program in two case reports of individual treatment of depressed children. Both improved substantially; but as there was no comparison condition and there were other treatment components, this report only gives preliminary encouragement.

Subsequently, Fine et al. (1991) compared two group therapies for adolescents who met DSM-III-R criteria for either major depression or dysthymia. The patients were referred for outpatient treatment and were then assigned to a 12-week therapy group using either "therapeutic support" (27 patients) or formal social skills training (20 patients). Forty-one percent of the patients were receiving concurrent treatment—psychotherapy, medication, or both.

At posttreatment, adolescents in the therapeutic support group were significantly *less* likely than those given social skills training to be diagnosed as depressed ($p < .03$) and had significantly lower scores on the CDI self-report measure of depression ($p < .05$). These group differences were no longer significant at follow-up, but this appeared to be a result of diminishing sample size as much as a change in relative rates of depression. As the authors point out, in the absence of an untreated control group, it is not possible to assert that the two treatments improved on the spontaneous remission rate; 68% of adolescents in the study were no longer diagnosable at 9-month follow-up, and in Kovacs and Gatsonis's (1989) study the median time to recovery was 9.5 months. This suggests a beneficial impact of therapy, but it is difficult to be sure how comparable the samples were. The high proportion of adolescents receiving other treatments also raises a major problem of interpretation.

Although this study has been regarded as supporting the use of social skills training for depressed adolescents, some reservations are expressed by the authors, who provide an interesting discussion of the unexpected superiority of the therapeutic support group over the "active" treatment. There were indications from process measures that adolescents in the social skills training group were less engaged and more avoidant. The authors suggest that social skills training may be too demanding for clinically depressed adolescents, but that they may be able to use some of the skills learned as they become less depressed (between posttreatment and follow-up). They suggest that a fruitful approach might be to offer therapeutic support that introduces social skills training at a later stage.

Interpersonal Psychotherapy

Interpersonal psychotherapy (IPT) is a brief treatment approach developed for adult patients (Klerman et al., 1984), which focuses on a specified range of interpersonal problems that may underlie the individual's depressed state. It has been tested in several clinical trials, notably the NIMH collaborative study of the treatment of depression (see Chapter 4; Elkin et al., 1989). The approach has quite recently been adapted for adolescents (IPT-A; Moreau et al., 1991). The authors are currently conducting a small, open trial using this modified, manualized approach; the results so far seem promising (Mufson et al., 1994).

Some other evidence on efficacy comes from a previous open trial (Robbins et al., 1989), this time applying the IPT approach for adults to a group of 38 adolescent inpatients diagnosed as suffering from major depression. It was not clear to what extent the procedures differed from those defined in the adult manual. Robbins et al. (1989) reported that 47% of patients showed clinically significant improvement with IPT alone. (Lack of response was associated with dexamethasone nonsuppression and "melancholic subtype.") The nonresponders were then treated with a combination of tricyclic antidepressant and this version of IPT; 92% then responded. This approach is interesting, but obviously needs further evaluation.

Psychodynamic Psychotherapy and Psychoanalysis

A chart review study of child psychoanalysis and psychotherapy (Target & Fonagy, 1994a), included 65 children and adolescents with dysthymia and/or major depression who had been treated for an average of 2 years; 82% of the cases no longer had these symptoms by the end of therapy, and in 75% of cases global adaptation (Children's Global Assessment Scale [CGAS] score; Shaffer et al., 1983) showed a reliable improvement. However, as major depression has been shown to run an episodic course, the absence of regular reassessment during and after treatment means that this study cannot be regarded as demonstrating the effectiveness of psychodynamic treatment for depression. One result is, however, worth noting—that children and adolescents with depressive disorders appeared to benefit more from intensive (four or five sessions per week) than from nonintensive (one or two sessions per week) therapy, after controlling for length of treatment and level of impairment at referral. This superiority of intensive treatment for depression is surprising in view of the fact that the depressed cases were mostly adolescents, who generally did not gain additional benefit from frequent sessions (Target & Fonagy, 1994b).

Summary

- There is some evidence of the effectiveness of cognitive-behavioral programs with depressed children and adolescents, although in the only study involving clinical levels of depression, over half the adolescents treated remained clinically depressed at termination.
- Social skills training has not yet been shown to be effective with clinical depression, and it may be better used when the patient has partially recovered.
- Interpersonal psychotherapy for adolescents (IPT-A) has not yet been evaluated, but preliminary evidence suggests that it may be helpful in about half of clinical cases.
- There is little evidence available on the psychodynamic treatment of depression in this age group, although there are suggestions from retrospective data that the majority of depressed children treated show clinically significant improvement, provided they receive frequent sessions.

Implications

- Very few studies have evaluated psychological treatments for clinical depression, and those that have been carried out suggest that

treatments tested with subclinical conditions (such as social skills training) are not always effective with disorders of clinical severity.
- While it seems to be a productive strategy to adapt treatments for depression developed for use with adults, these have yet to be demonstrated to be effective with children or adolescents.
- One common intervention for child and adolescent depression, psychodynamic psychotherapy, has barely been evaluated; this needs to be addressed alongside the continued evaluation of newer approaches.
- It is important to assess the usefulness of combined approaches, or of sequential strategies (as in the suggestion of following a supportive group with the more challenging social skills training).

Anxiety Disorders

Behavioral and Cognitive-Behavioral Treatments

This area has been reviewed by Kendall (1993). The early literature in this area consisted mostly of single-case reports of imaginal and *in vivo* desensitization for a variety of circumscribed phobias (see Morris & Kratochwill, 1991). However, these specific phobias (of dogs, dental treatment, small animals, etc.) are not a frequent cause of referral for treatment (Barrios & O'Dell, 1989), so the results were of theoretical rather than clinical interest.

The most systematic early study (Miller et al., 1972; Hampe et al., 1973) unfortunately gave inconclusive results; children with a variety of phobias (mostly school phobia) were recruited (not referred, but of "clinical severity"). They were then randomly assigned to either systematic desensitization, psychotherapy, or a waiting-list control condition. Both therapies were conducted three times a week for 8 weeks. Parental ratings of improvement showed that both active treatments were superior to the control condition, with no significant difference between them. However, ratings by a clinician (not the therapist, but also not blind to therapy assignment) showed no difference among the three groups. In fact, children in all three groups tended to improve over the therapy period; mean severity scores rated by the clinician fell by 45% in the desensitization group, 53% in the psychotherapy group, and 33% in the waiting-list group.

The strongest predictor of improvement was not treatment/control condition, but age: children under 11 years were significantly more likely to lose their phobic symptom. There were some indications of an interaction between age and treatment in that 96% of treated children under 11 improved, compared with 57% of the waiting-list cases; for children over 11, the figures were 20% and 17%, respectively. At 2-year follow-up, those who had improved in therapy generally remained well, and those who had not responded at the time had also improved; only 7% remained phobic. Thus, it seems that both of these brief forms of therapy accelerated improvement in children of primary school age, whereas neither was effective for older patients.

There is evidence that exposure treatments, involving rapid return to school, can be successful in managing school refusal. Blagg and Yule (1984) conducted a study of 66 school refusers, mostly of secondary school age, comparing behavioral treatment (BT) with inpatient treatment and home-tutoring of cases in a neighboring area. Children were not randomly assigned to groups, but were matched on relevant variables. Two important exceptions to the success of matching were that the BT group were significantly younger ($p < .01$) and had been away from school for somewhat less time. The behavioral treatment involved careful assessment and preparation of all concerned, followed by "flooding"—that is, forced return to school, with escort as long as necessary.

BT led to very much better rates of maintenance in school in the year following treatment; 93% were successful, compared with 38% and 10% in the other two groups. Separation anxiety was also successfully treated in that none of the BT cases showed separation anxiety at follow-up; hospital treatment also led to large improvements in this symptom, but two-thirds of the home-tutored children still showed significant difficulties with separation. The treatment was not only far more successful, but very rapid (2.5 weeks vs. around 1 year for the alternatives) and very much cheaper than the other forms of management.

The treatment of generalized anxiety states in children—although a frequent cause of referral for treatment (Last et al., 1987b)—has not been evaluated using behavioral or cognitive methods until recently. However, Kane and Kendall (1989) reported a multiple-baseline design study of cognitive-behavioral therapy (CBT) with four children diagnosed as suffering from overanxious disorder, which gave promising results. Recently, Kendall (1994) has reported results of a randomized clinical trial of a similar cognitive-behavioral program for 47 children aged 9–13 years, the majority of whom met diagnostic criteria for overanxious disorder (the remainder were diagnosed as showing separation anxiety disorder or avoidant disorder). A 16-session cognitive-behavioral treatment package was shown to be frequently successful in that there were significantly greater improvements in the treated group than in the waiting-list group on most measures. Nevertheless, over one-third of the treated children were still diagnosable after the course of treatment, and 22% of patients dropped out before it ended. The latter children were excluded from analyses of effectiveness.

One caution in interpreting the results of this impressive study is the possibility of bias due to expectations. Although the ratings of parents and children showed a significant effect of treatment, obviously neither of these informants was blind to treatment condition. Behavioral ratings of anxiety symptoms were also recorded by blind raters and showed a similar impact of treatment, but it is likely that the children who had been through the program would be less anxious performing on video in the clinic setting, as this was an important part of the therapy procedure. Waiting-list subjects had presumably not had comparable rehearsals.

A crucial question, therefore, is whether outside observers confirmed the improvement. Teachers were asked to rate the child's anxiety and other problems on the Teacher Report Form of the Child Behavior Checklist (Achenbach & Edelbrock, 1986), and their judgments unfortunately did not confirm the effectiveness of therapy. They judged all children to have improved, regardless of condition. Kendall points out that not all children were rated disturbed by teachers at the outset, but even when only cases initially rated as disturbed were included, there was no greater improvement among the treated group (in fact, scores on the relevant scale were lower in the waiting-list group). Nevertheless, in spite of this caveat, it does seem that CBT can be very helpful to some overanxious children, and for those who improved, the gains were very well maintained at follow-up.

The current status of treatment for childhood obsessive–compulsive disorder (OCD) has been reviewed by Wolff and Rapoport (1988) and Flament and Vera (1990), and most recently 32 studies of cognitive-behavioral methods have been carefully reviewed by March (1995). His conclusion was, "Although empirical support remains weak, CBT also may be the psychotherapeutic treatment of choice for children and adolescents with OCD [as for adults]" (p. 7). The vast majority of reports to date have been case reports; a few use systematic single-case experimental designs, or report the treatment of a group with a single treatment. There have been no reports contrasting treatment or components in different groups. Some of the important reports will be discussed below.

There are several case reports (e.g., Friedmann & Silvers, 1977; De Seixas Queiroz et al., 1981) of the successful treatment of children and adolescents with response prevention or thought stopping, often with simultaneous family therapy. In addition, Bolton et al. (1983) reported results from a series of 15 adolescents with moderate to severe, well-established OCD; they were mostly tertiary referrals, with a history of failed attempts to treat their symptoms elsewhere, and often needed to be treated as inpatients. The adolescents were treated primarily with response prevention, with family therapy used to support this (focusing mainly on obstacles to the response prevention approach); sometimes other treatments were required for associated symptoms (five patients received clomipramine to ease depression or anxiety, with mixed effects on the OCD symptoms). Treatment lasted for up to 4 years, although the successful outcomes were generally achieved within 1 year.

In eight of the 15 cases, symptoms were completely relieved at the end of treatment; six of these cases remained well at follow-up (between 1 and 4 years later), while the other two had relapsed quite severely. Three cases showed no response to treatment lasting between 5 months and 4 years, and the remaining four showed partial improvement. The authors offered a useful discussion of the factors that appeared to affect response to treatment. To summarize, it seemed from this small sample that poor adolescent motivation, primary obsessional ruminations, conduct disorder, and obsessional slowness were associated with the bad outcomes.

Although the use of different combinations of therapies in this series makes the results hard to interpret in terms of the effectiveness of individual components, it is a useful account of the effectiveness of response prevention treatment with a difficult group of severe obsessionals. Naturally, using such a sick group meant that the outcome could not be compared with no treatment, but this report shows that a naturalistic study with careful documentation of outcome, in the context of reasonably clear natural history, can indicate that the treatment helps most cases at least partly, and suggests factors associated with outcome.

One single-case study of childhood OCD with an experimental design is reported by Kearney and Silverman (1990). They treated a 14-year-old boy with severe OCD (the major symptom was checking the window for bats, and his own body for contamination) and a moderate major depressive disorder. The symptoms had been severe for 2 months before referral. Treatment consisted of alternating response prevention (without exposure) and cognitive therapy, with the aim of treating both the obsessional symptoms and the depressive disorder. Both checking rituals were eliminated by the end of the 24-session program; the two rituals seemed to respond selectively to one or other form of therapy. Rather surprisingly, anxiety symptoms were most responsive to cognitive therapy, and depression to response prevention.

The authors regarded the treatment as successful, and the boy clearly was functioning more normally after treatment and at 6-month follow-up. However, there have to be some reservations about this view, from a careful reading of the results.

1. Scores on the Children's Depression Inventory showed no improvement at all during treatment.
2. Self-esteem remained very impaired.
3. Symptoms of anxiety and depression (Internalizing scale on the Child Behavior Checklist) had moved half-way back to pretreatment levels at follow-up, mainly due to return of obsessive–compulsive features.
4. Most strikingly, the authors note that when either treatment was repeated for a second week rather than alternating, there were signs of deterioration.

For example, when response prevention was repeated in the middle of treatment, there was a dramatic relapse of anxiety and depression as rated by both parents and child. The authors suggest that this combined treatment works, but using consecutive weeks of the same approach leads to partial extinction! It is therefore important to note that this study does *not* confirm the efficacy of either response prevention or cognitive therapy alone, but only of the two in combination. Even then, there must be concern about the remaining depression and the tendency toward relapse of obsessional symptoms at follow-up.

An important recent study by March et al. (1994) used a manualized CBT package, combining anxiety-management techniques designed to appeal to children, and graded exposure with response prevention, in an open trial of 15 young people with DSM-III-R diagnoses of OCD. The treatment protocol used in this study introduced the important modification that exposure and goals were placed within the child's control; this seems likely to reduce the common problem of noncompliance with behavioral techniques among children. In their series of consecutive referrals, no patient refused treatment, although two did drop out before it was completed. Parents were heavily involved in the treatment regimen, which was conducted on an outpatient basis for an average of 8 months. Interpretation of this study is obscured by the fact that all but one of the cases were simultaneously treated with medication, and four cases received either family or individual dynamically oriented therapy.

The group on the whole did well: nine of the 15 were well at follow-up, although booster behavior therapy was required to wean these children from medication without relapse. Of the remaining six, two dropped out unimproved, three received prolonged treatment without benefit, and one was improved but still symptomatic. On average across the whole group, symptom ratings were halved between assessment and follow-up. Although, as has been mentioned, the concurrent use of other treatments limits the clarity of these results, it does appear that the combination was somewhat more effective than medication alone (average magnitude of improvement 37% in the multicenter child clomipramine trial; DeVeaugh-Giess et al., 1992).

Flament and Vera (1990) point out that OCD in children and adolescents is very similar to the disorder in adults, and believe that behavior therapy will prove to be similarly effective. Their recommendation is that behavior therapy should be offered alone for OCD unless depression or extreme anxiety makes it too difficult to carry out the therapy. In this case, clomipramine, which has been shown to be specifically effective in producing partial improvement in most cases (Flament et al., 1985; Leonard et al., 1988; DeVeaugh-Giess et al., 1992), is a useful adjunct to behavioral treatment. March (1995), in his recent review, suggested that many, if not most, patients benefit from medication alongside CBT, and he found that the drug could be discontinued later without a return of symptoms. At present, the effectiveness of behavior therapy with children and adolescents with OCD should be regarded as only provisionally established, whereas the effectiveness of medication (clomipramine) alone is well established but partial.

Psychodynamic Psychotherapy and Psychoanalysis

Psychodynamic psychotherapy is widely used in the treatment of anxious children; in the United Kingdom at least half the cases treated by over 200 child psychotherapists employed by statutory services present mainly with anxiety symptoms (Beedell & Payne, 1988). Nevertheless, there have been few attempts to evaluate the effectiveness of this treatment.

The studies by Heinicke and Ramsey-Klee (1986) and Moran and colleagues (1991), described later (under Specific Developmental Disorders and Disorders Associated with Physiological Disturbances), are relevant here, as most of the children treated showed clear symptoms of emotional disorders in addition to their learning difficulties or self-injurious behavior.

Another ongoing study should be mentioned for its effort to measure change in clinically meaningful ways and for its attention to a particularly needy (and costly) group. Lush et al. (1991) compared 35 children in psychotherapy who were fostered or adopted with 13 similar children for whom psychotherapy had been recommended but did not start. The children were aged 2 to 18 years, over half were girls, and they mostly received weekly sessions for at least 1 year. For ethical reasons, children could not be randomly allocated to treated and untreated groups; the study was naturalistic. A further drawback was that, because no measures suitable to the assessment of psychodynamic change existed, measures were developed specially for the study and used without prior evidence of reliability or validity. However, there are some indications that psychotherapy did benefit these deprived children. Preliminary results have been reported on the first 20 children to be treated. Sixteen cases made "good progress" as judged by therapists' ratings and generally confirmed by parents' and external clinicians' opinions. An informal comparison was made with seven similar (but not matched) control children; none of these had improved during the same period.

Further evidence suggestive of specific benefit for anxious children in psychodynamic treatment comes from a chart review study carried out at the Anna Freud Centre in London (Target & Fonagy, 1994a). In this study, children with anxiety disorders (with or without comorbidity) showed greater improvements than those with other conditions, and greater improvements than would probably be expected on the basis of studies of untreated outcome. Over 85% of 299 children with anxiety and depressive disorders no longer suffered any diagnosable emotional disorder after an average of 2 years' treatment.

Looking in more detail at specific diagnostic groups, it was found that phobias ($n = 48$), separation anxiety disorders ($n = 58$), and overanxious disorder ($n = 145$) were resolved in 85–87% of cases. OCD was more resistant, remaining at a diagnosable level in 30% of cases at the end of therapy. Although there are inevitable limitations to a retrospective study and there was no control group or follow-up, these rates of improvement are clearly above the level expected from recent longitudinal studies (see section on natural history of disorders). It appeared that children with severe or pervasive symptomatology, such as marked overanxious disorder, or comorbid disorders (anxiety with disruptive disorder, depression, learning difficulties, etc.) required more frequent therapy sessions, whereas focused anxiety symptoms, such as phobias or OCD, improved more or less equally with once- or twice-weekly sessions.

There are some indications that psychodynamic intervention is sometimes more acceptable to children and adolescents than is a cognitive-behavioral approach. For example, Apter and colleagues (1984) reported that hospitalized adolescent patients with OCD refused to cooperate with behavioral treatment but did accept and improve with supportive psychotherapy. This underlines the importance of trying to modify techniques so that they are not only effective but also acceptable to the patient, and it is very welcome that a number of manuals are being written (see Kendall, 1994; March et al., 1994) that describe child-oriented strategies and explanations, rather than applying techniques developed for adults to these young patients.

Summary

- Among behavior therapies, desensitization treatment for phobic states has not yet been conclusively shown to be effective; flooding, or rapid exposure, has shown very good results with school phobia.
- Cognitive-behavioral treatment for generalized anxiety shows much promise, but the only group study used behavioral measures tied to therapy activities, and teachers did not agree on the improvement.
- OCD can be successfully treated by behavioral or cognitive-behavioral techniques, although combinations of treatments may be required, relapse is relatively likely, and there are reports that children and adolescents frequently refuse to cooperate unless technique is substantially adapted from the adult model.
- Small-scale, controlled studies of psychodynamic treatment, and open trials, suggest that this therapy can show good results, possibly comparable with those obtained in behavioral treatment but requiring longer in therapy. More generalized anxiety, or severe anxiety with comorbidity, shows good response to intensive psychodynamic therapy.

Implications

- Behavioral treatments for circumscribed anxiety symptoms, such as phobias, are likely to be effective in younger children.
- In cases of school phobia, a short, sharp shock in the form of flooding therapy is far more effective than gentler strategies of home tuition or hospitalization. Similarly, OCD requires an intensive effort. In both cases, it is vital to involve parents, teachers, and any other carers so that therapy is consistent. It is also very important to engage the motivation of the child by careful tailoring of techniques to the appropriate developmental level.
- The treatment of generalized anxiety in children is an urgent problem needing further studies which emphasize independent measures and generalization of gains.
- Suggestive evidence of the impact of psychodynamic therapy, perhaps particularly on generalized anxiety, needs to be followed with a controlled study.
- With the information available to show that pervasive anxiety causes widespread effects on emotional and social adjustment, it is important that studies include wide-ranging measures of change.

Ideally, treatment should either have an impact on the other effects as well as on the anxiety, or be shown to lead to improvements at follow-up in these other areas, once anxiety has been alleviated.

Disruptive Behavioral Disorders, Excluding ADHD

Cognitive-Behavioral Interventions

In spite of wide consensus that disruptive disorders, especially conduct disorders, are very difficult to treat, two programs have been developed that appear to bring good results over a series of carefully conducted studies (Kazdin, 1993; see also review by Kendall, 1993). The two forms of treatment will be outlined, and then a study will be described that compared the outcomes of each approach.

Parent management training (PMT) is a form of behavioral treatment for conduct disorder in which the therapist works with the parents rather than the referred child. The parents are taught to observe and specify problem behavior systematically and to understand principles of social learning and behavior change. This particularly involves rewarding desired behavior and withdrawing attention and privileges following undesired behavior. Many studies have demonstrated the effectiveness of this form of treatment for disruptive behavior (e.g., Kazdin, 1987; McMahon & Wells, 1989; Miller & Prinz, 1990); the effects have been shown to persist for several months (Miller & Prinz, 1990) and in fact to be evident 10 and 14 years after treatment (Forehand & Long, 1988; Long et al., 1994). As well as reducing antisocial behavior in the target child, this form of treatment has been shown to reduce the likelihood of similar behavior in siblings (see Kazdin, 1985).

The second well-investigated form of treatment for disruptive behavior is problem-solving skills training (PSST). This treatment is founded on the assumption that antisocial behavior is due (at least in part) to cognitive processes, such as a tendency to attribute hostility to others inappropriately, and poor capacity to understand social situations and solve interpersonal problems (see Rubin et al., 1991). The treatment therefore focuses on how children think about and deal with the social situations they experience. Although most outcome studies have used nonclinical samples, the treatment has also been shown to be effective with referred children (e.g., Kazdin et al., 1989; Kendall et al., 1991). One difficulty with the outcome research here is that studies that have examined the cognitive changes assumed to underpin improvement have found little or no relationship between change in thinking and change in target behavior (see Kazdin, 1993c). A further problem is that although improvements have been demonstrated, these are often insufficient to achieve normal adaptation.

Kazdin et al. (1992) have compared the outcomes of PMT and PSST with 97 children aged 7–13, most of whom met DSM-III-R criteria for conduct or oppositional disorder. Children were assigned to PMT, PSST, or the two treatments in combination. The combination, in which both child and parents were directly treated, was most effective. At posttreatment assessment, 39, 33, and 64% of children were within the normal range, on the Child Behavior Checklist, in the three groups, respectively. Teachers' ratings showed much less difference between the groups. Changes were maintained over 1-year follow-up.

Family Therapy

Alexander and Parsons (1982) have conducted studies of functional family therapy, which have shown quite impressive results in the treatment of delinquent adolescents (a group with poor long-term response rates in studies of PMT [Bank et al., 1991], or behavior modification using a token economy approach [Fixsen et al., 1976]). The functional family therapy approach assumes that an adolescent's problem behavior is serving a necessary function, such as regulation of support or emotional distance between family members. Treatment focused on behavioral and cognitive as well as interactional aspects of family processes and was characterized by the authors as a "short-term behavioral family systems approach." This treatment was compared to two other forms of family therapy (client-centered and psychodynamic), as well as to a no-treatment condition. Functional family therapy achieved improvements on measures of family interaction, and these predicted recidivism rates 18 months later (Alexander & Parsons, 1973). Both target child and sibling offending (2–3 years later) were lower in the functional family therapy condition (Klein et al., 1977). The rates of target child reoffending at 6–18 months posttreatment were 50% with no treatment, 26% with the short-term behavioral family systems approach, 47% with client-centered family therapy, and 73% with eclectic/psychodynamic family therapy. Figures for sibling reoffending within the 2–3 years after treatment showed a similar pattern: 40%, 20%, 59%, and 63%, respectively. Thus, in this study, the behavioral family systems approach to family work showed a clear superiority over the two alternative family therapies, with eclectic/psychodynamic family therapy appearing to produce a worse outcome with this group of patients than no treatment, although this difference was apparently not significant.

A more recent example of the successful use of family therapy with children and adolescents with disruptive disorders is provided by a series of studies by Szapocznik and colleagues (1989, 1990; Szapocznik & Kurtines, 1989). These authors used structural family therapy with Hispanic families. In one study (Szapocznik et al., 1989), structural family therapy was compared with individual psychodynamic therapy and with a recreational control group. The treatment groups involved 12–24 sessions over up to 6 months. On parent-rated measures of child behavior, child psychodynamic functioning, and family functioning, both treatments led to significant gains and were not significantly different from each other. However, at 1-year follow-up, although child behavior was still improved in both treatment groups, family functioning had deteriorated in the individual therapy group, continued to improve in the family therapy group, and stayed the same in the control group. Other studies by this group have also provided interesting and surprising findings, such as that "family therapy"—that is, an approach based on understanding the family dynamics—can actually be successfully used with the child alone.

Psychodynamic Psychotherapy and Psychoanalysis

Some indication of the effectiveness of psychodynamic approaches to disruptive disorders is given by the Anna Freud Centre chart review study (Fonagy & Target, 1994). The limitations of this study, particularly the lack of a control group, have been mentioned previously; 135 children with disruptive behavioral disorders were included in this review, and results are reported for 93 cases who continued in therapy for at least a year. By the end of treatment, 69% no longer warranted any diagnosis. Children under 9 years showed significantly greater improvement (mean change in CGAS score 12 points vs. 6.6 in the older group, $p < .02$); they also gained extra benefit from intensive therapy, whereas this made little difference for older children. A probably related finding was that children with oppositional disorder were most likely to improve, those with the full syndrome of conduct disorder least likely, with ADHD cases falling in between. These rates of improvement appear to be better than would be expected on the basis of natural history studies. Predictors of improvement were examined, and the most important for disruptive children were the presence of an additional anxiety disorder (but absence of other comorbidity) and persisting with treatment. Another important influence was school difficulties, which made improvement less likely.

Prevention

Increasingly, it is recognized that although treatment of disruptive be-havior can be effective in children before adolescence, the best hope for reducing serious antisocial behavior in adolescence and early adulthood lies in preventive programs, and these are probably now the major focus of interest in the management of disruptive behavior disorders (see Tolan et al., 1995, and the special section on Prediction and Prevention of Child and Adolescent Antisocial Behavior, *Journal of Consulting and Clinical Psychology*, August 1995).

Summary

- Two cognitive-behavioral treatment packages for disruptive be-havior have been shown to be effective in both convenience and clinical samples of preadolescents. A combination of the two ap-proaches appears to be most effective.
- Functional or structural family therapies have shown impressive results in several studies, all the more since these involved delin-quent adolescents, who have not yet been found to respond well to cognitive-behavioral treatment.
- There is little evidence on the potential of psychodynamic therapy for this group. One uncontrolled, retrospective study suggests that younger and more anxious disruptive children do respond beyond the level expected from the natural history of these disor-ders. There were indications that more frequent sessions made it more likely that the therapy would be continued and would then bring about improvement.

Implications

- Disruptive disorders pose a serious problem at the levels of fami-lies, schools, and society at large. Intensive and systematic re-search has produced promising results in middle childhood, but the major problem exists in adolescence. Here, effective therapies are still being developed, but there is evidence that family therapy may be useful.
- Attrition is a major problem in delivering effective therapy, and recent research on this is welcomed.
- There is little evidence so far for the effectiveness of psychody-namic treatment with this group, although there are signs that anxiety, together with the antisocial behavior, is a positive factor.

Attention-Deficit/Hyperactivity Disorder

Although there is substantial comorbidity between the disorders, conduct disorders and attention-deficit/hyperactivity disorder (ADHD) have tended to be subjected to different forms of treatment and separate outcome evaluations. This is partly because, in the United States, stimulant medication is regarded as basic to the treatment of ADHD (King & Noshpitz, 1991; see study supporting this evaluation by Pelham et al., 1993). Nevertheless, medication does not entirely eliminate the deficits associated with ADHD, and there is a tendency for difficulties to return rapidly once it is stopped (see Kazdin, 1994). There has therefore been an impetus toward developing therapies that address different aspects of this severe problem, which can then be used in combination, in the hope of improving long-term outcome.

Cognitive-Behavioral Treatment

A treatment approach to ADHD that has generated much interest is self-instructional training (SIT; Meichenbaum & Goodman, 1971). Dush et al. (1989) reported a meta-analysis of 48 RCTs using this method with clinical samples. The overall effect size was 0.41 compared with no treatment; this is disappointingly much lower than the effect size of 0.81 reported in an earlier meta-analysis of adult SIT treatment (Dush et al., 1983). Better results were obtained with impulsive/hyperactive or anxious children than with aggressive children. Older children (11 years or older) improved more than younger, and group administration was just as effective as individual treatment, but there was an effect of therapist experience in that more experienced therapists got better results. A later meta-analysis (Baer & Nietzel, 1991) of cognitive-behavioral strategies with impulsivity gave similar results and added the findings that generalization was improved if training included interpersonal as well as paper-and-pencil tasks, and that a combination of operant training together with teaching of specific responses was more effective than SIT.

A number of reviews (e.g., Abikoff & Klein, 1992; Kendall, 1993) have reinforced earlier concern about generalization from cognitive-behavioral treatment to "on task" classroom behavior and to more manageable behavior in the home. It is therefore of limited value for ADHD as a whole (Spence, 1994).

Multimodal Treatment

Satterfield and colleagues have carried out a series of studies (Satterfield et al., 1981, 1987) with a large sample of 6- to 12-year-old hyperactive boys. Long-term multimodal treatment was compared with brief treatment and with stimulant medication alone. Assignment was not random, but differences between groups were carefully assessed. The actual components of treatment were individually tailored and modified as necessary (reflecting clinical practice), and might include individual psychodynamic treatment, family therapy, parent training, social casework, group therapy, or educational intervention. Families were treated for up to 2–3 years. It was found that longer treatment (at least 2 years) was associated with greater improvement on a variety of relevant measures of adjustment and behavior (Satterfield et al., 1981).

A later report (Satterfield et al., 1987) offers remarkable data from a 9-year follow-up, comparing multimodal treatment with stimulant medication alone. At 14–21 years, 30% of the drug-only cases had at least two arrests for felonies, as compared with 7% of the children given multimodal treatment. Other measures showed similarly wide divergence between the two groups, which were very comparable at the outset.

Summary

- Although stimulant medication is regarded as the standard treatment of ADHD in the United States, it is less widely used in other countries, such as the United Kingdom.
- Cognitively based therapies such as SIT have proved to be of modest benefit to children with ADHD, although there are suggestions that older children, like adults, can use these techniques well. Generalization is a particular problem, especially generalization to the home.
- There is evidence from one series of studies to show that long-term "multimodal" therapy (intensive treatment, involving several possible approaches, as in many clinics) can bring about substantial and long-term improvement in this severe disorder.

Implications

- A problem with Satterfield's studies is that, while the multimodal treatment is close to ordinary clinical practice in its flexibility, the criteria for deciding which combination of therapies to offer in particular cases were not clearly spelled out and would therefore be difficult to emulate in clinical practice or to replicate accurately in further studies. This is a task for future work, to identify the combinations that appear to be most effective with particular types of child, family, or symptomatology, or with children at different developmental stages.

Disorders Associated with Physiological Disturbances

Cognitive-Behavioral and Systemic Family Therapies

An early study of family therapy for physical illness in children involved the treatment of moderate to severe, chronic asthma in children of 4 to 14 years (Lask & Matthew, 1979). Eighteen children and their families were given six sessions of systemic family therapy as an adjunct to standard medical treatment; a well-matched (randomly allocated) control group of 16 children received only the medical treatment. Five parameters of asthma severity were monitored before treatment and a year later. Unfortunately, there was considerable attrition from the control group during the treatment and 1-year follow-up period, so that only 11 members remained. Three of the parameters of asthma severity showed no significant difference between groups (although all tended to favor the experimental group); two (thoracic gas volume and diary records of wheezing) were significantly improved in the experimental group compared with controls. As the authors pointed out, the numbers studied were very small, and a larger study controlling for amount of contact would seem very worthwhile.

A number of case reports (see Routh, 1988) have described the effectiveness of adding cognitive-behavioral therapy to medical management of physical, psychosomatic, and psychiatric disorders with physiological symptoms (for children, mainly eating and sleeping disorders). Generally, this therapy has been delivered either to the family as a whole or as a package involving the parents' cooperation.

An example is provided by a recent study of the management of recurrent abdominal pain in 47 children aged 7–14, whose disorder had persisted for an average of 3–4 years (Sanders et al., 1994). This disorder involves recurring pain with no demonstrable organic basis, which is severe enough to interfere with the child's normal activities. The disorder leads to much professional consultation, investigation, and sometimes fruitless surgical procedures (Barr & Feuerstein, 1983). Children were randomly assigned to either a six-session cognitive-behavioral family intervention (CBFI; Sanders & Dadds, 1993), or four to six sessions of pediatric education and advice. Both treatments were given to mother and child together. Mothers' expectation of success was found to be equivalent in the two groups. Families were followed up for 12 months after treatment.

Considerable improvements were seen in both groups, but significantly greater change, as judged by children's diaries and parent reports, occurred in the CBFI condition. This difference was maintained over the 12-month follow-up, when in the CBFI group 59% of children were pain-free by self-report, and 82% by parent observation (compared with 37% and 42%, respectively, in the pediatric care group). Relapse rates over the follow-up period, and parents' satisfaction with treatment, also favored the CBFI treatment. It was possible to predict a very high proportion (72%) of the variance in change in pain behavior. Over half of this variance was accounted for by pretreatment level of pain, but the remainder involved predictors based on the rationale of CBFI training (e.g., child's use of coping self-talk, parents' using recommended strategies for distraction). This is a particularly well-designed example of studies that point to the usefulness of applying behavioral strategies, in a family context, to the problems of unexplained physical symptoms in children.

Psychodynamic Treatment

Moran and Fonagy have reported three studies of psychoanalytic treatment with children suffering from so-called brittle diabetes. The first study (Moran & Fonagy, 1987) explored the relationship between metabolic control and the process of psychoanalysis in a single-case study of a diabetic adolescent girl. Process reports were rated for the presence of dynamic themes (symptomatic and conflictual). The association of these themes with independently obtained measures of diabetic control was demonstrated using time-series analysis. The second study by these authors (Moran et al., 1991) compared two equivalent groups of 11 diabetic children with grossly abnormal blood glucose profiles necessitating repeated admissions to the hospital. Patients in the treatment group were offered inpatient treatment which included intensive psychoanalytic psychotherapy. Patients in the comparison group were offered only the inpatient medical treatment. The children in the treatment group showed considerable improvements in diabetic control, maintained at 1-year follow-up. The comparison group children returned to pretreatment levels of metabolic control within 3 months of discharge from the hospital. The third of these reports (Fonagy & Moran, 1990) was a series of experimental single-case investigations. These assessed the impact of brief psychoanalytic treatment on growth rate (measured by changes in height and bone age) in three children whose height had fallen below the fifth percentile for age. In all three cases, treatment was associated with an acceleration of growth and a substantial increase in predicted adult height.

Summary

- The addition of forms of psychological treatment to the medical management of physical and psychosomatic illnesses has shown promising results across illnesses and forms of therapy.
- Family therapies based on both systemic and cognitive-behavioral principles have shown a significant impact on severe, chronic asthma, recurrent abdominal pain, and other disorders.
- Psychoanalytic psychotherapy has been demonstrated to bring about substantial improvements in diabetic control in children previously uncontrolled to a dangerous degree.

Implications

- There is great untapped potential in the contribution of psychotherapeutic approaches to the management of medical disorders. This has been more fully explored in the adult field, but it is evidently very relevant to children's illnesses also.
- These studies not only evaluate the efficacy of different therapies for particular illnesses. They also throw light on the mechanisms involved in both illness and treatment. This is easier in chronic physical disorders, such as those given as examples here, particularly because of the availability of objective physiological measures of improvement and the independence of measures of process and outcome.

Elimination Disorders (Enuresis and Encopresis)

Psychological and pharmacological treatments for nocturnal enuresis have been recently and comprehensively reviewed by Houts et al. (1994). The most widely used psychological treatment for nocturnal enuresis is the "bell and pad," which wakes the child immediately when he begins to wet the bed. The review by Houts et al. (1994) demonstrates that this is by far the most effective treatment, both at posttreatment and at follow-up. Across many studies, urine alarm treatment showed an average of 66% dry at night at posttreatment, and 51% still dry at follow-up. In comparison, tricyclic antidepressant medication (the treatment generally used by 60% of physicians in the United States; Foxman et al., 1986) achieved 40% success at posttreatment and 17% at follow-up, which was not significantly better than placebo. When urine alarm was used with other behavioral procedures, the success rate at posttreatment rose to 72%, and at follow-up to 56%.

There is some recent evidence for the idea that nocturnal enuresis reflects low functional bladder capacity, which can be increased by daytime training. The child increases fluid intake, then learns to delay urination for increasing periods. A 50% success rate has been reported from controlled studies (see King & Noshpitz, 1991).

Encopresis, or soiling, is a complex problem which often involves physical and family difficulties which may precede or follow the soiling symptoms. Many studies have reported success with behavioral retraining interventions (e.g., Wright & Walker, 1978; Levine, 1982). These programs tend to involve elements of punishment and shame (e.g., Doleys, 1983), and clinicians tend to prefer to avoid this as it is usually already occurring extensively at home. From 10–15% of families have also refused to enter on these programs (Wright & Walker, 1978). The Boston program (Levine, 1982) is more appealing in that it avoids blame and emphasizes education, self-control, and mastery. At 1-year follow-up, 51% were in complete remission, 27% showed marked improvement with only rare incontinence, 14% were partially improved, and 8% were unchanged. More severe and pervasive symptoms and comorbidity were associated with poorer outcome (Levine & Bakow, 1976). Reports from these programs emphasize that in some cases, individual emotional or family symptoms may need to be dealt with by concurrent psychotherapy for the child or family, or both.

Summary

- Behavioral retraining techniques appear to be helpful in cases of enuresis and encopresis, although the latter is often much more resistant to treatment and more complicated by other emotional and family problems. These may well require concurrent treatment if the primary therapy program is to work.
- There is virtually no evidence of the effectiveness of other psychological treatments for these disorders.

Implications

- Although many children are helped by behavioral programs, some remain incontinent for years, and this (particularly in the case of soiling) can cause secondary emotional problems. There is a need to evaluate other forms of treatment also (such as family therapy and individual psychotherapy), partly to assess their general efficacy and partly to find out what alternatives may be useful in the cases where retraining does not help.

Specific Developmental Disorders

There is evidence that disorders affecting specific areas of academic skills can impair emotional and social functioning, as well as restricting educational achievement (e.g., Rutter, 1989). The management of these disorders is normally thought of in terms of special educational provision, and there are few studies of psychological intervention (Lerner, 1989). An exception to this, using a psychoanalytic approach, is described below.

Heinicke (1965) reported a study of a sample of children aged 7–10 with developmental reading disorders linked to psychological disturbances. These children received psychoanalytic psychotherapy, either one or four sessions per week for 2 years. Greater improvement was found in the group receiving more frequent therapy. Heinicke and Ramsey-Klee (1986) extended this study, using the results of the first to try to maximize the impacts of different treatment frequencies. They introduced a third group, matched to the first two, who received therapy once a week for the first year and four times a week for the second. Outcome was measured in terms of the referral problem (reading level) and general academic performance, together with a standardized psychodynamic diagnostic profile. At termination of therapy, there were no significant differences between the groups, but at 1-year follow-up, the groups that had received treatment either four times a week throughout, or once a week followed by four times a week, showed continued improvements on all measures, beyond those of the once-a-week group. It therefore seemed that more intensive treatment in the second year of treatment had a beneficial effect.

This study was an impressive attempt to do three things: (1) to evaluate the effectiveness of intensive and nonintensive psychodynamic therapy for emotional and learning disturbances (which have been repeatedly shown to be intertwined); (2) to isolate the impact of treatment frequency, which is of interest in a variety of therapies, and particularly, for practical and theoretical reasons, in psychodynamic treatment; and (3) to measure change in both objective, service-relevant ways, and ways that reflected the theoretical perspective. In all these respects, the study broke new ground. There were some difficulties with it, reflecting the methods prevalent in all outcome research 30 years ago. Thus, diagnostic characteristics of the sample were rather poorly described, the projective tests and interview for eliciting diagnostic details were of unknown reliability, and the therapy was not fully specified but just stated to be analytically oriented.

Summary

- Little work has been done to evaluate psychological treatments for specific learning disorders, which are generally managed through special educational provision.
- There is evidence, from Heinicke and Ramsey-Klee (1986) that psychodynamic therapy, particularly if delivered intensively after the first stage, can have a beneficial impact on reading retardation.

Implications

- Disorders affecting specific areas of academic skills can be seriously disabling in emotional and social terms, as well as restricting educational achievement.
- It would be worthwhile to explore the possible contribution of psychotherapy further, perhaps in combination with educational measures, to find out whether certain children gain extra benefit from a psychodynamic or other psychological treatment approach.

Pervasive Developmental Disorders and Mental Retardation

The treatment of these conditions, often involving medication, forms of institutional care, and special education, has been reviewed by King and Noshpitz (1991). Although there are reports of effective psychodynamic treatment (e.g., Sinason, 1992), systematic outcome research has focused on behavioral training techniques (see Rutter, 1985b).

Operant Treatment

Using parents as therapists with autistic individuals has been found helpful in promoting verbal and nonverbal communication skills, and in reducing behavior such as stereotypies (Howlin & Rutter, 1987; Ollendick, 1986). The striking results that can be obtained using this approach are illustrated here with an account of one well-known study, described in detail because similar techniques have been applied (though less intensively) with individuals with learning disabilities or presenting a range of socially unacceptable behaviors.

This highly controversial study of operant treatment for autistic children was conducted by Lovaas (1987). He ran an extremely intensive behavior modification program for 19 children who were under 4 years at the time of referral, with a mental age of at least 11 months. The diagnosis of autism appears to have been strict and reliable. These children were treated individually for 40 hours per week over at least 2 years. Furthermore, the parents were trained to administer the same treatment for the remainder of the child's waking hours. The major treatment methods were (1) discouragement of disturbed (aggressive and self-stimulatory) behavior, if necessary by "physical aversives," a shouted "no," and slap on the thigh; and (2) teaching and rewarding positive behavior such as play and speech.

A further group of 19 similar children were assigned to a control group, which received 10 hours of similar treatment per week, but punishment was not used. It is not stated whether the parents of control group children were trained to use the treatment methods at other times. Assignment was not random, for ethical reasons, but appears to have been nearly so, determined before contact with the family by staff availability. Although the two groups were broadly similar at intake, the mean age was 6 months younger in the experimental group ($p < .05$), and their mean IQ was nonsignificantly (6 points) higher. (A third group of 21 children was also monitored; these children had been diagnosed at the same center, but not referred to the project, and were recruited to ensure that referral had not selected a biased group. Results for this group successfully replicated those for the main control group.) Children in the experimental group who were sufficiently improved to attend normal first grade schooling were reduced to 10 hours treatment per week. Those who improved less were treated intensively for over 6 years.

The results of this treatment were impressive, given the very poor prognosis of autistic disorder (see section on natural history). At 6–7 years of age, the experimental group were significantly superior on measures of educational attainment and IQ. Nine children had successfully attended normal first grade school and had recorded IQs of 94–120; eight had attended first grade in special classes for language-impaired children, and their IQs ranged from 56 to 95. Only two children had required special education for retarded/autistic children; their IQs were below 30. Corresponding figures for the combined control group were 1, 18, and 21. The IQs of children in the experimental group had increased by an average of 20 points; those of the control group children had decreased by an average of 10 points. IQ at referral was a strong predictor of improvement with treatment, but age (which had differed significantly between groups) was not related to outcome. A small study using systematic variations of treatment with eight children showed that the physical punishment procedure described earlier was crucial in reducing negative behavior and increasing positive alternatives.

McEachin et al. (1993) followed the children up when they were aged 13 years on average. The differences between experimental and control groups had been maintained at a similar level over some years without treatment. The nine children who had been well functioning at age 7 were examined very extensively. They had above-average IQs, and all but one were functioning within the normal range on developmental and personality tests. Although some methodological concerns have been raised about the study, it is generally seen as well designed and conservatively interpreted (see commentaries following McEachin et al., 1993), and in need of urgent replication.

Psychodynamic Psychotherapy

This form of therapy has not been extensively evaluated for severe, pervasive developmental disorders. The Anna Freud Centre chart review study showed very poor results from intensive, long-term psychoanalytic treatment (Fonagy & Target, 1996); though there are some clinical reports of good results, these remain to be demonstrated empirically.

Summary

- Behavioral (operant) treatment appears to be effective in eliminating undesirable features of autistic and similar disorders, such as uncontrollable aggression, self-mutilation, and stereotypies, and in increasing language, play, and educability. The dramatic and lasting results from one study need to be replicated. If reproducible, they offer the possibility of major improvements in the adaptation of autistic individuals, at the cost of several years' very intensive input.
- Successful operant treatment of autistic individuals appears to require the use of physical punishment as a last resort. The same

program without this element was ineffective in eliminating aggressive symptoms, and until these were reduced, positive behavior could not be built up.
- The claims of good results from psychodynamic and other therapies for this group have not been confirmed by systematic studies.

Implications

- If replicated by other groups, we may find that approximately half of the individuals diagnosed as autistic can be helped to achieve relatively normal functioning, through an extremely intensive operant program beginning well before school age. The results from the one study appear to be very stable into adolescence, so that *if confirmed by other work*, this approach could prove highly cost-effective as well as reduce suffering in the child and family. The wider application of this program would require an ethical decision about the acceptability of the methods used, which include some physical punishment.
- Research efforts must be continued to elucidate the psychological processes involved in autistic and similar disorders, so that further methods of therapy may be found to relieve this rare but profound disability.
- More work is also required to evaluate the reports from some experienced clinicians that these pervasive disorders are amenable to an intensive psychodynamic approach.

Community or School Interventions across Types of Disorders

The review does not cover community interventions in detail, as they are unlikely to be available, even in modified form, to purchasers of health care. However, the pioneering study of Kolvin et al. (1981) will be described as an example of what has been done in this area and for what it can tell us about the amenability of different groups of children to treatment, given its careful design and relatively large sample size.

The study compared four forms of school intervention for nearly 600 children, found to be showing either neurotic or conduct-type problems. These children were selected by screening 4,300 children in several schools. The aim was to assess ways of helping maladjusted children within school, without recourse to psychiatric referral. The children were dichotomized in two major ways; they were either 7–8 or 11–12 years old, and had either emotional or disruptive disorders. These disorders were not defined by psychiatric diagnosis but by extreme scores on measures of psychological adjustment in school, personality, and social acceptance by peers.

Children were randomly assigned to one of the four treatment conditions:

1. Parent counseling, teacher consultation: this was run by social workers offering casework with parents and consultation to teachers over one school year.
2. Group therapy: this was on a psychodynamic model, with the younger group playing and reflecting on feelings, with older children more traditional discussion of emotional issues. The program continued for 1 term only.
3a. Behavior modification, for the older children only, for two terms: attempts to alter behavior through systematic reinforcement, working toward specified individual goals.
3b. Nurture work, for younger children only, for five terms: enrichment of social experience in small group with leader selected for warmth and motherliness, some shaping of desirable behavior.
4. No-treatment control condition.

There were between 60 and 90 children in each age × treatment group. Outcome was assessed at 18 months after the beginning of treatment, and at 3 years. In line with other intervention studies, children with emotional disorders were found to have significantly better outcome on the whole than those with disruptive behavior, irrespective of age and treatment type. It was also found that girls had significantly better outcome across groups. Generally, psychotherapeutic work in a group and behavior modification for the older children were more effective than counseling parents and teachers, or no treatment. Interestingly and unexpectedly, these differences between treatment and control groups widened over time, so that the effect of intervention appeared to be increasingly evident, even 2 years after it had ended.

As Kolvin and colleagues note, the most effective interventions were in fact the briefest and therefore the most cost-effective. Group therapy, which appeared overall to have the best outcome, was carried out over just one term, but the effects were very clear 2.5 years later. This was a surprising finding, but it demonstrates the potential usefulness of certain interventions in the school setting, interventions that might not have had the same impact in a different context. Kolvin and colleagues amply achieved their aim of showing the potential of the school in delivering help to maladjusted children. School is a very important and familiar social context for children, one that may be able to facilitate *and sustain* considerable therapeutic impact. Similarly encouraging results have been reported in other, smaller-scale, more recent studies (e.g., Lochman et al., 1993).

Summary

- Intervention within the school system offers an innovative and promising approach to childhood emotional and disruptive disorders.
- As in other forms of therapy, children with neurotic disorders and girls did better (in comparison with untreated control) than disruptive children and boys.
- Group psychotherapy (playing or talking about emotional issues) for a single term appeared to have the greatest effect overall, and it was the most economical form of therapy offered. Behavior modification, focused on individual problem behavior, also had a substantial impact on older children. Any therapy, including consultation to parents and teachers, was more helpful than none.
- The effects of treatment, rather than wearing off, had an increasing impact over the following 2 years.

Implications

- While not at present likely to be available as an option to purchasers of health care for children, there are signs that school-based intervention may offer great potential for helping children.
- It is likely that most of the children reached through such programs would not otherwise obtain help (see earlier section on natural history).
- It is also likely that training teachers (as in this study) in the use of the more effective techniques would have spin-off benefits for other children under their care.
- The continuous, closely knit social environment of school may be more able to maintain changes achieved in treatment than may contact with a health professional seen solely for the referral problem, and for the duration of that problem.
- The study, which involved large numbers, a careful and comprehensive design, and both common forms of psychological distur-

bance, appears to justify initiatives to implement the more effective programs in schools, through training interested teachers.

SUMMARY

- Psychological disorders are very common in children and are less likely to clear up spontaneously than has traditionally been supposed.
- Research on the effectiveness of therapies for children has lagged far behind that on the treatment of adults, just as the development of diagnostic classifications and other measures of childhood functioning has been much slower.
- It has become clear that, while some therapies tested with adults are probably also useful with similar childhood disorders (e.g., behavioral treatment of anxiety disorders), other approaches do not work in the same way. This is well known to be the case in pediatric pharmacology, where anxiolytic and stimulant drugs can have paradoxical effects, and antidepressants can be both more toxic and less effective.
- There may be differences with some psychological therapies, where treatments known to work well with adults have as yet given only equivocal results in child studies. It is therefore important that treatments be separately evaluated for children and adolescents, not just adopted on the basis of experience with adults.
- On the whole, meta-analytic studies of treatments for children have led to only the broadest conclusion—that therapy seems to be better than no therapy, to a similar extent to that found in adults.
- At the level of specific disorders, or other characteristics of the child, results from different reviews have conflicted and little of practical application has emerged. Even the general result that behavioral treatment was more effective than nonbehavioral or family treatment has recently been convincingly challenged by more specific reviews. In the field of childhood disorders, there is therefore more to be learned by examining what is known about specific treatments and disorders separately.
- There are many more systematic studies of behavioral and cognitive-behavioral treatment than of family therapy or individual psychodynamic treatment. This does credit to the cognitive-behavior therapists, who have always been interested in evaluating effectiveness in systematic ways. It reflects less well on other

clinicians who, while providing a far greater proportion of services to children, have felt less need until recently to demonstrate effectiveness.

- It is fortunate that studies that have been carried out to investigate other treatments (e.g., the effectiveness of family strategies for children with disruptive disorders or psychosomatic illnesses, and the outcome of psychodynamic treatment for learning disorders and management of brittle diabetes) have been imaginative and well designed, so that the results have clearly and convincingly demonstrated that such therapies can be useful, at least under these circumstances. They have also performed a great service in showing that these therapies *can* be evaluated using the techniques and applying the standards of modern outcome research. Furthermore, they have tended to make efforts to investigate links between treatment process and outcome, which is of considerable interest practically as well as theoretically.
- Where both behavioral and nonbehavioral treatments have been investigated in relation to the same disorders, it seems in general that both approaches have contributions to make, although it has proved easier to demonstrate symptom change in more symptom-focused therapies.
- Studies demonstrate that, in evaluating therapeutic approaches, it is important to keep in mind the fact that children cannot be separated from their contexts. A treatment that might be offered to an adult individually, in a relatively standardized form, may need for a child to be offered through the family, by training the parents or teachers as therapists, etc. Often it becomes clear that a child cannot be offered a particular form of treatment, normally effective, because his environment cannot support it.

OVERALL IMPLICATIONS

- These contextual factors bring the family and the school into center stage and make them potentially powerful influences for change in either direction. They also mean that, in planning services for children, it is important that a variety of treatment approaches be maintained at an adequate level, so that clinicians have a choice in relation to a particular child's needs and family's circumstances. It is certainly not enough to provide simply the treatment that has come out best in research studies of nonreferred children with a single difficulty.

- A further consideration with children is that development is proceeding alongside the disorder and any treatment. In many cases, abnormal development *is* the major disorder, whether or not it has become entangled with neurotic or even psychotic symptoms.
- This brings into focus two requirements of research on the outcome of childhood disturbance: (1) Evaluation of change should take into account the natural history of disorders in relation to the child's developmental stage; and (2) standardized ways of measuring childhood functioning should be developed (and where necessary adapted for use in the United Kingdom), covering not only symptomatology but also developmental achievements and processes. These two areas of functioning are separated in both ICD-10 and DSM-IV, but they need to be integrated when thinking about a child's difficulties, as does the impact of treatments offered to the child or his family.
- It is very important that research studies reflect the balance of clinical provision more closely, so that the effectiveness of psychodynamic and family therapies, both very widely practiced in clinical services for this age group, can be rigorously assessed.

CHAPTER 16

Effectiveness of Psychological Interventions with Older People

ROBERT WOODS
ANTHONY ROTH

The literature on psychological interventions with older people "reflects a field still early in its conceptual and research development in which, even in the most explored areas, the research base is suggestive but not definitive" (Smyer et al., 1990). This may be related to the fact that older people are less likely to receive psychological treatment than younger adults, despite a similar prevalence of psychological problems (such as depression) and a greatly increased prevalence of the dementias, with their well-known impact on immediate family caregivers and the wider community.

PSYCHOLOGICAL PROBLEMS OF LATE LIFE

Definitions

The diagnostic criteria for functional disorders in the elderly are the same as those used elsewhere in this review. The purpose of treating this group separately rests on two considerations: (1) that the anticipated response to psychological interventions in the elderly cannot be assumed to be the same as in younger adult samples in the same way as the efficacy of treatments of childhood disorders is normally considered separately from their impacts with adults; and (2) that the higher prevalence of organic problems both of central nervous system (CNS) and non-CNS origin often complicate the application of psychological interventions, and hence necessitates separate evaluation.

321

Prevalence and Natural History

Lindesay et al. (1989) report the prevalence rates of depression and anxiety in an urban elderly population (Table 1). The zero prevalence of panic disorders reflects diagnostic criteria requiring three panic attacks in the preceding 3 weeks for the diagnosis to be made; older people may well prevent such attacks by avoidance strategies, but at the expense of greater dependency and disability (Livingston & Hinchliffe, 1993). There does, however, appear to be a lower prevalence of anxiety disorders in the elderly than in other age groups. Generalized anxiety disorder and specific phobias are the most common diagnosis, each of these conditions being extensively comorbid with depression (Flint, 1994).

In depression, a number of prognostic studies have been reported, although these reflect the usual treatment (nearly always medication) received. Around a third of patients with depression remain depressed 3 years later, with only around 20% sustaining a complete recovery (Livingston & Hinchliffe, 1993). In the shorter term, Burvill (1993) suggests that around a half (47%) make a complete recovery and do not relapse within a year; 18% recover but then relapse within 12 months; 24% remain depressed or make only a partial recovery; in this study 11% died within the year. Although there continues to be some debate regarding the interpretation of such figures (e.g., Baldwin, 1991), it is clear that a substantial number of older people with depression do not recover with the standard treatments and that relapse is a major issue.

The natural history of anxiety disorders in older people has not been adequately investigated. However, Sullivan et al. (1988) report a community survey of over 1,000 older people in Liverpool, showing

TABLE 1. Prevalence of Depression and Anxiety Disorders in an Urban Community Sample of Older People (Lindesay et al., 1989)

Disorder	Prevalence
Severe depression	4.3%
Mild/moderate depression	13.5%
Generalized anxiety	3.7%
Phobic disorder	
Agoraphobia	7.8%
Social phobia	1.3%
Specific phobia	2.1%
Total	10.0%
Total with co-occurring depression	6.1%
Panic disorder	0.0%

that 12.8% were taking benzodiazepine medication initially; at 3-year follow-up over 60% of these individuals continued to do so. At follow-up over a tenth of the total sample were taking benzodiazepines as a sleeping medication, reflecting the prevalence of sleep disorders in older people. Morgan (1987) reviews the prevalence of sleep disorders; surveys suggest that 20% of men and nearly 30% of women aged 70 and over report "trouble with sleeping often or all the time." In addition, around a further quarter of both men and women report sometimes having trouble with sleep. These figures are much higher than for younger age groups. They are reflected in studies showing that, "on average, about 10–15% of the elderly population living at home consume prescribed hypnotic drugs" (Morgan, 1987, p. 85).

The prevalence of the dementias has been the subject of numerous epidemiological studies internationally. While there are a number of differences between studies, there is broad agreement that the prevalence doubles for each increase of 5 years; 5% of the over-65s and 20% of the over 80s are widely accepted figures (Livingston & Hinchliffe, 1993; Paykel et al., 1994). The prognosis of the dementias should perhaps by definition be poor, and this is confirmed by most follow-up studies; however, where early cases are included, a proportion may show little deterioration for up to 4 years (Livingston & Hinchliffe, 1993).

The recognition of dementia as a major source of psychological dysfunction in older people also entails a broadening of the view of psychological treatment from a one-to-one, patient-and-therapist endeavor, to include families and other caregivers. Morris et al. (1988) review the impact in terms of strain and depression on family caregivers of older people with dementia, many of whom are themselves aged over 65. Estimates of levels of strain and depression in carers do show considerable variation, depending on sample characteristics and the measures used. Many samples have comprised those known to services, who may have come to attention through having high stress levels. Estimates from 14% to 40% are reported for depression and 33% to 68% for distress at a level of psychiatric "caseness" (using the General Health Questionnaire [GHQ]). Follow-up studies suggest an increase in GHQ scores, unless the person with dementia is admitted to long-term care (Levin et al., 1989).

It is worth considering why older people do not receive equitable access to psychological treatment. Taking contacts with British clinical psychologists as a crude index, in 1992/1993 less than 10% of initial contacts were aged 65 and over, although older people form 16% of the total population (Department of Health, 1994). Although blame is sometimes attributed to Freud himself for considering psychotherapy with older people inappropriate, other factors may be more relevant.

These include a reluctance by therapists themselves to treat older people, perhaps reflecting some of the complexities of their countertransference with older people who may be in poor physical health and be viewed as close to death (Weiss & Lazarus, 1993). In the United States, it is suggested that older people's psychological problems are not identified in primary care, and appropriate referrals are not made (Smyer et al., 1990). There is evidence from three surveys that family physicians in the United Kingdom are reasonably accurate in identifying depression and dementia in their patients. However, cases of depression were sometimes incorrectly identified as dementia, and there were indications of underdiagnosis, low rates of referral to tertiary care, and low use of antidepressant medication (O'Connor et al., 1988; Macdonald, 1986; Iliffe et al., 1991). Finally, older people themselves may be less psychologically minded and less likely to seek to initiate the referral themselves, though we may expect to see changing expectations with future generations of older people.

It is important to reflect that within the arbitrary category of older people (defined in the United Kingdom as over statutory retirement age) we are discussing a broad age band of 30 or so years, a diversity of life experiences and life stages; generalizations must be treated cautiously.

Treatment Approaches

Anxiety Disorders

There is a remarkable paucity of systematic work on anxiety, panic, and phobias in older people. A number of case studies suggest that procedures used with younger people may be used with little adaptation (see Woods & Britton, 1985), perhaps proceeding at a slightly slower pace and with less ambitious goals. In an important report, King and Barrowclough (1991) describe the use of cognitive-behavioral interventions with 10 outpatients suffering from generalized anxiety disorder and panic with a mean age of 73 (range 66–78). All 10 patients had a diagnosis including panic (five) or generalized anxiety disorder (two) or both (three). Seven also were judged to have depression, two of these also showing hypochondriasis. Six showed evidence of agoraphobia. Three had significant medical conditions. Seven of the patients had previously been treated with benzodiazepines or antidepressants with no effect. All lived in the community and were seen for an average of eight sessions.

In essence, the treatment involved assisting individuals to reinterpret their anxiety symptoms. Rather than perceiving them as life-threatening or catastrophic, they were encouraged to view them as nonthreatening, benign physical sensations. Techniques such as hyperventilation, provocation tests, and controlled breathing training—often used with younger patients experiencing panic attacks—were used to facilitate this process where appropriate. The outcome for these 10 patients was encouraging. All but one showed a decrease in symptoms following intervention, and these improvements were generally maintained at follow-up 3–6 months posttreatment, with eight patients showing no symptoms at all at that stage. A number of patients showed improvements posttreatment on standardized measures (the Beck Anxiety and Depression Inventories); five of the seven patients who were initially depressed moved into the nondepressed range, supporting the utility of this approach even where depression is also present. This study indicates that tackling the anxiety in its own right with techniques tried and tested with younger adults is a worthwhile endeavor, which could benefit a large number of older people.

Benzodiazepine Addiction

As noted above, a large number of older people (around 13%; Sullivan et al., 1988) are prescribed benzodiazepine medication, in many cases as an anxiolytic, often for a considerable period of time. Apart from a general concern about their long-term use, there are specific concerns about their use with older people, and possible links with falls and confusion (Higgitt, 1992). Some older people are responding to the widespread publicity, and themselves requesting help to withdraw from benzodiazepine use, and there is some evidence that psychological techniques such as anxiety management, support in gradual withdrawal, and reappraisal of symptoms are helpful to older people in assisting this process. Jones (1990, 1991) reports a randomized controlled trial in primary care settings; 227 patients completed the study; 39% of treated cases as compared with 20% of controls succeeded in reducing or stopping their medication over the 9-month period of the trial. Treatment was provided by a practice nurse offering counseling and relaxation therapy, under the supervision of a clinical psychologist.

Depression

Scogin and McElreath (1994) review 17 comparative trials of psychosocial treatments for depression in a total of 765 adults over 60. All studies included a control condition, which was either no-treatment or delayed treatment, a placebo condition or an alternative psychosocial intervention. However, only four (23%) of these studies included patients with a formal diagnosis of major depressive disorder; 10 (59%) included patients with clinical and subclinical levels of depression, and three (18%) focused only on patients with subclinical levels of depression. At least one study included patients with a diagnosis of dementia.

The mean effect size for any psychosocial treatment versus no-treatment or a placebo was 0.78. Comparison of the four studies using only clinically depressed patients with the remaining studies yielded almost exactly equivalent effect sizes (0.76 and 0.79, respectively). Estimates of improvement based on self-report yielded lower effect sizes than those based on clinician's ratings (0.69 vs. 1.15).

Because of the small number of studies, only limited exploration of the impact of specific therapies was possible. Cognitive therapy was employed in seven studies, yielding an effect size against no-treatment or placebo of 0.85. Based on data from eight trials, reminiscence therapy yielded an effect size of 1.05, again against no-treatment or placebo. Comparison between different therapies did not suggest any superiority for any one modality over the other. These effect sizes are comparable with those computed by Robinson et al. (1990) in their broader review of treatments for depression (discussed further in Chapter 4).

A major trial of acute and maintenance therapy for older people with recurrent depression is being conducted at the University of Pittsburgh. Reynolds et al. (1992) report preliminary results for 73 patients aged 60–80, treated with nortriptyline combined with weekly sessions of interpersonal psychotherapy (IPT). Once patients showed a good treatment response (defined as a Hamilton Rating Scale for Depression score ≤ 10), they were assigned to continuation therapy for a further 16 weeks, in which the frequency of sessions was reduced to monthly. At this point patients were assigned to one of four maintenance therapy conditions: receiving either nortriptyline or placebo, in combination with IPT, or to IPT alone over a period of 3 years. Although this trial is ongoing, preliminary results from the open-trial acute phase are promising; of the 61 completer patients, 48 (78.7%) met the criteria for treatment response. Of these, 41 (67.2%) met a stringent criteria of a Hamilton score of ≤ 6.

Individual Psychological Approaches

It has been the cognitive theories and therapies originating from Beck's work that have proved most influential in the development of psychological treatment approaches for older people with depression. Studies emanating from this approach have, in turn, shed light on other approaches, including psychodynamic psychotherapy.

In the United States Gallagher-Thompson, Thompson, and colleagues have carried out a systematic series of studies contrasting the efficacy of cognitive, behavioral, and eclectic/psychodynamic psychotherapies in the treatment of 91 elderly people suffering from depression in an outpatient setting. The behavioral treatment was based on the work of Lewinsohn, which conceptualizes depression as arising from a lack of social reinforcement. Therapy aims to help the person participate again in activities he or she enjoys, and hence to increase their level of reinforcement. The brief psychotherapy approach was described as eclectic and dynamic, relying on the "use of the therapeutic relationship to help patients gain insight into their problems and formulate plans for change." Generally, no specific skills were taught, and, in contrast to the other two modalities, structured homework assignments were not an integral part of the approach.

These three treatment approaches were compared to a waiting-list control group (Thompson et al., 1987). Elderly depressed outpatients received between 16 and 20 individual sessions of one of the three therapy modalities, either immediately or after a 4-month waiting-list period. There was a significant treatment effect compared with the waiting-list control group, but no differences in efficacy between groups were identified, either immediately after treatment, or at 1- and 2-year follow-ups. Over half (52%) of the 91 patients in the trial moved out of the depressed range following treatment, with a further 18% showing a substantial improvement on the various measures used (which included observer-rated as well as self-rated depression scales—the Hamilton Rating Scale, the Beck Depression Inventory, and the Geriatric Depression Scale). At 2-year follow-up (Gallagher-Thompson et al., 1990), 70% were no longer in the depressed range. Although far superior in methodology to any other outcome study in this field, as Weiss and Lazarus (1993) point out, a number of patients dropped out of treatment; for example, a quarter of those allocated to cognitive therapy were lost to treatment. Reasons for dropout tended to have as much to do with physical health and transportation problems as with dissatisfaction with the treatment. Further analyses have identified the factor of "patient commitment" (defined as motivation for, and involvement in, therapy) as a key predictor of clinical improvement (Marmar et al., 1989). Levels of the therapeutic alliance did not differ across the groups, with the level of alliance tending to predict improvement in depression better in the behavioral and cognitive therapy groups than in the brief psychotherapy condition (Gaston et al., 1991).

Some efforts have been made to identify the characteristics of those not responding to treatment. Those still depressed at 2 years tended to be those who had not responded initially to treatment. Despite receiving a variety of other treatments in the intervening period, their depression remained intractable. The presence of endogenous symptoms initially predicts poorer outcome (Gallagher & Thompson, 1983), but this is not a good indicator, as a substantial proportion of patients with such symptoms did recover or make significant improvements. Another suggestion is that a coexisting personality disorder may predict poor prognosis (Leung & Orrell, 1993; Thompson et al., 1988). Clearly there remains a need to develop more effective treatment strategies for these hard-to-treat patients.

Group Therapies

A number of studies on cognitive therapy with this age group have used a group format, with a detailed treatment manual being available (Yost et al., 1986). Psychodynamic and CBT group therapies were reported by Steuer et al. (1984) to be equally effective in reducing levels of depression, although there was a 40% dropout rate during the 9-month period of treatment. Of those who completed 9 months of therapy, 40% were in remission and 40% had some symptomatic reduction. In one of the few studies where CBT has been compared with a pharmacological treatment (Beutler et al., 1987), the attrition rate was lower in the group cognitive therapy condition during the 5 months of treatment. However, the relative effectiveness of CBT is difficult to evaluate, as the drug used, alprazolam, is not widely used as an antidepressant and certainly did not perform well in this trial; there was the most evidence of change among those receiving cognitive therapy. In both the Steuer et al. and the Beutler et al. studies, beneficial changes related to group cognitive therapy were particularly noted on the self-report Beck Depression Inventory rather than on the observer-rated Hamilton Rating Scale for Depression. Although a comparison of individual and group CBT has yet to be performed, the success rates in bringing elderly people into the nondepressed range do seem greater in the individual-therapy studies. This difference needs to be balanced against the possible greater input of therapeutic time needed in individual therapy.

It is in the sphere of relapse prevention that groups may prove to be most valuable. Several accounts are available of groups that provide long-term support, making use of the peer support available in a group context (Ong et al., 1987; Culhane & Dobson, 1991). For example, in a small randomized controlled study (10 patients in each group) Ong et al. (1987) reported significant differences in rereferral and readmission rates favoring those who attended a weekly support group over a period of a year. Seven of the control patients were rereferred to the hospital and six readmitted, despite receiving the usual support services available; none of the support group members were rereferred or readmitted.

Bibliotherapy

In addition to individual and group formats, cognitive and behavioral therapies have been compared through the use of self-help books with mildly or moderately depressed older people (Scogin et al., 1989). Compared with a waiting-list control, both books were effective in reducing depression, as measured by the Hamilton scale and a self-report measure; two-thirds of the subjects showed a clinically significant change. Treatment gains were maintained at 6-month and 2-year follow-ups, with over half of the follow-up sample reporting returning to the book in the intervening period (Scogin et al., 1990).

Relative Efficacy of Treatments with Older and Younger Client Groups

Are the effects of psychological therapy for depression reviewed here of the same level as for younger adults? Dobson (1989) reports a meta-analysis of cognitive therapy outcome studies, suggesting a significant negative correlation between amount of change and age of patients, with more clear-cut evidence for it being superior to other approaches in younger samples. However, Gallagher-Thompson et al. (1990) argue that their results "compare favorably with published reports on younger depressed patients." Knight (1988), evaluating a range of outpatient therapies, reports that the over-60 age group improved more than younger adults. Within the older age group, age was negatively related to change but was offset by longer courses of therapy. Thus an 80-year-old may show as much improvement as a 65-year-old, but would probably require more sessions of therapy over a longer period. Newton and Lazarus (1992) suggest that older patients do often require a longer-term involvement in therapy, but that after the initial treatment phase, contact can be relatively infrequent. Weiss and Lazarus (1993) also draw attention to the possibility that psychological treatment for older people may particularly reduce costs of later medical interventions; they quote a meta-analytic study (Mumford et al., 1984) as finding that "older subjects benefited even more from the specific modality of outpatient psychotherapy than those who were younger, enjoying a greater decrease both in rate and cost of subsequent medical care utilization."

Summary

- Prevalence rates of most functional disorders in older people are similar (although in some studies somewhat elevated), contrasted to younger age groups, though their natural history is less favorable.
- Older people appear to be less likely to be in receipt of psychological treatment. This may be a reflection both of patients' and clinicians' expectations of treatment outcome, and might also reflect problems in the detection of these disorders.
- There is relatively little research into the efficacy of treatments for functional disorders in older people.
- Data from case studies and open trials indicate that methods used in treating younger adults may be applicable to older people, though treatment may proceed at a slower pace.
- There is little research examining the efficacy of psychological treatments for anxiety disorders, although in a single, small-scale study, CBT appears to be effective.
- Treatment of anxiety with anxiolytics, although common, appears to be problematic.
- Data from controlled trials suggest that cognitive therapy, behavior therapy, and brief psychodynamic psychotherapy appear to be equally effective treatment modalities for depression in older people.
- Group therapies may be particularly helpful in preventing relapse for patients in this age group.
- Self-help books (bibliotherapy) may be helpful with mildly or moderately depressed older people.
- As many as 30% of patients with depression fail to respond to any type of treatment. A number of these have been described as having a personality disorder. The long-term effects of traumatic experiences in the person's life may also be relevant. Work on applying approaches to personality disorders in younger people to this population would be helpful.

ORGANIC DISORDERS

Sleep

Definitions

The essential feature of sleep disorders, as defined by DSM-IV, is a complaint of difficulty maintaining or initiating sleep, or of nonrestorative sleep that lasts for at least 1 month. Though there are some differences of detail between DSM-IV and DSM-III-R, both require that the level of sleep disturbance result in clinically significant distress or impairment in important areas of functioning. Because the depth and continuity of sleep deteriorate with age, age is always considered a factor in making this diagnosis.

Sleep Problems and Depression

Sleep problems are common in depression. However, in older people insomnia is not a good diagnostic index of depression (Morgan, 1992), as there are a number of other equally significant etiological factors. Early-morning waking is the classic sleep problem associated with depression; generally in older people, problems with broken sleep and in getting to sleep initially are more common.

Treatment Approaches

A number of psychological approaches are now available to assist with these difficulties, and may be of use for those mildly depressed patients where sleep disturbance is a major complaint. These approaches include relaxation methods, techniques for enhancing the connection between sleep and bed (Friedman et al., 1991), and CBT approaches. Expectations are important here; the well-documented changes in sleep patterns with age imply that individuals who believe that something is wrong unless they are having 8 hours sleep a night are very likely to be dissatisfied with their sleep, even though it may not be abnormal compared to other people of the same age.

This work implies that a number of interventions may be helpful, such as education on sleep in later life, sleep clinics in primary care, and review of repeat prescriptions for sleeping medication. However, the efficacy of such treatments remains untested.

Dementias

Definitions

As described by DSM-IV, the dementias are characterized by the development of multiple cognitive deficits (including memory impairment) that are due to the direct physiological effects of a general medical condition, to the persisting effects of a substance, or to multiple etiologies (such as the combined effects of cerebrovascular disease and Alzheimer's disease). Specific criteria are given for the diagnosis of dementia of the Alzheimer's type and vascular dementia (termed multi-infarct dementia within DSM-III-R), with the latter being diagnosed only where there is evidence of cerebrovascular disease.

Psychological Interventions

While there is a long history of psychological "treatments" for older people with dementia, their development has tended to be almost as much a matter of fashion as the result of empirical research. In part, this may be related to the intrinsic difficulty for care staff (who largely have the task of applying such methods) in perceiving whether or not the approach is helpful, in that it is applied against the backdrop of a natural history of progressive deterioration. Stability of function or slowing of decline may be an acceptable goal, but these are more difficult for the individual to discern without the benefit of a control group. Holden and Woods (1995) and Miller and Morris (1993) review many of the relevant studies.

The Care Environment. Two models are helpful in understanding the impact of the care environment on older people with dementia. Lawton's "environmental docility" model (Parmelee & Lawton, 1990) suggests that the person with lowered competence and function is more likely to be shaped by and vulnerable to environmental contingencies. Kitwood (1993) proposes that persons with dementia attract and are susceptible to the effects of a "malignant social psychology," where they are devalued, deskilled, and even dehumanized by the care environment. Both concepts lead to a situation where many people with dementia may be underfunctioning, withdrawing from an unhelpful, perplexing situation that does not support the remaining skills and abilities which the constraints of neurological impairment would allow. Such an understanding has led to attempts to develop more positive care environments, based on psychological principles. Examples of this would include "integrity-promoting care," from Sweden (Brane et al., 1989), and in the United Kingdom, the domus philosophy (Dean et al., 1993).

Evaluations of such approaches are producing promising results. For example, Dean et al. (1993) report improvements in cognitive function, self-care skills, and communications skills over the first year of operation of a domus for people with dementia. In addition, there were higher levels of activity and interactions in the domus. There was no control group in this study, and the comparison was made with the same patients when resident in a conventional psychogeriatric hospital setting; given the usual expectation of decline, such results are of great interest. Brane et al. (1989) compared patients receiving 3 months of "integrity-promoting care" with a control group receiving conventional care. Improvements were noted in performance of motor skills and in mood, with reduced distractibility. However, in such broad interventions it is naturally difficult to specify the key components, and more work is required to replicate such environments and their essential features.

On a smaller scale, there is continuing interest in assessing the impact of various forms of stimulation on patients, including those with the most severe degree of dementia, who generally appear to be unresponsive to most external stimuli. Studies that have attempted to evaluate the impact of offering particular forms of stimulation to patients with severe dementia include Norberg et al. (1986, employing music, touch, and various objects), Gaebler and Hemsley (1991) (music), and Haughie et al. (1992) (pet dogs). This last study, for example, showed an increase in interactions on a hospital ward for people with dementia when a dog was introduced. What are particularly notable from these studies are both the responsivity of patients with severe dementia to aspects of their environment, and the detailed, careful observation needed to identify this response. There is a real risk of patients being "written off" as completely unresponsive because the response is not immediately apparent.

Reality Orientation. Reality orientation (RO) is the most extensively evaluated of the psychological approaches to dementia. It has two main forms: (1) RO sessions taking the form of small structured group meetings, which use a variety of activities and materials to engage the patients with their surroundings and to maintain contact with the wider world, and (2) 24-hour RO involving environmental changes, with clear signposting and extensive use of memory aids, and a consistent approach by all staff in interacting with the person with dementia.

Holden and Woods (1995) review 21 controlled trials of varying methodological adequacy, including 677 people with dementia. In a variety of settings a small but significant effect of RO sessions on measures of verbal orientation has been reported, compared with untreated control groups or unstructured social groups. Changes in functional ability have been much more elusive, although reported in some earlier studies. Twenty-four-hour RO has been the subject of fewer evaluations, although there have been several studies, usually using single-case designs, demonstrating the efficacy of specific training sessions in helping disoriented patients find their way around the ward or home, often using signposting (e.g., Lam & Woods, 1986). Reeve and Ivison (1985) showed improvements in spatial orientation following the implementation of a 24-hour RO program. Similarly, Williams et al. (1987) showed significant cognitive and behavioral improvements associated with 24-hour RO.

Reminiscence. The use of past memories to foster contact has been often used in RO sessions and has attracted interest as an approach in its own right. Reminiscence therapy has been used with individuals and in small groups (Norris, 1986; Thornton & Brotchie, 1987; Woods et al., 1992; Gibson, 1994). Photographs, music, and archive recordings and items from the past are used to stimulate a variety of personal memories. Evaluative studies with people with dementia are few, and no clear picture has yet emerged of its effects. Head et al. (1990) found an increase in interaction in one group, compared with an alternative activity, but a group in another day center failed to show a differential benefit from involvement in reminiscence activities. Baines et al. (1987) similarly report results from two groups, with only one showing improvements in orientation and function outside the group. It is clearly an enjoyable activity for many older people with dementia, but there is little evidence of its impact continuing after the group session, or of its being more effective than other activities within a group in increasing interaction.

Validation Therapy. Dissatisfaction with RO, which can be applied in a rather rigid, unfeeling fashion if too much emphasis is put on "correcting" the person rather than seeking to understand his or her attempts at communication (Dietch et al., 1989), has led to increasing interest in validation therapy (Feil, 1993), where attempts are made to discern and respond to the emotional content of what the person says, rather than focusing on the factual content. Evaluative studies are beginning to appear (Morton & Bleathman, 1991; Bleathman & Morton, 1992), but to date the conclusion would have to be as for reminiscence—a useful addition to the repertoire of techniques for use in group and individual work with people with dementia, but with no clear evidence of persisting effects or of greater benefits generally than other approaches. Woods (1992) shows that the core techniques of validation therapy are not incompatible with the RO approach when it is used in a sensitive, individualized manner, and argues that to see alternative approaches as competitors may detract from the need to find the most effective strategy for working with a particular individual at a specific point in time.

Psychotherapy and CBT. People with dementia present with a broad range of functional abilities; increased public awareness of dementia as a disease may be leading to earlier recognition and diagnosis. A subgroup of patients are clearly aware that something is wrong, that they are not able to function as they did previously, and they may have awareness of others (often their relatives) who have had dementia; depression is perhaps a predictable consequence of such a scenario. Attempts are being made to apply psychotherapeutic (Hausman, 1992) and CBT approaches (Thompson et al., 1990) to older people with dementia, in the individual-therapy context. Clearly the presence of cognitive impairment must lead to some adaptations, and perhaps greater emphasis on "here and now" concerns, but case reports such as provided by Sinason (1992) suggest this is an area worthy of further development.

Behavior Modification. Despite considerable interest and speculation, there are still relatively few reports of the successful application of behavior modification to patients clearly identifiable as having dementia (Smyer et al., 1990; Holden & Woods, 1995; Woods & Britton, 1985). Successful interventions have included reduced wandering and other inappropriate and stereotyped behavior (Hussian, 1981; Mayer & Darby, 1991), increasing orientation (see section on RO), increasing social interaction and participation (Carstensen & Erickson, 1986), increasing mobility (Burgio et al., 1986), and increasing participation in activities (Burton, 1980). Eliciting the desired behavior through cueing or prompting, or providing a powerful discriminative stimulus for the behavior, has often proved to be the key element of the program, rather than the reinforcement schedule per se. For instance, progress in the Burgio (1986) study aimed at increasing mobility was so rapid that the authors concluded that the opportunity to walk must have been an important component. Presumably, environmental contingencies in this nursing home setting may have discouraged walking, with staff perhaps finding it more convenient to have residents in wheelchairs. This is a good example of the existence of "excess disabilities," where persons function at a worse level than that determined by their dementia, in response to the behavior and attitudes of their caregivers; this also exemplifies Kitwood's concept of a "malignant social psychology."

The common, and difficult to manage, problem of incontinence has been the subject of mixed results when behavioral approaches have been applied. Schnelle et al. (1989) and Burgio et al. (1988) successfully used a prompted voiding procedure, where nursing home residents are simply asked on a regular schedule, say hourly, whether they wish to use the toilet, and continence is systematically reinforced. The aim here is not independent toileting, and in fact self-initiated toileting became less frequent in the latter study. Rona et al. (1986) used a more complex procedure, aiming to increase independent toileting, with mixed results. Patients who had been incontinent less than once a day showed some improvements, while those who had been more frequently incontinent did not respond to the training program.

Continence requires a number of different skills—finding the toilet, recognizing it, adjusting clothing, and so on—and is affected in older people by a number of physical factors. Multimodal approaches, tackling physical, psychological, and environmental aspects, analyzing the factors leading to incontinence in each case, and adapting toileting regimens to individual patterns of micturition offer most help in this area (Hodge, 1984).

Working with Caregivers

Many of those providing care for older people with physical or mental health problems are themselves elderly, looking after their partner or other relative, or a very elderly parent. A number of studies have shown that levels of strain and depression are high, particularly in those caregivers in contact with service providers (Morris et al., 1988). This tends to be particularly the case where the cared-for person suffers from a dementia, perhaps reflecting the experience of loss, or "living bereavement," experienced by the caregiver.

A number of attempts have been made to reduce levels of strain and depression in caregivers (Brodaty, 1992), with rather mixed results. For example, Morris et al. (1992) showed increased reported use of a variety of coping strategies and increased knowledge of Alzheimer's disease following both problem-solving groups and information groups for caregivers of dementia sufferers, but no reduction in depression or strain was noted. Lovett and Gallagher (1988), however, report reductions in depression in caregivers, following a psychoeducational intervention, which included work on the caregiver's cognitions regarding their situation. The importance of the caregiver's perceptions in leading to depression has been highlighted by studies showing that strain is not related to objective burden *per se*, but is mediated by variables such as the caregiver's sense of control and their attributions about the situation (Pagel et al., 1985).

There is some preliminary evidence that the length of time for which clients have been caretakers may be significant in choosing intervention strategies. Gallagher-Thompson and Steffen (1994) contrasted cognitive-behavioral and brief psychodynamic treatments in 66 clinically depressed caregivers of frail, elderly relatives. At posttreatment the two therapies were equally effective overall; 71% of patients no longer met clinical criteria for depression. However, there was an interaction between outcome and longevity of caretaking. Patients who had been caretakers for a shorter period had a greater response to psychodynamic therapy, while those who had been caring for their relative for more than 3.5 years responded better to CBT. This interaction was less evident at 3- and 12-month follow-up. It is possible that more "chronic" carers have a greater need for support and structure (which CBT offers) and a corresponding difficulty in exploring problems that may themselves have left them emotionally depleted.

At least four specific strategies for psychological interventions involving family caregivers have been described. The first is to teach the caregiver to use behavioral techniques to modify the behavior of the person with dementia. Pinkston et al. (1988) used this approach with 66 carers, targeting a range of areas, including self-care, aggression, and walking; single-case designs were used to evaluate changes in target behaviors, with over 75% showing improvement. In an interesting single-case study, Green et al. (1986) taught a carer to use social reinforcement to increase the amount, spontaneity, and appropriateness of her cognitively impaired husband's verbal behavior. When this strategy is effective, it can also serve to help the caregiver feel a greater sense of control and less powerlessness, and could potentially improve their own mood. However, many relatives are first seen in a crisis, often when the strain is becoming unbearable. These techniques might be better taught earlier, while the strain is more manageable, or to supporters less emotionally involved. Other techniques, such as reminiscence, can be used to facilitate communication between elderly persons and their relatives (Davies, 1981; Bourgeois, 1990); family members are well placed to use personal prompts—photograph albums, heirlooms, and the like.

The second strategy focuses specifically on the caregiver's feelings of stress, by teaching the use of stress reduction approaches. Gendron et al. (1986) offered carers training sessions in relaxation and assertiveness and report benefits in stress reduction, assertiveness, and problem-solving skills compared with untreated control carers at 6-month follow-up. Sutcliffe and Larner (1988) taught a small group of carers anxiety management and anger control methods; this intervention was associated with greater strain reduction than the provision of information regarding dementia.

The third strategy is broadly educational. In addition to elements of the first two approaches, it also addresses cognitive factors (such as the caregiver's perceptions of and attributions about the situation) and ways of maximizing support from formal services and from family and friends. Lovett and Gallagher (1988) taught problem-solving skills in what they describe as a "psychoeducational intervention" and found reductions in levels of depression; however, not all studies have found improvements in the key variables of depression and strain when a control group has been used (e.g., Zarit et al., 1987). Knight et al. (1993) report a meta-analysis of nine controlled studies implementing such approaches. Mean effect sizes for group treatments were 0.15 for burden and 0.31 for depression; where individual treatment was offered, effect sizes were rather higher (0.41 and 0.58 for burden and depression, respectively). These effect sizes compare favorably in their impact on burden with interventions offering coordination of a variety of community services (0.15) and respite care (0.63), reviewed by the same authors.

Brodaty (1992) provides a helpful review of this literature and highlights the weaknesses of studies to date, which have often used training periods that are too brief and have not sufficiently targeted carers with high strain levels. Brodaty and Gresham (1989) brought both patient and carer into a special hospital unit, with carers receiving training in coping strategies while patients attended memory-retraining sessions. Carers reported less strain at 12-month follow-up compared with a control group of carers, whose relative had been admitted for an equivalent period without them, so that they had received respite rather than training. The control patients tended to enter institutional care at an earlier stage than the relatives of carers who had received training. Mittelman et al. (1993) also report an effect on delaying institutionalization of patients with Alzheimer's disease in a large-scale study including over 200 caregivers randomly allocated to treatment and control groups. Control patients were twice as likely to be institutionalized as those in the experimental group in the first year of the study. The treatment comprised individual and family counseling and support group participation; both groups had access to ad hoc consultation with counselors throughout.

Individual counseling and group approaches both have their advantages, and a strength of both the Brodaty and Gresham (1989) and the Mittelman et al. (1993) studies may be their combined use. The use of peer-group counselors (carefully trained and supervised), rather than professional therapists, has been evaluated by Toseland et al. (1989) and Toseland and Smith (1990); there appears to be scope for achieving greater cost-effectiveness through these means.

The fourth strategy seeks to mobilize family resources to tackle the difficulties experienced, using a family therapy framework (Benbow et al., 1993). There is increasing interest in applying family therapy to this stage of the life cycle and there are several descriptions of its application (e.g., Roper-Hall, 1993), but there is as yet little in the way of outcome research. The Mittelman et al. (1993) study was unusual in including this strategy.

Summary

- With the exception of reality orientation, there has been little systematic evaluation of interventions for people with dementia.
- A number of techniques have been employed to improve functioning in people with dementia (including modification of the care environment, reminiscence therapy, validation therapy, psychodynamic psychotherapy, cognitive therapy, and behavior modification). Though many of these techniques show promise in case reports and open trials, the absence of controlled studies makes it difficult to draw unequivocal conclusions about the efficacy of these interventions.
- Reality orientation shows small but significant benefits on measures of verbal orientation, but there is no evidence of functional improvement.
- Interventions are appropriately aimed at reducing strain and depression in caregivers of dementia sufferers, given that these are known complications of an increasingly common family circumstance.
- Interventions aimed at improving coping strategies have been examined; these include knowledge concerning the disorder (psychoeducation), psychodynamic and cognitive-behavioral treatments addressing depression, training in behavioral techniques to assist in the management of sufferers, and coping skills training (stress reduction, assertiveness, and problem-solving skills).
- Studies of the efficacy of these interventions show mixed but promising results which do not identify any single intervention as the treatment of choice.
- Many studies, however, suffer from methodological problems including a failure to target caregivers most needing input, a failure to offer intervention to caregivers at an early stage, employing group rather than individualized interventions, interventions that are too brief, and a lack of long-term follow-up.
- There are encouraging indications from studies in the United States and Australia that psychosocial interventions of sufficient intensity may have an impact in delaying institutionalization of the dementia sufferer.

OVERALL IMPLICATIONS

- There is justification for specialist psychotherapeutic services for older people, both to meet the need created by mental health problems in these individuals and to support, advise, and treat those who are involved in their care.

- Adequate services for this population will require specialist post-qualification training of mental health practitioners because of the particular obstacles faced in the treatment of functional disorders (such as lower response rates), the special problems presented by comorbid organic disorders, and the specific difficulties faced by those involved in the care of older people.
- Demographic, epidemiological, and financial imperatives highlight the need to encourage research into the psychotherapeutic care of the elderly; currently this is more a potential than an actual field of endeavor.
- Further developmental work is required in a number of areas including:
  - The application of family therapy and other psychological approaches to aid families where there is a sufferer from dementia, the use of psychological treatments addressing common issues in later life (particularly issues arising from physical health problems and bereavement), education of care staff and other professionals, and counseling of dementia sufferers.
  - Considerable work is required in evaluation of both existing programs and innovative ones, particularly trials comparing the use of psychological approaches with commonly used medical regimens for functional disorders, and the adjunctive use of psychological approaches with pharmacological treatment.
  - Research and evaluation addressing the maximization of functioning in people with dementias.
- There is some suggestion in the literature that early intervention for the person with dementia is likely to be important. Earlier detection of organic problems may help the dementia sufferer to cope better, and caregivers are more likely to manage and to provide effective care if emergent psychological problems are more rapidly identified and treated.
- Many of the approaches to dementia require taking a broader view of dementia care; they require the involvement of hard-pressed direct care staff. Further work on ways of supporting positive attitudes and behavior in such staff in the context of the unit in which they work is required for the widespread application of approaches that might benefit the function and well-being of many dementia sufferers.

CHAPTER 17

The Relationship between Outcome and Therapist Training, Experience, and Technique

Up to this point we have focused on the effectiveness of *specific* techniques with *particular* groups of psychiatric disorders. However, psychotherapy research over the past decades has demonstrated repeatedly that a substantial proportion of the variability in therapeutic outcomes is unexplained by differences between formally defined therapeutic procedures, differences between client groups, or (though less well examined) the interaction between these two factors (e.g., Garfield, 1994; Beutler et al., 1994). In this chapter we examine the contribution therapists make to treatment outcome, in terms of what they bring to the treatment situation by virtue of their training and experience, the techniques they apply, and the degree to which variation from the technique specified by their particular orientation has implications for effectiveness.

THE THERAPIST'S CONTRIBUTION TO EFFECTIVENESS

Luborsky et al. (1986) reanalyzed four major studies of psychotherapy outcome to compute the variance accounted for by therapists, finding that this was often larger than that claimed for between-treatment differences (even though all therapists in these trials were experienced). The studies examined were the Hopkins Psychotherapy Project (Nash et al., 1965), in which four therapists each treated patients with heterogeneous disorders using short-term psychodynamic treatment; the VA–Penn Psychotherapy Project, which contrasted supportive expressive psychotherapy (Luborsky, 1984), CBT (Beck & Emery, 1977) and drug counseling (Woody et al., 1977) over 6 months of treatment; the Pittsburgh psychotherapy project (Pilkonis et al., 1984), in which nine therapists offered either individual, conjoint, or group therapy; and the McGill psychotherapy project (Piper et al., 1984), in which three therapists offered individual or group therapies either in a short- or a long-term format.

The analysis examined differences between outcomes for each therapist and also explored any special patient–therapist matches that might account for this difference. Significant differences in therapist efficacy were found in all four studies on various measures. For some (but not all) therapists, the initial level of functioning of the patient influenced outcome, though for some this was a strong positive predictor and for others a negative predictor.

Although some therapists appeared to achieve consistently better outcomes, even those who performed poorly overall had some patients with good outcomes. More detailed examination indicated that there was some evidence that individual therapists achieved better effects in some domains than others—for example, that some therapists achieved better impacts on target symptoms, whereas others were more successful at increasing levels of interpersonal functioning.

Schaffer (1982) differentiates the therapist's contributions into three conceptual dimensions:

1. The therapeutic technique used
2. The "skillfulness" of the therapist, encompassing qualities such as persuasiveness, verbal ability, timeliness, the capacity for neutrality, and the capacity for reducing the discrepancy between the patient's and therapist's points of view
3. The personal qualities and interpersonal manner of the therapist, such as therapist warmth, capacity for empathy, likability, and perceived sincerity

Strupp (1986) suggests that the therapist's skill consists of an ability to create a particular interpersonal context, and within that context to foster certain kinds of learning. It is clear that technical prescriptions that follow from the models of intervention considered in previous sections are only one component of what an effective therapist needs to learn as part of their training. Therapy manuals, such as Beck's manual for cognitive therapy (Beck et al., 1979), Klerman et al.'s (1984) manual for interpersonal psychotherapy (IPT), Luborsky's (1984) manual for supportive–expressive therapy, or Strupp and Binder's (1984) manual for time-limited psychotherapy, provide an initial step toward operationalizing competently conducted psychotherapy. However, the degree of adherence to such manuals is only one indicator of the extent of a therapist's competence; other indicators of skillfulness and the personal qualities of therapists may be equally or even more important predictors of outcome.

THERAPIST EXPERIENCE

Although early studies suggested a clear relationship between outcome and experience, later studies have been more equivocal. Bergin (1971) coded studies according to the level of therapist experience in 48 studies of psychotherapy; 53% demonstrated positive results for more experienced therapists, while only 18% of trials using inexperienced therapists showed clear improvement. However, Smith and Glass's (1977) meta-analysis of 4,775 studies of therapy yielded a correlation of zero between experience and outcome, though most therapists in these studies were rather inexperienced and hence few contrasts were available for analysis. Shapiro and Shapiro (1982) obtained a similar result, noting that on average therapists had only 2.91 years of training plus experience. This restriction on experience level restricts the degree to which meta-analytic results can be meaningfully generalized.

A number of reviews have examined the impact of different levels of experience both directly and within (rather than across) studies. Anthony and Carkhuff (1977) concluded that therapist experience was not associated with better outcomes, though the review appears to have been based on studies of poor internal validity. Durlak (1979) reviewed 40 studies, again containing a high proportion of studies of poor methodological quality (Fisher & Nietzel, 1980; cited in Stein & Lambert, 1984). Auerbach and Johnson (1977) examined a narrower subset of comparative outcome studies. Professional trainees and novice therapists were contrasted with more senior psychotherapists; a modest but weak relationship was found between outcome and experience. Hattie et al. (1984) concluded that paraprofessionals were more likely to achieve therapeutic success than professionals. However, the systems used for coding of therapists as "professionals" and "paraprofessionals" may have led to some blurring of the distinction between the two groups, making their results difficult to interpret. Thus definitions of professionals did not differentiate between professional training and psychotherapeutic training, and in their coding of paraprofessionals some therapists were included who may indeed have received some psychotherapy training (such as nurses and social workers).

Berman and Norton (1985) carried out a meta-analysis of 32 studies of training, excluding those with poor methodology. Despite this greater selectivity, contrasting professionals with paraprofessionals yielded effect sizes close to zero, both at posttherapy and at follow-up.

Lyons and Woods (1991) report a meta-analysis of 70 studies of rational–emotive therapy; defining experience in terms of professional degree, therapist training was significantly correlated with treatment effects ($r = .3$). Balestrieri et al. (1988) examined studies contrasting outcomes in psychiatric patients after treatment by family physicians or specialist mental health workers, such as psychiatrists, psychologists, or social workers. Though all patients received medication (hence reducing likely differences between groups), better outcomes were achieved by specialist workers (effect size of 0.22).

In a careful review, Stein and Lambert (1984) sampled 41 studies, restricting their analysis to trials in which patients had clinically significant problems (hence excluding studies of interventions such as vocational and academic counseling and analogue interviews), and where enough therapists were included in each trial to enable meaningful comparison to be made. Again therapists tended to have limited experience—most having no more than 5 years in practice. Experience level was operationalized in a complex manner; three systems were employed to tap the impact of different codings:

1. A score based on training plus experience.
2. A "difference in experience" score, obtained by subtracting the years of experience of the experienced group from that of the inexperienced group.
3. A 5-point rating system on which, for example, 1 represented a lay person with no training and 5 a clinician with 3 or more years postgraduate training.

Overall the mean effect size for experience was zero. Regression analysis indicated that for some comparisons there was an association between experience and outcome, though for one comparison this favored experience, while in another, less-experienced therapists obtained better results. This rather confusing result may reflect methodological differences between studies.

Contrasting experience using the 5-point rating scale and examining the impact of increasing distance between therapist groups and the overall effect size yielded a significant but modest correlation of $r = .11$. In addition, the "difference in years of experience" measure was a significant predictor of more positive outcomes for more experienced therapists. Finally there was a trend for outcomes to be better for more experienced therapists when more disturbed patients were being seen (though of some interest in this debate, rather few studies included more distressed patients).

A further meta-analysis by Stein and Lambert (1995) reaches more definitive conclusions than earlier studies. As in their earlier study, Stein and Lambert restricted their analysis to trials of therapy for clinically relevant problems. These authors note that the codings of experience used by most studies make it difficult to distinguish between experience and training—for example, researchers frequently classify experience using global criteria, such as the type of degree held by a therapist. However, this may be misleading, since categorizing in this way will treat as homogeneous both newly degreed therapists and those who have been practicing for many years. These classificatory problems are likely to reduce the variance attributable to experience. Nonetheless, on the basis of 36 studies, moderate effect sizes were found for the relationship between experience and outcome, as measured both by pre–post measures of symptoms (0.3) and by clients (0.27).

While evidence for a relationship between therapist experience and outcome seems to be modest, this may reflect poor definitions of experience, a restriction in the range of experience in therapists surveyed, and (as indicated particularly by Stein & Lambert's [1984] study) methodological issues in the coding of experience. Stein and Lambert (1995) note that, given these problems, it is surprising that studies should attribute any variance to therapist experience. It may also be the case that experience is less relevant than expertise, and (as discussed below) a number of studies have linked this variable to outcomes.

THERAPIST EXPERIENCE AND DROPOUT FROM TREATMENT

The notion of premature dropout from therapy can be hard to define; for example, dropout immediately after assessment is different from a patient who leaves a planned long-term therapy after 6 months. Despite this methodological problem, the association between attrition and experience is reasonably consistent in the literature (e.g., Fiester, 1977; Levitz & Stunkard, 1974; Slipp & Kressel, 1978; Burlingame et al., 1989; Crits-Christoph et al., 1991) and is particularly evident with more psychodynamic therapies (e.g., Betz et al., 1979; Epperson, 1981; Krauskopf et al., 1981). Sue et al. (1976) report dropout rates for 13,000 patients in 17 community mental health centers, finding that patients were less likely to return after their initial interview or to terminate prematurely if seen by paraprofessionals (defined as therapists with less than graduate level training). This effect was evident even after statistical control for a variety of client factors. Data from Stein and Lambert's (1995) meta-analysis suggest that while there is no or little relationship between experience and dropout within university counseling centers (frequently the site for studies in this area), such effects become more prominent in other mental health settings. This observation may be relevant to

Wierzbicki and Pekarik's (1993) meta-analysis of 125 studies, which found no correlation between dropout and either the number of years of therapist experience or the professional degree gained by the therapist.

It is important to note that different rates of attrition between more and less experienced therapists makes it more difficult to interpret research that attempts to estimate the link between therapist experience and outcomes. As pointed out by Stein and Lambert (1995), the apparent efficacy of less experienced therapists will be increased if their clients drop out of treatment earlier (clients remaining in therapy may be unrepresentative of the original pool of untreated patients). An example of this is offered by Kopoian (1981; cited by Stein & Lambert, 1995), who contrasted therapists with graduate degrees with those with postgraduate degrees. Though the two groups achieved comparable outcomes, almost half the clients treated by less experienced therapists left the trial prematurely. This suggests that experienced and inexperienced therapists are best contrasted in terms of the probability that they will have a good outcome, rather than the absolute outcomes achieved—in other words, focusing on outcomes derived from intent to treat rather than completer samples.

PROFESSIONAL TRAINING AND OUTCOME

Orlinsky and Howard (1980) report the outcomes of 23 therapists offering verbal psychotherapy to 143 patients. Six therapists achieved success rates of 70% or more; five had a success rate of less than 50%, and more than 10% of their cases were rated as worse. Professional qualification was not associated with outcome, but greater experience was: therapists with more than 6 years' experience showed greater efficacy.

Some therapies showed a clearer impact of training than others, with psychodynamic therapy showing a trend toward better outcomes with more experienced therapists, an effect not observed for counseling or behavioral therapies. However, as part of their meta-analysis of behavioral treatments for agoraphobia, Trull et al. (1988) found that doctoral-level therapists achieved better results than nondoctoral.

Burns and Nolen-Hoeksema (1992) analyzed therapist effects in an open trial of 185 depressed patients treated with cognitive-behavioral therapy treated by 13 therapists ranging in experience from untrained "novices" to senior therapists (defined as those with more than 4 years' clinical experience with CBT). Measures were taken of the level of patient disturbance, compliance with homework tasks, and degree of therapist empathy. Controlling for these factors, the patients of novice therapists improved significantly less than did the patients of those with more experience.

THE RELATIONSHIP BETWEEN ADHERENCE TO MANUALIZED THERAPIES AND OUTCOME

Studies suggest that therapists vary considerably in the degree to which they adhere to therapy protocols. In one of the most extensive studies to date, Rounsaville et al. (1988) examined adherence to the IPT manual in 11 psychologists and psychiatrists, with an average of 15 years' experience. The average level of adherence did not change significantly throughout the study, which involved two or three training cases, and an additional five to 10 cases in the efficacy phase of the study. Although the severity of patient's pretreatment symptoms did not relate to adherence, there was a strong relationship between patient hostility and therapist adherence. More hostile patients with negative pretherapy expectations made adherence to the IPT protocol more difficult. General therapist qualities such as greater warmth and lower therapist expectations correlated both with therapist adherence to IPT and patient outcome. The authors suggest that this may represent a "good therapist" factor where the competent therapist is more capable of adapting techniques to conform to the dictates of the training manual. Similarly, Luborsky et al. (1985) found that personal qualities of the therapist (the level of personal adjustment and interest in helping the patient) and the quality of the helping alliance related significantly to therapy outcome. The authors conclude, "The major agent for effective psychotherapy is the personality of the therapist, particularly the ability to form a warm and supportive relationship" (Luborsky et al., 1985, p. 609). Interestingly, the extent to which therapists adhered to the techniques of either supportive–expressive therapy or cognitive-behavioral therapy ("purity") related to positive outcome. The authors argue that a good helping alliance may make adherence to a manualized treatment possible, either because the therapist who is able to establish an alliance can execute the intended therapy or because a good alliance enables the therapist to implement his or her intended technique.

DuRubeis and Feeley (1990) explored the impact of adherence to therapeutic technique in a study of CBT for depression. Twenty-five patients were treated by 14 therapists, most of whom were clinical psychologists in training. A significant correlation (0.53) was found between outcome and measures of adherence to symptom-focused cognitive technique in early sessions. "Facilitative conditions" of empathy, warmth, and genuineness were not related to change. However, these were present at high levels across all therapies, and as noted by Stiles and Shapiro (1989), a null finding under such conditions does not indicate the absence of an effect for these variables: if a process variable is present at high levels, it may well fail to correlate with outcome, not because it is unimportant but because its lack of variability across treatment conditions renders it "invisible" to statistical analysis.

O'Malley et al. (1988) examined the contribution of therapist competence to outcome in the NIMH treatment of depression collaborative study (Elkin, 1994). The performance of 11 therapists working with 35 patients who completed therapy was examined. Therapies were either CBT or IPT. Tape recordings of the fourth session of therapy were examined, together with therapist reports and ratings from supervisors. A correlation between competence and outcome was found for patient-rated change. However, there was also an association between patients' pretreatment social adjustment and change (in that the more maladjusted patients derived greater benefit). Controlling for this through regression analysis, initial patient functioning predicted 34% of outcome variance; the addition of therapist performance measures added a further 23% of variance beyond initial patient characteristics. A median split between therapists high and low in skill indicated significantly greater patient change in the more skilled group.

Although therapist competence was associated with patient-rated change, there was no evidence of such a relationship on measures of social adjustment, and only weak evidence of association on measures of depression. It should be noted that all therapists in this trial were chosen for their competence in delivering their therapy, reducing the variance attributable to this factor (though in contrast to most such studies, in the direction of a uniformly higher level of competence).

Frank et al. (1991) report data from a long-term maintenance study of depression (reviewed in detail in Chapter 4). Patients who had received IPT and had recovered from their index episode of depression were given monthly sessions of IPT over 3 years. The relationship between outcome and competence of delivery of IPT (or, more accurately, the degree of adherence to the IPT protocol) was examined in 38 patients who had complete therapy records. Sessions were analyzed for adherence to IPT, and sessions were divided into those above and below the median of adherence. Using this definition, patients in receipt of more accurately delivered therapy had a median survival time to relapse of 2 years; in contrast, those receiving less adherent therapy had a median time to relapse of 5 months.

It should be noted that this effect reflected the ability of therapists to establish the interpersonal focus specified by IPT, and was not a simple reflection of "better" or "worse" therapists. A rather similar interactive pattern has been reported by Foley et al. (1987). Although (as discussed above) competence of delivery of IPT was associated with greater patient change in the NIMH trials (O'Malley et al., 1988), more "difficult" patients were found significantly to decrease therapists performance. Taken together, these studies suggest that both patient and therapist factors, in interaction one with the other, will need to be considered in any assessment of the relationship between therapist competence and therapeutic efficacy.

Crits-Christoph et al. (1991) examined four variables related to therapist effects using meta-analytic techniques: (1) the use of a treatment manual; (2) the average level of therapist experience; (3) the length of treatment (on the perhaps rather dubious assumption that shorter therapies would show less therapist effects); and (4) the type of treatment. Fifteen outcome studies were selected for examination; though selection criteria are not clear from the paper, all were major studies of psychotherapy outcome.

Experience was coded in relation to the amount of exposure to psychotherapy, in contrast to many studies in which experience is coded only in terms of generic professional training. Calculation of the outcome variance attributable to differences between therapists suggested that this was smaller where therapy was manualized and more experienced therapists conducted the therapy. Logically, between-therapist variance increased when inexperienced therapists conducted therapies without a manual. Overall therapist-related impacts were equivalent to a medium effect size, though the size of this effect varied widely across studies, with the implication that such effects need to be minimized when examining between-therapy comparisons.

Other studies find lower correlations between adherence to a manual and therapist skills such as overall competence, use of language, attunement to the patient, timing and meaningfulness of intervention, openness to feedback, and avoidance of blaming (e.g., Henry et al., 1993a,b). Winston et al. (1987) report no significant association between adherence to the techniques of short-term psychodynamic psychotherapy or brief adaptational psychotherapy and outcome. Svartberg and Stiles (1994) examined the influence of both the therapeutic alliance and therapist competence on outcome in Sifneos's short-term anxiety-provoking therapy (STAP; Sifneos, 1987). Seven experienced therapists worked with 13 patients using STAP; on measures of symptomatic change, there was a negative correlation between adherence and outcome but a positive relationship between alliance and change. It is possible that these results reflect the nature of the techniques employed, which emphasize confrontation and might therefore increase the salience of the alliance in relation to their successful application.

In summary, there appears to be a complex relationship between adherence, skill, and outcome. The relationship between adherence (the implementation of technical training) and outcome is probably weak (e.g., Rounsaville et al., 1981) and may depend on the prior establishment of a helping alliance (Luborsky et al., 1985). There is an indication that more competent therapists are able to deviate appropriately from technical recommendations with more difficult patients (Rounsaville et al., 1988), and that these individuals are rated as more competent by their supervisors and produce greater improvement in their patients (O'Malley et al., 1988). This suggests that extensive training may be necessary not only in specific techniques, but also to indicate where deviations from prescriptive technique are desirable. These observations may be important in explaining some of the paradoxical associations between training, experience, and outcome, to be reviewed below.

The frequent use of experienced rather than inexperienced or novice therapists limits the implications for training that can be drawn from these studies. Conclusions from experienced therapists may not generalize, since novice therapists are far more amenable to suggestions regarding technique and style than experienced practitioners, who are likely to be quite comfortable with their approach. It should also be noted that many of the recommendations that emerge from these studies, such as the importance of establishing a working alliance with a patient, are hard to translate into specific skills which can be taught (Strupp et al., 1988). Adequate levels of personal adjustment and clinical sensitivity are also likely to be essential therapist characteristics, though there appears to be little evidence that personal therapy has the capacity to "teach" therapists appropriately to deal with chronic hostility and negativism from patients (Henry et al., 1986).

THERAPEUTIC ALLIANCE

The importance of the therapist–client relationship is widely recognized, and the findings of psychotherapy research have identified this factor as perhaps of the greatest importance alongside therapeutic technique. In this section we will review the evidence concerning the importance of establishing a good helping alliance and the qualities of both client and therapist which are likely to maximize the chances of a successful therapeutic relationship. This literature has implications not just for training but also for the selection of good practitioners and in the appraisal of the quality of psychotherapeutic services.

The notion of the therapeutic alliance originates from within a psychodynamic perspective. Freud (1940) underscored the importance of the "pact" between the analyst and the patient, who "band themselves together" with a common goal based on the demands of external reality. The term therapeutic alliance was coined by Zetzel (1956), who argued that in a successful therapy there is a conscious collaborative, rational agreement between therapist and client. Others (e.g., Bowlby, 1988) maintain that this alliance may in itself have a curative aspect in providing the patient with a new "healthier," positive relationship than he or she may have experienced in the past (see Gittleson, 1962; Horowitz, 1964). This emphasis is even stronger in the humanistic tradition, where the therapist's willingness to be empathic, congruent, and unconditionally accepting of the client is seen as a sufficient condition for therapeutic success (Rogers, 1951). From a more behavioral, social learning perspective, LaCrosse (1980) and Strong (1968) point to the importance of the client's perception of the therapist as expert, attractive, and trustworthy. These perceptions will strengthen the therapist's influence and thus predict the degree to which the patient is likely to benefit from therapy.

The importance of the therapeutic alliance is also emphasized by authors who adopt a less "school-based," more generic approach to psychotherapeutic treatment (e.g., Bordin, 1979). Horvath et al. (1993) distinguish three aspects of the therapeutic alliance from a pan-theoretical point of view:

1. The client's perception of the relevance and potency of the interventions offered.
2. The client's agreement with the therapist on reasonable and important expectations of the therapy in the short and medium term.
3. A cognitive and affective component, influenced by the client's ability to forge a personal bond with the therapist and the therapist's ability to present himself or herself as a caring, sensitive, and sympathetic, helping figure.

During the past two decades more than 100 research reports have been published on the alliance. These have been reviewed by Gaston (1990), Horvath and Symonds (1991), and Horvath et al. (1993). A meta-analytic study by Horvath and Symonds (1993) covered 24 studies, concluding that the average effect size linking quality of alliance to therapy outcome was 0.26. This figure may be an underestimate, because the meta-analysis coded all nonsignificant correlations as zero. Nevertheless, the finding implies that there is a 26% difference in the rate of therapeutic success related to the quality of the alliance. While there is an indication that measures of the alliance early in therapy are a particularly good predictor of therapeutic success, the strength of the alliance later in therapy shows less of an association. Studies of the evolution of the therapeutic alliance suggest that this may reflect the development of a nonlinear pattern of rupture/repair cycles in successful therapies (Safran et al., 1990), which would be predicted to reduce statistical associations.

Horvath and Symonds' (1993) analysis suggests that a strong alliance makes a positive contribution in all treatments, though a study by DeRubeis and Feeley (1991) implies that the alliance may be less predictive in highly structured forms of intervention. Horvath and Symonds' (1993) review also indicates that prediction is strongest for measures of outcome tailored to the individual client, such as target complaints measures.

Notwithstanding the apparently robust relationship between alliance and outcome, some caution should be exercised in interpreting these results. The client's positive orientation to therapy may itself be an index of the likelihood of improvement (e.g., Rounsaville et al., 1981). However, Horvath and Symonds' (1993) review provides no evidence that clients valued the results of intervention more positively or that they more favorably recall aspects of the treatment if the treatment outcome is good. Thus, available evidence indicates that the alliance–outcome relationship is more than a self-fulfilling prophecy. Evidence is also emerging that the association cannot be explained by early improvements (Gaston et al., 1991) and that outcome is most strongly linked to the successful repair of alliance ruptures (Safran et al., 1990; Horvath & Marx, 1991).

CLIENT CHARACTERISTICS, THERAPEUTIC ALLIANCE, AND OUTCOME

Unfortunately there is as yet insufficient evidence available concerning therapist characteristics pertinent to the development of a good alliance (Horvath et al., 1993). There is more information on client factor which predict the development of a favorable patient–therapist relationship. These include the client's motivation, their psychological status and quality of object relations, the quality of the client's social and family relations, and indices of stressful life events. Both interpersonal and intrapersonal factors appear to play a part. Thus, difficulty in maintaining relationships and poor family relations are both associated with poor alliance and poor outcome (Moras & Strupp, 1982; Kokotovic & Tracey, 1990). At the intrapersonal level, lack of hope, poor intrapsychic representations of others, and lack of psychological mindedness are often associated with poor outcome in terms of treatment alliance and therapeutic efficacy (Piper et al., 1991; Ryan & Cicchetti, 1985).

Piper et al. (1990) report data from 64 of 86 patients with mixed diagnoses who completed a trial of short-term dynamic therapy as described by Malan (1976) and Strupp and Binder (1984). Patients acted as their own controls during a waiting period. Patients' histories of stable and satisfying relationships were assessed using the Quality of Object Relationships (QOR) scale. Applying Jacobson and Revenstorf's (1988) criteria for the demonstration of clinically significant change across three measures (SCL-90, Beck Depression Inventory, and the Trait Anxiety Scale) suggested that patients with high QOR had better outcomes than those with low QOR: 70–83% of high-QOR patients, but only 12–32% of low-QOR patients, showed clinically significant change.

Similar evidence that patient characteristics may influence outcome in psychodynamic therapy comes from three further reports. Horowitz et al. (1984) describe outcome in 52 patients receiving 12 sessions of short-term therapy for bereavement, using principles described by Malan (1976). In this study, patients with higher levels of motivation for psychodynamic therapy and a more stable and coherent sense of self (perhaps broadly equivalent to high-QOR patients), responded better to dynamic exploration of their difficulties. In contrast, those with low levels of these qualities appeared to respond better to more supportive interventions. Somewhat more indirectly, Jones et al. (1988) examined transcripts of completed therapies from 40 patients, again undergoing 12 sessions of brief therapy following bereavement. A "psychotherapy Q sort" was used, in effect, to analyze the content of sessions and, in particular, the contributions of the therapist. Patients who showed the greatest distress and disturbance appeared to respond best to expressive techniques, whereas those with less distress had better outcomes with more supportive interventions. Horowitz et al. (1988, 1993) also present data suggesting that patients who describe their problems more in terms of interpersonal difficulties than symptoms tend to have better outcomes in psychodynamic psychotherapy.

These findings have important implications for the practice of therapy, suggesting that certain individuals may be more appropriately treated in psychotherapy than others (e.g., those with good inter- and intrapersonal relations). It also suggests that, all other factors being equal, clients who show early engagement in the therapeutic process are more likely to benefit from it. From a technical point of view, certain therapeutic interventions may facilitate the alliance:

1. A friendly, sympathetic attitude to the client (Adler, 1988; Kokotovic & Tracey, 1990).
2. The encouragement of a collaborative relationship (Horvath & Greenberg, 1989).

3. Therapist interventions aimed at addressing the client's negative feelings toward the therapist (Reandeu & Wampold, 1991).
4. Direct attention to the in-therapy relationship (Foreman & Marmar, 1985).

The frequency or accuracy of interventions by the therapist has not yet been shown to be linked to a positive alliance (Gaston & Ring, 1992; Crits-Christoph et al., 1988), although there is some suggestion that a curvilinear relationship may exist. Piper et al. (1990, 1993) made use of transcripts to explore the relationship between interpretation and outcome. The number of interpretations made in a session ("concentration") was distinguished from the degree to which these interpretations "correspond" to therapist's formulations—in other words, the degree to which interpretation was accurate. Correspondence was assessed using the Core Conflictual Relationship Theme method (Luborsky & Crits-Christoph, 1990), a technique for systematically and reliably formulating patients' difficulties.

Findings were complex. Overall there was an inverse relationship between the number of interpretations made per session and both outcome and the patient-rated alliance, an effect seen most clearly for patients with a high QOR. The impact of the correspondence (or accuracy) of interpretations differed according to the patient's QOR rating: when exposed to more correspondent interpretations, those with a low QOR tended to have poorer outcomes; in contrast, patients with a high QOR had better outcomes.

Correspondence and concentration were not correlated, suggesting that effects noted above were not simply a product of a high frequency of inaccurate interpretation. Regression analysis indicated an interaction between these factors and outcome in high-QOR patients, such that the best outcomes were seen in these patients when they were exposed to accurate interpretations at a lower concentration.

Although not directly intended as a study of the use of transference, further data from Henry et al. (1993a,b) also suggest that increased use of interpretation can lead to detrimental effects. This investigation was a study of the impact of training therapists in short-term dynamic therapy, as a part of which therapist adherence was measured and hence measures of transference interpretation were taken. Training seemed to have the consequence of increasing the rate of interpretation, though at the expense of decreasing supportive interventions and with some decrease in the therapeutic alliance. There was some evidence that poorer outcomes were associated with greater frequency of transference interpretation.

In summary, certain dynamic techniques, when used judiciously with an appropriate client group, appear to facilitate the development of a therapeutic relationship which, in its turn, is likely to influence outcome. Therapists with high levels of training are no more likely to be trusted or perceived as empathic than novices (Mallinckrodt & Nelson, 1991). However, with increased training and experience, therapists may develop a capacity for matching their client's progress and to time interventions appropriately, engage their patient, select appropriate goals, and develop a productive, collaborative relationship.

SUMMARY

- Studies that specifically examine the proportion of variance accounted for by client groups (such as type of disturbance), treatment technique (e.g., CBT vs. IPT), and their interaction have shown that there is considerable variability in the outcome of psychotherapy even from relatively homogeneous treatments. This variability cannot be accounted for in terms of client factors or treatment technique but seems, at least in part, to be associated with particular therapists.
- There is only a modest relationship between training and outcome, or between experience and outcome, although the evidence for the latter is stronger than that for the former.
- There is evidence that experience becomes a more important predictor of outcome with patients who are more severely disturbed.
- Training, and probably experience, may have specific importance in preventing early attrition and in retaining patients in treatment.
- Though professional qualification in and of itself seems to have little effect on outcome, if viewed as an indicator of experience, there is evidence for a positive association.
- Combining these factors, the tendency for more experienced therapists both to have less dropout and to retain more difficult patients in therapy may lead to poorer outcomes relative to inexperienced therapists. This effect may make it harder to detect differences attributable to experience in studies that do not control for the impact of attrition.
- There is strong evidence that training in specific therapeutic skills is possible and that adherence to a set of techniques embodied in psychotherapy manuals is measurable.
- Although adherence to technique is not generally a strong predictor of outcome, there is evidence that it is important in more difficult (severe and chronic) cases.
- The importance of training may be greater in some modes of therapy than others; in particular, psychodynamic therapies may require a fuller professional training.

- Expertise may become particularly important when therapists deviate from technical recommendations encoded in manuals of psychotherapy.
- The capacity to develop a treatment alliance is likely to be the most important mediator of therapist experience.
- Experience may therefore be important in dealing with cases where the patient's attitude is predominantly negative and hostile to the therapy.
- Client variables are also important in establishing a strong therapeutic alliance; both interpersonal and intrapersonal characteristics (such as good quality of object relationships and psychological mindedness) have been identified as particularly relevant factors.
- These client variables have been more systematically studied in the case of dynamic treatments than other approaches.
- Both therapist skills and therapist personal qualities play an important role in the evolution of a good therapist–client relationship.
- Concentration on the in-therapy relationship with clients who are more open to social relationships appears to facilitate the treatment alliance.
- Training and experience have a role in the therapist's ability to repair inevitable ruptures in the therapeutic relationship, with consequent gains in outcome.

IMPLICATIONS

- As therapeutic expertise, rather than experience, is an important predictor of the establishment of a productive treatment alliance (which is probably the single best predictor of outcome outside of client and orientation factors), the monitoring of individual therapist performance should be an important aspect of the evaluation of psychotherapy services.
- Though specialist professional training and clinical experience may be less relevant for first-time referrals in nonspecialist settings such as primary care, expertise is important for more "difficult" cases (chronic, negative, severe, or hostile patients). It follows that specialist psychotherapy centers should have adequate numbers of trained and experienced professionals who offer treatment to this group.
- Appropriate supervision, even of experienced therapists, is important in view of the likelihood of ruptures of the therapeutic

relationship and the adverse effect this may have on therapeutic outcome.

- There is evidence that manuals of psychotherapy have much to contribute to the training of psychotherapists. Models of good training practice could include acquainting candidates with training manuals and formally assessing their capacity to adhere to these.

- The literature clearly indicates that whereas good knowledge of the key components of a technique lays an important foundation for effective practice, expert practitioners are those who are able to use technical recommendations flexibly, and deviate and go beyond them at times when the clinical situation seems to require this.

- There is some limited evidence in the literature suggesting that in-depth training in multiple modalities may improve the therapeutic efficacy of individual practitioners. Further research needs to be undertaken to establish the value of training in multiple orientations for therapists.

CHAPTER 18

Conclusions and Implications

Previous chapters have presented an appraisal of research into psychological therapies for a range of conditions. Attempting to integrate our findings so that they can be constructively applied in service settings is a challenge. In the introduction to this book we drew attention to the complex relationship between efficacy as reported in research trials and clinical effectiveness in everyday practice. We also discussed a model (presented in Chapter 3) which locates the differing contributions of the researcher and the clinician within evidence-based practice. This model has utility for all stakeholders involved in improving and assuring the delivery of psychotherapy services, because it emphasizes the role of guidelines and protocols, derived from research but implemented through the clinical judgment of the therapist. The challenge is to achieve practice that is rooted in empirical findings but not circumscribed by them.

Before summarizing our findings and their implications, we explore further some methodological issues that constrain the generalizability of our findings.

METHODOLOGICAL LIMITATIONS ON THE GENERALIZABILITY OF RESEARCH

Our examination of research findings in adult and child psychotherapy suggests that their clinical impact may not reflect the promise of research. Some empirical support for this observation comes from a meta-analysis by Weisz et al. (1995), who in contrasting outcomes from research trials and clinical settings, find a large overall effect size for the former and a negligible effect size for the latter. While there are problems with this analysis, reliant as it is on the very small number of clinically based trials available for review, the disparity in results does point up the fact that though the technologies for investigating psychotherapy are increasingly sophisticated, they remain flawed, and this limits our capacity to generalize results.

We have already acknowledged some of the broad issues that might account for this. Patients who enter the protocols of RCTs may be unrepresentative of the general clinical population. Techniques used to enhance internal validity, such as diagnostically homogeneous patient samples, well-trained therapists, extensive monitoring of the patient's progress, and careful adherence to treatment protocols, may all serve to increase the apparent effectiveness of psychotherapeutic interventions. There are, however, some further constraints on generalization that are usefully discussed at this point.

The Absence of Long-Term Follow-Up Data

Throughout this book we have highlighted the chronic character of most psychological disorders. Unfortunately, few studies have investigated the capacity of psychological therapies to influence the long-term course of these disorders, and hence estimates of efficacy frequently relate only to short- or medium-term outcomes. It is important to recognize that there are practical as well as conceptual problems in achieving this information. Longer follow-up requires the expenditure of considerable effort and resources. Patient attrition inevitably increases over time, leading to problems of data interpretation. Additionally, longer follow-up periods are not necessarily informative of treatment effects unless there is some control on any additional therapies patients receive, and only rarely is this likely to be possible.

A further problem is that there is little consensus in the literature about how indicators of progress are to be defined and measured, though we noted in Chapter 2 that there are moves toward consistent use of terms such as relapse, recurrence, and remission. However, there is little sign of agreement over conventions that guide both how data is analyzed and how good outcomes are defined over follow-up—both factors that can alter the apparent efficacy of a trial. The significance of these issues is highlighted by Brown and Barlow (1995; reviewed in Chapter 6), who present 2-year outcomes for patients with panic disorder. Aggregated data suggested good results for a high percentage of patients, but this obscured shifts in symptomatic status by individual patients—because some patients improved, and others deteriorated, overall outcomes appeared more stable than was in fact the case. Secondly, decisions about the criteria for declaring high end-state functioning markedly altered apparent efficacy—long-term outcomes appeared much poorer when a criterion of "no panic attacks in the past year" was employed, contrasted to one of "no panic attacks in the past month."

The natural history of many mental health problems is both chronic and (in some cases) cyclic, and it is against this background that measures of improvement should be judged. Equally, however, the natural course of many disorders might suggest that overstringent criteria for high end-state functioning may be inappropriate; for example, improvement might be judged less by the presence or absence of symptoms than by the speed of improvements or the latency to relapse. Further work is required to agree on realistic standards by which longer-term outcomes may be judged.

Problems Arising from the Use of DSM

The structure of our review is strongly influenced by the *Diagnostic and Statistical Manual of Mental Disorders* of the American Psychiatric Association, which in our view represents a major advance in the classification of psychological disorders. This reflects our belief that no treatment will work for all problems, and that it is important to verify which interventions are most likely to be effective for which type of disorder. We have detailed the arguments for and against employing this system in Chapter 2, and recognize that such a framework is not accepted by therapists of all orientations. However, there remain two issues pertinent to problems of generalization, because our focus on DSM excludes them from consideration.

Subthreshold Cases

Many people present with psychosocial difficulties not categorizable within DSM, but which are nonetheless frequently treated within mental health services and which may be addressed by psychotherapy. For example, individuals confronted with major life difficulties, such as divorce, unemployment, or serious physical illness, may present with subthreshold conditions and make good use of psychological therapies (indeed it is possible that intervention might prevent the later emergence of major psychological difficulties). However, the potential need for psychological treatment almost certainly exceeds the capacity of currently available resources, even when these are calculated on the basis of diagnosable disorder, and it seems to us that using the latter as the criterion for consideration in this review is an acceptable compromise.

Comorbidity

Throughout we have noted and discussed the problem of comorbidity, which is a byproduct of using DSM as a classificatory system. RCTs may produce different outcomes depending on the patient mix, defined in terms of comorbidity, chronicity, and severity. This fact could be used to reject the application of findings of research trials. In our judgment this would be inappropriate, as we feel we have been able to demonstrate that the use of a diagnostic system can be helpful in identifying appropriate treatments for specific disorders.

While in our view none of the limitations of DSM, singly or in combination, invalidate our conclusions, they do imply that we should be cautious in interpreting the findings of research, particularly where radical revisions of services are contemplated. Restructuring a service on the basis of the profile of the scientific literature at any one point in time could lead to a profound distortion of psychological services, and could undermine future development by preventing the emergence of important new techniques. Thus we feel that the implications of our findings are much stronger insofar as they point to the way in which psychotherapy services should be provided rather than the precise nature of the therapy to be delivered.

The "File Drawer" Problem

It is a matter of common observation that researchers usually submit papers to journals when their trials show positive benefits for patients, though sometimes (but less frequently) null findings fit into a research context and are published. Only very rarely are findings presented that yield clear evidence of deterioration or positive damage to patients. Such trials, if they exist, are likely to languish in researchers' file drawers, leaving a potential but unknown skew in the literature. We have observed an absence of evidence in relation to some therapies, but from a scientific perspective this absence is informationally neutral. Only rarely are we able to suggest positively that a particular procedure is contraindicated. Unfortunately, it is not possible to say whether this is because psychological interventions are almost invariably benign, or whether it reflects, in effect, a suppression of data.

Meta-Analysis

We have made extensive use of meta-analytic reviews throughout this report. We wish to highlight some reservations concerning these techniques, in order to help readers make informed decisions concerning the implications of the studies we have reported.

Coverage

Meta-analytic reviews may not be fully comprehensive or representative, and consequently may present a biased picture of the field they claim to cover. There are several well-known selection biases (some detailed in Chapter 2). Some apply more particularly to meta-analyses performed prior to the mid-1980s, when certain reviews included analog rather than clinical populations, the latter showing smaller effect sizes than the former. Studies published in foreign-language journals are hard for reviewers to locate and evaluate adequately, leading to an overemphasis on studies published in English. An obvious point, but one that leads to further bias, is the necessity for studies to provide adequate information to calculate effect sizes; on occasion this can lead to inappropriately severe exclusion criteria (e.g., AHCPR; Depression Guidelines Panel, 1993b, reviewed in Chapter 4). Finally, a covert source of bias toward statistical significance is the so-called file drawer problem, noted above.

Quality

The quality of studies reviewed is often poor, but this can be disguised by their presentation within a meta-analysis. The difficulties may relate to problems we have already raised such as statistical validity or nonrepresentativeness of samples, or to others we have not had an opportunity to discuss, such as the poor qualifications of therapists, lack of relevant information concerning medication, and other factors essential for the interpretation of results.

This problem is not straightforward in its implications. Poor designs do not automatically mean poor information, and this can make interpretation difficult. For example, initial reports of the relationship between smoking and lung cancer suffered from major methodological flaws, yet proved to be accurate in their findings. Equally, other contemporary studies claiming links between environmental factors and disease have indeed proved inaccurate and are now forgotten. Within meta-analysis, strategies for resolving this issue have been developed and include the use of methodological criteria to select studies or examining the impact of methodological features on effect sizes as an independent variable. However, these enterprises are problematic. Kazdin (1988) has pointed out that methodological faults are so persistent and pervasive that any attempts at identifying variance attributable to them may be fruitless. Indeed, it could be argued that, since not all studies are flawed in the same way, meta-analysis offers a gain in information, since their deficiencies cancel each other out.

Statistical Problems

1. Meta-analyses make an assumption of homogeneity in combining studies statistically. Failures in relation to this criterion are particularly pertinent to some reviews; for example, Crits-Christoph et al.'s (1991) meta-analysis of psychodynamic psychotherapy violates this assumption by combining patient groups, treatments, and outcome measures. There are relatively few meta-analyses that fully meet the homogeneity assumption (e.g., Nietzel et al., 1987), and these tend to be based on a relatively small sample of studies, thus compromising other forms of validity.

2. Frequently, and appropriately, studies use multiple measures of outcome, though these may fail to yield a coherent prediction concerning efficacy. One approach to this problem is to average effect sizes across measures, which makes the assumption of homogeneity of measurement. An alternative is to compute independent effect sizes, although, because of the high correlation between outcome measures, this may be equally inappropriate. A further problem is added by studies that include the treatment of more or less the same patient group in a number of publications (e.g., Strupp's [1993] Vanderbilt study of 33 patients has been reported in a dozen publications).

3. An even more serious problem is posed by the incommensurability of studies. From both a logical and a statistical point of view, we know that we can only compare like with like. The classification of treatments within meta-analyses is frequently relatively subjective. For example, cognitive–analytic therapy (Ryle, 1989) contains elements of both cognitive therapy and psychodynamic treatments, which would make it difficult to locate in any future meta-analysis. The diversification of psychotherapeutic treatments can make it difficult to classify treatments reliably and hence to derive an average expectable outcome for therapeutic orientations. This factor in itself can be the basis for reviews reaching differing conclusions.

4. The conclusions of meta-analysis frequently have poor face validity, which leads many therapists to question the value of the approach. Some treatments emerge as effective that are known by clinicians to be outmoded or to have limited applicability (an example of which would be the AHCPR meta-analysis, which suggests greater efficacy for behav-

ioral than cognitive-behavioral treatments for depression). Even more relevant are the sometimes substantial disagreements between meta-analyses performed on overlapping samples of studies.

To summarize, meta-analyses cannot be thought of as settling the question of the superiority of one therapy over another. Rather, their utility may lie in the capacity to provide clues and broad indications concerning the relevant mode of treatment for specific disorders.

WHICH TREATMENTS HAVE BEEN EMPIRICALLY VALIDATED?

Our review has identified substantial progress in the literature on psychological treatments over the past 15 years. Research that dates back to the 1960s and 1970s, though significant in bulk, suffers from unacceptable limitations, such as:

- The inclusion of patients who were not seeking treatment for clinical problems
- A failure to apply diagnostic criteria
- Failing to standardize the treatments offered by using manuals that guide therapy
- Failing to monitor and evaluate adherence to treatment protocols
- Employing measures with an unacceptable degree of overlap with the treatment method provided

The criterion for treatment to be considered effective will always be to some degree arbitrary. Effectiveness begs the question of what is considered sufficient evidence, and what degree of change may be regarded as appropriate or significant. In considering treatments to be empirically validated, we identified the following criteria as important:

- *Replicated* demonstration of superiority to a control condition or another treatment condition, or a single high-quality randomized control trial
- The availability of a *clear description of the therapeutic method* (preferably but not necessarily in the form of a therapy manual), of sufficient clarity to be usable as the basis for training
- A *clear description* of the patient group to whom the treatment was applied

In addition, we felt it would be useful to identify treatments where research effort indicates some, but not conclusive, evidence of efficacy. Where these are innovative techniques, their inclusion indicates a promising line of intervention; where these are widely practiced methods, it may rather indicate only limited support for effectiveness.

Using these criteria we considered the following treatments to be either clearly effective (indicated by ▲) or promising/having limited support for their efficacy (indicated by ■ and italicized text). However, the list that follows is necessarily an attempt to simplify a complex set of findings and should not be considered a substitute for the more detailed appraisals of treatments found in the relevant chapters dealing with each disorder.

Depression

▲ Cognitive-behavioral therapy
▲ Interpersonal psychotherapy
■ *Psychodynamic psychotherapy*

Bipolar Disorder

Though there is tentative evidence of some benefit from psychological interventions, particularly in increasing adherence to medication regimens and reducing hospitalization, this is based on a very limited research base, and outcomes from more substantive trials in progress are needed before firmer conclusions are possible.

Anxiety

▲ Exposure therapy for specific and social phobias, and for agoraphobia/panic
▲ Cognitive therapy in combination with exposure for social phobia
▲ Cognitive-behavioral therapy for panic disorders with or without agoraphobia
▲ Panic control therapy
▲ Cognitive-behavioral therapy for generalized anxiety disorder
▲ Applied relaxation
■ *Applied tension and exposure for blood–injury phobia*

Obsessive–Compulsive Disorders

▲ Exposure and response prevention
■ *Cognitive restructuring and rational emotive–therapy in combination with exposure*

Posttraumatic Stress Disorder

▲ Stress inoculation therapy in combination with cognitive techniques and exposure
■ *Structured psychodynamic psychotherapy*

Eating Disorders

▲ Behavioral, cognitive, and eclectic psychotherapy, including dietary management, for anorexic patients
■ *Family therapy (particularly when offered to younger anorexic patients)*
▲ Cognitive-behavioral therapy, including dietary management, for patients with bulimia nervosa
▲ Interpersonal psychotherapy for bulimic patients

Schizophrenia

▲ Family intervention programs
■ *Cognitive therapy for delusions*

Personality Disorders

▲ Social skills training for avoidant personality disorder
▲ Dialectical behavior therapy
■ *Psychodynamic psychotherapy*

Alcohol Abuse

▲ Behavioral treatments aimed at enhancing social adaptation including social skills training, marital therapy, and community reinforcement packages
▲ Brief educational interventions, including motivational interviewing

Sexual Dysfunctions

▲ Behavioral and cognitive-behavioral treatment approaches aimed at reducing sexual anxiety and improving communication for erectile dysfunction
■ *Specific behavioral techniques for premature ejaculation*
▲ Exposure-based behavioral techniques for vaginismus

Counseling and Primary Care Treatments

The appropriate therapy depends on the form and severity of presentation, though more structured interventions based on theoretical models appear more effective than generic counseling.

Interventions with Children

▲ Behavior modification for enuresis and encopresis
▲ Parent training programs and cognitive-behavioral therapy for oppositional behavior
▲ Rapid exposure for school phobia
■ *Cognitive-behavioral treatment for GAD*
■ *Psychodynamic psychotherapy for GAD*
■ *Exposure and response prevention for OCD*
■ *Structural family therapies for disruptive disorders*
■ *Long-term multimodal therapy for ADHD*
▲ Family therapy for psychophysiological disorders
■ *Psychodynamic psychotherapy for psychophysiological disorder*
▲ Contingency management treatment of undesirable behavior in pervasive developmental disorders

Interventions with Older People

▲ Behavioral, cognitive-behavioral, and structured psychodynamic psychotherapy for depression
▲ Psychosocial interventions for carers
■ *Reality orientation for people with dementia*

We do not regard this list to be complete in any sense. There may be treatments that are efficacious but which have escaped our attention. Equally, studies are, to our knowledge, under way that may well lead to the inclusion of approaches and interventions other than those on this list. It is also important to emphasize the fact that there are a number of novel, integrative treatment approaches which (on the basis of clinical evidence and open trials) deserve serious consideration, but which could not be included in this list because controlled trials have not yet been carried out.

However, it can reasonably be concluded that nonspecific, poorly structured treatments, such as generic counseling, nonfocused psychodynamic therapy, and a variety of experiential therapies, are unlikely to be effective with severe presentations of the disorders we have considered in this review.

IMPLICATIONS FOR EVIDENCE-BASED PRACTICE

Having summarized the research evidence, we would like to draw out some implications of our review for psychological therapy services. As we indicated earlier, information from psychotherapy research should find its way into the organization of psychotherapy services via clinical consensus, which informs the construction of guidelines for clinical practice. What follows represents our personal view and is best seen as our contribution to this developing consensus.

THE ROLE OF MAINTENANCE TREATMENTS

It seems clear that patients with a range of disorders potentially benefit from short-term, structured treatments and that outcomes for some disorders (such as phobias, panic, PTSD, OCD), are characterized by relatively low or only moderate rates of relapse. Individuals with more acute and less severe presentations of many other disorders might also be expected to do well following brief interventions, using a variety of psychotherapeutic techniques. The situation may be somewhat different for chronic and severe disorders marked by a natural history indicating the probability of relapse, particularly when these conditions present in individuals with poor adaptation and a high level of comorbidity (especially when this includes many of the diagnoses within Axis II). For these patients the long-term outcome following brief treatments may be poor (even if their initial response is good) unless treatment is maintained over prolonged periods, albeit at low intensity. This observation almost certainly applies to patients who have a history of recurrent depression or to individuals with dysthymic disorder, but may be equally applicable to other groups.

The conditions treated in secondary or tertiary care are often chronic in character, and in this context psychological treatments may not be "curative," though they may improve an individual's adaptation, reduce symptomatology, and improve quality of life. Hence it may be inappropriate to see treatment as analogous to a surgical intervention. A better medical metaphor is offered by interventions for diabetes: here, though a patient might be discharged after stabilization of their condition, there will be provision for monitoring and continued contact, and the person is expected to return at times of crisis. It follows that even where psychotherapy services primarily offer short-term therapies, they need to recognize and plan for the likelihood of recurrence after short-term treatment for certain disorders. Further, relapse after recovery following psychotherapy should not necessarily contraindicate the appropriateness of further psychological intervention. In some cases, relapse could be seen as a predictable aspect of the disorder, and relapse prevention and management as an important component within a treatment package. Especially for chronic and severe cases, long-term maintenance therapy may be an appropriate and necessary treatment model.

THE ROLE OF ADJUNCTIVE PHARMACOLOGICAL AND PSYCHOLOGICAL TREATMENTS

The impact of pharmacological treatment in combination with psychological therapy varies according to the condition under examination, and has been detailed in the relevant sections of this report. In many cases the combination of these treatments seems more effective than either in isolation—particularly, for example, in some presentations of depression and anxiety.

There is little compelling evidence to routinely dictate a preference for one form of treatment over another. Clearly for some disorders, and for some individuals, medication may be indicated. For example, a patient with severe depression characterized by marked physiological symptoms and poor functioning might benefit from medication on the grounds of both likely rapidity of response and cost-effectiveness. However, for some patients, medication alone may not address or permit resolution of underlying psychological issues. Rates of relapse after such treatment suggest that combination therapy may have advantages in the medium to long term. It also seems reasonable to suggest that where either psychotherapy or psychopharmacological treatment is offered alone, and a patient is responding poorly, it may be hard to justify pursuing treatment without exploring the potential benefits of combination therapy.

Many psychological treatments may be more effective if patients are also receiving medication. This may be because they become accessible to intervention at a psychological level, because some of their more severe symptoms are being addressed pharmacologically. In addition, there is some evidence that adjunctive psychological treatment improves the response to a medical regimen, in some cases by improving compliance.

These observations suggest to us that services should offer both psychological and pharmacological modes of therapeutic intervention on the grounds that the availability of these modalities is (in appropriate cases) likely to improve outcomes, even where the primary focus of treatment lies within one or the other modality. Further, it seems reasonable that patients showing a poor response when treated by one modality of therapy alone should be offered combination treatments; it follows that the relationship between medical and psychological treatment services might need to be enhanced in some settings.

In reviewing studies of acute and chronically depressed clients, as well as in patients with schizophrenia and bipolar disorder, we have noted that medication compliance is often enhanced in trials that combine pharmacological treatment with "clinical management." This intervention includes factors often referred to as "common factors" of psychotherapy, such as reassurance, support, and hope. (There is also evidence that clinical management, in and of itself, has a therapeutic benefit for some [probably less distressed] patients [e.g., Elkin, 1994]). Even in the context of primarily psychopharmacological treatments, it may be worth exploring the benefits of clinical management, not only for its potential impact on compliance, but also because enhancing the therapeutic relationship may result in more rapid communication of information regarding factors such as relapse (a particularly pertinent issue in the management of people with psychotic disorders).

IMPLICATIONS FOR CLINICAL PRACTICE: THE ORGANIZATION OF SERVICES

A number of our findings may have relevance to the organization of psychotherapy services. We have found evidence to suggest that patients with relatively mild and acute disorders without comorbidity may be amenable to briefer treatments, and perhaps to more generic—though usually theory-based—therapies. In contrast, more severe and chronic disorders seem to require more specialized and possibly more lengthy treatments.

In the light of these observations, we see some merit in a "cascade" model of treatment, which employs broad criteria for assigning patients to care at primary, secondary, and tertiary levels, and within secondary and tertiary care might guide factors such as appropriate treatment length. (We acknowledge, however, that what follows is predicated on the presence of organized and clear referral procedures between primary and subsequent levels of care, and within specialized care on links between the differing components of mental health systems; these conditions will be met in some, but not all, contexts.)

Within this model, most patients in their first presentations, with mild and more acute disorders, could initially be offered brief interventions in primary care settings. While this is generally likely to be appropriate and sufficient for this group, some patients without obviously severe or chronic levels of symptomatology will require direct referral to more specialized care—for example, although they may have no previous psychiatric history, there may be elements to their presentation that suggest an elevated risk of self-harm, or there may be indications of more serious disorder than is apparent. For these individuals primary care treatment would be inappropriate. It follows that there needs to be a system for ensuring appropriate and rapid referral to secondary/tertiary care utilizing criteria based on severity, chronicity, and comorbidity. The principle is that patients should receive treatments of a suitable intensity conducted by therapists with a skill level appropriate to the patient's condition.

Patients who do not respond to primary care intervention could be referred to secondary/tertiary units; at this level (and where appropriate) shorter-term treatments may be offered initially, but with more skilled and expert therapists than at primary care level. However, it is important to note that longer treatments may also be justified on grounds of cost-efficiency,[1] particularly where research evidence suggest that short-term treatments are unlikely to be productive. For example, data from the Sheffield Psychotherapy Project (Shapiro et al., 1994, 1995) suggest that more seriously depressed individuals require longer treatments to achieve benefit.

Decisions about treatment length are difficult to make at the stage of assessment. The probable benefit of therapy for any individual patient is more likely to be demonstrated by their response to intervention than by prediction based on initial contact. Thus, though general decisions about the length of therapy could be made with regard to research-

---

[1] It should be noted that cost-effectiveness and cost-efficiency are not synonymous terms; this issue is discussed in the Introduction.

based criteria, decisions about individual patients might be better made with reference to their progress. A variety of research techniques are available for this purpose, though at present these are probably more applicable to research than to clinical settings. Nonetheless they do appear helpful in distinguishing slow but steady progress from therapies that are unlikely to lead to gains (e.g., Howard et al., 1993, 1995). However, some knowledge of "dose–response" relationships in therapy should influence clinical decision making in this area, since it should alert clinicians to the pattern of gains that most patients follow (see Howard et al., 1986, discussed in the Introduction to this book).

Finally, because specific therapies may be differentially effective not only for different client groups but also for particular individuals, the structure of services should assign patients to specific treatment modalities in a way that is consistent with the outcome literature, which is reflexive —in other words, sensitive to the individual client's response to treatment, and which, in the face of treatment failure, permits reallocation to alternative interventions—be it to another psychological therapy or to pharmacotherapy.

IMPLICATIONS FOR MONITORING AND AUDITING SERVICE DELIVERY

Although our review of the outcome literature offers considerable support for the efficacy of psychological and pharmacological interventions for mental health problems, most of the trials are unrepresentative of clinical practice, and they cannot be considered to guarantee the effectiveness of the same treatments in the framework of everyday service provision. Because of this gap, the safeguards established for the protection of clients must go beyond the claim of practicing a treatment of "known effectiveness," where known effectiveness was established in RCTs and research trials.

There is a risk that the broadly favorable tone of this review could be used to shield ineffective and potentially harmful treatment methods and practitioners from scrutiny. Our interpretation of the evidence is that a variety of techniques in the hands of well-trained and supervised practitioners, operating within a structured and controlled framework, may be both safe and effective. The context within which these studies were carried out should not be overlooked in interpreting these findings. The high level of training of diagnosticians and therapists in many of these trials, and the systematic way in which adherence to treatment protocols were assured may, in and of themselves, be factors critical to the efficacy of the treatment procedures under scrutiny. It follows that training alone in the same treatment methods may not be sufficient to assure standards of therapy delivery. In this respect, we feel that wherever possible, therapists should restrict the offer of treatment to interventions for which they are qualified by virtue of their training and experience.

There may be a number of useful and practical procedures for managing this problem. Professional supervision by a qualified and appropriately experienced mental health practitioner should be an essential prerequisite for the practice of psychotherapy, since this should improve standards of therapy delivery and also provide further training for therapists. Ideally, the effectiveness of treatment with each individual client should be monitored throughout, in terms of both its delivery and its outcome. However, monitoring procedures need to be achievable within the resources of services. Practical and workable systems could include the use of report card systems for "benchmarking" outcomes—contrasting the performance of local units with the outcomes achieved in similar service settings. Though systems have yet to be developed to accomplish this in practice, information might be collected on such factors as case mix, average length of treatment, percentage of patients improved (on some agreed, clinically significant criterion) after a set number of sessions, dropout rates, DNA rates, and skill mix. Simple methods are also needed to check that therapy is being delivered to an acceptable quality. This might begin by drawing up guidelines that specify the broad characteristics of an intervention, which can be used to check the integrity of therapy delivery, either by individual therapists or through a process of peer review or supervision.

IMPLICATIONS FOR TRAINING AND EDUCATION

Level of Training

We have presented evidence suggesting that therapist training and skill—particularly as reflected in the ability competently to deliver therapy-as-intended—become increasingly important the more severe or chronic the disorder. This factor is particularly significant in the context of specialist mental health services, but it may also be relevant even in the primary care setting. Though there is less evidence of a strong relationship between therapist skillfulness and outcome at this level (which may be attributable to the patient population), there is a need to ensure that workers in primary care are competent in recognizing when more specialized care is required.

Organization of Training

Our review provides good evidence for the efficacy of specific treatments for particular disorders. We could see this as implying two possible, and equally valid, models of training. While one would emphasize the need to learn specific techniques to a high standard, for application to particular groups, the other suggests that psychotherapists be trained in a number of models of treatment, in order to work effectively across a wide range of patients. Each model has its advantages and disadvantages, though in our judgment there may be arguments favoring training of clinicians in more than one modality (e.g., in both an exploratory and a more structured psychotherapy). There is some evidence to support this position, though it is as yet only suggestive and comes from a small number of studies, indicating that therapists may have better outcomes if they are able to adapt their technique to match client characteristics (which may at times mean employing a different modality of treatment).[2]

In view of the relatively clear demonstrations of efficacy of specific therapies for specific disorders, it seems to us important that training programs for psychological therapists should include material concerning these interventions. This could be facilitated if professional bodies kept a list of treatments meeting criteria for evidence of efficacy. It also seems appropriate to suggest that the training programs of relevant professional bodies should emphasize treatment programs of demonstrated validity, that their qualified trainees should have been observed to be competent at administering these treatments to acceptable criteria, and that such qualified individuals have good knowledge as to the range of conditions for which their techniques have been shown to be of demonstrable value and where they would be ill advised to apply them.

Researchers developing new and empirically validated treatment methods should ensure that their techniques are accessible to those involved in the training of clinicians. Equally, trainers should endeavor to follow the research literature closely, and acquire the necessary training to enable them to incorporate innovative methods in their programs.

Finally, within the evidence-based practice model, we consider that clinicians bear some responsibility to acquire up-to-date information which would enable them to apply their current clinical skills to the maximum benefit of patients and to acquire new skills which would enable them to deal more effectively with their clinical load. Relatedly, we would also like to see procedures established for exporting well-

---

[2] These studies are reviewed in Chapter 17.

developed research therapy programs from their laboratory base to service-oriented clinics. A number of studies have suggested that this can be practical and that the results obtained justify the additional resource implications, which may lie particularly in the area of training (see Weisz et al., 1995). As such, both of these endeavors are predicated on support for continuing professional development. We recognize that training has financial implications and can easily be neglected when time or money is short. However, managers and third-party payers should recognize the potential clinical and cost benefits of quality services offering treatments to the highest standards.

IMPLICATIONS FOR PSYCHOTHERAPY RESEARCH

In carrying out our review, we have become aware of many areas where further research is needed. Below we list research that we would particularly like to see carried out, covering the problem of underresearched or underdeveloped therapies, the exploration of therapy for difficult-to-treat or chronic conditions, and the development of research methods applicable in clinical settings.

First, we see an urgent need to examine the appropriateness to specific patient groups of frequently practiced, but insufficiently evaluated, models of care—in particular, psychodynamic approaches, but also methods which (at least in some countries) show increasing popularity, such as counseling. Research should also be carried out on newly emerging therapies, particularly those which attempt to integrate models of therapy. These provide a more formal theoretical framework for the "eclecticism" that often characterizes everyday clinical practice, with clear implications for efficacy.

We would like to see priority given to evaluating and encouraging the development of treatments for particularly costly disorders, such as those consequent on severe neglect and maltreatment in childhood, severe personality disorders, psychotic conditions, and depression. There would also be value in exploring the potential value of long-term treatment for populations that may require such approaches. Work could focus on developing models of treatment that incorporate principles of chronic disease management in a way that is cost-effective—for example, by sequential models of care, novel combinations of treatment modalities that may change over time, more rational integration of psychosocial and pharmacological treatments, or intermittent dosing strategies for both medication and psychotherapy.

The need for monitoring the outcome of psychotherapy, highlighted by both findings of effectiveness and ineffectiveness for many of the approaches reviewed, calls for research on an agreed set of evaluation tools for the measurement of psychotherapy outcome in clinical contexts. Such core measures would need to be reliable and valid as well as "user-friendly," and more work is needed to simplify the often complex and lengthy assessments used in research settings into practical measures.

In addition, further progress needs to be made with regard to extending measures relevant to treatment effectiveness. Current assessment procedures are adequate for assessing symptoms and have greatly improved. There are a number of procedures for gauging factors such as functional impairment, social performance, or quality of life. However, in other areas we are at some distance from arriving at suitable measures—for example, in the assessment of object relationships, mental representations of the self, the relationship of self and others, and other complex internal states that increasingly appear to be relevant to the prediction of individual outcomes.

At several points we have emphasized the importance of supervision and training in the psychotherapies. However, there is relatively little research on the impact of these processes, particularly in a form that examines the progress made by individual therapists over time; usually their gains are assessed by comparison across samples of therapists with different levels of experience and expertise. A longitudinal rather than a cross-sectional methodology might be more useful for assessing the impact of training and supervision on the development of, and outcomes from, clinical practice.

Finally, clinical protocols are central to our model of evidence-based practice. On the whole, those that have been developed seem to us to suffer from an underemphasis on the role of clinical judgment and formulation, and further work needs to be carried out to develop model guidelines for the treatment of disorders and the organization of services specific for each "family" of disorder, such as those considered in this review.

ACHIEVING EVIDENCE-BASED PRACTICE IN PSYCHOLOGICAL THERAPIES

Researchers often assume that their findings are readily absorbed into practice. This seems not to be the case; surveys repeatedly demonstrate that clinicians are ill informed about, and have limited interest in, findings from psychotherapy research (e.g., Morrow-Bradley & Elliot, 1986; Cohen et al., 1986). On the whole, research has only limited impact on services, perhaps for understandable reasons. Clinicians are experts in their field, and on many issues may be ahead of empirically generated research findings, but there is a tendency for them to limit their interest to the studies which apply directly to their current practice and to selectively disregard findings that would require of them substantial modification of their mode of work. This appears to be as true of behavior therapists as of psychodynamic clinicians (e.g., Raw, 1993; Suinn, 1993).

If findings from psychotherapy research are to be integrated into service provision, it may be necessary to create administrative structures to facilitate an exchange of knowledge between researchers and clinicians. For example, it would be useful for clinicians to have available summaries of important outcome research findings, organized on the basis of common clinical problems. We see an active role for professional bodies representing psychological therapies in the development of guidelines and clinical protocols that aim to integrate research findings with current practice. It would be useful if this work were not restricted to discipline-based organizations but included input from organizations representing specific therapeutic orientations, which will be able to speak more directly to clinicians with specific theoretical loyalties.

The problem of dissemination is even greater when it comes to users of psychotherapy services. Currently it is unlikely that patients have adequate information about the demonstrated efficacy of psychological treatments they may be offered. Most information is provided in a haphazard way through the media (particularly the press and television); often such information is unbalanced and misleading. We feel that it is important that the public be provided with accurate and readily comprehensible information concerning the availability of psychological help. For example, the education of users could begin with the provision of information sheets summarizing the nature of psychological disorders and available effective treatments. Active steps could be taken by professional organizations as well as public bodies to translate current knowledge about empirically validated psychotherapies into an accessible form, assuring that users can be given a genuinely informed choice about their treatment.

CONCLUDING COMMENTS

In conclusion, we have tried to present an overview of current findings from psychotherapy research and some of their implications for practice. We believe that an open examination of the evidence regarding methods of psychological intervention—both favorable and unfavorable—should lead to improvements in patient care. It can only do so, however, if it becomes subject to a process of critical examination by professional bodies and local service providers, who use their collective clinical experience to shape its findings into formats applicable in the field, but in a form that preserves the role of clinical judgment and thus safeguards the possibility of further innovation and development. This is a central issue; though we have aimed to present the current state of the art, there is a paradox inherent in this goal. In writing this book we became aware of the rapid growth of the field, which over time will modify the validity of our conclusions and recommendations. Yet this is as it should be—our model of evidence-based practice implies that the best results will be achieved through a process of continuous and reflexive refinements to technique and procedure. This is predicated on researchers, clinicians, service managers, professional bodies, funders, and users of services working together for the ultimate benefit of the mental well-being of society.

Appendix
Converting Effect Sizes to Percentiles

Effect sizes are computed using the formula

$$\text{Effect size} = \frac{M_1 - M_2}{SD}$$

where M_1 is the mean of the treatment group, M_2 is the mean of the control group, and SD is the pooled standard deviation. Converting scores to effect sizes assumes that the scores of the control group and the treatment group correspond to a normal distribution. It is assumed that, in all the contributing studies, patient scores will be distributed in this way.

As long as this assumption is correct, the equation above gives a numerical answer to the question, "How far apart are the means of the control group and the treated group?" on a common metric—the common metric being a standard score (known as a Z score). Data from many different studies can then be combined; effect sizes from each individual study contribute to a final overall effect size for the variable being examined.

As an example, imagine the effect size is being used to indicate the position of the average treated client relative to that of untreated clients. Figure 1 shows the (hypothetical) distributions of scores for treated and untreated patient groups and Table 1 the relationship of effect sizes to percentile scores .

If there were no difference between the treated and untreated group, the distribution of scores would be exactly the same; this would be indicated by an effect size of 0.0. This could be expressed in terms of percentiles; the average treated client would be at the 50th percentile of scores for the untreated client group.

An effect size of 1.0 indicates that the average treated patient will be placed at the 84th percentile of the scores for the untreated group. Similarly an effect size of 2.0 would indicate that the average client had a score at the 97th percentile of scores for the untreated group.

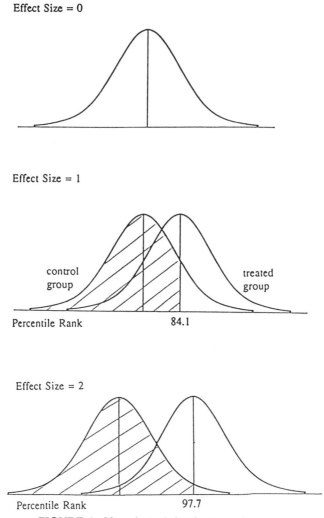

FIGURE 1. Hypothetical distributions of scores.

TABLE 1. Converting Effect Sizes into Percentiles

Effect size	Percentile	Effect size	Percentile	Effect size	Percentile
0.0	50.0	0.1	54.0	0.2	57.9
0.3	61.8	0.5	69.1	0.7	75.8
1.0	84.1	1.5	93.3	2.0	97.7

References

Abel, JL (1993) Exposure with response prevention and serotonergic antidepressants in the treatment of obsessive–compulsive disorder: A review and implications for interdisciplinary treatment. *Behaviour Research and Therapy, 31*, 463–478.

Abikoff, H, & Klein, RG (1992) Attention-deficit hyperactivity and conduct disorder: Comorbidity and implications for treatment. *Journal of Consulting and Clinical Psychology, 60*, 881–892.

Abramowitz, IA, & Coursey, RD (1989) Impact of an educational support group of family participants who take care of their schizophrenic relatives. *Journal of Consulting and Clinical Psychology, 57*, 232–236.

Abramowitz, SI, & Sewell, HH (1980) Marital adjustment and sex therapy outcome. *Journal of Sex Research, 16*, 325–337.

Achenbach, TM, & Edelbrock, CS (1983) *Manual for the child behavior checklist and revised child behavior profile.* Burlington, VT: TM Achenbach.

Achenbach, TM, & Edelbrock, CS (1986) *Manual for the teacher's report form and teacher version of the child behavior profile.* Burlington, VT: University of Vermont, Department of Psychiatry.

Achenbach, TM, & Edelbrock, CS (1987) *Manual for the youth self-report and profile.* Burlington, VT: University of Vermont, Department of Psychiatry.

Achenbach, TM, Edelbrock, C, & Howell, CT (1987) Empirically based assessment of the behavioral/emotional problems of 2- and 3-year-old children. *Journal of Abnormal Child Psychology, 15*, 629–650.

Acierno, R, Hersen, M, Van Hasselt, VB, & Tremont, G (1994) Review of the validation and dissemination of eye-movement desensitization and reprocessing: A scientific and ethical dilemma. *Clinical Psychology Review, 14*, 287–299.

Adler, JV (1988) *A study of the working alliance in psychotherapy.* Unpublished doctoral dissertation, University of British Columbia.

Agras, WS, Chapin, HH, & Oliveau, D (1972) The natural history of phobias: Course and prognosis. *Archives of General Psychiatry, 26*, 315–317.

Agras, WS, Rossiter, EM, Arnow B, & Schneider, JA, et al. (1992) Pharmacologic and cognitive-behavioral treatment for Bulimia Nervosa: A controlled comparison. *American Journal of Psychiatry, 149*, 82–87.

Agras, WS, Rossiter, EM, Arnow, B, Telch, CF, Raeburn, SD, Bruce, B, & Koran, LM (1994) One year follow-up of psychosocial and pharmacologic treatments for bulimia. *Journal of Clinical Psychiatry, 55,* 179–183.

Agras, WS, Schneider, JA, Arnow, B, Raeburn, SD, & Telch, CF (1989) Cognitive-behavioral and response-prevention treatments for Bulimia Nervosa. *Journal of Consulting and Clinical Psychology, 57,* 778–779.

Alanen, YO, Rakkozainen, Y, & Riija, R, et al. (1985) Psychotherapeutically oriented treatment of schizophrenia: Results of a five year follow-up. *Acta Psychiatrica Scandinavica, 71,* 31–49.

Alden, LE (1989) Short-term structured treatment for avoidant personality disorder. *Journal of Consulting and Clinical Psychology, 56,* 756–764.

Alden, LE, & Capreol, MJ (1993) Avoidant personality disorder: Interpersonal problems as predictors of treatment response. *Behavior Therapy, 24,* 357–376.

Alexander, F, & French, TM (1946) *Psychoanalytic therapy: Principles and applications.* New York: Ronald Press.

Alexander, JF, & Parsons, BV (1973) Short-term behavioral intervention with delinquent families: Impact on family process and recidivism. *Journal of Abnormal Psychology, 81,* 219–225.

Alexander, JF, & Parsons, BV (1982) *Functional family therapy.* Monterey, CA: Brooks/Cole.

Alford, BA, & Correia, CJ (1994) Cognitive therapy of schizophrenia: Theory and empirical status. *Behavior Therapy, 25,* 17–33.

Al-Kubaisy, T, Marks, IM, Logsdail, S, Marks, MP, Lovell, K, Sungur, M, & Araya, R (1992) Role of exposure homework in phobia reduction: A controlled study. *Behavior Therapy, 23,* 599–621.

Allsop, S, & Saunders, B (1989) Relapse and alcohol problems. In M Gossop (Ed.), *Relapse and addictive behaviour.* London: Tavistock/Routledge.

Althof, SE, Turner, LA, Levine, SB, Risen, CB, Bodner, D, Kursh, ED, & Resnick, MI (1991) Sexual psychological and marital impact of self-injection of papaverine and phentolamine: A long-term prospective study. *Journal of Sex and Marital Therapy, 17,* 101–112.

Ambrosini, PJ, Bianchi, MD, & Rabinovitch, H, et al. (1993) Antidepressant treatments in children and adolescents. *Journal of the American Academy of Child and Adolescent Psychiatry, 32,* 483–493.

American Psychiatric Association (1980) *Diagnostic and statistical manual of mental disorders* (3rd ed.). Washington, DC: Author.

American Psychiatric Association (1987) *Diagnostic and statistical manual of mental disorders* (3rd ed., rev.). Washington, DC: Author.

American Psychiatric Association (1993) Practice guidelines for major depressive disorder in adults. *American Journal of Psychiatry, 150,* 1–26.

American Psychiatric Association (1994) *Diagnostic and statistical manual of mental disorders* (4th ed.). Washington, DC: Author.

Anderson, JC, Williams, S, McGee, R, & Silva, PA (1987) DSM-III disorders in preadolescent children; prevalence in a large sample from the general population. *Archives of General Psychiatry, 44,* 69–76.

Angst, J (1992) Epidemiology of depression. *Psychopharamacology, 106,* 571–574.

Angst, J, Doblar-Mikola, A, & Schbniedegger, P (1985) The Zurich study: Anxiety and phobia in young adults. *European Archives of Psychiatric and Neurological Sciences, 235,* 171–178.

Angst, J, & Dobler-Mikola, A (1983) Anxiety states, panic and phobia in a young general population. In P Pichot, R Beiner, R Wolf, & K Thaw (Eds.), *Psychiatry: The state of the art. Proceedings of the World Psychiatry Congress, Vienna.* New York: Plenum Press.

Anthony, WA, & Carkhuff, RR (1977) The functional professional therapeutic agent. In AS Gurman & AM Razin (Eds.), *Effective psychotherapy.* New York: Pergamon Press.

Apfelbaum, B (1984) The ego-analytic approach to individual body-work sex therapy: Five case examples. *Journal of Sex Research, 20,* 44–70.

Apter, A, Bernhour, E, & Tyano, S (1984) Severe obsessive compulsive disorder in adolescence. A report of eight cases. *Journal of Adolescence, 7,* 349–358.

Archibald, HC, & Tuddenham, RD (1965) Persistent stress reaction after combat. *Archives of General Psychiatry, 12,* 475–481.

Argyle, M, Bryant, BM, & Trower, P (1974) Social skills training and psychotherapy: A comparative study. *Psychological Medicine, 4,* 435–443.

Aronson, TA (1987) Follow-up of two panic disorders–agoraphobic study populations. *Journal of Nervous and Mental Disease, 175,* 595–598.

Asarnow, JR, Goldstein, MJ, Carlson, GA, Perdue, S, Bates, S, & Keller, J (1988) Childhood-onset depressive disorders: A follow-up study of rates of rehospitalization and out-of-home placement among child psychiatric in-patients. *Journal of Affective Disorders, 15,* 245–253.

Ashurst, PM, & Ward, DF (1983) *An evaluation of counselling in general practice: Final report of the Leverholme project.* London: Mental Health Foundation.

Auerbach, AH, & Johnson, M (1977) Research on the therapists level of experience. In AS Gurman & AM Razin (Eds.), *Effective psychotherapy.* New York: Pergamon Press.

Auerbach, R, & Kilmann, PR (1977) The effects of group systematic desensitization on secondary erectile failure. *Behavior Therapy, 8,* 330–339.

Austad, CS, & Berman, WH (1991) Managed health care and the evolution of psychotherapy. In CS Austad & WH Berman (Eds.), *Psychotherapy in managed health care.* Washington DC: American Psychological Association.

Azrin, NH, Sisson, RW, Meyers, R, & Godley, M (1982) Alcoholism treatment by disulfiram and community reinforcement therapy. *Journal of Behavior Therapy and Experimental Psychiatry, 13,* 105–112.

Azrin, NH (1976) Improvements in the community reinforcement approach to alcoholism. *Behaviour Research and Therapy, 6,* 7–12.

Baer, RA, & Nietzel, MT (1991) Cognitive and behavioral treatment of impulsivity in children: A meta-analytic review of the outcome literature. *Journal of Clinical Child Psychology, 20,* 400–412.

Baines, S, Saxby, P, & Ehlert, K (1987). Reality orientation and reminiscence therapy: A controlled cross-over study of elderly confused people. *British Journal of Psychiatry, 151,* 222–231.

Baldwin, B (1991). The outcome of depression in old age. *International Journal of Geriatric Psychiatry, 6,* 395–400.

Balestrieri, M, William, P, & Wilkinson, G (1988) Specialist mental health treatment in general practice: A meta-analysis. *Psychological Medicine, 18,* 711–717.

Bancroft, J, & Coles, L (1976) Three years experience in a sexual problems clinic. *British Medical Journal, 1976*(1), 1575–1577.

Bancroft, J, Dickerson, M, Fairburn, CG, Gray, J, Greenwood, J, Stevenson, N, & Warner, P (1986) Sex therapy outcome research: A reappraisal of methodology. *Psychological Medicine, 16,* 851–863.

Bandura, A (1977) *Social learning theory.* Englewood Cliffs, NJ: Prentice-Hall.

Bank, L, Marlowe, JH, Reid, JB, Patterson, GR, & Weinrott, MR (1991) A comparative evaluation of parent-training interventions for families of chronic delinquents. *Journal of Abnormal Child Psychology, 19,* 15–33.

Banta, HD, & Saxe, L (1983) Reimbursement for psychotherapy: Linking efficacy research and public policymaking. *American Psychologist, 38,* 918–923.

Barker, WA, Scott, J, & Eccleston, D (1987) The Newcastle chronic depression study: Results of a treatment regime. *International Clinical Psychopharmacology, 2,* 261–272.

Barkham, M, Rees, A, Shapiro, DA, Agnew, RM, Halstead, J, & Culverwell, A (1994) Effects of treatment method and duration and severity of depression on the effectiveness of psychotherapy: Extending the Second Sheffield Psychotherapy Project to NHS settings. Sheffield University *SAPU Memo 1480.*

Barkley, RA (1977) A review of stimulant drug research with hyperactive children. *Journal of Child Psychology, 18,* 137.

Barlow, DH (1988) *Anxiety and its disorders: The nature and treatment of anxiety and panic.* New York: Guilford Press.

Barlow, DH (1994) Comorbidity in social phobia: Implications for cognitive-behavioral treatment. *Bulletin of the Menninger Clinic, 58* (Suppl. A), 43–57.

Barlow, DH, Craske, MG, Cerny, JA, & Klosko, JS (1989) Behavioral treatment of panic disorder. *Behavior Therapy, 20,* 261–282.

Barr, RG, & Feuerstein, M (1983). Recurrent abdominal pain syndrome: How appropriate are our basic clinical assumptions? In PJ McGrath & P Firestone (Eds.), *Pediatric and adolescent behavioral medicine.* New York: Springer.

Barrett, CJ, Hampe, IE, & Miller, LC (1978) Research on child psychotherapy. In SG Garfield & AE Bergin (Eds.), *Handbook of psychotherapy and behavior change* (2nd ed.). New York: Wiley.

Barrios, BA, & O'Dell, SL (1989). Fears and anxieties. In EJ Mash & RA Barkley (Eds.), *Treatment of childhood disorders.* New York: Guilford Press.

Barrnett, RJ, Docherty, JP, & Frommelt, GM (1991) A review of psychotherapy research since 1963. *Journal of the American Academy of Child and Adolescent Psychiatry, 30*(1).

Barrowclough, C, & Tarrier, N (1984) Psychosocial intervention with families and their effects on the course of schizophrenia: A review. *Psychological Medicine, 14,* 629–642.

Barrowclough, C, Tarrier, N, Watts, S, Vaughn, C, Bamrah, JS, & Freeman, HL (1987) Assessing the functional value of relatives knowledge about schizophrenia: A preliminary report. *British Journal of Psychiatry, 151,* 1–8.

Baruch, G (1995, January) *Evaluating the outcome of a community-based psychoanalytic psychotherapy service for young people between 12 and 25 years old: Work in progress.* Paper presented at day conference on audit and psychoanalytic psychotherapy services, Tavistock Clinic, London.

Basoglu, M, Lax, T, Kasvikis, Y, & Marks, IM (1988) Predictors of improvement in obsessive–compulsive disorder. *Journal of Anxiety Disorders, 2,* 299–317.

Basoglu, M, Marks, IM, Kilic, C, Swinson, RP, Noshirvani, H, Kuch, K, & O'Sullivan, G (1994) Relationship of panic, anticipatory anxiety, agoraphobia and global improvement in panic disorder with agoraphobia treated with Alprazolam and exposure. *British Journal of Psychiatry, 164,* 647–652.

Baum, CG, & Forehand, R (1981) Long-term follow-up assessment of parent training by use of multiple outcome measure. *Behavior Therapy, 12,* 643.

Bebbington, PE, Bruha, T, & McCarthy, B, et al. (1988) The Camberwell collaborative depression study 1: Depressed probands, adversity and the form of depression. *British Journal of Psychiatry, 152,* 754–765.

Bebbington, P, & Kuipers, L (1994) The positive utility of expressed emotion in schizophrenia: An aggregate analysis. *Psychological Medicine, 24,* 707–718.

Beck, AT (1967) *Depression: Clinical, experimental, and theoretical aspects.* New York: Harper & Row.

Beck, AT (1976) *Cognitive therapy and the emotional disorders.* New York: International Universities Press.

Beck, AT (1987) Cognitive models of depression. *Journal of Cognitive Psychotherapy, 1,* 5–37.

Beck, AT, & Emery, GD (1977) *Individual treatment manual for cognitive behavioral psychotherapy for drug abuse.* Unpublished manuscript, University of Pennsylvania.

Beck, AT, Rush, AJ, Shaw, BF, & Emery, G (1979) *Cognitive therapy of depression.* New York: Guilford Press.

Beck, AT, Hollon, SD, & Young, JE, et al. (1985) Treatment of depression with cognitive therapy and amitriptyline. *Archives of General Psychiatry, 42,* 142–148.

Beck, AT, Sokol, L, Clark, DA, Berchick, R, & Wright, F (1992) A crossover study of focused cognitive therapy for panic disorder. *American Journal of Psychiatry, 149,* 778–783.

Beck, JG, Stanley, MA, Baldwin, LE, Deagle, EA, & Averill, PM (1994) Comparison of cognitive therapy and relaxation training for panic disorder. *Journal of Consulting and Clinical Psychology, 62,* 818–826.

Becker, JV, & Abel, GG (1981) Behavioral treatment of victims of sexual assault. In SM, Turner, KS, Calhoun, & HE, Adams (Eds.), *Handbook of clinical behavior therapy.* New York: Wiley.

Becker, RE, Heimberg, RG, & Bellack, AS (1987) *Social skills training treatment for depression.* New York: Pergamon Press.

Beedell, C, & Payne, S (1989) *Making the case for child psychotherapy: A survey of the membership and activity of the Association of Child Psychotherapists.* Bristol, UK: University of Bristol School of Applied Social Studies.

Bellack, AS, Hersen, M, & Himmelhoch, JM (1981) Social skills training compared with pharmacotherapy and psychotherapy for depression. *American Journal of Psychiatry, 138,* 1562–1567.

Belsher, G, & Costello, CG (1988) Relapse after recovery from unipolar depression: A critical review. *Psychological Bulletin, 104,* 84–96.

Benbow, SM, Marriott, A, Morley, M, & Walsh, S (1993) Family therapy and dementia: Review and clinical experience. *International Journal of Geriatric Psychiatry, 8,* 717–725.

Benson, R (1975) The forgotten treatment modality in bipolar illness: Psychotherapy. *Diseases of the Nervous System, 36,* 634–638.

Bentall, RP, Haddock, G, & Slade, P (1994) Cognitive behavior therapy for persistent auditory hallucinations: From theory to therapy. *Behavior Therapy, 25,* 51–66.

Benton, MK, & Scroeder, HE (1990) Social skills training with schizophrenics: A meta-analytic evaluation. *Journal of Consulting and Clinical Psychology, 58,* 741–747.

Berelowitz, M, & Tarnapolsky, A (1993) The validity of borderline personality disorder: An updated review of recent research. In P Tyrer & G Stein (Eds.), *Personality disorder reviewed.* London: Gaskell.

Berg, CZ, Rapoport, JL, Whitaker, A, et al. (1989) Childhood obsessive–compulsive disorder: A two-year prospective follow-up of a community sample. *Journal of the American Academy of Child and Adolescent Psychiatry, 28,* 528–533.

Bergin, AE (1971) The evaluation of therapeutic outcomes. In AE Bergin & SL Garfield (Eds.), *Handbook of psychotherapy and behavior change.* New York: Wiley.

Berkowitz, R, Eberlein-Friess, R, Kuipers, L, & Leff, J (1984) Educating relatives about schizophrenia. *Schizophrenia Bulletin, 10,* 418–429.

Berman, JS, & Norton, NC (1985) Does professional training make a therapist more effective? *Psychological Bulletin, 98,* 401–407.

Berney, T, Kolvin, I, Bhate, SR, Garside, RF, Jeans, J, Kay, B, & Scarth, L (1981) School phobia: A therapeutic trial with clomipramine and short-term outcome. *British Journal of Psychiatry, 138,* 110–118.

Bernstein, GA, & Borchardt, CM (1991) Anxiety disorders of childhood and adolescence: A critical review. *Journal of the American Academy of Child and Adolescent Psychiatry, 30,* 519–532.

Bernstein, GA, Garfinkel, BD, & Borchardt, CM (1987) *Imipramine versus alprazolam for school phobia.* Paper presented at the annual meeting of the American Academy of Child and Adolescent Psychiatry, Washington, DC.

Betz, NE, & Shullman, SL (1979) Factors related to client return following intake. *Journal of Counselling Psychology, 26,* 542–545.

Beutler, LE, Scogin, F, Kirkish, P, Schretlen, D, Corbishley, A, Hamblin, D, Meredith, K, Potter, R, Bamford, CR, & Levenson, AI (1987) Group cognitive therapy and alprazolam in the treatment of depression in older adults. *Journal of Consulting and Clinical Psychology, 55,* 550–556.

Beutler, LE, Machado, PPP, & Neufeldt, SA (1994) Therapist variables. In AE Bergin & SL Garfield (Eds.), *Handbook of psychotherapy and behavior change* (4th ed.). New York: Wiley.

Bhugra, D, & Cordle, C (1988) A case control study of sexual dysfunction in Asian and non-Asian couples 1981–1985. *Sexual and Marital Therapy*, *3*, 71–76.

Bien, TH, Miller, WR, & Tonigan, JC (1993) Brief interventions for alcohol problems: A review. *Addiction*, *88*, 315–336.

Billings, AG, & Moos, RH (1983) Psychosocial processes of recovery among alcoholics and their families: Implications for clinicians and program evaluators. *Addictive Behaviors*, *8*, 205–218.

Bird, HR, Gould, MS, Yager, T, Staghezza, B, & Canino, G (1989) Risk factors for maladjustment in Puerto Rican children. *Journal of the American Academy of Child and Adolescent Psychiatry*, *28*, 847–850.

Blackburn, IM, Bishop, S, Glen, AIM, Whalley, LJ, & Christie, JE (1981) The efficacy of cognitive therapy in depression: A treatment trial using cognitive therapy and pharmacotherapy, each alone and in combination. *British Journal of Psychiatry*, *139*, 181–189.

Blackburn, IM, Eunson, KM, & Bishop, S (1986) A two-year naturalistic follow-up of depressed patients treated with cognitive therapy, pharmacotherapy and a combination of both. *Journal of Affective Disorders*, *10*, 65–75.

Blackburn, IM (1988) An appraisal of comparative trials of cognitive therapy in depression. In C Perris, IM Blackburn, & H Perris (Eds.), *Cognitive psychotherapy: Theory and practice*. Heidelberg: Springer-Verlag.

Blagg, NR, & Yule, W (1984) The behavioral treatment of school refusal—A comparative study. *Behaviour Research and Therapy*, *22*, 119–127.

Bland, RC, Newman, SC, & Orn, H (1988) Age of onset of psychiatric disorders. *Acta Psychiatrica Scandinavica*, *77*, 43–49.

Blazer, DG, Hughes, D, George, LK, Swartz, M, & Boyer, R (1991) Generalized anxiety disorder. In LN Robins & DA Regier (Eds.), *Psychiatric disorders in America: The Epidemiological Catchment Area Study*. New York: Free Press.

Blazer, DG, Kessler, RC, McGonagle, KA, & Swartz, MS (1994) The prevalence and distribution of major depression in a national community sample: The National Comorbidity Survey. *American Journal of Psychiatry*, *151*, 979–986.

Bleathman, C., & Morton, I (1992) Validation therapy: Extracts from 20 groups with dementia sufferers. *Journal of Advanced Nursing*, *17*, 658–666.

Blue, FR, McKnight, DL, Rau, BW, & Fulcher, RB (1987) A multidisciplinary approach to an individual with severe ritualistic behaviors. *Psychological Reports*, *61*, 407–410.

Boersma, K, den Hengst, S, Dekker, J, & Emmelkamp, PMJ (1976) Exposure and response prevention in the natural environment: A comparison with obsessive compulsive patients. *Behaviour Research and Therapy*, *14*, 19–24.

Boland, FJ, Mellor, CS, & Revusky, S (1978) Chemical aversion treatment of alcoholism: Lithium as the aversive agent. *Behaviour Research and Therapy*, *16*, 401–409.

Bolton, D, Collins, S, & Steinberg, D (1983) The treatment of obsessive–compulsive disorder in adolescence: A report of fifteen cases. *British Journal of Psychiatry*, *142*, 456–464.

Bolton, D, Luckie, M, & Steinberg, D (1995) Long-term course of obsessive–compulsive disorder treated in adolescence. *Journal of the American Academy of Child and Adolescent Psychiatry, 34,* 1441–1450.

Bond, CR, & McMahon, RJ (1984) Relationships between marital distress and child behavior problems, maternal personal adjustment, maternal personality, and maternal parenting behavior. *Journal of Abnormal Psychology, 93,* 348–351.

Bordin, ES (1979) The generalizability of the psychoanalytic concept of the working alliance. *Psychotherapy, 16,* 252–260.

Borkovec, TD, & Mathews, AM (1988) Treatment of nonphobic anxiety disorders: A comparison of nondirective, cognitive and coping desensitization therapy. *Journal of Consulting and Clinical Psychology, 56,* 877–884.

Borkovec, TD, & Costello, E (1993) Efficacy of applied relaxation and cognitive-behavioral therapy in the treatment of Generalized Anxiety Disorder. *Journal of Consulting and Clinical Psychology, 61,* 611–619.

Borkovec, TD, Abel, JL, & Newman, H (1995) Effects of psychotherapy on comorbid conditions in Generalized Anxiety Disorder. *Journal of Consulting and Clinical Psychology, 63,* 479–483.

Bornstein, MR, Bellack, AS, & Hersen, M (1977) Social skills training for unassertive children: A multiple baseline analysis. *Journal of Applied Behavior Analysis, 10,* 183–195.

Boudewyns, PA, & Hyer, L (1990) Physiological response to combat memories and preliminary treatment outcome in Vietnam veteran PTSD patients treated with direct therapeutic exposure. *Behavior Therapy, 21,* 63–87.

Boudewyns, PA, Hyer, L, Woods, MG, Harrison, WR, & McCranie, E (1990) PTSD among Vietnam veterans: An early look at treatment outcome using direct therapeutic exposure. *Journal of Traumatic Stress, 3,* 359–368.

Boudewyns, PA, Stwertka, LA, Hyer, JW, Albrecht, X, & Sperr, EG (1993) Eye-movement desensitization for PTSD of combat: A treatment outcome pilot study. *Behavior Therapist, 16,* 29–33.

Boulougouris, JC (1977) Variables affecting outcome in obsessive–compulsive patients treated by flooding. In JC Bolougiouris & AD Rabevillas (Eds.), *Treatment of phobic and obsessive–compulsive disorders.* Oxford: Pergamon Press.

Bourgeois, MS (1990) Enhancing conversational skills in patients with Alzheimer's disease using a prosthetic memory aid. *Journal of Applied Behavior Analysis, 23,* 29–42.

Bowden, C, Brugger, A, Swan, A, Calabrese, J, Janicek, P, Petty, F, Dilsaver, S, Davis, J, Rush, J, Small, J, Garva-Trevine, E, Risch, S, Goodnick, P, & Morris, D (1994) Efficacy of divalproax sodium vs lithium and placebo in the treatment of mania. *Journal of the American Medical Association, 271,* 918–924.

Bowen, GR, & Lambert, JA (1986) Systematic desensitization therapy with PTSD cases. In CR Figley (Ed.), *Trauma and its wake II.* New York: Brunner/Mazel.

Bowers, WA (1990) Treatment of depressed in-patients: Cognitive therapy plus medication, relaxation plus medication and medication alone. *British Journal of Psychiatry, 156,* 73–78.

Bowlby, J (1988) *A secure base: Clinical applications of attachment theory.* London: Routledge.

Brandsma, JM, Maultsby, MC, & Welsh, RJ (1980) *The outpatient treatment of alcoholism: A review and a comparative study.* Baltimore, University Park Press.

Brane, G, Karlsson, I, Kihlgren, M, & Norberg, A (1989) Integrity-promoting care of demented nursing home patients: Psychological and biochemical changes. *International Journal of Geriatric Psychiatry, 4,* 165–172.

Breslau, N, & Davis, GC (1985) DSM-III generalized anxiety disorder: An empirical investigation of more stringent criteria. *Psychiatry Research, 14,* 231–238.

Breslau, N, Davis, CG, Andreski, P, & Petrerson, E (1991) Traumatic events and PTSD in an urban population of young adults. *Archives of General Psychiatry, 40,* 216–222.

Brewin, CR, & Bradley, C (1989) Patient preferences and randomized controlled trials. *British Medical Journal, 233,* 313–315.

Brinkley, JR, Beitman, BD, & Friedal, RO (1979) Low-dose neuroleptic regimes in the treatment of borderline patients. *Archives of General Psychiatry, 36,* 319–326.

Brodaty, H, (1992) Carers: Training informal carers. In T Arie (Ed.), *Recent advances in psychogeriatrics—2.* Edinburgh: Churchill Livingstone.

Brodaty, H, & Gresham, M (1989) Effect of a training programme to reduce stress in carers of patients with dementia. *British Medical Journal, 299,* 1375–1379.

Brom, D, Kleber, RJ, & Defares, PB (1989) Brief psychotherapy for PTSD. *Journal of Consulting and Clinical Psychology, 57,* 607–612.

Brooker, C, Tarrier, N, Barrowclough, C, Butterworth, A, & Goldberg, D (1992) Training community psychiatric nurses for psychosocial intervention: Report of a pilot study. *British Journal of Psychiatry, 160,* 836–844.

Brooker, C, Falloon, I, Butterworth, A, Goldberg, D, Graham-Hole, V, & Hillier, V (1994) The outcome of training community psychiatric nurses to deliver psychosocial interventions. *British Journal of Psychiatry, 165,* 222–230.

Brown, GW, Birley, JLT, & Wing, JK (1972) Influence of family life on the course of schizophrenic disorders; replication. *British Journal of Psychiatry, 121,* 241–258.

Brown, J (1987) A review of meta-analyses conducted on psychotherapy outcome research. *Clinical Psychology Review, 7,* 1–23.

Brown, TA, & Barlow, DH (1992) Comorbidity among anxiety disorders: Implications for treatment and DSM-IV. *Journal of Consulting and Clinical Psychology, 60,* 835–844.

Brown, TA, Antony, MM, & Barlow, DH (1995) Diagnostic comorbidity in panic disorder: Effect on treatment outcome and course of comorbid diagnoses following treatment. *Journal of Consulting and Clinical Psychology, 63,* 408–418 .

Brown, TA, & Barlow, DH (1995) Long-term outcome in cognitive-behavioral treatment of panic disorder: Clinical predictors and alternative strategies for assessment. *Journal of Consulting and Clinical Psychology, 63,* 754–765.

Burgio, LD, Burgio, KL, Engel, BT, & Tice, LM (1986) Increasing distance and independence of ambulation in elderly nursing home residents. *Journal of Applied Behavior Analysis, 19,* 357–366.

Burgio, L, Engel, BT, McCormick, K, Hawkins, A, & Scheve, A. (1988) Behavioral treatment for urinary incontinence in elderly inpatients: Initial attempts to modify prompting and toileting procedures. *Behavior Therapy, 19,* 345–357.

Burke, KC, Burke, JD, Rae, DS, & Regier, DA (1991) Comparing age at onset of major depression and other psychiatric disorders by birth cohorts in five US community populations. *Archives of General Psychiatry, 48,* 789–795.

Burlingame, GM, Fuhriman, A, Paul, S, & Ogles, B (1989) Implementing a time-limited therapy program: Differential effects of training and experience. *Psychotherapy, 26,* 303–313.

Burns, DD, & Nolen-Hoeksema, S (1992) Therapeutic empathy and recovery from depression in cognitive-behavioral therapy: A structural equation model. *Journal of Consulting and Clinical Psychology, 60,* 441–449.

Burton, M (1980) Evaluation and change in a psychogeriatric ward through direct observation and feedback. *British Journal of Psychiatry, 137,* 566–571.

Burvill, PW (1993) Prognosis of depression in the elderly. *International Review of Psychiatry, 5,* 437–443.

Butler, G, Cullington, A, Mumby, M, Amies, P, & Gelder, M (1984) Exposure and anxiety management in the treatment of social phobia. *Journal of Consulting and Clinical Psychology, 52,* 642–650.

Butler, G, Cullington, A, & Hibbert, G, et al. (1987) Anxiety management for persistent generalised anxiety. *British Journal of Psychiatry, 151,* 535–542.

Butler, G, Fennell, M, Robson, P, & Gelder, M (1991) Comparison of behavior therapy and cognitive behavior therapy in the treatment of generalized anxiety disorder. *Journal of Consulting and Clinical Psychology, 59,* 167–175.

Bystritsky, A, & Waikar, SV (1994) Inert placebo versus active medication: Patient blindability in clinical pharmacological trials. *Journal of Nervous and Mental Disease, 182,* 485–487.

Cade, JFL (1949) Lithium salts in the treatment of psychotic excitement. *Medical Journal of Australia, 3,* 349–352.

Cadogan, DA (1973) Marital group therapy in the treatment of alcoholism. *Quarterly Journal of Studies on Alcohol, 34,* 1187–1194.

Campbell, M, & Spencer, EK (1988) Psychopharmacology in child and adolescent psychiatry: A review of the past five years. *Journal of the American Academy of Child and Adolescent Psychiatry, 32,* 269–279.

Campbell, SB (1990) *Behavior problems in preschool children: Clinical and developmental issues.* New York: Guilford Press.

Campbell, SB (1995) Behavior problems in preschool children: A review of recent research. *Journal of Child Psychology and Psychiatry, 36,* 113–149.

Campbell, SB, & Ewing, LJ (1990) Hard-to-manage preschoolers: Adjustment at age nine and predictors of continuing symptoms. *Journal of Child Psychology and Psychiatry, 31 ,* 871–889.

Cannon, DS, & Baker, TB (1981) Emetic and electric shock aversion therapy: Assessment of conditioning. *Journal of Consulting and Clinical Psychology, 49,* 20–33.

Cannon, DS, Baker, TB, & Wehl, CK (1981) Emetic and electric shock aversion therapy: Six and twelve month follow-up. *Journal of Consulting and Clinical Psychology, 49,* 360–368.

Cantwell, DP, & Baker, L (1989) Stability and natural history of DSM-III childhood diagnoses. *Journal of the American Academy of Child and Adolescent Psychiatry, 28,* 691–700.

Cappe, RF, & Alden, LE (1986) A comparison of treatment strategies for clients functionally impaired by extreme shyness and social avoidance. *Journal of Consulting and Clinical Psychology, 54,* 796–801.

Cardin, VA, McGill, CW, & Falloon, IRH (1986) An economic analysis: Costs benefits and effectiveness. In IRH Falloon (Ed.), *Family management of schizophrenia.* Baltimore: Johns Hopkins University Press.

Caron, C, & Rutter, M (1991) Comorbidity in child psychopathology: Concepts, issues and research strategies. *Journal of Child Psychology and Psychiatry, 32,* 1063–1080.

Carpenter, WT, Gunderson, JG, & Strauss, JS (1977) Considerations of the borderline syndrome: A longitudinal comparative study of borderline and schizophrenic patients. In P Hartocollis (Ed.), *Borderline personality disorders.* New York: International Universities Press.

Carstensen, LL, & Erickson, R (1986) Enhancing the social environments of elderly nursing home residents: Are high rates of interaction enough? *Journal of Applied Behavior Analysis, 19,* 349–355.

Carter, FA, & Bulik, CM (1994) Exposure treatments for bulimia nervosa: Procedure, efficacy, and mechanisms. *Advances in Behavior Research and Therapy, 16,* 77–129.

Caserta, MS, & Lund, DA (1993) Intrapersonal resources and the effectiveness of self-help groups for bereaved older adults. *Gerontologist, 33,* 619–629.

Casey, RJ, & Berman, JS (1985) The outcome of psychotherapy with children. *Psychological Bulletin, 98,* 388–400.

Castle, DJ, Deane, A, Marks, IM, Cutts, F, Chadboury, Y, & Stewart, A (1994) Obsessive–compulsive disorder: Prediction of outcome from behavioral psychotherapy. *Acta Psychiatrica Scandinavica, 89,* 393–398.

Catalan, J, Gath, D, Edmonds, G, & Ennis, J (1984a) The effects of non-prescibing of anxiolytics in general practice. I. Controlled evaluation of psychiatric and social outcome. *British Journal of Psychiatry, 144,* 593–602.

Catalan, J, Gath, D, Bond, A, & Martin, P (1984b) The effects of non-prescribing of anxiolytics in general practice. II. Factors associated with outcome. *British Journal of Psychiatry, 144,* 603–610.

Catalan, J, Gath, DH, Anastasiades, P, Bond, SA, Day, A, & Hall, L (1991) Evaluation of a brief psychological treatment for emotional disorders in primary care. *Psychological Medicine, 21,* 1013–1018.

Catalan, J, Hawton, K, & Day, A (1990) Couples referred to a sexual dysfunction clinic: Psychological and physical morbidity. *British Journal of Psychiatry, 156,* 61–67.

Cerbone, M, Mayo, J, Cuthbertson, B, & O'Connell, R (1992) Group therapy as an adjunct to medication in the management of affective disorder. *Group, 16,* 174–187.

Chadwick, PDJ, & Lowe, CF (1990) Measurement and modification of delusional beliefs. *Journal of Consulting and Clinical Psychology, 58,* 225–232.

Chadwick, PDJ, & Birchwood, M (1994) The omnipotence of voices: A cognitive approach to auditory hallucinations. *British Journal of Psychiatry, 164,* 190–201.

Chadwick, PDJ, & Lowe, CF (1994) A cognitive approach to measuring and modifying delusions. *Behaviour Research and Therapy, 32,* 355–367.

Chambless, DL, & Gillis, MM (1993) Cognitive therapy of anxiety disorders. *Journal of Consulting and Clinical Psychology, 61,* 248–260.

Chambless, DL, Renneberg, B, Goldstein, A, & Gracely, EJ (1992) MCMI-diagnosed personality disorders among agoraphobic outpatients: Prevalence and relationship to severity and treatment outcome. *Journal of Anxiety Disorders, 6,* 193–211.

Chaney, EF, O'Leary, MR, & Marlatt, GA (1978) Skill training with alcoholics. *Journal of Consulting and Clinical Psychology, 46,* 1092–1104.

Channon, S, DeSilva, P, Hemsley, D, & Perkins, R (1989) A controlled trial of cognitive-behavioral and behavioral treatment of anorexia nervosa. *Behaviour Research and Therapy, 27,* 529–535.

Chapman, PLH, & Huygens, I (1988) An evaluation of three-month treatment programmes for alcoholism: An experimental study with 6 and 18 month follow-ups. *British Journal of Addiction, 83,* 67–81.

Chazan, M, & Jackson, S (1974) Behavior problems in the infant school: Changes over two years. *Journal of Child Psychology and Psychiatry, 15,* 33–46.

Chess, LK, & Thomas, CG (1979) *Childhood pathology and later adjustment.* New York: Wiley.

Chick, J, Lloyd, G, & Crombie, E (1985) Counselling problem drinkers in medical wards: A controlled study. *British Medical Journal, 290,* 965–967.

Chick, J, Ritson, B, Connaughton, J, Stewart, A, & Chick, J (1988) Advice versus extended treatment for alcoholism: A controlled study. *British Journal of Addictions, 83,* 159–170.

Christensen, H, Hadzi, P, Andrews, G, & Mattick, R (1987) Behavior therapy and tricyclic medication ion the treatment of obsessive–compulsive disorder: A quantitative review. *Journal of Consulting and Clinical Psychology, 55,* 701–711.

Cicchetti, D (1990) An historical perspective on the discipline of development psychopathology. In J Rolfe, et al. (Eds.), *Risk protection factors in the development of psychopathology.* New York: Cambridge University Press.

Clark, DB, Smith, MG, Neighbors, BD, Skerlec, LM, & Randall, J (1994) Anxiety disorders in adolescence: Characteristics, prevalence, and comorbidities. *Clinical Psychology Review, 14,* 113–137.

Clark, DM, Salkovskis, PM, Hackmann, A, Middleton, H, Anastasiades, P, & Gelder, M (1994) A comparison of cognitive therapy, applied relaxation and imipramine in the treatment of panic disorder. *British Journal of Psychiatry, 164,* 759–769.

Clarkin, JF, Glick, ID, Haas, GL, Spencer, JH, Lewis, AB, Peyser, J, DeMane, N, Good-Ellis, M, Harris, E, & Lestelle, V (1990) A randomized clinical trial of inpatient family intervention. *Journal of Affective Disorders, 18,* 17–28.

Clarkin, JF (1994, March) *Psychodynamically informed investigation of the borderline personality disorder.* Paper delivered at the IPA Fourth Psychoanalytic Research Conference: Clinical Applications of Current Research in Borderline Disorders, London.

Clarkin, JF, & Kendall, PC (1992) Comorbidity and treatment planning: Summary and future directions. *Journal of Consulting and Clinical Psychology, 60,* 904–908.

Clement, U, & Schmidt, G (1983) The outcome of couple therapy for sexual dysfunctions using three different formats. *Journal of Sex and Marital Therapy, 9,* 67–78.

Clum, GA (1989) Psychological interventions vs drugs in the treatment of panic. *Behavior Therapy, 20,* 429–457.

Clum, GA, Clum, GA, & Surls, R (1993) A meta-analysis of treatments for panic disorder. *Journal of Consulting and Clinical Psychology, 61,* 317–326.

Coccaro, EF (1993) Psychopharmacologic studies in patients with personality disorders: Review and perspective. *Journal of Personality Disorder, 7* (Suppl.), 181–192.

Coccaro, EF, Astill, JL, Herbert, JL, & Schut, AG (1990) Fluoxetine treatment of impulsive aggression in DSM-III-R personality disorder patients. *Journal of Clinical Pharmacology, 10,* 373–375.

Cochran, S (1984) Preventing medical non-compliance in the out-patient treatment of bipolar affective disorder. *Journal of Consulting and Clinical Psychology, 52,* 873–878.

Cohen, J (1962) The statistical power of abnormal-social psychological research: A review. *Journal of Abnormal and Social Psychology, 65,* 145–153.

Cohen, J (1969) *Statistical power analysis for the behavioral sciences.* San Diego, CA: Academic Press.

Cohen, J (1990) Things I have learned (so far). *American Psychologist, 45,* 1304–1312.

Cohen, LH, Sargenet, MM, & Sechrest, LB (1986) Use of psychotherapy research by professional psychologists. *American Psychologist, 41,* 198–206.

Cohen, P, Cohen, J, Kasen, S, Velez, CN, Hartmark, C, Johnson, J, Rojas, M, Brook, J, & Streuning, EL (1993a) An epidemiological study of disorders in late childhood and adolescence: I. Age- and gender-specific prevalence. *Journal of Child Psychology and Psychiatry, 34,* 851–865.

Cohen, P, Cohen, J, & Brook, J (1993b) An epidemiological study of disorders in late childhood and adolescence. II. Persistence of Disorders. *Journal of Child Psychology and Psychiatry, 34,* 869–897.

Cohen, P, Kasen, S, Brook, JS, & Struening, EL (1991) Diagnostic predictors of treatment patterns in a cohort of adolescents. *Journal of the American Academy of Child and Adolescent Psychiatry, 30,* 989–993.

Cohen, S, Tyrell, DAG, & Smith AP (1991) Psychological stress and susceptability to the common cold. *New England Journal of Psychiatry, 325,* 606.

Cole, M (1986) Socio-sexual characteristics of men with sexual problems. *Sexual and Marital Therapy, 1,* 89–108.

Collings, S, & King, M (1994) Ten year follow-up of 50 patients with bulimia nervosa. *British Journal of Psychiatry, 164,* 80–87.

Connolly, J, Hallam, RS, & Marks, I (1976) Selective association of fainting with blood-injury-illness fear. *Behavior Therapy, 7,* 8–13.

Conte, HR, Plutchik, R, Wild, KV, & Karasu, TB (1986) Combined psychotherapy and pharmacotherapy for depression. *Archives of General Psychiatry, 43,* 471–479.

Cook, TD, & Campbell, DT (Eds.) (1979) *Quasi-experimentation: Design and analysis issues for field settings.* Chicago: Rand-McNally.

Coolidge, JC, Brodie, RD, & Feeney, B (1964) A ten year follow up study of sixty six school children. *American Journal of Orthopsychiatry, 34,* 675–684.

Cooper, AJ (1969) Clinical and therapeutic studies in premature ejaculation. *Comprehensive Psychiatry, 10,* 285.

Cooper, B, Harwin, BG, Depla, C, & Shepherd, M (1975) Mental health care in the community: An evaluative study. *Psychological Medicine, 5,* 372–380.

Cooper, JE (1990) The classification of anxiety states in the International Classification of Diseases. In N Sartorius, V Andreoli, L Eisenberg, P Kielholtz, P Pancheri, & G Racagni (Eds.), *Anxiety: Psychobiological and clinical perspectives.* Washington, DC: Hemisphere Publishing Company.

Cooper, NA, & Clum, GA (1989) Imaginal flooding as a supplementary treatment for PTSD in combat veterans: A controlled study. *Behavior Therapy, 20,* 381–391.

Corder, BF, Corder, RF, & Laidlaw, ND (1972) An intensive treatment program for alcoholics and their wives. *Quarterly Journal of Studies on Alcohol, 33,* 1114–1146.

Cornelius, JR, Soloff, PH, Perel, JM, & Ulrich, RF (1990) Fluoxetine trial in borderline personality disorder. *Psychopharmacology Bulletin, 26,* 151–154.

Cornelius, JR, Soloff, PH, Perel, JM, & Ulrich, RF (1993) Continuation pharmacotherapy of borderline personality disorder with Haloperidol and phenelzine. *American Journal of Psychiatry, 150,* 1843–1848.

Corney, RH (1987) Marital problems and treatment outcome in depressed women: A clinical trial of social work intervention. *British Journal of Psychiatry, 151,* 652–659.

Corney, RH (1990) Counselling in general practice—does it work? Discussion paper. *Journal of the Royal Society of Medicine, 83,* 253–257.

Coryell, W, & Noyes, R (1988) Placebo response in panic disorder. *American Journal of Psychiatry, 145,* 1138–1140.

Coryell, W, Endicott, J, Andreason, NC, Keller, MB, Clayton, PJ, Hirschfeld, RMA, Schefter, WA, & Winokur, G (1988) Depression and panic attacks: The significance of overlaps as reflected in follow-up and family study data. *American Journal of Psychiatry, 145,* 293–300.

Costello, EJ (1989a) Child psychiatric disorders and their correlates: A primary care paediatric sample. *Journal of the American Academy of Child and Adolescent Psychiatry, 28,* 851–855.

Costello, EJ (1989b) Developments in child psychiatric epidemiology. *Journal of the American Academy of Child and Adolescent Psychiatry, 28,* 836–841.

Costello, EJ, Costello, AJ, & Edelbrock, C, et al. (1988) Psychiatric disorders in pediatric primary care. *Archives of General Psychiatry*, 45, 1107–1116.

Cottraux, J, Mollard, E, Bouvard, M, Marks, I, Sluys, M, Nury, AM, Douge, R, & Ciadella, P (1990) A controlled study of fluvoxamine and exposure in obsessive–compulsive disorder. *International Journal of Clinical Pharmacotherapy*, 5, 17–30.

Cottraux, J, Messy, PM, Marks, IM, Mollard, E, & Bouvard, M (1993) Predictive factors in the treatment of obsessive–compulsive disorders with fluvoxamine and or behavior therapy. *Behavioural Psychology*, 21, 45–50.

Covi, L, & Lipman, RS (1987) Cognitive-behavioral group psychotherapy combined with imipramine in major depression. *Psychopharmacology Bulletin*, 23, 173–176.

Cowdrey, RW, & Gardener, DL (1988) Pharmacotherapy of borderline personality disorder: Alprazolam, carbamazepine, trifluperazine and trancypromine. *Archives of General Psychiatry*, 45, 111–119.

Cox, BJ, Ballenger, JC, Laraia, M, Hobbs, WR, Peterson, GA, & Hucek, A (1988) Different rates of improvement of different symptoms in combined pharmacological and behavioral treatment of agoraphobia. *Journal of Behavior Therapy and Experimental Psychiatry*, 19, 119–126.

Cox, BJ, Endler, NS, & Lee, PS (1992) A meta-analysis of treatments for panic disorder with agoraphobia: Imipramine, alprazolam and *in vivo* exposure. *Journal of Behavior Therapy and Experimental Psychiatry*, 23, 175–182.

Cozolino, LJ, Goldstein, MJ, Nuechterlein, KH, West, KL, & Synder, KS (1988) The impact of education about schizophrenia on relatives varying in expressed emotion. *Schizophrenia Bulletin*, 14, 675–687.

Craighead, LW, & Agras, WS (1991) Mechanisms of action in cognitive-behavioral and pharmacological interventions for obesity and bulimia nervosa. *Journal of Consulting and Clinical Psychology*, 59, 115–125.

Craske, MG, Brown, TA, & Barlow, DH (1991) Behavioral treatment of panic disorder: A two year follow-up. *Behavior Therapy*, 22, 289–304.

Creamer, M (1987) Cognitive interventions in the treatment of obsessive compulsive disorder. *Behavior Change*, 4, 20–27.

Crisp, AH (1980) *Anorexia nervosa: Let me be.* London: Academic Press.

Crisp, AH, Kalucy, RS, Lacey, JH, & Harding, B (1977) The long-term prognosis in anorexia nervosa: Some factors predictive of outcome. In RA Vigersky (Ed.), *Anorexia nervosa.* New York: Raven Press.

Crisp, AH, Norton, K, Gowers, S, Halek, C, Bowyer, C, Yeldham, D, Levett, G, & Bhat, A (1991) A controlled study of the effect of therapies aimed at adolescent and family psychopathology in anorexia nervosa. *British Journal of Psychiatry*, 159, 325–333.

Crits-Christoph, P (1992) The efficacy of brief dynamic psychotherapy: A meta-analysis. *American Journal of Psychiatry*, 149, 151–158.

Crits-Christoph, P, Cooper, A, & Luborsky, L (1988) The accuracy of therapists' interpretations and the outcome of dynamic psychotherapy. *Archives of General Psychiatry*, 56, 490–495.

Crits-Christoph, P, Baranackie, K, Kurcias, JS, Beck, AT, Carroll, K, Perry, K, Luborsky, L, McLellan, Woody, GE, Thompson, L, Gallagher, D, &

Zitrin, C (1991) Meta-analysis of therapist effects in psychotherapy outcome studies. *Psychotherapy Research*, *1*, 81–91.

Crits-Christoph, P, Frank, E, Chambless, DL, Brody, C, & Karp, JF (1995) Training in empirically validated treatments: What are clinical psychology students learning? *Professional Psychology: Research and Practice*, *26*, 514–522.

Crowe, MJ, Gillan, P, & Golombok, S (1981) Form and content in the conjoint treatment of sexual dysfunction: A controlled study. *Behaviour Research and Therapy*, *19*, 47–54.

Crumbach, JC, & Carr, GL (1979) Treatment of alcoholics with logotherapy. *International Journal of the Addictions*, *14*, 847–853.

Cryer, L, & Beutler, L (1980) Group therapy: An alternative approach for rape victims. *Journal of Sex and Marital Therapy*, *6*, 40–46.

Csillag, ER (1976) Modification of penile erectile response. *Journal of Behavior Therapy and Experimental Psychiatry*, *7*, 27–29.

Culhane, M, & Dobson, H (1991) Groupwork with elderly women. *International Journal of Geriatric Psychiatry*, *6*, 415–418.

Cullen, K (1976) A six year controlled trial of prevention of children with behavioral disorders. *Journal of Pediatrics*, *88*, 662.

Cummings, NA (1987) The future of psychotherapy: One psychologist's perspective. *American Journal of Psychotherapy*, *41*, 349–360.

Curran, PS, Bell, P, Murray, G, Loughrey, G, Roddy, R, & Rocke, LG (1990) Psychological consequences of the Enniskillen bombing. *British Journal of Psychiatry*, *156*, 478–482.

Curson, DA, Barnes, TRE, & Bamber, RW et al. (1985) Long term depot maintenance of chronic schizophrenic outpatients. *British Journal of Psychiatry*, *146*, 464–480.

Curson, DA, Patel, M, & Liddle, PF, et al. (1988) Psychiatric morbidity of a long stay hospital population with chronic schizophrenia and implications for future community care. *British Medical Journal*, *297*, 819–822.

Dahl, EK, Cohen, DJ, & Provence, S (1986). Clinical and multivariate approaches to nosology of pervasive developmental disorders. *Journal of the American Academy of Child Psychiatry*, *25*, 170–180.

Dar, R (1987) Another look at Meehl, Lakatos and the scientific practices of psychologists. *American Psychologist*, *42* , 145–151.

Dar, R, Serlin, RC, & Omer, H (1994) Misuse of statistical tests in three decades of psychotherapy research. *Journal of Consulting and Clinical Psychology*, *62*, 75–82.

Dare, C (1992) Change the family, change the child? *Archives of Disease in Childhood*, *67*, 643–648.

Dauw, DC (1988) Evaluating the effectiveness of the SECS surrogate-assisted sex therapy model. *Journal Sex Research*, *24*, 269–275.

Davanloo, H. (Ed.) (1978) *Basic principles and techniques in short-term dynamic therapy*. New York: SP Medical and Scientific Books.

Davenport, Y, Ebert, M, Adland, M, & Goodwin, F (1977) Couples group therapy as an adjunct to lithium maintenance in the manic patient. *Journal of Orthopsychiatry*, *47*, 495–502.

Davidson, JR, Kudler, HS, & Smith, R, et al. (1990) Treatment of PTSD with amitriptyline and placebo. *Archives of General Psychiatry, 47,* 259–266.

Davidson, JR, Hughes, D, Blazer, DG, & George, LK (1991) Post-traumatic stress disorder in the community: An epidemiological study. *Psychological Medicine, 21,* 713–721.

Davies, ADM (1981) Neither wife nor widow: An intervention with the wife of a chronically handicapped man during hospital visits. *Behaviour Research and Therapy, 19,* 449–451.

Deahl, MP, Gillham, AB, Thomas, J, Searle, MM, & Srinivasan, M (1994) Psychological sequelae following the Gulf War: Factors associated with subsequent morbidity and the effectiveness of psychological debriefing. *British Journal of Psychiatry, 165,* 60–65.

De Amicis, LA, Goldberg, DC, LoPiccolo, J, Friedman, J, & Davies, L (1985) Clinical follow-up of couples treated for sexual dysfunction. *Archives of Sexual Behavior, 14,* 467–489.

Dean, C, Surtees, PG, & Sashisharan, SP (1983) Comparison of research diagnostic systems in an Edinburgh community sample. *British Journal of Psychiatry, 142,* 247–256.

Dean, R, Briggs, K, & Lindesay, J (1993) The domus philosophy: A prospective evaluation of two residential units for the elderly mentally ill. *International Journal of Geriatric Psychiatry, 8,* 807–817.

De Jong, R, Treiber, R, & Henrich, G (1986) Effectiveness of two psychological treatments for inpatients with severe and chronic depressions. *Cognitive Therapy and Research, 10,* 645–663.

Dekker, J, Dronkers, J, & Staffeleu, J (1985) Treatment of sexual dysfunctions in male-only groups: Predicting outcome. *Journal of Sex and Marital Therapy, 11,* 80–90.

DeLeon, PH, VandenBos, GR, & Cummings, NA (1983) Psychotherapy—Is it safe, effective and appropriate? *American Psychologist, 38,* 907–911.

DeLeon, PH, Uyeda, MK, & Welch, B (1985) Psychology and HMOs: New partnership or new adversary? *American Psychologist, 40,* 1122–1124.

Delong, GR, & Aldersdorf, AL (1987) Long-term experience with lithium treatment in childhood: Correlation with clinical diagnosis. *Journal of the American Academy of Child and Adolescent Psychiatry, 26,* 489.

Department of Health (1994) *Clinical psychology services 1992–93: Summary information from Form KT24 England.* London: Government Statistical Service, DH Statistics Division 2B.

Depression Guideline Panel (1993a) *Depression in primary care: Vol. 1. Diagnosis and detection.* Clinical Practice Guideline No. 5, AHCPR publication No. 93–0550. Rockville, MD: US Department of Health and Human Services, Public Health Service, Agency for Health Care Policy and Research.

Depression Guideline Panel (1993b) *Depression in primary care: Vol 2. Treatment of major depression.* Clinical Practice Guideline No. 5, AHCPR publication No. 93–0551. Rockville, MD: US Department of Health and Human Services, Public Health Service, Agency for Health Care Policy and Research.

Depression Guideline Panel (1993c) *Depression in primary care: Detection, diagnosis and treatment: Quick reference guide for clinicians.* Clinical Practice Guideline No. 5, AHCPR publication No. 93–0552. Rockville, MD: US Department of Health and Human Services, Public Health Service, Agency for Health Care Policy and Research.

Derogatis, LR (1977) *SCL-90: Administration and procedure manual for the revised version.* Baltimore: Clinical Psychometrics Research.

DeRubeis, RJ, & Feeley, M (1991) Determinants of change in cognitive therapy for depression. *Cognitive Therapy and Research, 14,* 469–482.

De Seixas Queiroz, LO, Motta, MA, & Pinho Madi, MBB, et al. (1981) A functional analysis of obsessive–compulsive problems with related therapeutic procedures. *Behaviour Research and Therapy, 19,* 377–388.

DeVeaugh-Geiss, J, Moroz, G, & Biederman, J, et al. (1992) Clomipramine hydrochloride in childhood and adolescent obsessive–compulsive disorder: A multicenter trial. *Journal of the American Academy of Child and Adolescent Psychiatry, 31,* 45–49.

Dietch, JT, Hewett, LJ, & Jones, S (1989) Adverse effects of reality orientation. *Journal of the American Geriatrics Society, 37,* 974–976.

Diguer, L, Barber, JP, & Luborsky, L (1993) Three concomitants: Personality disorders, psychiatric severity and outcome of dynamic psychotherapy of major depression. *American Journal of Psychiatry, 150,* 1246–1248.

Dische, S, Yule, W, Corbett, J, & Hand, D (1983) Childhood nocturnal enuresis: Factors associated with outcome of treatment with an enuretic alarm. *Developmental Medicine and Child Neurology, 25,* 67–80.

Dobson, KS (1989). A meta-analysis of the efficacy of cognitive therapy for depression. *Journal of Consulting and Clinical Psychology, 57,* 414–419.

Dobson, KS, & Shaw, BF (1986) Cognitive assessment with major depressive disorders. *Cognitive Therapy and Research, 10,* 13–29.

Doleys, DM (1983) Enuresis and encopresis. In TH Ollendick & M Hersen (Eds.), *Handbook of child psychopathology.* New York: Plenum Press.

Donabedian, A (1980) Basic approaches to assessment. In *The definition of quality and approaches to its assessment.* Ann Arbor, MI: Health Administration Press.

Donahoe, CP, & Driesenga, SA (1989) A review of social skills training with chronic mental patients. *Progress in Behavior Modification, 21,* 131–164.

Dorus, W, Ostrow, DG, Anton, R, Cushman, P, Collins, PF, Schaefer, M, Charles, Hl, Desai, P, Hayashida, M, Malkerneker, U, Willenbring, O, Fiscella, R, & Sather, M (1989) Lithium treatment of depressed and non-depressed alcoholics. *Journal of the American Medical Association, 262,* 1646–1652.

Drake, RE, 7 Sedere, LI (1986) The adverse effects of intensive treatment of schizophrenia. *Comprehensive Psychiatry, 27,* 313–326.

Dreessen, L, Arntz, A, Luttels, C, & Sallaerts, S (1994) Personality disorders do not influence the results of cognitive behavior therapies for anxiety disorders. *Comprehensive Psychiatry, 35,* 265–274.

Drury, V, Birchwood, M, Cochrane, R, & Macmillan, F (in press a) Cognitive therapy and recovery from acute psychosis: A controlled trial I: Impact on psychotic symptoms. *British Journal of Psychiatry.*

Drury, V, Birchwood, M, Cochrane, R, & Macmillan, F (in press b) Cognitive therapy and recovery from acute psychosis: A controlled trial II: Impact on recovery time. *British Journal of Psychiatry*.

Durham, RC, & Allan, T (1993) Psychological treatment of generalized anxiety disorder: A review of the clinical significance of outcome studies since 1980. *British Journal of Psychiatry, 163*, 19–26.

Durham, RC, & Turvey, AA (1987) Cognitive therapy vs behavior therapy in the treatment of chronic general anxiety. *Behaviour Research and Therapy, 25*, 229–234.

Durlak, JA (1979) Comparative effectiveness of paraprofessional and professional helpers. *Psychological Bulletin, 86*, 80–92.

DuRubeis, RJ, & Feeley, M (1990) Determinants of change in cognitive therapy for depression. *Cognitive Therapy and Research, 14*, 469–482.

Dush, DM, Hirt, ML, & Schroeder, HE (1983) Self-statement modification with adults: A meta-analysis. *Psychological Bulletin, 94*, 408–422.

Dush, DM, Hirt, ML, & Schroeder, HE (1989) Self-statement modification in the treatment of child behavior disorders: A meta-analysis. *Psychological Bulletin, 106*, 97–106.

Earll, L, & Kincey, J (1982) Clinical psychology in general practice: A controlled trial evaluation. *Journal of the Royal College of General Practitioners, 32*, 32–37.

Eaton, WW, Dryman, A, & Weissman, MM (1991) Panic and phobia. In LN Robins & DA Regier (Eds.), *Psychiatric disorders in America: The Epidemiologic Catchment Area Study*. New York: Free Press.

Eddy, DM, Hasselbad, V, & Schacter, R (1990) A Bayseian method for synthesizing evidence: The confidence profile method. *International Journal of Technology Assessment in Health Care, 6*, 31–55.

Edelbrock, C, Costello, A, Dulcan, M, Conover, N, & Kala, R (1986) Parent–child agreement on child psychiatric symptoms assessed via structured interview. *Journal of Child Psychology and Psychiatry, 27*, 181–190.

Edwards, G, Orford, J, Egert, S, Guthrie, S, Hawker, A, Hensman, C, Mitcheson, M, Oppenheimer, E, & Taylor, C (1977) Alcoholism: A controlled trial of "treatment" and "advice." *Journal of Studies on Alcohol, 38*, 1004–1031.

Elkin, I (1994) The NIMH treatment of depression collaborative research program: Where we began and where we are. In AE Bergin & SL Garfield (Eds.), *Handbook of psychotherapy and behavior change* (4th ed.). New York: Wiley.

Elkin, I, Pilkonis, PA, Docherty, JP, & Sotsky, SM (1988a) Conceptual and methodological issues in comparative studies of psychotherapy and pharmacotherapy. I: Active ingredients and mechanisms of change. *American Journal of Psychiatry, 145*, 909–917.

Elkin, I, Pilkonis, PA, Docherty, JP, & Sotsky, SM (1988b) Conceptual and methodological issues in comparative studies of psychotherapy and pharmacotherapy. II: Nature and timing of treatment effects. *American Journal of Psychiatry, 145*, 1070–1076 .

Elkin, I, Shea, MT, Watkins, JT, Imber, SD, Sotsky, SM, Collins, JF, Glass, DR, Pilkonis, PA, Leber, WR, Docherty, JP, Fiester, SJ, & Parloff, MB

(1989) National Institute of Mental Health Treatment of Depression Collaborative Program: General effectiveness of treatments. *Archives of General Psychiatry*, 46, 971–982.

Elkin, I, Gibbons, RD, Shea, MT, Sotsky, SM, Watkins, JT, Pilkonis, PA, & Hedeker, D (1995) Initial severity and differential treatment outcome in the National Institute of Mental Health Treatment of Depression Collaborative Research Program. *Journal of Consulting and Clinical Psychology*, 63, 841–847.

Elkins, RL (1980) Covert sensitization treatment of alcoholism: Contributions of successful conditioning to subsequent abstinence maintenance. *Addictive Behaviors*, 5, 67–89.

Elkins, RL, & Murdoch, RP (1977) The contribution of successful conditioning to abstinence maintenance following covert sensitization (verbal aversion) treatment of alcoholism. *IRCS Medical Science: Psychology and Psychiatry: Social and Occupational Medicine*, 5, 167.

Ellis, A (1987) Integrative developments in rational–emotive therapy (RET). *Journal of Integrative and Eclectic Therapy*, 6, 470–479.

Elvy, GA, Wells, JE, & Baird, KA (1988) Attempted referral as intervention for problem drinking in the general hospital. *British Journal of Addiction*, 83, 83–89.

Emmelkamp, PM, Mersch, PP, Vissia, E, & Van der Helm, M (1985) Social phobia: A comparative evaluation of cognitive and behavioural interventions. *Behaviour Research and Therapy*, 23, 365–369.

Emmelkamp, PMG (1982) *Phobic and obsessive compulsive disorders: Theory, research and practice.* New York: Plenum Press.

Emmelkamp, PMG (1994) Behavior therapy with adults. In AE Bergin & SL Garfield (Eds.), *Handbook of psychotherapy and behavior change* (4th ed.). New York: Wiley.

Emmelkamp, PMG, & Beens, H (1991) Cognitive therapy with obsessive–compulsive disorder: A comparative evaluation. *Behaviour Research and Therapy*, 29, 293–300.

Emmelkamp, PMG, & Giesselbach, P (1981) Treatment of obsessions: Relevant vs irrelevant exposure. *Behavioural Psychotherapy*, 9, 322–329.

Emmelkamp, PMG, & Kwee, K (1977) Obsessional ruminations: A comparison between thought-stopping and prolonged exposure in imagination. *Behaviour Research and Therapy*, 15, 441–444.

Emmelkamp, PMG, & van der Hayden, H (1980) Treatment of harming obsessions. *Behavior Analysis Modification*, 4, 28–35.

Emmelkamp, PMG, van der Helm, M, van Zanten, BL, & Plocgh, I (1980) Treatment of obsessive–compulsive patients: The contribution of self-instructional training to the effectiveness of exposure. *Behaviour Research and Therapy*, 18, 61–66.

Emmelkamp, PMG, Visser, S, & Hoekstra, RJ (1988) Cognitive therapy vs exposure in-vivo in the treatment of obsessive–compulsive disorder. *Cognitive Therapy and Research*, 12, 103–114.

Ends, EJ, & Page, CW (1957) Group therapy and concomitant psychological change. *Psychological Monographs*, 73 (serial number 480).

Enright, SJ (1991) Group treatment for obsessive–compulsive disorder: An evaluation. *Behavioral Psychotherapy*, 19, 183–192.

Epperson, DL (1981) Counsellor gender and early premature termination from counselling: A replication and extension. *Journal of Counselling Psychology, 28*, 349–356.

Esser, G, Schmidt, MI, & Woerner, W (1990) Epidemiology and course of psychiatric disorders in school-age children. *Journal of Child Psychology and Psychiatry, 31*, 243–263.

Evans, MD, Hollon, SD, DuRubeis, RJ, Piasecki, JM, Grove, WM, Garvey, MJ, & Tuason, VB (1992) Differential relapse following cognitive therapy and pharmacotherapy for depression. *Archives of General Psychiatry, 49*, 802–808.

Everaerd, W, & Dekker, J (1985) Treatment of male sexual dysfunction: Sex therapy compared with systematic desensitisation and rational emotive therapy. *Behaviour Research and Therapy, 23*, 13–25.

Everaerd, W, et al. (1982) Treatment of homosexual and heterosexual sexual dysfunction in male-only groups of mixed sexual orientation. *Archives of Sexual Behavior, 11*, 1–10.

Eysenck, HJ (1952) The effects of psychotherapy. *Journal of Consulting and Clinical Psychology, 16*, 319–324.

Eysenck, HJ (1978) An exercise in megasilliness. *American Psychologist, 35*, 517.

Fairburn, CG (1985) Cognitive-behavioral treatment for bulimia. In DM Garner & PE Garfinkel (Eds.), *Handbook of psychotherapy for anorexia and bulimia.* New York: Guilford Press.

Fairburn, CG, Kirk, J, O'Connor, M, & Cooper, PJ (1986) A comparison of two psychological treatments for bulimia nervosa. *Behaviour Research and Therapy, 24*, 629–643.

Fairburn, CG, & Beglin, SJ (1990) Studies of the epidemiology of bulimia nervosa. *American Journal of Psychiatry, 147*, 401–408.

Fairburn, CG, Jones, R, Peveler, R, & Carr, S, et al. (1991) Three psychological treatments for bulimia nervosa: A comparative trial. *Archives of General Psychiatry, 48*, 463–469.

Fairburn, CG, Agras, WS, & Wilson, GT (1992) The research on the treatment of bulimia nervosa: Practical and theoretical considerations. In GH Anderson & SH Kennedy (Eds.), *The biology of feast and famine: Relevance to eating disorders.* San Diego, CA: Academic Press.

Fairburn, CG, Jones, R, Peveler, R, Carr, S, Hope Ra, & O'Connor, M (1993) Psychotherapy and bulimia nervosa: Longer term effects of interpersonal psychotherapy, behavior therapy, and cognitive behavior therapy. *Archives of General Psychiatry, 50*, 41–428.

Fairburn, CG, Norman, PA, Welch, SL, O'Connor, ME, Doll, HA, & Peveler, RC (1995) A prospective study of outcome in bulimia nervosa and the long term effects of three psychological treatments. *Archives of General Psychiatry, 52*, 304–312.

Falloon, IRH, Boyd, JL, McGill, CW, Ranzini, J, Moss, HB, & Gilderman, AM (1982) Family management in the prevention of exacerbation in schizophrenia: A controlled study. *New England Journal of Medicine, 306*, 1437–1440.

Falloon, IRH, Boyd, J, & McGill, C (1984) *Family care of schizophrenia: A problem-solving approach to the treatment of mental illness.* New York: Guilford Press.

Falloon, IRH, Boyd, JL, McGill, CW, Williamson, M, Ranzini, J, Moss, HB, Gilderman, AM, & Simpson, GM (1985) Family management in the prevention of morbidity of schizophrenia: Clinical outcome of a two year longitudinal study. *Archives of General Psychiatry, 42,* 887–896.

Falloon, IRH, McGill, CW, Boyd, JL, & Pederson, J (1987) Family management in the prevention of morbidity of schizophrenia: Social outcome of a two year longitudinal study. *Psychological Medicine, 17,* 59–66.

Fauber, RL, & Long, N (1991) Children in context: The role of the family in child psychotherapy. *Journal of Consulting and Clinical Psychology, 59,* 813–820.

Fawcett, J, Zajecka, M, & Kravitz, M (1989) Fluoxetine vs amitryptiline in adult outpatients with major depression. *Current Therapy Research, 46,* 821–832.

Feighner, J, Robins, E, & Guze, S (1972) Diagnostic criteria for use in psychiatric research. *Archives of General Psychiatry, 26,* 57–63.

Feil, N (1993) *The validation breakthrough: Simple techniques for communicating with people with "Alzheimer's type dementia."* Baltimore: Health Professions Press.

Fennel, MJ, & Teasdale, JD (1982) Cognitive therapy with chronic drug refractory depressed outpatients: A note of caution. *Cognitive Therapy and Research, 6,* 455–460.

Ferrell, WL, & Galassi, JP (1981) Assertion training and human relations training in the treatment of chronic alcoholics. *International Journal of the Addictions, 16,* 959–968.

Fichten, CS, Libman, E, & Brender, W (1986) Measurement of therapy outcome and maintenance of gains in the behavioral treatment of secondary orgasmic dysfunction. *Journal of Sex and Marital Therapy, 12,* 22–34.

Fiester, A (1977) Clients' perceptions of therapists with high attrition rates. *Journal of Consulting and Clinical Psychology, 43,* 528–535.

Fine, S, Forth, A, Gilbert, M, & Haley, G (1991) Group therapy for adolescent depressive disorder: A comparison of social skills and therapeutic support. *Journal of the American Academy of Child and Adolescent Psychiatry, 30,* 79–85.

Fiorot, M, Boswell, P, & Murray, EJ (1990) Personality and response to psychotherapy in depressed women. *Behavior Health and Ageing, 1,* 51–63.

Fischer, M, Rolf, JE, Hasazi, JE, & Cummings, L (1984) Follow-up of a preschool epidemiological sample: Cross-age continuities and predictions of later adjustment with internalizing and externalizing dimensions of behavior. *Child Development, 55,* 137–150.

Fischer, M, Barkley, RA, Fletcher, KE, & Smallish, L (1993) The adolescent outcome of hyperactive children: Predictors of psychiatric, academic, social, and emotional adjustment. *Journal of the American Academy of Child and Adolescent Psychiatry, 32,* 324–331.

Fixsen, DL, Phillips, EL, Phillips, EA, & Wolf, MM (1976). The teaching-family model of group home treatment. In WE Craighead, AE Kazdin, & MJ Mahoney (Eds.), *Behavior modification: Principles, issues, and applications.* Boston: Houghton Mifflin.

Flakierska, N, Lindstrom, M, & Gillberg, C (1988). School refusal: A 15–20 year follow-up study of 35 Swedish urban children. *British Journal of Psychiatry, 152,* 834–837.

Flament, MF, & Vera, L (1990) Treatment of childhood obsessive–compulsive disorder. A review in the light of recent findings. In JG Simeon & HB Ferguson (Eds.), *Treatment strategies in child and adolescent psychiatry.* New York: Plenum Press.

Flament, M, Rapoport, JL, & Berg, CJ, et al. (1985) Clomipramine treatment of childhood obsessive compulsive disorder: A double-blind controlled study. *Archives of General Psychiatry, 42,* 977.

Flament, MF, Koby, E, Rapoport, JL, Berg, CJ, Zahn, T, Cox, C, Denckla, M, & Lenane, M (1990) Childhood compulsive disorder: A prospective follow-up study. *Journal of Child Psychology and Psychiatry, 31,* 363–380.

Flament, MF, Whitaker, A, & Rapoport, JL, et al. (1988) Obsessive–compulsive disorder in adolescence: An epidemiological study. *Journal of the American Academy of Child and Adolescent Psychiatry, 27,* 764–771.

Fleiger, DL, & Zingle, HW (1973) Covert sensitisation treatment with alcoholics. *Canadian Counsellor, 7,* 269–277.

Flick, SN (1988) Managing attrition in clinical research. *Clinical Psychology Review, 8,* 499–515.

Flint, AJ (1994) Epidemiology and comorbidity of anxiety disorders in the elderly. *American Journal of Psychiatry, 151,* 640–649.

Foa, EB (1979) Failure on treating obsessive–compulsives. *Behaviour Research and Therapy, 17,* 169–176.

Foa, EB, Steketee, G, & Milby, JB (1980) Differential effects of exposure and response prevention in obsessive–compulsive washers. *Journal of Consulting and Clinical Psychology, 48,* 71–79.

Foa, EB, Steketee, G, Grayson, JB, & Doppelt, HG (1983) Treatment of obsessive–compulsives: When do we fail? In EB Foa & PMG Emmelkamp (Eds.), *Failures in behavior therapy.* New York: Wiley.

Foa, EB, Steketee, G, Grayson, JB, & Latimer, PR (1984) Deliberate exposure and blocking of obsessive–compulsive rituals: Immediate and long-term effects. *Behavior Therapy, 15,* 450–472.

Foa, EB, Rothbaum, BO, Riggs, DS, & Murdoch, TB (1991) Treatment of PTSD in rape victims: A comparison between cognitive-behavioral procedures and counselling. *Journal of Consulting and Clinical Psychology, 59,* 715–723.

Foa, EB, Davidson, J, & Rothbaum, BO (1995) Treatment of post-traumatic stress disorder. In GO Gabbard (Ed.), *Treatment of psychiatric disorders: The DSM-IV edition.* Washington, DC: American Psychiatric Press.

Foa, EB, & Kozac, MJ (in press) Obsessive–compulsive disorder: Long-term outcome of psychological treatment. In Mavissaklian & Prien (Eds.), *Long-term treatments of anxiety disorders.* Washington, DC: American Psychiatric Press.

Foley, SH, O'Malley, S, Rounsaville, B, Prusoff, BA, & Weissman, MM (1987) The relationship of patient difficulty to therapist performance in interpersonal psychotherapy of depression. *Journal of Affective Disorders, 12,* 207–217.

Folger, R (1989) Significance tests and the duplicity of binary decision. *Psychological Bulletin, 106,* 155–160.

Fombonne, E (1994) Increased rates of depression: Update of epidemiological findings and analytical problems. *Acta Psychiatrica Scandinavica, 90,* 145–156.

Fonagy, P, & Higgitt, A (1989) Evaluating the performance of departments of psychotherapy. *Psychoanalysis and Psychotherapy, 4,* 121–153.

Fonagy, P, & Moran, GS (1990) Studies on the efficacy of child psychoanalysis. *Journal of Consulting and Clinical Psychology, 58*(6), 684–694.

Fonagy, P, & Moran, GS (1993) A psychoanalytical approach to the treatment of brittle diabetes in children and adolescents. In J Wardle & S Pearce (Eds.), *The practice of behavioral medicine.* Oxford: Oxford University Press.

Fonagy, P, Moran, GS, Edgcumbe, R, Kennedy, H, & Target, M (1993). The roles of mental representations and mental processes in therapeutic action. *Psychoanalytic Study of the Child, 48,* 9–48.

Fonagy, P, Moran, GS, & Higgitt, A (1989) Psychological factors in the self-management of insulin-dependent diabetes mellitus in children and adolescents. In J Wardle & S Pearce (Eds.), *The practice of behavioral medicine.* Oxford: Oxford University Press.

Fonagy, P, & Moran, G (1993) Selecting single case designs for clinicians. In NE Miller, L Luborsky, JP Barber, & JP Docherty (Eds.), *Psychodynamic treatment research: A handbook for clinical practice.* New York: Basic Books.

Fonagy, P, & Target, M (1994) The efficacy of psychoanalysis for children with disruptive disorders. *Journal of the American Academy of Child and Adolescent Psychiatry, 33,* 45–55.

Fonagy, P, & Target, M (1996) Predictors of outcome in child psychoanalysis: A retrospective study of 763 cases at the Anna Freud Centre. *Journal of the American Psychoanalytic Association, 44,* 27–77.

Forehand, R, & Long, N (1988). Outpatient treatment of the acting out child: Procedures, long-term follow-up data, and clinical problems. *Advances in Behavior Research and Therapy, 10,* 129–177.

Foreman, S, & Marmar, RC (1985) Therapist actions that address initially poor therapeutic alliance in psychotherapy. *American Journal of Psychiatry, 142,* 922–926.

Foulkes, SH (1975) *Group analytic psychotherapy.* London: Gordon and Breach.

Fournier, JP, Garfinkel, BD, Bond, A, Beauchesne, H, & Shapiro, SK (1987) Pharmacological and behavioral management of enuresis. *Journal of the American Academy of Child and Adolescent Psychiatry, 26,* 849–853.

Fowler, D, & Morley, S (1989) The cognitive-behavioral treatment of hallucinations and delusions: A preliminary study. *Behavioral Psychotherapy, 17,* 267–282.

Fowler, D, Garety, PA, & Kuipers, L (in preparation) *Cognitive behaviour therapy for people with psychosis: A clinical handbook.* Chichester: Wiley.

Foxman, B, Valdex, RB, & Brook, RH (1986) Childhood enuresis: Prudence, perceived impact and treatments. *Pediatrics, 77,* 482–487.

Frame, C, Matson, JL, Sonis, WA, Fialkov, MJ, & Kazdin, AE (1982) Behavioral treatment of depression in a prepubertal child. *Journal of Behavior Therapy and Experimental Psychiatry, 3,* 239–243.

Frances, A, Pincus, H, Widiger, T, Davis, W, & First, M (1990) DSM-IV: Work in progress. *American Journal of Psychiatry, 147,* 1439–1448.

Francis, G, & Ollendick, TH (1986) Anxiety disorders. In CL Frame & JL Matson (Eds.), *Handbook of assessment in child psychopathology: Applied issues in differential diagnosis and treatment evaluation*. New York: Plenum Press.

Frank, AF, & Gunderson, JG (1990) The role of the therapeutic alliance in the treatment of schizophrenia: Relationship to course and outcome. *Archives of General Psychiatry*, 47, 228–238.

Frank, E, & Kupfer, DJ (1976) In every marriage there are two marriages. *Journal of Sex and Marital Therapy*, 2, 137–143.

Frank, E, & Stewart, DB (1984) Depressive symptoms in rape victims. *Journal of Affective Disorders*, 1, 269–277.

Frank, E, Anderson, B, Stewart, BD, & Dancu, C, et al. (1988) Efficacy of behavior therapy and systematic desensitization in the treatment of rape trauma. *Behavior Therapy*, 19, 403–420.

Frank, E, Kupfer, DJ, & Perel, JM (1989) Early recurrence in unipolar depression. *Archives of General Psychiatry*, 46, 397–400.

Frank, E, Kupfer, DJ, Perel, JM, Jarrett, DB, Mallinger, AG, Thase, ME, McEachran, AB, & Grochocinski, CJ (1990) Three year outcomes for maintenance therapies in recurrent depression. *Archives of General Psychiatry*, 47, 1093–1099.

Frank, E, Kupfer, DJ, Wagner, EF, McEachrn, AB, & Cornes, C (1991) Efficacy of interpersonal therapy as a maintenance treatment of recurrent depression. *Archives of General Psychiatry*, 48, 1053–1059.

Frank, E, & Kupfer, DJ (1994) reply to GJ Barnes & Q Jones. Maintenance therapy in depression. *Archives of General Psychiatry*, 51, 504–505.

Frank, JD (1961) *Persuasion and healing*. Baltimore: Johns Hopkins University Press.

Freedberg, EJ, & Johnson, WE (1978) *The effects of assertion training within the context of a multi-modal alcoholism treatment programme for employed alcoholics* (substudy 998). Toronto, Ontario: Alcoholism and Drug Addiction Research Foundation.

Freeman, CPL, Barry, R, Dunkeld-Turnbull, J, & Henderson, A (1988) Controlled trial of psychotherapy for bulimia nervosa. *British Medical Journal*, 296, 521–525.

Freud, A (1965) *Normality and pathology in childhood*. Harmondsworth: Penguin Books.

Freud, S (1940) The technique of psychoanalysis. In J Strachey (Ed.), *Standard edition of the complete psychological works of Sigmund Freud*. London: Hogarth Press.

Freud, S, & Breuer, J (1895/1955) studies on hysteria. In J Strachey (Ed.), *The standard edition of the complete psychological works of Sigmund Freud*. London: Hogarth Press.

Friedman, AS (1975) Interaction of drug therapy with marital therapy in depressive patients. *Archives of General Psychiatry*, 32, 619–637.

Friedman, CJ, Shear, MK, & Frances, AJ (1987) DSM-III personality disorders in panic patients. *Journal of Personality Disorders*, 1, 132–135.

Friedmann, CTH, & Silvers, FM (1977) A multimodal approach to inpatient treatment of obsessive–compulsive disorder. *American Journal of Psychotherapy*, 31, 456–465.

Friedman, L, Bliwise, DL, Yesavage, JA, & Salom, SR (1991) A preliminary study comparing sleep restriction and relaxation treatments for insomnia in older adults. *Journal of Gerontology, 46,* 1–8.

Fuller, RK, & Roth, HP (1979) Disulfiram for the treatment of alcoholism: An evaluation in 128 men. *Annals of Internal Medicine, 90,* 901–904.

Fuller, RK, Branchey, L, Brightwell, DR, Derman, RM, Emrick, DC, Iber, FL, James, KE, Lacoursiere, RB, Lee, KK, Lowenstam, I, Maany, I, Neidershiser, D, Nocks, II, & Shaw, S (1986) Disulfiram treatment of alcoholism: A Veterans Administration cooperative study. *Journal of the American Medical Association, 256,* 1449–1455.

Gabbard, GO, Takahashi, T, Davidson, J, Bauman-Bork, M, & Ensroth, K (1991) A psychodynamic perspective on the clinical impact of insurance review. *American Journal of Psychiatry, 148,* 318–323.

Gaebler, HC, & Hemsley, DR (1991) The assessment and short-term manipulation of affect in the severely demented. *Behavioural Psychotherapy, 19,* 145–156.

Gallagher, DE, & Thompson, LW (1983) Effectiveness of psychotherapy for both endogenous and non-endogenous depression in older adult outpatients. *Journal of Gerontology, 38,* 707–712.

Gallagher-Thompson, D, Hanley-Peterson, P, & Thompson, L (1990) Maintenance of gains versus relapse following brief psychotherapy for depression. *Journal of Consulting and Clinical Psychology, 58,* 371–374.

Gallagher-Thompson, D, & Steffen, AM (1994) Comparative effects of cognitive-behavioral and brief psychodynamic psychotherapies for depressed family caregivers. *Journal of Consulting and Clinical Psychology, 62,* 543–549.

Gallant, DM, Bishop, MP, Camp, E, & Tisdale, C (1968) A six-month controlled evaluation of metronidazole (Flagyl) in chronic alcoholic patients. *Current Therapeutic Research, 10,* 82–87.

Garb, HN (1989) Clinical judgment, clinical training, and professional experience. *Psychological Bulletin, 105,* 387–396.

Garber, J, Kriss, MR, Koch, M, & Lindholm, L (1988) Recurrent depression in adolescents: A follow-up study. *Journal of the American Academy of Child and Adolscent Psychiatry, 27,* 49–54.

Gardener, DL, & Cowdrey, RW (1985) Alprazolam induced dyscontrol in borderline personality disorder. *American Journal of Psychiatry, 142,* 98–100.

Garety, PA, Kuipers, L, Fowler, D, Chamberlain, F, & Dunn, G (1994) Cognitive behavioral therapy for drug-resistant psychosis. *British Journal of Psychiatry, 67,* 259–271.

Garfield, SL (1994) Research on client variables in psychotherapy. In AE Bergin & SL Garfield (Eds.), *Handbook of psychotherapy and behavior change* (4th ed.). New York: Wiley.

Garner, DM, Rockert, W, Davis, R, & Garner, MD (1993) A comparison between CBT and supportive expressive therapy for bulimia nervosa. *American Journal of Psychiatry, 150,* 37–46.

Gaston, L (1990) The concept of the alliance and its role in psychotherapy: Theoretical and empirical considerations. *Psychotherapy, 27,* 143–153.

Gaston, L, Marmar, CR, Gallagher, D, & Thomson, LW (1991) Alliance prediction of outcome beyond in-treatment symptomatic change as psychotherapy progresses. *Psychotherapy Research, 1,* 104–112.

Gaston, L, & Ring, JM (1992) Preliminary results on the Inventory of Therapeutic Strategies. *Journal of Psychotherapy Research and Practice, 1,* 1–13.

Gazzaniga, MS (1992) *Nature's mind.* New York: Basic Books.

Gelenberg, AJ, & Hopkins, HS (1993) Report on efficacy of treatments for bipolar disorder. *Psychopharmacology Bulletin, 29,* 447–456.

Gelernter, CS, Uhde, TW, & Cimbolic, P (1991) Cognitive-behavioral and pharmacological treatments for social phobia: A controlled study. *Archives of General Psychiatry, 48,* 938–945.

Gendron, CE, Poitras, LR, & Engels, ML (1986) Skills training with supporters of the demented. *Journal of the American Geriatrics Society, 34,* 875–880.

Gerrein, JR, Rosenberg, CM, & Manohar, V (1973) Disulfiram maintenance in outpatient treatment of alcoholism. *Archives of General Psychiatry, 28,* 633–635.

Ghosh, A, Marks, IM, & Carr, AC (1988) Therapist contact and outcome of self-exposure treatment for phobias: A controlled study. *British Journal of Psychiatry, 152,* 234–238.

Gibson, F (1994) What can reminiscence contribute to people with dementia? In J Bornat (Ed.), *Reminiscence reviewed: Evaluations, achievements, perspectives.* Buckingham: Open University Press.

Gillberg, C (1991) Outcome in autism and autistic-like conditions. *Journal of the American Academy of Child and Adolescent Psychiatry, 30,* 375–381.

Gillberg, C, Hellgren, L, & Gillberg, C (1993) Psychotic disorders diagnosed in adolescence. Outcome at age 30 years. *Journal of Child Psychology and Psychiatry, 34,* 1173–1185.

Gittelman, R, & Klein, DF (1984) Relationship between separation anxiety and panic and agoraphobic disorders. *Psychopathology, 17* (Suppl.), 56–65.

Gittleson, M (1962) The curative functions in psychotherapy. *International Journal of Psychoanalysis, 43,* 194–205.

Glick, ID, Clarkin, JF, Haas, GL, & Spencer, JH (1993) Clinical significance of inpatient family intervention: Conclusions from a clinical trial. *Hospital and Community Psychiatry, 44,* 869–873.

Goldberg, D, & Huxley, P (1980) *Mental illness in the community: The pathway to psychiatric care.* London: Tavistock Publications.

Goldeberg, SC, Schulz, SC, Schulz, PM, Resnick, RJ, Hamer, RM, & Friedel, RO (1986) Borderline and schizotypal personality disorders treated with low dose thiothoxine versus placebo. *Archives of General Psychiatry, 43,* 680–686.

Goldfried, MR (1995) *From cognitive therapy to psychotherapy integration.* New York: Springer.

Goldstein, MJ (1991) Psychosocial (nonpharmacologic) treatments for schizophrenia. *Review of Psychiatry, 10,* 116–135.

Gomes-Schwartz, B (1979) The modification of schizophrenic behavior. *Behavior Modification, 3,* 439–468.

Gonzales, LR, Lewinsohn, PM, & Clarke, GN (1985) Longitudinal follow-up of unipolar depressives: An investigation of predictors of relapse. *Journal of Consulting and Clinical Psychology, 53,* 461–469.

Goodwin, FK, & Jamison, KR (1990) *Manic-depressive illness.* New York: Oxford University Press.

Gournay, K, & Brooking, J (1994) Community psychiatric nurses in primary health care. *British Journal of Psychiatry, 165,* 231–238.

Gowers, S, Norton, K, Halek, C, & Crisp, AH (1994) Outcome of outpatient psychotherapy in a random allocation treatment study of anorexia nervosa. *International Journal of Eating Disorders, 15,* 165–177.

Graham, PJ (1993) Treatment of child psychiatric disorders: Types and evidence for effectiveness. *International Journal of Mental Health, 22,* 67–82.

Grayson, JB, Foa, EB, & Skeketee, GS (1986) Exposure in-vivo of obsessive-compulsives under distraction and attention focussing conditions: Replication and extension. *Behaviour Research and Therapy, 24,* 475–479.

Graziano, AM, & Mooney, KC (1982) Behavioral treatment of 'night-fears' in children: Maintenance of improvement at 2– to 3–year follow-up. *Journal of Consulting and Clinical Psychology, 50,* 598–599.

Green, GR, Linsk, NL, & Pinkston, EM (1986) Modification of verbal behavior of the mentally impaired elderly by their spouses. *Journal of Applied Behavior Analysis, 19,* 329–336.

Greenberg, RP, Bornstein, RF, Greenberg, MD, & Fisher, S (1992) A meta-analysis of antidepressant outcome under "blinder" conditions. *Journal of Consulting and Clinical Psychology, 60,* 664–669.

Greenberg, RP, & Fisher, S (1989) Examining antidepressant effectiveness: findings, ambiguities and some vexing puzzles. In S Fisher & RP Greenberg (Eds.), *The limitations of biological treatments for psychological distress; comparisons with psychotherapy and placebo.* Hillsdale, NJ: Earlbaum.

Gregoire, A (1992) New treatments for erectile impotence. *British Journal of Psychiatry, 160,* 315–326.

Grenier, G, & Byers, ES (1995) Rapid ejaculation: A review of conceptual, etiological, and treatment issues. *Archives of Sexual Behavior, 24,* 447–472.

Grigsby, JP (1987) The use of imagery in the treatment of PTSD. *Journal of Nervous and Mental Disease, 175,* 55–59.

Grunhaus, L (1988) Clinical and psychobiological characteristics of simultaneous panic disorder and major depression. *American Journal of Psychiatry, 145,* 1214–1221.

Gunderson, JG, Frank, AF, & Katz, HM, et al. (1984) Effects of psychotherapy in schizophrenia: II. Comparative outcome of two forms of treatment. *Schizophrenia Bulletin, 10,* 564–598.

Gunderson, JG, Frank, AF, Ronningstam, EF, Wachter, S, Lynch, VJ, & Wolf, PJ (1989) Early discontinuance of borderline patients from psychotherapy. *Journal of Nervous and Mental Disease, 177,* 38–42.

Gurman, AS, Kniskern, DP, & Pinsof, WM (1986) Research on the process and outcome of marital and family therapy. In SL Garfield & AE Bergin (Eds.), *Handbook of psychotherapy and behavior change.* New York: Wiley.

Hacker-Hughes, JGH, & Thompson, J (1994) Post-traumatic stress disorder: An evaluation of behavioral and cognitive-behavioral interventions and treatments. *Clinical Psychology and Psychotherapy, 1,* 125–142.

Hackman, A, & McLean, C (1975) A comparison of flooding and thought stopping in the treatment of obsessional neurosis. *Behaviour Research and Therapy, 13,* 263–269.

Halford, WK, & Haynes, R (1991) Psychosocial rehabilitation of chronic schizophrenic patients: Recent findings on social skills training and family psychoeducation. *Clinical Psychology Review, 11,* 23–44.

Hall, A, & Crisp, AN (1987) Brief psychotherapy in the treatment of anorexia nervosa. *British Journal of Psychiatry, 151,* 185–191.

Hall, W, & Heather, N (1991) The issue of statistical power in comparison of minimal and intensive controlled drinking interventions. *Addictive Behaviors, 16,* 83–87.

Hampe, E, Noble, H, Miller, LC, & Barrett, CL (1973) Phobic children one and two years posttreatment. *Journal of Abnormal Psychology, 82,* 446–453.

Hanna, GL (1995) Demographic and clinical features of obsessive–compulsive disorder in children and adolescents. *Journal of the American Academy of Child and Adolescent Psychiatry, 34,* 19–27.

Harpin, RE, Liberman, RP, Marks, I, Stern, S, & Bohannon, WE (1982) Cognitive-behavior therapy for chronically depressed patients: A controlled pilot study. *Journal of Nervous and Mental Disease, 170,* 295–301.

Harrington, R (1993) *Depressive disorder in childhood and adolescence.* Chichester: Wiley.

Harrington, R, Fudge, H, Rutter, M, Pickles. A, & Hill, J (1990) Adult outcomes of childhood and adolescent depression. *Archives of General Psychiatry, 47,* 465–473.

Harrington, R, Fudge, H, Rutter, M, Pickles, A, & Hill, J (1991) Adult outcomes of childhood and adolescent depression: II. Links with antisocial disorders. *Journal of the American Academy of Child and Adolescent Psychiatry, 30,* 434–439.

Harrington, R, Bredenkamp, D, Groothues, C, Rutter, M, Fudge, H, & Pickles, A (1994) Adult outcomes of childhood and adolescent depression. III. Links with suicidal behaviors. *Journal of Child Psychology and Psychiatry, 35,* 1309–1319.

Harrow, M, & Silverstein, ML (1977) Psychotic symptoms in schizophrenia after the acute phase. *Schizophrenia Bulletin, 3,* 608–616.

Hartman, LM, & Daly, EM (1983) Relationship factors in the treatment of sexual dysfunction. *Behaviour Research and Therapy, 21,* 153–160.

Hartman, WE, & Fithian, MA (1972) *Treatment of sexual dysfunctions: A biopsychosocial approach.* Long Beach, CA: Center for Marital and Sexual Studies.

Hartmann, A, Herzog, T, & Drinkman, A (1992) Psychotherapy of bulimia nervosa: What is effective? A meta-analysis. *Journal of Psychosomatic Research, 36,* 159–167.

Hartmann, U, & Langer, D (1993) Combination of psychosexual therapy and intrapenile injections in the treatment of erectile dysfunctions: Rationale and predictors of outcome. *Journal of Sex Education and Therapy, 19,* 1–12.

Hattie, JA, Sharpley, CF, & Rogers, HJ (1984) Comparative effectiveness of professional and paraprofessional helpers. *Psychological Bulletin, 95,* 534–541.

Hatzenbuehler, LC, & Schroeder, HE (1978) Desensitization procedures in the treatment of childhood disorders. *Psychological Bulletin, 85,* 831–844.

Haughie, E, Milne, D, & Elliott, V (1992) An evaluation of companion dogs with elderly psychiatric patients. *Behavioural Psychotherapy, 20,* 367–372.

Hausman, C (1992) Dynamic psychotherapy with elderly demented patients. In G Jones & BML Miesen (Eds.), *Care-giving in dementia: Research and applications.* London: Routledge.

Hawton, K, Catalan, J, & Fagg, J (1992) Sex therapy for erectile dysfunction: Characteristics of couples, treatment outcome, and prognostic factors. *Archives of Sexual Behavior, 21,* 61–175.

Hawton, K, & Catalan, J (1990) Sex therapy for vaginismus: Characteristics of couples and treatment outcome. *Sexual and Marital Therapy, 5,* 39–48.

Hawton, K (1985) *Sex therapy: A practical guide.* Oxford: Oxford University Press.

Hawton, K, & Catalan, J (1986) Prognostic factors in sex therapy. *Behaviour Research and Therapy, 24,* 377–385.

Hawton, K (in press) Treatment of sexual dysfunctions by sex therapy and other approaches. *British Journal of Psychiatry.*

Hazelrigg, MD, Cooper, HM, & Borduin, CM (1987) Evaluating the effectiveness of family therapies: An integrative review and analysis. *Psychological Bulletin, 101,* 428–442.

Head, D, Portnoy, S, & Woods, RT (1990). The impact of reminiscence groups in two different settings. *International Journal of Geriatric Psychiatry, 5,* 295–302.

Healy, A, & Knapp, M (1994) *Economic evaluation and psychotherapy: A review for the Department of Health.*

Heather, N, Robertson, I, MacPherson, B, Allsop, S, & Fulton, A (1987) The effectiveness of a controlled drinking self-help manual: One year follow-up results. *British Journal of Clinical Psychology, 26,* 279–287.

Heather, N, Campion, PD, Neville, RG, & MacCabe, D (1987) Evaluation of a controlled drinking minimal intervention for problem drinkers in general practice (the DRAMS scheme). *Journal of the Royal College of General Practitioners, 37,* 358–363.

Hegel, MT, Ravaris, CL, & Ahles, TA (1994) Combined cognitive-behavioral and time-limited Alprazolam treatment of panic disorder. *Behavior Therapy, 25,* 183–195.

Heiman, JR, & LoPiccolo, J (1983) Clinical outcome of sex therapy: Effects of daily v weekly treatment. *Archives of General Psychiatry, 40,* 443–449.

Heimberg, RG (1989) Cognitive and behavioral treatments for social phobia: A critical analysis. *Clinical Psychology Review, 9,* 107–128.

Heimberg, RG, Dodge, CS, & Beccker, RE (1987) Social phobia. In L Mitchelson & LM Ascher (Eds.), *Anxiety and stress disorders: Cognitive-behavioral assessment and treatment.* New York: Guilford Press.

Heimberg, RG, Dodge, CS, & Hope, DA (1990) Cognitive behavioral treatment of social phobia: Comparison to a credible placebo control. *Cognitive Therapy and Research, 14,* 1–23.

Heimberg, RG, & Juster, HR (1994) Treatment of social phobia in cognitive-behavioral groups. *Journal of Clinical Psychiatry, 55* (Suppl.). 38–46.

Heinicke, CM, & Ramsey-Klee, DM (1986) Outcome of child psychotherapy as a function of frequency of sessions. *Journal of the American Academy of Child Psychiatry, 25,* 247–253.

Heinicke, CM (1965) Frequency of psychotherapeutic session as a factor affecting the child's developmental status. *Psychoanalytic Study of the Child, 20,* 42–98.

Heinicke, CM, & Strassman, LH (1975) Toward more effective research on child psychotherapy. *Journal of the American Academy of Child and Adolescent Psychiatry, 4,* 561–588.

Helzer, JE, Robins, LN, & McEvoy, L (1987) Post-traumatic stress disorder in the general population: Findings of the epidemiological catchment area survey. *New England Journal of Medicine, 317,* 1630–1634.

Henry, WP, Schacht, TE, & Strupp, HH (1986) Structural analysis of social behavior: Application to a study of interpersonal process of differential therapeutic outcome. *Journal of Consulting and Clinical Psychology, 54,* 27–31.

Henry, WP, Schacht, TE, & Strupp, H (1990) Patient and therapist introject, interpersonal process and differential outcome. *Journal of Consulting and Clinical Psychology, 58,* 768–774.

Henry, WP, Schacht, TE, Strupp, HH, Butler, SF, & Binder, JL (1993a) Effects of training in time-limited psychotherapy: Mediators of therapists responses to training. *Journal of Consulting and Clinical Psychology, 61,* 441–447.

Henry, WP, Strupp, HH, Butler, SF, Schacht, TE, & Binder, JL (1993b) The effects of training in time-limited psychotherapy: Changes in therapists behavior. *Journal of Consulting and Clinical Psychology, 61,* 434–440.

Hermesh, H, Shahar, A, & Munitz, H (1987) Obsessive–compulsive disorder and borderline personality disorder. *American Journal of Psychiatry, 144,* 120–121.

Hersen, M (1970) Behavior modification approach to a school phobia case. *Journal of Clinical Psychology, 26,* 128–132.

Hersen, M, Bellack, AS, Himmelhoch, JM, & Thase, ME (1984) Effects of social skills training, amitriptyline and psychotherapy in unipolar depressed women. *Behavior Therapy, 15,* 21–40.

Herzog, DB, Keller, MB, & Lavori, PW (1988) Outcome in anorexia nervosa and bulimia nervosa: A review of the literature. *Journal of Nervous and Mental Disease, 176,* 131–143.

Herzog, DB, Keller, MB, Lavori, PW, Sacks, NR (1991) The course and outcome of bulimia nervosa. *Journal of Clinical Psychiatry, 52 (10, suppl),* 4–8.

Higgitt, A (1992) Dependency on prescribed drugs. *Reviews in Clinical Gerontology, 2,* 151–155.

Higgitt, A, & Fonagy, P (1993) Psychotherapy in borderline and narcissistic personality disorder. In P Tyrer & G Stein (Eds.), *Personality disorder reviewed.* London: Gaskell.

Hill, J, Harrington, RC, Fudge, H, Rutter, M, & Pickles, A (1989) Adult Personality Functioning Assessment (APFA): An investigation based standardised interview. *British Journal of Psychiatry, 161,* 24–35.

Hiss, H, Foa, EB, & Kozac, MJ (1994) Relapse prevention program for treatment of obsessive–compulsive disorder. *Journal of Consulting and Clinical Psychology, 62*, 801–808.

Hoagwood, K, Hibbs, E, Brent, D, & Jensen, P (1995) Introduction to the Special Section: Efficacy and effectiveness in studies of child and adolescent psychotherapy. *Journal of Consulting and Clinical Psychology, 63*, 683–687.

Hodge, J (1984) Towards a behavioral analysis of dementia. In I Hanley & J Hodge (Eds.), *Psychological approaches to the care of the elderly*. London: Croom Helm.

Hodgson, RJ (1992) Alcohol dependence treatments: Research and policy connections. In *The quality assurance handbook II: On advising purchasers*. Leicester: British Psychological Society.

Hogarty, GE, Anderson, CM, Reiss, DJ, Kornblith, SJ, Greebwald, DP, Javana, CD, & Madsonia, MJ (1986) Family psychoeducation, social skills training and maintenance chemotherapy in the aftercare treatment of schizophrenia. *Archives of General Psychiatry, 43*, 633–642.

Hogarty, GE, Anderson, CM, & Reiss, DJ (1987) Family psychoeducation, social skills training and medication in schizophrenia; the long and short of it. *Psychopharmacology Bulletin, 23*, 12–13.

Holden, JM, Sagovsky, R, & Cox, JL (1989) Counselling in a general practice setting: Controlled study of health visitor intervention in treatment of postnatal depression. *British Medical Journal, 298*, 223–226.

Holden, NL (1990) Is anorexia nervosa an obsessive–compulsive disorder? *British Journal of Psychiatry, 157*, 1–5.

Holden, UP, & Woods, RT (1995) *Positive approaches to dementia care* (3rd ed.). Edinburgh: Churchill Livingstone.

Holder, H, Longabaugh, R, Miller, WR, & Rubois, AV (1991) The cost-effectiveness of treatment for alcoholism: A first approximation. *Journal of Studies on Alcohol, 52*, 517–520.

Holder, HD, & Blose, JO (1992) The reduction of health care costs associated with alcoholism treatment: A 14 year longitudinal study. *Journal of Studies on Alcohol, 53*, 293–302.

Holen, A. (1990) *A long term outcome study of survivors from a disaster: The Alexander L. Kielland disaster in perspective*. Monograph. University of Oslo.

Hollingsworth, CE, Tanguey, P, Grossman, L, & Pabst, P (1980) Long term outcome of obsessive–compulsive disorder in children. *Journal of the American Academy of Child and Adolescent Psychiatry, 19*, 134–144.

Hollon, SD, DuRubeis, RJ, Evans, MD, Weimer, MJ, Garvey, MJ, Grove, WM, & Tuason, VB (1992) Cognitive therapy and pharmacotherapy for depression: Singly or in combination. *Archives of General Psychiatry, 49*, 774–781.

Hollon, SD, & Beck, AT (1994) Cognitive and cognitive-behavioral therapies. In AE Bergin & SL Garfield (Eds.), *Handbook of psychotherapy and behavior change* (4th ed.). New York: Wiley.

Honig, A, Hofman, A, Hilwig, M, Noorthoorn, E, & Ponds, R (1995) Psychoeducation and expressed emotion in bipolar disorder: Preliminary findings. *Psychiatry Research, 56*, 299–301.

Hoogduin, CAL, & Duivenvoorden, HJ (1988) A decision model in the treatment of obsessive-compulsive neurosis. *British Journal of Psychiatry, 152,* 516–521.

Hoogduin, CAL, Duivenvoorden, H, Schaap, C, & de Haan, E (1989) On the outpatient treatment of obsessive–compulsives: Outcome, prediction of outcome and follow-up. In PMG Emmelkamp, WT Evaraerd, F Kraaimaaat, & M van Son (Eds.), *Fresh perspectives on anxiety disorders.* Amsterdam: Swets.

Hooley, JM, Orley, J, & Teasdale, J (1986) Levels of expressed emotion and relapse in depressed patients. *British Journal of Psychiatry, 148,* 642–647.

Hope, DA, Heimberg, RG, & Bruch, MA (1990, March) *The importance of cognitive interventions in the treatment of social phobia.* Paper presented at the annual meeting of the Phobia Society of America, Washington, DC.

Hope, DA, Heimberg, RG, & Bruch, MA (1995) Dismantling cognitive-behavioral group therapy for social phobia. *Behaviour Research and Therapy, 33,* 637–650.

Horowitz, LM, Rosenberg, SE, Baer, BA, Ureño, G, & Villaseñor, G (1988) Inventory of interpersonal problems: Psychometric properties and clinical applications. *Journal of Consulting and Clinical Psychology, 56,* 885–892.

Horowitz, LM, Rosenberg, S, Ureño, G, Kalehzan, B, & O'Halloran, P (1989) Psychodynamic formulation, consensual response method and interpersonal problems. *Journal of Consulting and Clinical Psychology, 57,* 599–606.

Horowitz, LM, Rosenberg, SE, & Bartholomew, K (1993) Interpersonal problems, attachment styles and outcome in brief dynamic therapy. *Journal of Consulting and Clinical Psychology, 61,* 549–560.

Horowitz, MJ (1989) Relationship schema formulation: Role relationship models and intrapsychic conflicts. *Psychiatry, 52,* 260–274.

Horowitz, MJ, Marmar, C, Weiss, DS, DeWitt, KN, & Rosenbaum, R (1984) Brief psychotherapy of bereavement reactions: The relationship of process to outcome. *Archives of General Psychiatry, 41,* 438–448.

Horvath, AO, & Greenberg, LS (1989) The development and validation of the working alliance inventory. *Journal of Consulting and Clinical Psychology, 36,* 223–233.

Horvath, AO, & Marx, RW (1991) The development and decay of the working alliance during time-limited counselling. *Canadian Journal of Counselling, 24,* 240–259.

Horvath, AO, & Symonds, BD (1991) Relation between working alliance and outcome in psychotherapy: A meta-analysis. *Journal of Consulting and Clinical Psychology, 38,* 139–149.

Horvath, AO, Gaston, L, & Luborksy, L. (1993) The therapeutic alliance and its measures. In NE Miller, L Luborsky, Barber JP, & Docherty JP (Eds.), *Psychodynamic treatment research: A handbook for clinical practice.* New York: Basic Books.

Hout, MA van den, Emmelkamp, PMJ, Kraaykamp, J, & Griez, E (1988) Behavioral treatment of obsessive–compulsives: In-patient vs out-patient. *Behaviour Research and Therapy, 26,* 331–332.

Houts, AC, Berman, JS, & Abramson, H (1994) Effectiveness of psychological and pharmacological treatments for nocturnal enuresis. *Journal of Consulting and Clinical Psychology, 62*, 737–745.

Howard, KI, Krause, MS, & Orlinsky, DE (1986) The dose-effect relationship in psychotherapy. *American Psychologist, 41*, 159–164.

Howard, KI, Lueger, RJ, Marling, MS, & Martinovich, Z (1993) A phase model of psychotherapy outcome: Causal mediation of change. *Journal of Consulting and Clinical Psychology, 61*, 678–685.

Howard, KI, Orlinsky, DE, & Lueger, RJ (1995) The design of clinically relevant outcome research: Some considerations and an example. In M Aveline & DA Shapiro (Eds.), *Research foundations for psychotherapy practice*. Chichester: John Wiley.

Howland, RH (1991) Pharmacotherapy of dysthymia: A review. *Journal of Clinical Psychopharmacology, 11*, 83–92.

Howlin, P, & Rutter, M (1987) *Treatment of autistic children*. New York: Wiley.

Hsu, LKG (1988) The outcome of anorexia nervosa: A re-appraisal. *Psychological Medicine, 18*, 807–812.

Hsu, LKG (1990) *Eating disorders*. New York: Guilford Press.

Hsu, LKG (1991) Outcome studies in patients with eating disorders. In SM Mirin, JT Gossett, & MC Grob (Eds.), *Psychiatric treatment: Advances in outcome research*. Washington, DC: American Psychiatric Press.

Hunt, GM, & Azrin, NH (1973) A community reinforcement approach to alcoholism. *Behaviour Research and Therapy, 11*, 91–104.

Husain, SA, & Kashani, JH (1992) *Anxiety disorders in children and adolescents*. Washington, DC: American Psychiatric Press.

Hussian, RA (1981) *Geriatric psychology: A behavioral perspective*. New York: Van Nostrand Reinhold.

Iliffe, S, Haines, A, Gallivan, S, Booroff, A, Goldenberg, E, & Morgan, P (1991) Assessment of elderly people in general practice. I. Social circumtances and mental state. *British Journal of General Practice, 41*, 9–12.

Inouye, DK (1983) Mental health care: Access, stigma and effectiveness. *American Psychologist, 38*, 912–917.

Jackson, P, & Oei, TPS (1978) Social skills training and cognitive restructuring with alcoholics. *Drug and alcohol dependence, 3*, 369–374.

Jacobsen, W, & Cooper, AM (1993) Psychodynamic diagnosis in the era of the current DSM's. In NE Miller, L Luborsky, JP Barber, & JP Docherty (Eds.), *Psychodynamic treatment research: A handbook for clinical practice*. New York: Basic Books.

Jacobson, NS, Follette, WC, & Revenstorf, D (1984) Psychotherapy outcome research: Methods for reporting variability and evaluating clinical significance. *Behavior Therapy, 15*, 336–352.

Jacobson, NS, & Revenstorf, D (1988) Statistics for assessing the clinical significance of psychotherapy techniques: Issues, problems and new developments. *Behavioral Assessment, 10*, 133–145.

Jacobson, NS, Wilson, L, & Tupper, C (1988) The clinical significance of treatment gains resulting from exposure-based interventions for agoraphobia: A re-analysis of outcome data. *Behavior Therapy, 19*, 539–554.

Jacobson, NS, & Truax, P (1991) Clinical significance: A statistical approach to defining meaningful clincal change in psychotherapy research. *Journal of Consulting and Clinical Psychology, 59*, 12–19.

James, I, & Blackburn, I (1995) Cognitive therapy with obsessive–compulsive disorder. *British Journal of Psychiatry, 166*, 444–450.

Jannoun, L, Oppenheimer, C, & Gelder, M (1982) A self-help treatment program for anxiety state patients. *Behavior Therapy, 13*, 103–111.

Jansen, A, Broekmate, J, & Heymans, M (1992) Cue exposure vs self-control in the treatment of binge eating: A pilot study. *Behaviour Research and Therapy, 30*, 235–241.

Jansen, A, van den Hout, MA, de Loof, C, Zandenbergen, J, & Griez, E (1989) A case of bulimia successfully treated by cue exposure. *Journal of Behavior Therapy and Experimental Psychiatry, 20*, 327–332.

Jansson, L, & Öst, LG (1982) Behavioral treatments for agoraphobia: An evaluative review. *Clinical Psychology Review, 2*, 311–336.

Jarrett, RB, & Down, M (in press) Psychotherapy for adults with major depressive disorder. In Depression Guideline Panel, *Depression in primary care: Detection, diagnosis and treatment. Guideline Report No. 5*. Rockville, MD: US Department of Health and Human Services, Public Health Service, Agency for Health Care Policy and Research.

Jenike, MA, Baer, L, Minichiello, WE, Schwartz, CE, & Carey, RJ (1986) Concomitant obsessive–compulsive disorder and schizotypal personality disorders. *American Journal of Psychiatry, 143*, 530–532.

Jenike, MA (1989) Obsessive–compulsive and related disorders: A hidden epidemic. *New England Journal of Medicine, 321*, 539–541.

Jenike, MA (1990) Predictors of treatment failure. In MA Jenike, L Baer, & WE Minichiello (Eds.), *Obsessive–compulsive disorders: Theory and management*. Chicago: Year Book Medical.

Johnson, CH, Gilmore, JD, & Shenoy, RZ (1982) Use of a feeding procedure in the treatment of a stress related anxiety disorder. *Journal of Behavior Therapy and Experimental Psychiatry, 13*, 235–237.

Johnson, JAW (1976) The duration of maintenance therapy in chronic schizophrenia. *Acta Psychiatrica Scandinavica, 53*, 298–301.

Johnson, SL, & Roberts, JE (1995) Life events and bipolar disorder: Implications from biological theories. *Journal of Consulting and Clinical Psychology, 117*, 434–449.

Jones, D (1990/1991) Weaning elderly patients off psychotropic drugs in general practice: A randomized controlled trial. *Health Trends, 22*, 164–166.

Jones, EE, Cumming, JD, & Horowitz, MJ (1988) Another look at the nonspecific hypothesis of therapeutic effectiveness. *Journal of Consulting and Clinical Psychology, 56*, 48–55.

Judd, FK, & Burrows, GD (1986) Panic and phobic disorders—Are psychological or pharmacological treatments effective? *Australian and New Zealand Journal of Psychiatry, 20*, 342–348.

Kahn, JS, Jenson, WR. & Kehle, TJ (1988, November) *Assessment and treatment of depression among early adolescents*. Paper presented at the meeting of the Association for Advancement of Behavior Therapy, New York.

Kandel, DB, & Davies, M (1986) Adult sequelae of adolescent depressive symptoms. *Archives of General Psychiatry, 43,* 255–262.

Kane, M, & Kendall, P (1989) Anxiety disorders in children: Evaluation of a cognitive-behavioral treatment. *Behavior Therapy, 20,* 499–508.

Kaplan, HS (1974) *The new sex therapy.* New York: Times Books.

Karno, M, Golding, JM, Sorenson, SB, & Burnham, MA (1988) The epidemiology of OCD in five US communities. *Archives of General Psychiatry, 45,* 1094–1099.

Karno, M, & Golding, JM (1991) Obsessive–compulsive disorder. In LN Robins & DA Reiger (Eds.), *Psychiatric disorders in America: The epidemiological catchment area study.* New York: Free Press.

Kashani, JH, & Orvaschel, H (1990) A community study of anxiety in children and adolescents. *American Journal of Psychiatry, 147,* 313–318.

Kasvikis, Y, & Marks, IM (1988) Clomipramine, self-exposure and therapist accompanied exposure in obsessive–compulsive ritualizers: Two year follow-up. *Journal of Anxiety Disorders, 2,* 291–298.

Katon, WJ (1991) Psychiatry and primary care. *General Hospital Psychiatry, 13,* 9.

Kavanagh, DJ (1990) Towards a cognitive-behavioral intervention for adult grief reactions. *British Journal of Psychiatry, 157,* 373–383.

Kazdin, AE (1985) *Treatment of antisocial behavior in children and adolescents.* Homewood, IL: Dorsey Press.

Kazdin, AE (1986) Comparative outcome studies of psychotherapy: Methodological issues and strategies. *Journal of Consulting and Clinical Psychology, 54,* 95–105.

Kazdin, AE (1987) Treatment of antisocial behavior in children: Current status and future directions. *Psychological Bulletin, 102,* 187–203.

Kazdin, AE (1988) *Child psychotherapy. Developing and identifying effective treatment.* New York: Pergamon Press.

Kazdin, AE (1994) Psychotherapy for children and adolescents. In AE Bergin & SL Garfield (Eds.), *Handbook of psychotherapy and behavior change* (4th ed.). New York: Wiley.

Kazdin, AE (1990a) Childhood depression. *Journal of Child Psychology and Psychiatry, 31,* 121–160.

Kazdin, AE (1990b) Premature termination from treatment among children referred for antisocial behavior. *Journal of Child Psychology and Psychiatry, 31,* 415–425.

Kazdin, AE (1990c) Psychotherapy for children and adolescents. *Annual Review of Psychology, 41,* 21–54.

Kazdin, AE (1991) Treatment research: The investigation and evaluation of psychotherapy. In M Hersen, AE Kazdin, & AS Bellack (Eds.), *The clinical psychology handbook* (2nd ed.). New York: Wiley.

Kazdin, AE (1993a) Psychotherapy for children and adolescents: Current progress and future research directions. *American Psychologist, 48,* 644–657.

Kazdin, AE (1993b) Adolescent mental health: Prevention and treatment programs. *American Psychologist, 48,* 127–141.

Kazdin, AE (1993c) Treatment of conduct disorder: Progress and directions in psychotherapy research. *Development and Psychopathology, 5,* 277–310.

Kazdin, AE, Bass, D, Siegel, TC, & Thomas, C (1989) Cognitive-behavioral therapy and relationship therapy in the treatment of children referred for antisocial behavior. *Journal of Consulting and Clinical Psychology, 57*, 522–535.

Kazdin, AE, Siegel, TC, & Bass, D (1990) Drawing on clinical practice to inform research on child and adolescent psychotherapy: Survey of practitioners. *Professional Psychology: Research and Practice, 21*, 189–198.

Kazdin, AE, Siegel, TC, & Bass, D (1992) Cognitive problem-solving skills training and parent management training in the treatment of antisocial behavior in children. *Journal of Consulting and Clinical Psychology, 60*, 733–747.

Kazdin, AE, Bass, D, Ayers, WA, & Rodgers, A (1990) Empirical and clinical focus of child and adolescent psychotherapy research. *Journal of Consulting and Clinical Psychology, 58*, 729–740.

Keane, TM, Fairbank, JA, Caddell, JM, & Zimering (1989) Implosive therapy reduces symptoms of PTSD in Vietnam combat veterans. *Behavior Therapy, 20*, 245–260.

Keane, TM, & Wolfe, J (1990) Comorbidity in post-traumatic stress disorder: An analysis of community and clinical studies. *Journal of Applied Social Psychology, 20*, 1776–1778.

Kearney, CA & Silverman, WK (1990) Treatment of an adolescent with obsessive–compulsive disorder by alternating response prevention and cognitive therapy: An empirical analysis. *Journal of Behavior Therapy and Experimental Psychiatry, 21*, 39–47.

Keisjers, GPJ, Hoogduin, CAL, & Schaap, CPD (1994) Predictors of treatment outcome in the behavioral treatment of obsessive–compulsive disorder. *British Journal of Psychiatry, 165*, 781–786.

Keller, MB, Shapiro, RW, Lavori, PW, & Wolfe, N (1982) Relapse in major depressive disorder. *Archives of General Psychiatry, 39*, 911–915.

Keller, MB, & Shapiro, RW (1982b) Double depression; superimposition of acute depressive episodes on chronic depressive disorders. *American Journal of Psychiatry, 139*, 438–442.

Keller, MB, Lavori, PW, Endicott, J, Coryell, W, & Klerman, GL (1983) Double depression: Two year follow-up. *American Journal of Psychiatry, 140*, 689–694.

Keller, MB, Lavori, PW, Friedman, BL, Nielson, E, McDonald-Scott, P, Andreason, NC, & Endicott, J (1987) The LIFE-II: A comprehensive method for assessing outcome in prospective longitudinal studies. *Archives of General Psychiatry, 44*, 540–549.

Kelly, T, Soloff, PH, Cornelius, J, George, A, Lis, JA, & Ulrich, R (1992) Can we study (treat) borderline patients? Attrition from research and open treatment. *Journal of Personality Disorders, 6*, 417–433.

Kendall, PC (1993) Cognitive-behavioral therapies with youth: Guiding theory, current status and emerging developments. *Journal of Consulting and Clinical Psychology, 61*, 235–247.

Kendall, PC (1994) Treating anxiety disorders in children: Results of a randomized clinical trial. *Journal of Consulting and Clinical Psychology, 62*, 100–110.

Kendall, PC, & Braswell, L (1985) *Cognitive-behavioral therapy for impulsive children.* New York: Guilford Press.

Kendall, PC, Howard, GL, & Epps, J (1988) The anxious child: Cognitive-behavioral treatment strategies. *Behavior Modification, 12,* 281–310.

Kendall, PC, Ronan, KR, & Epps, J (1991) Aggression in children/adolescents: Cognitive-behavioral treatment perspectives. In DJ Pepler & KH Rubin (Eds.), *The development and treatment of childhood aggression.* Hillsdale, NJ: Erlbaum.

Kendall, PC, Kortlander, E, Chansky, TE, & Brady, EU (1992) Comorbidity of anxiety and depression in youth: Treatment implications. *Journal of Consulting and Clinical Psychology, 60,* 869–880.

Kendall, PC, & Southam-Gerow, MA (1995) Issues in the transportability of treatment: The case of anxiety disorders in youths. *Journal of Consulting and Clinical Psychology, 63,* 702–708.

Kendall, RE (1993) Schizophrenia: Clinical features. In R Michels (Ed.), *Psychiatry.* Philadelphia: J.B. Lippincott.

Kennedy, H, & Moran, G (1991) Reflections on the aims of child psychoanalysis. *Psychoanalytic Study of the Child, 46,* 181–198.

Kernberg, O, Selzer, M, Koenigsberg, HW, Carr, A, & Appelbaum, A (1989) *Psychodynamic psychotherapy of borderline patients.* New York: Basic Books.

Kessler, RC, McGonagle, KA, Zhao, S, Nelson, CB, Hughes, M, Eshleman, S, Wittchen, H-U, & Kendler, KS (1994) Lifetime and 12-month prevalence of DSM-III-R psychiatric disorders in the United States. *Archives of General Psychiatry, 51,* 8–19.

Kilmann, PR, & Auerbach, R (1979) Treatments of premature ejaculation and psychogenic impotence: A critical review of the literature. *Archives of Sexual Behavior, 8,* 81–100.

Kilmann, PR, Mills, KH, Caid, C, Davidson, E, Bella, B, Milan, R, Drose, G, Boland, J, Follingstad, D, Montgomery, B, & Wanlass, R (1986) Treatment of secondary orgasmic dysfunction: An outcome study. *Archives of Sexual Behavior, 15,* 211–229.

Kilmann, PR, Milan, RJ, Boland, JP, Nankin, HR, Davidson, E, West, MO, Sabalis, RF, Caid, C, & Devine, JM (1987) Group treatment of secondary erectile dysfunction. *Journal of Sex and Marital Therapy, 13,* 168–182.

Kilpatrick, DG, & Resnick, HS (1993) PTSD associated with exposure to criminal victimization in clinical and community populations. In JRT Davidson & EB Foa (Eds.), *PTSD in review: DSMIV and beyond.* Washington, DC: American Psychiatric Press.

Kinder, BN, & Curtiss, G (1988) Specific components in the etiology, assessment and treatment of male sexual dysfunctions: Controlled outcome studies. *Journal of Sex and Marital Therapy, 14,* 40–48.

King, LJ, & Pittman, GD (1970) A six-year follow-up of 65 adolescent patients. *Archives of General Psychiatry, 22,* 230–236.

King, MB (1989) Eating disorders in a general practice population: Prevalence, characteristics, and follow-up at 12 to 18 months. *Psychological Medicine, 22,* 951–959.

King, MB (1991) The natural history of eating pathology in attenders to primary care. *International Journal of Eating Disorders, 10,* 379–387.

King, M, Broster, G, Lloyd, M, & Horder, J (1994) Controlled trials in the evaluation of counselling in general practice. *British Journal of General Practice, 44,* 229–232.

King, P, & Barrowclough, C (1991). A clinical pilot study of cognitive-behavioral therapy for anxiety disorders in the elderly. *Behavioural Psychotherapy, 19,* 337–345.

King, RA, & Noshpitz, JD (1991) *Pathways of growth.* Vol. 2. *Psychopathology.* New York: Wiley.

Kingdon, DG, & Turkington, D (1991) The use of CBT with a normalizing rationale in schizophrenia—preliminary report. *Journal of Nervous and Mental Disease, 179,* 207–211.

Kirk, JW (1983) Behavioral treatment of obsessive–compulsive patients in routine clinical practice. *Behaviour Research and Therapy, 21,* 57–62.

Kirley, BG, Schneider, JA, Agras, WS, & Bachman, JA (1985) Comparison of two group treatments for bulimia. *Journal of Consulting and Clinical Psychology, 53,* 43–48.

Kissel, S (1972) Systematic desensitization therapy with children: A case study and some suggested modifications. *Professional Psychology, 3,* 164–169.

Kissin, B, & Gross, MM (1968) Drug therapy in alcoholism. *American Journal of Psychiatry, 125,* 31–41.

Kissin, B, Platz, A, & Su, WH (1970) Social and psychological factors in the treatment of chronic alcoholism. *Journal of Psychiatric Research, 8,* 13–27.

Kitwood, T (1993) Towards a theory of dementia care: the interpersonal process. *Ageing and Society, 13,* 51–67.

Klein, DF (1968) Psychiatric diagnosis and a typology of clinical drug effects. *Psychopharmacology, 13,* 359–386.

Klein, NC, Alexander, JF, & Parsons, BV (1977) Impact of family systems intervention on recidivism and sibling delinquency: A model of primary prevention and program evaluation. *Journal of Consulting and Clinical Psychology, 45,* 469–474.

Klein, RG, & Last, CG (1989) *Anxiety disorders in children.* London: Sage Publications.

Klerman, GL (1983) The efficacy of psychotherapy as the basis for public policy. *American Psychologist, 38,* 929–934.

Klerman, GL, Weissman, MM, Rounsaville, BJ, & Chevron, ES (1984) *Interpersonal therapy of depression.* New York: Basic Books.

Klerman, GL, Budman, S, Berwick, D, Weisman, MM, Damico-White, J, Denby, A, & Feldstin, M (1987) Efficacy of a brief psychosocial intervention of symptoms of stress and distress among patients in primary care. *Medical Care, 25,* 1078–1088.

Klerman, GL, & Weissman, MM (1989) Increasing rates of depression. *Journal of the American Medical Association, 261,* 2229–2235.

Klerman, GL, Weissman, MM, Markowitz, J, Glick, I, Wilner, P, Mason, B, & Shear, MK (1994) Medication and psychotherapy. In AE Bergin & SL Garfield (Eds.), *Handbook of psychotherapy and behavior change* (4th ed.). New York: Wiley.

Klosko, JS, Barlow, DH, Tassinari, R, & Cerny, JA (1990) A comparison of alprazolam and behavior therapy in treatment of panic disorder. *Journal of Consulting and Clinical Psychology, 58,* 77–84.

Kluznik, JC, Speed, N, Van Valkenburg, C, & Magraw, R (1986) 40 year follow-up of United States prisoners of war. *American Journal of Psychiatry, 143,* 1443–1446.

Knight, BG (1988) Factors influencing therapist-rated change in older adults. *Journal of Gerontology, 43,* 111–112.

Knight, BG, Lutzky, SM, & Macofsky-Urban, F (1993) A meta-analytic review of interventions for caregiver distress: Recommendations for future research. *Gerontologist, 33,* 240–248.

Knitzer, J (1982) *Unclaimed children.* Washington, DC: Children's Defense Fund.

Kocsis, JH, Frances, AJ, Voss, C, & Mason, BJ (1988) Imipramine and social vocational adjustment in chronic depression. *American Journal of Psychiatry, 145,* 997–999.

Kohut, H (1977) *The restoration of the self.* New York: International Universities Press.

Kokotovic, AM, & Tracey TJ (1990) Working alliance in the early phase of counselling. *Journal of Counselling Psychology, 37,* 16–21.

Kolada, JL, Bland, RC, & Newman, SC (1994) Obsessive–compulsive disorder. (Suppl. 376), *Acta Pyschiatrica Scandinavica,* 24–35.

Kolko, DJ, & Kazdin, AE (1993) Emotional/behavioral problems in clinic and nonclinic children: Correspondence among child, parent and teacher reports. *Journal of Child Psychology and Psychiatry, 34,* 991–1006.

Kolvin, I, Garside, RF, Nicol, AR, MacMillan, A, Wolstenholme, F, & Leitch, IM (1981) *Help starts here: The maladjusted child in the ordinary school.* London: Tavistock.

Kolvin, I, Taunch, J. Currah, J, Garside, RF, Nolan, J, & Shaw, WB (1972) Enuresis: A descriptive analysis and a controlled trial. *Developmental Medicine and Child Neurology, 14,* 715–726.

Kolvin, I, MacMillan, A, & Wrate, RM (1988). Psychotherapy is effective. *Journal of the Royal Society of Medicine, 81,* 261–266.

Koocher, GP, & Pedulla, BM (1977) Current practices in child psychotherapy. *Professional Psychology, 8,* 275–287.

Koot, HM (1993) *Problem behavior in Dutch preschoolers.* Unpublished doctoral dissertation, Erasmus University, Rotterdam.

Kornblith, SJ, Rehm, LP, O'Hara, MW, & Lamparski, DM (1983) The contribution of self-reinforcement training and behavioral assignments to the efficacy of self-control therapy for depression. *Cognitive Therapy and Research, 7,* 499–528.

Kottgen, C, Sonnichsen, I, Mollenhauser, K, & Jurth, R (1984) Group therapy with families of schizophrenia patients: Results of the Hamburg Camberwell family interview study III. *International Journal of Family Psychiatry, 5,* 84–94.

Kovacs, M, Rush, AJ, Beck, AT, & Hollon, SD (1981) Depressed outpatients treated with cognitive therapy and pharmacotherapy: A one year follow-up. *Archives of General Psychiatry, 38,* 33–39.

Kovacs, M, Feinberg, TL, Crouse-Novak, MA, Paulauskas, SL, Pollock, M, & Finkelstein, R (1984) Depressive disorders in childhood. II: A longitudinal study of the risk for a subsequent major depression. *Archives of General Psychiatry, 41*, 643–649.

Kovacs, M (1986) A developmental perspective on methods and measures in the assessment of depressive disorders: A clinical interview. In M Rutter, C Izard, & P Read (Eds.), *Depression in young people: Developmental and clinical perspectives*. New York: Guilford Press.

Kovacs, M, & Gatsonis, C (1989) Stability and change in childhood-onset depressive disorders: longitudinal course as a diagnostic validator. In LN Robins & JE Barrett (Eds.), *The validity of psychiatric diagnosis*. New York: Raven Press.

Kovacs, M, Gatsonis, C, Paulauskas, S, & Richards, C (1989) Depressive disorders in childhood, IV: A longitudinal study of comorbidity with and risk for anxiety disorders. *Archives of General Psychiatry, 46*, 776–782.

Krauskopf, C, Baumgardner, A, & Mandraccia, S (1981) Return rate following intake revisited *Journal of Counselling Psychology, 28*, 519–521.

Kreipe, RE, Churchill, BH, & Strauss, J (1989) Long-term outlook in adolescents with anorexia nervosa. *American Journal of Diseases of Children, 143*, 1322–1327.

Kripke, D, & Robinson, D (1985) Ten years with a lithium group. *McLean Hospital Journal, 10*, 1–11.

Kristenson, H, Ohlin, H, Hulten-Nosslin, MB, Trell, E, & Hood, B (1983) Identification and intervention of heavy drinking in middle-aged men: Results and follow-up of 24–60 months of long-term study with randomized controls. *Alcoholism: Clinical and Experimental Research, 7*, 203–209.

Krupnick, JL, & Pincus, HA (1992) The cost-effectiveness of psychotherapy: A plan for research. *American Journal of Psychiatry, 149*, 1295–1305.

Kuhn, T (1970) *The structure of scientific revolutions*. Chicago: University of Chicago Press.

Kuipers, L, & Bebbington, P (1988) Expressed emotion research in schizophrenia: Theoretical and clinical implications. *Psychological Medicine, 18*, 893–909.

Kukla, A (1989) Nonempirical issues in psychology. *American Psychologist, 44*, 785–794.

Kupfer, DJ, & Frank, E (1987) Relapse in recurrent early depression. *American Journal of Psychiatry, 144*, 86–88.

Kupfer, DJ, Frank, E, Perel, JM, Cornes, Mallinger, AG, Thase, ME, McEachran, AB, & Grochocinski, CJ (1992) Five year outcome for maintenance therapies in recurrent depression. *Archives of General Psychiatry, 49*, 769–773.

Kuruvilla, K (1984) Treatment of single impotent males. *Indiana Journal of Psychology, 26*, 160–163.

Kutcher, SP (1990) *A controlled treatment study of adolescent major depression*. Child Depression Consortium Meeting, Pittsburgh, PA.

LaCrosse, MB (1980) Perceived counsellor social influence and counselling outcomes: Validity of the counsellor rating form. *Journal of Consulting and Clinical Psychology, 27*, 320–327.

Ladd, GW, & Mize, J (1983) A cognitive-social learning model of social skill training. *Psychological Review, 90,* 127–157.

Laessle, RG, Kittl, S, & Fichter, M (1987) Major affective disorders in anorexia nervosa and bulimia: A descriptive diagnostic study. *Psychiatry, 151,* 785–789.

Laessle, RG, Zoettl, C, & Pirke, K-M (1987) Meta-analysis of treatment studies for bulimia. *International Journal of Eating Disorders, 5,* 647–653.

Lam, DH (1991) Psychosocial family intervention in schizophrenia: A review of empirical studies. *Psychological Medicine, 21,* 423–441.

Lam, DH, & Woods, RT (1986) Ward orientation training in dementia: A single-case study. *International Journal of Geriatric Psychiatry, 1,* 145–147.

Lambert, MJ (1976) Spontaneous remission in adult neurotic disorders: A revision and a summary. *Psychological Bulletin, 83,* 107–119.

Lambert, MJ (1989) The individual therapists contribution to psychotherapy process and outcome. *Clinical Psychology Review, 9,* 469–485.

Lambert, MJ, Hatch, DR, Kingston, MD, & Edwards, BC (1986) Zung Beck and Hamilton rating scales as measures of treatment outcome: A meta-analytic comparison. *Journal of Consulting and Clinical Psychology, 54,* 54–59.

Lambert, MJ, & Bergin, AE (1994) The effectiveness of psychotherapy. In AE Bergin & SL Garfield (Eds.), *Handbook of psychotherapy and behavior change* (4th ed.). New York: Wiley.

Lask, B, & Matthew, D (1979) Childhood asthma. A controlled trial of family psychotherapy. *Archives of Disease in Childhood, 54,* 116–119.

Last, CG (1987) Developmental considerations. In CG Last & M Hersen (Eds.), *Issues in diagnostic research.* New York: Plenum Press.

Last, CG, Hersen, M, & Kazdin, AE, et al. (1987a) Comparison of DSM-III separation anxiety and overanxious disorders: Demographic characteristics and patterns of co-morbidity. *Journal of the American Academy of Child and Adolescent Psychiatry, 26(4),* 527–531.

Last, CG, Phillips, JE, & Statfeld, A (1987b) Childhood anxiety disorders in mothers and their children. *Child Psychiatry and Human Development, 18,* 103–117.

Laverty, SG (1966) Aversion therapies in the treatment of alcoholism. *Psychosomatic Medicine, 28,* 651–666.

Leahey, T (1980) The myth of operationalism. *Journal of Mind and Behavior, 1,* 127–143.

Leff, JP, & Wing, JK (1971) Trial of maintenance therapy in schizophrenia. *British Medical Journal, 3,* 599–604.

Leff, JP, Kuipers, L, Berkowitz, R, & Sturgeon, D (1982) A controlled trial of social intervention in schizophrenia families. *British Journal of Psychiatry, 141,* 121–134.

Leff, JP, & Vaughn, C (1985) *Expressed emotion in families.* New York: Guilford Press.

Leff, JP, Kuipers, L, Berkowitz, R, & Sturgeon, D (1985) A controlled trial of social intervention in the families of schizophrenia patients; two year follow-up. *British Journal of Psychiatry, 146,* 594–600.

Leff, JP, Berkowitz, R, Shavit, N, Strachan, A, Glass, I, & Vaughn, C (1988) A trial of family therapy vs a relatives group for schizophrenia. *British Journal of Psychiatry, 153,* 58–66.

Leff, JP, Berkowitz, R, Shavit, N, Strachan, A, Glass, I, & Vaughn, C (1990) A trial of family therapy vs a relatives group for schizophrenia; two year follow-up. *British Journal of Psychiatry, 157,* 571– 577.

Lefkowitz, MM, Eron, LD, Walder, LO, & Heussmann, LR (1977). *Growing up to be violent: A longitudinal study of aggression.* Oxford: Pergamon Press.

LeGrange, D, Eisler, I, Dare, C, & Russell, GF (1992) Evaluation of family treatments in adolescent anorexia nervosa: A pilot study. *International Journal of Eating Disorders, 12,* 347–357.

Lehrman, LJ, Sirluck, H, Black, BJ, & Glick, SJ (1949) *Success and failure of treatment of children in the child guidance clinics of the Jewish Board of Guardians, New York City.* New York: Jewish Board of Guardians.

Leiblum, SR, Rosen, RC, & Pierce, D (1976) Group treatment format: Mixed sexual dysfunction. *Archives of Sexual Behavior, 5,* 313–322.

Leigh, G, Osborne, AC, & Cleland, P (1984) Factors associated with patient drop-out from an out-patient alcoholism treatment service. *Journal of Studies on Alcohol, 45,* 359–362.

Leitenberg, H, Rosen, J, Gross, J, Nudelman, S, & Vara, LS (1988) Exposure plus response prevention treatment of bulimia nervosa. *Journal of Consulting and Clinical Psychology, 56,* 535–541.

Leitenberg, H, Rosen, JC, Wolf, J, Vara, LS, Detzer, MJ, & Srebnik, D (1994) Comparison of cognitive-behavior therapy and desipramine in the treatment of bulimia nervosa. *Behaviour Research and Therapy, 32,* 37–45.

Lelliot, PT, Marks, IM, Monteiro, WO, Tsakiris, F, & Noshirvani, H (1987) Agoraphobics 5 years after imipramine and exposure. *Journal of Nervous and Mental Disease, 175,* 599–605.

Lelliot, PT, Noshirvani, HF, Basoglu, M, Marks, IM, & Monteiro, WO (1988) Obsessive–compulsive beliefs and treatment outcome. *Psychological Medicine, 18,* 697–702.

Leonard, H, Swedo, S, Rapoport, JL, Koby, EV, Lenane, M, Cheslow, DL, & Hamburger, SD (1988) Treatment of obsessive–compulsive disorder with clomipramine and desmethylimipramine: A double-blind crossover comparison. *Psychopharmacology Bulletin, 24,* 93–95.

Leone, NF (1982) Response of borderline patents to loxapine and chlorpromazine. *Journal of Clinical Psychiatry, 43,* 148–150.

Lerner, JW (1989) Educational interventions in learning disabilities. *Journal of the American Academy of Child and Adolescent Psychiatry, 28,* 326–331.

Lesser, IM, Rubin, RT, & Pecknold, JC (1988) Secondary depression in panic disorder and agoraphobia. *Archives of General Psychiatry, 45,* 437.

Leung, SNM, & Orrell, MW (1993) A brief cognitive-behavioral therapy group for the elderly: Who benefits? *International Journal of Geriatric Psychiatry, 8,* 593–598.

Levin, E, Sinclair, I, & Gorbach, P (1989) *Families, services and confusion in old age.* Aldershot, UK: Gower Press.

Levine, MD, & Bakow, H (1976) Children with encopresis: A study of treatment outcome. *Pediatrics, 58,* 845–852.

Levine, MD (1982) Encopresis: Its potentiation, evaluation, and alleviation. *Pediatric Clinics of North America, 29,* 315–330.

Levinson, T, & Sereny, G (1969) An experimental evaluation of insight therapy for the chronic alcoholic. *Canadian Psychiatric Association Journal, 14,* 143–146.

Levitt, EE (1957) The results of psychotherapy with children: an evaluation. *Journal of Consulting Psychology, 21,* 186–189.

Levitt, EE (1963) Psychotherapy with children: A further evaluation. *Behaviour Research and Therapy, 60,* 326–329.

Levitt, EE (1971) Research on Psychotherapy with children. In AE Bergin & S Garfield (Eds.), *Handbook of psychotherapy and behavior change.* New York: Wiley.

Levitz, LS, & Stunkard, AJ (1974) A therapeutic coalition for obesity: Behavior modification and patient self-help. *American Journal of Psychiatry, 131,* 423–427.

Lewinsohn, PM, Clarke, GN, Hops, H, & Andrews, J (1990) Cognitive-behavioural treatment for depressed adolescents. *Behaviour Therapy, 21,* 385–401.

Lewinsohn, PM, Clarke, GN, Seeley, JR, & Rohde, P (1994) Major depression in community adolescents: Age of onset, episode duration, and time to recurrence. *Journal of the American Academy of Child and Adolescent Psychiatry, 33,* 809–818.

Liberman, RP (1994) Psychosocial treatments for schizophrenia. *Psychiatry, 57,* 104–114.

Liberman, RP, & Eckman, T (1981) Behavior therapy vs insight oriented therapy for repeated suicide attempters. *Archives of General Psychiatry, 38,* 1126–1130.

Libman, E, Fichten, CS, Brender, W, Burstein, R, Cohen, J, & Binik, YM (1984) A comparison of three therapeutic formats in the treatment of secondary orgasmic dysfunction. *Journal of Sex and Marital Therapy, 10,* 147–159.

Liddell, A, di Fazio, L, Blackwood, J, & Ackerman, C (1994) Long-term follow-up of treated dental phobics. *Behaviour Research and Therapy, 32,* 605–610.

Likierman, H, & Rachman, S (1982) Obsessions: An experimental investigation of thought stopping and habituation training. *Behavioral Psychotherapy, 10,* 324–338.

Lindesay, J, Briggs, K, & Murphy, E (1989) The Guys/Age Concern survey: Prevalence rates of cognitive impairment, depression and anxiety in an urban elderly community. *British Journal of Psychiatry, 155,* 317–329.

Lindsay, WR, Gamsu, CV, McLaughlin, E, Hood, EM, & Espie, CA (1987) A controlled trial of treatments for generalized anxiety. *British Journal of Clinical Psychology, 26,* 3–15.

Lindy, JD, Green, BL, Grace, M, & Tichener, J (1983) Survivors of the Beverly Hills supper-club fire. *American Journal of Psychotherapy, 4,* 593–610.

Linehan, MM (1993) *The skills training manual for treating borderline personality disorder.* New York: Guilford Press.

Linehan, MM, Armstrong, HE, Suarez, A, Allmon, D, & Heard, H (1991) Cognitive-behavioral treatment of chronically parasuicidal borderline patients. *Archives of General Psychiatry, 48,* 1060–1064.

Linehan, MM, Heard, H, & Armstrong, HE (1993) Naturalistic follow-up of a behavioral treatment for chronically parasuicidal borderline patients. *Archives of General Psychiatry, 50,* 971–974.

Links, PS, Steiner, M, Boigo, I, & Irwin, D (1990) Lithium therapy for borderline patients: Preliminary findings. *Journal of Personality Disorders, 4,* 173–181.

Lipman, RS, Covi, I, & Shapiro, AK (1979) The Hopkins symptom check list: Factors derived from the HSCL-90. *Journal of Affective Disorders, 1,* 9–24.

Little, RJA, & Rubin, DB (1987) *Statistical analysis with missing data.* New York: Wiley.

Livingston, G, & Hinchliffe, AC (1993) The epidemiology of psychiatric disorders in the elderly. *International Review of Psychiatry, 5,* 317–326.

Long, P, Forehand, R, Wierson, M, & Morgan, A (1994) Moving into adulthood: Does parent training with young noncompliant children have long-term effects? *Behaviour Research and Therapy, 32,* 101–107.

LoPiccolo, J (1985) Diagnosis and treatment of male sexual dysfunction. *Journal of Sex and Marital Therapy, 11,* 215–232.

LoPiccolo, J, Heiman, JR, Hogan, DR, & Roberts, CW (1985) Effectiveness of single therapists versus cotherapy teams in sex therapy. *Journal of Consulting and Clinical Psychology, 53,* 287–294.

LoPiccolo, J, & Stock, WE (1986) Treatment of sexual dysfunctions. *Journal of Consulting and Clinical Psychology, 54,* 158–167.

Lovaas, OI (1987) Behavioral treatment and normal educational/intellectual functioning in young autistic children. *Journal of Consulting and Clinical Psychology, 55,* 3–9.

Lovell, K, Marks, IM, Noshirvani, H, & O'Sullivan, G (1994) Should treatment distinguish anxiogenic from anxiolytic obsessive–compulsive ruminations? *Psychotherapy and Psychosomatics, 61,* 150–155.

Lovett, S, & Gallagher, D (1988) Psychoeducational interventions for family caregivers: Preliminary efficacy data. *Behavior Therapy, 19,* 321–330.

Luborsky, L (1984) *Principles of psychoanalytic psychotherapy: A manual for supportive–expressive treatment.* New York: Basic Books.

Luborsky, L (1992) *Can psychotherapy make you healthier?* Paper presented at the meeting of the American Psychological Association, Washington, DC.

Luborsky, L, McLellan, AT, Woody, GE, O'Brien, CP, & Auerbach, A (1985) Therapists success and its determinants. *Archives of General Psychiatry, 42,* 602–611.

Luborsky, L, Crits-Christoph, P, McLellan, T, Woody, G, Piper, W, Liberman, B, Imber, S, & Pilkonis, P (1986) Do therapists vary much in their success? Findings from four outcome studies. *American Journal of Orthopsychiatry, 51,* 501–512.

Luborsky, L, Crits-Christoph, P, Mintz, J, & Auerbach, A (1988) *Who will benefit from psychotherapy? Predicting therapeutic outcomes.* New York: Basic Books .

Luborsky, L, & Crits-Christoph, P (1990) *Understanding transference—The CCRT method (The Core Conflictual Relationship Theme).* New York: Basic Books.

Luborsky, L, Popp, C, & Barber, JP (1994) Common and special factors in different transference-related measures. *Psychotherapy Research, 4,* 277–286.

Lush, D, Boston, M, & Grainger, E (1991) Evaluation of psychoanalytic psychotherapy with children: Therapists' assessments and predictions. *Psychoanalytic Psychotherapy, 5,* 191–234.

Lyons, LC, & Woods, PJ (1991) The efficacy of rational–emotive therapy: A quantitative review of the outcome research. *Clinical Psychology Review, 11,* 357–369.

Macdonald, AJD (1986) Do general practitioners miss depression in elderly patients? *British Medical Journal, 292,* 1365–1367.

Mahrer, AR (1989) *The integration of psychotherapies.* New York: Human Sciences.

Malan, D (1976) *The frontiers of brief psychotherapy.* New York: Plenum Press.

Malan, D, & Osimo, F (1992) *Psychodynamics, training and outcome in brief psychotherapy.* London: Butterworth-Heinemann.

Mallinckrodt, B, & Nelson, ML (1991) Counsellor training level and the formulation of the therapeutic working alliance. *Journal of Consulting and Clinical Psychology, 38,* 14–19.

Mann, AH, Jenkins, R, & Belsey, E (1981) The twelve-month outcome of patients with neurotic illness in general practice. *Psychological Medicine, 11,* 535–550.

Manning, DW, Markowitz, JC, & Frances, AJ (1992) A review of combined psychotherapy and pharmacotherapy in the treatment of depression. *Journal of Psychotherapy Practice and Research, 1,* 103–116.

Mansdorf, IJ, & Lukens, E (1987) Cognitive-behavioral psychotherapy for separation anxious children exhibiting school phobia. *Journal of the American Academy of Child and Adolescent Psychiatry, 26,* 222–225.

March, JS (1995) Cognitive-behavioral psychotherapy for children and adolescents with OCD: A review and recommendations for treatment. *Journal of the American Academy of Child and Adolescent Psychiatry, 34,* 7–18.

March, JS, Mulle, K, & Herbel, B (1994) Behavioral psychotherapy for children and adolescents with obsessive–compulsive disorder: An open trial of a new protocol-driven treatment package. *Journal of the American Academy of Child and Adolescent Psychiatry, 33,* 333–341.

Margraf, J, Barlow, DH, Clark, DM, & Telch, MJ (1993) Psychological treatment of panic: Work in progress on outcome, active ingredients and follow-up. *Behaviour Research and Therapy, 31,* 1–8.

Mari de Jesus, J, & Streiner, DL (1994) An overview of family interventions and relapse on schizophrenia: Meta-analysis of research findings. *Psychological Medicine, 24,* 565–578.

Markovitz, PJ, Calabrese, JR, Schulz, SC, & Meltzer, HY (1990, May) *Fluoxetine in borderline and schizotypal personality disorder.* Paper presented at the Society of Biological Psychiatry 45th Annual Meeting, New York.

Markovitz, PJ, Calabrese, JR, Schulz, SC, & Meltzer, HY (1991) Fluoxetine treatment of borderline and schizotypal personality disorder. *American Journal of Psychiatry, 148,* 1064–1067.

Markowitz, JC (1994) Psychotherapy of dysthymia: Is it effective? *American Journal of Psychiatry, 151,* 1114–1121.

Markowitz, JC, Moran, ME, Kocsis, JH, & Frances, AJ (1992) Prevalence and co-morbidity of dysthymic disorder among psychiatric outpatients. *Journal of Affective Disorders, 24,* 63–71.

Marks, IM (1985) Controlled trial of psychiatric nurse therapists in primary care. *British Medical Journal, 290,* 1181–1184.

Marks, IM (1986) The epidemiology of anxiety. *Social Psychiatry*, *21*, 167–171.

Marks, IM (1987) *Fears, phobias and rituals.* Oxford: Oxford University Press.

Marks, IM (1989) Behavioral psychotherapy for generalized anxiety disorder. *International Review of Psychiatry*, *1*, 235–244.

Marks, IM, Hodgson, R, & Rachman, S (1975) Treatment of chronic obsessive–compulsive neurosis by in-vivo exposure. *British Journal of Psychiatry*, *127*, 349–364.

Marks, IM, & Mathews, AM (1979) Brief standard self-rating for phobic patients. *Behaviour Research and Therapy*, *17*, 263–267.

Marks, IM, Stern, RS, Mawson, D, Cobb, J, & McDonald, D (1980) Clomipramine and exposure for obsessive–compulsive rituals. *British Journal of Psychiatry*, *152*, 522–534.

Marks, IM, Gray, S, & Cohen, D (1983) Imipramine and brief therapist-aided exposure in agoraphobics having self-exposure homework. *Archives of General Psychiatry*, *40*, 153–162.

Marks, IM, & O'Sullivan, G (1988) Drugs and psychological treatments for agoraphobia/panic and obsessive–compulsive disorders: A review. *British Journal of Psychiatry*, *153*, 650–658.

Marks, IM, Swinson, RP, Basoglu, M, Kuch, K, Noshirvani, H, O'Sullivan, G, Lelliot, PT, Kirby, M, McNamee, G, Sengun, S, & Wickwire, K (1993a) Alprazolam and exposure alone and combined in panic disorder with agoraphobia. *Journal of Psychiatry*, *162*, 776–787.

Marks, IM, Swinson, RP, Basoglu, M, Kuch, K, Noshirvani, H, Kuch, K, O'Sullivan, G, & Lelliot, PT (1993b) Reply to comment on the London/Toronto study. *British Journal of Psychiatry*, *162*, 790–793.

Markus, E, Lange, A, & Pettigrew, TF (1990) Effectiveness of family therapy—a meta analysis. *Journal of Family Therapy*, *12*, 205–221.

Marmar, CR, Gaston, L, Gallagher, D, & Thompson, LW (1989) Alliance and outcome in late-life depression. *Journal of Nervous and Mental Disease*, *177*, 464–472.

Marshall, WL (1985) Variable exposure in flooding. *Behaviour Research and Therapy*, *23*, 117.

Marshall, WL (1988) Behavioural indices of habituation and sensitisation during exposure to phobic stimuli. *Behaviour Research and Therapy*, *26*, 67–77.

Martin, C, & Tarrier, N (1992) The importance of cultural factors in exposure to obsessive ruminations: A case example. *Behavior Psychotherapy*, *20*, 181–184.

Marzillier, JS, Lambert, C, & Kellett, J (1976) A controlled evaluation of systematic desensitization and social skills training for socially inadequate psychiatric patients. *Behaviour Research and Therapy*, *14*, 225–238.

Mason, BJ, Markowitz, JC, & Klerman, GL (1993) IPT for dysthymic disorder. In GL Klerman & MM Weissman (Eds.), *New applications of interpersonal therapy.* Washington, DC: American Psychiatric Press.

Masters, WH, & Johnson, VE (1966) *Human sexual response.* Boston: Little, Brown.

Masters, WH, & Johnson, VE (1970) *Human sexual inadequacy.* Boston: Little, Brown.

Mathews, A, Bancroft, J, Whitehead, A, Hackmann, A, Julier, D, Bancroft, J, Gath, D, & Shaw, P (1976) The behavioral treatment of sexual inadequacy: A comparative study. *Behaviour Research and Therapy, 14,* 427–436.

Matson, JL (1989) *Treating depression in children and adolescents.* New York: Pergamon Press.

Matsuura, M, Okubo, Y, Kojima, T, Takahashi, R, Wang, Y-F, Shen, Y-C, & Lee, CK (1993) A cross-national prevalence study of children with emotional and behavioral problems—a WHO collaborative study in the Western Pacific region. *Journal of Child Psychology and Psychiatry, 34,* 307–316.

Mattick, RP, & Peters, L (1988) Treatment of severe social phobia: Effects of guided exposure with and without cognitive restructuring. *Journal of Consulting and Clinical Psychology, 56,* 251–260.

Mattick, RP, Peters, L, & Clarke, JC (1989) Exposure and cognitive restructuring for social phobia: A controlled study. *Behavior Therapy, 20,* 3–23.

Mattick, RP, Andrews, G, Hadzi-Pavlovic, D, & Christensen, H (1990) Treatment of panic and agoraphobia: An integrative review. *Journal of Nervous and Mental Disease, 178,* 567–576.

Mattick, RP, & Newman, CR (1991) Social phobia and avoidant personality disorder. *International Journal of Psychiatry, 3,* 163–173.

Mattick, RP, & Jarvis, T (Eds.) (1993) *An outline for the management of alcohol problems: Quality assurance in the treatment of drug dependence project.* Monograph series No. 20. Canberra: Australian Government Publishing Service.

Mavissakalian, M (1993) Combined behavioral and pharmacological treatment of anxiety disorders. In JM Oldham et al. (Eds.), *Review of psychiatry.* Washington, DC: American Psychiatric Press.

Mavissakalian, M, & Michelson, L (1986) Two year follow-up of exposure and imipramine treatment of agoraphobia. *American Journal of Psychiatry, 143,* 1106–1112.

Mavissakalian, M, & Michelson, M (1986) Agoraphobia: Relative and combined effectiveness of therapist-assisted in-vivo exposure and imipramine. *Journal of Clinical Psychiatry, 47,* 117–122.

Mavissakalian, M, & Hamann, MS (1988) Correlates of DSM-III personality disorder in panic disorder and agoraphobia. *Comprehensive Psychiatry, 29,* 535–544.

Mawson, D, Marks, IM, & Ramm, L (1982) Clomipramine and exposure for chronic obsessive–compulsive rituals III: Two year follow-up and further findings. *British Journal of Psychiatry, 140,* 11–18.

Mayer, R, & Darby, S (1991) Does a mirror deter wandering in demented older people? *International Journal of Geriatric Psychiatry, 6,* 607–609.

Mayes, LC, & Spence, DP (1994) Understanding therapeutic actions. *Journal of the American Psychoanalytic Association, 42,* 789–818.

McAuley, R (1992) Counseling parents in child behavior therapy. *Archives of Disease in Childhood, 67,* 536–542.

McCrady, BS, Paolino, TJ, Longaborough, R, & Rossi, J (1979) Effects of joint hospital admission and couples treatment for hospitalized alcoholics: A pilot study. *Addictive Behaviors, 4,* 1244–1250.

McCullough, JP, Klein, DN, Shea, MT, & Miller, I (1992, September) *Review of DSM-IV mood disorder data in the field trials.* Paper presented at the 100th Meeting of the American Psychological Association, Washington, DC.

McCullough, JP (1991) Psychotherapy for dysthymia: A naturalistic study of ten patients. *Journal of Nervous and Mental Disease, 179,* 734–740.

McDermott, JF Jr, Werry, J, & Petti, T, et al. (1989). Anxiety disorders of childhood or adolescence. In *Treatments of psychiatric disorders: A task force report of the American Psychiatric Association* (Vol. I). Washington, DC: American Psychiatric Association.

McEachin, JJ, Smith, T, & Lovaas, OI (1993) Long-term outcome for children with autism who received early intensive behavioral treatment. *American Journal of Mental Retardation, 97,* 359–372.

McGee, R, Feehan, M, Williams, S, Partridge, F, Silva, PA, & Kelly, J (1990) DSM-III disorders in a large sample of adolescents. *Journal of the American Academy of Child and Adolescent Psychiatry, 29,* 611–619.

McGee, R, Partridge, F, Williams, S, & Silva, PA (1991) A twelve-year follow-up of preschool hyperactive children. *Journal of the American Academy of Child and Adolescent Psychiatry, 30,* 224–232.

McGill, CW, Falloon, IRH, Boyd, JL, & Wood-Siverio, C (1983) Family educational intervention in the treatment of schizophrenia. *Hospital and Community Psychiatry, 34,* 934–938.

McGlashan, T (1986) The Chestnut Lodge follow-up study III: Long-term outcome of borderline personalities. *Archives of General Psychiatry, 43,* 2–30.

McGrady, BS, Moreau, J, Paolino, TJ, & Longabaugh, R (1982) Joint hospitalization and couples therapy for alcoholism: A four year follow-up. *Journal of Studies on Alcohol, 43,* 1244–1250.

McGrady, BS, Longabaugh, R, Fink, E, & Stout, R (1986) Cost-effectiveness of alcoholism treatment in partial hospital versus in-patient settings after brief in-patient treatment: 12 month outcomes. *Journal of Consulting and Clinical Psychology, 54,* 708–713.

McLean, PD, & Hakstian, AR (1979) Clinical depression: Comparative efficacy of outpatient treatments. *Journal of Consulting and Clinical Psychology, 47,* 818–836.

McLean, PD, & Hakstian, AR (1990) Relative endurance of unipolar depression treatment effects: Longitudinal follow-up. *Journal of Consulting and Clinical Psychology, 58,* 482–488.

McLean, PD, & Taylor, S (1992) Severity of depression and choice of treatment. *Behaviour Research and Therapy, 30,* 443–451.

McMahon, RJ, & Wells, KC (1989) Conduct disorders. In EJ Mash & RA Barkley (Eds.), *Treatment of childhood disorders.* New York: Guilford Press.

McNamee, G, O'Sullivan, G, Lelliot, P, & Marks, IM (1989) Telephone-guided treatment for housebound agoraphobics with panic disorder: Exposure vs relaxation. *Behavior Therapy, 20,* 491–497.

McNeilly, CL, & Howard, KI (1991) The effects of psychotherapy: A re-evaluation based on dosage. *Psychotherapy Research, 1,* 74–78.

Meehl, PE (1978) Theoretical risks and tabular asterisks: Sir Karl, Sir Ronald and the slow progress of soft psychology. *Journal of Consulting and Clinical Psychology, 46,* 806–834.

Meichenbaum, D & Goodman, J (1971) Training impulsive children to talk to themselves: A means of developing self control. *Journal of Abnormal Psychology*, 77, 115–126.

Melman, A, Tiefler, L, & Pederson, R (1988) Evaluation of first 406 patients in urology department based center for male sexual dysfunction. *Urology*, 32, 6–10.

Mercier, MA, Stewart, JW, & Quitkin, FM (1992) A pilot sequential study of cognitive therapy and pharmacotherapy of atypical depression. *Journal of Clinical Psychiatry*, 53, 166–170.

Merckelbach, H, Hout, MA van den, Hoekstra, R, & van Oppen, P (1988) Are prepared fears less severe but more resistant to treatment? *Behaviour Research and Therapy*, 26, 527–530.

Merry, J, & Whitehead, A (1968) Metronidazole and alcoholism. *British Journal of Psychiatry*, 114, 859–861.

Mersch, PA (1995) The treatment of social phobia: The differential effectiveness of exposure in vivo and an integration of exposure in vivo, rational emotive therapy and social skills training. *Behaviour Research and Therapy*, 33, 259–269.

Meterissian, GB, & Bradwejn, J (1989) Comparative studies on the efficacy of psychotherapy, pharmacotherapy, and their combination in depression: Was adequate pharmacotherapy provided? *Journal of Clinical Psychopharmacology*, 9, 334–339.

Meyer, JK, Schmidt, CW, & Wise, TN (1983) *Clinical management of sexual disorders*. Baltimore: Williams and Wilkins.

Meyer, RE (1989) Prospects for a rational pharmacotherapy of alcoholism. *Journal of Clinical Psychiatry*, 50, 403–412.

Michelson, L, & Wood, R (1980) Behavioral assessment and training of children's social skills. In M Hersen, R Eisler, & PM Miller (Eds.), *Progress in behavior modification* (Vol. 9). New York: Academic Press.

Michelson, L, & Mavissakalian, M (1983) Temporal stability of self-report measures in agoraphobia research. *Behaviour Research and Therapy*, 21, 695–698.

Miklowitz, D, & Goldstein, M (1990) Behavioural family treatment for patients with bipolar affective disorder. *Behaviour Modification*, 14, 457–489.

Miklowitz, D, Goldstein, M, Nuechterlein, K, Snyder, K, & Mintz, J (1988) Family factors and the course of bipolar affective disorder. *Archives of General Psychiatry*, 45, 225–231.

Milan, RJ, Kilmann, PR, & Boland, JP (1988) Treatment outcome of secondary orgasmic dysfunction: A two to six year follow-up. *Archives of Sexual Behavior*, 17, 463–480.

Miller, E, & Morris, R (1993) *The psychology of dementia*. Chichester: Wiley.

Miller, GE, & Prinz, R J (1990) The enhancement of social learning family interventions for childhood conduct disorders. *Psychological Bulletin*, 108, 291–307.

Miller, IW, Bishop, SB, Norman, WH, & Keitner, GI (1985) Cognitive behavioral therapy and pharmacotherapy with chronic drug-refractory depressed in-patients: A note of optimism. *Behavioural Psychotherapy*, 13, 320–327.

Miller, IW, Norman, WH, Keitner, GI, Bishop, S, & Dow, MG (1989) Cognitive-behavioral treatment of depressed in-patients. *Behavior Therapy*, 20, 25–47.

Miller, LC, Barrett, CL, Hampe, E, & Noble, H (1972) Comparison of reciprocal inhibition psychotherapy and waiting list control of phobic children. *Journal of Abnormal Psychology, 79,* 269–279.

Miller, NE, & Magruder, KM (Eds.) (1996) *The cost-effectiveness of psycotherapy: A guide for practitioners, researchers, and policy-makers.* New York: Wiley.

Miller, WR (1983) Motivational interviewing with problem drinkers. *Behavioural Psychotherapy, 11,* 147–172.

Miller, WR, Taylor, CA, & West, JC (1980) Focused versus broad-spectrum behavior therapy for problem drinkers. *Journal of Consulting and Clinical Psychology, 48,* 590–601.

Miller, WR, & Hester, RK (1986) The effectiveness of alcoholism treatment: What research reveals. In WR Miller & N Heather (Eds.), *Treating addictive behaviors; the process of change.* New York: Plenum Press.

Miller, WR, & Sanchez, VC (1993) Motivating young adults for treatment and lifestyle change. In G Howard (Ed.), *Issues in alcohol use and abuse in young adults.* Notre Dame, IN: University of Notre Dame Press.

Millon, T (1981) The avoidant personality. In JR Lion (Ed.), *Personality disorders: Diagnosis and treatment, revised for DSM-III-R.* Baltimore: Williams and Wilkins.

Millon, T (1987) Concluding commentary. *Journal of Personality Disorders, 1,* 110–112.

Milne, D, & Souter, K (1988) A re-evaluation of the clinical psychologist in general practice. *Journal of the Royal College of General Practitioners, 38,* 457–460.

Minichiello, W, Baer, L, & Jenike, MA (1987) Schizotypal personality disorder: A poor prognostic indicator for behavior therapy in the treatment of obsessive–compulsive disorder. *Journal of Anxiety Disorders, 1,* 273–276.

Mintz, J (1981) Measuring outcome in psychodynamic psychotherapy. *Archives of General Psychiatry, 38,* 503–506.

Mitchell, JE (1991) A review of the controlled trials of psychotherapy for bulimia nervosa. *Journal of Psychosomatic Research, 35,* 23–31.

Mitchell, JE, Specker, SM, & de Zwaan, M (1991) Comorbidity and medical complications of bulimia nervosa. *Journal of Clinical Psychiatry, 52* (10, Suppl.), 13–20.

Mitchell, JE, Pyle, RL, Eckert, ED, & Hatsukami, D, et al. (1990) A comparison study of antidepressants and structured intensive group psychotherapy in the treatment of bulimia nervosa. *Archives of General Psychiatry, 47,* 149–157.

Mitchell, JT, & Everly, GS (1994) *Critical incident stress debriefing: CISD—an operations manual for the prevention of traumatic stress among emergency service and disaster workers.* Baltimore: Chevron Publishing Corporation.

Mittelman, MS, Ferris, SH, Steinberg, G, Shulman, E, Mackell, JA, Ambinder, A, & Cohen, J (1993) An intervention that delays institutionalization of Alzheimer's disease patients: Treatment of spouse-caregivers. *Gerontologist, 33,* 730–740.

Mohr, DC, & Beutler, LE (1990) Erectile dysfunction: A review of diagnostic and treatment procedures. *Clinical Psychology Review, 10,* 123–150.

Montgomery, RW, & Allyon, T (1994) Eye movement desensitization across subjects: Subjective and physiological measures of treatment efficacy. *Journal of Behavior Therapy and Experimental Psychiatry, 25,* 217–230.

Moore, KA, & Burrows, GD (1991) Hypnosis in the treatment of obsessive–compulsive disorder. *Australian Journal of Clinical and Experimental Hypnosis.*

Moran, GS, & Fonagy, P (1987) Psychoanalysis and diabetic control: A single-case study. *British Journal of Medical Psychology, 60,* 357–372.

Moran, GS, Fonagy, P, Kurtz, A, Bolton, A & Brook, C (1991) A controlled study of the psychoanalytic treatment of brittle diabetes. *Journal of the American Academy of Child and Adolescent Psychiatry, 30,* 926–935.

Moras, K, & Strupp, HH (1982) Pretherapy interpersonal relations, patient's alliance and the outcome in brief psychotherapy. *Archives of General Psychiatry, 39,* 397–402.

Moreau, D, Mufson, L, Weissman, MM, & Klerman, GL (1991) Interpersonal psychotherapy for adolescent depression: Description of modification and preliminary application. *Journal of the American Academy of Child and Adolescent Psychiatry, 30,* 642–651.

Moreno, JL (1953) *Who shall survive?* New York: Beacon House.

Morgan, K (1987) *Sleep and ageing.* London: Croom Helm.

Morgan, K (1992) Sleep, insomnia, and mental health. *Reviews in Clinical Gerontology, 2,* 246–253.

Morley, S (1987) Single case methodology in behavior therapy. In SJ Lindsay & GE Powell (Eds.), *A handbook of clinical adult psychology.* London: Gower Press.

Morley, S (1989) Single case research. In G Parry & FN Watts (Eds.), *Behavioral and mental health research: A handbook of skills and methods.* Hillsdale NJ: Erlbaum.

Morris, RG, Morris, LW, & Britton, PG (1988) Factors affecting the emotional well-being of the caregivers of dementia sufferers. *British Journal of Psychiatry, 153,* 147–156.

Morris, RJ, & Kratochwill, TR (1991) In TR Kratochwill & RJ Morris (Eds.), *The practice of child therapy* (2nd ed.). Elmsford, NY: Pergamon Press.

Morris, RG, Woods, RT, Davies, KS, Berry, J, & Morris, LW (1992) The use of a coping strategy focused support group for carers of dementia sufferers. *Counselling Psychology Quarterly, 5,* 337–348.

Morrow-Bradley, C, & Elliot, R (1986) Utilization of psychotherapy research by practicing psychotherapists. *American Psychologist, 41,* 188–197.

Morton, I, & Bleathman, C (1991) The effectiveness of validation therapy in dementia: A pilot study. *International Journal of Geriatric Psychiatry, 6,* 327–330.

Mueser, KT, & Berenbaum, H (1990) Psychodynamic treatment of schizophrenia: Is there a future? *Psychological Medicine, 20,* 253–62.

Mufson, L, Moreau, D, Weissman, MM, & Wickramaratne, P (1994) Modification of interpersonal psychotherapy with depressed adolescents. *Journal of the American Academy of Child and Adolescent Psychiatry, 33,* 695–705.

Müller-Oerlinghausen, B, Ahrens, B, Grof, E, Grof, P, Lenz, G, Schou, M, Simhandl, C, Thau, K, Volk, J, Wolf, R, & Wolf, T (1992) The effect of long-term lithium treatment on the mortality of patients with manic-depressive and schizoaffective illness. *Acta Psychiatrica Scandinavica, 86,* 218–222.

Mumford, E, Schlesinger, HJ, Glass, GV, Patrick, C, & Cuerdon, T (1984) A new look at evidence about reduced cost of medical utilization following mental health treatment. *American Journal of Psychiatry, 141,* 1145–1158.

Munjack, DJ, Schlaks, A, Sanchez, VC, Usigli, R, Zulueta, A, & Leonard, M (1984) Rational emotive therapy in the treatment of erectile dysfunction: An initial study. *Journal of Sex and Marital Therapy, 10,* 170–175.

Munoz, RF, Hollon, SD, McGrath, E, Rehm, L, & Vanden Bos, GR (1994) On the AHCPR depression in primary care guidelines. *American Psychologist, 49,* 42–61.

Murphy, GE, Simons, AD, Wetzel, RD, & Lustman, PJ (1984) Cognitive therapy and pharmacotherapy; singly and together in the treatment of depression. *Archives of General Psychiatry, 41,* 33–41.

Murray, JB (1993) Post-traumatic stress disorder: A review. *Genetic, Social, and General Psychology Monographs, 118,* 315–338.

Myers, JK, Weissman, MM, & Tischler, GL, et al. (1984) Six month prevalence of psychiatric disorders in three communities. *Archives of General Psychiatry, 41,* 959–967.

Nagy, LM, Krystal, JH, Woods, SW, & Charney, DS (1989) Clinical and medication outcome after short term alprazolam and behavioral group treatment in panic disorder. *Archives of General Psychiatry, 46,* 993–999.

Nash, EH, et al. (1965) Systematic preparation of patients for short-term psychotherapy II: Relation to characteristics of patient, therapist, and the psychotherapeutic process. *Journal of Nervous and Mental Disease, 140,* 374–383.

Neitzel, MT, Russell, RL, Hemmings, KA, & Gretter, ML (1987) Clinical significance of psychotherapy for unipolar depression: A meta-analytic approach to social comparison. *Journal of Consulting and Clinical Psychology, 55,* 156–161.

Nelson, H, Thrasher, S, & Barnes, TR (1991) Practical ways of alleviating auditory hallucinations. *British Medical Journal, 302,* 327.

Newman, C, & Beck, AT (1993) *Cognitive therapy of rapid cycling bipolar affective disorder—Treatment manual.* Philadelphia: Center for Cognitive Therapy, University of Pennsylvania.

Newman, FL, & Howard, KI (1986) Therapeutic effort, treatment outcome, and national health policy. *American Psychologist, 41,* 181–187.

Newton, NA, & Lazarus, LW (1992) Behavioral and psychotherapeutic interventions. In JE Birren, RB Sloane, & GD Cohen (Eds.), *Handbook of mental health and ageing* (2nd ed.). San Diego, CA: Academic Press.

Nezirogulu, F (1979) A combined behavioural pharmacotherapy approach to obsessive compulsive disorders. In J Oriols, C Ballus, M Gonzales, & J Prijol (Eds.), *Biological psychiatry today.* Amsterdam: Elsevier, North Holland.

NIMH (1994) NIMH workshop report on the treatment of bipolar disorder, April 6–7, Bethesda, MD.

Nofzinger, EA, Thase, ME, Reynolds, CF, Frank, E, Jennings, JR, Garamoni, GL, Fasicka, A, & Kupfer, DA (1993) Sexual functioning in depressed men: Assessment using self-report, behavioral and nocturnal penile tumescence measures before and after treatment with cognitive behavioral therapy. *Archives of General Psychiatry, 50,* 24–30.

Norberg, A, Melin, E, & Asplund, K (1986) Reactions to music, touch, and object presentation in the final stage of dementia: An exploratory study. *International Journal of Nursing Studies, 23,* 315–323.

Norden, MJ (1989) Fluoxetine in borderline personality disorder. *Progress in Neuropsychopharmacology and Biological Psychiatry, 13,* 885–893.

Norris, A (1986) *Reminiscence.* London: Winslow Press.

Nurnberg, HG, Raskin, M, Levine, PE, Pollack, S, Prince, R, & Siegal, O (1989) Borderline personality disorder as a negative prognostic factor in anxiety disorders. *Journal of Personality Disorders, 3,* 205– 216.

Oakley-Brown, M (1991) The epidemiology of anxiety disorders. *International Journal of Psychiatry, 3,* 243–252.

O'Connor, DW, Pollitt, PA, Hyde, JB, Brook, CPB, Reiss, BB, & Roth, M (1988) Do general practitioners miss dementia in elderly patients? *British Medical Journal, 297,* 1107–1110.

Oei, TPS, & Jackson, PR (1980) Long-term effects of group and individual social skills training with alcoholics. *Addictive Behaviors, 5,* 129–136.

Oei, TPS, & Jackson, PR (1982) Social skills and cognitive behavioral approaches to the treatment of problem drinking. *Journal of Studies on Alcohol, 43,* 532–547.

O'Farrell, TJ, & Cutter, HS (1982) Evaluating behavioral therapy for alcoholics: Procedures and preliminary results. In LA Hamerlynck (Ed.), *Essentials of behavior treatments for families.* New York: Brunner/Mazel.

O'Farrell, TJ, Cutter, HS, & Floyd, FJ (1984) Evaluating behavioral marital therapy for male alcoholics: Effects on marital adjustment and communication before and after treatment. *Behavior Therapy, 15.*

Office of Technology Assessment (1980) *The efficacy and cost effectiveness of psychotherapy.* Washington, DC: US Government Printing Office.

Offord, DR, Boyle, MH, & Racine, Y (1989) Ontario Child Health Study: Correlates of disorder. *Journal of the American Academy of Child and Adolescent Psychiatry, 28,* 856–860.

Offord, DR, & Bennett, KJ (1994) Conduct disorder: Long-term outcomes and intervention effectiveness. *Journal of the American Academy of Child and Adolescent Psychiatry, 33,* 1069–1078.

Ogles, BM, Lambert, MJ, & Sawyer, JD (1995) Clinical significance of the National Institute of Mental Health Treatment of Depression Collaborative Research Program data. *Journal of Consulting and Clinical Psychology, 63,* 321–326.

Ollendick, TH (1986) Child and adolescent and behavior therapy. In SL Garfield & AE Bergin (Eds.), *Handbook of psychotherapy and behavior change* (3rd ed.). New York: Wiley.

Ollendick, TH, & King, NJ (1991) Fears and phobias of childhood. In M Herbert (Ed.), *Clinical child psychology.* Chichester: Wiley.

Ollendick, TH, & King, NJ (1994) Diagnosis, assessment, and treatment of internalizing problems in children: The role of longitudinal data. *Journal of Consulting and Clinical Psychology, 62,* 918–927.

O'Malley, SS, Foley, SH, Rounsaville, BJ, Watkins, JT, Imber, SD, Sotsky, SM, & Elkin, I (1988) Therapist competence and patient outcome in interpersonal psychotherapy of depression. *Journal of Consulting and Clinical Psychology, 56,* 496–501.

O'Malley, SS, Jaffe, AJ, Chang, G, Schottenfeld, RS, Meyer, R, & Rounsaville, B (1992) Naltrexone and coping skills therapy for alcohol dependence. *Archives of General Psychiatry, 49,* 881–887.

Ong, Y, Martineau, F, Lloyd, C, & Robbins, I (1987) A support group for the depressed elderly. *International Journal of Geriatric Psychiatry, 2,* 119–123.

Orford, J, & Edwards, G (1977) Alcoholism: A comparison of treatment and advice. *Maudsley Monograph No. 26* London: Oxford University Press.

Orlinsky, DE, & Howard, KI (1986) Process and outcome in psychotherapy. In AE Bergin & SL Garfield (Eds.), *Handbook of psychotherapy and behavior change* (3rd ed.). New York: Wiley.

Orlinsky, DE, Grawe, K, & Parks, BK (1994) Process and outcome in psychotherapy. In AE Bergin & SL Garfield (Eds.), *Handbook of psychotherapy and behavior change* (4th ed.). New York: Wiley.

Osborn, M, Hawton, K, & Gath, D (1988) Sexual dysfunction among middle aged women in the community. *British Medical Journal, 296,* 959–962.

Öst, LG (1987) Applied relaxation: Description of a coping technique and a review of controlled studies. *Behaviour Research and Therapy, 25,* 397–409.

Öst, LG (1988) Applied relaxation vs progressive relaxation in the treatment of panic disorder. *Behaviour Research and Therapy, 26,* 13–22.

Öst, LG (1989) One session treatment for specific phobias. *Behaviour Research and Therapy, 27,* 1–7.

Öst, LG (1989) A maintenance programme for behavioural treatment of anxiety disorders. *Behaviour Research and Therapy, 27,* 123–130.

Öst, LG, Jerramalm, A, & Johansson, J (1981) Individual response patterns and the effects of different behavioral methods in the treatment of social phobia. *Behaviour Research and Therapy, 19,* 1–16.

Öst, LG, Lindahl, IL, Sterner, U, & Jerremalm, A (1984) Exposure in-vivo vs applied relaxation in the treatment of blood phobia. *Behaviour Research and Therapy, 22,* 205.

Öst, LG, Sterner, U, & Fellenius, J (1989) Applied tension, applied relaxation in the treatment of blood phobia. *Behaviour Research and Therapy, 27,* 109.

Öst, LG, Salkovskis, P, & Hellstrom, K (1991) One session therapist directed exposure vs self-exposure in the treatment of spider phobia. *Behavior Therapy, 22,* 407–422.

Öst, LG, & Westling, BE (1995) Applied relaxation vs cognitive behavior therapy in the treatment of panic disorder. *Behaviour Research and Therapy, 33,* 145–158.

O'Sullivan, G, & Marks, IM (1990) Long-term outcome of phobic and obsessive–compulsive disorders after treatment. In R Noyes, M Roth, & GD Burrows (Eds.), *Handbook of anxiety:* Vol. 4. *The treatment of anxiety.* Amsterdam: Elsevier Science Publishers.

Ownby, R (1983) A cognitive behavioral intervention for compulsive hand-washing in a 13 year old boy. *Psychology in the Schools, 20,* 219–222.

Pagel, MD, Becker, J, & Coppel, DB (1985) Loss of control, self-blame, and depression: An investigation of spouse caregivers of Alzheimer's disease patients. *Journal of Abnormal Psychology, 94,* 169–182.

Palmer, AG, Williams, H, & Adams, M (1995) CBT in a group format for bipolar affective disorder. *Behavioral and Cognitive Psychotherapy, 23,* 153–168.

Paris, J, Brown, R, & Nowlis, D (1987) Long term follow-up of borderline patients in a general hospital. *Comprehensive Psychiatry, 28*, 530–535.

Parkes, CM (1992) Bereavement and mental health in the elderly. *Reviews in Clinical Gerontology, 2*, 45–51.

Parmelee, PA, & Lawton, MP (1990) The design of special environments for the aged. In JE Birren & KW Schaie (Eds.), *Handbook of the psychology of ageing* (3rd ed.). San Diego, CA: Academic Press.

Parry, G (1986) The case of the anxious executive: A study from the research clinic. *British Journal of Medical Psychology, 59*, 221–233.

Parry, G (1992) Improving psychotherapy services: Applications of research, audit and evaluation. *British Journal of Clinical Psychology, 31*, 3–19.

Parry, G (1996) Psychotherapy services in the English National Health Service. In NE Miller & KM Magruder (Eds.), *The cost-effectiveness of psychotherapy: A guide for practitioners, researchers and policy-makers*. New York: Wiley.

Parsons, B, Quitkin, FM, McGrath, PJ, Stewart, JW, Tricarno, E, Ocepek-Welikson, K, Harrison, W, Rabkin, J, Wagner, SG, & Nuries, E (1989) Phenelzine, imipramine and placebo in borderline patients meeting criteria for atypical depression. *Psychopharmacology Bulletin, 25*, 524–534.

Patience, DA, McGuire, RJ, Scott, AIF, & Freeman, CPL (1995) The Edinburgh primary care depression study: Personality disorders and outcome. *British Journal of Psychiatry, 167*, 324–330.

Patmore, C, & Weaver, T (1991) *Community mental health teams: Lessons for planners and managers*. London: Good Practices in Mental Health.

Pato, MT, Zoka-Kadouch, R, Zohar, J, & Murphy, DL (1988) Return of symptoms after desensitization of clomipramine in patients with obsessive–compulsive disorder. *American Journal of Psychiatry, 145*, 1521–1525.

Patterson, GR (1982) *Coercive family processes*. Aegean, OR: Castilia Publishing.

Pattison, EM, Brissenden, A, & Wohl, T (1967) Assessing specific aspects of in-patient group psychotherapy. *International Journal of Group Psychotherapy, 17*, 283–297.

Paykel, ES (1989) Treatment of depression: The relevance of research for clinical practice. *British Journal of Psychiatry, 155*, 754–763.

Paykel, ES, & Tanner, J (1976) Life events, depressive relapse and maintenance treatment. *Psychological Medicine, 6*, 481–485.

Paykel, ES, Brayne, C, Huppert, FA, Gill, C, Barkley, C, Gehlbaar, E, Beardsall, L, Girling, DM, Pollitt, P, & O'Connor, D (1994) Incidence of dementia in a population older than 75 years in the United Kingdom. *Archives of General Psychiatry, 51*, 325–332.

Peachey, JE, Annis, HM, Bornstein, ER, Sykora, K, Maglana, SM, & Shamai, S (1989) Calcium carbimide in alcoholism treatment. Part 1: A placebo controlled double-blind clinical trial of short-term efficacy. *British Journal of Addiction, 84*, 877–887.

Pelham, WE, Carlson, CL, Sams, SE, & Vallano, G (1993) Separate and combined effects of methylphenidate and behaviour modification on boys with hyperactivity disorder in the classroom. *Journal of Consulting and Clinical Psychology, 61*, 506–515.

Peniston, EG (1986) EMG biofeedback assisted desensitization treatment for Vietnam combat veterans PTSD. *Clinical Biofeedback and Health, 9*, 35–41.

Pennebaker, JW (1990) *Opening-up: The healing power of confiding in others.* New York: William Morrow.

Pepler, DJ, & Rubin, KH (Eds.) (1991) *The development and treatment of childhood aggression.* Hillsdale, NJ: Erlbaum.

Perl, M, Westlin, AB, & Peterson, LG (1985) The female rape survivor: Time limited therapy with female/male co-therapists. *Journal of Psychosomatic Obstetrics and Gynaecology, 4,* 197–205.

Perris, C, & Skagerlind, L (1994) Cognitive therapy with schizophrenic patients. *Acta Psychiatrica Scandinavica, 89(suppl 382),* 65–70.

Perry, JC (1985) Depression in borderline personality disorders: Lifetime prevalence at interview and longitudinal course of symptoms. *American Journal of Psychiatry, 142,* 15–21.

Perry, JC, Augusto, F, & Cooper, SH (1989) Assessing psychodynamic conflicts: 1. Reliability of the idiographic conflict formulation method. *Psychiatry, 52,* 289–301.

Perry, S (1990) Combining anti-depressants and psychotherapy: Rationale and strategies. *Journal of Clinical Psychiatry, 51*(suppl), 16–20.

Persaud, R, & Marks, IM (1995) A pilot study of exposure control of chronic auditory hallucinations in schizophrenia. *British Journal of Psychiatry, 167,* 45–50.

Perse, T (1988) Obsessive–compulsive disorder: A treatment review. *Journal of Clinical Psychiatry, 49,* 48–55.

Persons, J (1989) *Cognitive therapy in practice: The case formulation approach.* New York: Norton.

Persons, JB (1991) Psychotherapy outcome studies do not accurately represent current models of psychotherapy: A proposed remedy. *American Psychologist, 46,* 99–106.

Phares, V, Compas, BE, & Howell, DC (1989) Perspectives on child behavior problems: Comparisons of children's self-reports with parent and teacher reports. *Journal of Consulting and Clinical Psychology, 1,* 68–71.

Piccinelli, M, & Wilkinson, G (1994) Outcome of depression in psychiatric settings. *British Journal of Psychiatry, 164,* 297–304.

Piccinelli, M, Pini, S, Bellantuono, C, & Wilkinson, G (1995) Efficacy of drug treatment in obsessive–compulsive disorder: A meta-analytic review. *British Journal of Psychiatry 166* 424–443.

Pilkonis, P, et al. (1984) A comparative outcome study of individual, group and conjoint therapy. *Archives of General Psychiatry, 41,* 431–437.

Pinkston, EM, Linsk, NL, & Young, RN (1988) Home-based behavioral family treatment of the impaired elderly. *Behavior Therapy, 19,* 331–344.

Piorkowsky, GK, & Mann, ET (1975) Issues in treatment efficacy research with alcoholics. *Perceptual and Motor Skills, 41,* 695–700.

Piper, WE, Debbane, EG, Bienvenu, JP, & Garant, J (1984) A comparative study of four forms of psychotherapy. *Journal of Consulting and Clinical Psychology, 52,* 268–279.

Piper, WE, Azim, HFA, Joyce, AS, McCallum, M, Nixon, GWH, & Segal, PS (1991) Quality of object relations vs interpersonal functioning as a predictor of the therapeutic alliance and psychotherapy outcome. *Journal of Nervous and Mental Disease, 179,* 432–438.

Piper, WE, Joyce, AS, McCallum, M, & Azim, HFA (1993) Concentration and correspondence of transference interpretations in short term therapy. *Journal of Consulting and Clinical Psychology, 61,* 586–595.

Piper, WE, Joyce, AS, Azim, HFA, & Rosie, JS (1994) Patient characteristics and success in day treatment. *Journal of Nervous and Mental Disease, 182,* 381–386.

Pittman, DJ, & Tate, RL (1972) A comparison of two treatment programs for alcoholics. *International Journal of Social Psychiatry, 18,* 183–193.

Polanyi, M (1958) *Personal knowledge.* Chicago: University of Chicago Press.

Pomerleau, O, Pertshuk, M, Adkins, D, & d'Aquili, E (1978) Treatment for middle-income problem drinkers. In PE Nathan, GA Marlatt, & T Loberg (Eds.), *Alcoholism: New directions in behavioral research and treatment.* New York: Plenum Press.

Pope, HG, Jonas, MJ, & Hudson, JI (1983) The validity of DSM-III borderline personality disorders. *Archives of General Psychiatry, 40,* 23–30.

Power, KG, Simpson, RJ, Swanson, V, & Wallace, LA (1990) A controlled comparison of cognitive-behavior therapy, diazepam, and placebo, alone and in combination, for the treatment of generalized anxiety disorder. *Journal of Anxiety Disorders, 4,* 267–292.

Price, SC, Reynolds, BS, Cohen, BD, & Anderson, AJ (1981) Group treatment of erectile dysfunction for men without partners: A controlled evaluation. *Archives of Sexual Behavior, 8,* 127–138.

Prien, RF, Kupfer, DJ, Mansky, PA, Small, JG, Tuason, VB, Voss, CB, & Johnson, WE (1984) Drug therapy in the prevention of recurrences in unipolar and bipolar affective disorders. *Archives of General Psychiatry, 41,* 1096–1104.

Prien, RF, & Potter, WZ (1990) NIMH workshop report on treatment of bipolar disorder. *Psychopharmacology Bulletin, 26,* 409–427.

Prien, RF, Carpenter, LL, & Kupfer, DJ (1991) The definition and operational criteria for treatment outcome of major depressive disorder. *Archives of General Psychiatry, 48,* 796–800.

Prioleau, L, Murdoch, M, & Brody, N (1983) An analysis of psychotherapy versus placebo studies. *Behavioral and Brain Sciences, 6,* 275–310.

Prochaska, JO (1984) *Systems of psychotherapy: A transtheoretical analysis* (2nd ed.). Homewood, IL: Dorsey.

Puig-Antich, J, Perel, JM, Lupatkin, W, Chambers, WJ, Tabrizi, MA, King, J, Goetz, R, Davies, M, & Stiller, RL (1987) Imipramine in prepubertal major depressive disorders. *Archives of General Psychiatry, 44,* 81–89.

Pyle, RL, Mitchell, JE, Eckert, ED, & Hatsukami, D, et al. (1990) Maintenance treatment and six month outcome for bulimic patients who respond to initial treatment. *American Journal of Psychiatry, 147,* 871–875.

Quality Assurance Project (1983) A treatment outline for depressive disorders. *Australian and New Zealand Journal of Psychiatry, 17,* 129–146.

Quality Assurance Project (1985) Treatment outlines for the management of anxiety states. *Australian and New Zealand Journal of Psychiatry, 19,* 138–151.

Rabavilas, AD, Boulougouris, JC, & Stefanis, C (1979) Duration of flooding sessions in the treatment of obsessive–compulsive patients. *Behaviour Research and Therapy, 14,* 349–355.

Rabiner, CJ, & Klein, DF (1969) Imipramine treatment of school phobia. *Comprehensive Psychiatry*, *10*, 387–390.

Rachman, S, Marks, IM, & Hodgson, R (1973) The treatment of obsessive–compulsive neurotics by modelling and flooding in-vivo. *Behaviour Research and Therapy*, *11*, 463–471.

Rachman, S, Cobb, J, Grey, B, McDonald, D, Mawson, D, Sartory, G, & Stern, RS (1979) The behavioral treatment of obsessive disorders with and without clomipramine. *Behaviour Research and Therapy*, *17*, 467–478.

Rachman, SJ (1983) Obstacles to the successful treatment of obsessions. In E Foa & P Emmelkamp (Eds.), *Failures in behavior therapy*. New York: Wiley.

Ramsay, R (1990) Post-traumatic stress disorder: A new clinical entity? *Journal of Psychosomatic Research*, *34*, 355–365.

Randolph, ET, Eth, S, Glynn, SM, Paz, GG, Leong, GB, Shaner, AL, Strachan, A, van Vort, W, Escobar, JI, & Liberman, RP (1994) Behavioral family management in schizophrenia: Outcome of a clinic-based intervention. *British Journal of Psychiatry*, *164*, 501–506.

Rapaport, MH, & Maser, JD (1992) Secondary depression: Definition and treatment. *Pharmacology Bulletin*, *28*, 27–33.

Raphael, B (1979) Preventative intervention with the recently bereaved. *Archives of General Psychiatry*, *34*, 1450–1454.

Ratnasuriya, RH, Eisler, I, Szmukler, GI, & Russell, GFM (1991) Outcome and prognostic factors after 20 years. *British Journal of Psychiatry*, *158*, 495–502.

Raw, SD (1993) Does psychotherapy research teach us anything about psychotherapy? *Behavior Therapist*, March, 75–76.

Reandeu, SG, & Wampold, BE (1991) Relationship of power and involvement to working alliance: A multiple case sequential analysis of brief therapy. *Journal of Consulting and Clinical Psychology*, *38*, 107–114.

Reed, GF (1983) Obsessive compulsive disorder: A cognitive/structural approach. *Canadian Psychology*, *24*, 169–180.

Rees, DW, & Farmer, R (1985) Health beliefs and attendance for specialist alcoholism treatment. *British Journal of Psychiatry*, *147*, 317–319.

Reeve, W, & Ivison, D (1985) Use of environmental manipulation and classroom and modified informal reality orientation with institutionalized, confused elderly patients. *Age and Ageing*, *14*, 119–121.

Regier, DA, Boyd, JH, & Burke, JD (1988) One month prevalence of mental disorders in the United States. *Archives of General Psychiatry*, *45*, 977.

Regier, DA, Farmer, ME, & Goodwin, FK (1992) Comorbidity of mental and substance abuse disorders. In R Michaels (Ed.), *Psychiatry*. Philadelphia: Lippincott.

Rehm, LP (1977) A self-control model of depression. *Behavior Therapy*, *8*, 787–804.

Rehm, LP, & Kaslow, NJ (1984) Behavioral approaches to depression: Research results and clinical recommendations. In CM Franks (Ed.). *New developments in behavior therapy*. New York: Haworth Press.

Reich, JH (1986) The epidemiology of anxiety. *Journal of Nervous and Mental Disease*, *174*, 129–136.

Reich, JH (1988) DSM-III personality disorders and the outcome of treated panic disorder. *American Journal of Psychiatry, 145,* 1149–1152.

Reich, JH (1990) The effect of personality on placebo response in panic patients. *Journal of Nervous and Mental Disease, 187,* 699–702.

Reich, JH, & Green, AI (1991) Effect of personality disorders on outcome of treatment. *Journal of Nervous and Mental Disease, 179,* 74–82.

Reich, JH, & Vasile, RG (1993) Effect of personality disorders on the treatment outcome of Axis I conditions: An update. *Journal of Nervous and Mental Disease, 181,* 475–484.

Reinert, RE (1958) A comparison of reserpine and disulfiram in the treatment of alcoholism. *Quarterly Journal of Studies on Alcohol, 19,* 617–622.

Reinherz, HZ, Giaconia, RM, Lefkowitz, ES, Pakiz, B, & Frost, AK (1993) Prevalence of psychiatric disorders in a community population of older adolescents. *Journal of the American Academy of Child and Adolescent Psychiatry, 32,* 369–377.

Reist, C, Kauffman, CD, & Haier, RJ, et al. (1989) A controlled trial of desipramine in 18 men with PTSD. *American Journal of Psychiatry, 146,* 513–516.

Renfrey, G, & Spates, CR (1994) Eye movement desensitization: A partial dismantling study. *Journal of Behavior Therapy and Experimental Psychiatry, 25,* 231–239.

Renneberg, B, Goldstein, AM, Phillips, D, & Chambless, DL (1990) Intensive behavioral group treatment of avoidant personality disorder. *Behavior Therapy, 21,* 363–377.

Renouf, AG, & Kovacs, M (1994) Concordance between mothers' reports and children's self-reports of depressive symptoms: A longitudinal study. *Journal of the American Academy of Child and Adolescent Psychiatry, 33,* 208–216.

Resick, PA, Jordan, CG, Girelli, SA, Hutter, CK, & Marhoefer-Dvorak, S (1988) A comparative outcome study of behavioral group therapy for sexual assault victims. *Behavior Therapy, 19,* 385–401.

Resick, PA, & Schnicke, MK (1992) Cognitive processing therapy for sexual assault victims. *Journal of Consulting and Clinical Psychology, 60,* 784–756.

Reynolds, BS (1982) Biofeedback and facilitation of erection in men with erectile dysfunction. *Archives of Sexual Behavior, 9,* 101–113.

Reynolds, BS, Cohen, BD, Shochet, BV, Price, SC, & Anderson, AJ (1981) Dating skills training in the group treatment of erectile dysfunction for men without partners. *Journal of Sex and Marital Therapy, 7,* 184–194.

Reynolds, BS (1991) Psychological treatment of erectile dysfunction in men without partners: Outcome results and a new direction. *Journal of Sex and Marital Therapy, 17,* 136–146.

Reynolds, CF, Frank, E, Perel, JM, Imber, S, Cornes, C, Morycz, RK, Mazumdar, S, Miller, MD, Pollock, BG, Rifai, AH, Stack, JA, George, CJ, Houck, PR, & Kupfer, DJ (1992) Combined pharmacotherapy and psychotherapy in the acute and continuation treatment of elderly patients with recurrent major depression: A preliminary report. *American Journal of Psychiatry, 149,* 1687–1692.

Reynolds, WM, & Coats, KI (1986) A comparison of cognitive-behavioral therapy and relaxation training for the treatment of depression in adolescents. *Journal of Consulting and Clinical Psychology, 54,* 653–660.

Richards, DA, Lovell, K, & Marks, IM (1994) Post-traumatic stress disorder: Evaluation of a treatment program. *Journal of Traumatic Stress*, 7, 319–325.

Richardson, P (1989) Placebos: Their effectiveness and modes of action. In AK Broome (Ed.), *Health psychology: Process and applications*. London: Chapman and Hall.

Richman, N, Stevenson, J, & Graham, PJ (1982) *Pre-school to school: A behavioral study*. London: Academic Press.

Riddle, MA, Scahill, L, & King, RA (1992) Double-blind cross-over trial of fluoxetine and placebo in children and adolescents with obsessive–compulsive disorder. *Journal of the American Academy of Child and Adolescent Psychiatry*, *31*, 1062.

Robbins, DR, Allessi, NE, & and Colfer, MV (1989) Treatment of adolescents with major depression: Implications of the DST and the melancholic clinical subtype. *Journal of Affective Disorders*, *17*, 99–104.

Robins, LN, & Rutter, M (Eds.) (1990) *Straight and devious pathways from childhood to adulthood*. London: Oxford University Press.

Robins, LN (1981) Epidemiological approaches to natural history research: Antisocial disorders in children. *Journal of the American Academy of Child and Adolescent Psychiatry*, *20*, 566–580.

Robins, LN (1966) *Deviant children grown-up*. Baltimore: Williams and Wilkins.

Robins, LN, & Regier, DA (Eds.) (1991) *Psychiatric disorders in America: The Epidemiologic Catchment Area Study*. New York: Free Press.

Robinson, LA, Berman, JS, & Neimeyer, RA (1990) Psychotherapy for the treatment of depression: A comprehensive review of controlled outcome research. *Psychological Bulletin*, *108*, 30–49.

Robinson, S, Birchwood, M, & Eastman, C (submitted) A trial of group cognitive therapy for panic disorder with agoraphobia in a dedicated service setting.

Robson, MH, France, R, & Bland, M (1984) Clinical psychologist in primary care: Controlled clinical and economic evaluation. *British Medical Journal*, *288*, 1805–1808.

Robson, RAH, Paulus, I, & Clarke, GG (1965) An evaluation of the effects of a clinic program on the rehabilitation of chronic alcoholic patients. *Quarterly Journal of Studies on Alcohol*, *26*, 264–278.

Rogers, CR (1951) *Client-centered therapy*. Cambridge, MA: Riverside Press.

Rona, D, Wylie, B, & Bellwood, S. (1986) Behavior treatment of day-time incontinence in elderly male and female patients. *Behavioural Psychotherapy*, *14*, 13–20.

Roper, G, Rachman, S, & Marks, IM (1975) Passive and participant modelling in exposure treatment of obsessive–compulsive neurotics. *Behaviour Research and Therapy*, *13*, 271–279.

Roper-Hall, A (1993) Developing family therapy services with older adults. In J Carpenter & A Treacher (Eds.), *Using family therapy in the nineties*. Oxford: Blackwell.

Rosenberg, SD (1974) Drug maintenance in the outpatient treatment of chronic alcoholics. *Archives of General Psychiatry*, *30*, 373–377.

Rosenstiel, SK, & Scott, DS (1977) Four considerations in imagery techniques with children. *Journal of Behavior Therapy and Experimental Psychiatry*, *8*, 287–290.

Ross, D, Ross, S, & Evans, TA (1971) The modification of extreme social withdrawal by modification with guided practice. *Journal of Behavior Therapy and Experimental Psychiatry*, 2, 273–279.

Ross, M, & Scott, M (1985) An evaluation of the effectiveness of individual and group cognitive therapy in the treatment of depressed patients in an inner city health centre. *Journal of the Royal College of General Practitioners*, 35, 239–242.

Rosser, RM, Birch, S, Bond, , Denford, J, & Schachter, J (1987) Five year follow-up of patients treated with psychotherapy at the Cassel Hospital for nervous diseases. *Journal of the Royal Society of Medicine*, 80, 549–555.

Rossiter, EM, Agras, WS, Losch, M, & Telch, CF (1988) Dietary restraint of bulimic subjects following cognitive behavioral or pharmacological treatment. *Behaviour Research and Therapy*, 26, 495–432.

Rossiter, EM, & Wilson, GT (1985) Cognitive restructuring and response prevention in the treatment of bulimia nervosa. *Behaviour Research and Therapy*, 23, 349–359.

Roth, AD, & Church, JA (1994) The use of revised habituation in the treatment of obsessive–compulsive disorders. *British Journal of Clinical Psychology*, 33, 201–204.

Rothbaum, BO, Foa, EB, Riggs, DS, Murdock, T, & Walsh, W (1992) A prospective examination of PTSD in rape victims. *Journal of Traumatic Stress*, 5, 455–475.

Rounsaville, BJ, Weissman, MM, & Prusoff, BA (1981) Psychotherapy with depressed outpatients: Patient and process variables as predictors of outcome. *British Journal of Psychiatry*, 13, 67–74.

Rounsaville, BJ, O'Malley, S, Foley, S, & Weissman, MM (1988) Role of manual guided training in the conduct and efficacy of interpersonal therapy for depression. *Journal of Consulting and Clinical Psychology*, 56, 681–688.

Routh, DK (Ed.) (1988) *Handbook of pediatric psychology*. New York: Guilford Press.

Roy-Burne, PP, & Katon, W (1987) An update on treatment of the anxiety disorders. *Hospital and Community Psychiatry*, 38, 835–843.

Rubin, KH, Bream, LA, & Rose-Krasnor, L (1991) Social problem-solving and aggression in childhood. In DJ Pepler & KH Rubin (Eds.), *The development and treatment of childhood aggression*. Hillsdale, NJ: Erlbaum.

Rush, AJ (1993) Clinical practice guidelines: Good news, bad news, or no news? *Archives of General Psychiatry*, 50, 483–490.

Rush, AJ, Beck, AT, Kovacs, M, & Hollon, SD (1977) Comparative efficacy of cognitive therapy and imipramine in the treatment of depressed patients. *Cognitive Therapy and Research*, 1, 17–37.

Russell, GFM, Szmukler, GI, Dare, C, & Eisler, I (1987) An evaluation of family therapy in anorexia nervosa and bulimia nervosa. *Archives of General Psychiatry*, 44, 1047–1056.

Rutter, M (1985a) Infantile autism and other pervasive developmental disorders. In M Rutter & L Hersov (Eds.), *Child and adolescent psychiatry: Modern approaches*. Oxford: Blackwell.

Rutter, M (1985b) The treatment of autistic children. *Journal of Child Psychology and Psychiatry*, 26, 193–214.

Rutter, M (1987) Temperament, personality and personality disorder. *British Journal of Psychiatry, 150,* 443–458.

Rutter, M (1988) Depressive disorders. In M Rutter, AH Tuma, & IS Lann (Eds.), *Assessment and diagnosis in child psychopathology.* New York: Guilford Press.

Rutter, M (1989a) Annotation: Child psychiatric disorders in ICD-10. *Journal of Child Psychiatry, 30*(4), 499–513.

Rutter, M (1989) Isle of Wight revisited: Twenty-five years of child psychiatric epidemiology. *Journal of the American Academy of Child and Adolescent Psychiatry, 28,* 633–653.

Rutter, M (1994) Beyond longitudinal data: Causes, consequences, changes, and continuity. *Journal of Consulting and Clinical Psychology, 62,* 928–940.

Rutter M (in press) Continuities, transitions and turning points in development. In M Rutter & DS Hay (Eds.), *Development through life: A handbook for clinicians.* Oxford: Blackwell Scientific Publications.

Rutter, M, Tizard, J, & Whitmore, K (Eds.) (1970) *Education, health and behaviour.* London: Longmans.

Rutter, M, Tizard, J, & Whitmore, K (Eds.) (1981). *Education, health and behavior.* New York: Krieger.

Ryan, ER, & Cicchetti, DV (1985) Predicting quality of alliance in the initial psychotherapy interview. *Journal of Nervous and Mental Disease, 173,* 717–725.

Ryan, ND, Puig-Antich, J, Cooper, T, et al. (1986) Imipramine in adolescent major depression: Plasma level and clinical response. *Acta Psychiatrica Scandinavica, 73,* 289.

Ryle, A (1990) *Cognitive analytic therapy: Active participation in change.* Chichester: Wiley.

Safran, JD, Crocker, P, McMain, S, & Murray, P (1990) The therapeutic alliance rupture as a therapy event for empirical investigation. *Psychotherapy, 27,* 154–165.

Safran, JD, & Segal, ZV (1990) *Interpersonal process in cognitive therapy.* New York: Basic Books.

Salkovskis, PM (1995) Demonstrating specific effects in cognitive and behavioral therapy. In M Aveline & D Shapiro, *Research foundations for psychotherapy practice.* Chichester: Wiley.

Salkovskis, PM & Clark, D (1991) Cognitive therapy for panic attacks. *Journal of Cognitive Psychotherapy, 5,* 215–226.

Salkovskis, PM, & Westbrook, D (1989) Behavior therapy and obsessional ruminations: Can failure be turned into success? *Behaviour Research and Therapy, 27,* 149–160.

Sanderson, A, & Carpenter, R (1992) Eye movement desensitization versus image confrontation: A single session crossover study of 58 phobic subjects. *Journal of Behavioral Therapy and Experimental Psychiatry, 23,* 269–275.

Sanders, MR, & Dadds, MR (1993) *Behavioral family intervention.* Needham Heights, MA: Allyn and Bacon.

Sanders, MR, Shepherd, RW, Cleghorn, G, & Woolford, H (1994) The treatment of recurrent abdominal pain in children: A controlled comparison of cognitive-behavioral family intervention and standard pediatric care. *Journal of Consulting and Clinical Psychology, 62,* 306–314.

Satterfield, JH, Satterfield, BT, & Cantwell, DP (1981) Three-year multimodality treatment study of 100 hyperactive boys. *Journal of Pediatrics, 98,* 650–655.

Satterfield, JH, Satterfield, BT, & Schell, AM (1987) Therapeutic interventions to prevent delinquency in hyperactive boys. *Journal of the American Academy of Child and Adolescent Psychiatry, 26,* 56–64.

Saxe, LM, Cross, T, & Silverman, N (1986) *Children's mental health: Problems and services: Background paper,* Washington, DC: US Government Printing Office.

Schaffer, ND (1982) Multi-dimensional measures of therapist behavior as a predictor of outcome. *Psychological Bulletin, 92,* 670–681.

Scheidlinger, S (1994) On overview of nine decades of group psychotherapy. *Hospital and Community Psychiatry, 45,* 217–225.

Schenk, J, Pfang, H, & Rausche, A (1983) Personality traits versus the quality of the marital relationship as the determinant of marital sexuality. *Archives of Sexual Behavior, 12,* 31–42.

Schnelle, JF, Traughber, B, Sowell, VA, Newman, DR, Petrilli, CO, & Ory, M (1989) Prompted voiding treatment of urinary incontinence in nursing home patients: A behavior management approach for nursing home staff. *Journal of the American Geriatrics Society, 37,* 1051–1057.

Schnier, F, Johnson, J, & Hornig, CD (1992) Social phobia: Co-morbidity, and morbidity in an epidemiological sample. *Archives of General Psychiatry, 49,* 282.

Schmidt, U, & Marks, IM (1988) Cue exposure to food plus response prevention of binges for bulimia: A pilot study. *International Journal of Eating Disorders, 7,* 663–672.

Schmidt, U, & Marks, IM (1989) Exposure plus prevention of binging vs exposure plus prevention of vomiting in bulimia nervosa. *Journal of Nervous and Mental Disease, 177,* 259–266.

Scholing, A, & Emmelkamp, PMG (1993) Exposure with and without cognitive therapy for generalized social phobia; effects of individual and group treatment. *Behaviour Research and Therapy, 31,* 667–681.

Schover, LR, & LoPiccolo, J (1982) Treatment effectiveness for dysfunctions of sexual desire. *Journal of Sex and Marital Therapy, 8,* 179–197.

Schover, LR, & Leiblum, SR (1994) Commentary: The stagnation of sex therapy. *Journal of Psychology and Human Sexuality, 6,* 5–30.

Schulberg, HC, & Rush, JA (1994) Clinical practice guidelines for managing major depression in primary care practice: Implications for psychologists. *American Psychology, 49,* 34–41.

Schulze-Mönking, H (1994) Self-help groups for families of schizophrenic patients: Formation, development and therapeutic impact. *Social Psychiatry and Psychiatric Epidemiology, 29,* 149–154.

Schwartz, DM, & Thompson, MG (1981) Do anorectics get well? Current research and future needs. *American Journal of Psychiatry, 138,* 319–323.

Schwartz, MA (1991) The nature and classification of the personality disorders: A re-examination of basic premises. *Journal of Personality Disorders, 5,* 25–30.

Schwartz, MA, & Wiggins, OP (1986) Logical empiricism and psychiatric classification. *Comprehensive Psychiatry, 27,* 101–114.

Scogin, F, Jamison, C, & Gochneaur, K (1989) Comparative efficacy of cognitive and behavioral bibliotherapy for mildly and moderately depressed older adults. *Journal of Consulting and Clinical Psychology, 57,* 403–407.

Scogin, F, Jamison, C, & Davis, N (1990) Two-year follow-up of bibliotherapy for depression in older adults. *Journal of Consulting and Clinical Psychology, 58,* 665–667.

Scogin, F, & McElreath, L (1994) Efficacy of psychosocial treatments for geriatric depression: A quantitative review. *Journal of Consulting and Clinical Psychology, 62,* 69–74.

Scott, AIF, & Freeman, CPL (1992) Edinburgh primary care depression study: Treatment outcome, patient satisfaction and costs after 16 weeks. *British Medical Journal, 304,* 883–887.

Scott, J (1992) Chronic depression: Can cognitive therapy succeed when other treatments fail? *Behavioural Psychotherapy, 20,* 25–36.

Scott, J (1995) Psychotherapy for bipolar disorder: An unmet need? *British Journal of Psychiatry, 167,* 581–588.

Scott, J (in press) Bipolar disorder. In D Tantum (Ed.), *Clinical topics in psychotherapy.*

Segraves, KA, Segraves, RT, & Schoenberg, HW (1987) Use of sexual history to differentiate organic from psychogenic impotence. *Archives of Sexual Behavior, 9,* 457–575.

Segraves, RT, Knopf, J, & Cammic, P (1982) Spontaneous remission in erectile dysfunction. *Behaviour Research and Therapy, 20,* 89–91.

Segraves, RT, Camic, P, & Ivanoff, J (1985) Spontaneous remission in erectile dysfunction: A partial replication. *Behaviour Research and Therapy, 23,* 203–204.

Sellwood, W, Haddock, G, Tarrier, N, & Yusupoff, L (1994) Advances in the psychological management of positive symptoms of schizophrenia. *International Review of Psychiatry, 6,* 201–215.

Serlin, RC, & Lapsley, DK (1985) Rationality in psychological research: The good-enough principle. *American Psychologist, 40,* 73–83.

Shadler, J, Mayman, M, & Manis, M (1993) The illusion of mental health. *American Psychologist, 48,* 1117–1131.

Shaffer, D, Gould, MS, Brasie, J, Ambrosini, P, Fisher, P, Bird, H, & Aluwahlia, S (1983) A children's global assessment scale (CGAS). *Archives of General Psychiatry, 40,* 1228–1231.

Shakir, S, Volkmar, F, Bacon, S, & Pfefferbaum, A (1979) Group psychotherapy as an adjunct to lithium maintenance. *American Journal of Psychiatry, 136,* 455–456.

Shapiro, B (1943) Premature ejaculation: A review of 1130 cases. *Journal of Urology, 50,* 374–379.

Shapiro, DA, & Shapiro, D (1982) Meta-analysis of comparative outcome studies: A replication and refinement. *Psychological Bulletin, 92,* 581–604.

Shapiro, DA, Barkham, M, Rees, A, Hardy, GE, Reynolds, S, & Startup, M (1994) Effects of treatment duration and severity of depression on the effectiveness of cognitive/behavioral and psychodynamic/interpersonal psychotherapy. *Journal of Consulting and Clinical Psychology, 62,* 522–534.

Shapiro, DA, Rees, A, Barkham, M, Hardy, G, Reynolds, S, & Startup, M (1995) Effects of treatment duration and severity of depression on the maintenance of gains following cognitive behavioral and psychodynamic interpersonal psychotherapy. *Journal of Consulting and Clinical Psychology, 63,* 378–387.

Shapiro, ES, Shapiro, AK, & Fulop, G, et al (1989) Controlled study of haloperidol, pimozide, and placebo for the treatment of Gilles de la Tourette's syndrome. *Archives of General Psychiatry, 44,* 722.

Shapiro, F (1989a) Eye movement desensitization: A new treatment for post-traumatic stress disorder. *Journal of Behavior Therapy and Experimental Psychiatry, 20,* 211–217.

Shapiro, F (1989b) Efficacy of the eye movement desensitization procedure in the treatment of traumatic memories. *Journal of Traumatic Stress, 2,* 199–223.

Shapiro, T (1991) Psychoanalytic classification and empiricism with borderline personality disorder as a model. *Journal of Consulting and Clinical Psychology, 57,* 187–194.

Shaw, BF (1989) Cognitive-behavior therapies for major depression: Current status with an emphasis on prophylaxis. *Psychiatric Journal of the University of Ottowa, 14,* 403–408.

Shaw, BF (1977) Comparison of cognitive therapy and behavior therapy in the treatment of depression. *Journal of Consulting and Clinical Psychology, 45,* 543–551.

Shaw, E (1986) Lithium noncompliance. *Psychiatric Annals, 16,* 583–587.

Shea, MT (1993) Psychosocial treatment of personality disorder. *Journal of Personality Disorders, 7* (Suppl.), 167–180.

Shea, MT, Pilkonis, PA, Beckham, E, Collins, JF, Elkin, I, Sotsky, SM, & Docherty, J (1992a) Personality disorders and treatment outcome in the NIMH treatment of depression collaborative research program. *American Journal of Psychiatry, 147,* 711–718.

Shea, MT, Widiger, TA, & Klein, MH (1992b) Comorbidity of personality disorders and depression: Implications for treatment. *Journal of Consulting and Clinical Psychology, 60,* 857–868.

Shea, MT, Elkin, I, Imber, SD, Sotsky, SM, Watkins, JT, Collins, JF, Pilkonis, PA, Beckham, E, Glass, DR, Dolan, RT, & Parloff, MB (1992c) Course of depressive symptoms over follow-up: Findings from the NIMH treatment of depression collaborative research program. *Archives of General Psychiatry, 49,* 782–787.

Shear, MK, Pilkonis, PA, Cloitre, M, & Leon, AC (1994) Cognitive behavioral treatment compared with non-prescriptive treatment of panic disorder. *Archives of General Psychiatry, 51,* 395–401.

Sheldon, T, Freemantle, N, House, A, Adams, CE, Mason, JM, Song, F, Long, A, & Watson, P (1993) Examining the effectiveness of treatments for depression in general practice. *Journal of Mental Health, 2,* 141–156.

Shepherd, M, Oppenheim, B, & Mitchell, S (1971) *Childhood behaviour and mental health.* London: University of London Press.

Shepherd, M, Watt, D, Falloon, I, & Smeeton, N (1989) The natural history of schizophrenia: A five year follow-up of outcome and prediction in a representative sample of schizophrenics. In *Psychological Medicine Monograph 16.* Cambridge: Cambridge University Press.

Shestatsky, M, Greenberg, D, & Lerer, B (1988) A controlled trial of phenelzine in PTSD. *Psychiatry Research, 24,* 149–155.

Shore, JH, Vollmer, WM, & Tatum, EL (1986) Community patterns of post-traumatic stress disorders. *Journal of Nervous and Mental Disease, 177,* 681–685.

Siever, LJ, Klar, J, & Coccaro, E (1985) Psychobiologic substrates of personality. In LS Siever & H Klar (Eds.), *Biologic response styles: Clinical implications.* Washington, DC: APA Press.

Shirk, SR, & Russell, RL (1992) A reevaluation of estimates of child therapy effectiveness. *Journal of the American Academy of Child and Adolescent Psychiatry, 31,* 703–709.

Sibbald, B, Addington-Hall, J, Brennerman, D, Freeling, P (1993) Counsellors in English and Welsh general practices: Their nature and distribution. *British Medical Journal, 306,* 29–33.

Sifneos, PE (1972) *Short-term psychotherapy and emotional crisis.* Cambridge, MA: Harvard University Press.

Sifneos, PE (1987) *Short-term dynamic psychotherapy: Evaluation and technique.* (2nd ed.). New York: Plenum Press.

Silver, L, & Silver, B (1983) Clinical practice of child psychiatry: A survey. *Journal of the American Academy of Child and Adolescent Psychiatry, 22,* 573–579.

Silverman, WK, & Kearney, CA (in press). Behavioral treatment of childhood anxiety. In V. B. Van Hasselt & M Hersen (Eds.), *Handbook of behavior therapy and pharmacotherapy for children: A comparative analysis.* New York: Grune and Stratton.

Silverstein, ML, & Harrow, M (1978) First-rank symptoms in the post-acute schizophrenic: A follow-up study. *American Journal of Psychiatry, 135,* 1481–1486.

Simeon, JG, & Ferguson, HB (1987). Alprazolam effects in children with anxiety disorders. *Canadian Journal of Psychiatry, 32,* 570–574.

Simons, AD, Murphy, GE, Levine, JE, & Wetzel, RD (1986) Cognitive therapy and pharmacotherapy for depression; sustained improvement over one year. *Archives of General Psychiatry, 43,* 43–48.

Simons, AD, & Thase, ME (1992) Biological markers, treatment outcome and one year follow-up of endogenous depression: Electroencephalographic studies sleep studies and response to cognitive therapy. *Journal of Consulting and Clinical Psychology, 60,* 392–401.

Sinason, V (1992) The man who was losing his brain. In V Sinason (Ed.), *Mental handicap and the human condition: New approaches from the Tavistock.* London: Free Association Books.

Sinason, V (1992) *Mental handicap and the human condition.* London: Free Association Books.

Skodol, AE, Buckley, P, & Charles, E (1983) Is there a characteristic pattern to the treatment history of clinic patients with borderline personality? *Journal of Nervous and Mental Disease, 171*, 405–410.

Slavson, SR (1964) *A textbook in analytic group psychotherapy.* New York: International Universities Press.

Slipp, S, & Kressel, K (1978) Difficulties in family therapy evaluation I: A comparison of insight vs problem solving II: Design, critique, and recommendations. *Family Process, 17*, 409–422.

Smart, RG, & Gray, G (1978) Minimal, moderate and long-term treatment for alcoholism. *British Journal of Addiction, 73*, 35–38.

Smith, J, & Birchwood, MJ (1987) Specific and non-specific effects of educational interventions with families living with schizophrenic relatives. *British Journal of Psychiatry, 150*, 645–652.

Smith, JW, & Fawley, PJ (1990) Long-term abstinence from alcohol in patients receiving aversion therapy as part of a multimodal in-patient program. *Journal of Substance Abuse Treatment, 7*, 77–82.

Smith, ML, & Glass, GV (1977) Meta-analysis of psychotherapy outcome studies. *American Psychologist, 32*, 752–760.

Smith, ML, Glass, GV, & Miller, TI (1980) *The benefits of psychotherapy.* Baltimore: Johns Hopkins University Press.

Smith, TA, Kroeger, RF, Lyon, HE, & Mullins, MR (1990) Evaluating a behavioral method to manage dental fears: A two year study of dental practices. *Journal of the American Dental Association, 121*, 525–530.

Smyer, MA, Zarit, SH, & Qualls, SH (1990) Psychological intervention with the ageing individual. In JE Birren & KW Schaie (Eds.), *Handbook of the psychology of ageing* (3rd ed.). San Diego, CA: Academic Press.

Snow, J, & Paternite, C (1986) Individual and family therapy in the treatment of children. *Professional Psychology: Research and Practice, 17*, 242–250.

Soloff, PH (1994) Is there any drug treatment of choice for the borderline patient? *Acta Psychiatrica Scandinavica, 89* (Suppl. 379), 50–55.

Soloff, PH, George, A, Nathan, RS, Schulz, PM, Cornelius, JR, Herring, J Ulrich, RF, & Perel, JM (1989) Amitripyline versus haloperidol in borderlines: Final outcomes and predictors of response. *Journal of Clinical Pharmacology, 9*, 238–246.

Soloff, PH, George, A, Nathan, RS, Schulz, PM, Ulrich, RF, & Perel, JM (1986) Progress in the pharmacotherapy of borderline disorders: A double blind study of amitriptyline, haloperidol, and placebo. *Archives of General Psychiatry, 43*, 691–697.

Solomon, SD, Gerrity, ET, & Muff, AM (1992) Efficacy of treatments for post-traumatic stress disorder. *Journal of the American Medical Association, 268*, 633–638.

Spector, IP, & Carey, MP (1990) Incidence and prevalence of the sexual dysfunctions: A critical review of the empirical literature. *Archives of Sexual Behavior, 19*, 389–408.

Speigal, DA, Roth, M, & Weissman, M, et al. (1993) Comment on the London/Toronto study of alprazolam and exposure in panic disorder with agoraphobia. *British Journal of Psychiatry, 162*, 788–789.

Speilberger, CG, Gorsuch, RL, & Lushene, R (1983) *Manual for the state–trait anxiety inventory.* Palo Alto, CA: Consulting Psychologists Press.

Spence, SH (1994) Practitioner review: Cognitive therapy with children and adolescents: From theory to practice. *Journal of Child Psychology and Psychiatry, 35,* 1191–1228.

Spiegal, D, Bloom, JR, Kraemer, HC, & Hottheil, E (1989) Effect of psychosocial treatment on survival of patients with metastatic breast cancer. *Lancet, 14,* 888–891.

Spitzer, RD, Endicott, J, & Ronin, E (1978) Research diagnostic criteria. *Archives of General Psychiatry, 35,* 773–782.

Stallard, P, & Law, F (1994) Screening and psychological debriefing of adolescent survivors of life-threatening danger. *British Journal of Psychiatry, 163,* 660–665.

Stanley, L (1980) Treatment of ritualistic behavior in an eight-year-old girl by response prevention: A case report. *Journal of Child Psychology and Psychiatry, 21,* 234–251.

Stark, KD (1990) *Childhood depression: School-based intervention.* New York: Guilford Press.

Stark, KD, Reynolds, WM, & Kaslow, N (1987) A comparison of the relative efficacy of self-control therapy and a behavioral problem-solving therapy for depression in children. *Journal of Abnormal Child Psychology, 15,* 91–113.

Stein, DM, & Lambert, MJ (1984) On the relationship between therapist experience and psychotherapy outcome. *Clinical Psychology Review, 4,* 127–142.

Stein, DM, & Lambert, MJ (1995) Graduate training in psychotherapy: Are therapy outcomes enhanced? *Journal of Consulting and Clinical Psychology, 63,* 182–196.

Stein, G (1993) Drug treatment of the personality disorders. In P Tyrer & G Stein (Eds.), *Personality disorder reviewed.* London: Gaskell.

Stein, G (1994) Physical treatments of the personality disorders. *Current Opinion in Psychiatry, 7,* 129–136.

Steinbruek, SM, Maxwell, SE, & Howard, GS (1983) A meta-analysis of psychotherapy and drug therapy in the treatment of unipolar depression with adults. *Journal of Consulting and Clinical Psychology, 51,* 856–863.

Steinhausen, HCH, Ruass-Mason, C, & Seidal, R (1991) Follow-up studies of anorexia nervosa: A review of four decades of outcome research. *Psychological Medicine, 21,* 447–454.

Steketee, G (1990) Personality traits and disorder in obsessive–compulsives. *Journal of Anxiety Disorders, 4,* 351–364.

Steketee, G, & Shapiro, LJ (1995) Predicting behavioral treatment outcome for agoraphobia and obsessive–compulsive disorder. *Clinical Psychology Review, 15,* 317–346.

Stephens, JH, & Schaffer, JW (1970) A controlled study of the effects of diphenylhydantoin on anxiety, irritability and anger in neurotic outpatients. *Psychopharmacologica (Berlin), 17,* 169–181.

Stern, R, Lipsedge, M, & Marks, IM (1973) Obsessive ruminations; a controlled trial of thought stopping techniques. *Behaviour Research and Therapy, 11,* 659–662.

Steuer, J, Mintz, J, Hammen, C, Hill, MA, Jarvik, LF, McCarley, T, Motoike, P, & Rosen, R (1984) Cognitive-behavioral and psychodynamic group psychotherapy in treatment of geriatric depression. *Journal of Consulting and Clinical Psychology, 52,* 180–192.

Stevenson, J, & Meares, R (1992) An outcome study of psychotherapy for patients with borderline personality disorder. *American Journal of Psychiatry, 149,* 358–362.

Stewart, JW, Mercier, MA, Agosti, V, Guardino, M, & Quitkin, FM (1993) Imipramine is effective after unsuccessful cognitive therapy: Sequential use of cognitive therapy and imipramine in depressed outpatients. *Journal of Clinical Psychopharmacology, 13,* 114–119.

Stiles, WB, & Shapiro, DA (1989) Abuse of the drug metaphor in psychotherapy process-outcome research. *Clinical Psychology Review, 9,* 521–543.

St Lawrence, JS, & Madakasira, S (1992) Evaluation and treatment of premature ejaculation: A critical review. *International Journal of Psychiatry in Medicine, 22,* 77–97.

Stone, MH (1990) *The fate of borderline patients.* New York: Guilford Press.

Stone, MH (1993) Long-term outcome in personality disorders. In P Tyrer & G Stein (Eds.), *Personality disorder reviewed.* London: Gaskell.

Strachan, AM (1986) Family intervention for the rehabilitation of schizophrenia; towards protection and coping. *Schizophrenia Bulletin, 12,* 678–698.

Strauss, CC, Last, CG, & Hersen, M, et al. (1988) Association between anxiety and depression in children and adolescents with anxiety disorders. *Journal of Abnormal Child Psychology, 16,* 57–68.

Stravynski, A (1986) Indirect behavioral treatment of erectile failure and premature ejaculation in a man without a partner. *Archives of Sexual Behavior, 15,* 355–361.

Stravynski, A, Belisle, M, Marcouiller, M, Lavallée, YJ, & Elie, R (1994) The treatment of avoidant personality disorder by social skills training in the clinic or in real-life settings. *Canadian Journal of Psychiatry, 39,* 377–383.

Stravynski, A, & Greenberg, D (1989) Behavioral psychotherapy for social phobia and dysfunction. *International Review of Psychiatry, 1,* 207–218.

Stravynski, A, & Greenberg, D (1990) The treatment of sexual dysfunction in single men. *Sexual and Marital Therapy, 5,* 115–122.

Stravynski, A, Marks, I, & Yule, W (1982) Social skills problems in neurotic outpatients: social skills training with and without cognitive modification. *Archives of General Psychiatry, 39,* 1378–1385.

Stravynski, A, Sahar, A, & Verreault, R (1991) A pilot study of the cognitive treatment of dsythymic disorder. *Behavioural Psychotherapy, 4,* 369–372.

Strong, SR (1968) Counselling: An interpersonal influence process. *Journal of Consulting and Clinical Psychology, 15,* 215–224.

Stroudemire, A, Frank, R, Hedemark, N, Kamlet, M, & Blazer, D (1986) The economic burden of depression. *General Hospital Psychiatry, 8,* 387–394.

Strupp, HH (1978) Psychotherapy research and practice—an overview. In AE Bergin & SL Garfield (Eds.), *Handbook of psychotherapy and behavior change* (2nd ed.). New York: Wiley.

Strupp, HH (1993) The Vandebilt psychotherapy studies: Synopsis. *Journal of Consulting and Clinical Psychology, 61,* 431–433.

Strupp, HH (1986) Psychotherapy: Research, practice, and public policy (How to avoid dead-ends). *American Psychologist, 41,* 120–130.

Strupp, HH, & Binder, J (1984) *Psychotherapy in a new key: A guide to time limited dynamic psychotherapy.* New York: Basic Books.

Strupp HH, Butler, SF, & Rosser, CL (1988) Training in psychodynamic psychotherapy. *Journal of Consulting and Clinical Psychology, 56,* 689–695.

Subotnik, L (1975) Spontaneous remission of emotional disorder in a general medical practice. *Journal of Nervous and Mental Disease, 161,* 239–244.

Sue, S, McKinney, H, & Allan, D (1976) Predictors of duration of therapy for clients in the community mental health system. *Community Mental Health Journal, 12,* 365–375.

Suinn, RM (1993, February) Psychotherapy: Can the practitioner learn from the researcher? *Behavior Therapist,* 47–49.

Sullivan, CF, Copeland, JRM, Dewey, ME, Davidson, IA, McWilliam, C, Saunders, P, Sharma, VK, & Voruganti, LNP (1988) Benzodiazepine usage amongst the elderly: Findings of the Liverpool community survey. *International Journal of Geriatric Psychiatry, 3,* 289–292.

Sullivan, HS (Ed.) (1953) *The interpersonal theory of psychiatry.* New York: Norton.

Sullivan, PF, Joyce, PR, & Mulder, RT (1994) Borderline personality disorder in major depression. *Journal of Nervous and Mental Disease, 182,* 508–516.

Sutcliffe, C, & Larner, S (1988) Counselling carers of the elderly at home: A preliminary study. *British Journal of Clinical Psychology, 27,* 177–178.

Svartberg, M, & Stiles, TC (1994) Therapeutic alliance, therapist competence and client change in short-term anxiety-provoking psychotherapy. *Psychotherapy Research, 4,* 20–33.

Swartz, M, Blazer, D, & Winfield, I (1990) Estimating the prevalence of borderline personality disorder in the community. *Journal of Personality Disorders, 4,* 257.

Szapocznik, J, & Kurtines, W (1989) *Breakthroughs in family therapy with drug-abusing and problem youth.* New York: Springer.

Szapocznik, J, Kurtines, W, Santisteban, DA, & Rio, A (1990) Interplay of advances between theory, research, and application in treatment interventions aimed at behavior problem children and adolescents. *Journal of Consulting and Clinical Psychology, 58,* 696–703.

Szapocznik, J, Rio, A, Murray, E, Cohen, R, Scopetta, M, Rivas-Valquez, A, Hervis, O, Posada, V, & Kurtines, W (1989). Structural family versus psychodynamic child therapy for problematic Hispanic boys. *Journal of Consulting and Clinical Psychology, 57,* 571–578.

Takefman, J, & Brender, W (1984) An analysis of the effectiveness of two components in the treatment of erectile dysfunction. *Archives of Sexual Behavior, 13,* 321–340.

Target, M, & Fonagy, P (1994a) The efficacy of psychoanalysis for children with emotional disorders. *Journal of the American Academy of Child and Adolescent Psychiatry, 33,* 361–371.

Target, M, & Fonagy, P (1994b) The efficacy of psychoanalysis for children: Prediction of outcome in a developmental context. *Journal of the American Academy of Child and Adolescent Psychiatry, 33,* 1134–1144.

Tarrier, N (1991a) Some aspects of family intervention programmes in schizophrenia. I: Adherence to intervention programmes. *British Journal of Psychiatry, 159,* 475–480.

Tarrier, N (1991b) Some aspects of family intervention programmes in schizophrenia. II: Financial considerations. *British Journal of Psychiatry, 159,* 481–484.

Tarrier, N (1992) Management and modification of residual psychotic symptoms. In M Birchwood & N Tarrier (Eds.), *Innovations in the psychological management of schizophrenia.* Chichester: Wiley.

Tarrier, N, Barrowclough, C, Vaughn, C, Bamrah, JS, Porceddu, K, Watts, S, & Freeman, HL (1988) The community management of schizophrenia: A controlled trial of a behavioral intervention with families to reduce relapse. *British Journal of Psychiatry, 153,* 532–542.

Tarrier, N, Barrowclough, C, Vaughn, C, Bamrah, JS, Porceddu, K, Watts, S, & Freeman, HL (1989) The community management of schizophrenia: A two year follow-up of a behavioral intervention with families. *British Journal of Psychiatry, 154,* 625–628.

Tarrier, N, Beckett, R, Harwood, S, Baker, A, Yusupoff, L, & Ugarterburu, I (1993a) A trial of two cognitive-behavioral methods of treating drug-resistant residual psychotic symptoms in schizophrenic patients: I. Outcome. *British Journal of Psychiatry, 162,* 524–532.

Tarrier, N, Sharpe, L, & Beckett, R (1993b) A trial of two cognitive-behavioral methods of treating drug-resistant residual psychotic symptoms in schizophrenic patients: II. Treatment specific changes in coping and problem solving skills. *Social Psychiatry and Psychiatric Epidemiology, 28,* 5–10.

Task Force on Promotion and Dissemination of Psychological Procedures (1995) Training in and dissemination of empirically-validated psychological procedures: Report and recommendations. *Clinical Psychologist, 48,* 3–23.

Taube, CA, & Barrett SA (1985) *Mental Health, United States 1985.* National Institute of Mental Health, DHHS Pub. No. (ADM) 85–1378. Washington, DC: Superintendent of Documents, US Government Printing Office.

Taylor, E, Sandberg, S, Thorley, G, & Giles, S (1991) *The epidemiology of childhood hyperactivity.* Institute of Psychiatry Maudsley Monographs. London: Oxford University Press.

Taylor, FG, & Marshall, WL (1977) Experimental analysis of cognitive-behavioral therapy for depression. *Cognitive Therapy and Research, 1,* 59–72.

Teasdale, JD, Fennell, MJ, Hibbert, GA, & Amies, PL (1984) Cognitive therapy for major depressive disorder in primary care. *British Journal of Psychiatry, 144,* 400–406.

Telch, MJ, Agras, WS, & Taylor, CB (1985) Combined pharmacological and behavioral treatment for agoraphobia. *Behaviour Research and Therapy, 23,* 325–335.

Temple, MT, & Leino, EV (1989) Long-term outcomes of drinking: A 20 year longitudinal study of men. *British Journal of Addiction, 84,* 889–899.

Thase, M, Bowler, K, & Harden, T (1991) Cognitive behavior therapy of endogenous depression. Part 2: Preliminary findings in 16 unmedicated inpatients. *Behavior Therapy*, *22*, 469–477.

Thase, ME, Simons, AD, & Reynolds, CF (1993) Psychobiological correlates of poor response to cognitive behavior therapy: Potential indications for antidepressant pharmacotherapy. *Psychopharmacology Bulletin*, *29*, 293–301.

Thom, B, Browne, C, Drummond, DC, Edwards, G, & Mullan, M (1992) Engaging patients with alcohol problems in treatment: The first consultation. *British Journal of Addiction*, *87*, 601–611.

Thom, B, Foster, R, Keaney, F, & Salazar, C (1994, February) *Alcohol treatment since 1983: A review of the research literature.* Report to the Alcohol Education and Research Council.

Thompson, JA, Charlton, PFC, Kerry, R, Lee, D, & Turner, SW (1995) An open trial of exposure therapy based on deconditioning for post-traumatic stress disorder. *British Journal of Clinical Psychology*, *34*, 407–416.

Thompson, LW, Gallagher, D, & Czirr, R (1988) Personality disorder and outcome in the treatment of late-life depression. *Journal of Geriatric Psychiatry*, *21*, 133–146.

Thompson, LW, Gallagher, D, & Breckenridge, JS (1987) Comparative effectiveness of psychotherapies for depressed elders. *Journal of Consulting and Clinical Psychology*, *55*, 385–390.

Thompson, LW, Wagner, B, Zeiss, A, & Gallagher, D (1990). Cognitive/ behavioral therapy with early stage Alzheimer's patients: An exploratory view of the utility of this approach. In E Light & BD Lebowitz (Eds.), *Alzheimers disease: Treatment and family stress.* New York: Hemisphere.

Thompson, RJ, Gil, KM, Burbach, DJ, Keith, BR, & Kinney, TR (1993) Role of child and maternal processes in the psychological adjustment of children with sickle cell disease. *Journal of Consulting and Clinical Psychology*, *61*, 468–474.

Thomsen, PH, & Mikkelsen, HU (1995) Course of obsessive–compulsive disorder in children and adolescents: A prospective follow-up study of 23 Danish cases. *Journal of the American Academy of Child and Adolescent Psychiatry*, *34*, 1432–1440.

Thomson, R (1982) Side effects and placebo amplification. *British Journal of Psychiatry*, *140*, 64–68.

Thornton, S, & Brotchie, J (1987) Reminiscence: A critical review of the empirical literature. *British Journal of Clinical Psychology*, *26*, 93–111.

Thyer, BA (1985) Audiotaped exposure therapy in a case of obsessional neurosis. *Journal of Behavior Therapy and Experimental Psychiatry*, *16*, 271–273.

Tolan, PH, Guerra, NG, & Kendall, PC (1995) Introduction to Special Section: Prediction and prevention of antisocial behavior in children and adolescents. *Journal of Consulting and Clinical Psychology*, *63*, 515–517.

Tomsovic, M (1970) A follow-up study of discharged alcoholics. *Hospital and Community Psychiatry*, *21*, 94–97.

Toseland, RW, Rossiter, CM, & Labrecque, MS (1989) The effectiveness of peer-led and professionally led groups to support family caregivers. *Gerontologist*, *29*, 465–471.

Toseland, RW, & Smith, GC (1990) Effectiveness of individual counselling by professional and peer helpers for family caregivers of the elderly. *Psychology and Ageing, 5,* 256–263.

Tramontana, MG (1980) Critical review of research on psychotherapy outcome with adolescents: 1967–1977. *Psychological Bulletin, 88,* 429–450.

Treasure, J, Todd, G, Brolly, M, Tiller, J, Nehmed, A, & Denman, F (1995) A pilot study of a randomised trial of cognitive analytical therapy versus educational behavioral therapy for adult anorexia nervosa. *Behaviour Research and Therapy, 33,* 363–367.

Trower, P, Yardley, K, Bryant, BM, & Shaw, P (1978) The treatment of social failure: A comparison of anxiety reduction and skills acquisition procedures on two social problems. *Behaviour Modification, 2,* 41–60.

Trull, TJ, Nietzel, MT, & Main, A (1988) The use of meta-analysis to assess the clinical significance of behavior therapy for agoraphobia. *Behavior Therapy, 19,* 527–538.

Tucker, L, Bauer, SF, Wagner, S, Harlam, D, & Sher, I (1987) Long-term hospital treatment of borderline patients: A descriptive outcome study. *American Journal of Psychiatry, 144,* 1443–1448.

Tuma, JM (1989) Mental health service for children: The state of the art. *American Psychologist, 44,* 188–199.

Turkat, ID, & Maisto, SA (1985) Personality disorders: Application of the experimental method to the formulation of personality disorders. In DH Barlow (Ed.), *Clinical handbook of psychological disorders.* New York: Guilford Press.

Turner, RM (1987) The effects of personality disorder diagnosis on the outcome of social anxiety symptom reduction. *Journal of Personality Disorders, 1,* 136–143.

Turner, S (1996) Common sense and novel treatments. In BA Van der Kolk, AC McFarlane, & L Weisaeth (Eds.), *Traumatic stress: The effects of overwhelming experience on mind, body, and society.* New York: Guilford Press.

Turner, SM, Beidel, DC, Dancu, CV, & Keys, DJ (1986) Psychopathology of social phobia and comparison to avoidant personality disorder. *Journal of Abnormal Psychopathology, 95,* 389–394.

Turner, SM, Beidel, DC, & Jacob, RG (1994) Social phobia: A comparison of behavior therapy and atenolol. *Journal of Consulting and Clinical Psychology, 62,* 350–358.

Turner, SM, Beidel, DC, Cooley, MR, Woody, SR, & Messer, SC (1994) A multi-component behavioral treatment for social phobia: Social effectiveness therapy. *Behaviour Research and Therapy, 32,* 381–390.

Turner, SM, Beidel, DC, & Cooley-Quille, MR (1995) Two-year follow-up of social phobics treated with social effectiveness therapy. *Behaviour Research and Therapy, 33,* 553–555.

Tyrer, P (1989) Clinical importance of personality disorder. *Current Opinion in Psychiatry, 2,* 240–243.

Tyrer, P, Seivewright, N, Ferguson, B, Murphy, S, Darling, C, Brothwell, J, Kingdon, D, & Johnson, AL (1990) The Nottingham study of neurotic disorder: Relationship between personality status and symptoms. *Psychological Medicine, 20,* 423–431.

Tyrer, P, Seivewright, N, Ferguson, B, Murphy, S, & Johnson, AL (1993) The Nottingham study of neurotic disorder: Effect of personality status on response to drug treatment, cognitive therapy and self-help over two years. *British Journal of Psychiatry, 162,* 219–226.

Tyrer, P, Merson, S, Onyett, S, & Johnson, T (1994) The effect of personality disorder on clinical outcome, social networks and adjustment: A controlled clinical trial of psychiatric emergencies. *Psychological Medicine, 24,* 731–740.

Uhlenhuth, EH, Balter, MB, & Mellinger, GD et, al. (1983) Symptom checklist syndromes in the general population: Correlations with psychotherapeutic drug use. *Archives of General Psychiatry, 40,* 1167–1172.

Ultee, CA, Griffiaen, D, & Schellekens, J (1982) The reduction of anxiety in children: A comparison of the effects of systematic desensitisation in vitro and systematic desensitization in vivo. *Behaviour Research and Therapy, 20,* 61–67.

Vaal, JJ (1973) Applying contingency contracting to a school phobic: A case study. *Journal of Behavior Therapy and Experimental Psychiatry, 4,* 371–737.

Van Balkom, AJLM, van Oppen, P, Wermeulen, AWA, van Dyck, R, Nauta, MCE, & Vorst, HCM (1994) Meta-analysis on the treatment of obsessive–compulsive disorder: A comparison of antidepressants, behavior, and cognitive therapy. *Clinical Psychology Review, 14,* 359–381.

Van Balkom, AJLM, Nauta, MCE, & Bakker, A (1995) Meta-analysis on the treatment of panic disorder with agoraphobia: Review and examination. *Clinical Psychology and Psychotherapy, 2,* 1–14.

Vanderhoof, JC, & Campbell, P (1967) Evaluation of an aversive technique as a treatment for alcoholism. *Quarterly Journal of Studies on Alcoholism, 28,* 476–485.

Van Gent, EM, & Zwart, FM (1994) A long follow-up after group therapy in conjunction with lithium prophylaxis. *Nordic Journal of Psychiatry, 48,* 9–12.

Van Hasselt, VB, Hersen, M, Bellack, AS, Rosenbloom, N, & Lamparski, D (1979) Tripartite assessment of the effects of systematic desensitization in a multiphobic child: An experimental analysis. *Journal of Behavior Therapy and Experimental Psychiatry, 10,* 57–66.

Van Oppen, P, De Haan, E, Van Balkom, AJLM, Spinhoven, P, Hoogduin, K, & Van Dyck, R (1995) Cognitive therapy and exposure in vivo in the treatment of obsessive–compulsive disorder. *Behaviour Research and Therapy, 33,* 379–390.

Vaughn, CE, & Leff, JP (1976) The influence of family and social factors on the course of psychiatric illness. *British Journal of Psychiatry, 129,* 125–137.

Vaughn, K, Armstrong, MS, Gold, R, O'Connor, N, Jenneke, W, & Tarrier, N (1994b) A trial of eye movement desensitization compared to image habituation training and applied muscle relaxation training in PTSD. *Journal of Behavior Therapy and Experimental Psychiatry, 25,* 283–291.

Vaughn, K, & Tarrier, N (1992) The use of image habituation training with PTSD. *British Journal of Psychiatry, 161,* 658–664.

Vaughn, K, Weise, M, Gold, R, & Tarrier, N (1994a) Eye movement desensitization: Symptom change in PTSD. *British Journal of Psychiatry, 164,* 533–541.

Velez, CN, Johnson, J, & Cohen, P (1989) Longitudinal analyses of selected risk factors for childhood psychopathology. *Journal of the American Academy of Child and Adolescent Psychiatry, 28,* 861–864.

Verhulst, FC, & van der Ende, J (1993) "Comorbidity" in an epidemiological sample: A longitudinal perspective. *Journal of Child Psychology and Psychiatry, 34,* 767–784.

Visser, S, Hoekstra, RJ, & Emmelkamp, PMG (1991) Long-term follow-up of obsessive–compulsive patients after exposure treatment. In A Ehlers (Ed.), *Perspectives and promises of clinical psychology.* New York: Plenum Press.

Volkmar, F, Shakir, S, Bacon, S, & Pfefferbaum, A (1981) Group psychotherapy in the management of manic-depressive illness. *American Journal of Psychotherapy, 35,* 226–234.

Volpicelli, JR, Alterman, AI, Hayashida, M, & O'Brien, CP (1992) Naltrexone in the treatment of alcohol dependence. *Archives of General Psychiatry, 49,* 876–880.

Waddington, CH (1966) *Principles of development and differentiation.* New York: Macmillan.

Waldinger, MD, Hengeveld, MW, & Zwinderman, AH (1994) Paroxetine treatment of premature ejaculation: A double-blind, randomized, placebo-controlled study. *American Journal of Psychiatry, 151,* 1377–1379.

Waldinger, RJ, & Frank, AF (1989) Clinicians' experiences in combining medication and psychotherapy in the treatment of borderline patients. *Hospital and Community Psychiatry, 40,* 712–718.

Waldinger, RJ, & Gunderson, JG (1984) Completed therapies with borderline patients. *American Journal of Psychotherapy, 38,* 190–202.

Wallace, CJ, Nelson, CJ, Liberman, RP, Aitchison, RA, Lukoff, D, Elder, JP, & Ferris, C (1980) A review and critique of social skills training with schizophrenics. *Schizophrenia Bulletin, 6,* 42–63.

Wallace, P, Cutler, S, & Haines, A (1988) Randomized controlled trial of general practitioner intervention in patients with excessive alcohol consumption. *British Medical Journal, 297,* 663–668.

Wallerstein, RS (1989) The psychotherapy research project of the Menninger Foundation: An overview. *Journal of Consulting and Clinical Psychology, 57,* 195–205.

Wallerstein, RS, Chotlos, JW, Friend, MB, Hammersley, DW, Perlswig, EA, & Winship, GM (1957) *Hospital treatment of alcoholism: A comparative experimental study.* New York: Basic Books.

Wardle, J (1990) Behavior therapy and benzodiazepines: Allies or antagonists? *British Journal of Psychiatry, 156,* 163–168.

Wardle, J, Hayward, P, Higgitt, A, Stabl, M, Blizard, R, & Gray, J (1994) Effects of concurrent diazepam treatment on the outcome of exposure therapy in agoraphobia. *Behaviour Research and Therapy, 32,* 203–215.

Warheit, GJ, & Auth, JB (1993) Epidemiology of alcohol abuse in adulthood. In R Michaels (Ed.), *Psychiatry.* Philadelphia: Lippincott.

Waring, EM, Chamberlaine, CH, McCrank, EW, Stalker, CA, Carver, C, Fry, R, & Barnes, S (1988) Dysthymia: A randomised study of cognitive marital therapy and antidepressants. *Canadian Journal of Psychiatry, 33,* 96–99.

Warner, P, Bancroft, J, & Members of the Edinburgh Human Sexuality Group (1987) A regional clinical service for psychosexual problems: A three year study. *Sex and Marital Therapy, 2,* 115–126.

Watson, JP, & Brockman, B (1982) A follow-up of couples attending a psychosexual problems clinic. *British Journal of Clinical Psychology, 21,* 143–144.

Weiden, P, & Havens, L (1994) Psychotherapeutic management techniques in the treatment of outpatients with schizophrenia. *Hospital and Community Psychiatry, 45,* 549–555.

Weisaeth, L (1989) Importance of high response rates in traumatic stress research. *Acta Psychiatrica Scandinavica* (Suppl.), *355,* 131–137 .

Weiss, B, & Weisz, JR (1990) The impact of methodological factors on child psychotherapy outcome research: A meta-analysis for researchers. *Journal of Consulting and Clinical Psychology, 54,* 789–795.

Weiss, B, & Weisz, JR (1995) Relative effectiveness of behavioral and non-behavioral child psychotherapy. *Journal of Consulting and Clinical Psychology, 63,* 317–320.

Weiss, G, & Hechtman, LT (1986) *Hyperactive children grown up.* New York: Guilford Press.

Weiss, LJ, & Lazarus, LW (1993) Psychosocial treatment of the geropsychiatric patient. *International Journal of Geriatric Psychiatry, 8,* 95–100.

Weissman, MM (1993) The epidemiology of personality disorders. In R Michels (Ed.), *Psychiatry.* Philadelphia: Lippincott.

Weissman, MM, Leaf, PJ, Holzer, CE, & Merikangas, KR (1985) Epidemiology of anxiety disorders. *Psychopharmacology Bulletin, 26,* 543–545.

Weissman, MM, Leaf, PJ, & Blaser, DG (1986) Panic disorder: Clinical characteristics, epidemiology and treatment. *Psychopharmacology Bulletin, 22,* 787.

Weissman, MM, Leaf, PJ, & Tishler, GL et, al. (1988a) Affective disorders in five communities. *Psychological Medicine, 18,* 141–153.

Weissman, MM, Leaf, PJ, Bruce, ML, & Florio, L (1988b) The epidemiology of dysthymia in five communities; rate, risks, comorbidity, and treatment. *American Journal of Psychiatry, 145,* 815–819.

Weissman, MM, Prusoff, BA, & DiMascio, A (1979) The efficacy of drugs and psychotherapy in the treatment of acute depressive episodes. *American Journal of Psychiatry, 136,* 555–558.

Weissman, MM, Wickramaratne, P, Adams, PB, Lish, JD, Horwarth, E, Charney, D, Woods, SW, Leeman, E, & Frosch, E (1993) The relationship between panic disorder and major depression. *Archives of General Psychiatry, 50,* 767–780.

Weissman, MM, & Markowitz, J (1994) Interpersonal psychotherapy—current status. *Archives of General Psychiatry, 51,* 599–606.

Weisz, JR, Donenberg, GR, Han, SS, & Weiss, B (1995) Bridging the gap between laboratory and clinic in child and adolescent psychotherapy. *Journal of Consulting and Clinical Psychology, 63,* 688–701.

Weisz, JR, Weiss, B, Alicke, MD, & Klotz, ML (1987) Effectiveness of psychotherapy with children and adolescents: Meta-analytic findings for clinicians. *Journal of Consulting and Clinical Psychology, 55,* 542–549.

Weisz, JR, & Weiss, B (1989) Assessing the effects of clinic-based psychotherapy with children and adolescents. *Journal of Consulting and Clinical Psychology*, 57, 741–746.

Weisz, JR, & Weiss, B (1991) Studying the "referrability" of child clinical problems. *Journal of Consulting and Clinical Psychology*, 59, 266–273.

Weisz, JR, Weiss, B, Morton, T, Granger, D, & Han S (1992a) *Meta-analysis of psychotherapy outcome research with children and adolescents*. Unpublished manuscript, University of California, Los Angeles.

Weisz, JR, Weiss, B, & Donenberg, GR (1992b) The lab versus the clinic: Effects of child and adolescent psychotherapy. *American Psychologist*, 47, 1578–1585.

Weisz, JR, & Weiss, B (1993) *Effects of psychotherapy with children and adolescents*. Newbury Park, CA: Sage Publications.

Wells, JE, Bushnell, JA, Hornblow, AR, Joyce, PR, & Oakley-Browne, MA (1989) Christchurch psychiatric epidemiology study: Methodology and lifetime prevalence for specific psychiatric disorders. *Australian and New Zealand Journal of Psychiatry*, 23, 315–326.

Wells, KB (1985) *Depression as a tracer condition for the National Study of Medical Care outcomes; background review*. Santa Monica, CA: Rand Corporation R-3293 RWJ/HJK.

Wells, KB, Burnam, MA, & Rogers, W, et al. (1992) The course of depression in adult outpatients: Results from the medical outcomes study. *Archives of General Psychiatry*, 49, 788–794.

Werble, B (1970) Second follow-up of borderline patients. *Archives of General Psychiatry*, 23, 3–7.

Werkman, S (1987) Anxiety disorders. In HI Kaplan, AM Freedman, & BJ Sadock (Eds.), *Comprehensive textbook of psychiatry* (Vol. III). Baltimore: Williams and Wilkins.

Werry, JS, & McClellan, JM (1992) Predicting outcome in child and adolescent (early onset) schizophrenia and bipolar disorder. *Journal of the American Academy Child and Adolescent Psychiatry*, 31, 147–150.

Werry, JS, McClellan, JM, & Chard, L (1991) Childhood and adolescent schizophrenia, bipolar and schizoaffective disorders: A clinical and outcome study. *Journal of the American Academy of Child and Adolescent Psychiatry*, 30, 457–465.

Werry, JS, & Wollersheim, JP (1989) Behavior therapy with children and adolescents: A twenty-year overview. *Journal of the American Academy of Child and Adolescent Psychiatry*, 28, 1.

West, DJ, & Farrington, DP (1973) *Who becomes delinquent?*. London: Heinemann Educational.

Western, D, Moses, MJ, Silk, KR, Lohr, NE, Cohen, R, & Segal, H (1992) Quality of depressive experience in borderline personality disorder and major depression: When depression is not just depression. *Journal of Personality Disorders*, 6, 382–393.

Wexler, BE, & Cicchetti, DV (1992) The outpatient treatment of depression; implications of outcome research for clinical practice. *Journal of Nervous and Mental Disease*, 180, 277–286.

White, J, Moffitt, TE, Earls, F, Robins, L, & Silva, P (1990) How early can we tell? Pre-school predictors of boys' conduct disorder and delinquency. *Criminology, 28,* 507–533.

Whitehead, A, Mathews, A, & Ramage, M (1987) The treatment of sexually unresponsive women: A comparative evaluation. *Behaviour Research and Therapy, 25,* 195–205.

Wierson, M, & Forehand, R (1994) Introduction to special section: The role of longitudinal data with child psychopathology and treatment: Preliminary comments and issues. *Journal of Consulting and Clinical Psychology, 62,* 883–886.

Wierzbicki, M, & Pekarik, G (1993) A meta-analysis of psychotherapy dropout. *Professional Psychology: Research and Practice, 24,* 190–195.

Wilfley, DE, Agras, WS, Telch, CF, Rossiter, EM, Schneider, JA, Golomb, AG, Sifford, LA, & Raeburn, SD (1993) Group cognitive behavioral therapy and group interpersonal psychotherapy for the non-purging bulimic individual: A controlled comparison. *Journal of Consulting and Clinical Psychology, 61,* 296–303.

Williams, JM (1992) *Psychological treatment of depression.* London: Routledge.

Williams, R, Reeve, W, Ivison, D, & Kavanagh, D (1987) Use of environmental manipulation and modified informal reality orientation with institutionalized confused elderly subjects: A replication. *Age and Ageing, 16,* 315–318.

Willmuth, ME (1988) Cognitive behavioral and insight oriented psychotherapy of an 11 year old boy with obsessive compulsive disorder. *American Journal of Psychotherapy, 42,* 472–478.

Wilson, A, White, J, & Lange, DE (1978) Outcome evaluation of a hospital-based alcoholism treatment programme. *British Journal of Addiction, 73,* 39–45.

Wilson, GT, & Rachman, SJ (1983) Meta-analysis and the evaluation of psychotherapy outcome: Limitations and liabilities *Journal of Consulting and Clinical Psychology, 51,* 54–64.

Wilson, GT, Rossiter, EM, Kleinfield, EI, & Lindholm, L (1986) Cognitive-behavioral treatment of bulimia-nervosa: A controlled evaluation. *Behaviour Research and Therapy, 24,* 277–288.

Wilson, GT, Eldredge, KL, Smith, D, & Niles, B (1991) Cognitive behavioral treatment with and without response prevention for bulimia. *Behaviour Research and Therapy, 129,* 575–583.

Wilson, GT, & Fairburn, CG (1993) Cognitive treatments for eating disorders. *Journal of Consulting and Clinical Psychology, 61,* 261–269.

Wilson, M (1993) DSM-III and the transformation of American psychiatry. *American Journal of Psychiatry, 150,* 399–410.

Wilson, PH, Goldin, JC, & Charbonneau-Powis, M (1983) Comparative efficacy of behavioral and cognitive treatments of depression. *Cognitive Therapy and Research, 7,* 111–124.

Wing, JK, Cooper, JE, & Sartorius, N (1974) *Measurement and classification of psychiatric symptoms.* Cambridge: Cambridge University Press.

Winston, A, Flegheimer, W, Pollack, J, Laikin, M, Kestenbaum, R, & McCullough, L (1987, June) *A brief psychotherapy fidelity scale—reliability, validity and relation to outcome.* Abstracts from the Society for Psychotherapy Research 18th Annual Meeting, Ulm, West Germany.

Winston, A, Pollack, J, McCullough, L, Flegenheimer, W, Kestenbaum, R, & Trujillo, M (1991) Brief psychotherapy of personality disorders. *Journal of Nervous and Mental Disease, 179*, 188–193.

Winston, A, Laikin, M, Pollack, J, Samstag, LW, McCullough, L, & Muran, JC (1994a) Short-term psychotherapy of personality disorders. *American Journal of Psychiatry, 151*, 190–194.

Winston, A, Laikin, M, Pollack, J, Samstag, LW, McCullough, L, & Muran, JC (1994b) Short-term psychotherapy of personality disorders. *American Journal of Psychiatry, 151*, 190–194.

Witmer, HL, & Keller, J (1942) Outgrowing childhood problems: A study in the value of child guidance treatment. *Smith College Studies in Social Work, 13*, 74–90.

Wittchen, HU (1988) Natural course and spontaneous remission of untreated anxiety disorders: Results of the Munich follow-up study. In I Hand & HU Wittchen (Eds.), *Panic and phobias* (2nd ed.). Heidelberg: Springer.

Witzum, E, Dasberg, H, & Shefler, G (1989) A two year follow-up of time limited therapy in a community mental health centre in Jerusalem. *Israel Journal of Psychiatry, 4*, 244–258.

Wittchen, HU, Essau, CA, & Krieg, C (1991) Comorbidity: Similarities and differences in treated and untreated groups. *British Journal of Psychiatry, 159* (Suppl.), 23.

Wittchen, H-U, Zhao, S, Kessler, RC, & Eaton, WW (1994) DSM-III-R generalized anxiety disorder in the National Comorbidity Survey. *Archives of General Psychiatry, 51*, 355–364.

Wolfe, BE, & Maser, JD (Eds.) (1994) *Treatment of panic disorder: A consensus development conference*. Washington, DC: American Psychiatric Press.

Wolff, R, & Rapoport, J (1988) Behavioral treatment of childhood obsessive–compulsive disorder. *Behavior Modification, 12*, 252–266.

Woods, RT, Portnoy, S, Head, D, & Jones, G (1992) Reminiscence and life-review with persons with dementia: Which way forward? In G Jones & B Miesen (Eds.), *Care-giving in dementia*. London: Routledge.

Woods, RT, & Britton, PG (1985) *Clinical psychology with the elderly*. London: Croom Helm/Chapman Hall.

Woods, RT (1992) What can be learned from studies on reality orientation? In G Jones & B Miesen (Eds.), *Care-giving in dementia*. London: Routledge.

Woody, GE, Stockdale, D, & Hargrove, E (1977) *A manual for drug counseling*. Unpublished manuscript, University of Pennsylvania.

Woody, GE, McLellan, T, Luborsky, L, & O'Brien, CP (1985) Sociopathy and psychotherapy outcome. *Archives of General Psychiatry, 179*, 188–193.

World Health Organization (1978) *International classification of diseases* (9th rev.). Geneva: World Health Organization.

Wright, DM, Moelis, I, & Pollack, LJ (1976) The outcome of individual child psychotherapy: Increments at follow-up. *Journal of Child Psychology and Psychiatry, 17*, 275–285.

Wright, J, Perreault, R, & Mathieu, M (1977) The treatment of sexual dysfunction. *Archives of General Psychiatry, 34*, 881–890.

Wright, L, & Walker, CE (1978) A simple behavioral treatment program for psychogenic enuresis. *Behaviour Research and Therapy, 16*, 209–212.

Wulpsin, L, Bachop, M, & Hoffman, D (1988) Group therapy in manic-depressive illness. *American Journal of Psychotherapy, 42,* 263–271.

Yalom, I (1975) *The theory and practice of group psychotherapy.* New York: Basic Books.

Yost, EB, Beutler, LE, Corbishley, MA, & Allender, JR (1986) *Group cognitive therapy: A treatment approach for depressed older adults.* Oxford: Pergamon Press.

Young, JE, Lindemann, Md (1992) An integrative schema-focused model for personality disorders. *Journal of Cognitive Psychotherapy, 6,* 11–23.

Yule, W (1981) The epidemiology of child psychopathology. In BB Lahey & AE Kazin (Eds.), *Advances in clinical child psychology* (Vol 4). New York: Plenum Press.

Yulis, S (1976) Generalization of therapeutic gain in the treatment of premature ejaculation. *Behavior Therapy, 7,* 355–358.

Zahner, GEP, Jacobs, JH, Freeman, DH, & Trainor, KF (1993) Rural–urban child psychopathology in a northeastern U.S. state: 1986–1989. *Journal of the American Academy of Child and Adolescent Psychiatry, 32,* 378–387.

Zanarini, MC, Frakenberg, FR, & Gunderson, JG (1988) Pharmacotherapy of borderline patients. *Comprehensive Psychiatry, 29,* 372–378.

Zarit, SH, Anthony, CR, & Boutselis, M (1987) Interventions with caregivers of dementia patients: Comparison of two approaches. *Psychology and Aging, 2,* 225–232.

Zeiss, AM, Lewinsohn, PM, & Munoz, RF (1979) Non-specific improvement effects in depression using interpersonal, cognitive, and pleasant events focused treatments. *Journal of Consulting and Clinical Psychology, 47,* 427–439.

Zetin, M, & Kramer, MA (1992) Obsessive compulsive disorder. *Hospital and Community Psychiatry, 43,* 689–699.

Zetzel, ER (1956) Current concepts of transference. *International Journal of Psychoanalysis, 37,* 369–376.

Zill, N, & Schoenborn, CA (1990) Developmental, learning, and emotional problems: Health of our nation's children. United States 1988. *Advance Data: National Center for Health Statistics,* Number 190.

Zimberg, S (1974) Evaluation of alcoholism treatment in Harlem. *Quarterly Journal of Studies on Alcohol, 35,* 550–557.

Zimmer, D (1987) Does marital therapy enhance the effectiveness of treatment for sexual dysfunction? *Journal of Sex and Marital Therapy, 13,* 193–209.

Zimmerman, M, & Coryell, WH (1990) Diagnosing personality disorders within the community: A comparison of self-report and interview measures. *Archives of General Psychiatry, 47,* 527.

Zitrin, CM, Klein, DF, & Woerner, MG (1980) Treatment of agoraphobia with group exposure in vivo and imipramine. *Archives of General Psychiatry, 37,* 63–72.

Zitrin, CM, Klein, DF, Woerner, MG, & Ross, DC (1983) Treatment of phobias. *Archives of General Psychiatry, 40,* 125–138.

Zweben, A, Pearlan, S, & Li, S (1988) A comparison of brief advice and conjoint therapy in the treatment of alcohol abuse: The results of the marital systems study. *British Journal of Addiction, 83,* 899–916.

Author Index

If a text citation has more than one author or editor, the work is indexed only under the name of the first author or editor.

Subject Index